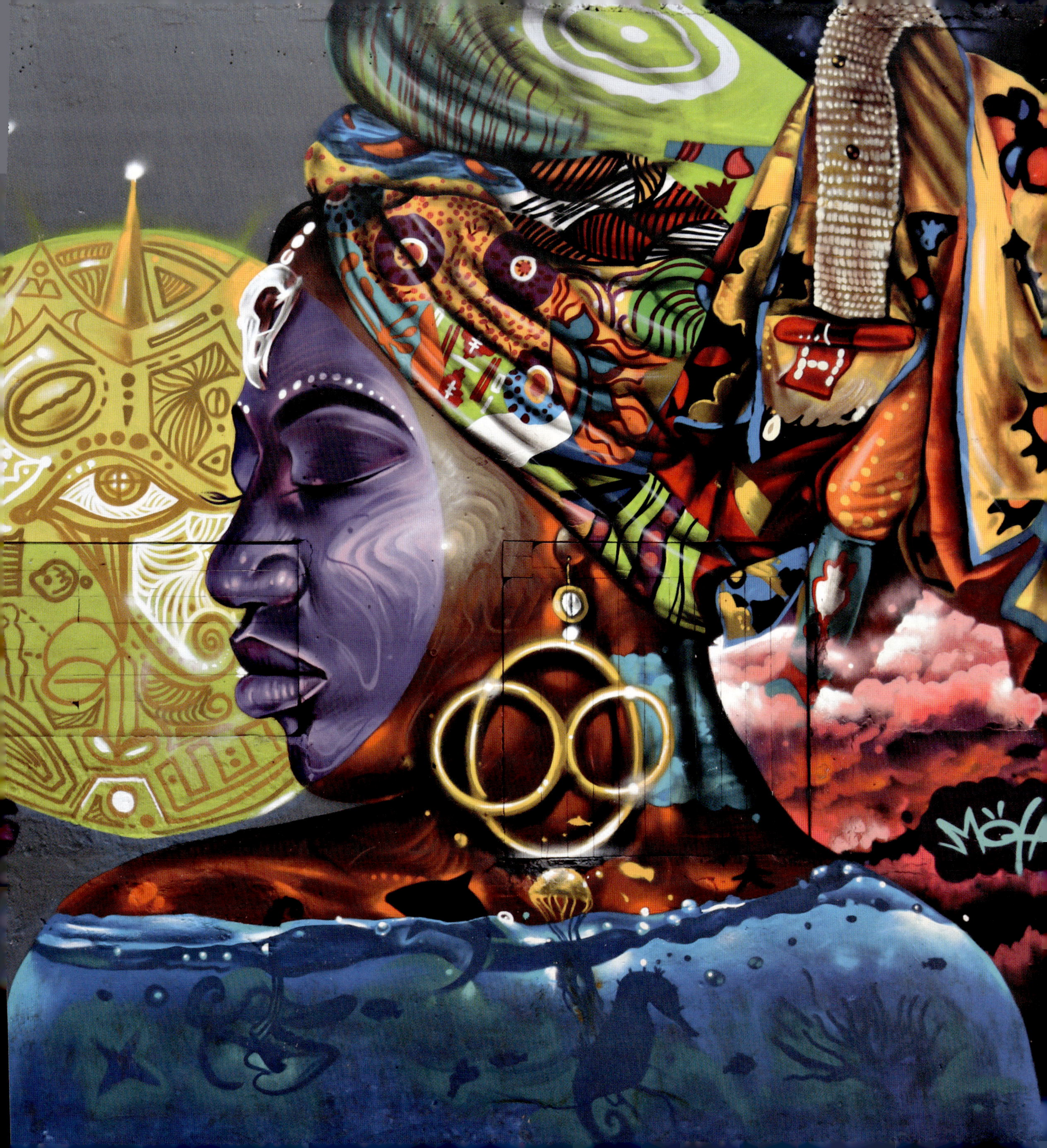

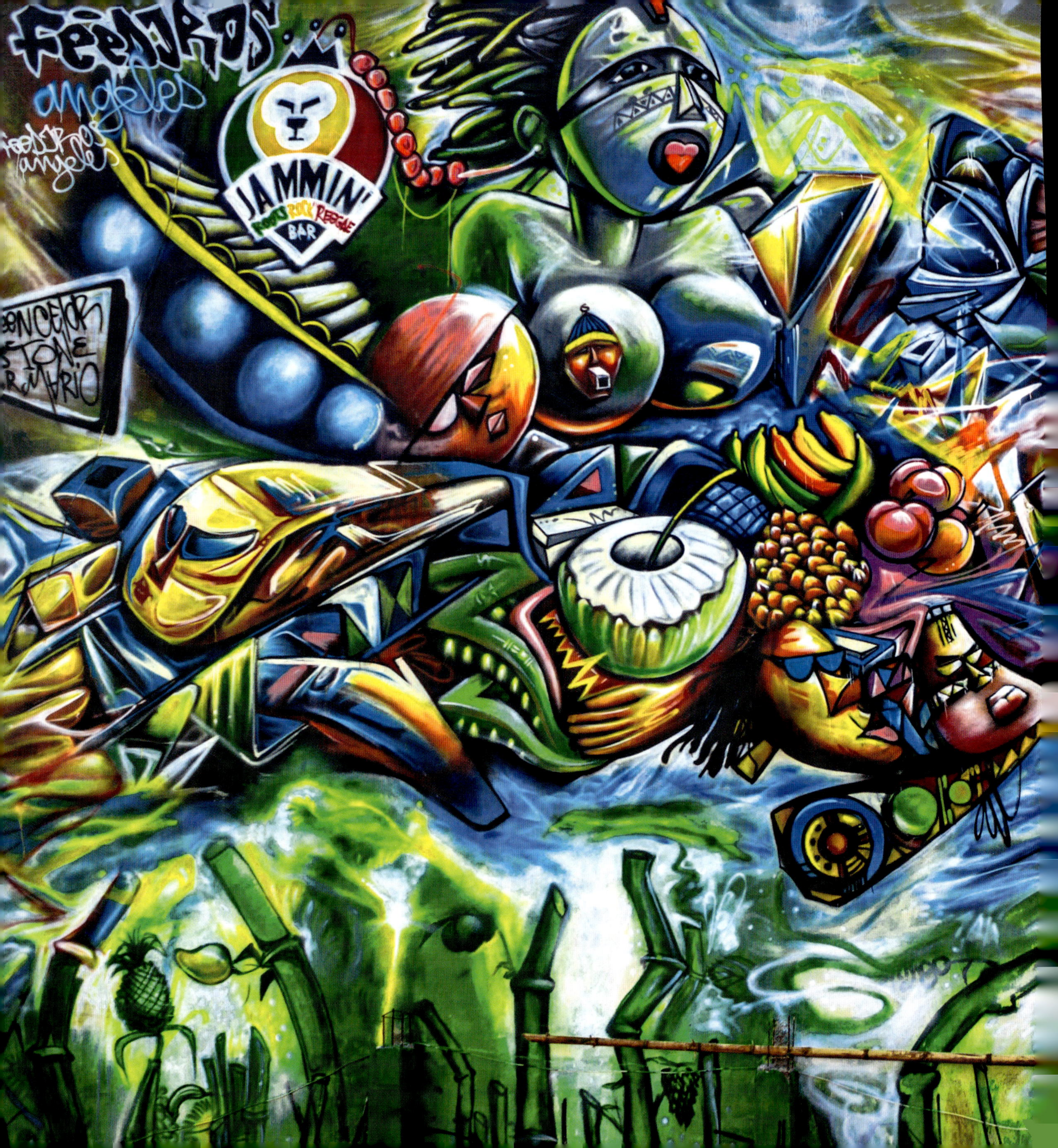
FEELJROS
angeles
feeljros
angeles
JAMMIN'
ROCK REGGAE
BAR
CONCEPCION
STONE
R. DARIO

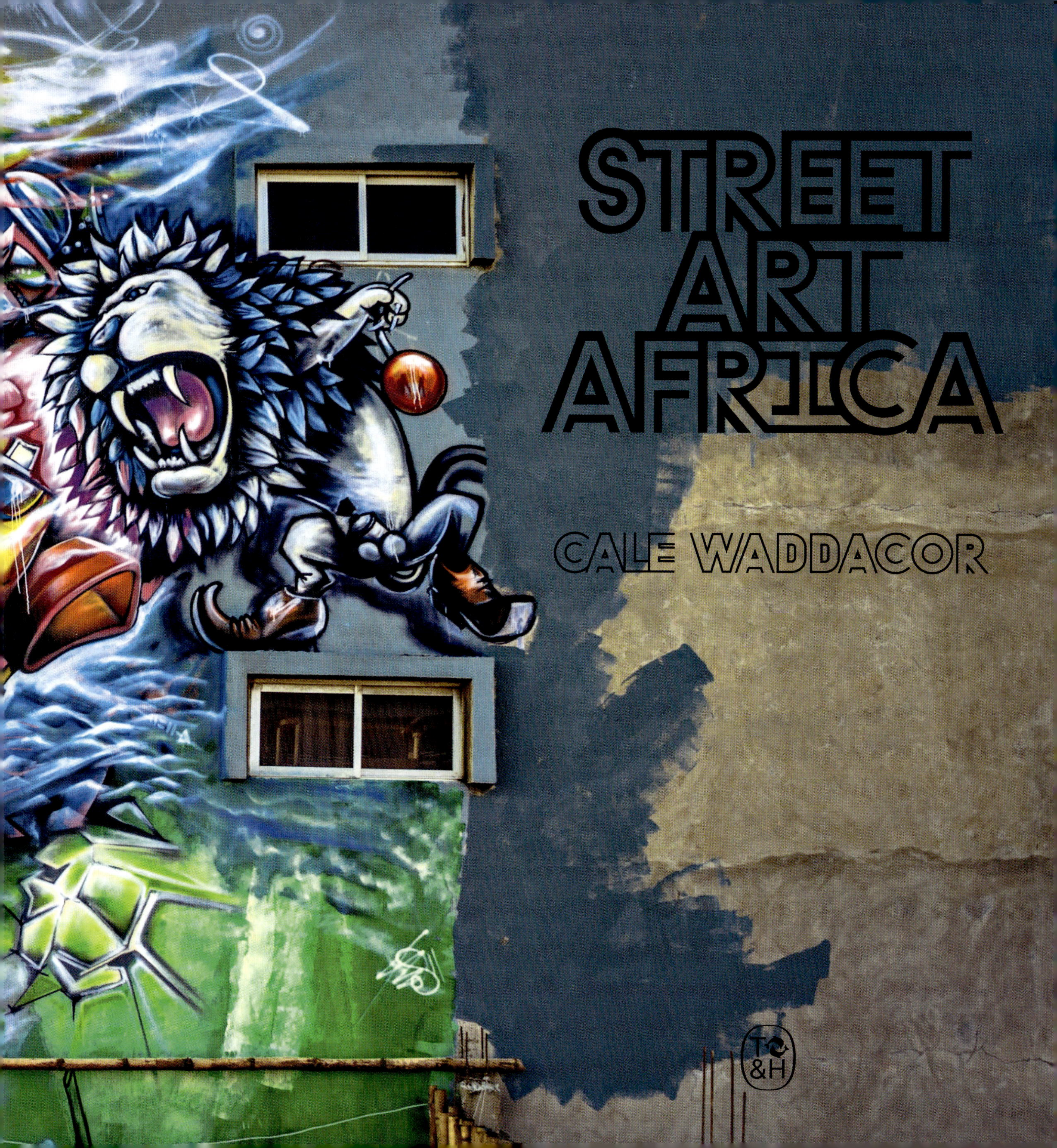

STREET ART AFRICA

CALE WADDACOR

CONTENTS

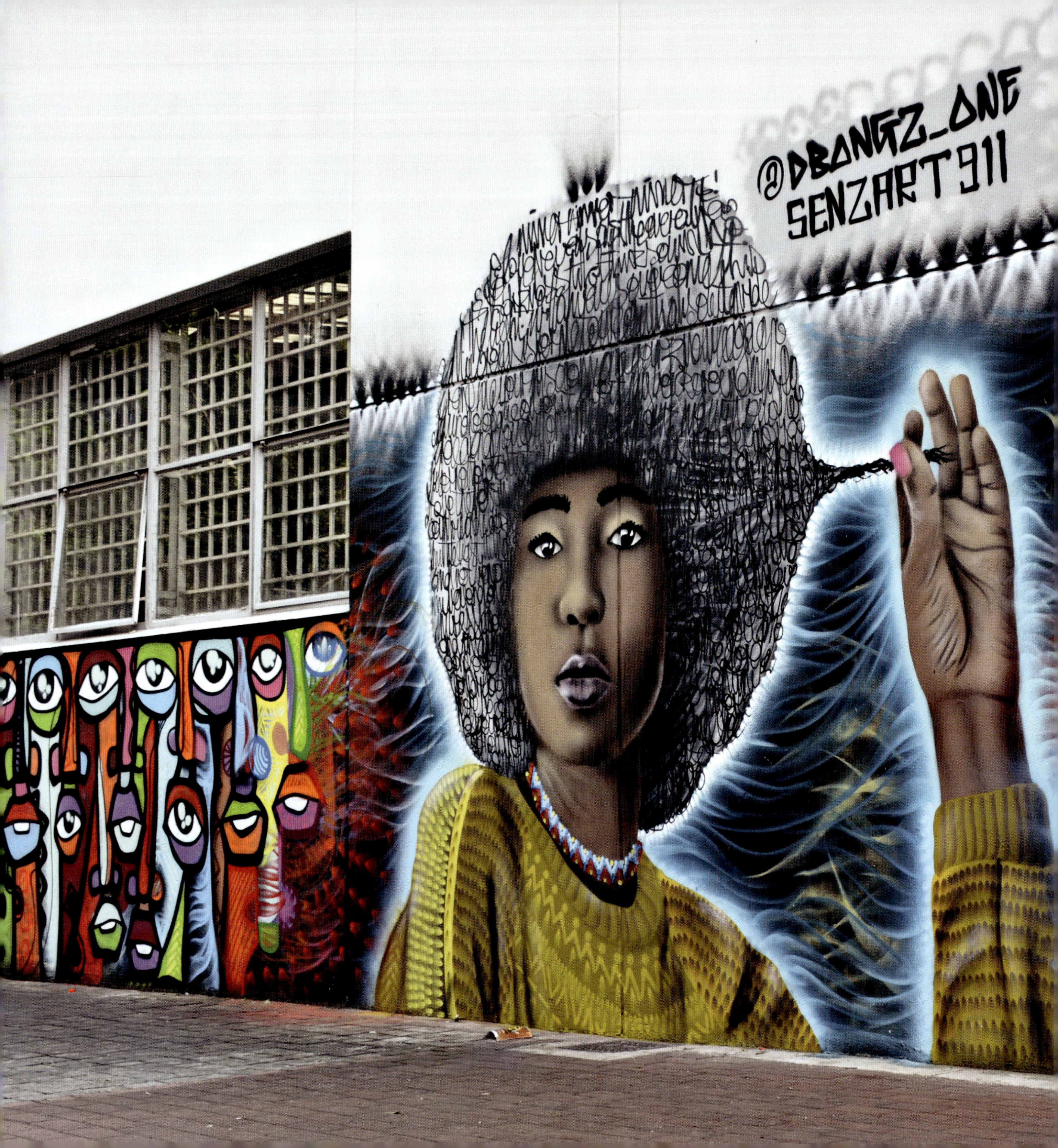

@DBONGZ_ONE
SENZART911

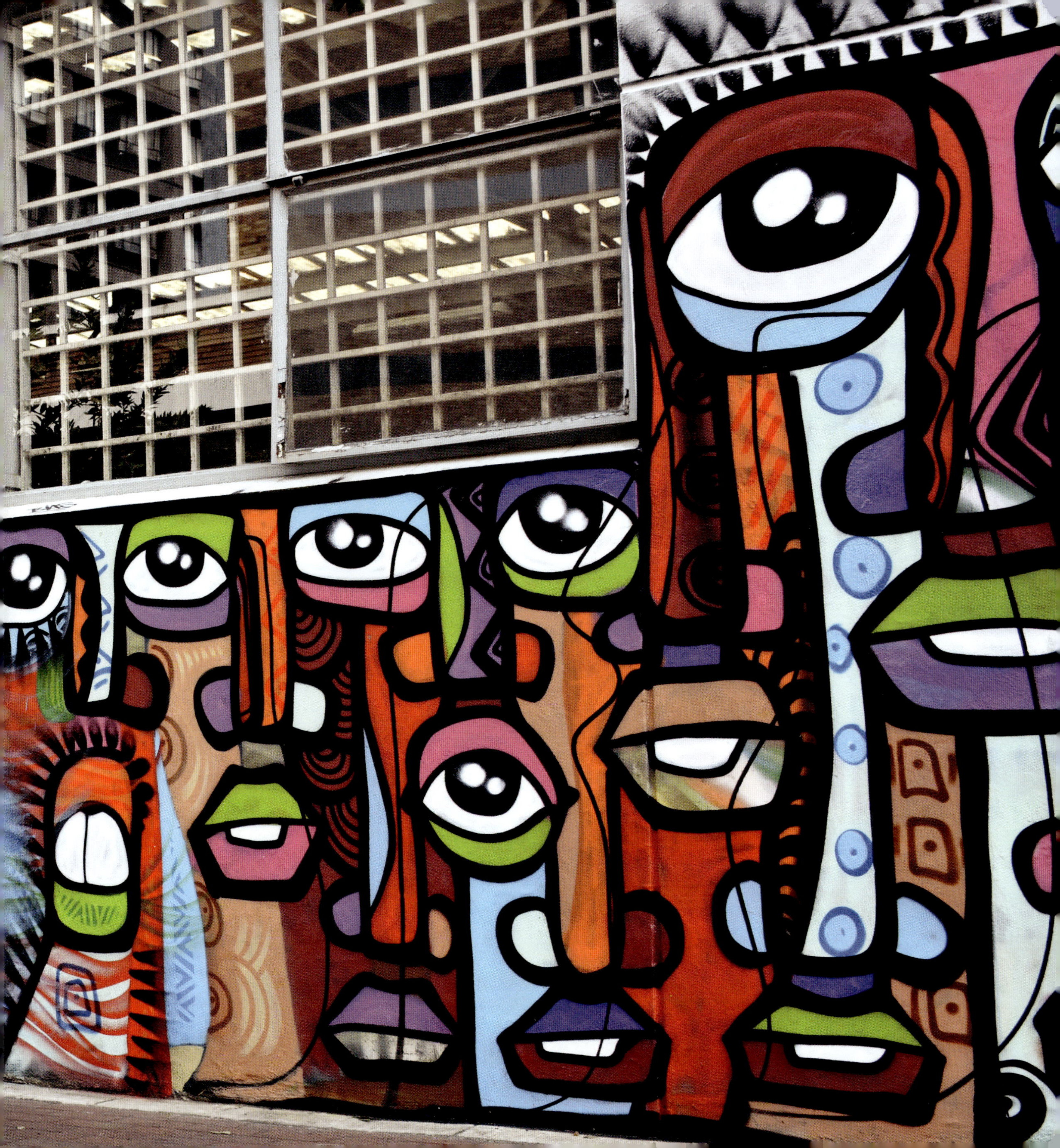

INTRODUCTION

Street art is a global movement that continually defies the limitations of what is possible within the urban environment – constantly expanding into every sphere, reinventing itself and putting its stamp on the world. Present in some form in almost every city, this far-reaching spectacle continues to relentlessly thread its way into the fabric of our daily lives. Over the past sixty years, unsightly scrawls and innocent drawings have developed into elaborate murals and witty sociopolitical commentary pieces. From nothing, a counterculture was born, to grow steadily into one of the most relevant art forms of our time. This urban artwork renaissance, unfolding before our eyes, embodies the essence of modern expression, and its daily evolution is considered by many to be a significant phenomenon in art history.

In Africa, street art is flourishing and strengthening graffiti's global takeover with the addition of new artists, styles, locations and admirers as it thrives in the public realm for all to see. Since the dawn of time, humans have been telling stories and passing knowledge and experiences from person to person, generation to generation. The desire to share these stories and ideas caused primitive civilizations to experiment with stones and bones, hairs and feathers, and pigments from the earth, drawing and scratching symbols and elementary narratives into rock. Mark making and proto-writing can be traced back to prehistoric times, with Africa being home to many of the oldest and grandest discoveries. From the caves of Southern Africa to the deserts of the Sahara and the hieroglyphs of the ancient Egyptians, many of these communications were sealed in a time capsule, only to pique interest centuries later. These inscriptions – and other forms of expression – were always present through the ages, but were not always appreciated or considered significant. Tens of thousands of years later, this deep-rooted urge to make marks would see new light on the North American East Coast in Philadelphia and New York City in the late 1960s – owing much to the invention of the aerosol spray can.

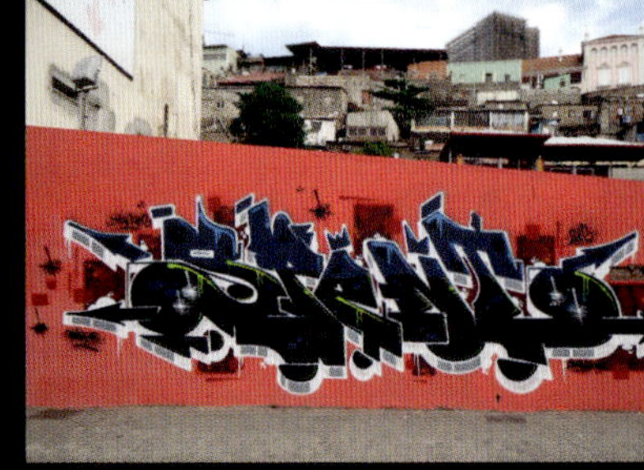

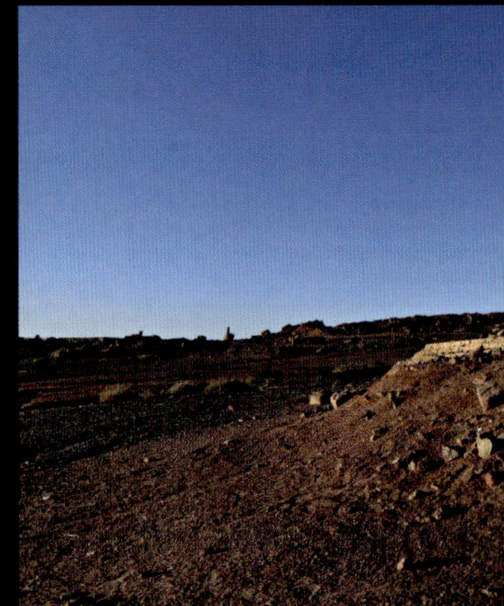

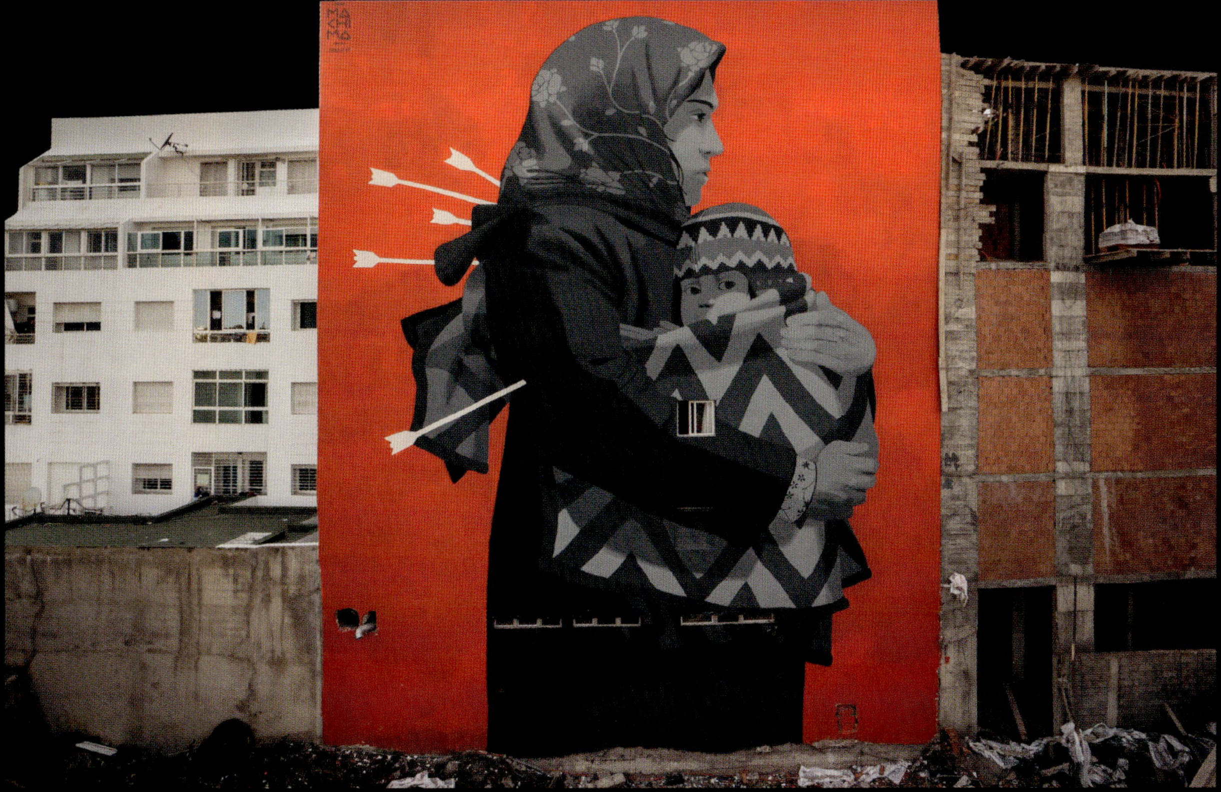

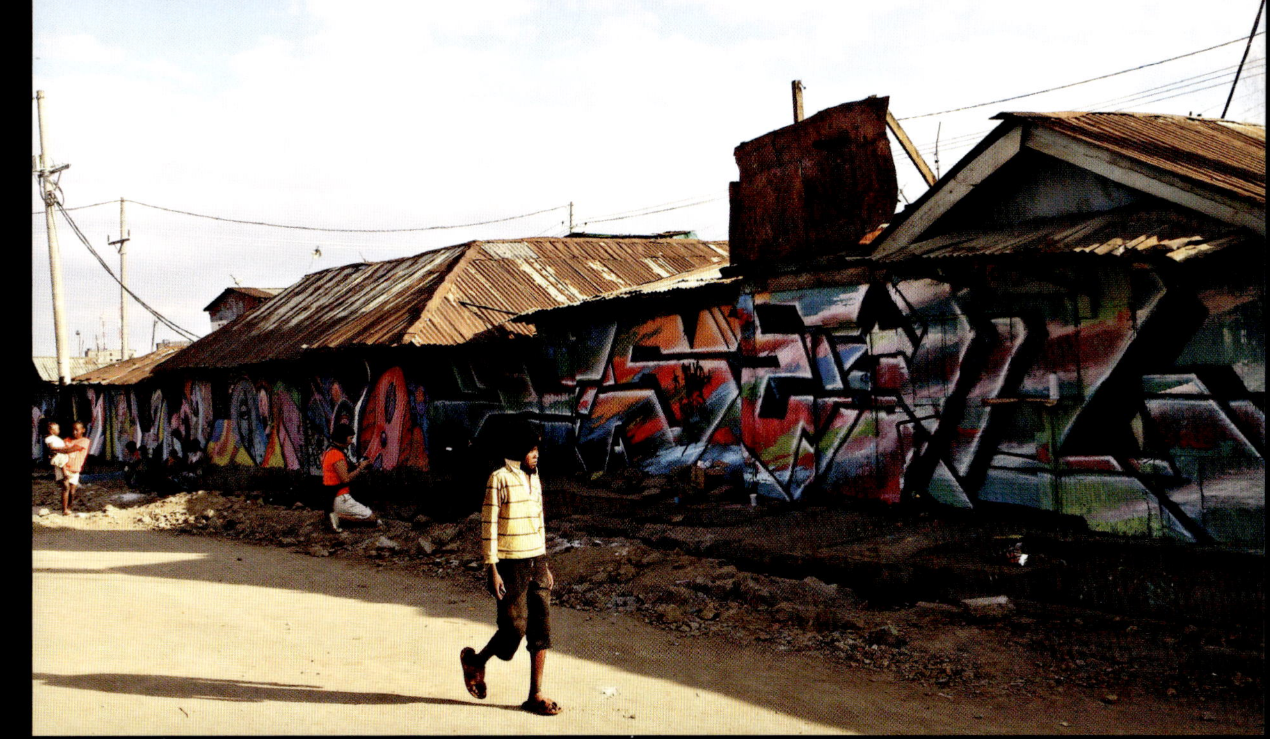
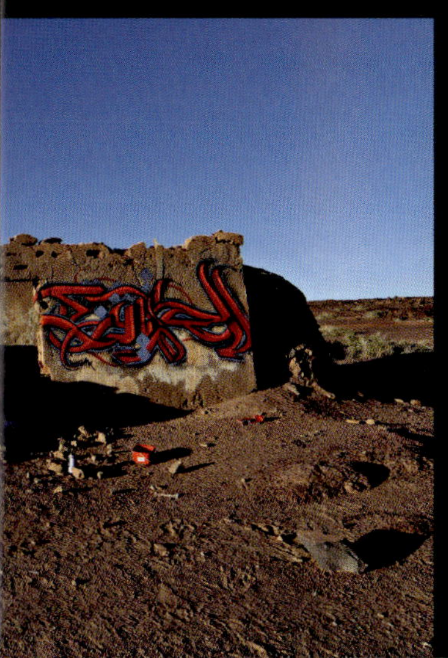

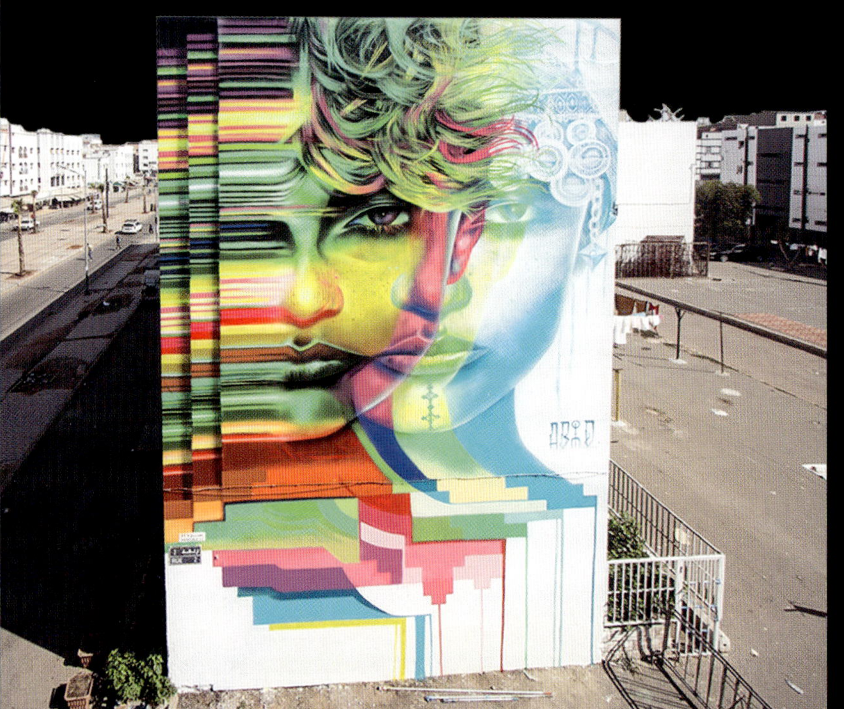

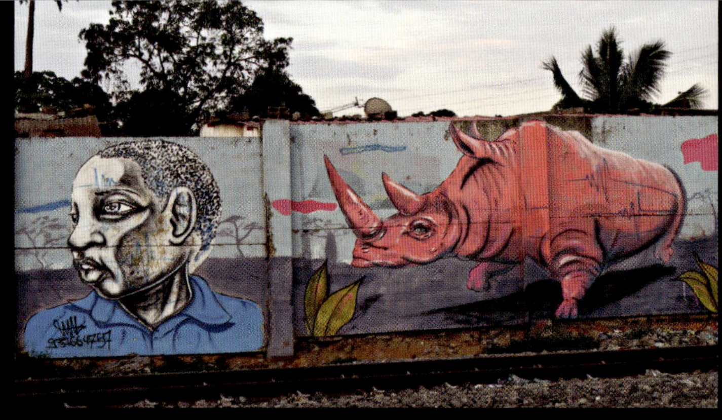

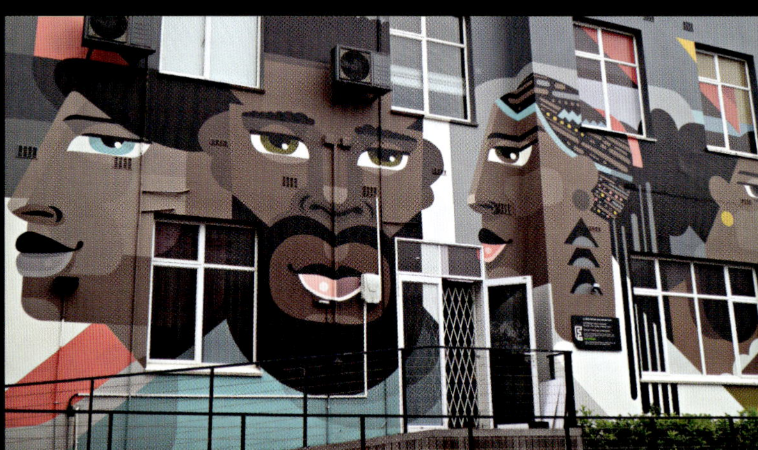

The act of marking one's surroundings was a natural urge and in modern times became the foundation for the ultimate form of expression. Traditional graffiti was born as an act of rebellion and echoed worldwide, evolving faster and further. American hip-hop culture was a major catalyst and people around the globe embraced the movement for its expressive traits. Devoted MCs, DJs, breakdancers and graffiti artists began to profess their love for an urban lifestyle that now dominates mass media. The age of street art followed at the turn of the millennium, conjuring up a new energy that was relevant to the time and place: the inherent visual power brightens forgotten corners of a city, stimulates and reinvigorates, bringing with it a refreshed lease on life. This art is accessible, relevant and free, devoid of elitist values, raising the bar for self-expression.

As the movement filtered into more parts of the world, Africa slowly caught on and impassioned youths actively sought to bolster their own creative exploits. Although ephemeral in nature, this ever-present impulse of humans to make their mark in society continues to exist and adapt. Graffiti seemed a lot more interesting than the usual traditional art, and African practitioners began to borrow from what they saw in books, magazines and music videos. However, they faced challenges as few references existed around them in the physical space, on the streets; and modern technology and art supplies were even more scarce. Africa's graffiti pioneers persisted through pure dedication, adapting to their

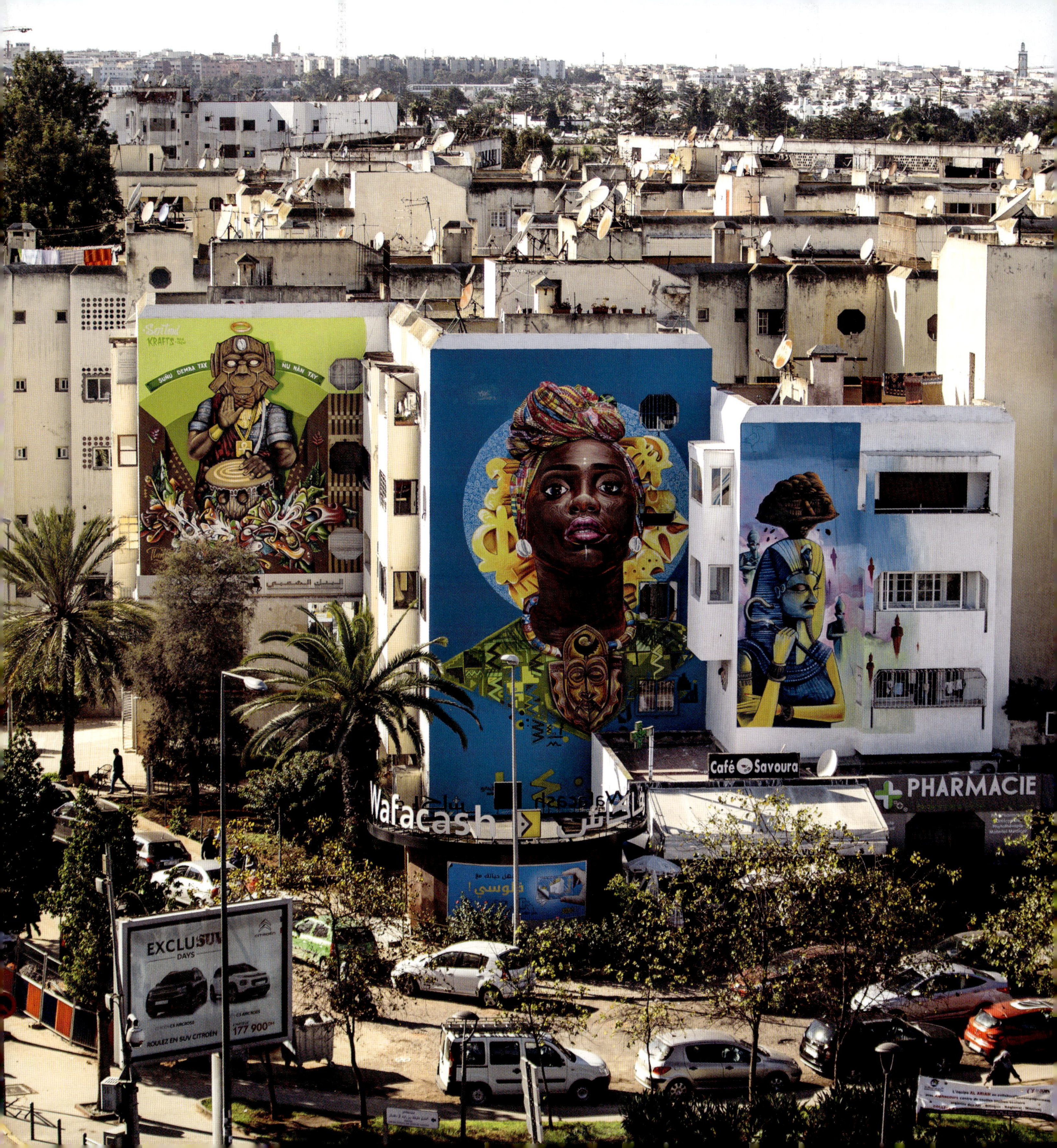

KRAFTS
SUNU DEMBA TAY NU NAN TAY
Wafacash
Café Savoura
+ PHARMACIE
EXCLUSIV DAYS
177 900
ROULEZ EN SUV CITROËN

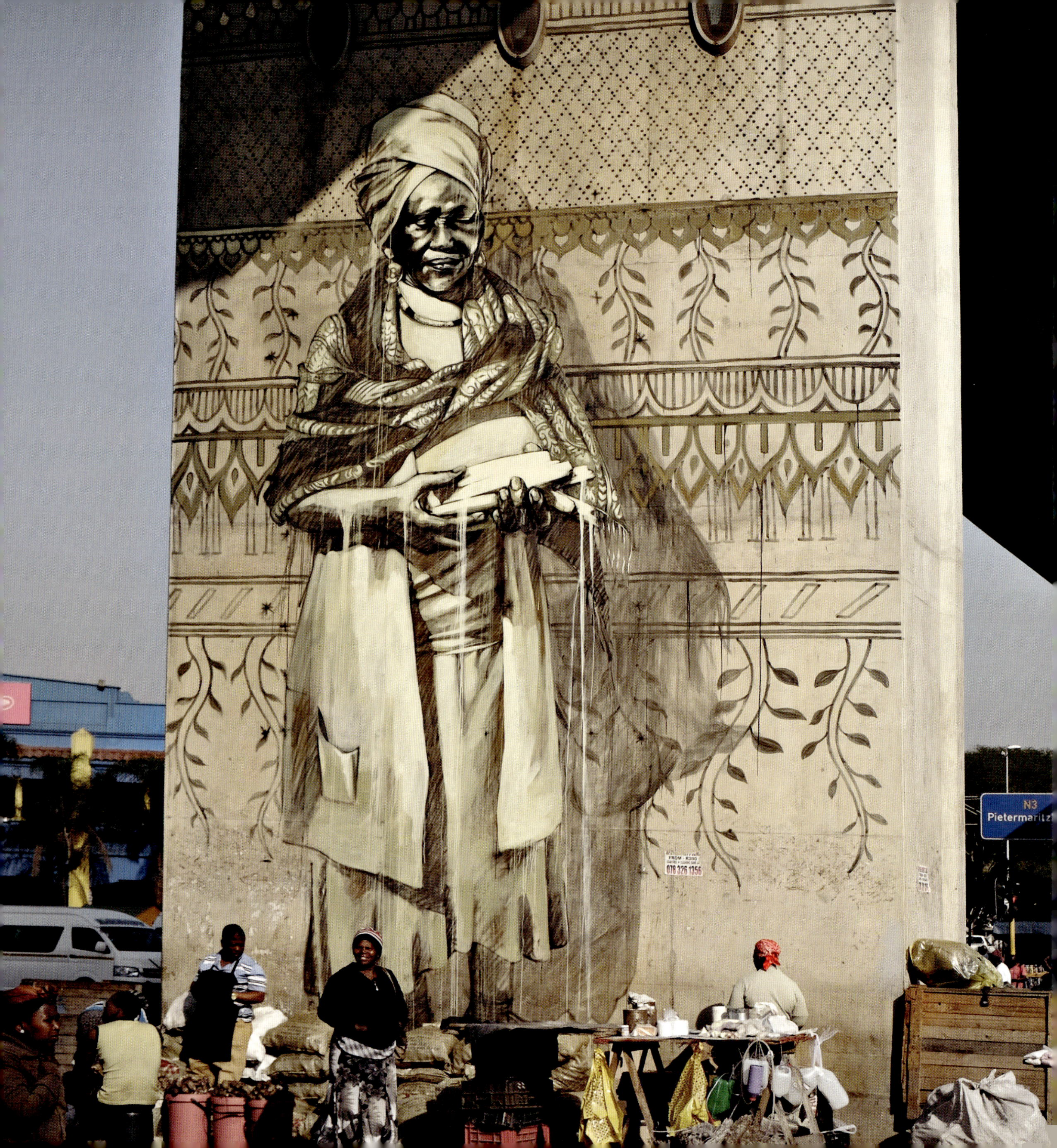

078 326 1356
N3
Pietermaritz

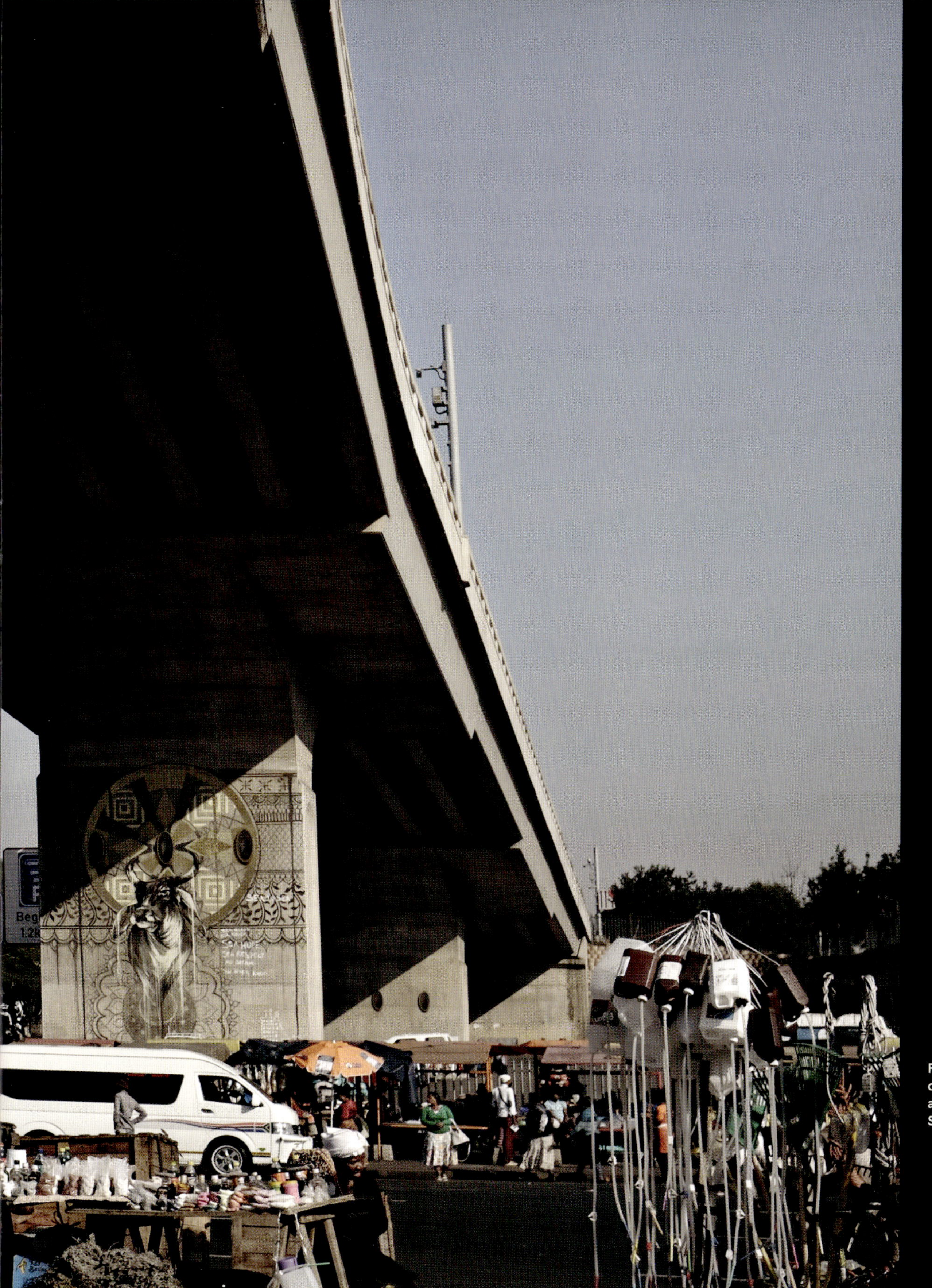

Faith XLVII. 'A Study of Warwick Triangle at Rush Hour', Durban, South Africa, 2014

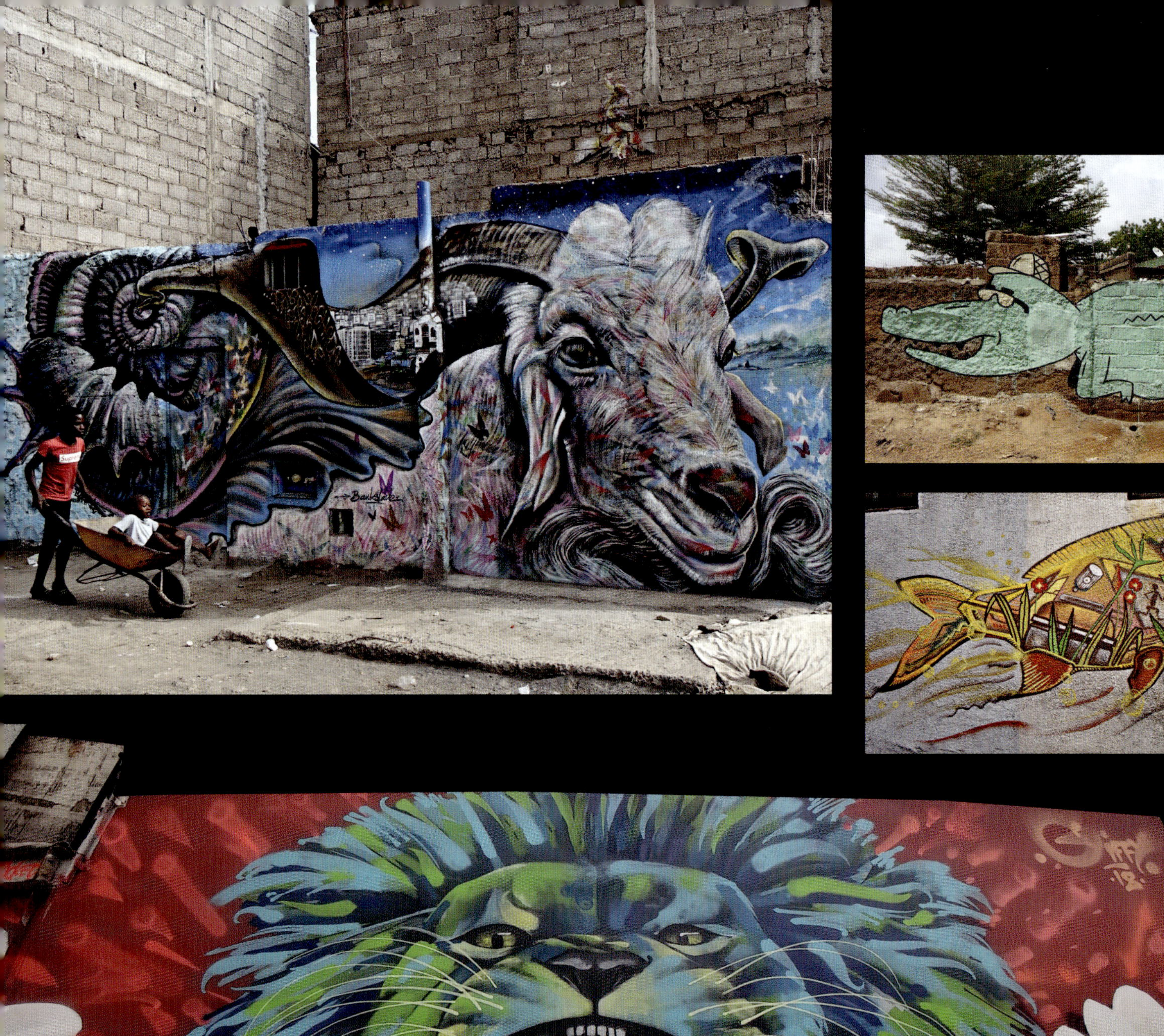

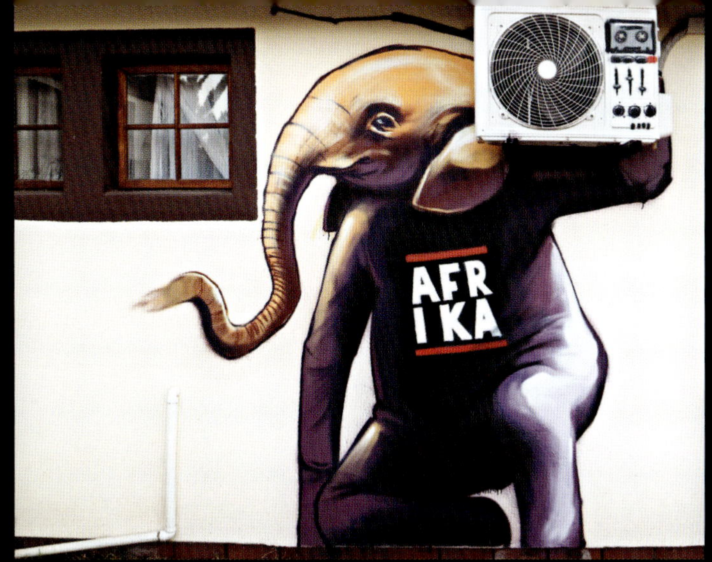

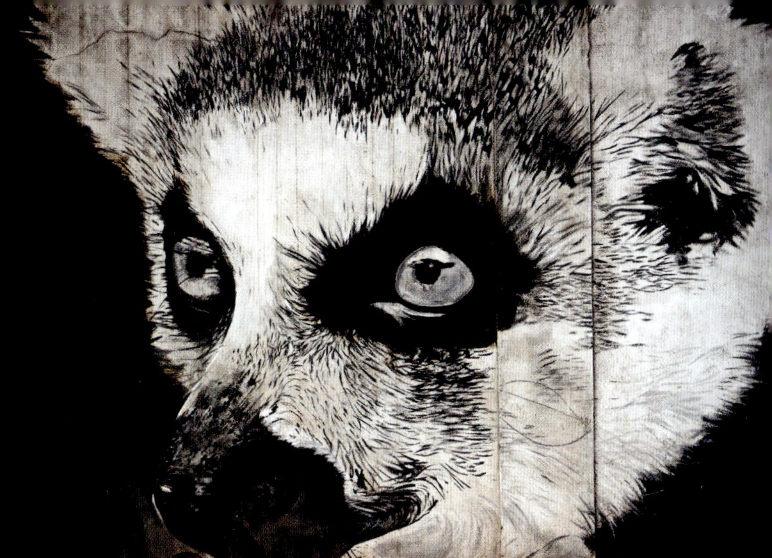

conditions and experimenting in any way possible. The shaping of the art form over the past two to three decades has culminated in what we see now.

Each region of Africa operates with its own distinct characteristics – a melange of cultures, ethnicities, languages and religions. In Western Africa, graffiti artists choose to paint words with deeper meaning instead of their tag names, thus dispelling any negative connotations during the inception stage, as many inhabitants were new to the idea of graffiti. Although many retain their signature style in terms of letter structures, serifs or colour use, their approach reflects a sense of pride that defies the norms of international style-writing. Western African artists eschew vandalism, maintaining it is not necessary to deface their environment. By bringing beauty to their surroundings and promoting the art form in a positive way, often focusing on their ancestry, they add intrinsic value to the environment and their graffiti is perceived as an important tool for civil cohesion. Certain advanced practitioners still enforce the use of complex letter forms for their own artistic growth, but fuse key words and historical figures (sometimes with denotations) for the public to understand the context. In Senegal, the practice was further enhanced by Set Setal, a youth movement of the 1980s that encouraged cleanliness. By being socially conscious and actively maintaining a sanitary community, artists and residents alike were able to keep the quality of life high.

Whereas most graffiti artists concentrate on letter forms, writing their names repeatedly in a stylized manner, often painting for their own enjoyment and that

Graffiti is growing steadily due to the increasing number of live art events, ease of access to the Internet, infrastructure development and the emergence of more artistic hubs. Graffiti techniques are similar worldwide, but style is personal. African artists weave their own stories within portraits, murals and graffiti-style letters.' SWIFT9

of other graffiti 'writers', street artists fuse more elements and techniques, taking the environment into consideration, adding and influencing, sparking a greater conversation with a broader audience. The art form is relatively new in Africa, and both sects exist in a conglomerate of styles; however, there is a greater preponderance of traditional graffiti because of its association with hip-hop, and its long-standing appeal. As the worldwide movement splits into two more clearly defined genres (both under the urban art umbrella), artists in Africa mix the concepts in order to remain relevant in their unique environments.

Graffiti-writers in the Arabic regions in Northern Africa have a strong script style, often referred to as 'calligraffiti'. Notable political revolutions also evoked an outburst of alternative mediums – stencils and wheatpastes, something that is not as common across the continent as artworks painted with aerosol or brush paint. This spurt of activism bolstered the urban art scene across the region and nowadays one can find a growing spectrum of large-scale murals. The themes expressed in these powerful pieces aim to enrich the social structure, teaching others about graffiti's positive nature and how it can empower and uplift society.

Festivals and events play an integral role across the continent, with more transnational gatherings at play each year, bringing artists together. Initiatives such as Festigraff, Effet Graff, Murais da Leba, JIDAR – Toiles de Rue, Graff Up Festi and Afri-Cans Street Art Festival are advancing graffiti's footprint and birthing new generations of artists while also considering their direct environments and the people who exist there. In Eastern and Central Africa, artists tackle social issues and exhibit their cultural background, incorporating African motifs such as masks. Festivals are becoming more prominent in the calendar year and many artists dedicate themselves to these platforms as a beacon of change. Despite the high cost and lack of quality spray paint in many parts of the continent, creative solutions are found to keep up productivity, and the movement is progressing faster with a rising number of active artists and increasing demand for work from corporate businesses and commercial events. There is a greater familiarity with work and a visible shift in what is possible. African graffiti artists are reinventing the process, constructing a solid foundation for the future and garnering wider acceptance. A once uneconomical hobby now

Opposite, clockwise from top left
La Main Du Peuple. 'Antidiotique', Taghit, Algeria, 2018

Evan Sohun. 'The Gate', Port Louis, Mauritius, 2019

Grocco. 'Karakayn', Mohammedia, Morocco, 2019

Kouka (France/Congo), Barkinado Bocoum. The Play Wall (2nd edn), Dakar, Senegal, 2019

r1. 'Hidden Trophy', artwork formed with 100 chevron signs to create a hidden mandala of a buffalo, Johannesburg, South Africa, 2015

Following spread
Ammar Abo Bakr. Cairo, Egypt, 2013

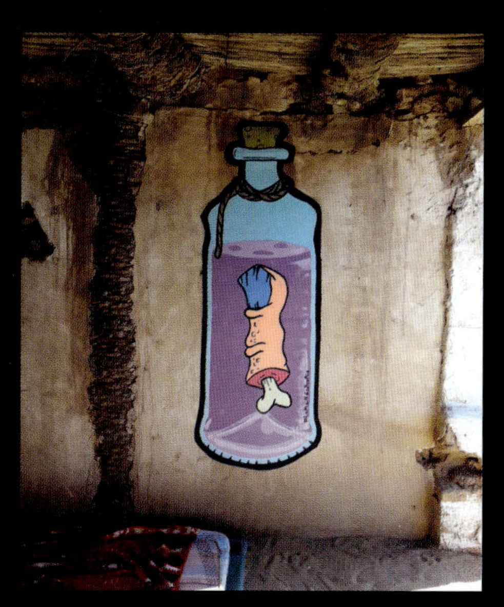
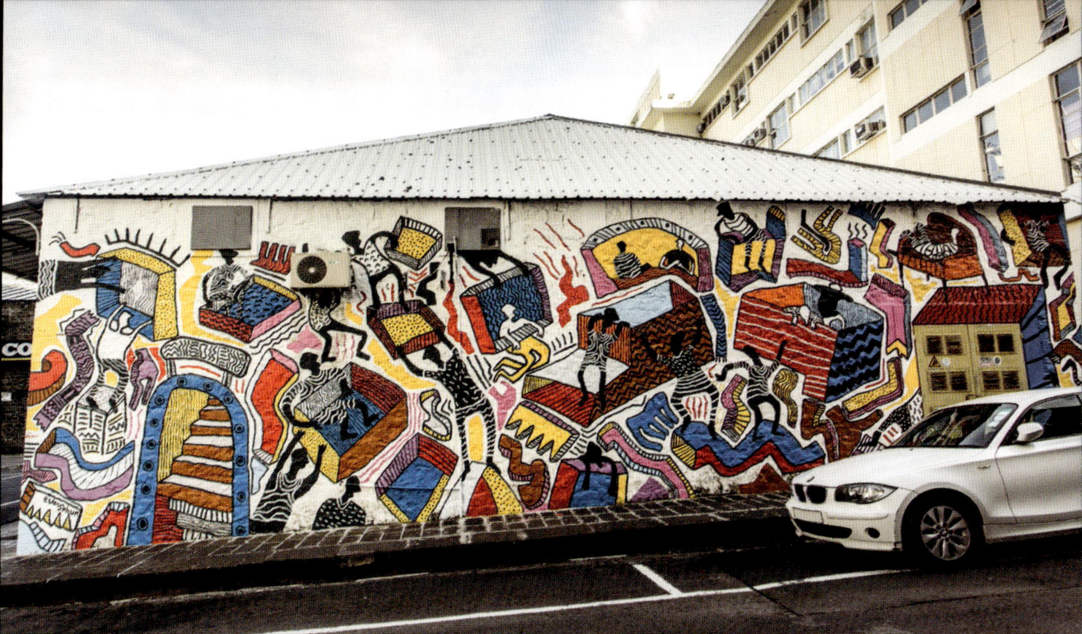
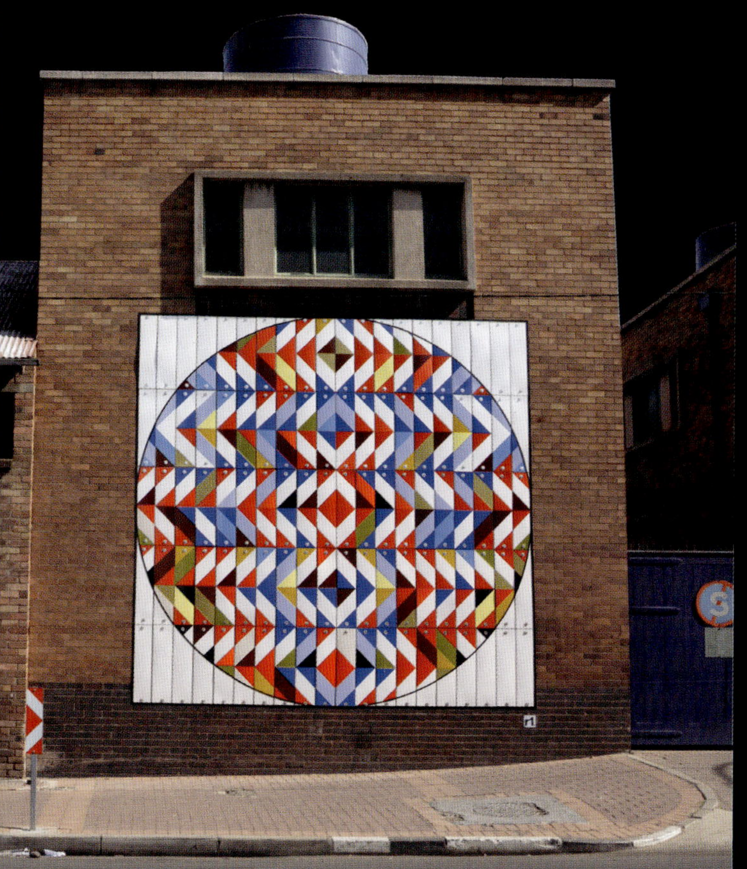
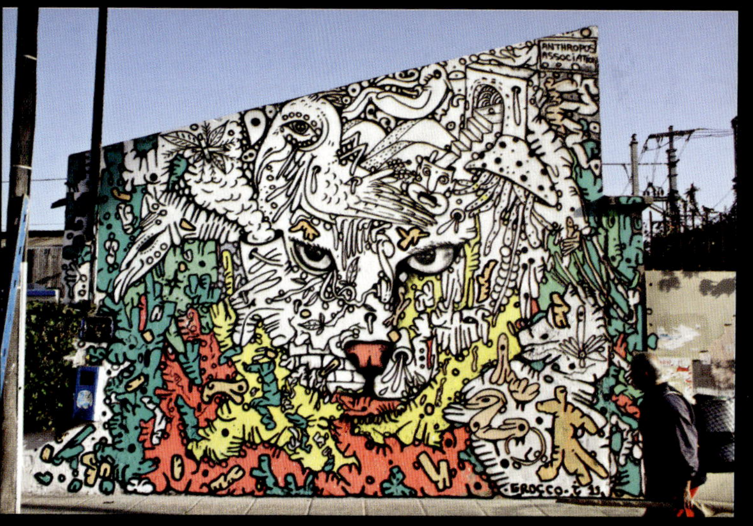

ANTHROPS ASSOCIATION
CROCCO

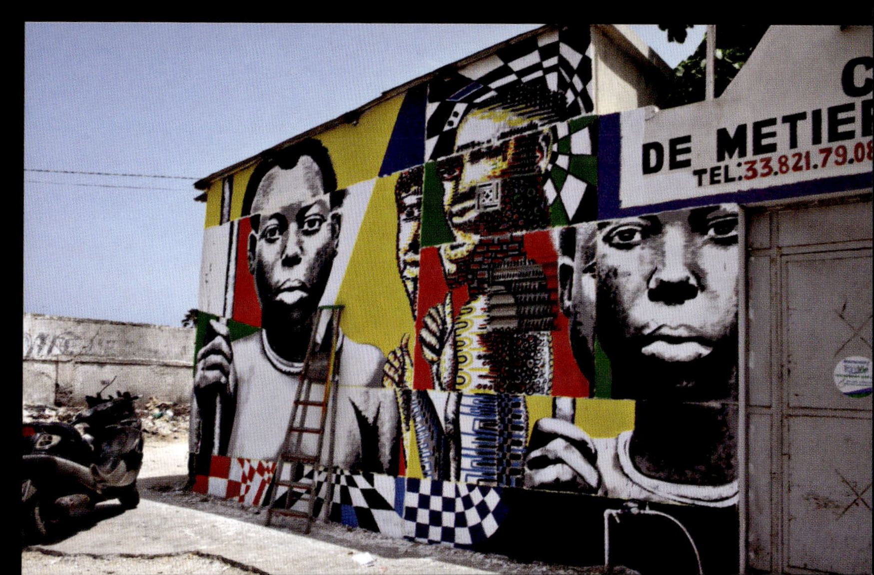

DE METIER
TEL:33.821.79.08

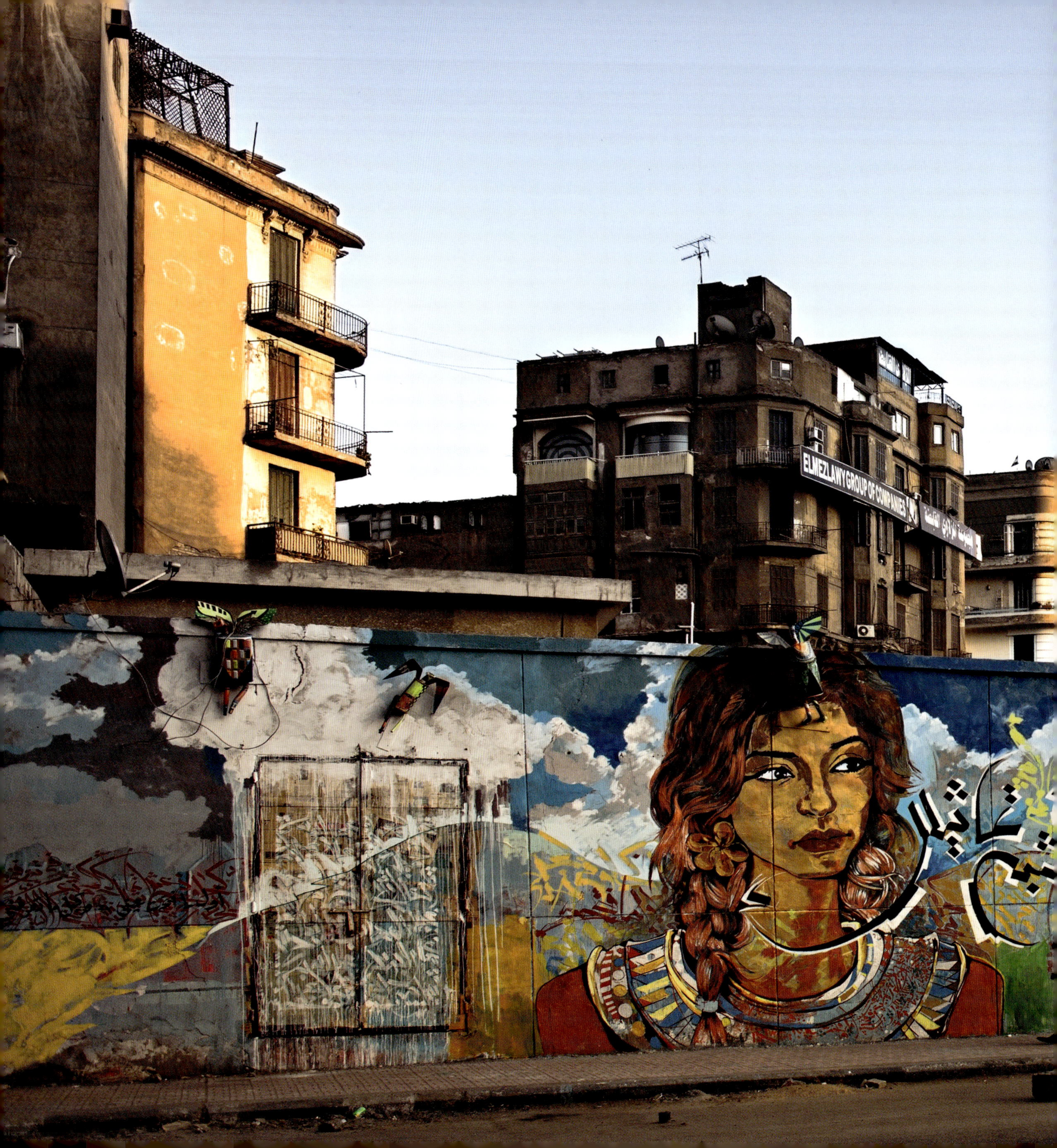

ELMEZLAWY GROUP OF COMPANIES

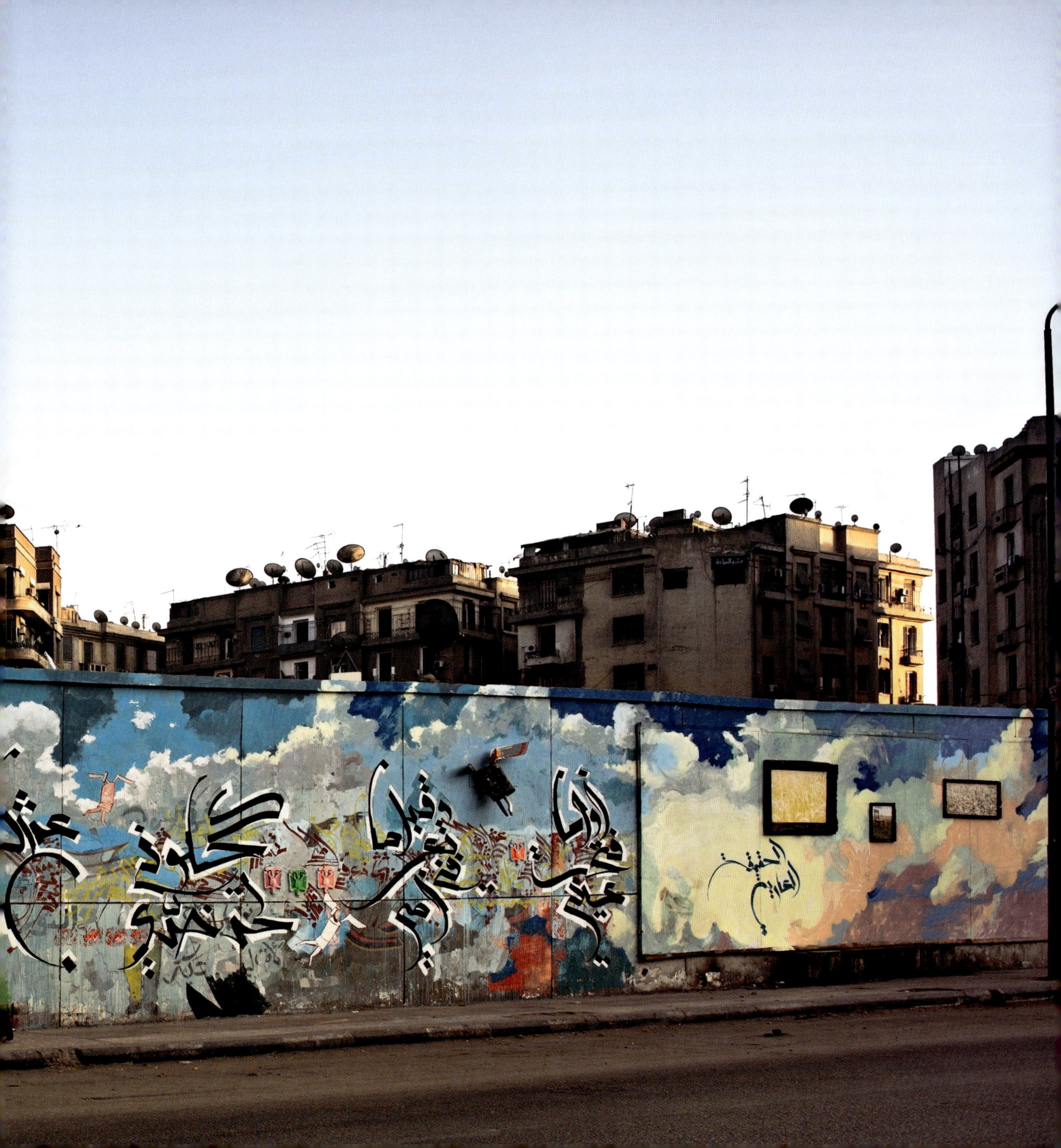

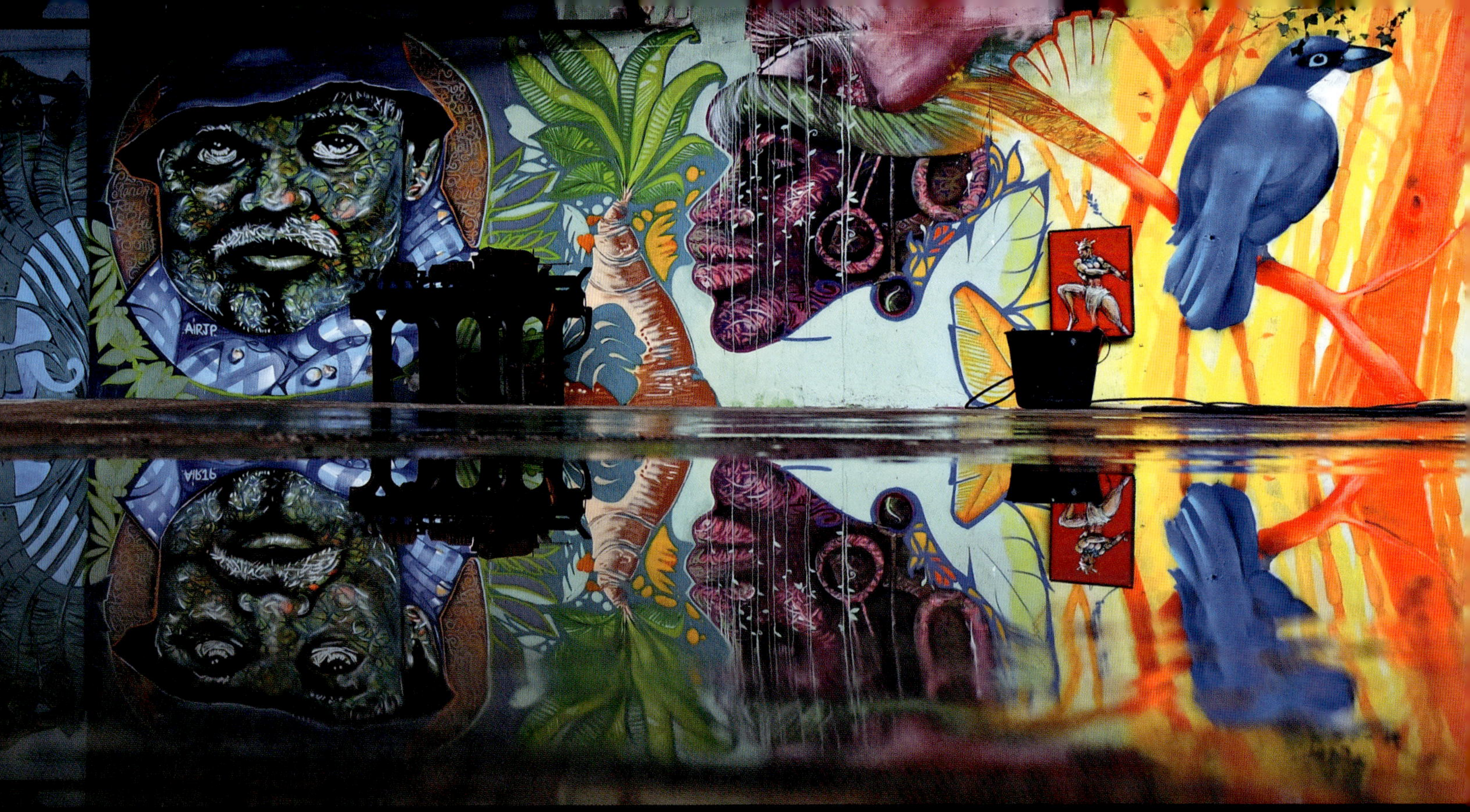

has value and substance. Raw talent is being unlocked through workshops and other outlets, and more work exists on the street as inspiration for newcomers.

Urbanization is a driving force and graffiti is usually limited to major metropolises, but South African artists are fostering dialogues in the broader vicinity, as well as in more rural areas, to showcase the importance of art through outreach programmes as an educational tool. Foreign artists also contribute directly to the expansion of graffiti in Africa every time they visit or traverse the continent for personal or commissioned projects. Locals are able to learn techniques as they witness international dexterity first-hand. African graffiti is forging its own imprint and formulating its own string of successful endeavours to compete with top street art destinations.

Street Art Africa celebrates the continent's burgeoning graffiti arena, shining light on the talented African artists who deserve to be globally recognized. The book is a window on the subject, recording its expansion and significance and, most importantly, its ensuing direction. Africa is a leader in art, fashion, music and science, rapidly growing into a powerhouse – an unfamiliar voice in an ever-changing world, a medley of inspiration: the new vanguard. Transcending the constraints deriving from the distresses of the continent's colonial history, artists from assorted backgrounds are free-spirited and imaginative, incorporating

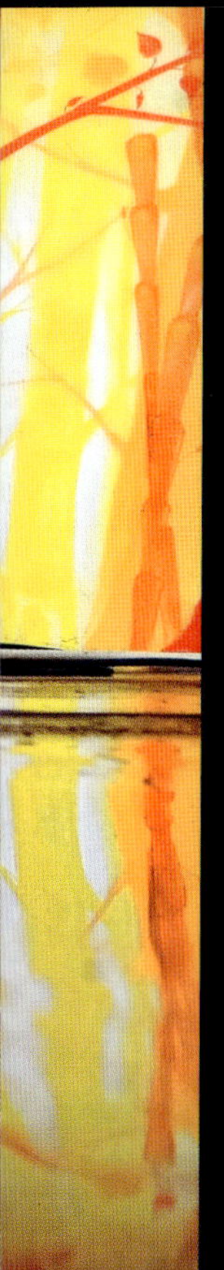

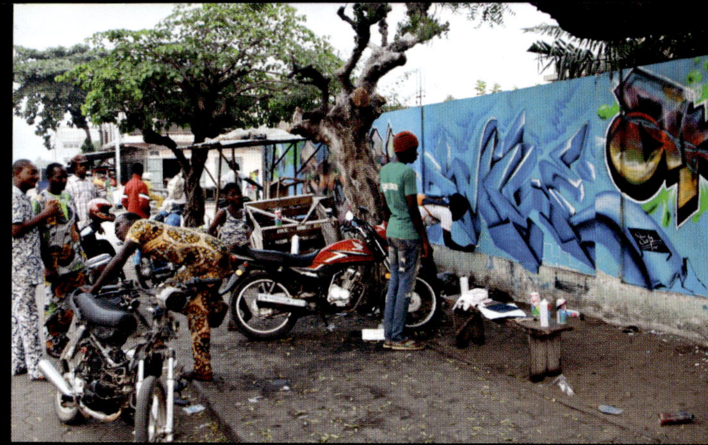

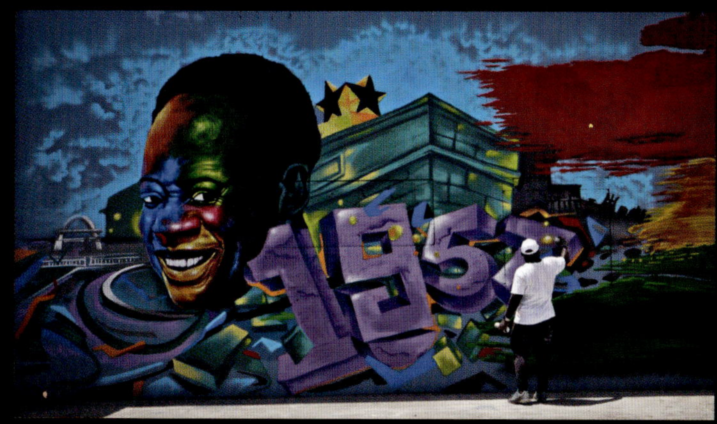

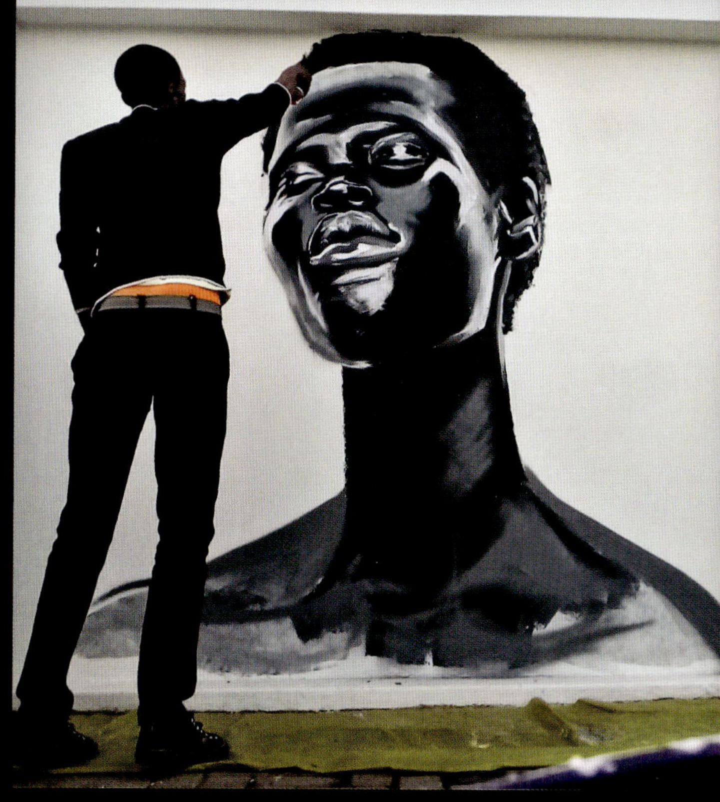

intrinsic values and adding African aesthetics into the melting pot. The landscape, natural resources, wildlife, beliefs and societies are unlike those found anywhere else in the world, and wide-ranging artworks reveal this.

By connecting with thousands of individuals in the world of African graffiti and street art, from artists and photographers to event organizers, project directors, fan pages and friends, no stone has been left unturned in researching this book. Delivering a retrospective that highlights key developments, the content has been curated to reflect the spirit of the African urban art universe and focus on prominent artists across all regions, with some sharing their unique perspectives.

Street art and graffiti continue to expand organically, both universally and multiculturally. As a new wave of contemporary muralism permeates the

Top left
SMI, Bandi (Switzerland), Mr Stone, Akira (Germany). Cotonou, Benin, 2015

Bottom left
Moh Awudu. Accra, Ghana, 2018

Above
Khwezi. Gaborone, Botswana, 2019

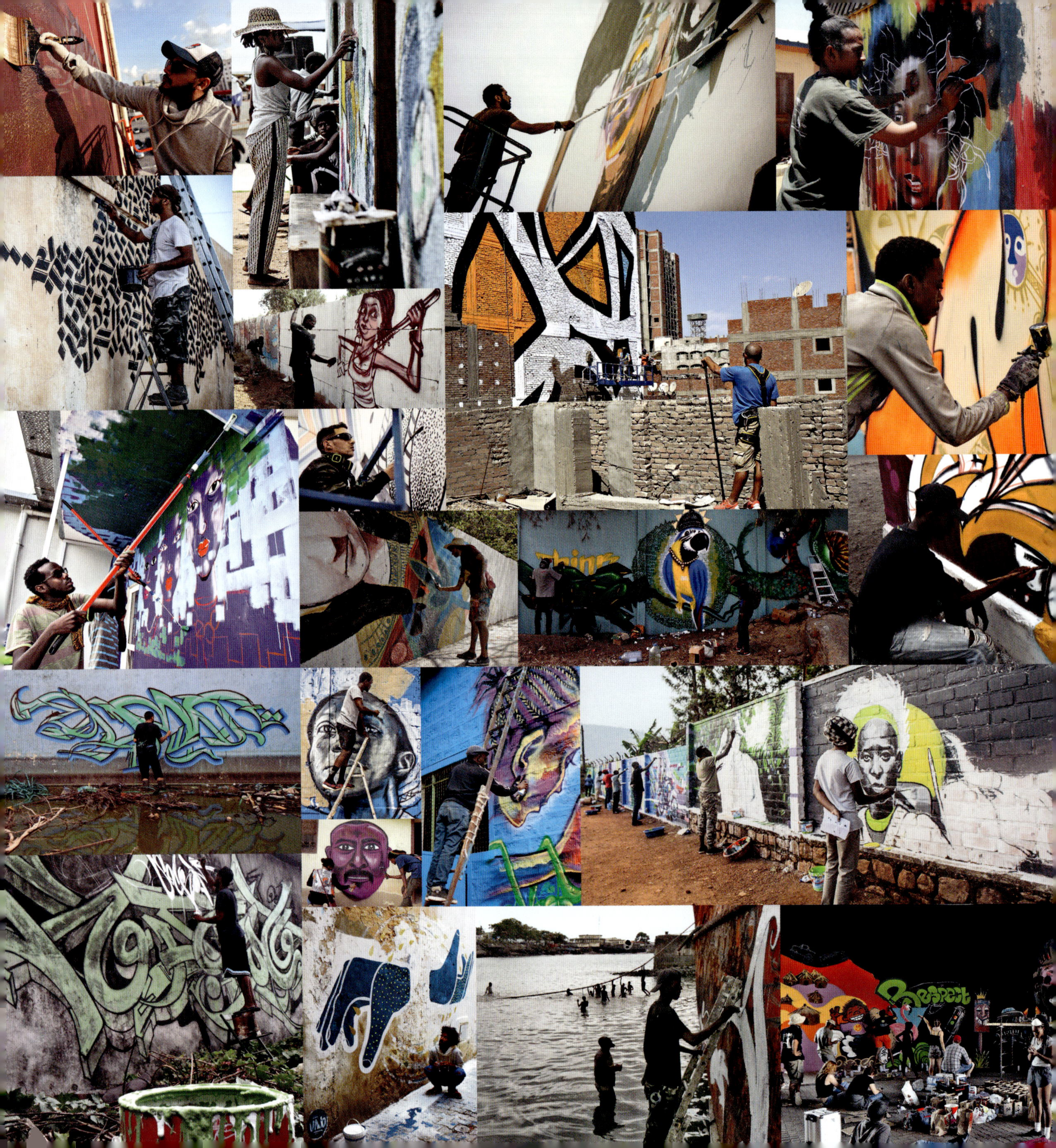

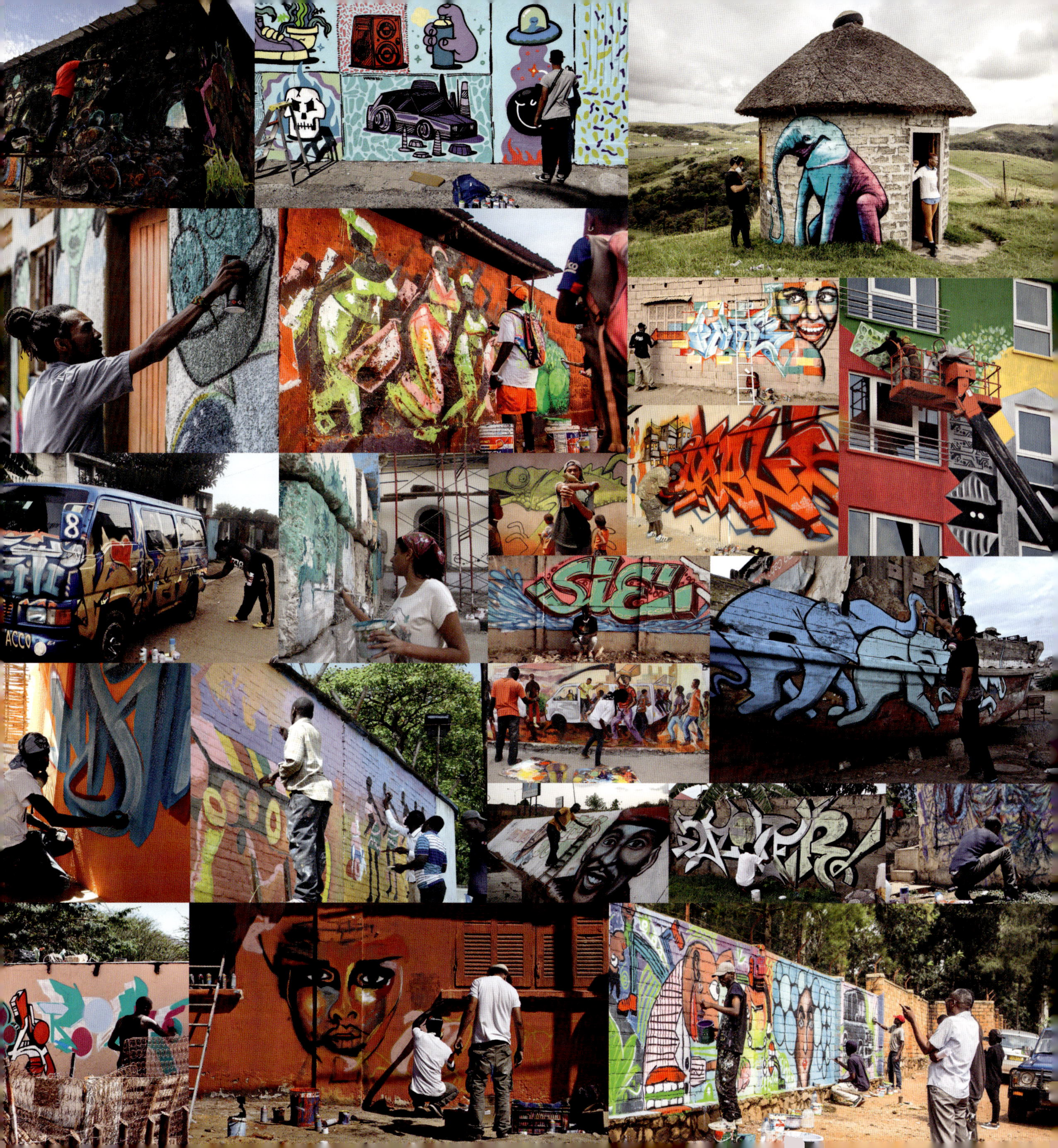

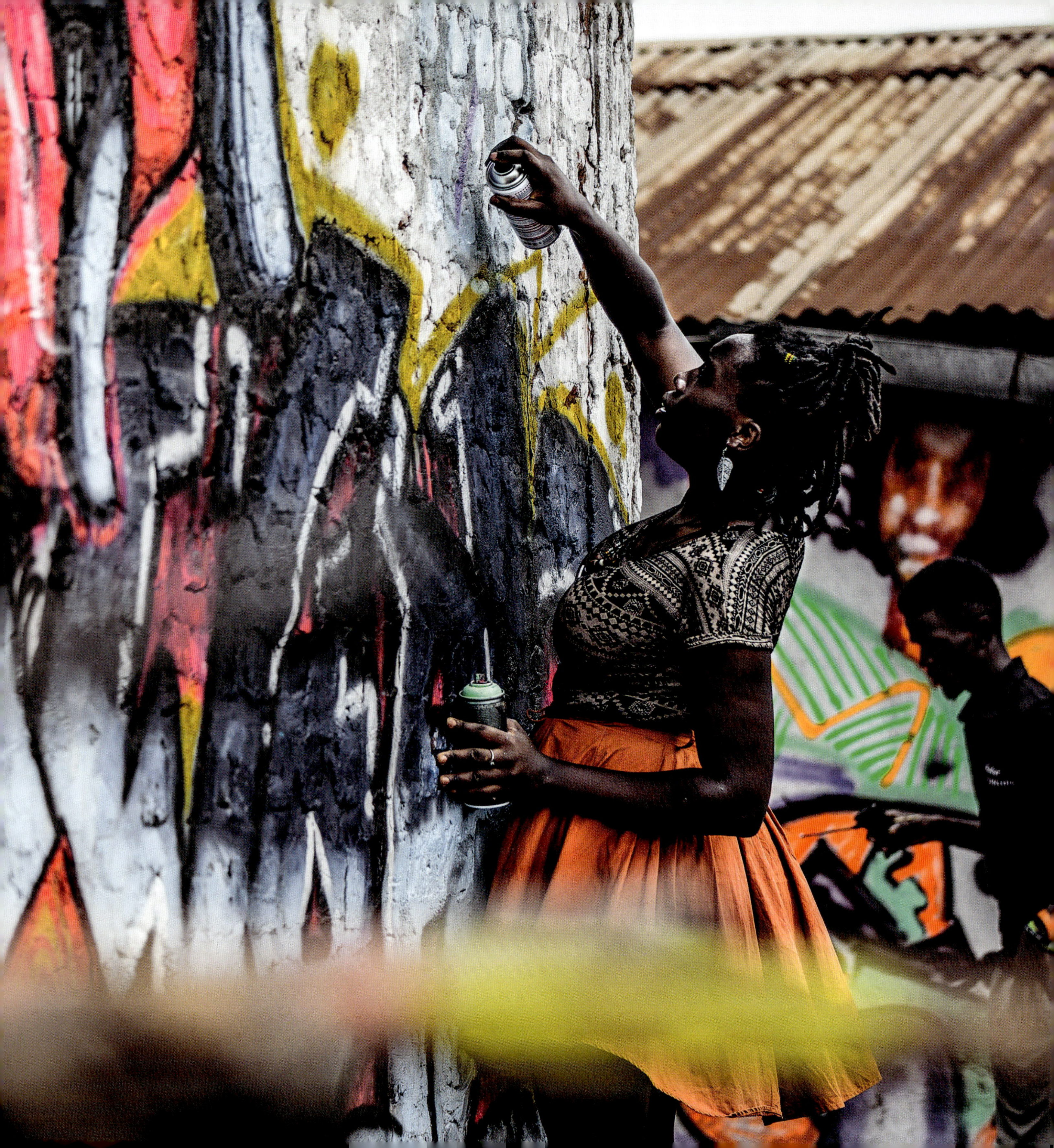

EASTERN AFRICA

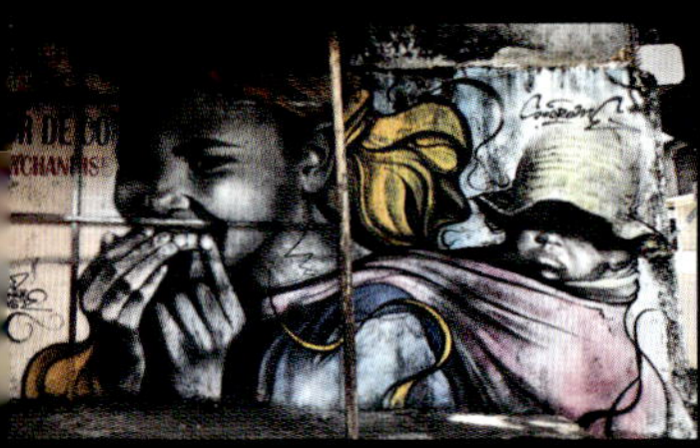
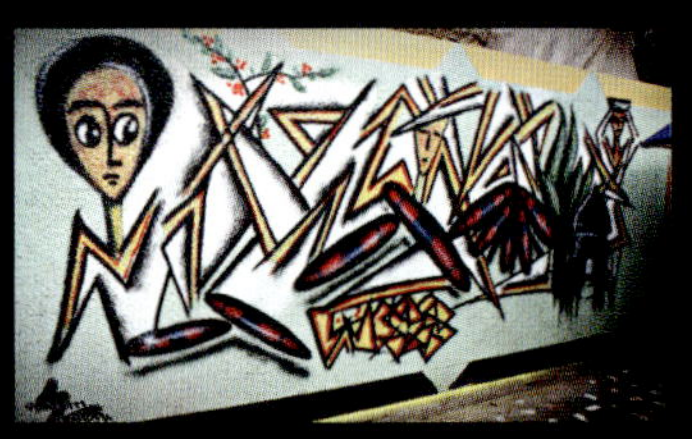
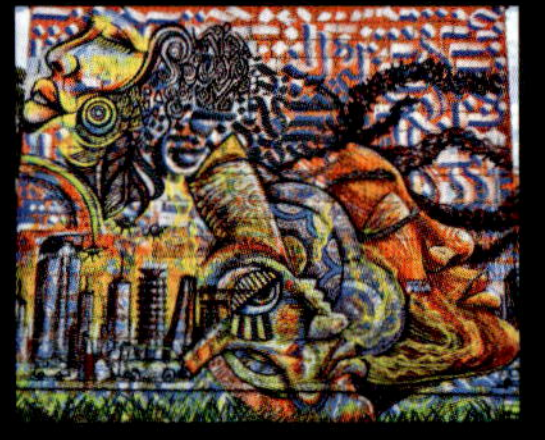
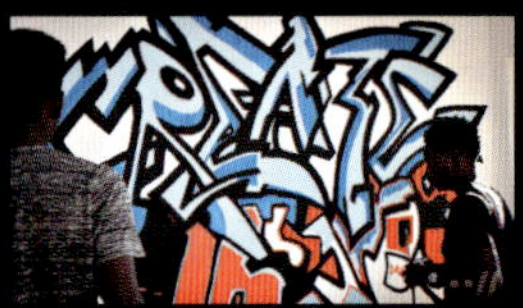
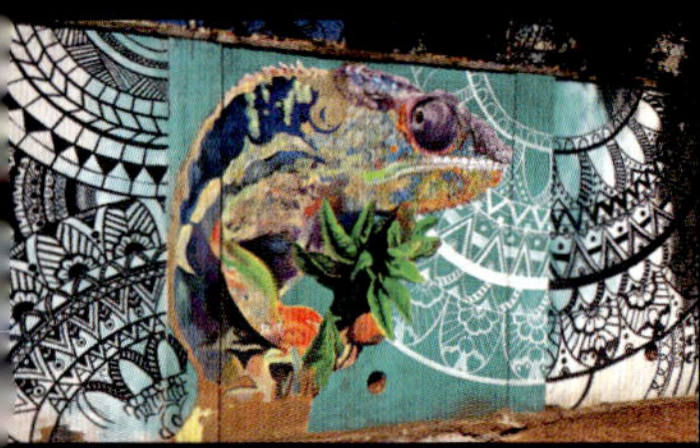
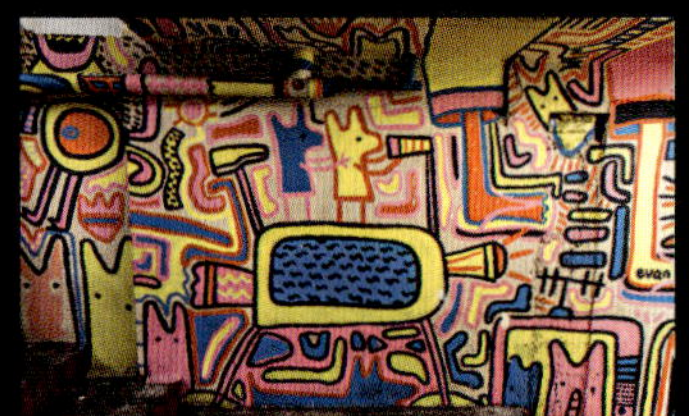

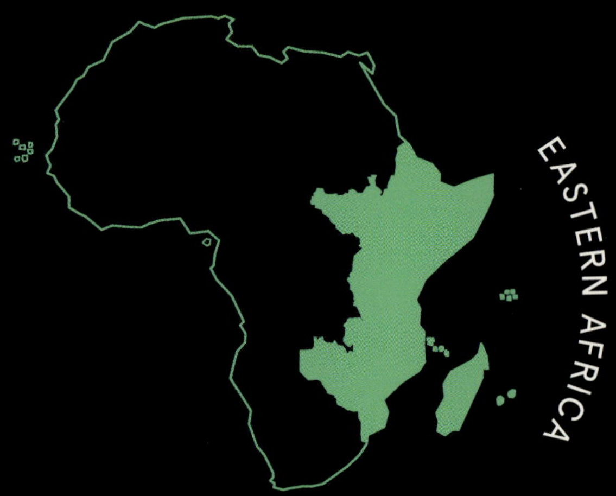

Festivals

❶ **Afri-Cans Street Art Festival**
pp. 56–59

❷ **Stritarty** p. 67

❸ **Porlwi** p. 68

❹ **Festival d'Art Urbain** pp. 70–71

Projects

① **WaPi** pp. 28, 45

② **Kurema Kureba Kwiga** pp. 34, 76

③ **Mother Tongue Colours** p. 38

④ **Taninjanaka** p. 66

Page 24
Chela. Afri-Cans Festival (2nd edn), Kampala, Uganda, 2018

Left, from top
Socrome. Moroni, Comoros, 2018

Behulum. 'Rokobote', Yirga Alem, Ethiopia, 2014

Swift9, BSQ Crew: Thufu-B, Msaleh, Kaymist4. Nairobi, Kenya, 2018

Zaluso Arts. Lilongwe, Malawi, 2018

RinaArt, Naty Kaly. Antananarivo, Madagascar, 2016

Evan Sohun. 'Manghalkan', Curepipe, Mauritius, 2017

Opposite, from top
Wise Two, Fred Kagame, JMV Munezero, Muntu 621, Crista Uwase, Jean Baptiste Rukundo, Djamal Ntagara, Shadrack Kayiranga, Dolph Kayitannkore, Ben Rusagara, Kevin Gahima. 'The HAPPI Generation', a project by Kurema Kureba Kwiga, Kigali, Rwanda, 2015

Mrock. Tofo, Mozambique, 2013

Wachata Crew. 'Equality', Dar es Salaam, Tanzania, 2019

Hatimax256. Kampala, Uganda, 2018

Lo, Take. Lusaka, Zambia, 2019

Kause263, Lotus. Bulawayo, Zimbabwe, 2015

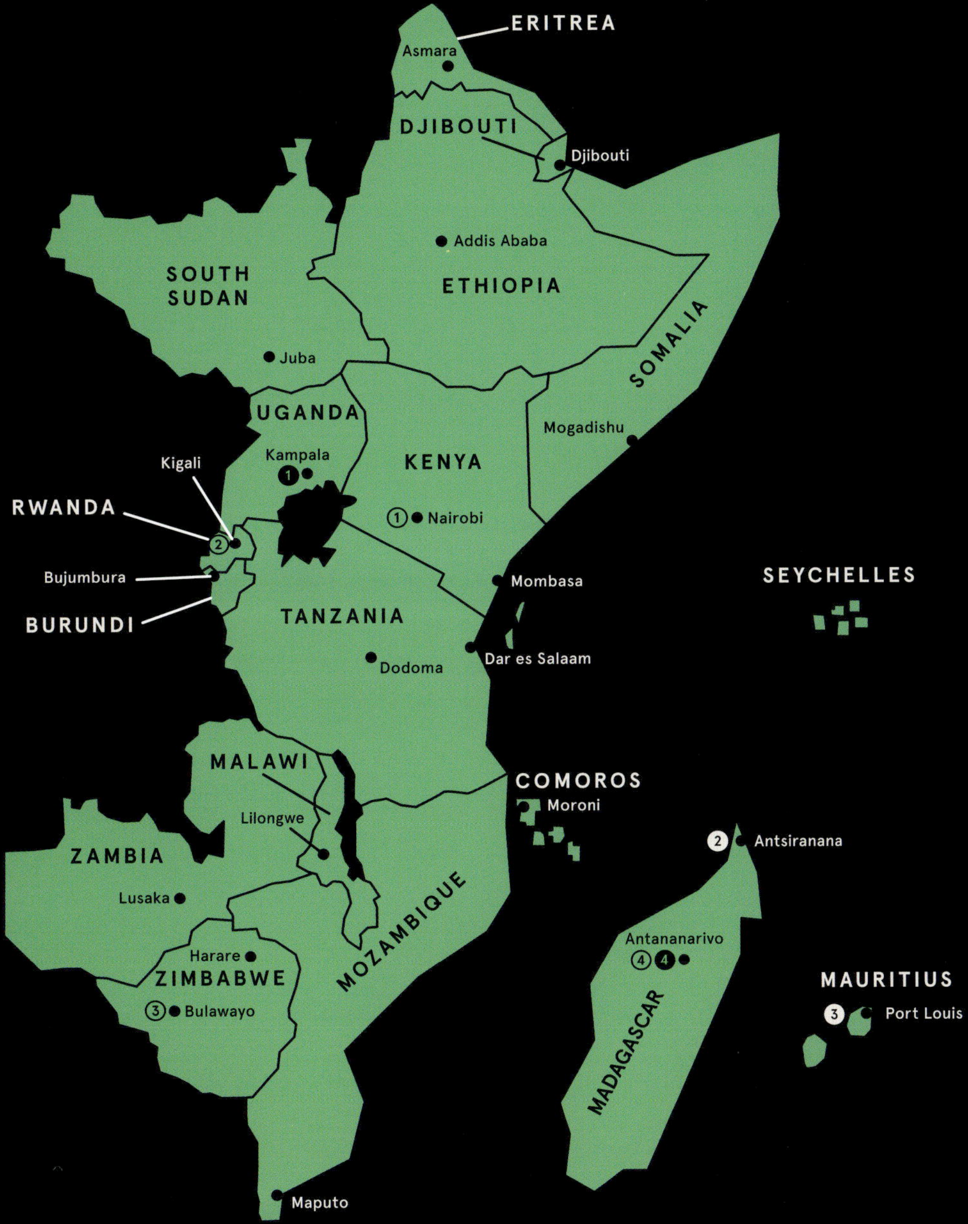

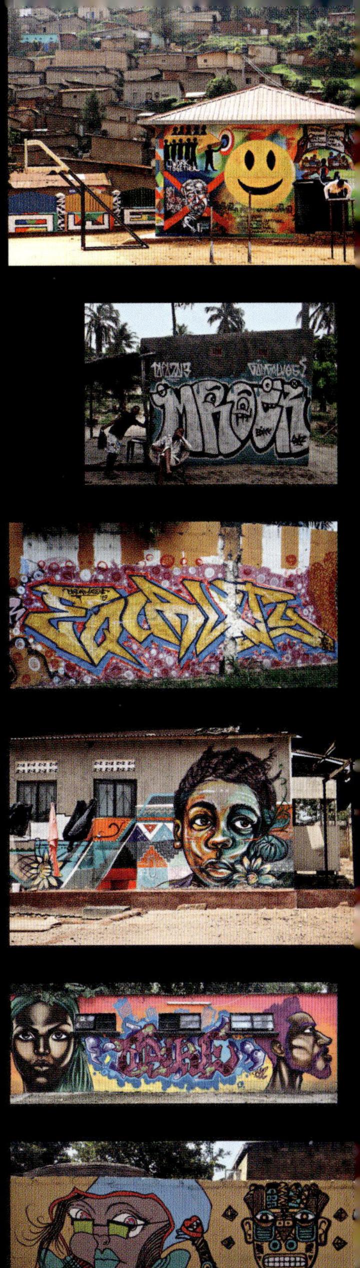

ERITREA
Asmara
DJIBOUTI
Djibouti
Addis Ababa
ETHIOPIA
SOUTH
SUDAN
SOMALIA
Juba
UGANDA
Mogadishu
Kampala
Kigali
KENYA
RWANDA
Nairobi
Bujumbura
SEYCHELLES
BURUNDI
Mombasa
TANZANIA
Dar es Salaam
Dodoma
MALAWI
COMOROS
Moroni
Antsiranana
Lilongwe
ZAMBIA
Antananarivo
Lusaka
MAURITIUS
Harare
MOZAMBIQUE
ZIMBABWE
Bulawayo
MADAGASCAR
Port Louis
Maputo

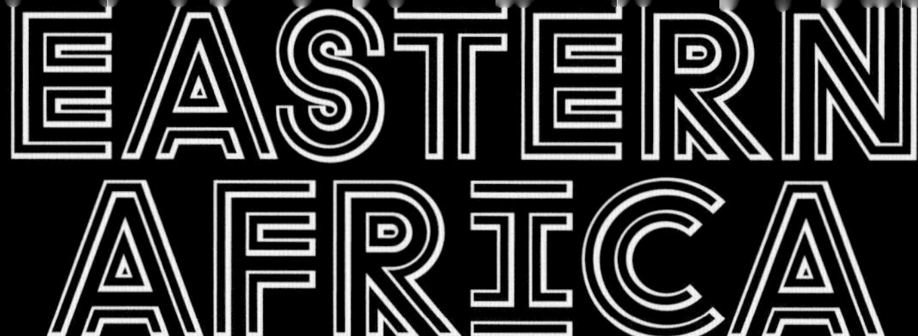

Eastern Africa, home to various indigenous tribes and a large concentration of wildlife, including the celebrated Masai Mara National Reserve and the Serengeti National Park, is also a thriving arts and culture hub. Cities are alive with a constant hustle and bustle; colourful matatu buses dart through Nairobi's congested streets in Kenya, while, in Uganda and Rwanda, studios are filled with freshly painted canvases. Artists are hard at work defining their personal styles and creating a look for the future of African street art.

Kenya boasts the most renowned graffiti scene in the region, having existed for more than twenty years. Kenyan artists now travel regularly to Europe, North America and Australia on invitation. However, the stage remains relatively underground and small-scale, with only about thirty active artists in the capital, Nairobi, and the port city of Mombasa. Parochial stigmas exist around the art form, with many murals being defaced, yet art in public is powerful and serves its purpose. In shanty towns, such as Kibera, graffiti is always welcomed and artists donate their time and skills to bring colour to the community. Themes in the artworks address education, cleanliness, peace and unity, and create a more vibrant atmosphere.

Many first-generation Kenyan graffiti artists cite the monthly WaPi (Words and Pictures) events of the mid-2000s as a turning point for the culture. Through these get-togethers, artists formed bonds that would last for years, regardless of tribal or political affiliations. Graffiti was relatively new and by painting work legally – with the wall owners' permission instead of 'bombing' – artists were able to advance spray-painting as an art form, and many began to earn a living from it.

WaPi was not limited only to Kenya. The social fixture reached other African countries, such as neighbouring Tanzania, where Mejah Mbuya established WCT (Wachata Crew), Tanzania's first official graffiti crew, in Dar es Salaam in 2007.

Opposite, top to bottom
Bantu.Moja, Swift9. Nairobi, Kenya, 2018

Tak1, Ican, Bantu.Moja, Bankslave, Smok ('Mzalendo'), Shakes ('Umoja'), Detail 7 ('Africa'), Esen ('Rauka'). Jamhuri Jam, Nairobi, Kenya, 2015

Deepsea Studios production by Viktart and Kerosh (assisted by Eileen Tamining, Alvin Mwangi, Mwakisha Makoko, Angela Wambui and Huldah Njeru). Nairobi, Kenya, 2019

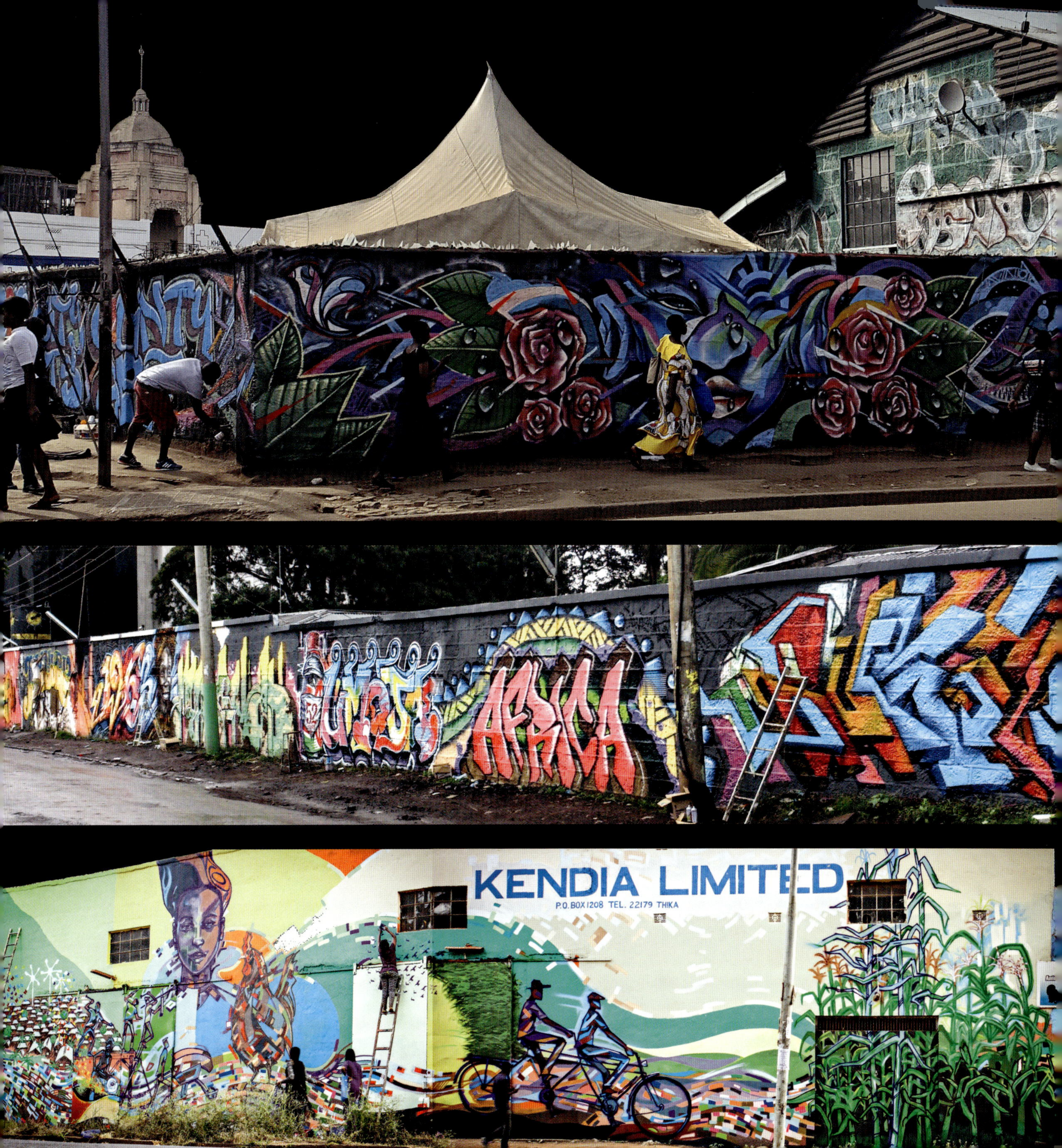

KENDIA LIMITED
P.O. BOX 1208 TEL. 22179 THIKA
AFRICA

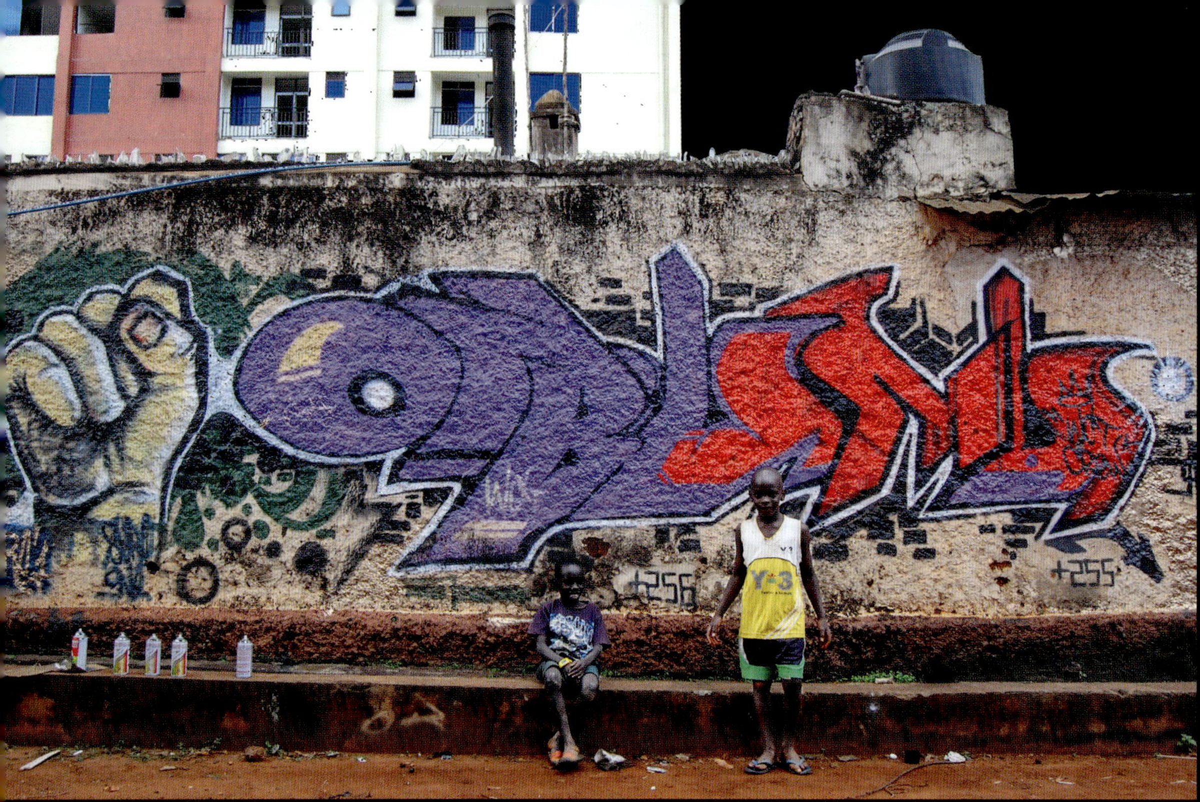

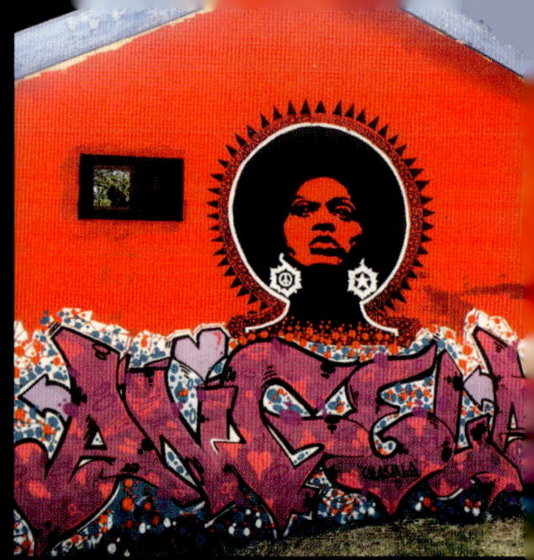

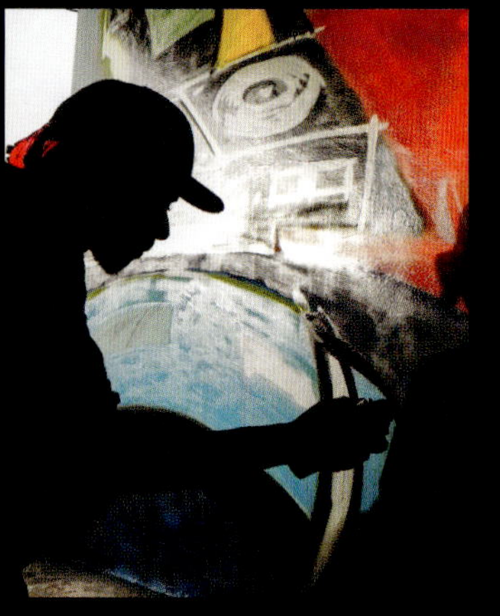

Kala Singa, Local Ism and Maubaka joined later, and at one time there were more than a dozen members, but the difficulty and cost meant that many left. Still Wachata pressed on and validated the movement as demand for graffiti work grew. They also began to host their own workshops, exhibitions and events. Their name is an ode to the country's real graffiti roots: mark-making with charcoal, when throughout the 1970s and 1980s, youths seeking a better life elsewhere would stow away on ships bound for Europe, leaving their name, nickname or message along the way. This charcoal graffiti became known as 'chata', derived from the English word 'charter', with 'Wachata' meaning 'We Graffiti'. Today a new wave of painters has emerged thanks to Wachata's tutelage and long-term presence, although they are not very active. These graffiti artists include Stanfox Def, EWC (East Wallz Crew) and the duo of Sistadada and 3rdeyegoof known as DMT (Doing More Together).

Ethiopia, situated in the Horn of Africa, has just a handful of working street artists – but an interesting take on the format. Residents of the region speak the Ethiopian Semitic language Amharic, which uses the Ge'ez script and is written from left to right. In a way that is reminiscent of the logograms of Chinese and Japanese writing, Ethiopian artists have fused this local language with graphic elements of graffiti, adding a drop shadow to construct their own inherent font system. Behulum Mengistu, aka Woes97, from Awasa (or Hawassa), south of the capital Addis Ababa, was at the forefront of this development. Woes (which translates to 'Words') had been drawing throughout his teenage years and

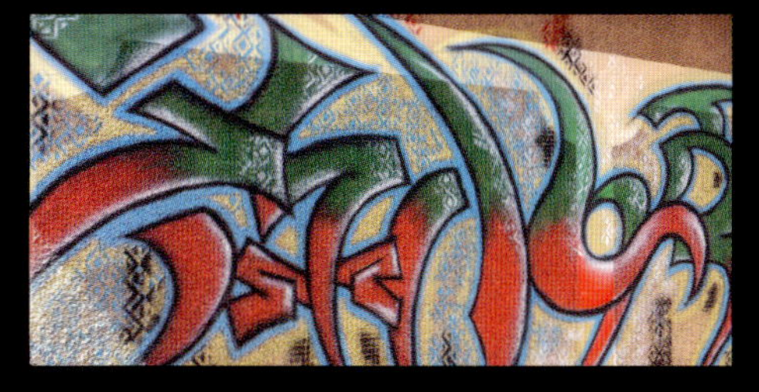

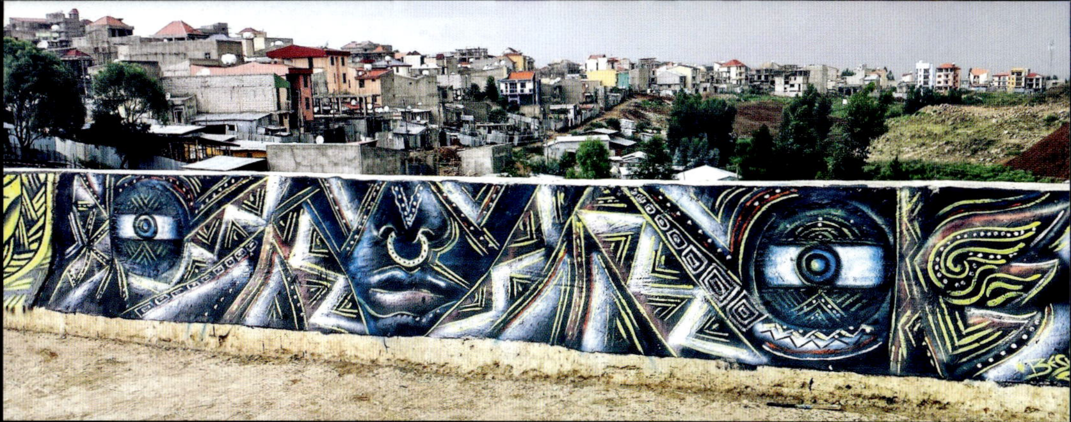

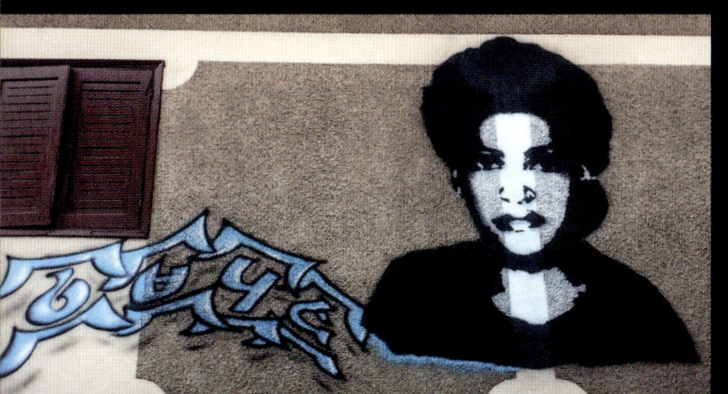

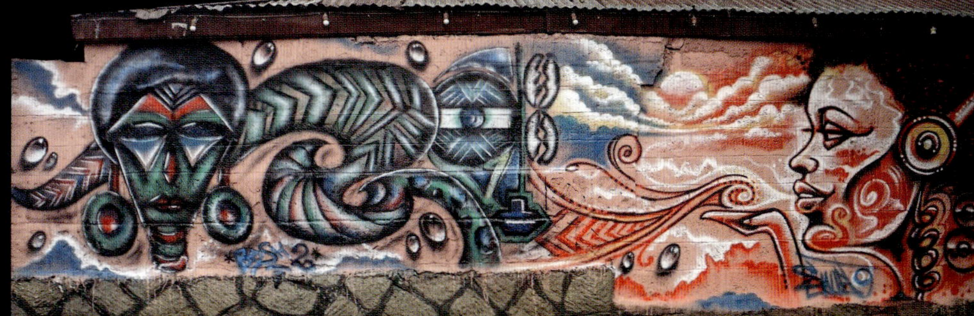

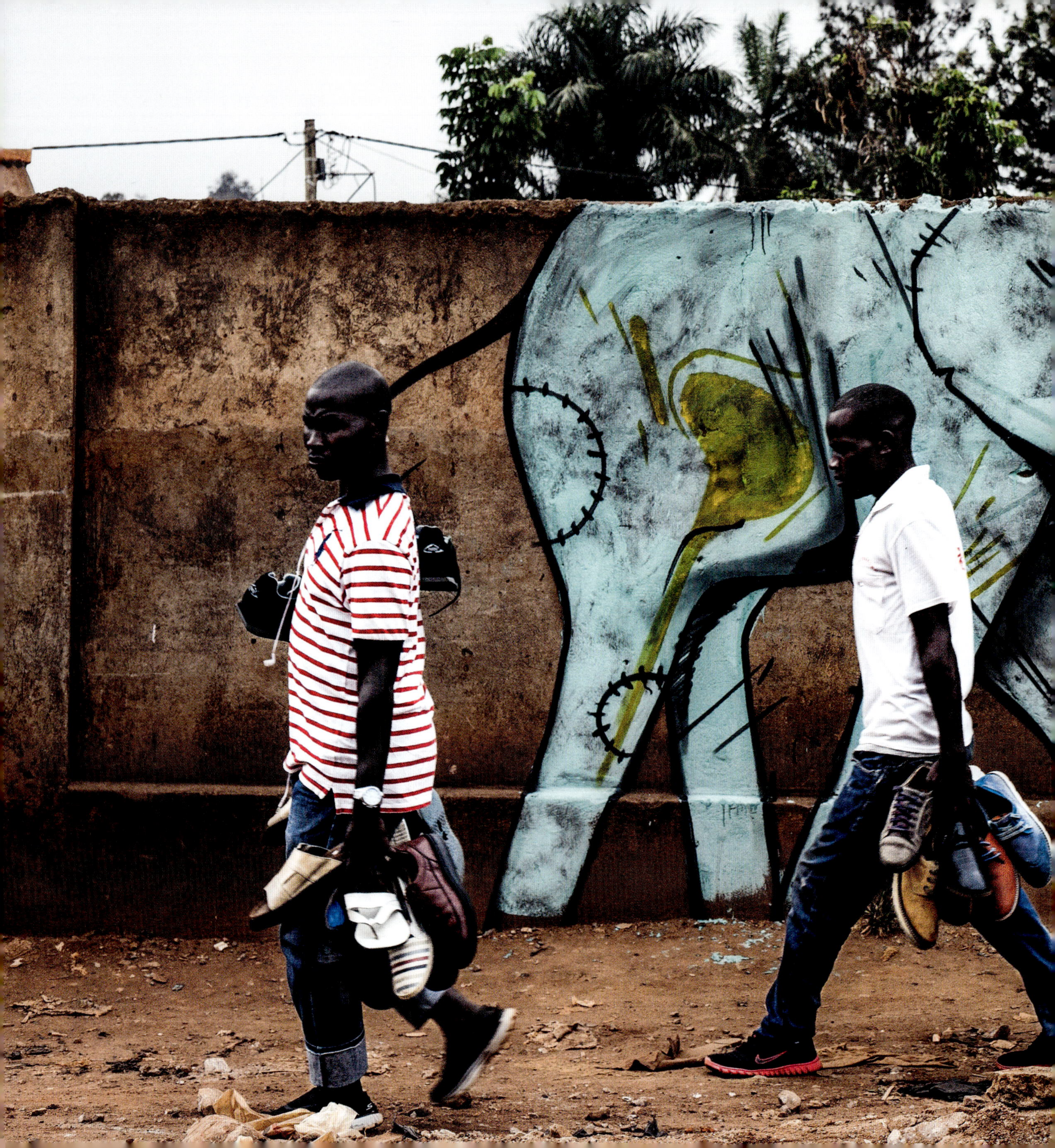

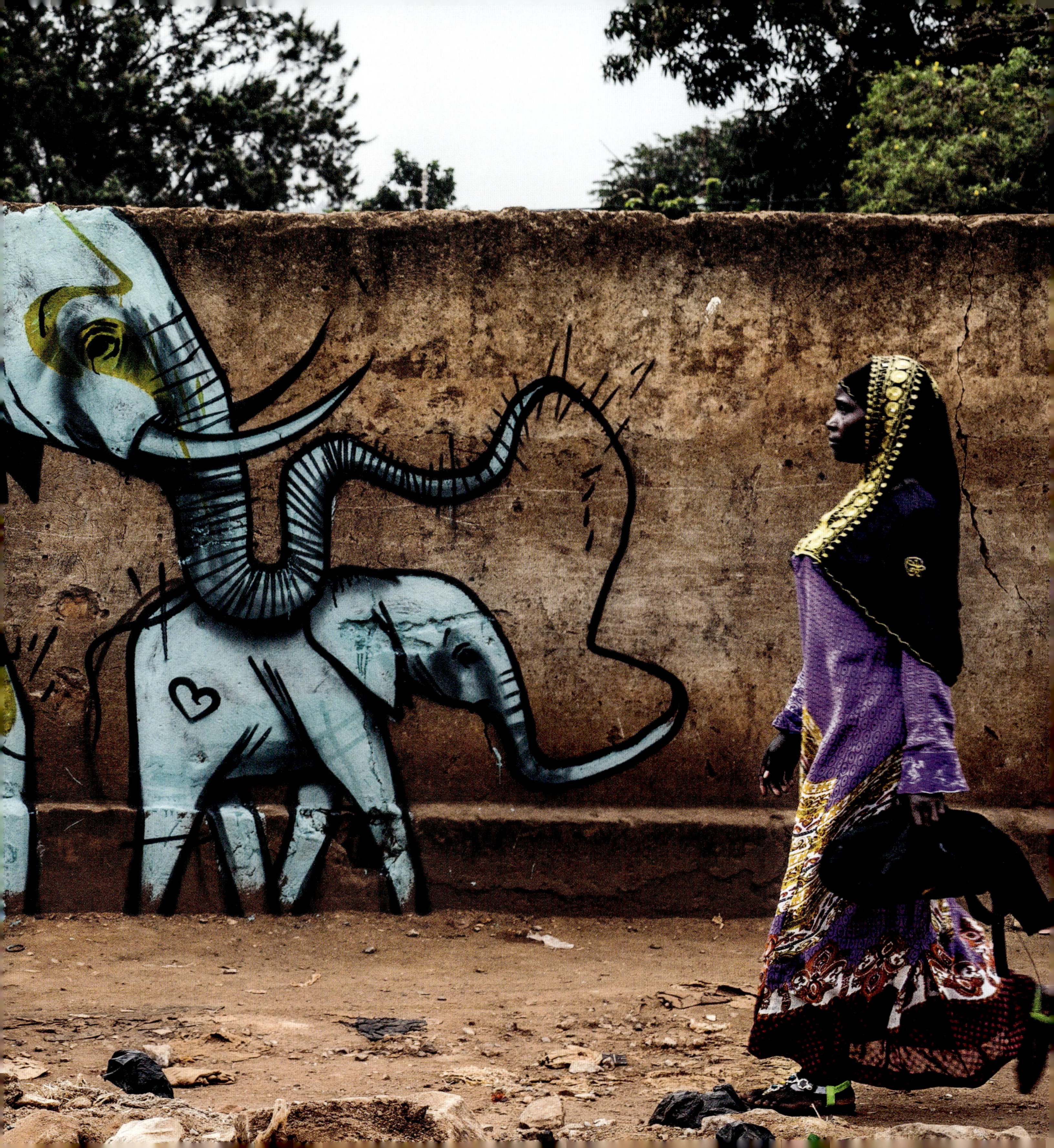

'What makes African graffiti unique is the fact that most graffiti artists explore their personal stories. They involve their cultural backgrounds in their themes and concepts and communicate with people. The visual aspect creates a connection; a deeper contact and understanding.' JOBRAY

Monk256 Crew formed and became a well-known collective of urban artists. Other graffiti artists and fine art painters including Destreet, Hatimax256, Kwiz Era, Hamza Kimera, Rawdney, Doddridge, JK Jaymore and Wamala Art have since appeared and have contributed to the arena. Afri-Cans Street Art Festival was established in 2017 to further strengthen the regional community, while an influx of international artists also plays a positive role in the overall dynamics of the small scene. Many Ugandan artists, such as the accomplished Xenson, have attracted the attention of international galleries and have undertaken successful art residencies in Europe, proving there are no boundaries.

The use of community murals to promote well-being is in full force in Rwanda. Artists often engage with public art projects to bring gallery art to the streets and create a thoroughfare that is vibrant and inspirational for a broader audience. The organization Kurema Kureba Kwiga (meaning 'To Create, To See, To Learn') is leading these activities, nourishing a street art drive that goes beyond the usual hand-painted signage and corporate advertising that exist in the capital city, Kigali. Judith Kaine, founder and director of Kurema Kureba Kwiga, initiated the project in 2013 after she discovered a collective of professional fine artists, including the enthusiastic and talented Ngabonziza Bonfils. Kaine's desire to bring positive visual stimuli to the city's streets, paired with her leadership skills and background in public health, was welcomed by the government. The social enterprise creates site-specific murals, art events and workshops for the benefit of a wholesome community, targeting all districts, while remaining empathetically close to its core values. Topics range from water and sanitation to HIV/AIDS, formal education, women's empowerment and the environment. Through self-generated or commissioned projects, grants or sponsorships, it strives to empower local artists and elevate the population, instilling dignity and an overarching sense of value, bringing colour to a country that is usually stereotyped for its violent history.

Opposite, clockwise from top
Wise Two, Kerosh. Kampala, Uganda, 2017
Hatimax256. Kampala, Uganda, 2018
Xenson. Kampala, Uganda, 2015
Xenson. Jinja, Uganda, 2012

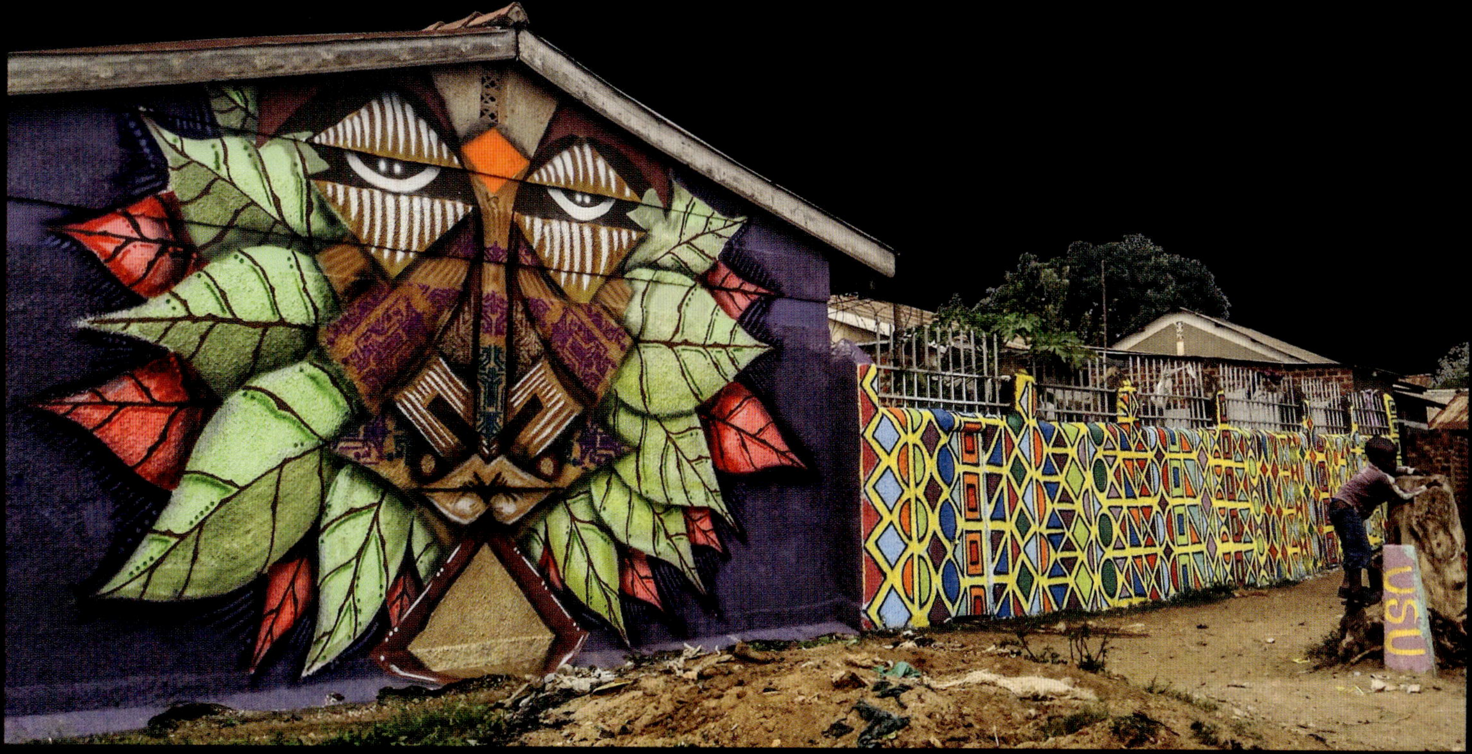

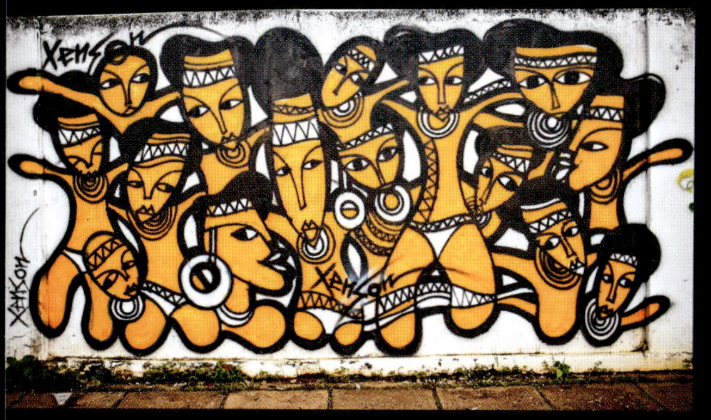
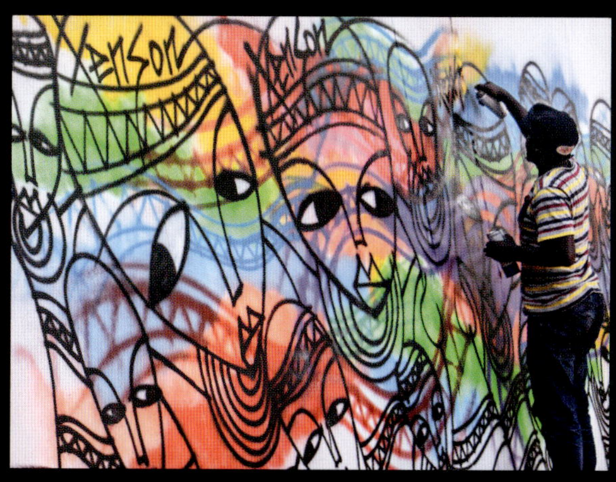
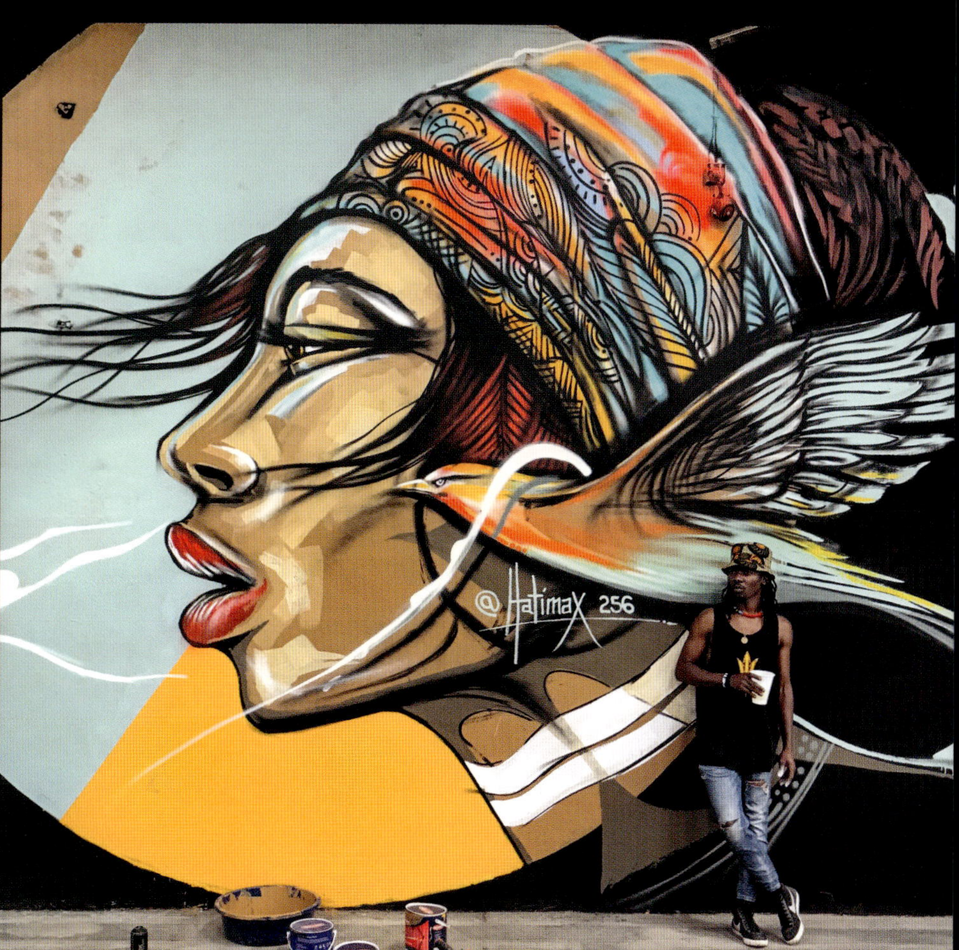

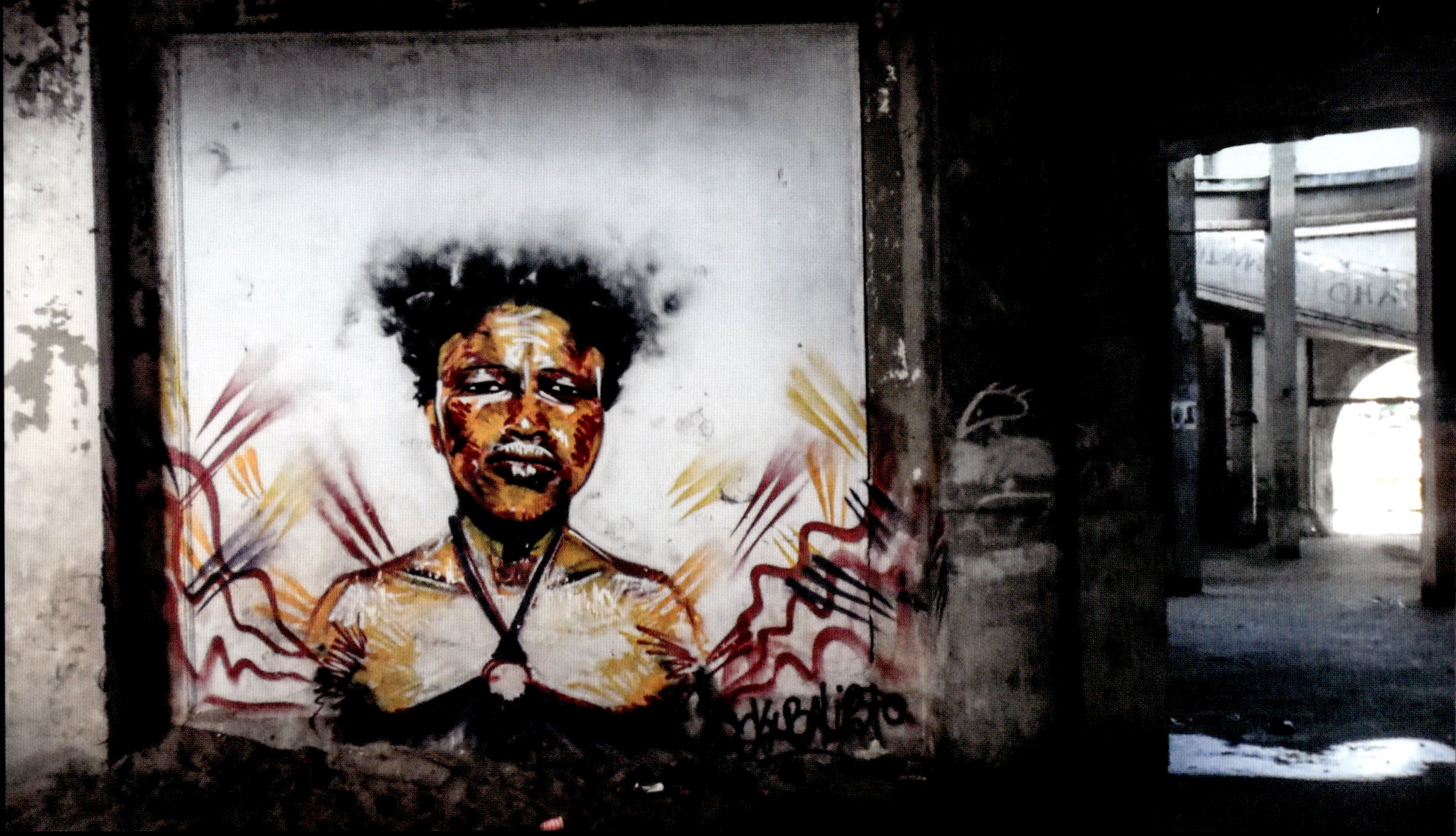

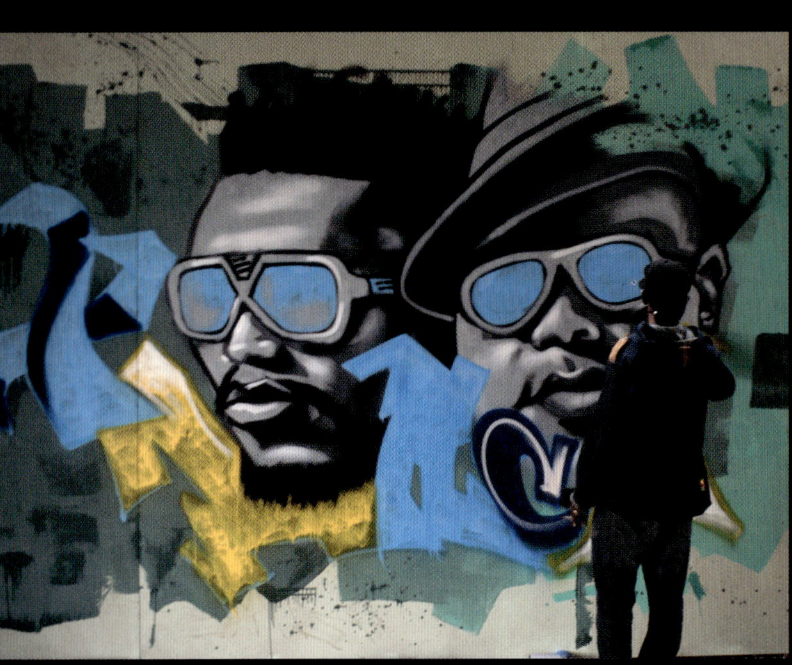

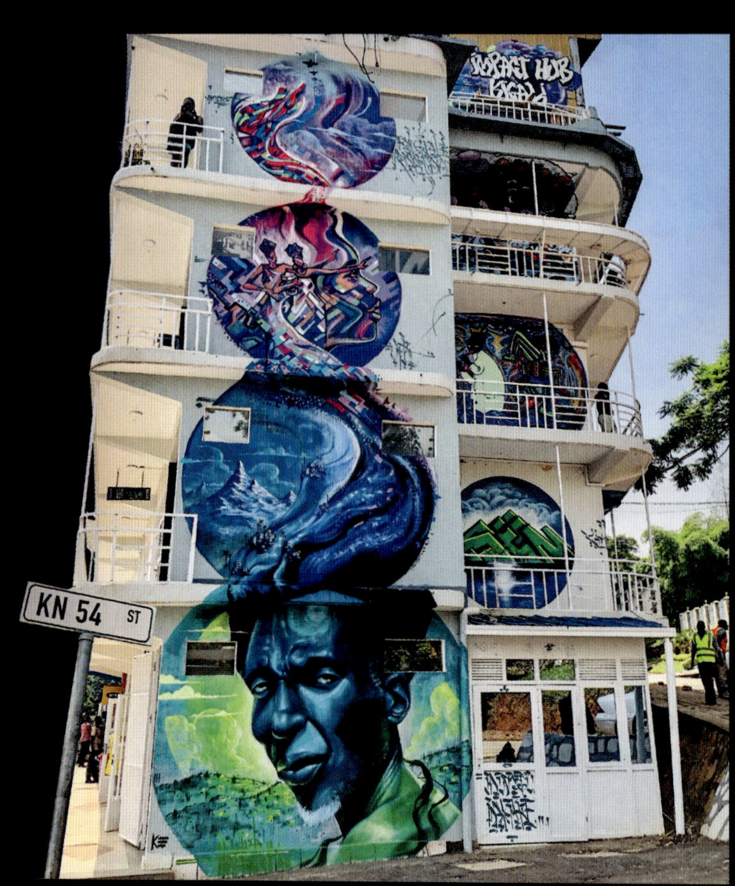
KN 54 ST

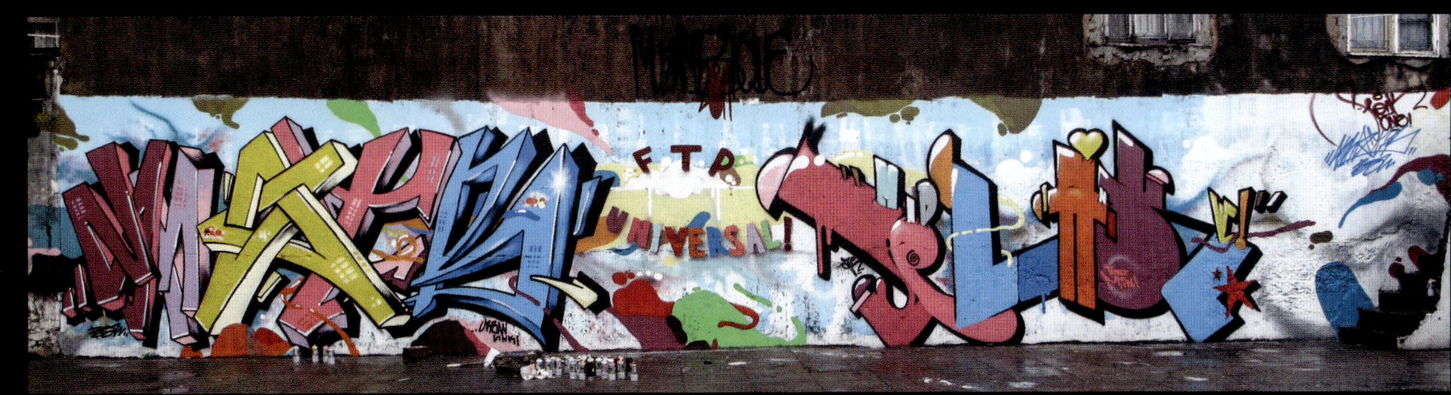

Bound to Kurema Kureba Kwiga's magic wand is a new wave of young artists who are now able to voice their stories on the walls and transform the look and feel of a space. Umuhire Isakari (aka Muntu 621) used the distinct energy that graffiti evokes to take his art further. The self-taught artist is now one of Rwanda's first true street artists, along with fellow muralist and painter Willy Karekezi, who has exhibited his work extensively in Europe. Visiting international artists also accelerate Rwanda's urban arts boom, turning lifeless structures into sites of wonder and emphasizing the general growth in the Land of a Thousand Hills.

Further south, in Zambia, past highlights include a multi-week festival and environmental event by Greenpop that produced a mural about protecting bees with a local artist, Mwamba Chikwemba; and Modzi Arts, founded in 2016, which devotes itself to the cultivation of the country's contemporary art scene. Through its Afro Luso programme, Modzi Arts aims to spark a dialogue within the SADC (Southern African Development Community) and has worked with Zambian graffiti artists Take and Lo, as well as Jarell Thompson and Chibale Kapumpa (aka CrossOver). Take is a full-time artist who is dubbed Zambia's graffiti pioneer; graffiti was nonexistent in the capital, Lusaka, but a trip to Johannesburg, South Africa, consolidated his interest. Take often collaborates with Lo, a comic artist who has invested time in developing his street art persona since 2016 because it is more visible to the public. As both follow their journeys of discovery, they explore styles, techniques and materials, becoming paragons in the process.

Traditional art has always had a place in Africa. In Malawi one can find urban centres that cater for art education and business opportunities, such as the growing tourist market. Institutions and collectives like Zaluso Arts, 7 Seals Arts and Nthililo Studios Art Gallery and School (NSAGAS) now dip their creative

Opposite, clockwise from top
Skubalisto. The Bridge Tour, Beira, Mozambique, 2014

Viktart, Muntu 621, Monk.E (Canada), with Ngabonziza Bonfils, Dolph Kayitannkore, Brave Tangz, Isaac Iirumva, Shingiro Ntigurirwa and Pruzz. GaraGara250 project, Kigali, Rwanda, 2018

Shot B. Maputo, Mozambique, *c.* 2013

Above
Shot B, Spank One (Sweden/ Spain). First international collaboration in Mozambique using a popular global brand of spray paint. Maputo, Mozambique, 2011

Most communities in Europe and America are saturated with graffiti and the negative connotations that precede it, but in Africa we as artists have the unique opportunity to mould perceptions of how it will be initially perceived. We can use graffiti as a positive tool to uplift communities.' TAKE

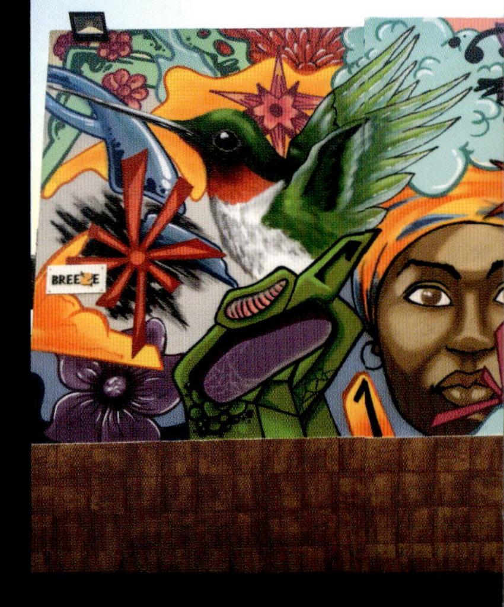

Opposite, top
Take, Lo. Lusaka, Zambia, 2019

Opposite, bottom left
Kause263, Lotus. Mother Tongue Colours project, Bulawayo, Zimbabwe, 2015

Opposite, bottom right
Lotus. Bulawayo, Zimbabwe, 2015

Following spread
Mozer, Nino, Blue, featuring BM Souljah. 'Colourful People', Stritarty Festival (3rd edn), Antsiranana, Madagascar, 2018

toes into mural projects, producing the few works in the cities of Blantyre and Lilongwe. Njelele Art Station is doing interesting projects in and outside Zimbabwe despite debilitating factors – following years of mismanagement and dictatorship, Zimbabwe was driven into a harrowing state of decline. The cost of bread and fuel skyrocketed, with the price of art supplies also being affected. Nonetheless, visual art still exists in both formal and informal spaces.

While traditional art thrives, the street art scene in Zimbabwe remains paltry, with only a handful of committed artists. Kause263 is a leading graffiti artist and member of TUNE KRU with SUP (Still Using Pressure) and SEH137 (Street Elevated Hieroglyphics). His Mother Tongue Colours project with Lotus in Makokoba Township in Bulawayo was a huge success, as they were inundated with requests to decorate people's houses. Visual artist Tinofireyi Zhou (aka Aero5ol) focuses on fine art, but occasionally explores the medium of urban art as a personal experiment, crafting custom works with stencils on laptops or handbags. Aero5ol and Kause263 are often employed for live events and other projects. The Dutch artist Karski painted some of the only large-scale street art murals in Zimbabwe as part of HIFA (Harare International Festival of the Arts). Over three consecutive editions he collaborated with other international artists, Olivier Schimmel (the Netherlands) in 2010 and 2011, and SatOne (Germany) in 2012.

In neighbouring Mozambique, there are few street pieces; however, Shot B, out of Maputo, is Mozambique's long-standing king of graffiti writing. A household name in the local hip-hop scene, the accomplished graffiti artist and rapper makes his way around the country for commissioned jobs, art exhibitions, live event paintings and workshops. Since the early 2000s, he has exhibited in South Africa and Portugal. Finally, across the Mozambique Channel, in the Indian Ocean, Eastern African graffiti can be found thriving in its own world on a set of islands, including Madagascar, Mauritius and the Comoros.

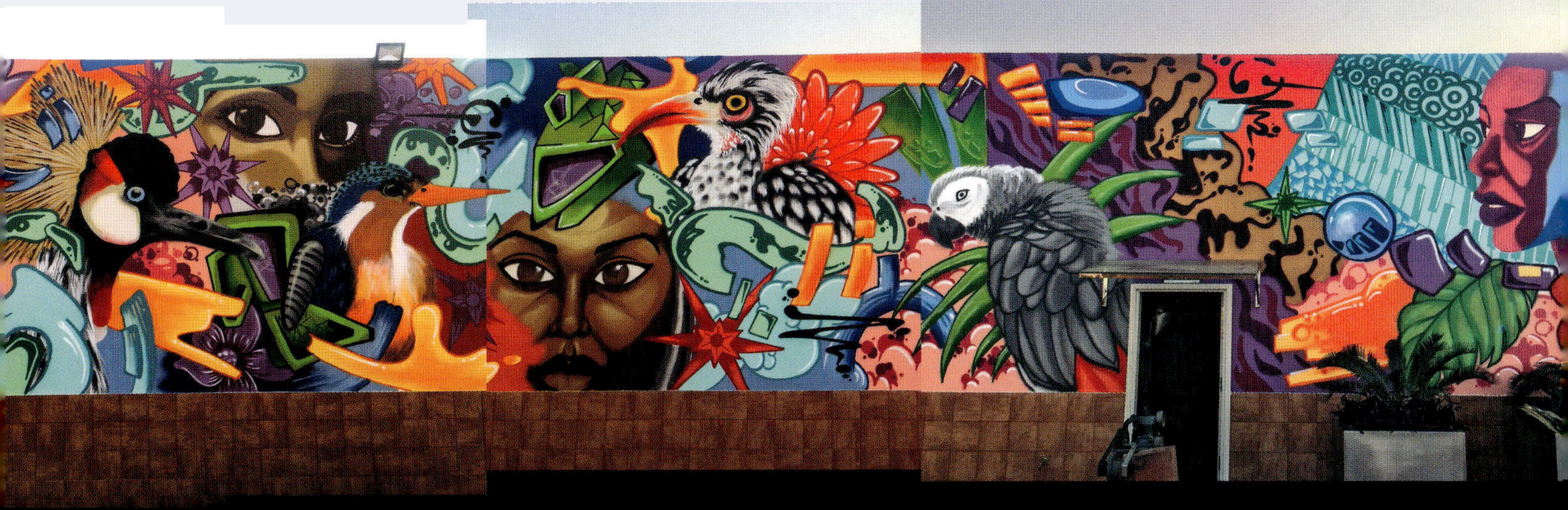

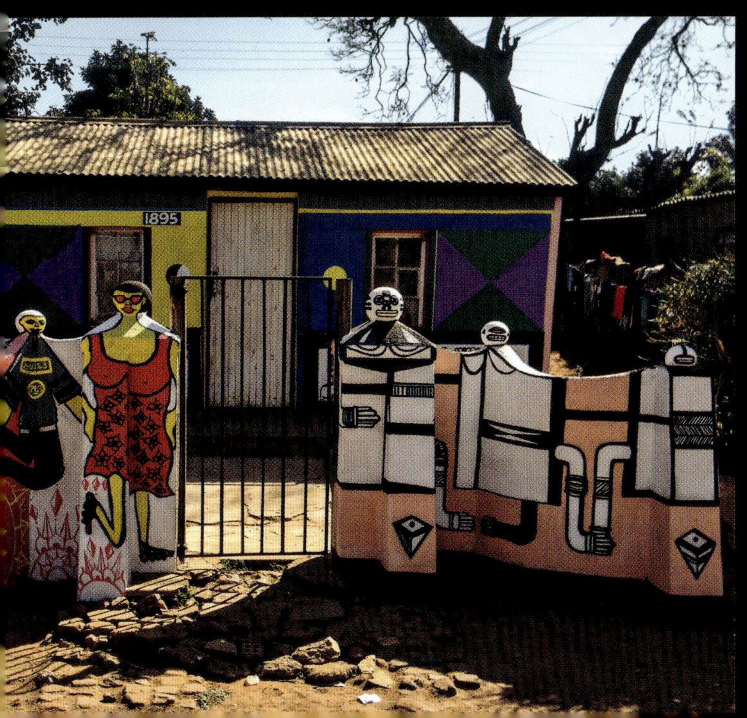

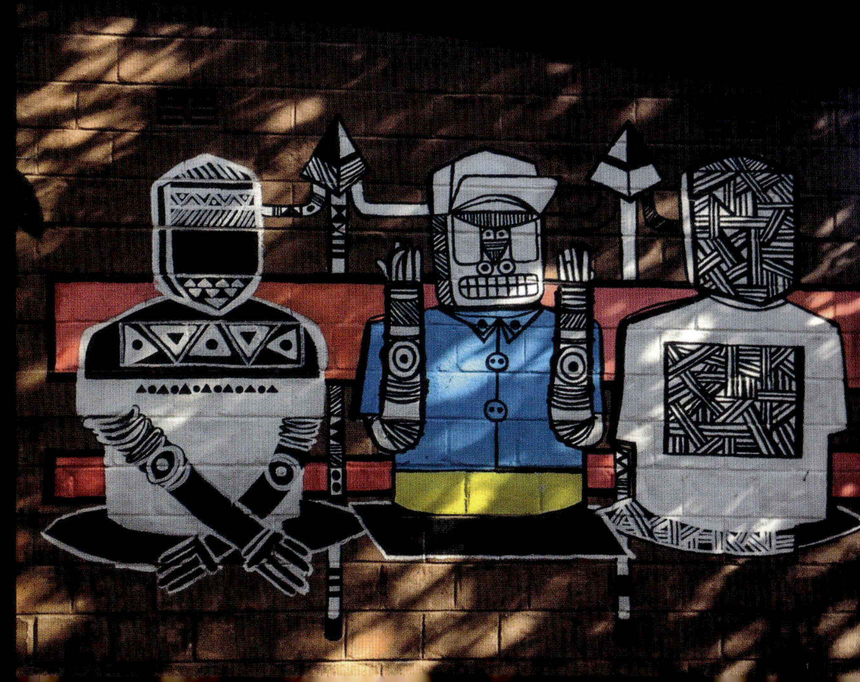

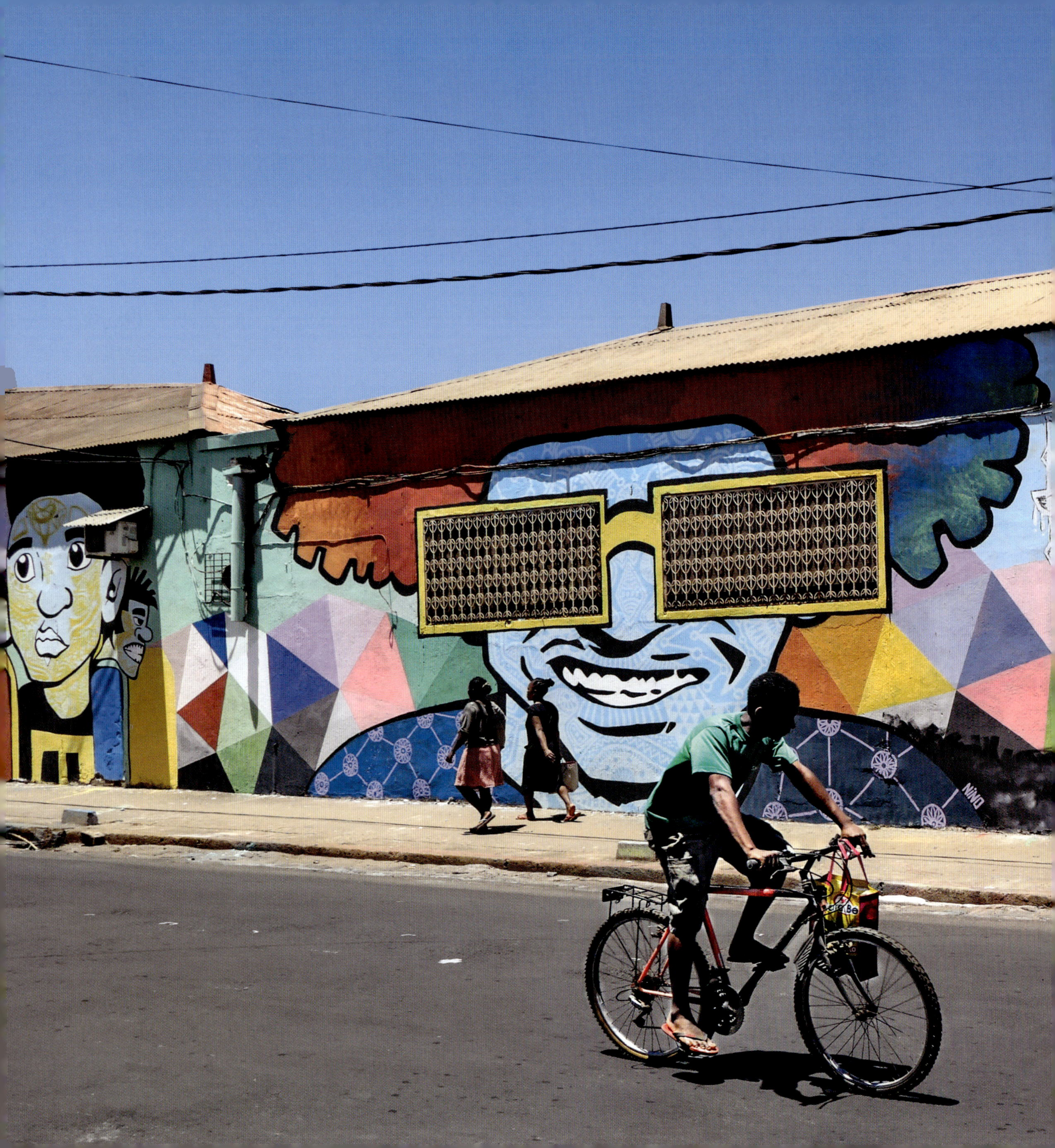

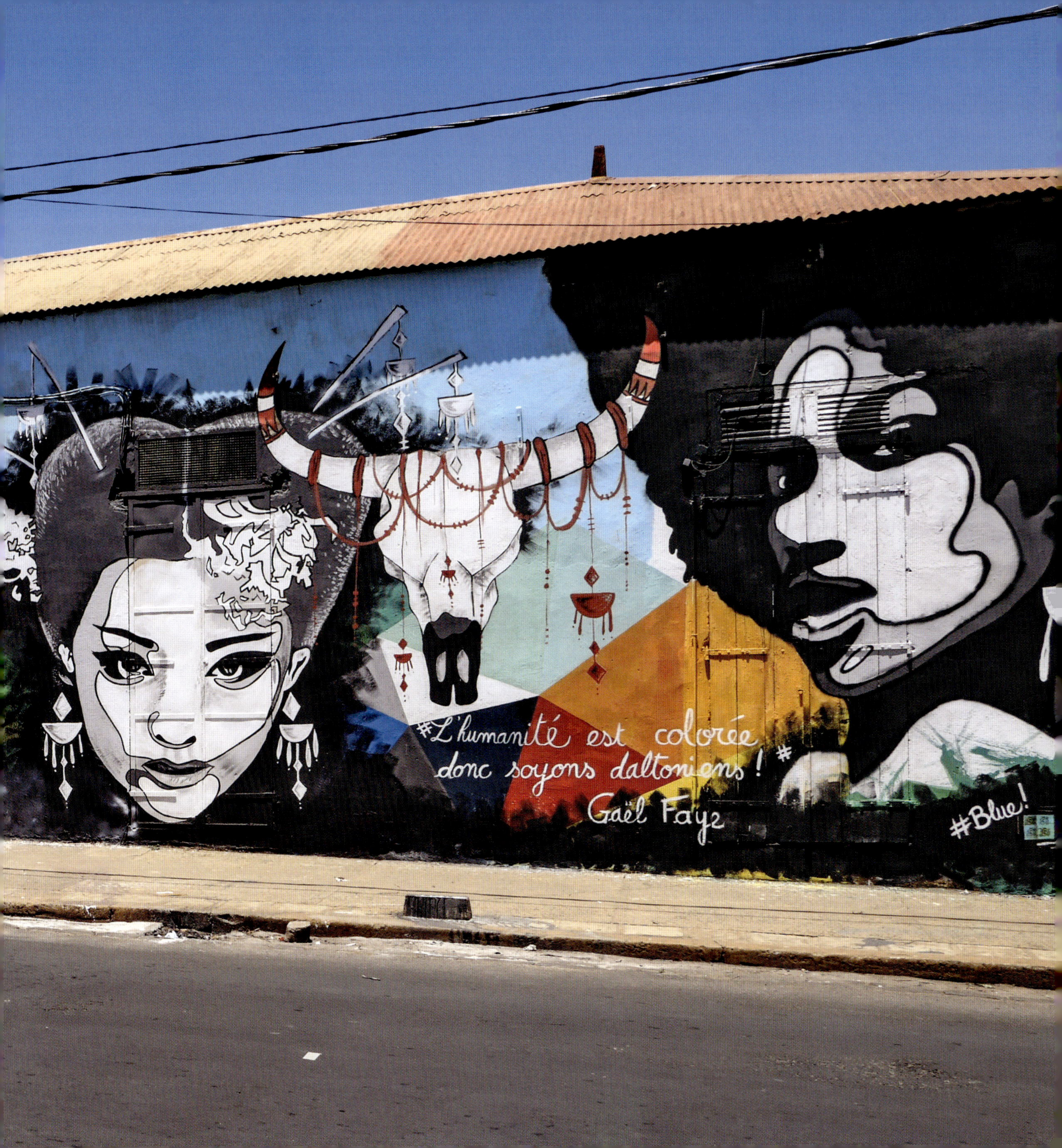

#L'humanité est colorée
donc soyons daltoniens ! #
Gaël Faye
#Blue!

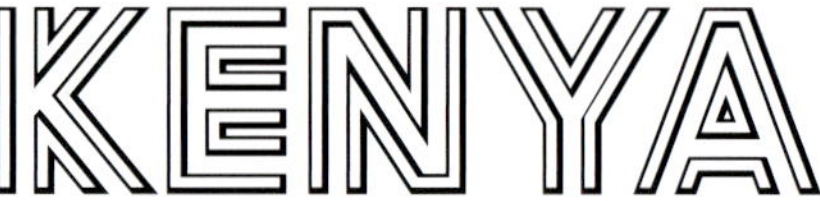

KENYA

IN FOCUS

Kenya is home to a diverse blend of cultures, ethnicities and traditions. Famed for vibrant wildlife and majestic scenery, this Eastern African nation has emerged as a popular tourist destination, and its cosmopolitan capital, Nairobi, is a thriving business and media centre. African crafts, including beadwork and wooden sculpture, are widely produced, while music and sport also contribute to the cultural landscape. Although much of the country remains rural, the lure of the big city for better employment opportunities and higher income has contributed to mass urbanization. This expansion has stimulated other social and urban phenomena, including graffiti, thus advancing Kenya's street art scene.

Graffiti in Kenya is often compared to the graphics decorating matatus – the flamboyant minibuses that originated in the 1960s. Matatu drivers compete for clients by customizing their rides with stylish airbrush and vinyl artwork, often featuring iconography from popular culture. They adorn their vehicles with endearing nicknames or slogans, while some install state-of-the-art sound systems and on-board Wi-Fi for passengers. Although matatu 'pimping' is deemed obscene or unsafe by many – including the government, which once banned the practice for several years – the culture is noteworthy and creates a platform for up-and-coming artists and musicians. These urban art-mobiles,

Below left
**Bankslave, Monk.E
(Canada). 'Kibera',
Nairobi, Kenya, 2015**

Below right
**Shakes. 'Swag',
Mombasa, Kenya, 2018**

Opposite, top
**Bantu.Moja, Nairobi,
Kenya, 2017**

Opposite, bottom
**Swift9, Bantu.Moja,
Bankslave, featuring
Msaleh and Smok.
Nairobi, Kenya, 2018**

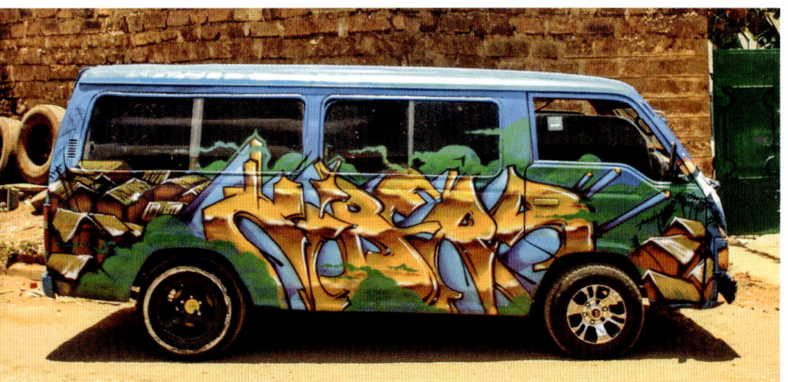

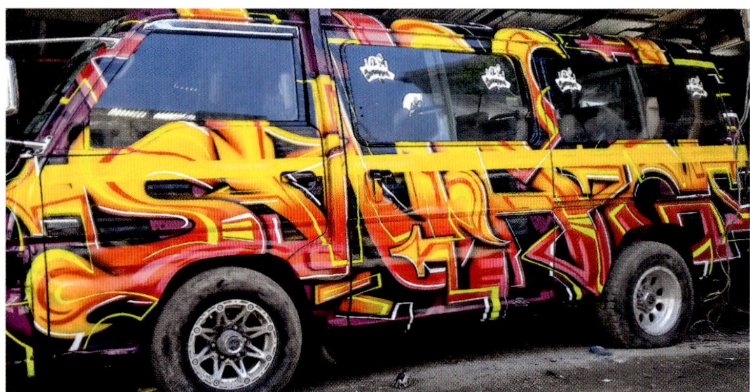

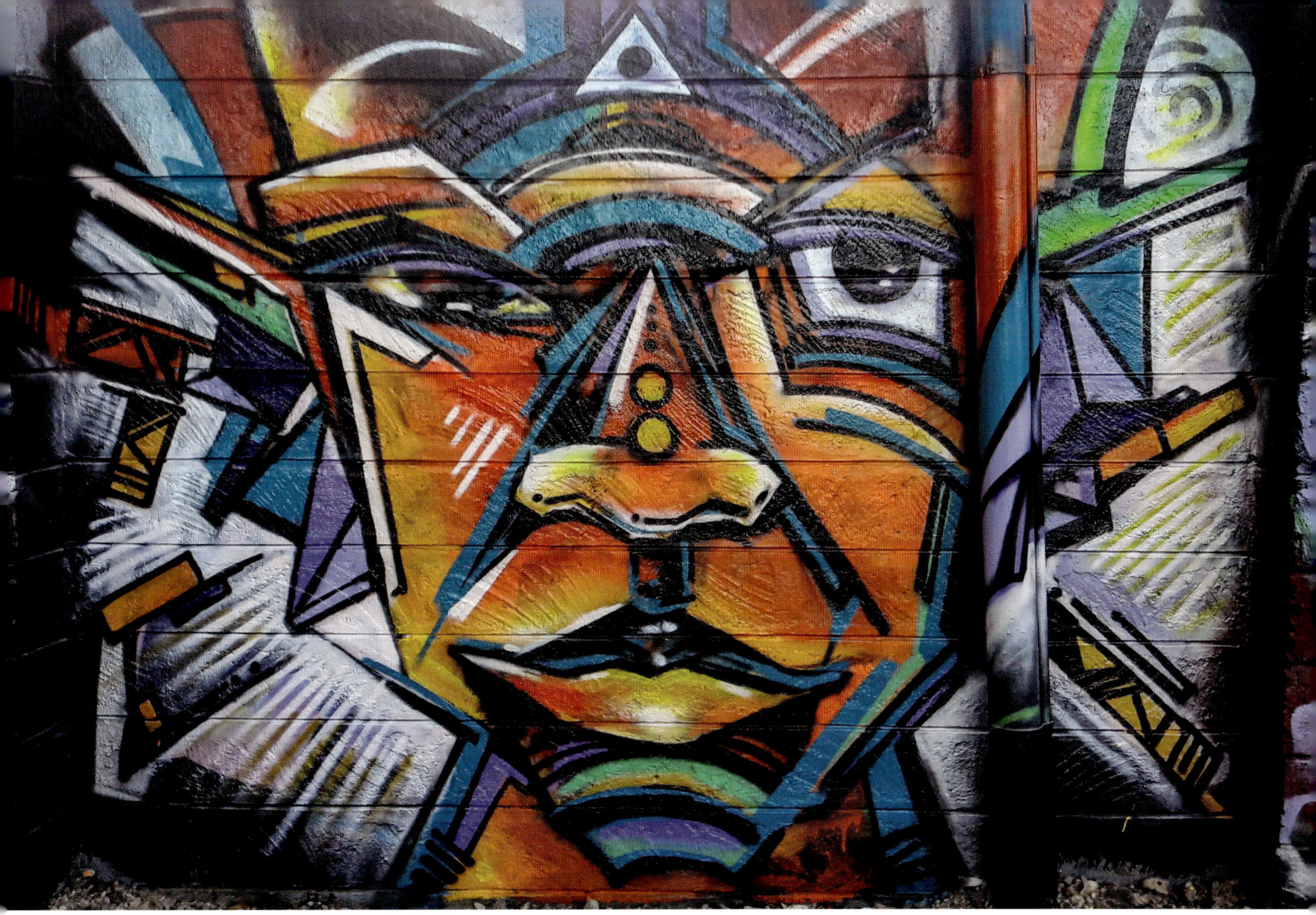

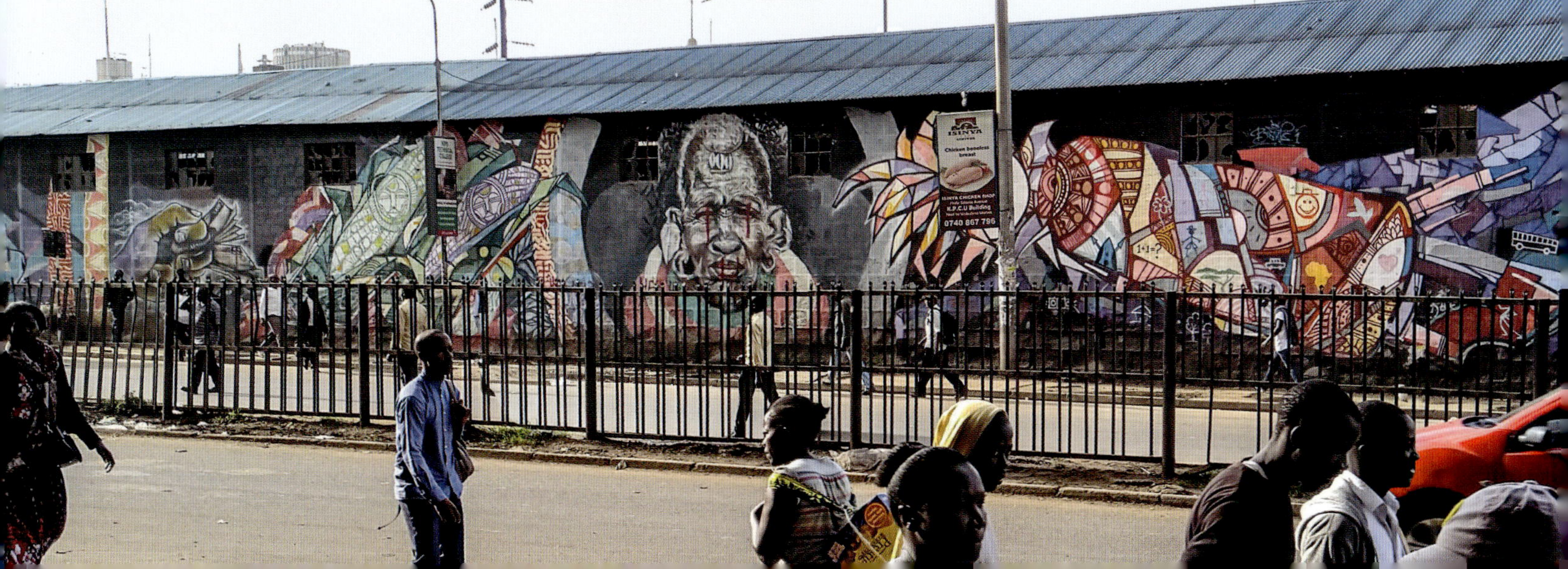

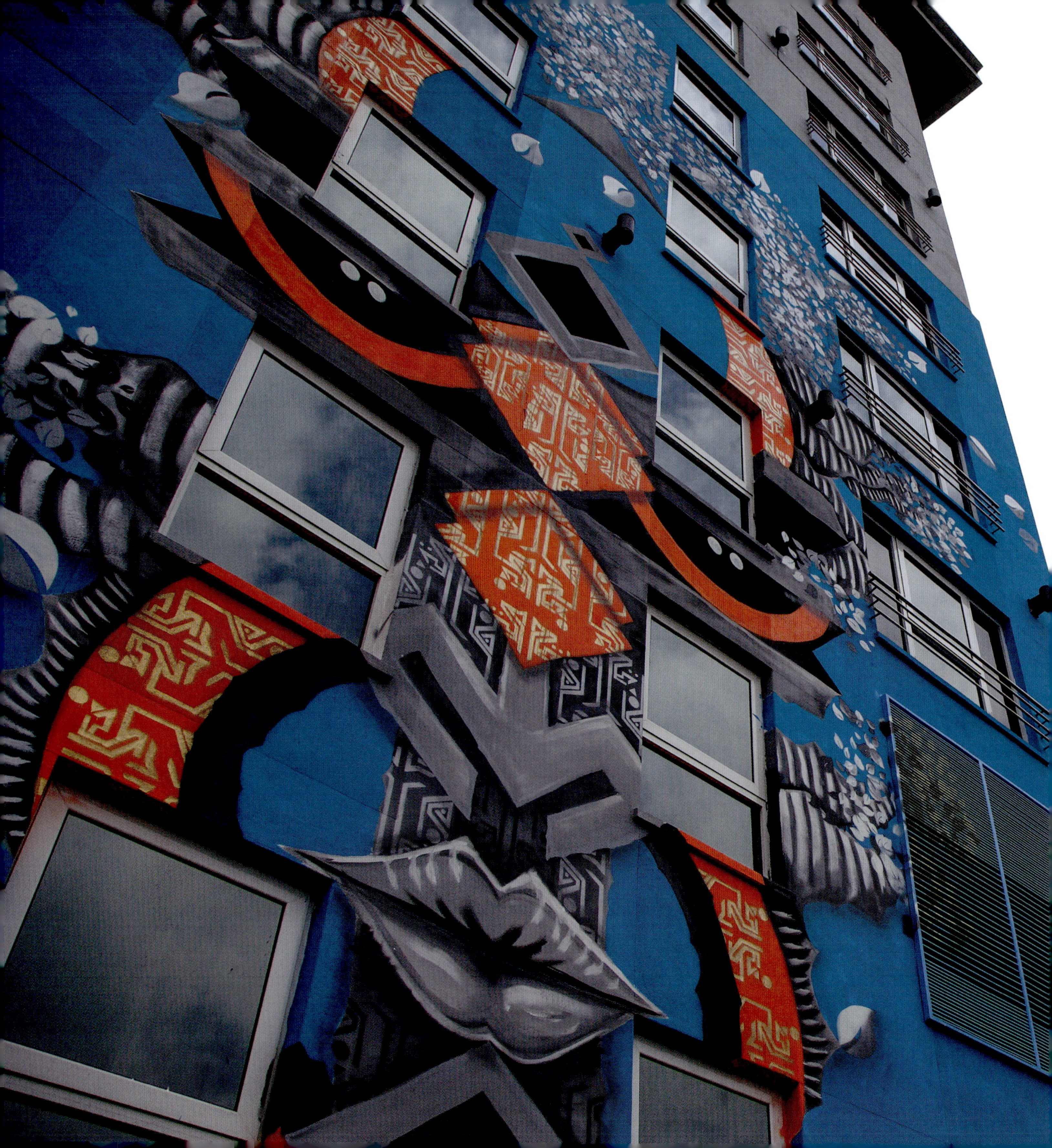

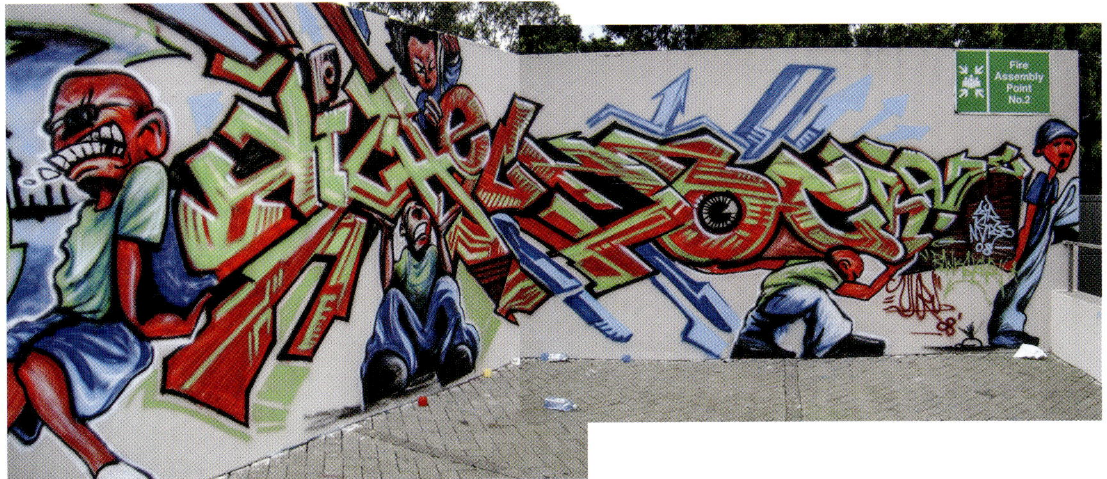

or 'nganyas' in local street slang, existed before the graffiti movement originated around 1998.

Some of the early forms of graffiti (besides political slogans) were visible in matatu culture and in bars and barbershops decorated by signwriters. Informal graffiti also popped up in Nairobi neighbourhoods such as Eastlands, Ngara, Parklands, South C and Nairobi West by local rap groups representing their 'hoods', often with brush paint, as spray cans were expensive. Although they did not fully engage with the graffiti subculture, they laid the foundations for artists such as Phiks, who originated from the matatu industry. Phiks played a part in both scenes in the 2000s, empowering himself with knowledge and skills that he would implement as a graffiti pioneer. Other early graffiti artists, including Lithium, advanced to become famous in the matatu art world.

From 2001 to 2005, the true graffiti scene was cultivated when artists such as Tak1, Felok, Ican, Bankslave, Swift9, Uhuru B, Smokillah and Esen emerged. Tak1 (aka Sea4 for stencils) and Ican founded one of the first crews, SIAFU (meaning 'Safari Ants' in Swahili), and would experiment with stencils, characters and wildstyle letter pieces. Their first big piece inspired many others within the pioneering generation to take their work from sketchbooks to the streets. Eventually they would all meet at the landmark WaPi (Words and Pictures) events in the mid-2000s. This monthly showcase gave audio and visual artists a platform, soon becoming the most significant catalyst for the rise of Kenya's hip-hop world.

Young graffiti artists also began to showcase their talent at a local arts centre in Nairobi. In 2005, the walls were blessed by visiting South African graffiti stars Faith XLVII and Falko One, as part of the Lines of Attitude project with Phiks and Dreph (UK). These interactions were fundamental, as Kenyan graffiti had had little exposure to the international scene. Graffiti was in its infancy and, because the public was unfamiliar with the process, artists could paint freely if they did not appear ill-intentioned. Abu, Fingaz, Shan, Nef, Ash, Mush, Hue, Scopt, 3rdm, Tyso,

Opposite
Wise Two. Nairobi, Kenya, 2017

Above
Uhuru B, Bankslave, SirNare. Walls in the British Council parking lot filled with graffiti from the acclaimed WaPi event, Nairobi, Kenya, 2008

Following spread
BSQ Crew. Jamhuri Jam, Nairobi, Kenya, 2015

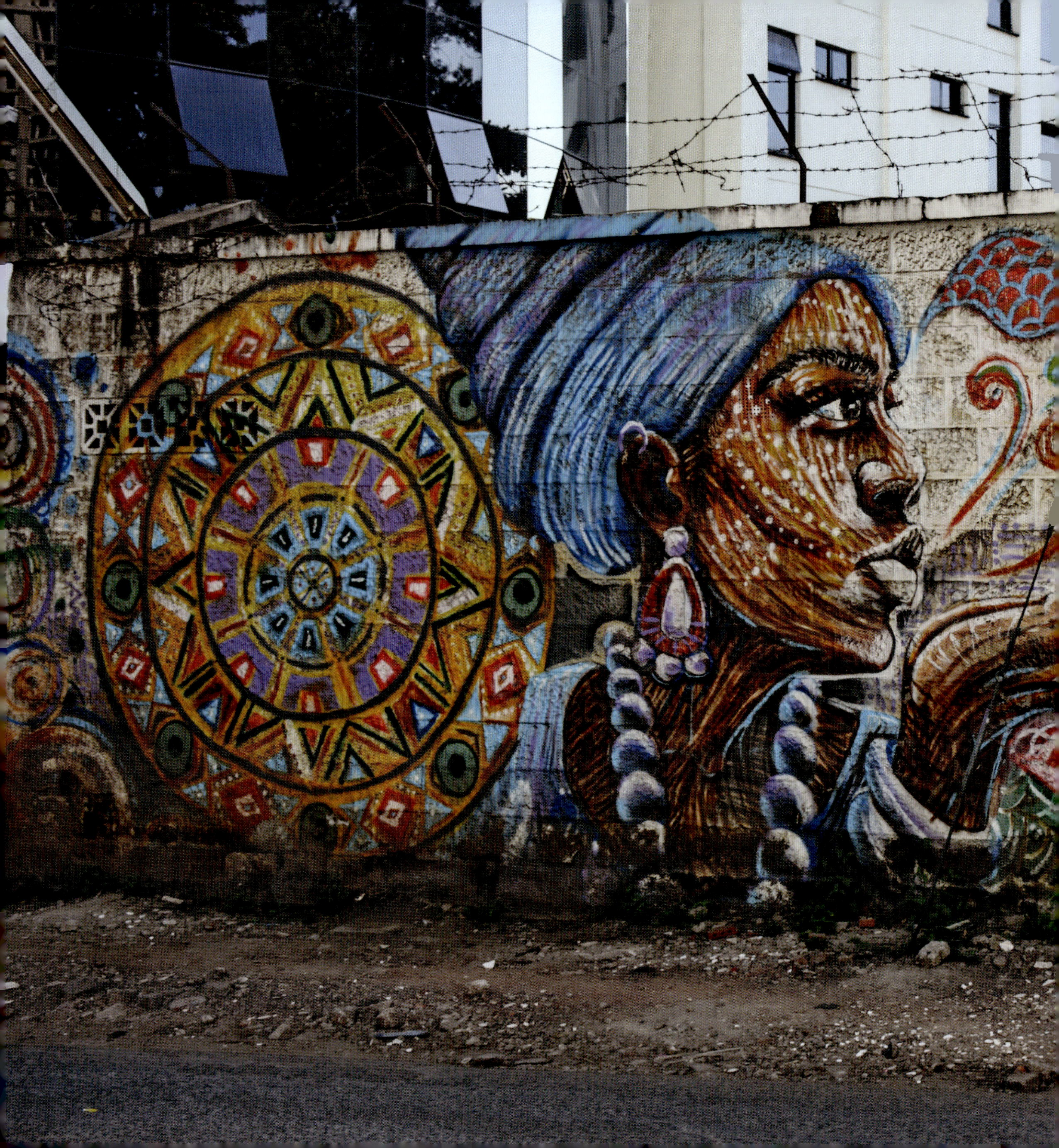

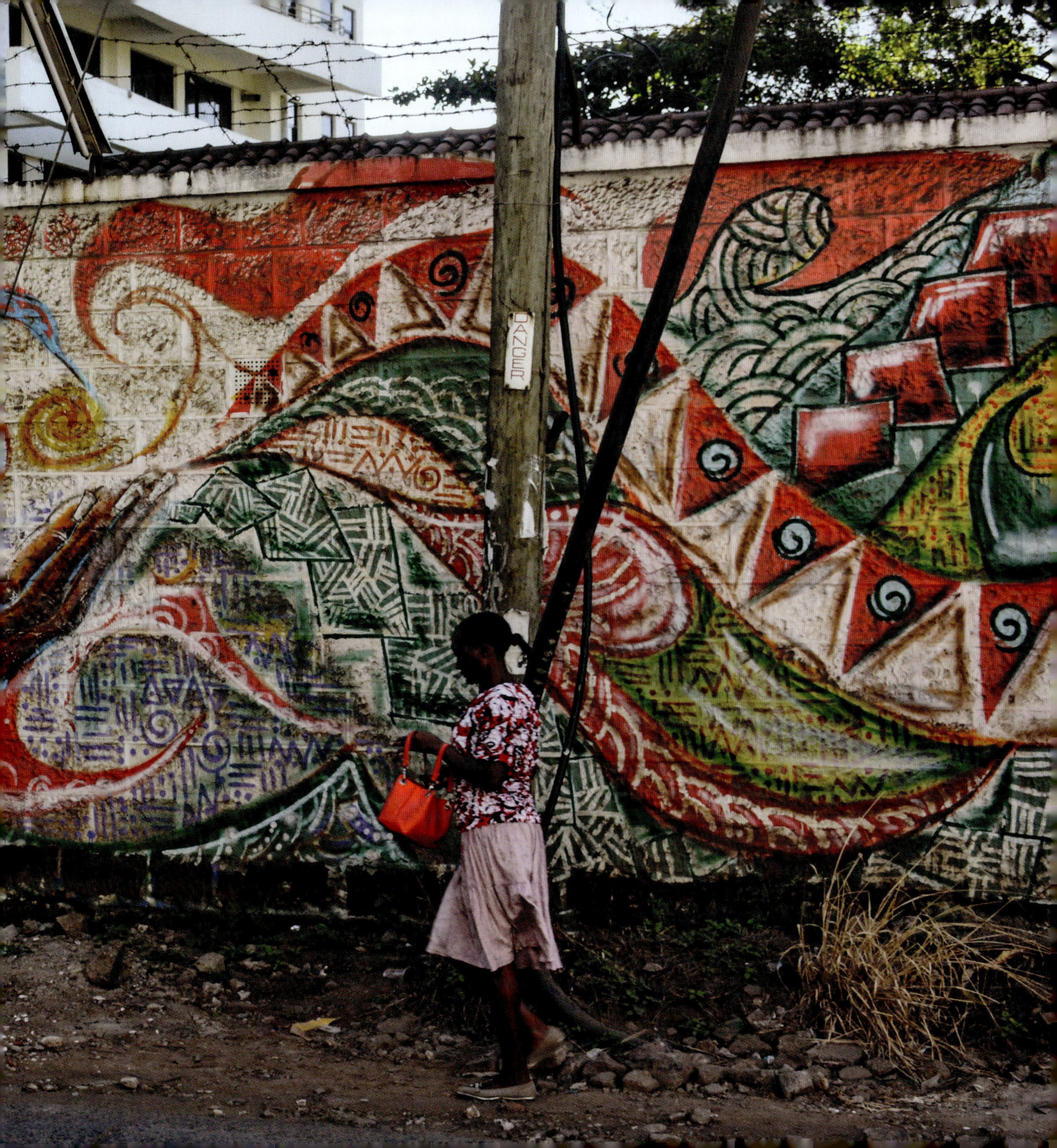

DANGER

Jkello, Diaz, Skim, Detail7, Giza, Relik and Wise Two were part of the following generation, while Bantu.Moja, Kerosh, Porsh, Slick Weasol, Minz, Vandal and SermOne came after them. Various crews appeared, including 3WG (Third World Graffiti), composed of Esen, Wise Two, Kerosh and Bantu.Moja; and SPU (Spray Uzi), with members Bankslave, Swift9, Smokillah and Uhuru B. These two crews became the leaders, painting commissioned work indoors and garnering experience on the streets.

Spray Uzi, previously known as GAS (Graffiti Afrisociation/Afrikan Society), was formed in 2009 by a lively mix of personas who grew up in different parts of Nairobi. Many of the members attended art classes in high school or studied art at tertiary level, but through hip-hop they found the most suitable outlet: graffiti. Over the years they experimented with styles, from characters and photo-realism to 3D, wildstyle, tags and throw-ups. As with most of the artists in Spray Uzi Crew, Bankslave could not afford spray paint when he first began in the early 2000s and resorted to charcoal and other paraphernalia. Through sheer dedication he overcame all obstacles and took his graffiti onto an international stage, painting in Australia, Europe and the USA. At home he has won competitions and participated in numerous projects, where he paints both graffiti and traditional African art to pay his bills. His recent quest to stand out from the crowd led him to experiment with fat caps, the nozzle that sprays a thicker line, to produce variegated triangular flares in his realist portraits.

Co-member Swift9 also pays close attention to the tricks of the trade and has mastered painting with any brand of spray paint, yielding flares and glows as he

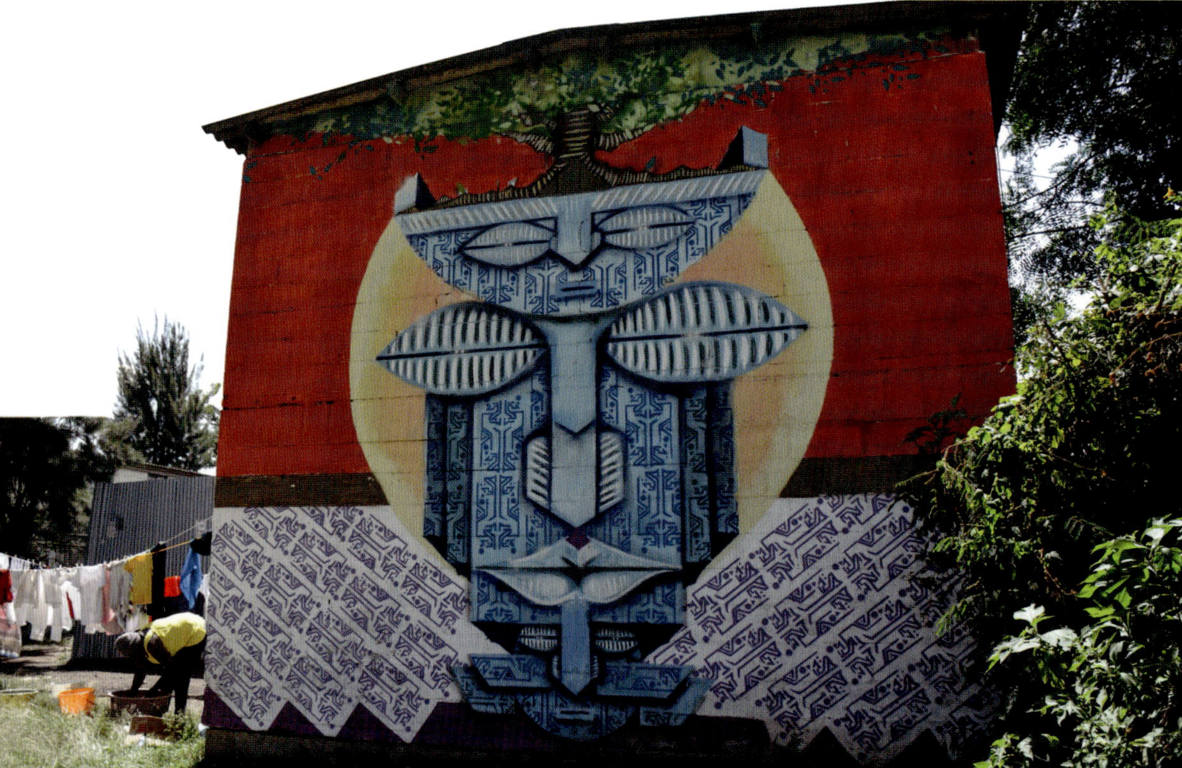

Wise Two. Nairobi, Kenya, 2018

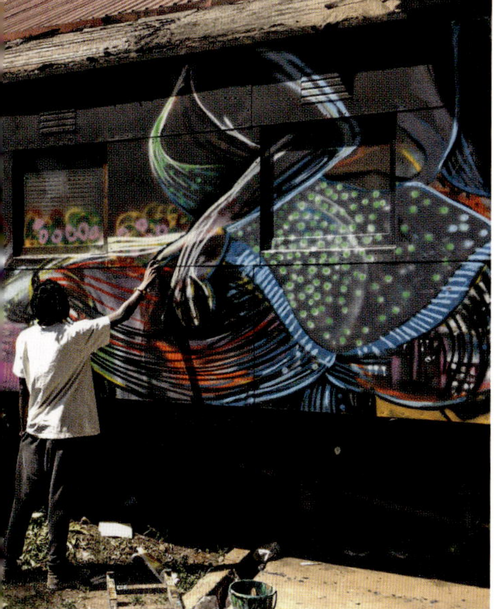

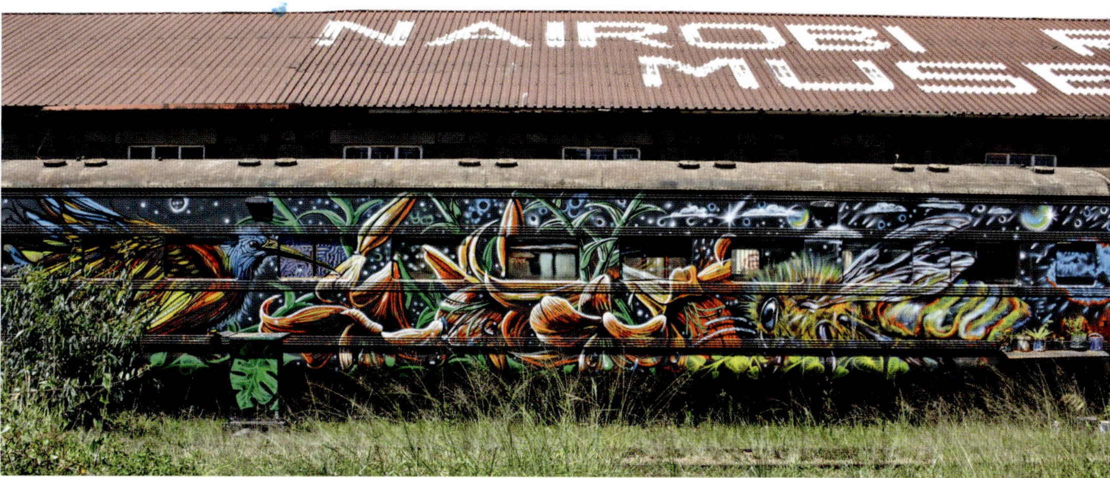

constantly pushes his craft to new heights. This mindset has aided his artistic advancement and enabled him to travel the world. Swift9 embeds Afro-futuristic elements and often collaborates with artists from other crews. Smokillah (aka Smok and Hemp) pushes his constantly evolving personal style and is a fervent believer in utilizing graffiti to effect positive change in the environment. In 2015 Smok launched Graffiti Girls Kenya to introduce more female artists to the culture and tackle issues that affect women in society. Uhuru B (aka Afro Ink) also became a graffiti mentor, successfully teaching the younger generation, which led to new crews such as BSQ dominating the Kenyan scene. Unlike overseas, where graffiti is more competitive, Uhuru believes collaboration and accessibility are key elements to grow the scene and harness collective energies. He endeavoured to find an identity for African graffiti – a look that would define it globally. Fusing African elements like fabric prints, patterns, lines, dots and splashes related to the continent, as well as wooden masks, Uhuru ran with what would best boost the graffiti arsenal, and his rogue approach elevated everyone.

Esen was gaining traction as a rapper, but switched lanes after being inspired by graffiti in South Africa and abroad via the Internet. He formed IAS (Ill Art Squad) with Felok in 2006 and briefly teamed up with GAS, later forming ICG (Intense Cities Group) with Ash, Nef, Ican and Swift9, and then 3WG when ICG disbanded. (ICG was a super-crew involving multiple crews, including Bandits, Wagani, Abyss and 3000BC, having more than twenty members at its peak.) Esen is an advocate for graffiti in Eastern Africa and has been involved in many uplifting projects. Wise Two, one of Africa's most formidable street artists, began to paint graffiti after he met Esen and Swift9 at a WaPi event. Often experimenting with his real name in typographical and wildstyle fonts, he soon found lettering too technical and searched for inspiration elsewhere, cutting stencils and using a central, symmetrical figure in all his pieces. His style became an amalgamation of African, Aztec and Maya influences, while his 'glyph' stencils form textures. Wise Two has travelled extensively, painting at festivals and exhibiting his work internationally.

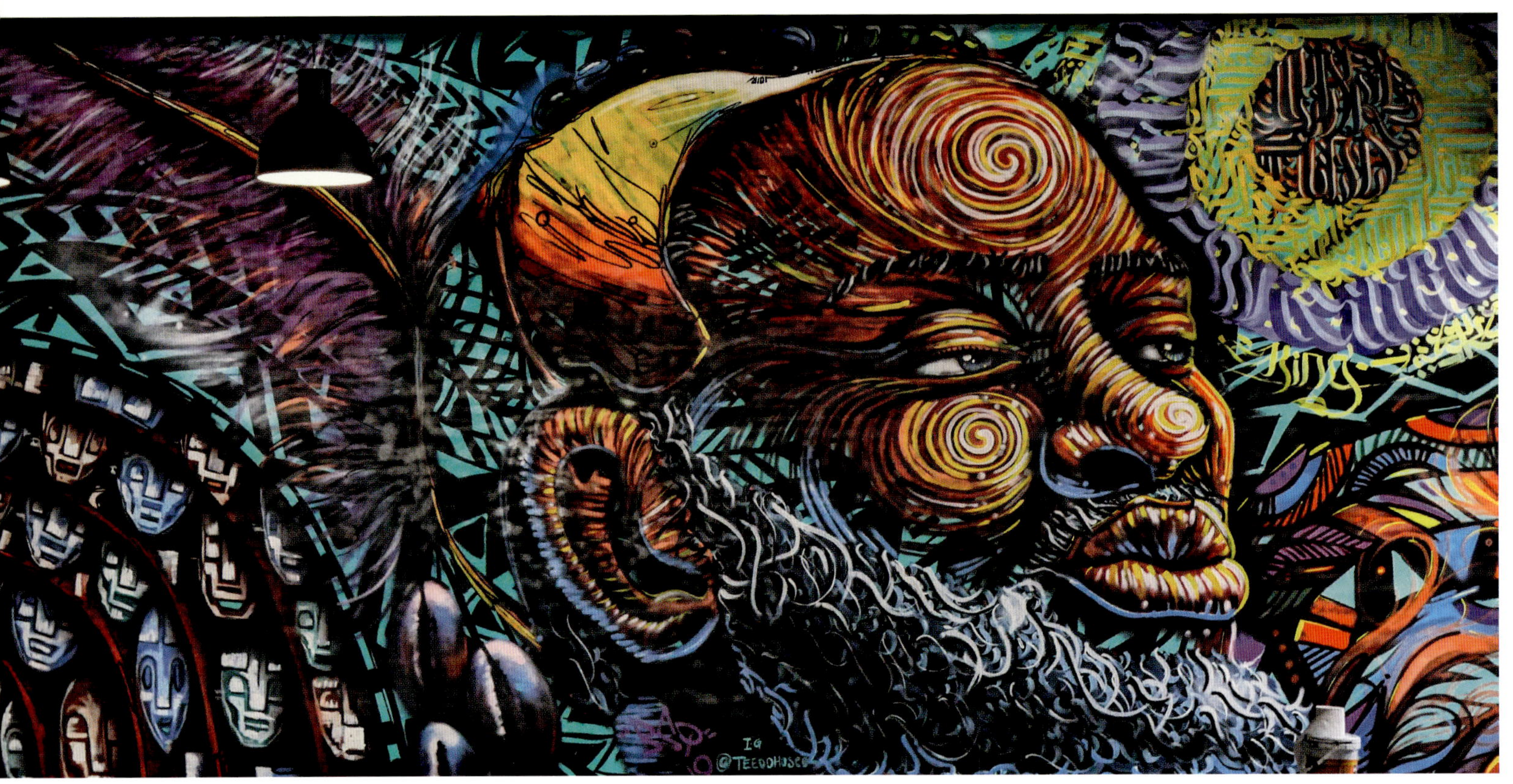

Between 2011 and 2014, BSQ (Bomb Squad) Crew was introduced to graffiti under the guidance of Uhuru B and Swift9. Through their teaching, Kaymist4, Msaleh and Thufu-B have attained prominence. The crew is amassing more members, such as Ibrah/E-Bruh, Nyeks and Stic One, while the original members display their talent through large commissioned works in a recognizable style. Each member is proficient with portraiture: Thufu-B paints with line streaks and adds patterns and floral elements, Msaleh plays with abstract calligraphy fonts and calligrams (which he terms *grafikali*), while Kaymist4 weaves bold, black linework along the structures of faces and animals, sometimes adding technological features such as bolts or gears. The crew currently works in a train coach-cum-art studio at the Nairobi Railways Museum where it hosts numerous exhibitions and regularly adds to one of the longest graffiti walls of the region. BSQ is now mentoring the next generation and hoping to strengthen graffiti's foothold.

Projects such as Spray for Change, MaVulture and Kibera Walls for Peace were created to tackle issues relating to the country's political climate. Politicians often pay people to scrawl their names around the city to solicit votes, and many of those in power are allegedly corrupt, using state funds for personal gain. The MaVulture project by Boniface Mwangi saw a group of unnamed graffiti artists portray these officials as vultures in caustic figurative murals, while Spray for Change was a commercially backed campaign to spread messages of hope and

Above
**BSQ Crew, Teeoohusee.
Nairobi, Kenya, 2019**

Opposite
Chela. Nairobi, Kenya, 2019

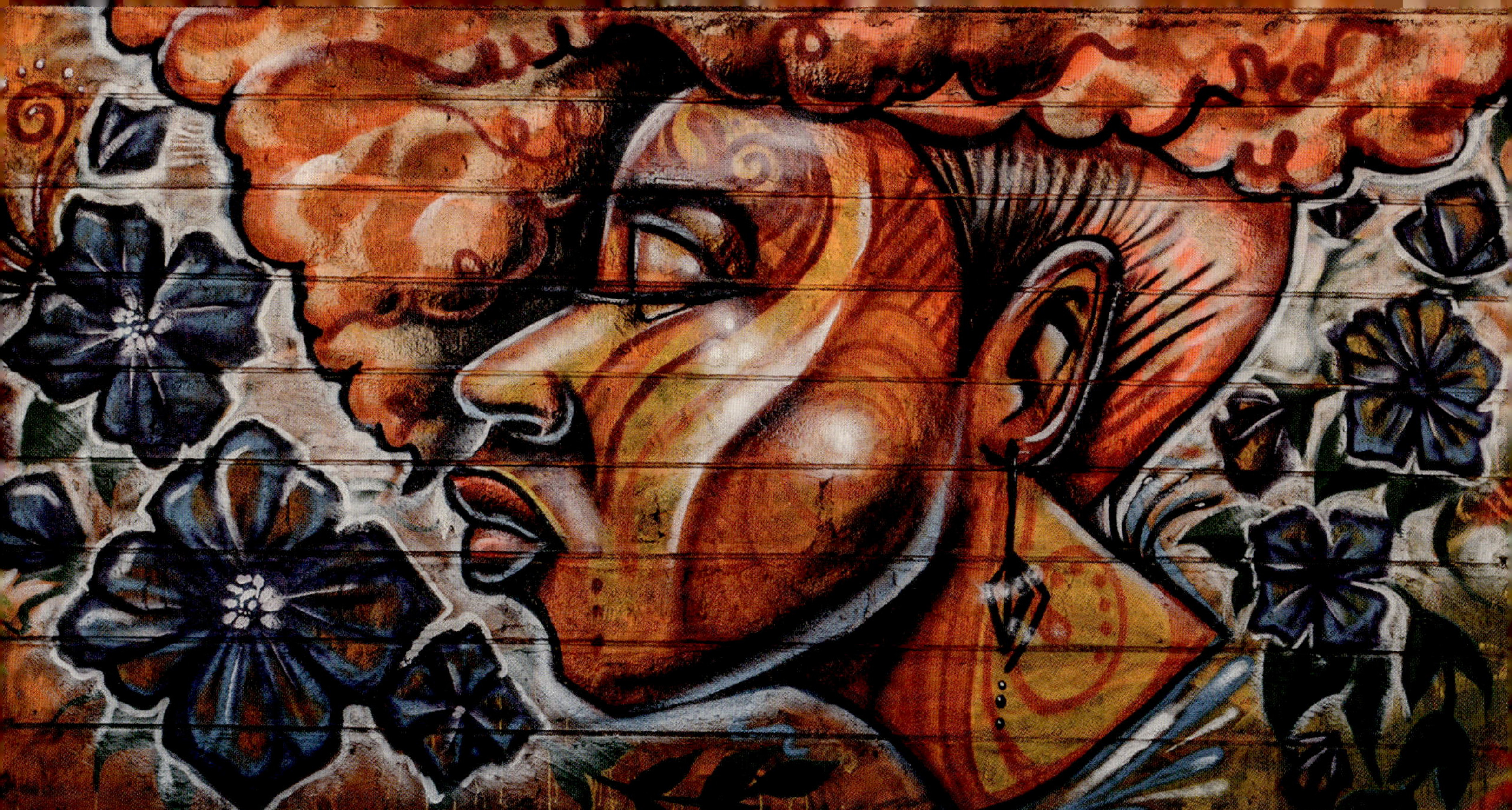

positivity. During pre-elections in 2013, many Kenyans did not want to relive 2007 and 2008's violent clashes between opposing tribes. Walls encouraging *amani* (peace) and unity were painted by visiting American artist Joel Bergner together with locals for the Walls for Peace public art project. The programme culminated in the decoration of a passenger train, a significant rolling artwork featuring a portrait of then American president Barack Obama, an international symbol of transformation who was born to Kenyan parents. Non-graffiti artists like Solo7 launched their own tag campaigns to further promote peace; there is no corner of the Kibera settlement, Africa's largest slum, without one of Solo7's messages.

Other talents, for example Blaine29, Chela and Shakes, also contribute to the scene. Shakes is based in Mombasa, Kenya's second-largest city, with a long history as a trade port. He paints pieces with positive words like 'umoja' (unity), 'focus', 'power' and 'rise up', and is part of West Indies Crew with Moha. Jonari is another Mombasa-based graffiti artist. Although Kenyan graffiti is sometimes misunderstood – with many artists choosing to paint permission walls during daylight to avoid harassment from private security – the urban art scene remains vigorous, with an increasing number of practising artists and a strong focus on togetherness. Pioneer Tak1 continues to make his mark in Kenya and other African countries, while newer additions, including Ohmz, Garuk87, Mutua Arts, Daddo Omutitii, Kazoga, Viktart and 8ToWn Crew, are breaking new ground.

BANKSLAVE

Tell me about your introduction to graffiti.
When I was a kid my mom would brag to her friends about my drawings. I had potential, and later, in school, I was the best in my art classes. I just kept going because art is my strength, my forte, my own superpower. I learned graffiti from *The Source* magazine with its single-page article in every issue. I started doing graffiti backdrops for music videos, and corporate work later enabled me to fund my personal painting projects.

Tell me about painting in the community, especially on your own.
My artwork needs to be outside and seen by everyone, not just in a gallery where few people see it. Art in the streets can be experienced by all. There is also an opportunity for me to express myself, whether it is something political or anything I want to share with the world. I choose to paint spots with a big audience and am very careful with what I put up in order to receive a good response.

Do people in Kenya understand graffiti, especially the letter forms?
Some people do not understand graffiti, but I try to make it clear for the layman. Kenya is a conservative country and there is a lot of religion. People could consider it to be devilish, so I keep things legible or Igo more abstract. I want to avoid a lot of questions about it, and it getting buffed the next day. I want my piece to stay up longer and create something that relates to the people in the area. I do a lot of

research before I go to a specific wall, that is why many of my pieces are still around. I feel like my art is a media tool that can reach the masses in a different way; if I feel like sending a message, I go ahead and do it.

Quality spray paint is limited in Africa. How has this influenced your painting style?
We still produce and find ways around it. We use both spray paint and tub paint for a bolder, stronger pigment. They are privileged in Europe where they make the paint, but we cannot be mad with what we do not have. It becomes easier and is an advantage.

You have ventured outside of Africa to global street art festivals. How has this grown your artistic endeavours?
It has been a positive thing, an eye opener. Being able to travel and view the international graffiti world in real life is inspirational, and painting with artists who look up to is an achievement. I receive exposure and take it home to do big murals around my city.

Tell me about your crew and its influence on the Kenyan graffiti scene.
Our crew, Spray Uzi, formed in Nairobi in 2006 through a platform called WaPi and we have motivated other young kids to paint graffiti in Kenya. I also represent global crews such as Ghetto Pimps in Germany and Grown From Concrete in the USA. Kenyan graffiti artists are

upping the game and guys like Bantu.Moja, Wise Two, BSQ Crew and many others are finding their style. Back in the day I was relying on artists from abroad for inspiration but now I get it naturally. Studying a piece by another local artist motivates me to find other angles and styles to explore.

Do you think it's important to showcase Africa in your work?
Bringing out Africa is very important because it is a distinguishing factor. It makes my work stand out globally and showcases where I am from, both for me and for my people.

Tell me about your signature style.
I realized that portraiture artists often create work that is similar, so I began to add flares and bring in an element that is mine – my uniqueness, to stand out from everyone else around the world. Anyone

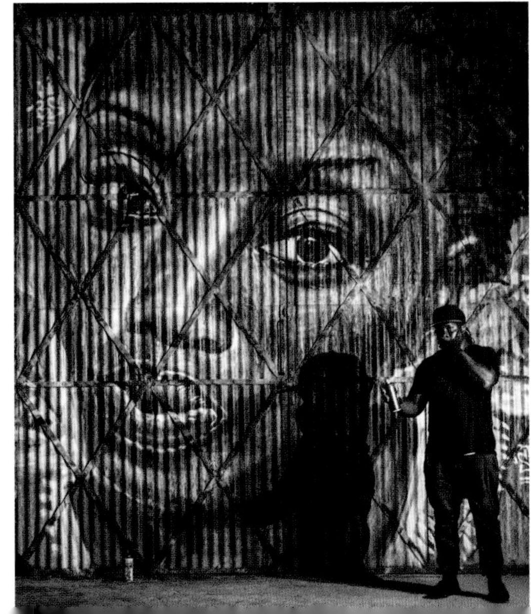

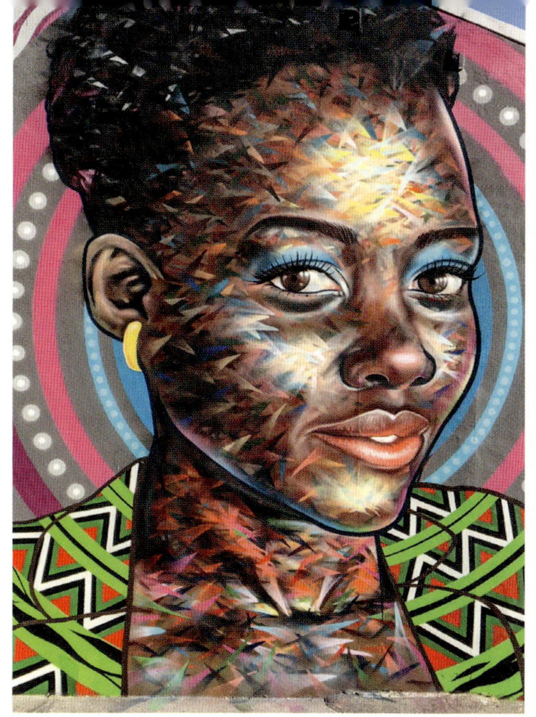

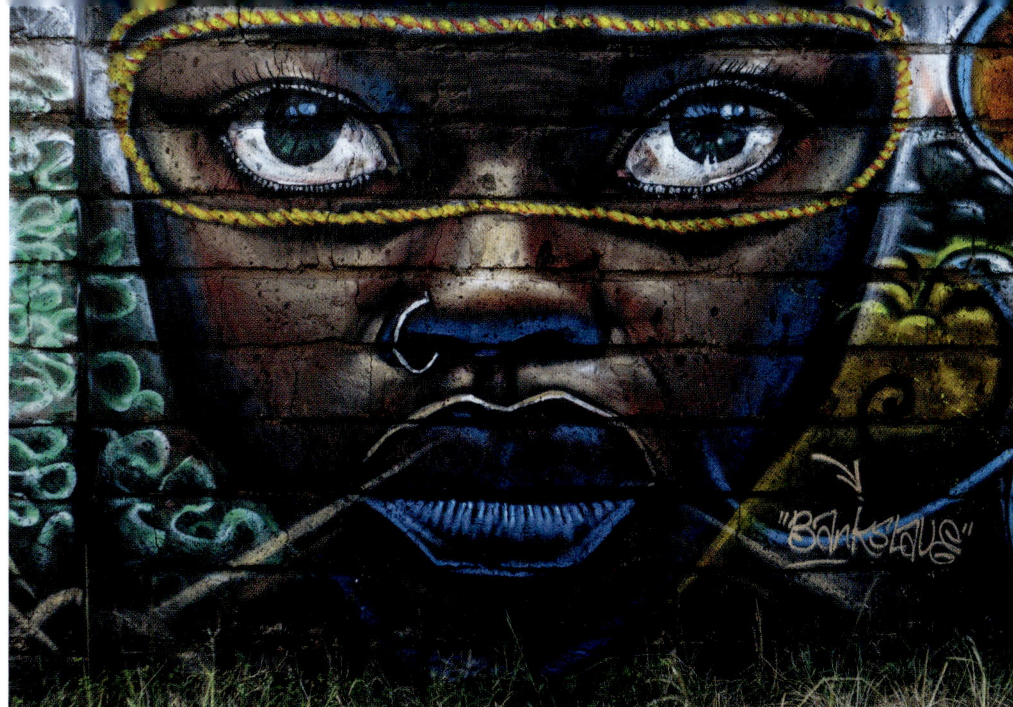

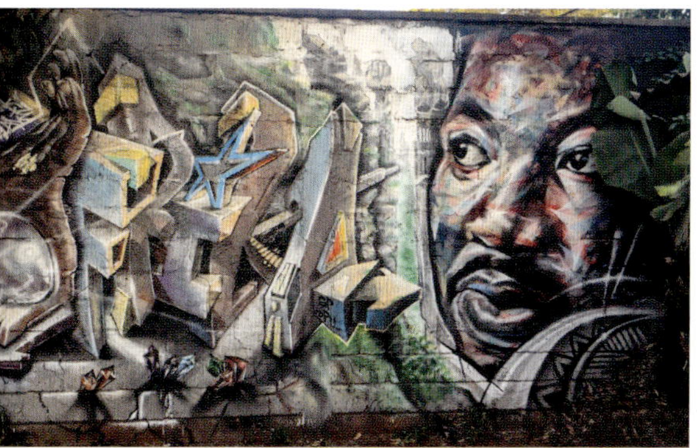

Opposite
**Bankslave. Jinja,
Uganda, 2018**

Above, clockwise from top
**Bankslave, with Vans
the Omega (Australia).
Sanaa Festival, Adelaide,
Australia, 2018**

**Bankslave. Nairobi,
Kenya, 2016**

**Bankslave. 'Afrika' piece
with Martin Luther King,
Nairobi, Kenya, 2019**

can take a picture and blow it up, but adding stylistic elements helps to define your personal style.

How do you get inspired and conceptualize your next piece?

I mostly sketch for better preparation because you can choose what is best suited to the new wall. The sketches are only the concepts and it might change if the wall dictates what it wants to be. I often cannot sketch the flare effect because I use a fat cap, so I just go with it.

What do you think about the importance of sharing your work, especially online?

You already share your work once you paint in the streets. Online is good because there is a broader audience for you. It feels good when one of my posted pieces is reshared – I want to keep pushing myself.

Where else have you painted in Africa?

I have only been to Uganda and Tanzania in the east, Zimbabwe further south and Senegal and Cabo Verde in the west.

We have similarities, using whatever we have to produce artworks. It is growing and is only going to get bigger.

Bankslave is a renowned Kenyan graffiti artist who paints expressive realist portraits and graffiti letter studies. A self-professed rebel against the capitalist system, he paints figures who are historically or culturally relevant, combining art and activism. His portraits include Nelson Mandela, Dedan Kimathi, Malcolm X and many more African heroes. His influence is not limited to Eastern Africa and his work leaves an impression on everyone. He has been painting since 2001.

SPRAY PAINT INNOVATION

STYLES & TECHNIQUES

In some areas of Africa, graffiti is almost twenty years behind the rest of the world, although the large gap is closing. The main reason for delayed development is the paint supplies, which generally cost more but are essentially inferior. Aerosol technology is limited to a small colour palette with low coverage and a watery appearance, intended for tasks like respraying a bicycle. The advancement of paint quality, tonal range, nozzles and ease of use has many benefits, now seen in the rapid spurt of global graffiti in the past two decades. The restrictions placed on African artists have caused them to invent their own techniques or hacks to get things done, birthing artists with great perseverance who continually break the mould. Kenyan artist Bankslave burns a needle into the exit hole of the nozzle to produce a skinnier line. The paint is thrust along the needle's edge before landing on the wall surface – a similar result to a stencil cap. His crew mate Swift9 pokes a hole in a small piece of polythene paper, which he wedges between the can and the nozzle, thus reducing pressure for longevity and ease of use. Many artists also mix spray paint with roller paint to get the job done. More professional artist's spray paint is slowly becoming more common.

Opposite, clockwise from top left
BSQ Crew: Thufu-B, Kaymist4, Msaleh. Nairobi, Kenya, 2019

Resko. Porlwi by Light Festival, Port Louis, Mauritius, 2015

Swift9, Thufu-B, Smok. Nairobi, Kenya, 2019

Smok, Swift9. Nairobi, Kenya, 2018

Bankslave burns a needle into the nozzle to gain a special effect with the spray can. Nairobi, Kenya, 2019

'We are taken back in time to New York's train era – they were using the kind of paint we use today!' WISE TWO

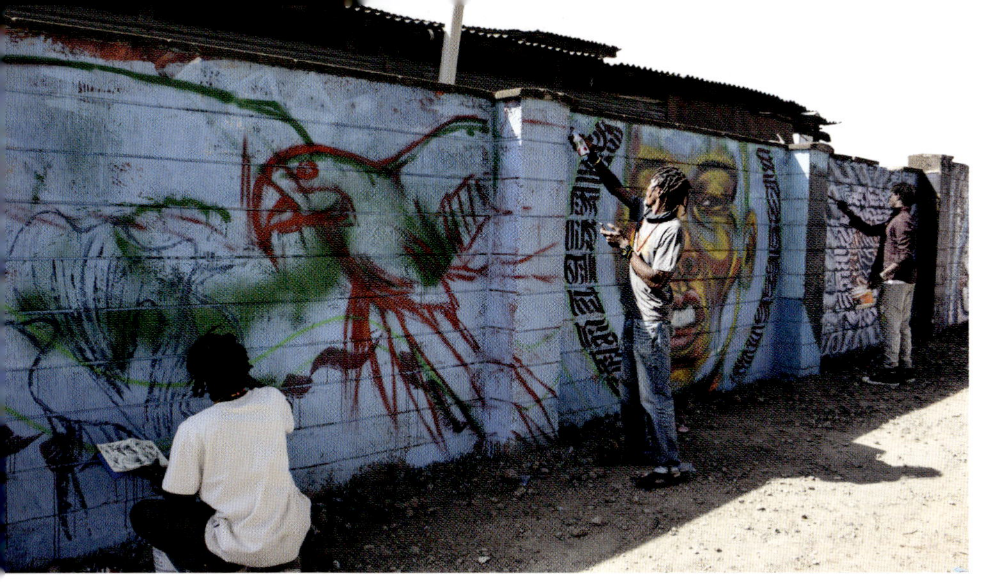
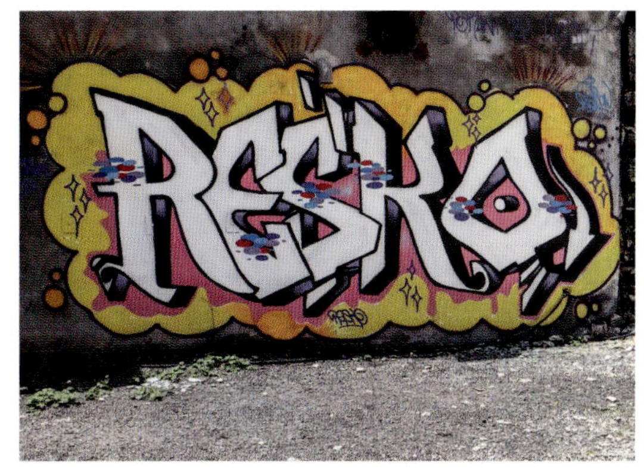
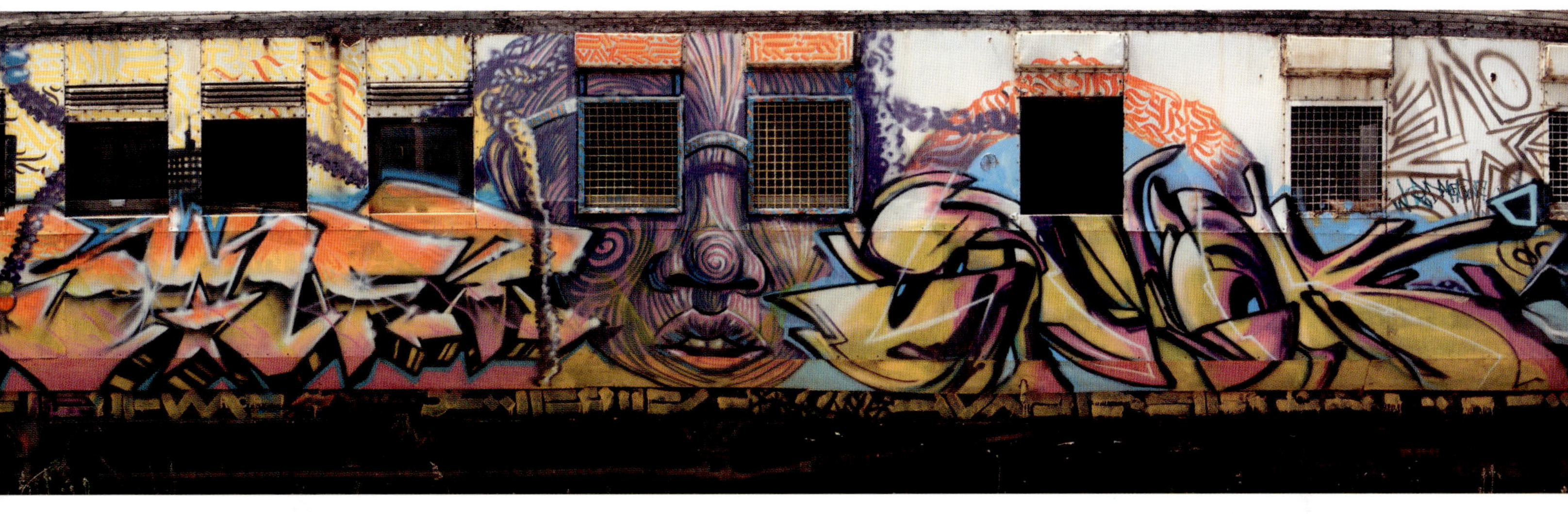
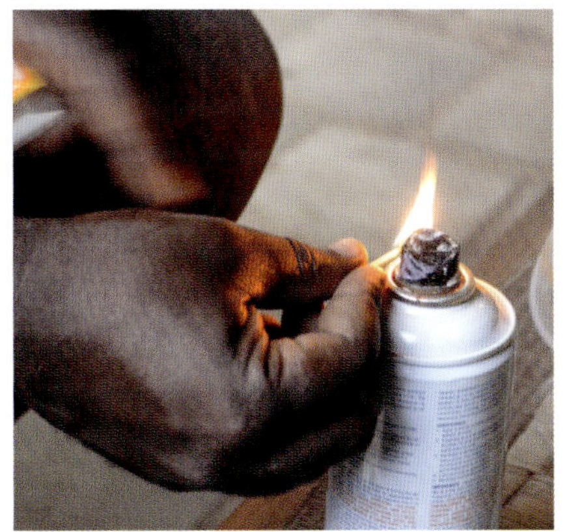
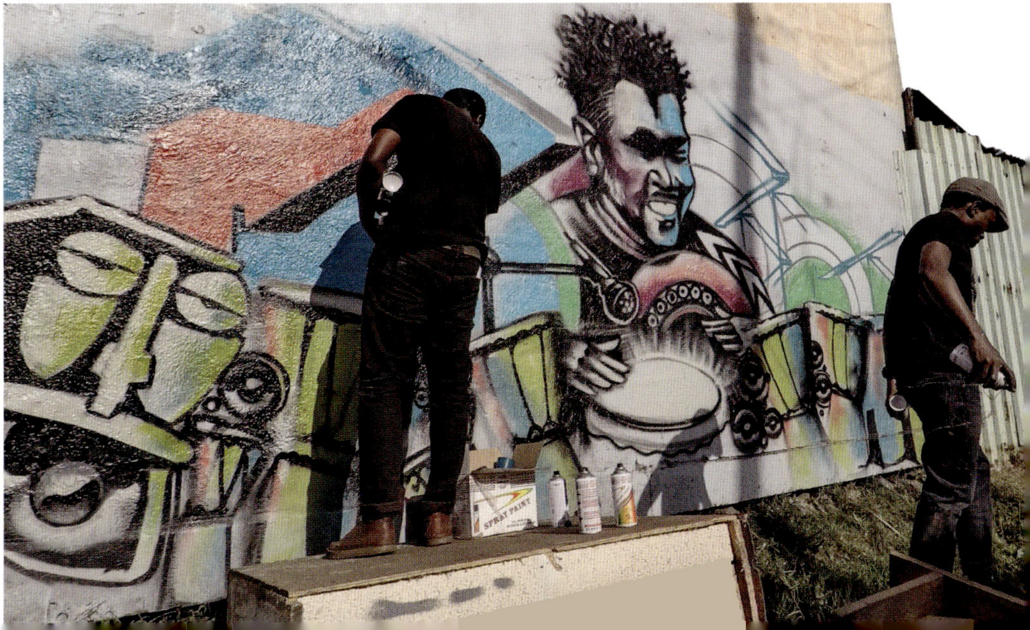

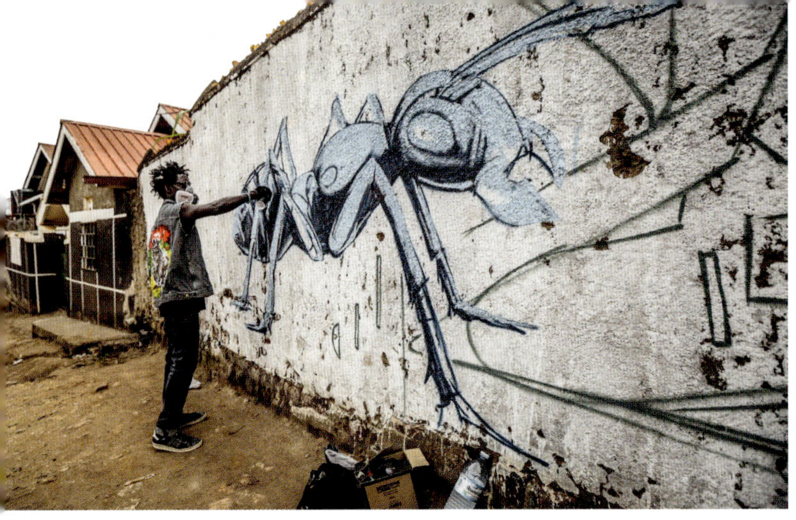
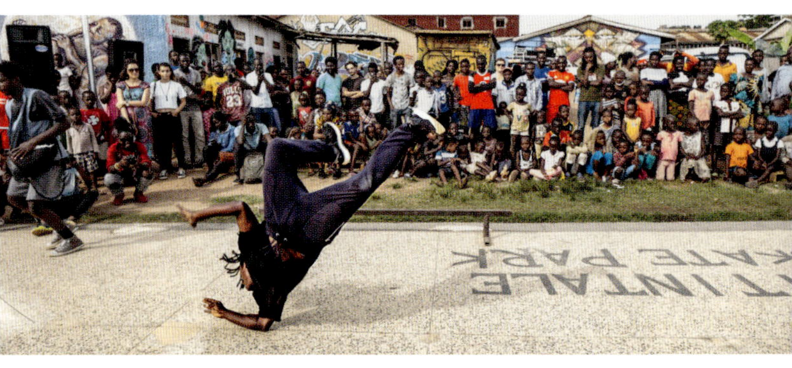
TINTALE
KATE PARK
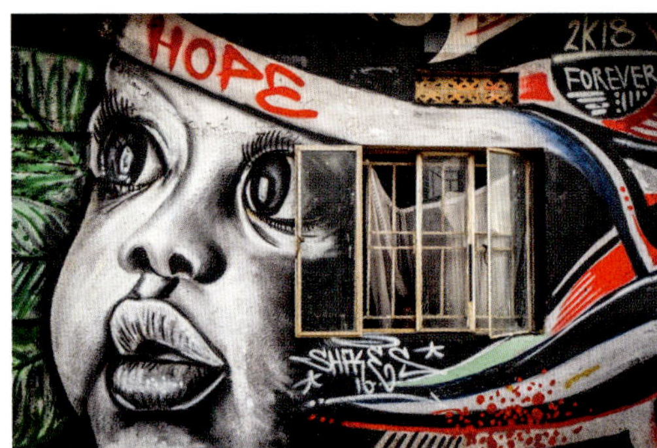
HOPE
2K18
FOREVER
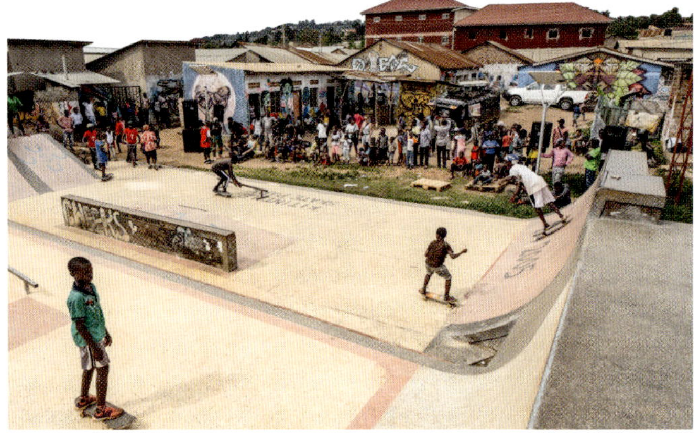

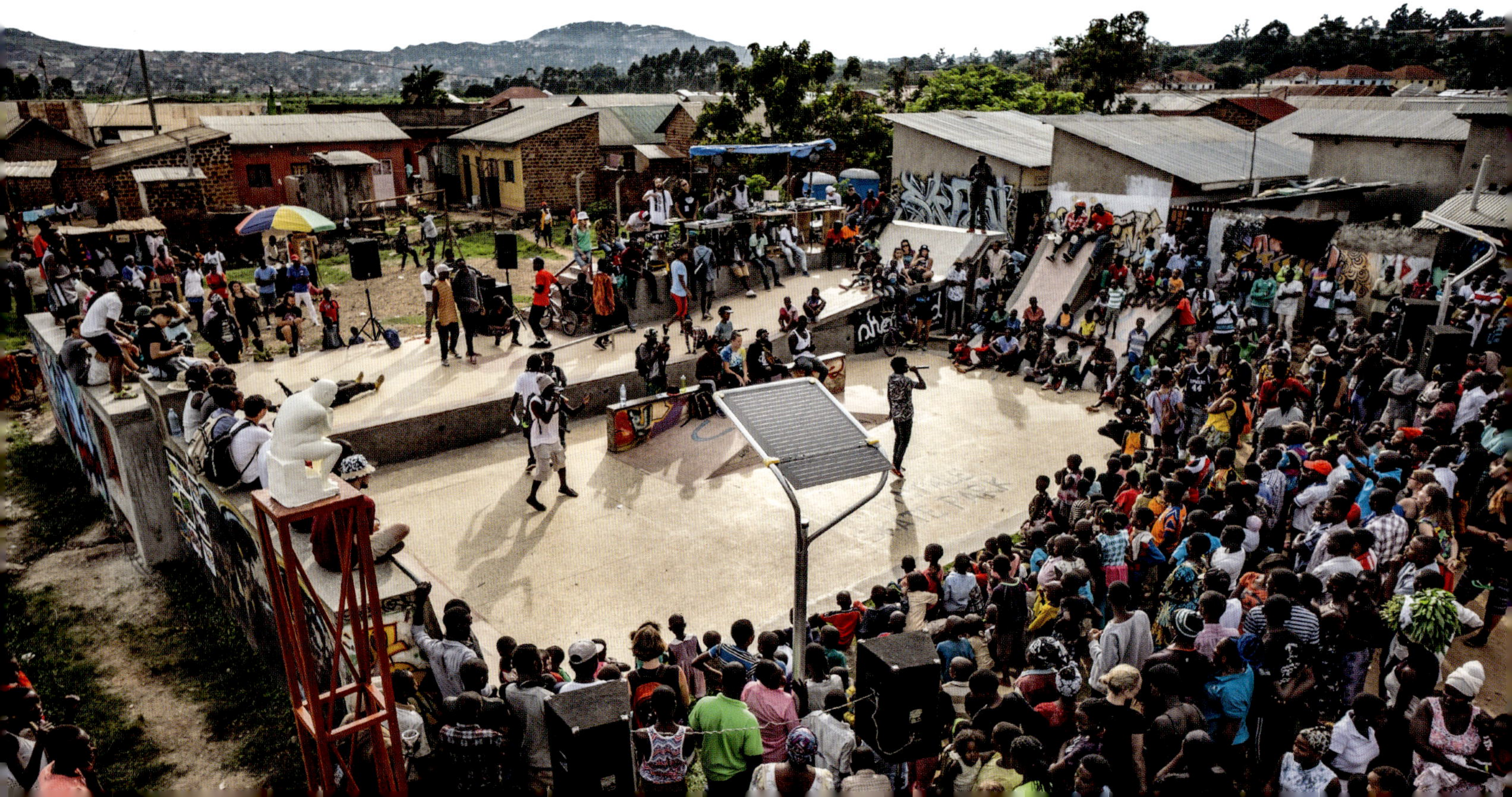

AFRI-CANS STREET ART FESTIVAL

FESTIVALS & CULTURE

The Afri-Cans Street Art Festival in Kampala, Uganda, founded by Sparrow and Mos Opten in 2017, aims to nurture and grow graffiti while beautifying select spaces of the city. Music, breakdancing, tattoos and workshops also play a role, while the festivities unite artists from all over Eastern Africa. It is one of the only events to feature prominent and up-and-coming urban artists from Kenya, Tanzania, Rwanda, Zambia and Uganda. In 2019 the festival included events in Kigali, Rwanda, and it plans to further extend its footprint in the region.

Opposite, clockwise from top left
Jobray. 2nd edn, Kampala, Uganda, 2018

Breakdancing during the festival. 2nd edn, Kampala, Uganda, 2018

Skateboarders at the festival. 2nd edn, Kampala, Uganda, 2018

The crowd enjoying a performance. 2nd edn, Kampala, Uganda, 2018

Shakes. 2nd edn, Kampala, Uganda, 2018

Right
Passers-by learning how to spray; Ohmz and Garuk87 painting in the background. 2nd edn, Kampala, Uganda, 2018

Page 58, top
Bankslave, Hatimax256. 2nd edn, Kampala, Uganda, 2018

Page 58, bottom
Take, Lo. 2nd edn, Kampala, Uganda, 2018

Page 59, top
Ngabonziza Bonfils, Muntu 621, Xenson. 2nd edn, Kampala, Uganda, 2018

Page 59, bottom
Rawdney, Willy Karekezi. 2nd edn, Kampala, Uganda, 2018

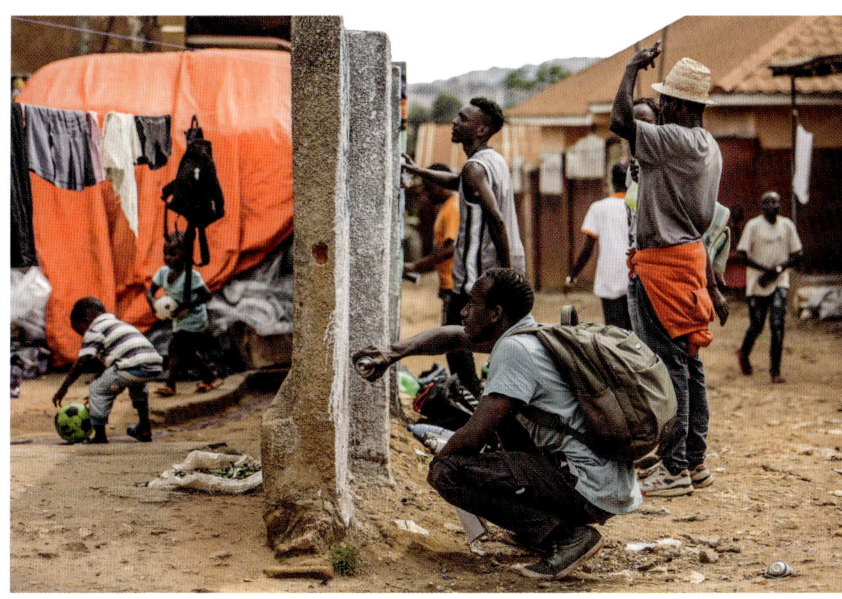

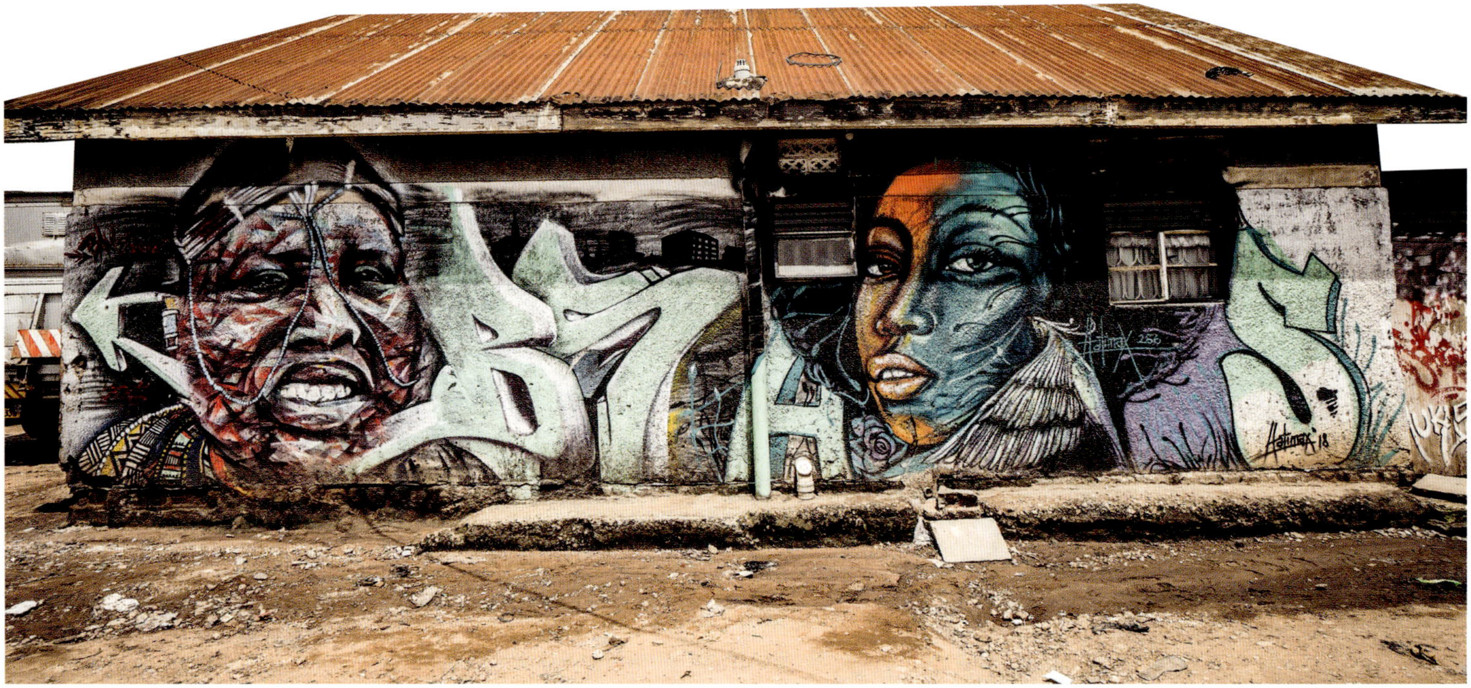

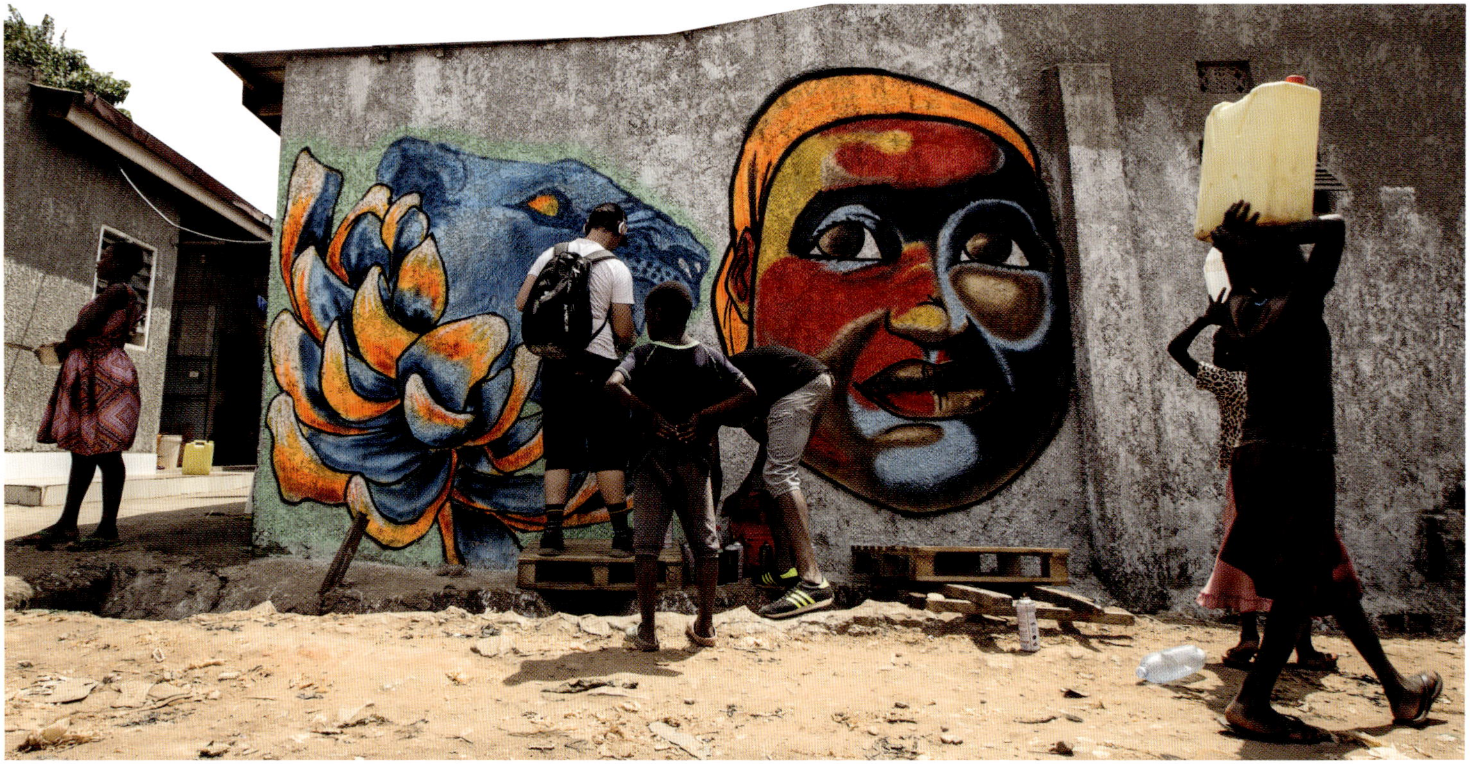

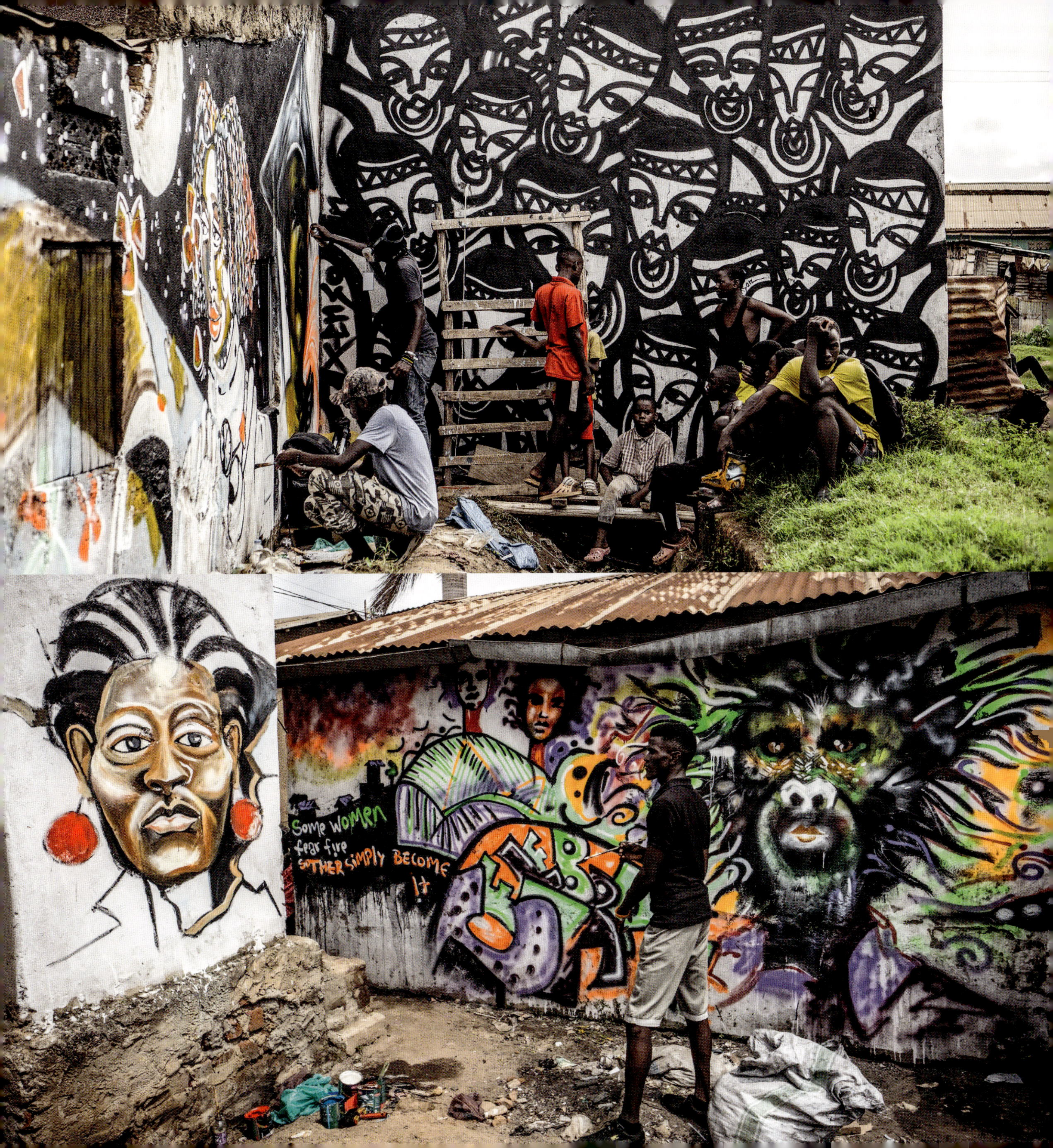

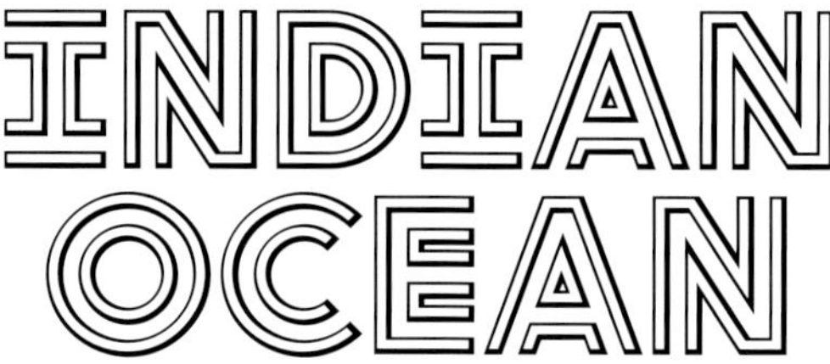

Off the east coast of Africa, the Indian Ocean features a scattering of several islands, including Mauritius, the Seychelles, the Comoros and Madagascar – the fourth largest island in the world. Other islands include Réunion and Mayotte, which are still administered by France. Unsurprisingly, street art has wandered into these remote patches of paradise, where it is relatively abundant. French is commonly spoken among the islanders and Réunion in particular has an incredibly developed urban arts movement.

In the Comoros, Socrome has pioneered a small community of graffiti artists. He first began doodling graffiti around 1999 in Moroni, the capital city, and refined his practice when he moved to mainland France. In 2003, he created LCN (Le Chat Noir) with Öpse One, and by the time he was a teenager, having moved back after spending a few years abroad, he became the first bona fide graffiti artist on the Comoro Islands. Socrome's name is an anagram of Comoros (Les Comores in French), a true dedication to his home country. Gathering momentum in his art, Socrome enlisted a few young, motivated boys to mentor in 2007, teaching them how to wield a can of paint and write their names in graffiti.

The cluster of islands forming the Comoros is an amalgamation of African, French and Arabic culture and heritage, therefore Arabic script also makes an appearance. In 2010, Socrome met the artists Saïd Omar and Hamou (who he still works with today), who were part of an association of calligraphers called Calcamart. Socrome fused Western graffiti with the Arabic calligraphic style invented by Calcamart known as 'Hattul Camart'. Together they initiated a variety of self-produced projects, including urban interventions on multi-storey walls and even on ships. Over the years they have collaborated with other artists, both local and international, such as Amir, Cheikn, Papadjo, Keal, Medo, Nakib and Servz 3HS. To ferment the brew and take the scene to even greater heights, in 2017 Socrome founded a domestic crew called Swana Studio.

Opposite
Swana Studio. 'Coelacanth' – a rare fish, an important symbol of the Comoros, Moroni, Comoros, 2017

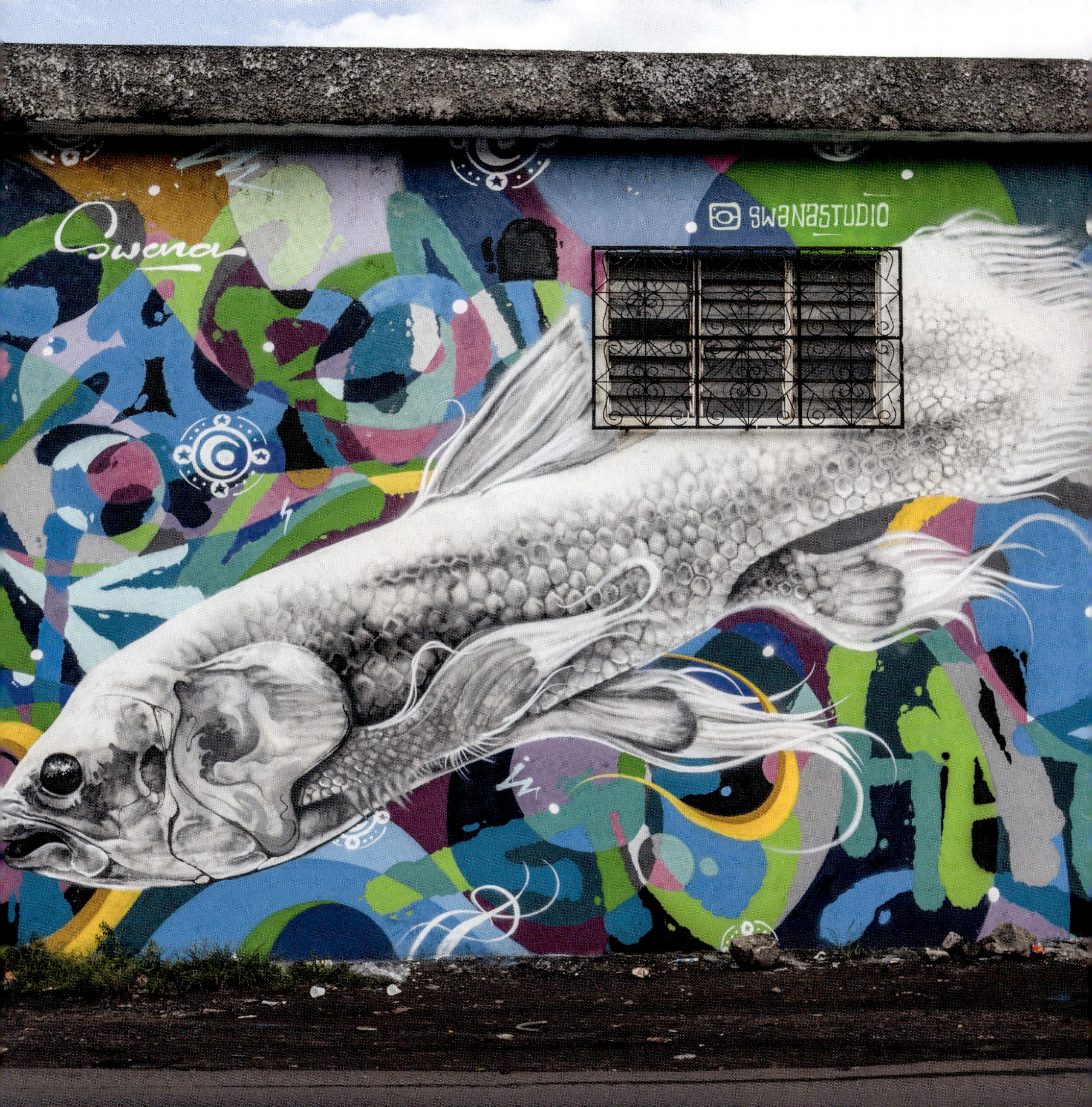
Swana
SWANASTUDIO

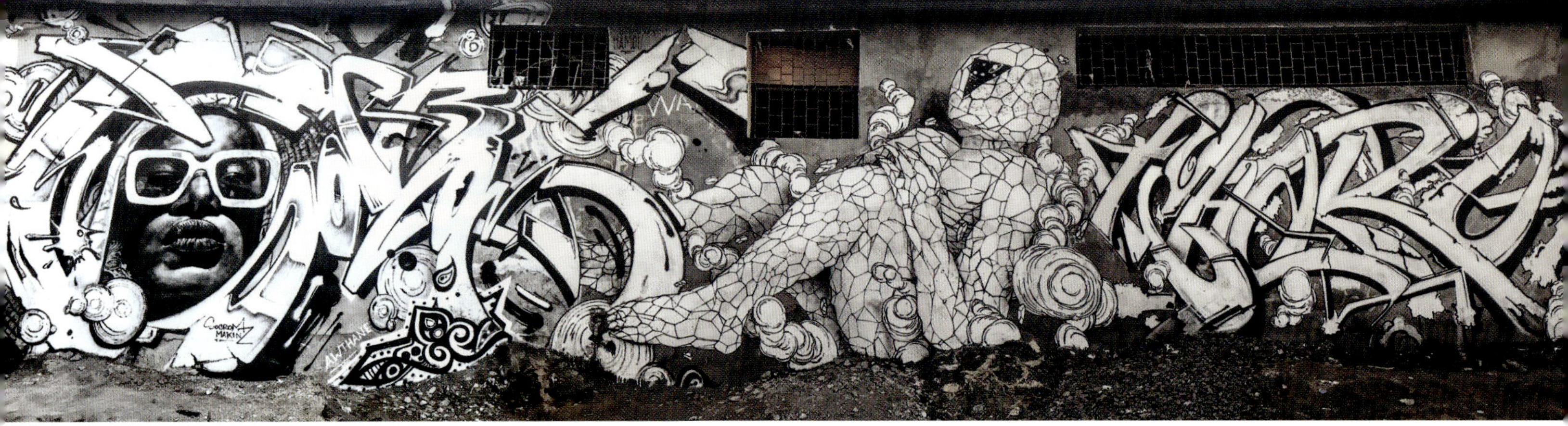

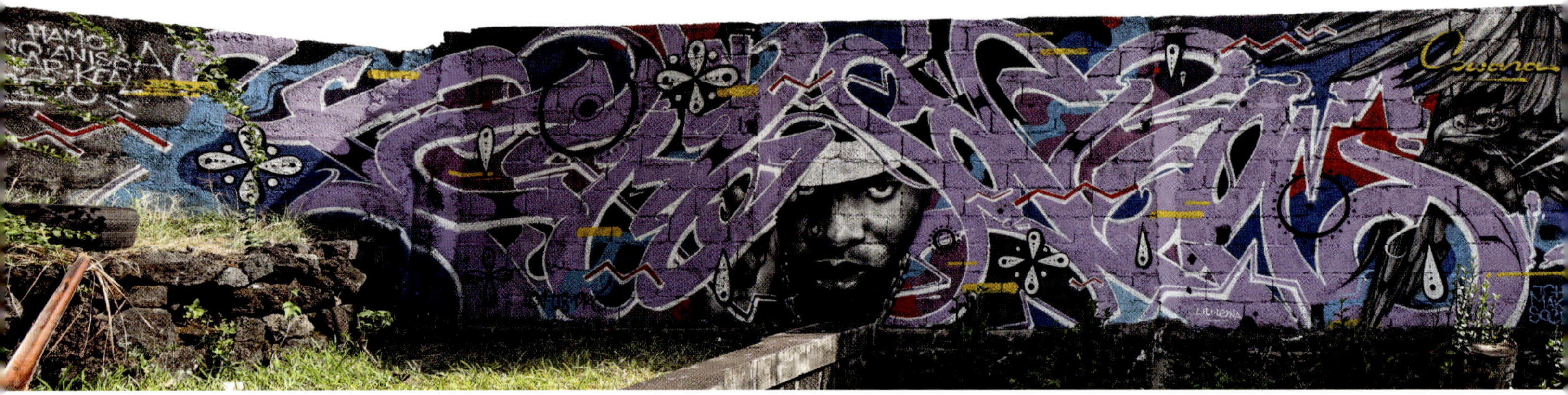

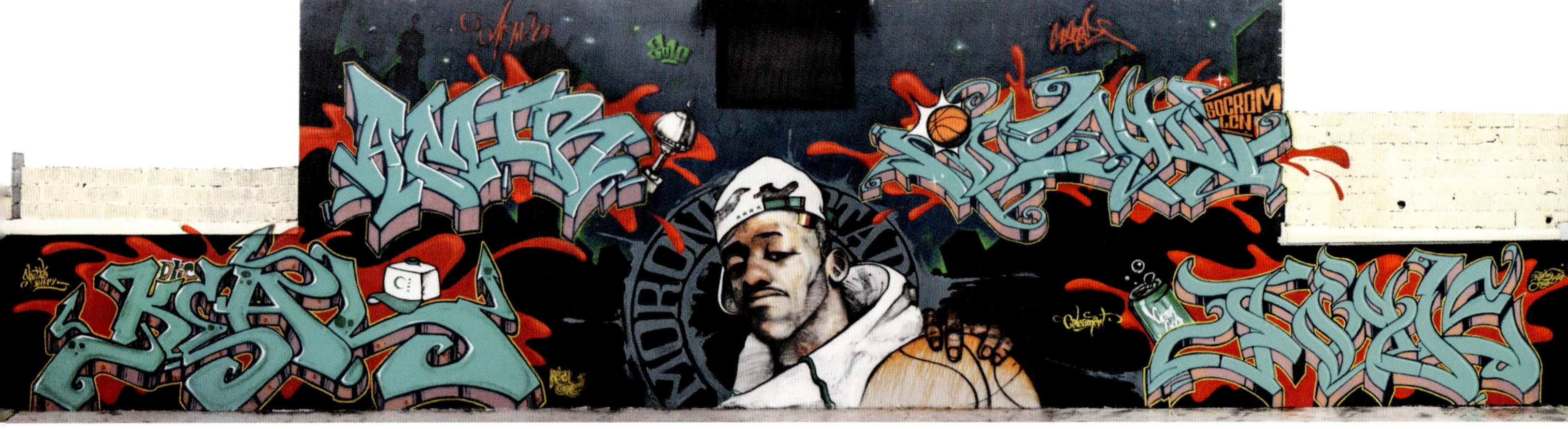
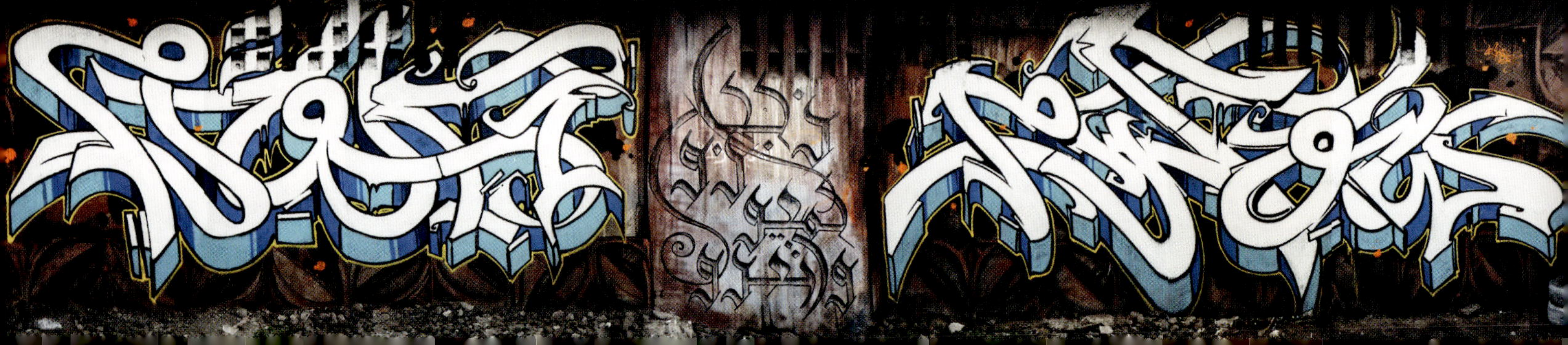

Swana Studio features motivated Comoros-bred artists: Makinz – who is focused on characters; Tcharo – who flows with letters; and the calligrapher Hamou. The collective is now an accomplished design studio and business-based enterprise, with their workmanship ranging from graphic and packaging design to decor murals and other illustration work. They also create many personal, large-scale mural projects and run several art workshops with young people. The Comoros is teeming with talented dancers, designers, rappers and urban street artists, even though quality materials are limited.

The large island nation of Madagascar is home to one of the world's most diverse ecosystems, with thousands of endemic species of fauna and flora. Visual artists often feature the vivid wildlife, such as lemurs and chameleons, in their works. Early settlers originated from Southeast Asia and Eastern Africa, resulting in a unique ethnic group, the Malagasy people. Although the country was colonized by the French, it is now independent and the Malagasy retain many traditional cultural beliefs, as well as their own language. Most of the land remains rural, but is under threat owing to deforestation and the rising human population. Following years of recurrent political unrest, the country is still very poor, and for young artists there are few opportunities or tertiary courses. Nevertheless, many of them manage to harness the expressive nature of graffiti to empower themselves and their communities.

When hip-hop culture first arrived in Madagascar it was like a benign invasion; yet despite the baggy pants and rapping in English, hip-hop had to adopt the Malagasy way of life. An infamous group, MCM Boys (later Da Hopp), was the catalyst for the urban movement, but graffiti had a belated genesis. After an explosion of hand-painted signage, advertisements became part of the cityscape, but graffiti was slower to acclimatize. Graffiti was misunderstood and inhabitants did not comprehend why someone would paint something on a wall without making money from the advertisers. But exponents blended their native tongue with the concept and the movement began to grow in numbers.

By the early 2000s, the graffiti scene started to take shape with the emergence of pioneers such as Sk4rz Tsijonriake and AIRJP Tagman. Sk4rz had immersed himself in hip-hop while studying abroad in France in the late 1990s. On his return to Antananarivo, Madagascar's capital, in 2001, he began to consult within the local 'haintso haintso' (Malagasy hip-hop) scene and explore the artistic mediums available to him. He wanted to transform his surroundings and began to paint graffiti on his city's streets, which he still does today. AIRJP Tagman lived in the countryside, and became interested in comic books while studying in Ambositra, his nearest town. Soon he was painting speech bubbles on walls together with his hip-hop friends, earning his nickname 'Tagman'. In 2007 he joined a collective of comic artists in Antananarivo, where he participated in many events, and by 2008 he was painting graffiti pieces. With the hip-hop dancer Anansi Dzao, in 2009 he co-created the diverse collective Motion Nation, which also includes singers and circus artists. During the political crisis of that year they gathered

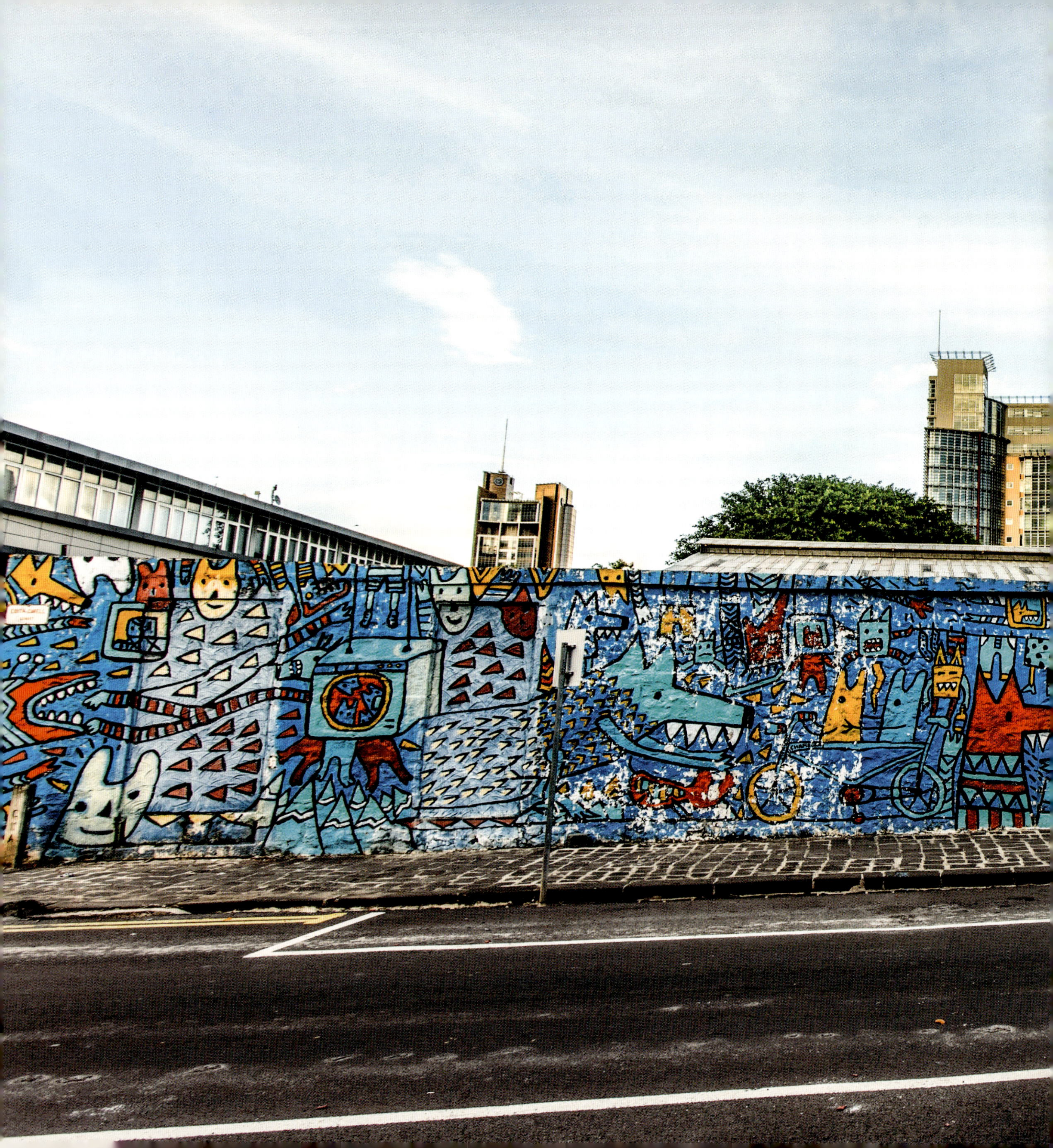

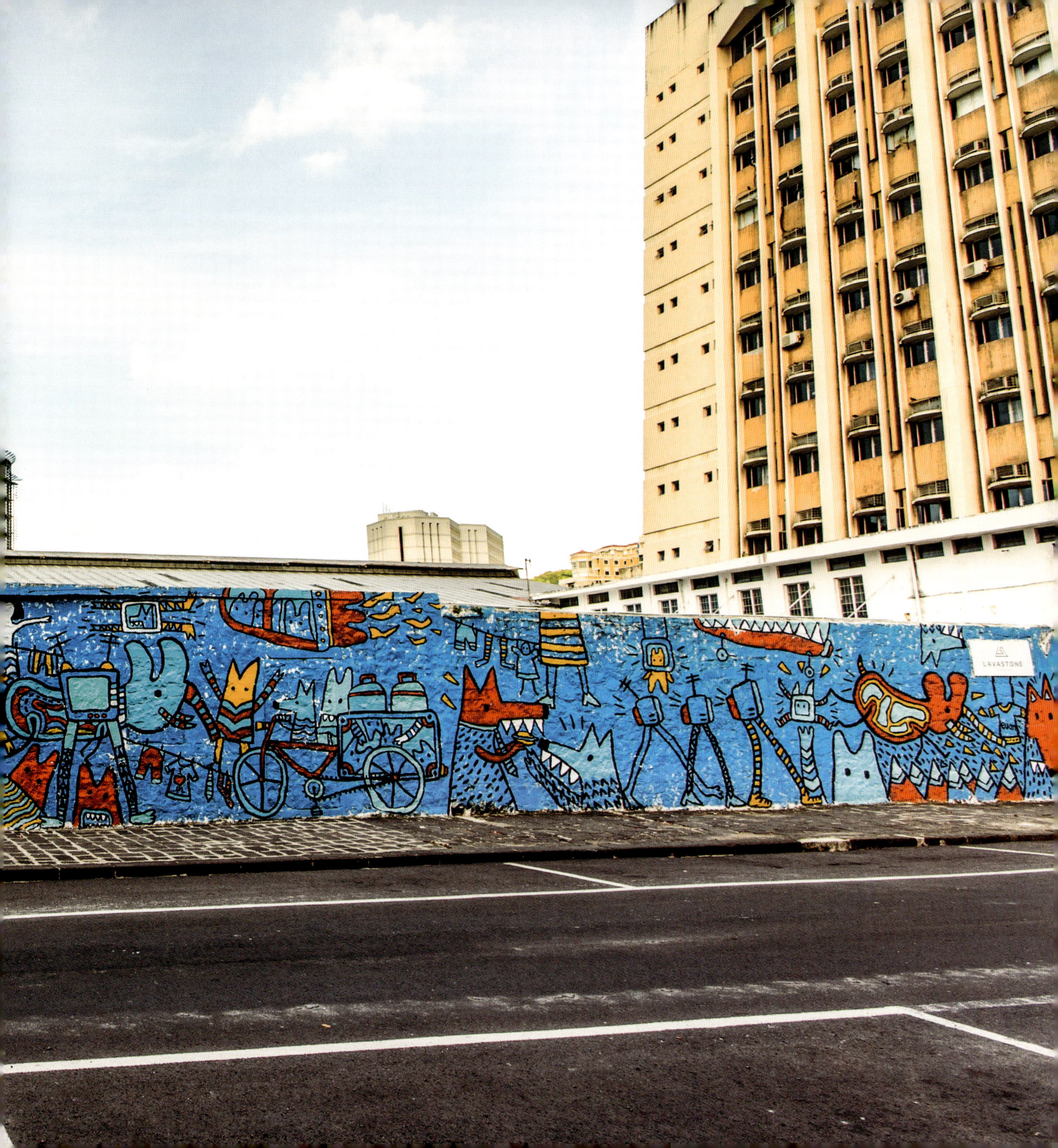

 NATY KALY

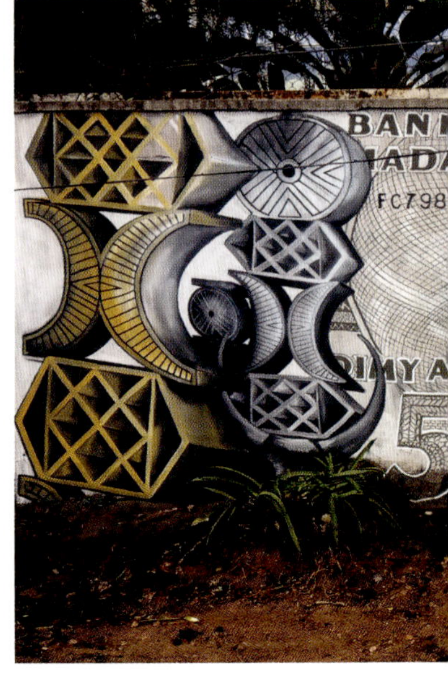

weekly to promote peace, in partnership with 2HY-faire lien, an association that nurtures sustainable development through arts and culture. In 2011, AIRJP Tagman began travelling between France and Madagascar, connecting with artists from Marseille, with whom he realized several murals in both countries. AIRJP's artworks embody his outlook on life, portraying the relationship between humans and the environment and often featuring his iconic chameleon and other signature elements from his native land.

Jamerla Koonaction is a respected group of Malagasy artists and artisans, musicians, chefs, mechanics and more, including some of the country's finest muralists. Formally established in 2013, the graffiti crew features many who were closely linked to the emergence of hip-hop in the early 2000s. Naty Kaly, BM Souljah, RinaArt, Clipse Teean, Isaac, Ponk and close associate Taka Andrianavalona make up the talented squad, many of whom initially tried their luck at other disciplines within the hip-hop culture, such as MCing and B-boying, before settling on street art as their chosen means of expression. Many members first dabbled with graffiti around 2006, some experimenting with charcoal, later buying paint to colour the Ampefiloha neighbourhood. Today the association paints long stretches of walls for its Taninjanaka project, which offers glimpses of local life, painted in the group's signature style. These artists too are considered pioneers and innovators in the Madagascan scene.

An inspiring undertaking by a visiting artist from the island of Réunion, Jace, put Malagasy graffiti on the world map. His 2011 personal project saw him paint the

Naty Kaly, RinaArt. Taninjanaka project, Antananarivo, Madagascar, 2017

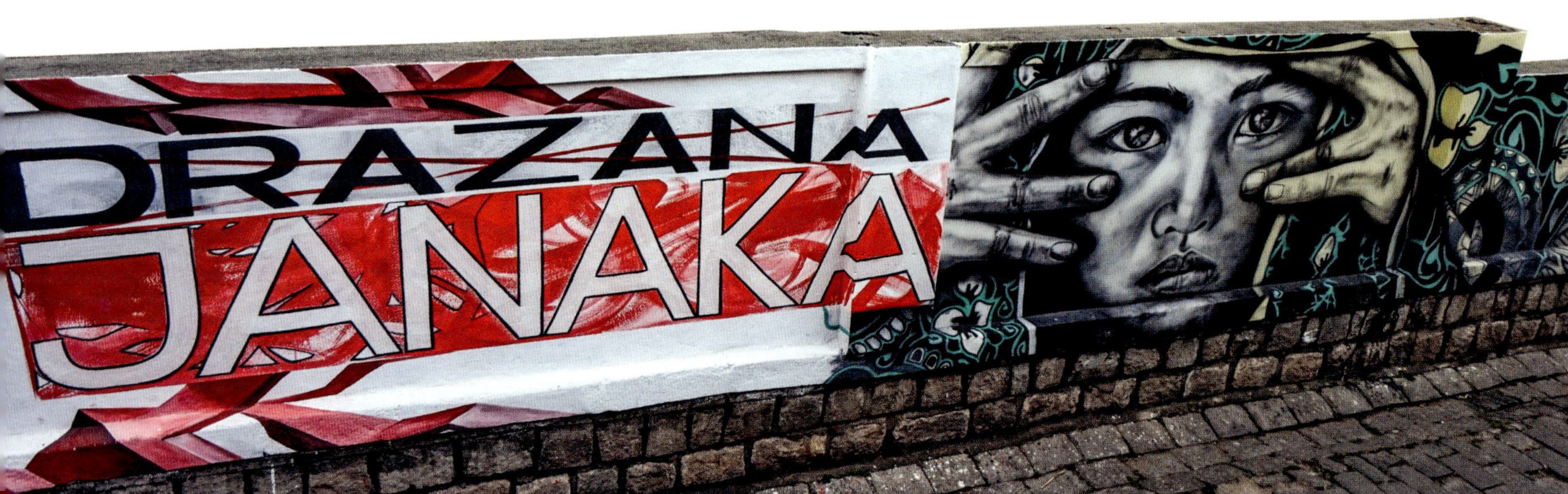

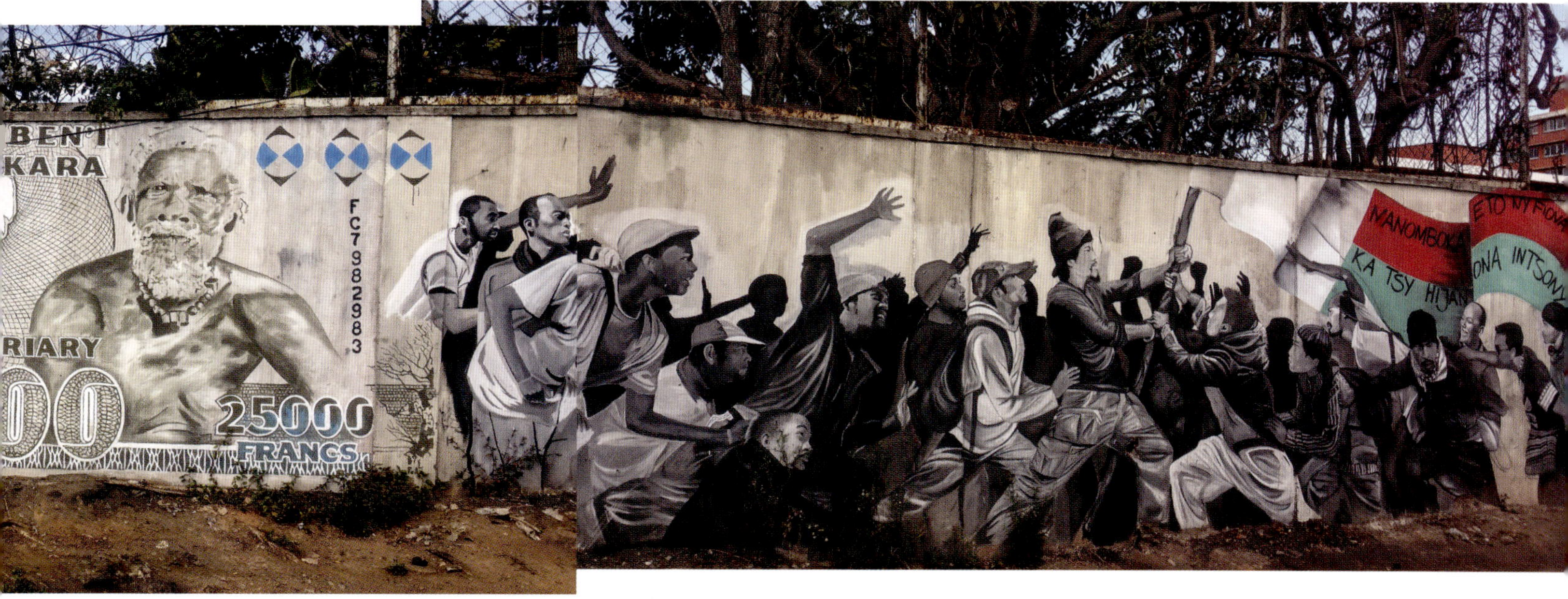

RinaArt, Naty Kaly.
Taninjanaka project,
'Manomboka Eto Ny Fiovana
Ka Tsy Hijanona Intsony'
(Changes Start Here and
Will Never Stop; according
to the artist, the phrase
signifies unity), Antananarivo,
Madagascar, 2016

boat sails of the Vezo people, a fishing community, and he later returned with
a stream of international stalwarts for the project Du Graffiti dans les Voiles
(Graffiti in the Sails). Other artists and organizations are also encouraging an
active arts circuit through dynamic festivals. Is'Art Galerie, a leading art centre
in Antananarivo, collaborated with ANAE (AfricaINosy Art Echange) to establish
Festival d'Art Urbain (Urban Art Festival) in 2014. The annual event strives to build
an exchange between the local arts scene, the neighbouring Indian Ocean scene
and the bigger and more active scene on mainland Africa. Since its formation, the
festival has continued to expose new minds to the constructive characteristics
of urban art in the capital city with wall paintings, art classes, street performances
and further collaborative exploits, while also infiltrating other parts of the country.

The fourth edition of Festival d'Art Urbain joined forces with Stritarty, another
annual event, in the northern port city of Antsiranana (also known as Diego
Suarez). Founded in 2016 by Alliance Française and the Dsary collective, Stritarty:
Le Festival des Arts Urbains is a platform for free expression and intercultural
exchange through graffiti, dance, slam poetry and more. It encompasses
multiple disciplines of underground art forms as live musicians, DJs, BMXers,
skateboarders and parkour enthusiasts all perform in the streets. Stritarty aims
to connect the public by creating dialogue and meaningful encounters while
beautifying dreary urban centres. In Antananarivo, practitioners such as Sleeping
Pop dedicate their time to paint in public spaces to enrich the landscape,
especially in neglected back alleys. Spreading their love for art, they aim to teach
citizens to take pride in their surroundings while changing perceptions of graffiti.
Mat Li, Nino, Mozeration and Maherisoa Rakotomalala are other active local
artists, while Blue (originally from France) has also made Madagascar her home.

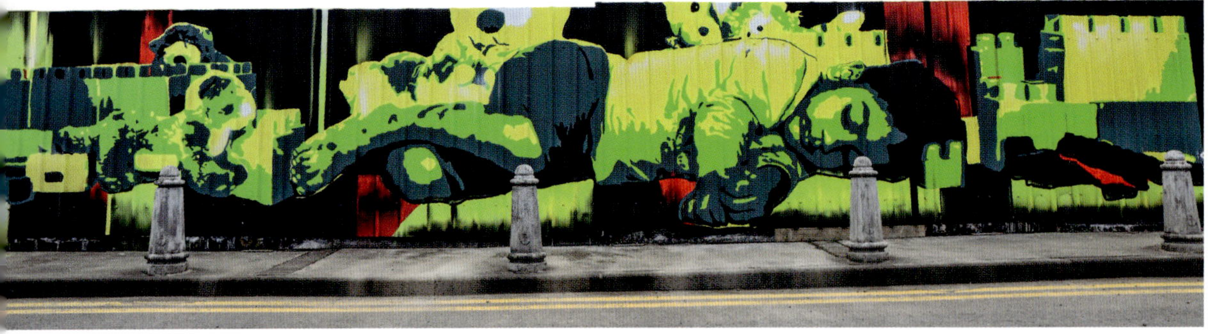

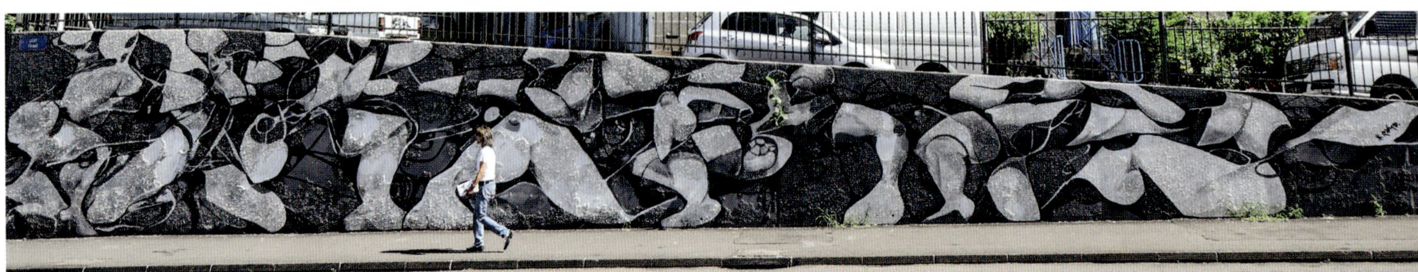

Islands are now recognized 'spraycation' destinations within graffiti circles and the tropical paradise of Mauritius is no different. World renowned for its white sand beaches, the isle boasts a small artists' community and a festival that has placed its street art on the map. Porlwi Festival was launched in 2015 to revitalize the city centre of Port Louis. Over three consecutive years, Porlwi changed the face of the country's capital by means of street arts, including live performances of mural painting and dance, as well as video mapping and projections, thus generating new interest in the area. The event primarily took place at nighttime, with a relevant theme for each edition – Porlwi by Light (2015), Porlwi by People (2016) and Porlwi by Nature (2017). Organizers invited national, regional and international artists to create large-scale masterpieces, also drafting in select local fine artists who had no previous experience in painting walls. The event was a major success and stimulated a revival of construction in the central business district soon afterwards. Porlwi also ignited a fire within many of the Mauritian artists, as they continue to produce murals.

Practising muralists in Mauritius often choose to use brushes, even though imported spray paint is readily available. Graffiti writer Resko was invited to Porlwi thanks to his local reputation on the island, while artists such as Brian Lamoureux, Evan Sohun, RYMD and Dévid were selected for their exciting potential – something that has certainly paid off. Other street artists, such as Joshila Dhaby, who works with stencils, have ventured overseas to paint at formidable gatherings such as Upfest in Bristol, UK, and Art Basel in Miami, USA. Each artist tells a zestful story through a balance of colours and techniques, as demand for their work grows. Overall, the Indian Ocean area is becoming a dynamic showground for contemporary art.

Top
Joshila Dhaby. 'Sleep. Dream. Play.', Port Louis, Mauritius, 2017

Above
RYMD. 'The 2100', Porlwi by People Festival, Port Louis, Mauritius, 2016

Opposite, top
Naty Kaly. Taninjanaka project, Antananarivo, Madagascar, 2016

Opposite, bottom
Naty Kaly. Taninjanaka project, Antananarivo, Madagascar, 2016

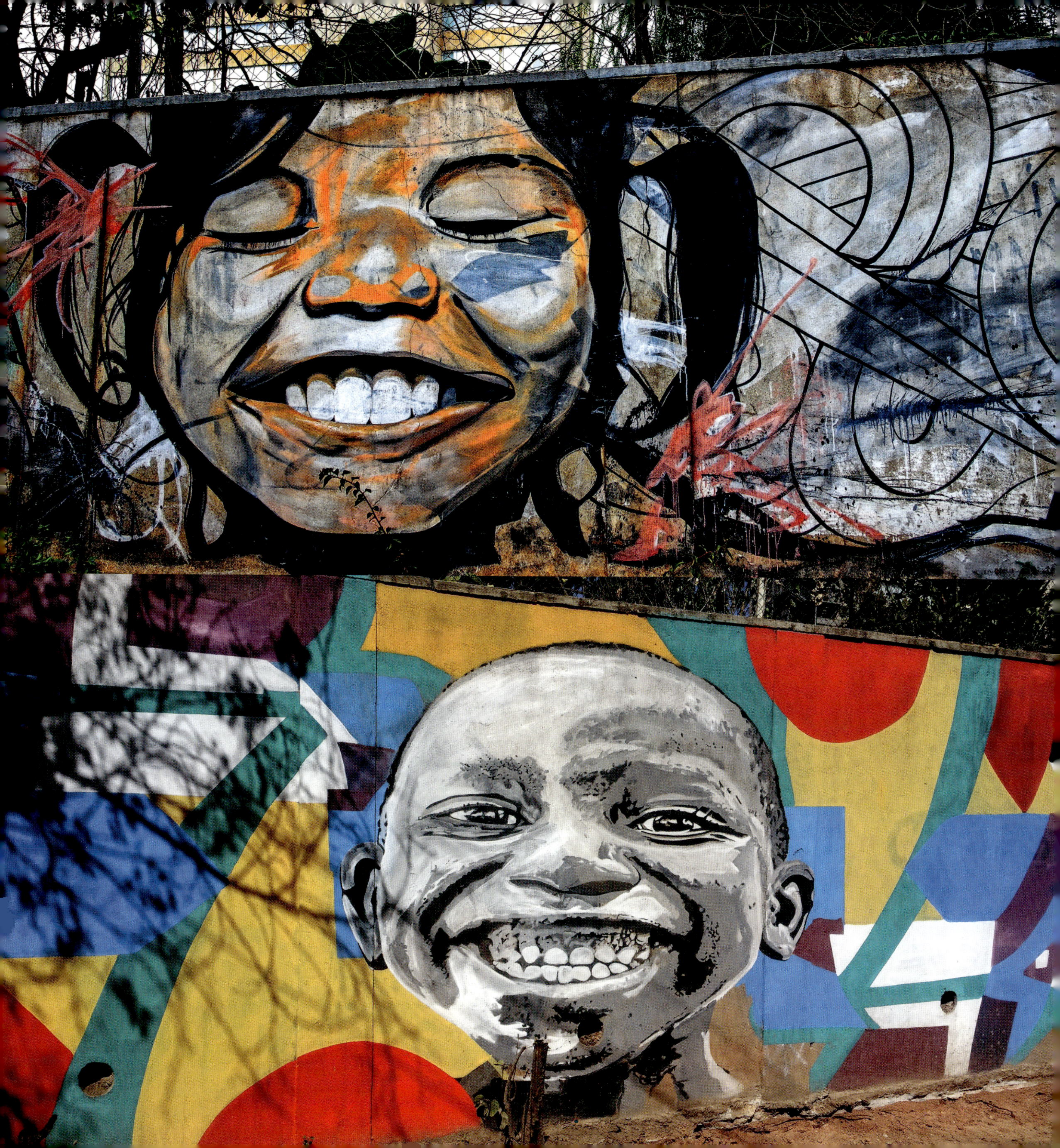

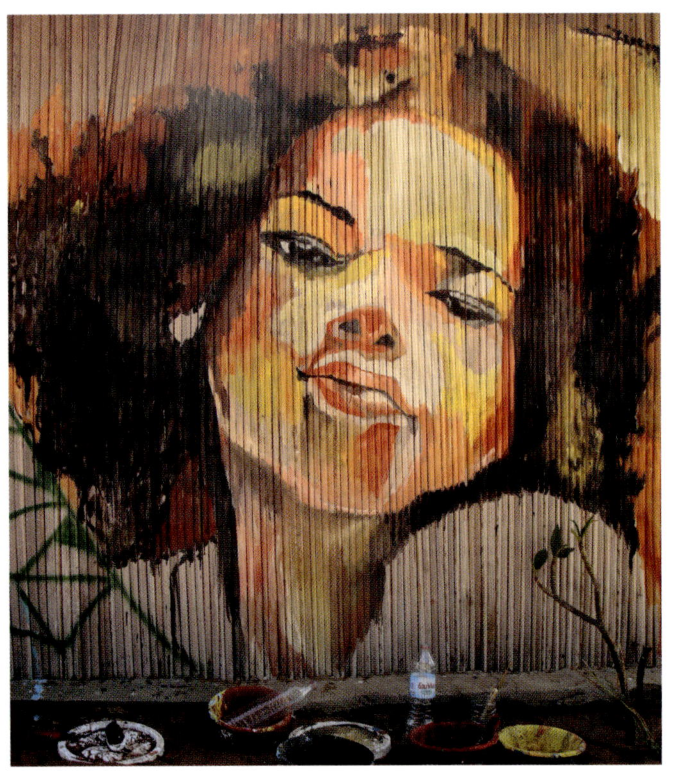

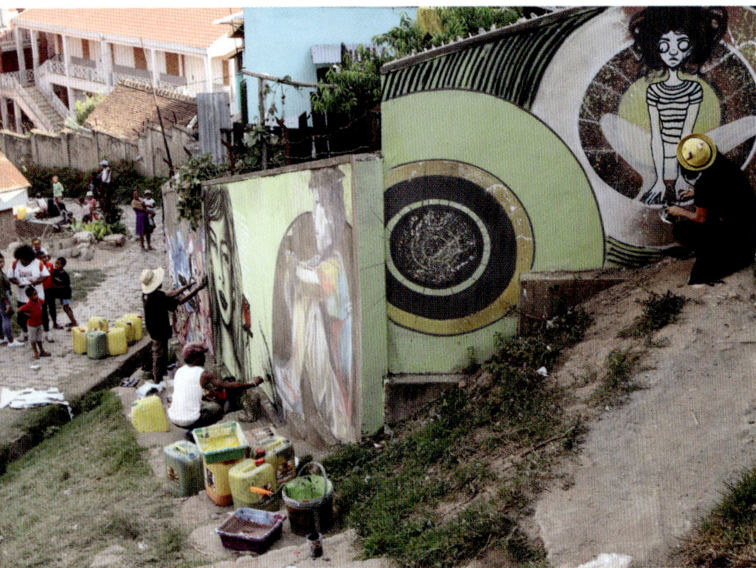

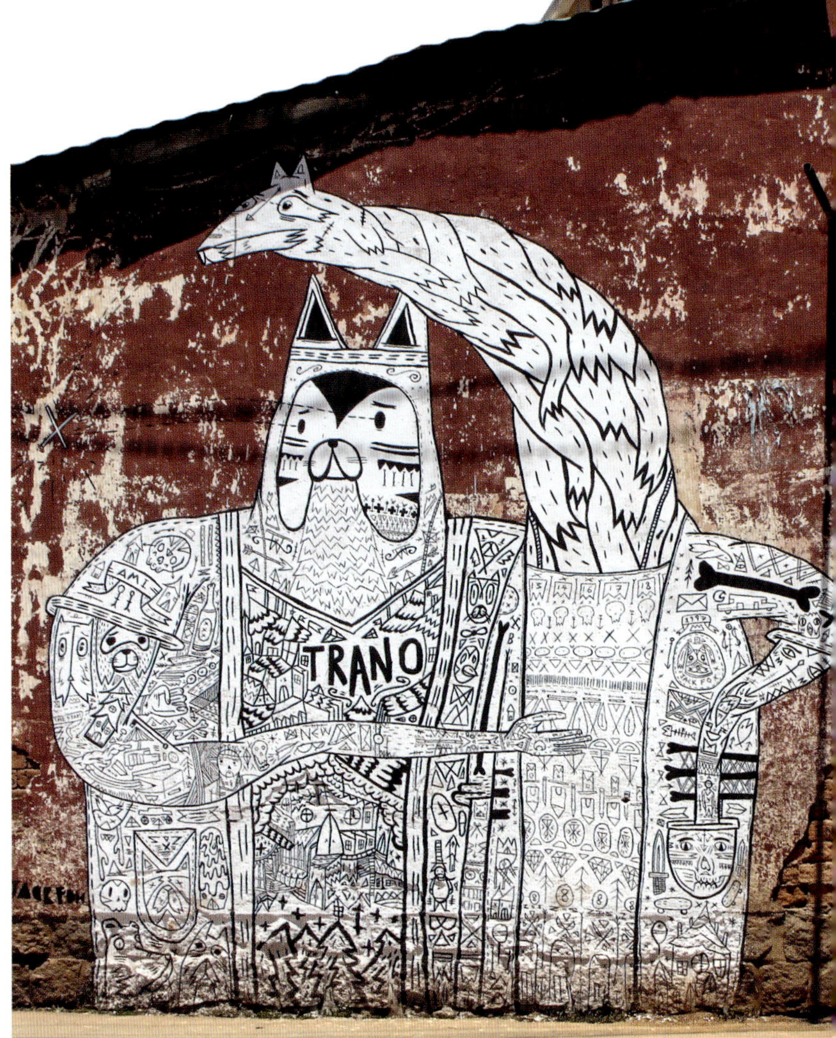
TRANO

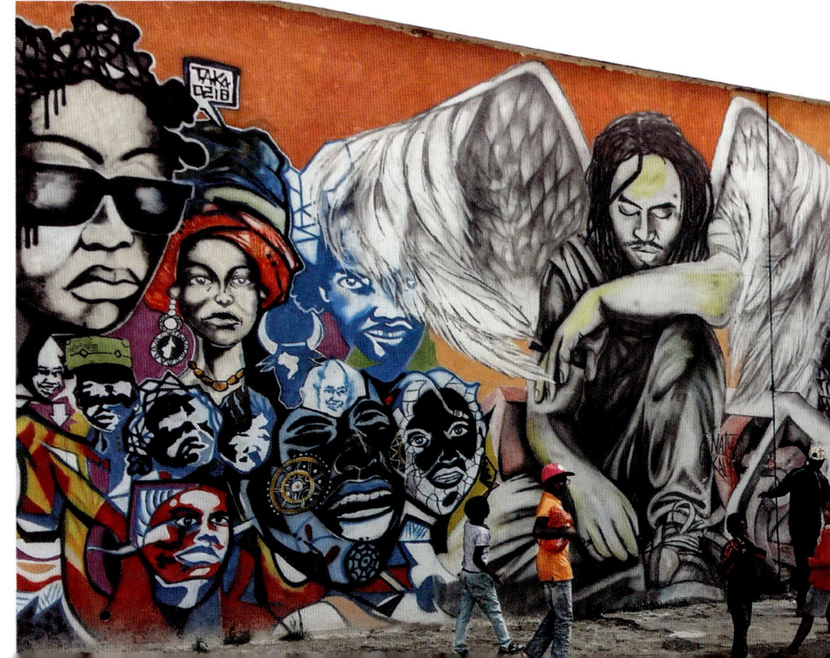
TAKA
0218

FESTIVAL D'ART URBAIN

Clockwise from top left
**Naty Kaly. 4th edn,
Ramena, Madagascar, 2017**

**Jack Fox. 1st edn,
Antananarivo,
Madagascar, 2014**

**Maherisoa Rakotomalala.
3rd edn, Mahajunga,
Madagascar, 2016**

**Taka Andrianavalona,
Naty Kaly, RinaArt.
5th edn, Antananarivo,
Madagascar, 2018**

**Taka Andrianavalona,
Clipse Teean, Naty
Kaly, Mat Li, Vanii Suki.
5th edn, Antananarivo,
Madagascar, 2018**

Madagascar's arts circuit is developing rapidly as many foreign cultural agents invest in its growth. Festival d'Art Urbain was established in 2014 by Is'Art Galerie in Antananarivo. Local artists collaborate on mural paintings while invited guests facilitate workshops to provide further stimulation and cultural exchange. Since its inception, the festival has welcomed artists from Réunion, the Comoros, the Seychelles, Benin, Kenya, Zambia, the DRC (Democratic Republic of the Congo) and South Africa, including starlets such as Faith XLVII, Ricky Lee Gordon, Keya Tama (fka Jack Fox) and Jarrett Erasmus (of Burning Museum), among others. Working independently, and with the help of foreign institutions like Pro Helvetia Swiss Council, Festival d'Art Urbain has continued to expose the constructive characteristics of urban art to new minds, while also infiltrating other parts of the island.

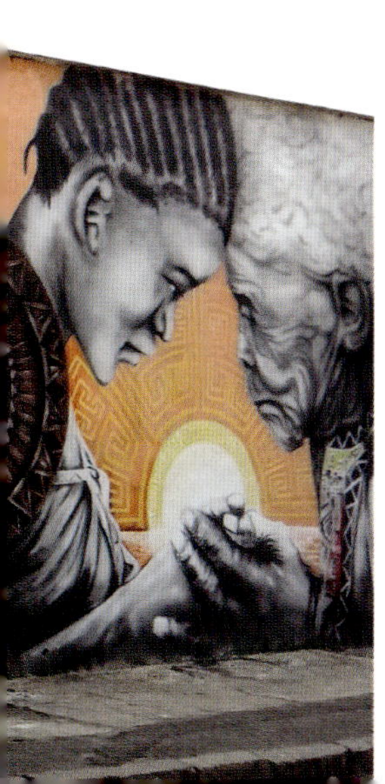

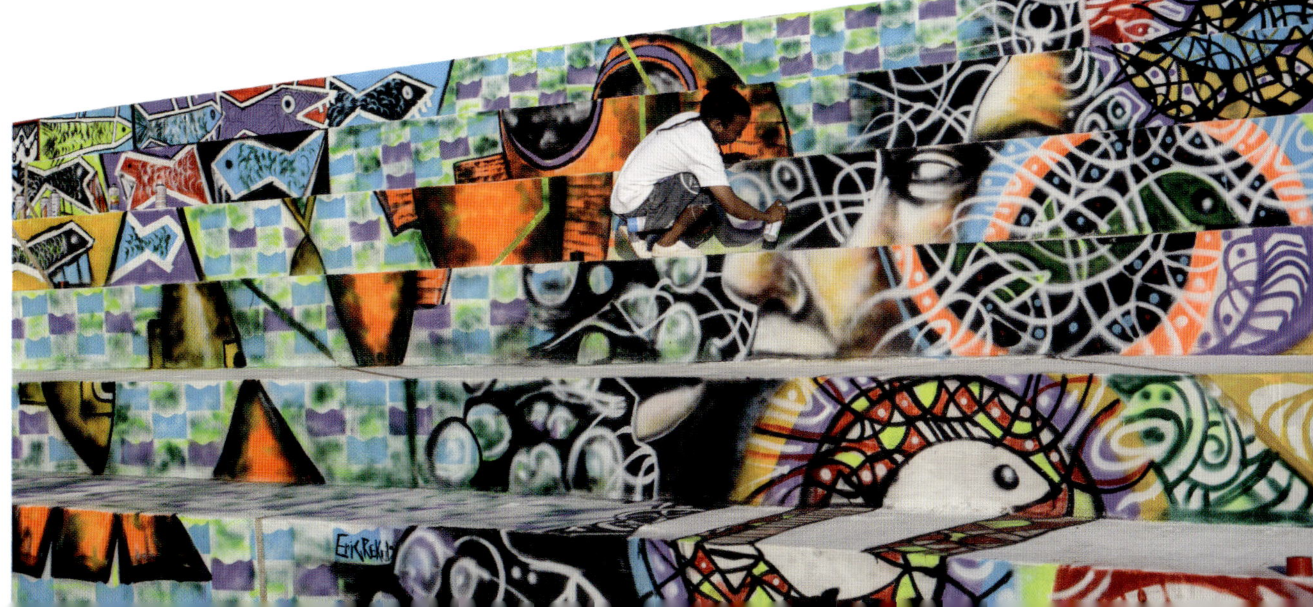

AIRJP TAGMAN

Tell me about your introduction to art and your passion for graffiti.

Growing up, my house was filled with family portraits and I was fascinated by these drawings – there was already a whole generation of artists and painters in our tribe. My childhood was built around my father's passion for art and he encouraged me to take this path in life. My love for graffiti came later when I discovered comic books: I tell stories through my art, no matter what medium. My strong love for colours and the need to draw keeps me passionate – in my bubble, a world where everything is possible, I can express anything and bring my imagination to life. It brings great joy to myself and those around me when I create.

Tell me about your style and the way you paint.

I do not have a precise style but I always work with the same themes. Graffiti is an experiment, like being in a laboratory where I search, invent, test and analyse.

Among my art styles, I developed what I call 'signaturism': a way for me to draw with signatures to form a complete figure. I also make 'ekologik'art', which are murals made with ecological materials, like soil or natural pigments. Graffiti is an experience and I like to paint freestyle, going wherever my painting takes me, without thinking too much.

Do you have any particular meaning behind your work?

Every work of mine has its own story. I paint to tell my history and that of others. I work with two specific themes: humans (man) and the environment (animals). Humans: I tell my story and the stories of those who I have met – and also Malagasy culture, tribes, traditions and daily life. Environment: I paint a lot of Madagascar's endemic fauna and flora, like the chameleon, lemur and zebu. Each piece is an endless story, like a book; sometimes inexplicable, joyful, sad, revolting, committed or simply decorative, depending on how people will interpret it. My artworks are like a crossroads between my imagination and the reality of the viewer. Sometimes we can understand each other, but sometimes our perspectives differ. If I have a message to convey, it is to be human and live in harmony with nature.

Tell me about your crew or the people you paint with. Are you in a crew?

In 2009, I painted with my crew named Motion Nation, based in Antananarivo, and in 2011 I started to work with a Marseille-based collective called TCK (The Colorz Kings) with Fresk and KidR.

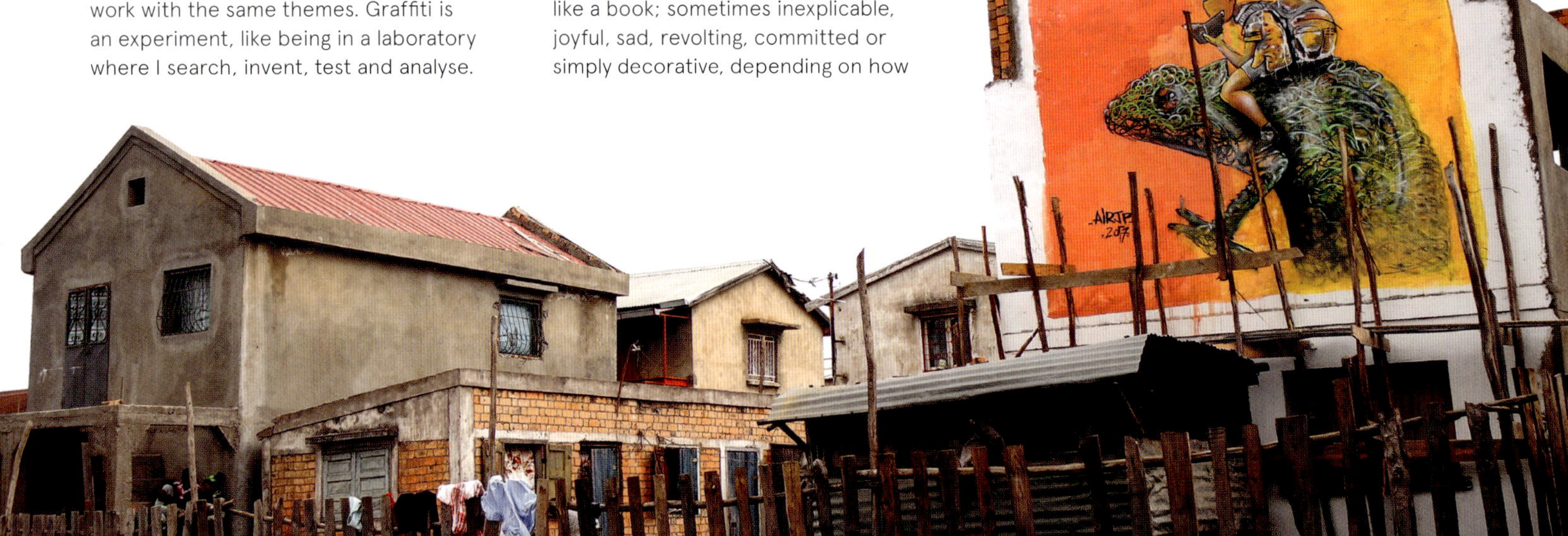

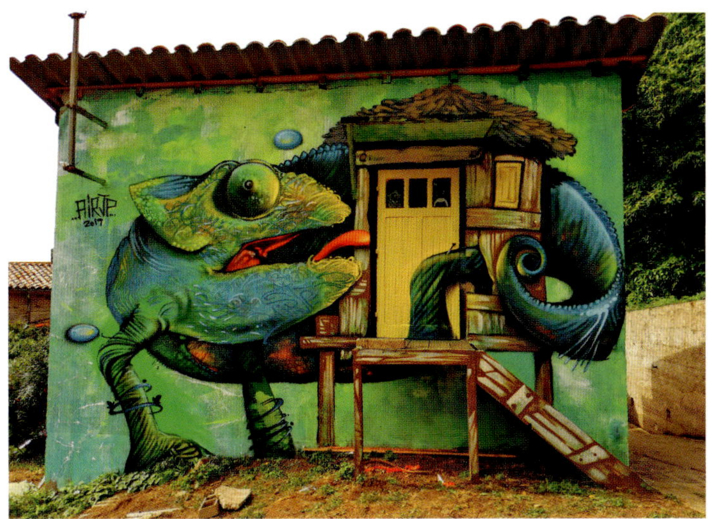
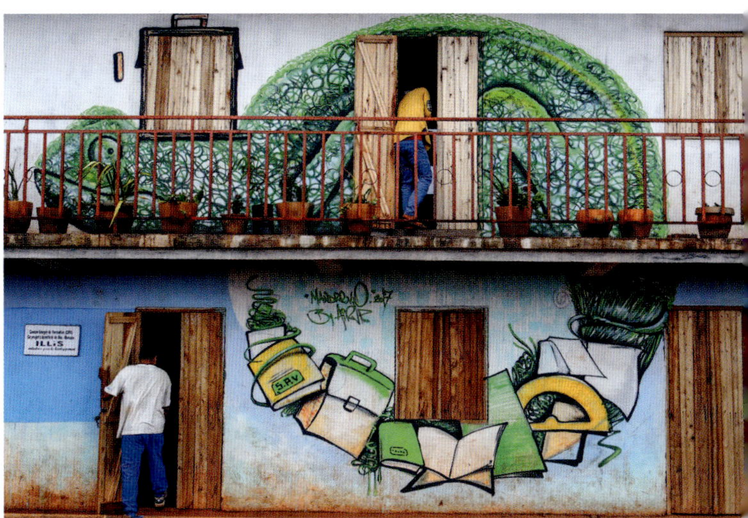

What is the graffiti scene like in Madagascar? How has it grown in recent years?

When I first started to paint graffiti in Madagascar, people did not know what it was. Many thought we were wasting our money, while some liked the idea of bringing colours to the city. Graffiti plays an important role because artists can use it to communicate about politics and social discontent. It also allows us to share art with the people, no matter their social status. Nowadays, a lot of Malagasy comic book artists are becoming graffiti artists; there are more than twenty active street artists.

What would you say is unique about graffiti in Madagascar?

Graffiti in Madagascar is inspired by its culture, endemic animals and many cultural and traditional items like hairstyle, dressing, beliefs (*fombafomba*) and taboos (*fady*). Malagasy graffiti talks about its rich culture, music and rhythm with lots of colours.

Can you compare African graffiti to that of the rest of the world, places such as Europe and America?

African graffiti and street art is on a par with the rest of the planet, but the lack of painting materials is significant. It is difficult to find good-quality paints for economic reasons, but we manage to get by with what we have. Artistic ingenuity is at the core of the creation process and materials are just tools to facilitate the realization of the imagination. Many graffiti artists have remarkable determination and use oil paint and natural pigments. Despite the high number of African graffiti artists, we unfortunately do not see much of them on the international art market.

How has graffiti affected your life?

I have had many encounters and adventures, as well as a good artistic experience overall. Thanks to my art I have travelled and met people easily, no matter their origins or culture. Graffiti breaks down barriers, even if it may only be a smile or a stare. I never stop learning, experimenting and discovering. Every day I progress a little bit more, whether it is aspiration or on a technical level.

What is the most important thing about painting graffiti?

Every step is important, but it depends on what you want to achieve. If I paint for pleasure, the result is not important because gratification is found in the moment. It is meditative, like therapy, and my mind travels elsewhere – I am in a place of well-being. If I paint to convey a message, the result is very valuable and I must first study how to enhance the subject matter for the audience. I need to keep it simple and effective, in the perfect location.

AIRJP Tagman is from Madagascar and holds a deep fascination for his native roots. Telling stories and promoting sustainable development through his artworks, he aims to bridge the divide between urban and rural inhabitants. Based in France, he travels back and forth often.

Opposite
AIRJP Tagman. Antananarivo, Madagascar, 2017

Above left
AIRJP Tagman. Lespinassière, France, 2019

Above right
AIRJP Tagman. Graffiti Nomad project, Antsirabe, Madagascar, 2017

Following spread
AIRJP Tagman. Zion Expo, Montolieu, France, 2015–19

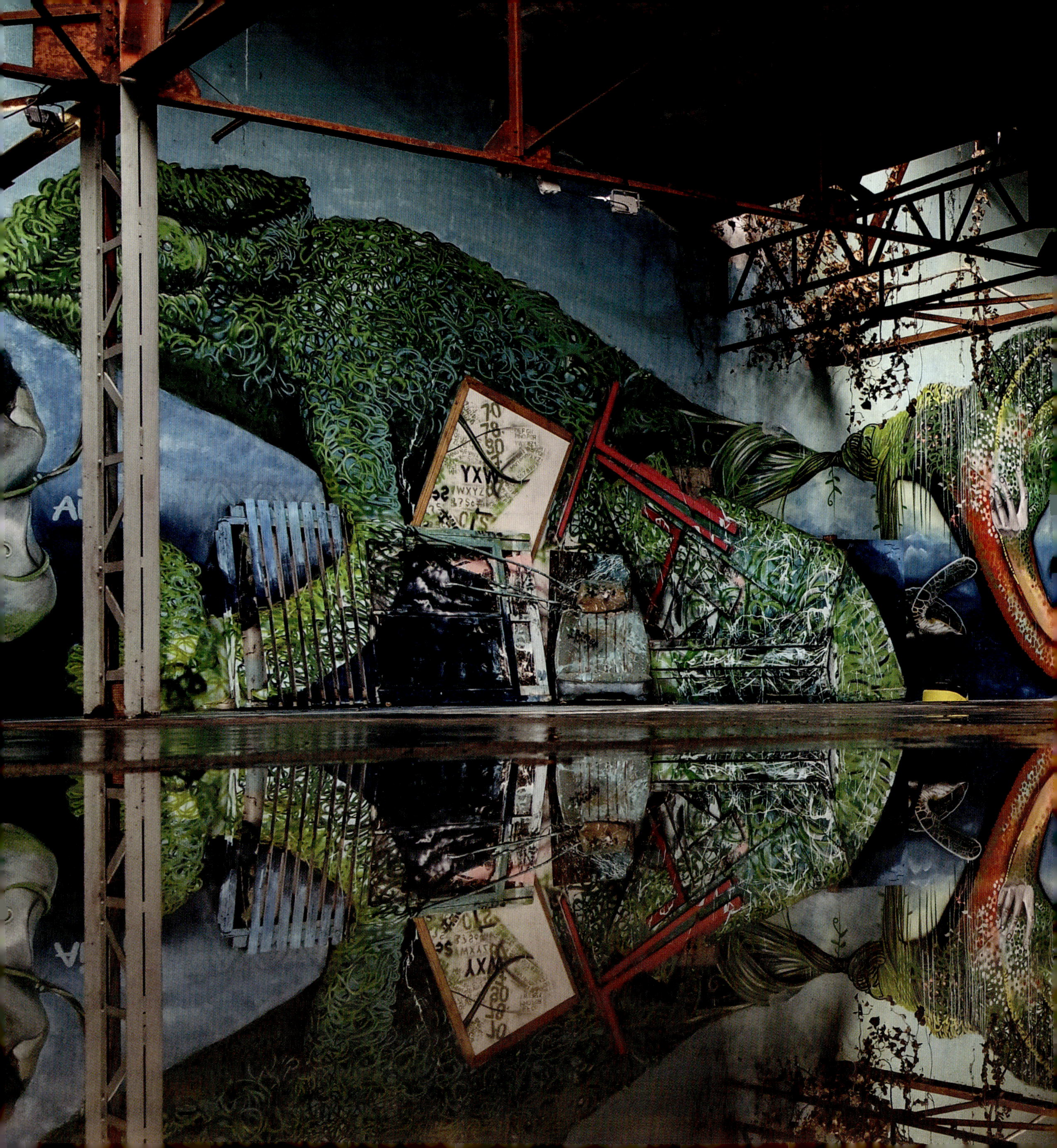
70
79
90
YXXY
WXYZ
STORS

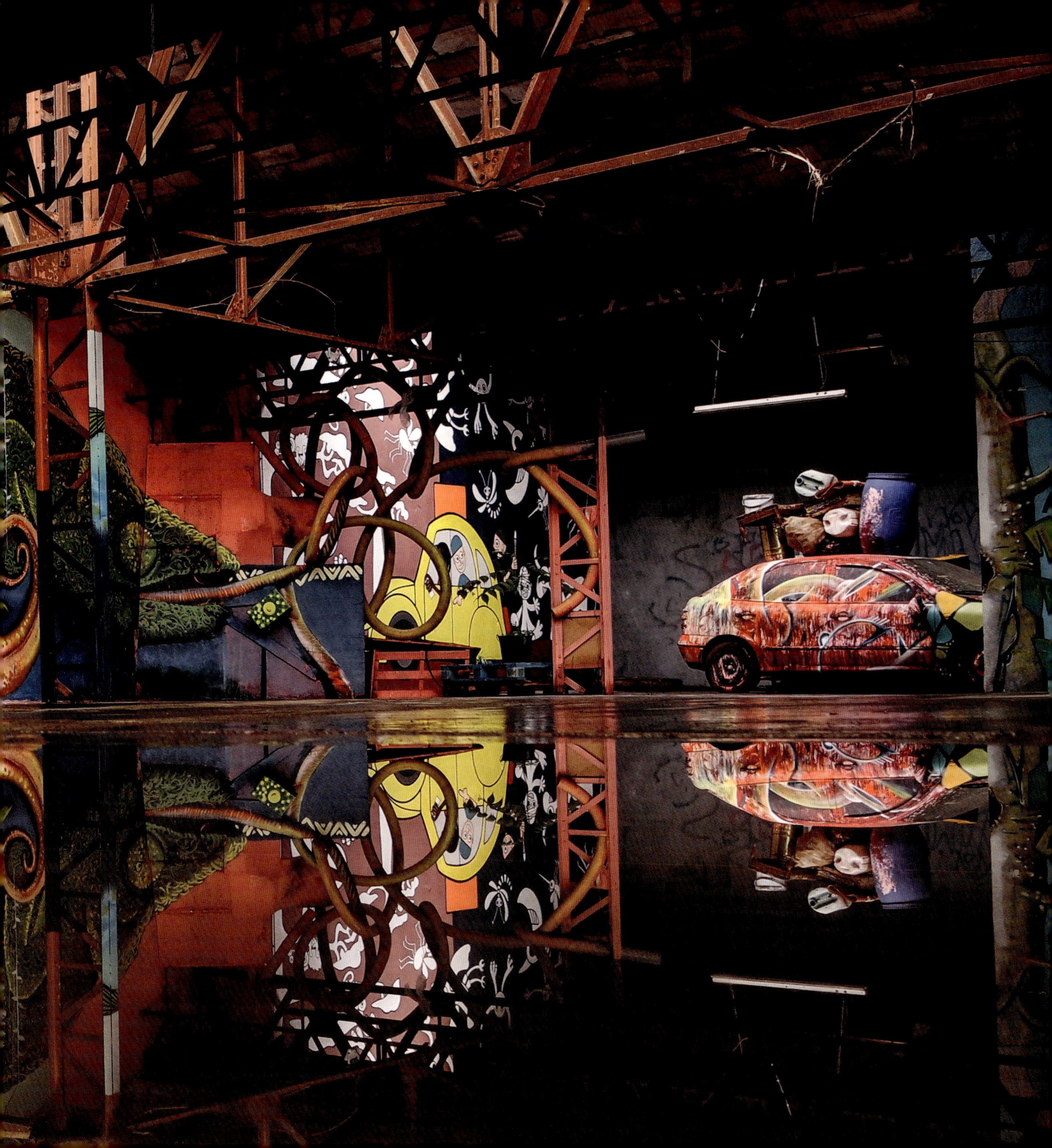

THE AGRESTIC AESTHETIC

ART ON THE GROUND

Rapid urbanization is sweeping across Africa, although the continent still remains mostly rural. Cities are becoming modernized and Western cultures appropriated. Street art is a powerful tool connecting people and places, manifesting ideas, highlighting issues and redefining the achievable. In shanty towns and poverty-stricken neighbourhoods, from Khayelitsha in South Africa to Kibera in Kenya, and from Nima in Ghana to Imbaba in Egypt, artists are using their prowess to beautify neglected spaces. A little paint and a profusion of colour can bring about change, and these receptive communities can attest to that. Many artists in Africa come from harsh backgrounds and are focused on spreading positive messages to inspire. Their actions are breaking down barriers and engaging at a grassroots level. Young people are motivated and stimulated while social ills are addressed.

Many murals scattered throughout rural areas are realized during community-based projects that seek to enhance the milieu. Artists travel off the beaten track to escape the norm and give back to the community, often growing their artistic footprint and awakening further potential. Projects are directly related to the needs of communities that require a new spin on life – otherwise artists are just looking for the perfect canvas to tackle. Initiatives in Uganda raise awareness about water and sanitation in Kampala, while in Rwanda, Kurema Kureba Kwiga touch on a broad range of topics in Kigali. Further south in Lilongwe, Malawi (where street art is not common), Zaluso Arts are beginning to create murals more frequently. They were commissioned to produce a mural campaign, called 'Zathu', for the Girl Effect organization, to promote freedom of expression among young people, who are often excluded by the older generation. Mook Lion, from South Africa, brought his unique lino-cut style to Lake Malawi, collaborating with locals by using one of their paintings as the main reference for the mural. The artwork was site-specific and participatory – unlike when graffiti artists impose on an environment with which they have no connection.

Opposite, clockwise from top
Zaluso Arts. 'Nanenso Ndifuna Ndimvedwe' (I Too Want To Be Heard), Zathu project, Lilongwe, Malawi, 2017

Mook Lion, with Thom Symon, Listen Kanthiti, Chris Sambani. Mangochi, Malawi, 2015

Innocent Buregeya, Muntu 621, Jobray. A community mural art project by Kurema Kureba Kwiga, Kigali, Rwanda, 2016

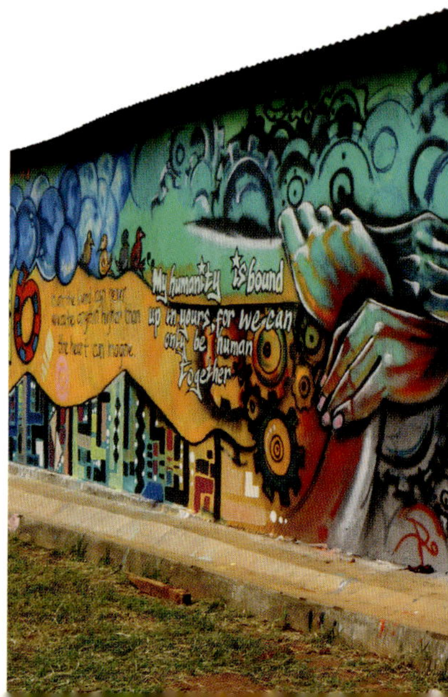

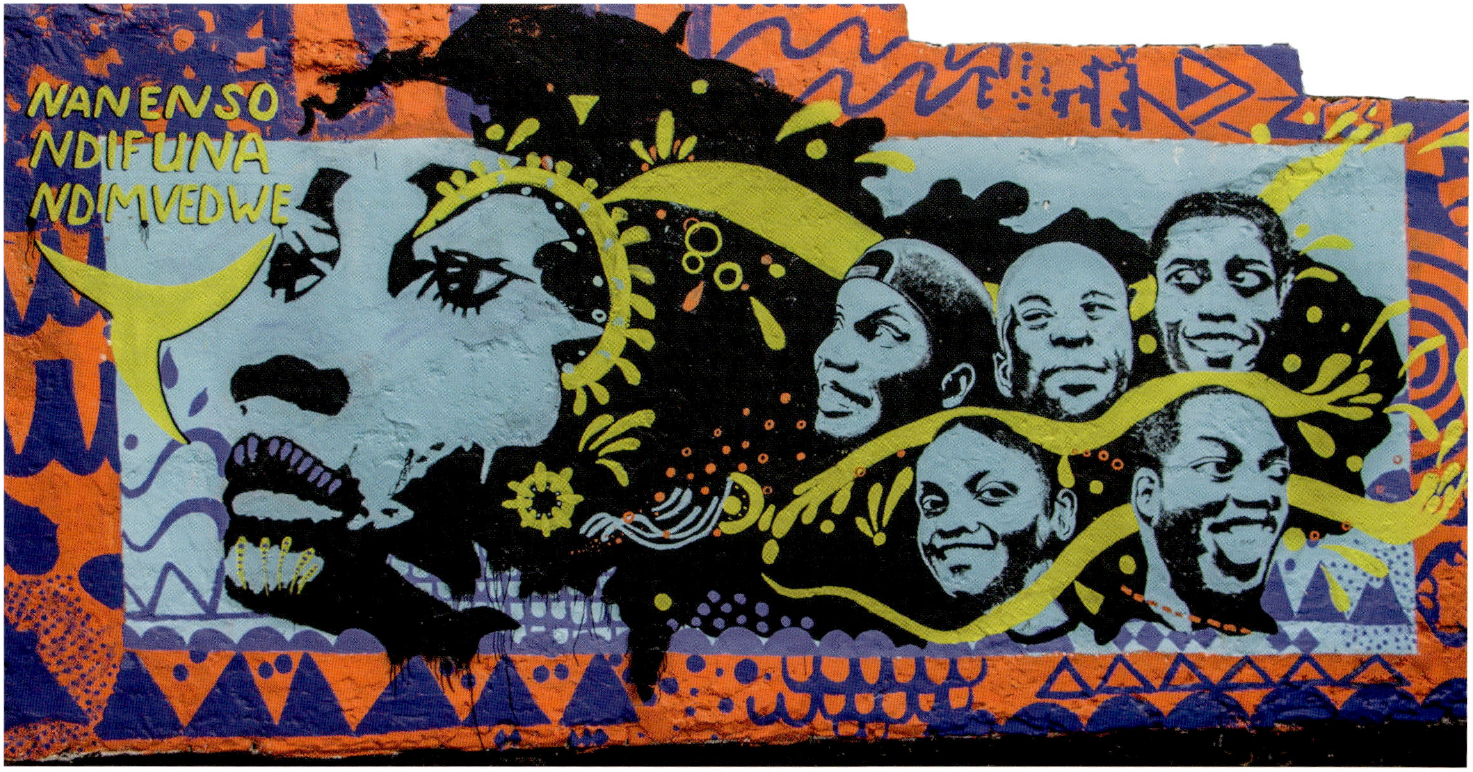

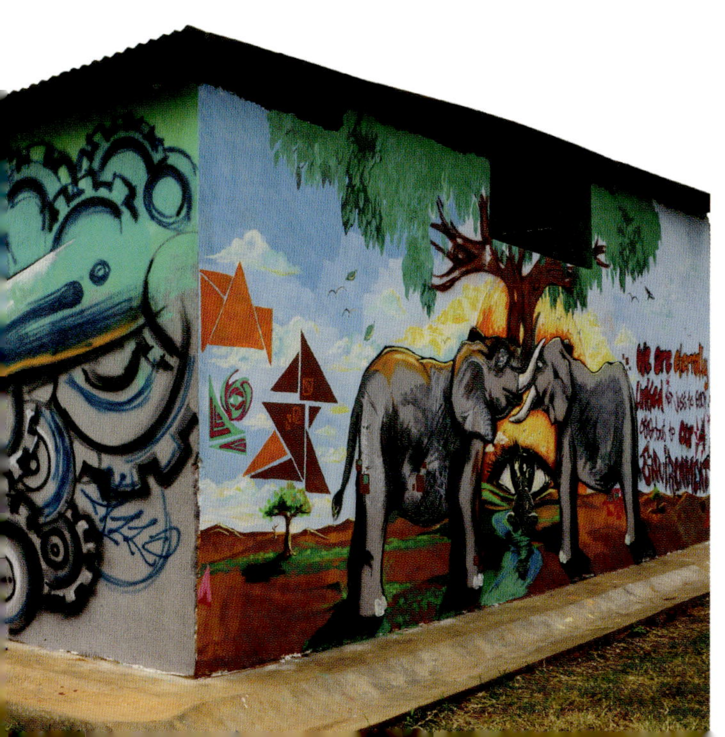

NANENSO
NDIFUNA
NDIMVEDWE

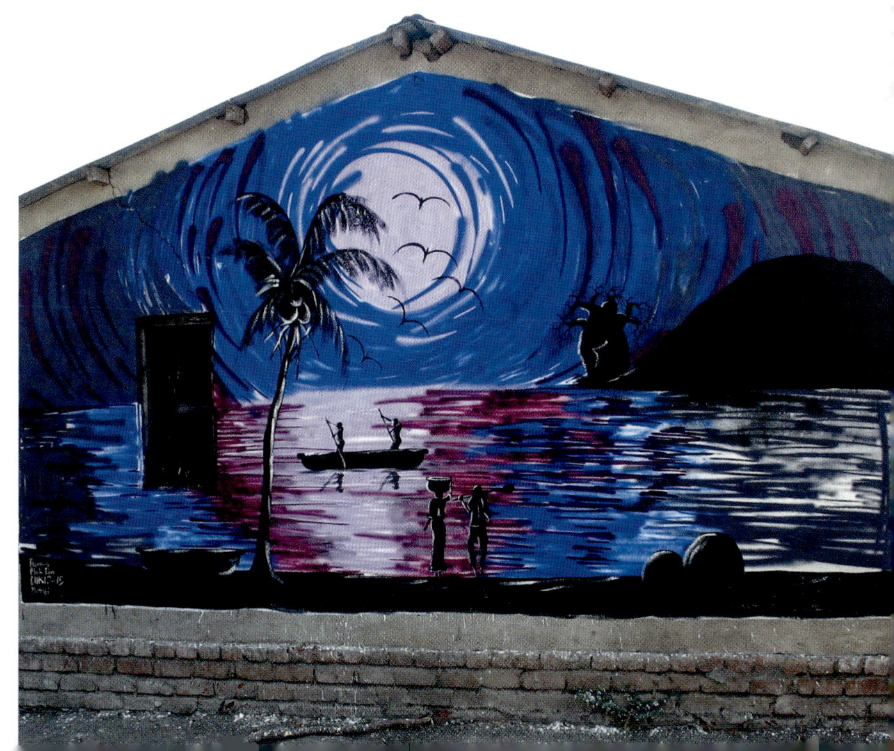

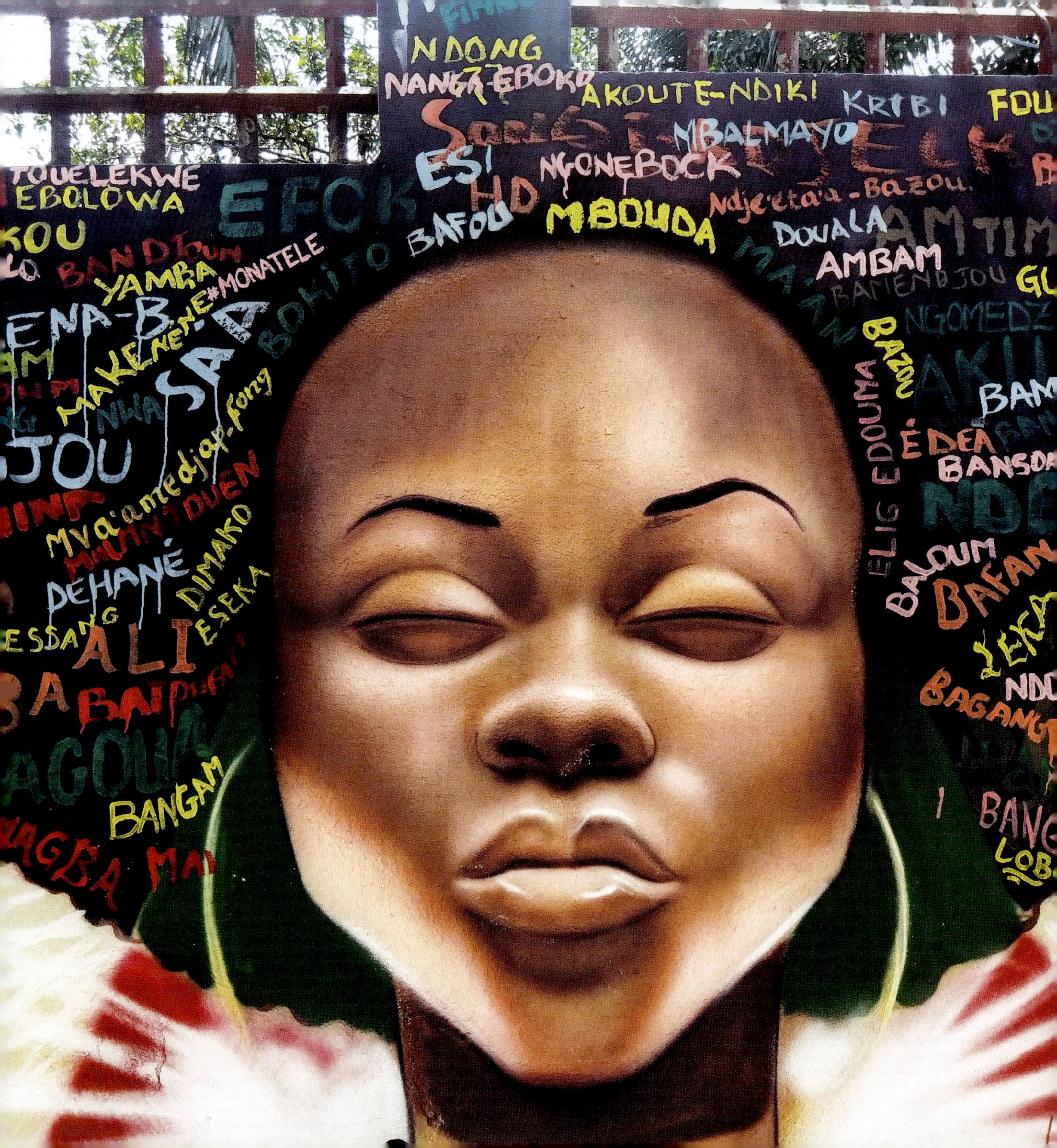
FIMNG
NDONG
NANGA-EBOKO
AKOUTE-NDIKI
KRIBI
FOU
MBALMAYO
TOUELEKWE
EBOLOWA
EFCK
ESI
NGONEBOCK
HD
Ndje'eta'a-Bazou
KOU
BAFOU
MBOUDA
DOUALA
AMTIM
BANDOUN
AMBAM
YAMBA
BAMENBJOU
GO
ENA-B
MAKENENE*MONATELE
BOKITO
NGOMEDZ
SAP
BAZOU
AKU
NWA
Mva'amedjap-fong
ELIG EDOUMA
BAM
JOU
DEA
MVANTDUEN
BANSOA
DEHANÉ
DIMAKO
NDE
ESSANG
ESEKA
BALOUM
BAFAM
ALI
EKA
BAIPUM
NDO
BAGANG
GOUA
BANGAM
BANG
AGBA MA
LOB

CENTRAL AFRICA

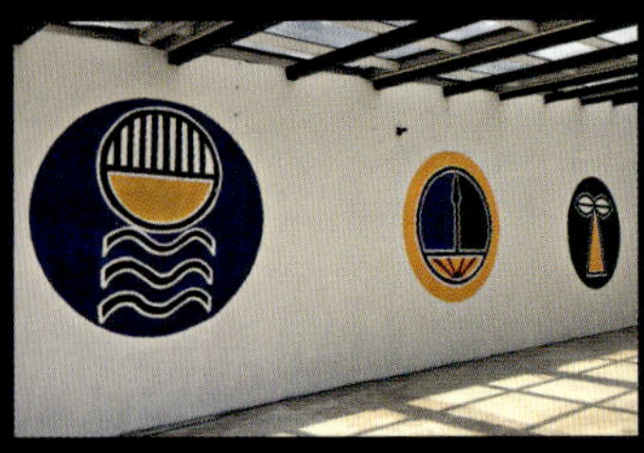
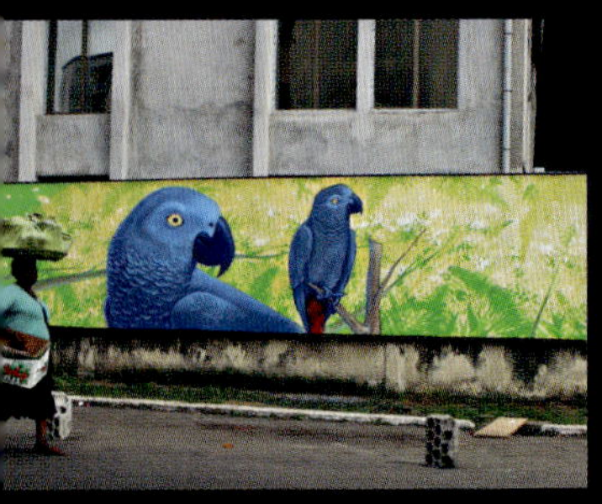
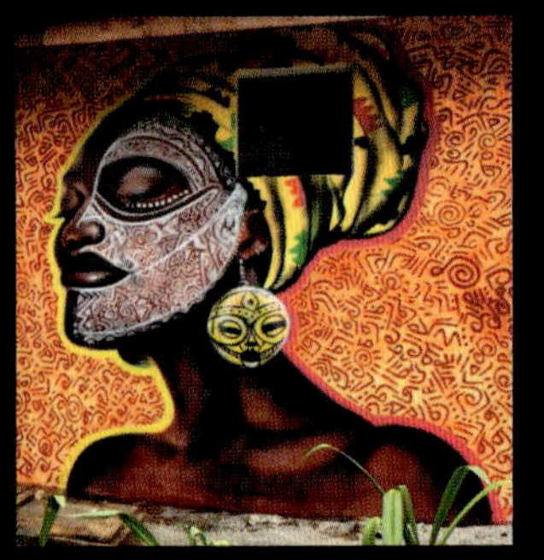
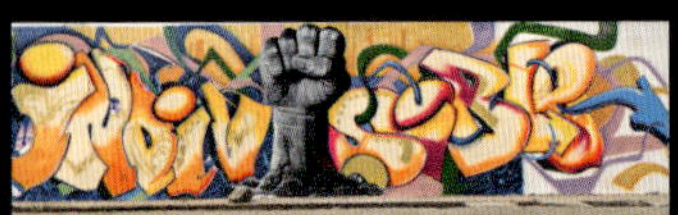
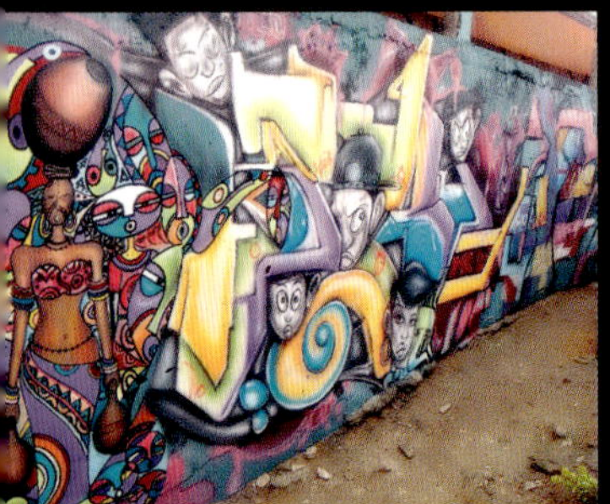

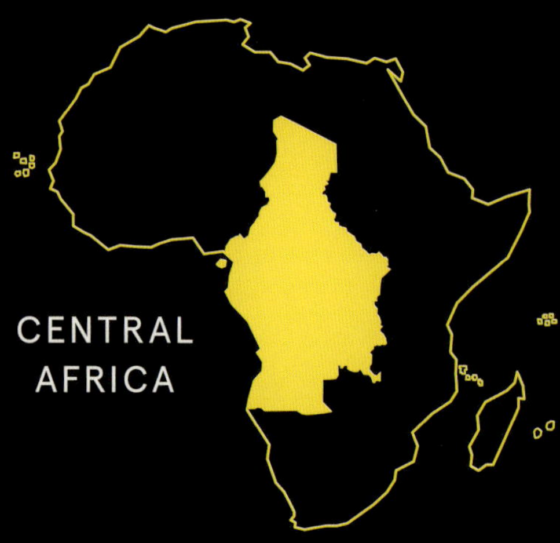

Festivals

❶ **Kin-Graff** p. 85

❷ **237 Five Colors Festival** pp. 88, 90

❸ **Graff Up Festi** pp. 92–93

Projects

① **Naxixi Street** p. 98

② **Murais da Leba** pp. 104–7

Page 78
**Nems. 237 Five Colors Festival,
Yaoundé, Cameroon, 2019**

Left, from top
**Buntu Fihla. 'Future Tribe
Watch (Over Our) Land',
Libreville, Gabon, 2017**

**Monk.E (Canada). Libreville,
Gabon, 2015**

**Tetebotan Kali. Correia,
São Tomé and Príncipe, 2020**

**MOC. 'Indivisible', Graff
Up Festi (2nd edn), Douala,
Cameroon, 2018**

**Kayaman, P3pe Art2dieu,
MOC. Douala, Cameroon, 2018**

Opposite, from top
**Señor Poste. Naxixi
Street Festival, Luanda,
Angola, 2019**

**Rómulo De Santa Rita.
Naxixi Street Festival,
Luanda, Angola, 2019**

**Unknown artist. Kin-Graff
Festival (1st edn), Kinshasa,
Democratic Republic of
the Congo, 2013**

**Collectif Moyindo Tag.
Kinshasa, Democratic
Republic of the Congo, 2019**

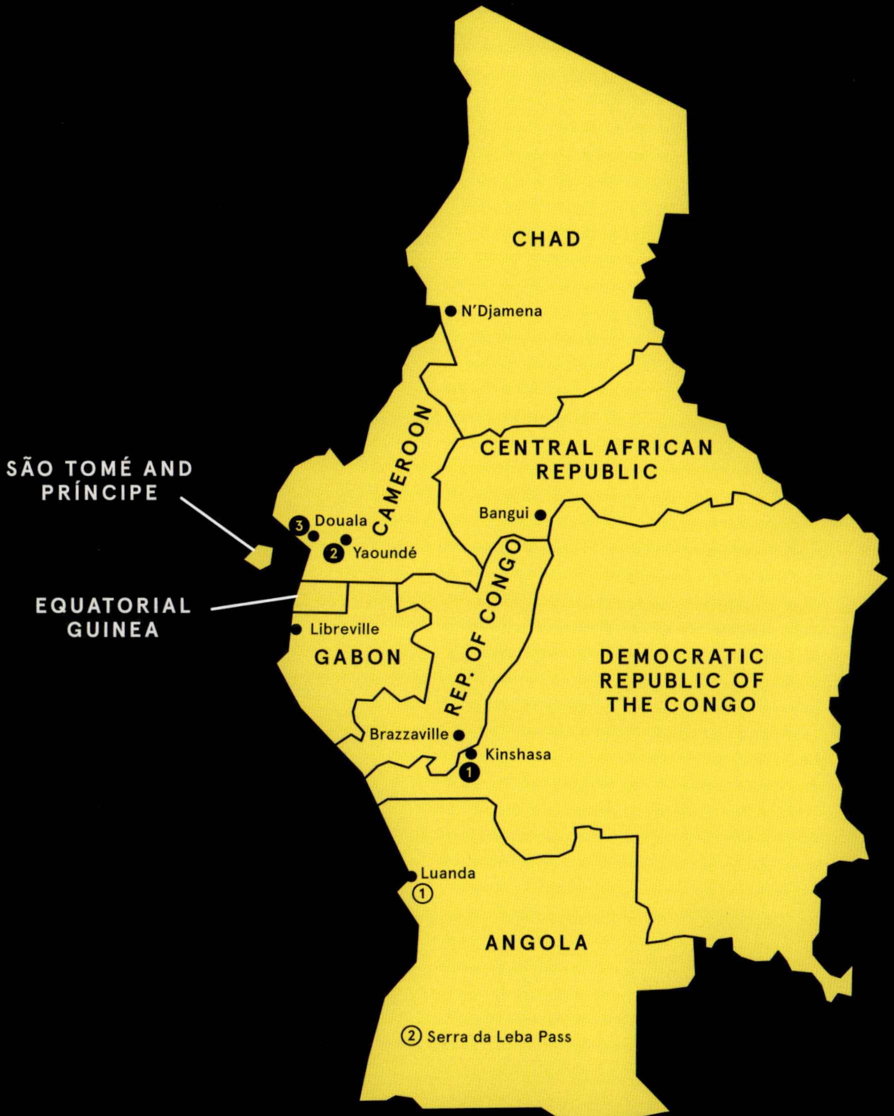

CHAD
N'Djamena
CAMEROON
CENTRAL AFRICAN
REPUBLIC
SÃO TOMÉ AND
PRÍNCIPE
Douala
Bangui
Yaoundé
REP. OF CONGO
EQUATORIAL
GUINEA
Libreville
DEMOCRATIC
REPUBLIC OF
THE CONGO
GABON
Brazzaville
Kinshasa
Luanda
ANGOLA
Serra da Leba Pass

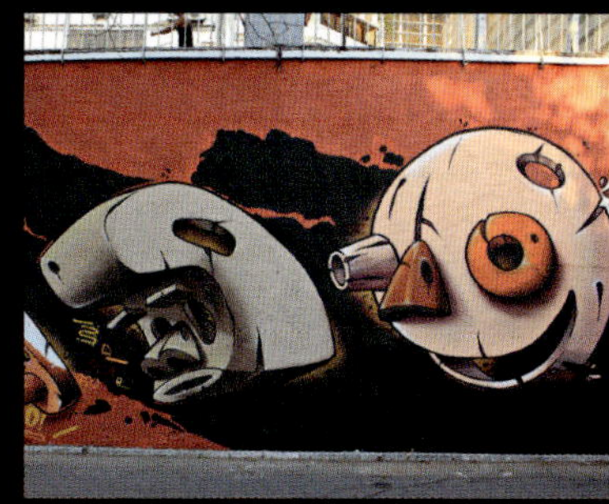

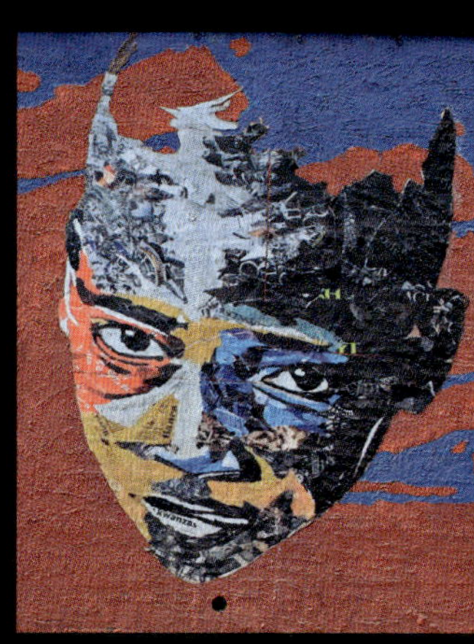

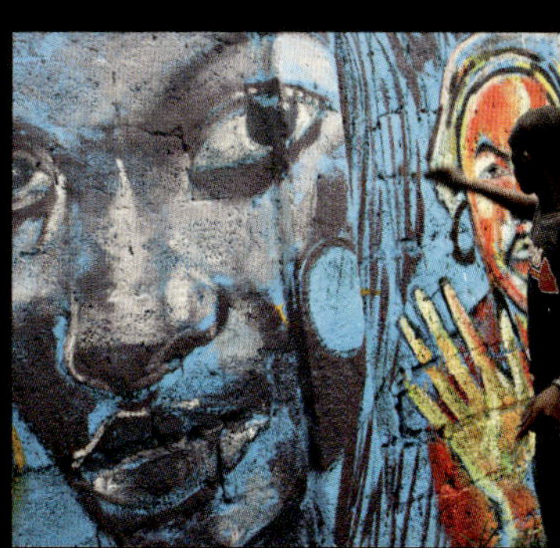

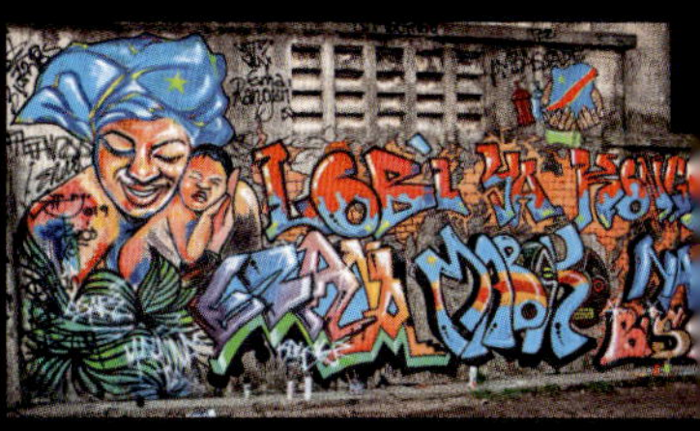

CENTRAL AFRICA

The central region of Africa has the lowest output of graffiti in comparison to other areas of the continent. Negative factors such as past conflicts and outbreaks of disease have hindered, among many other things, the growth of urban street art, with many countries still recovering or even still affected. Angola, however, has witnessed a rising affinity for street art culture, while Cameroon is beginning to showcase its expertise with a conglomerate of multidisciplinary artists, including airbrush, tattoo and body-painting artists. Traditional fine arts and murals have existed before, but graffiti is now more relevant and in demand. Artists are being commissioned by bars, clubs and restaurants to create works for decoration or advertising, as well as painting live at events or for government-funded projects. Despite the various drawbacks, including poor-quality spray paint, a lack of paint in a multitude of colours, and no Internet access when the Cameroon government shuts it down, artists continue to produce dynamic work with true African aesthetics, often relying on alternative mediums such as airbrush guns with compressors and common household paints with brushes.

Although African artists tend to yield a smaller output than their international counterparts, the final artworks are often uniquely linked to their causes. Sedulously working on new proposals or concepts in their sketchbooks or earning income by selling canvases and merchandise to raise funds for their

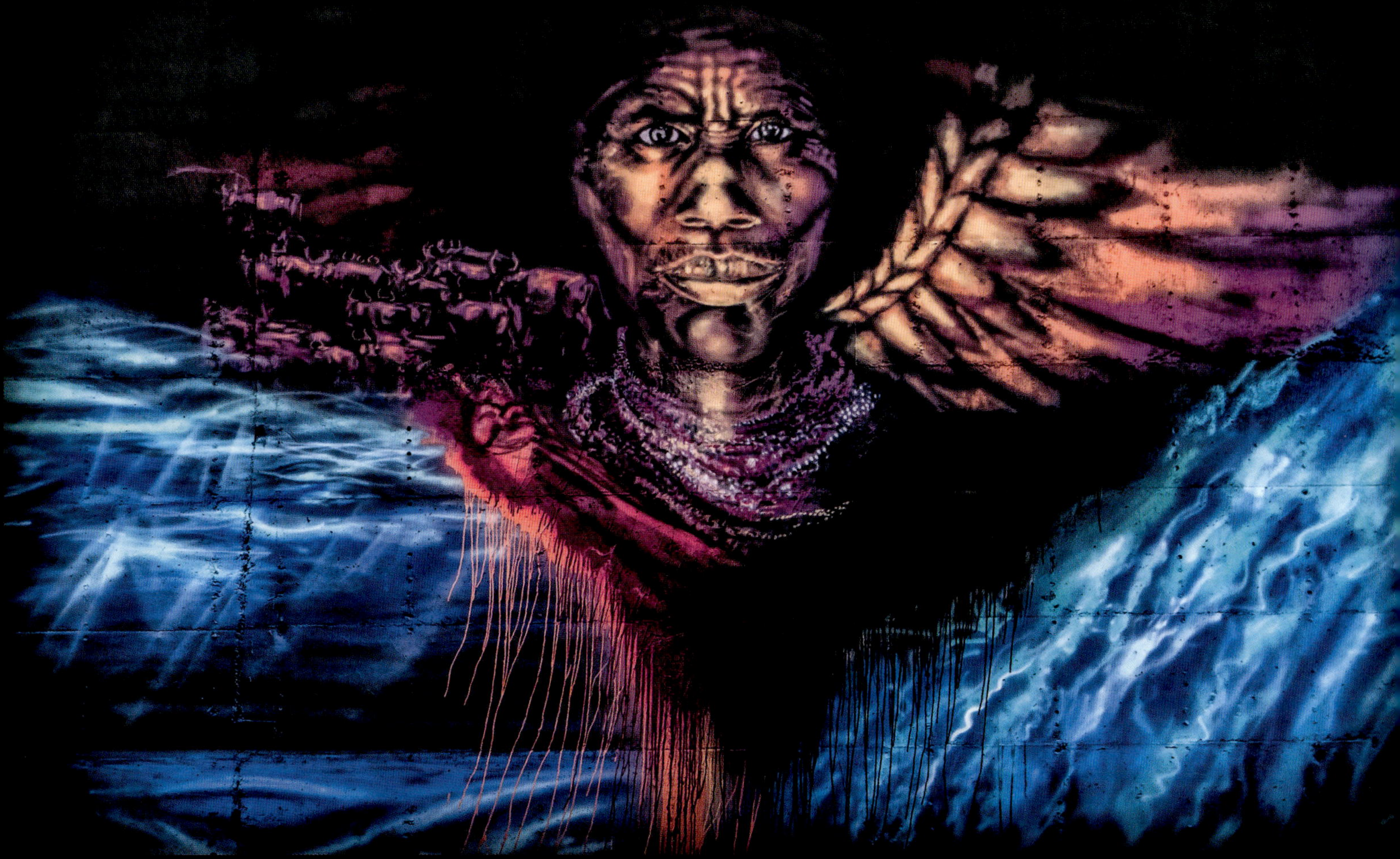

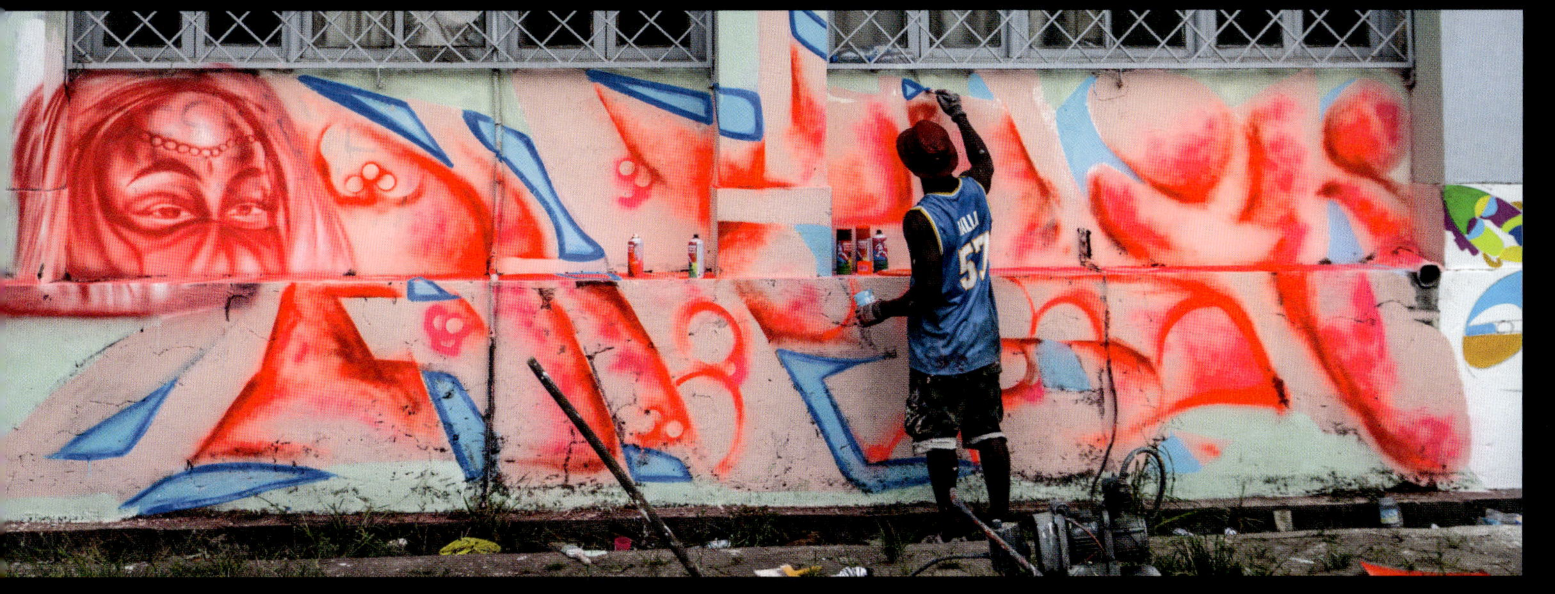

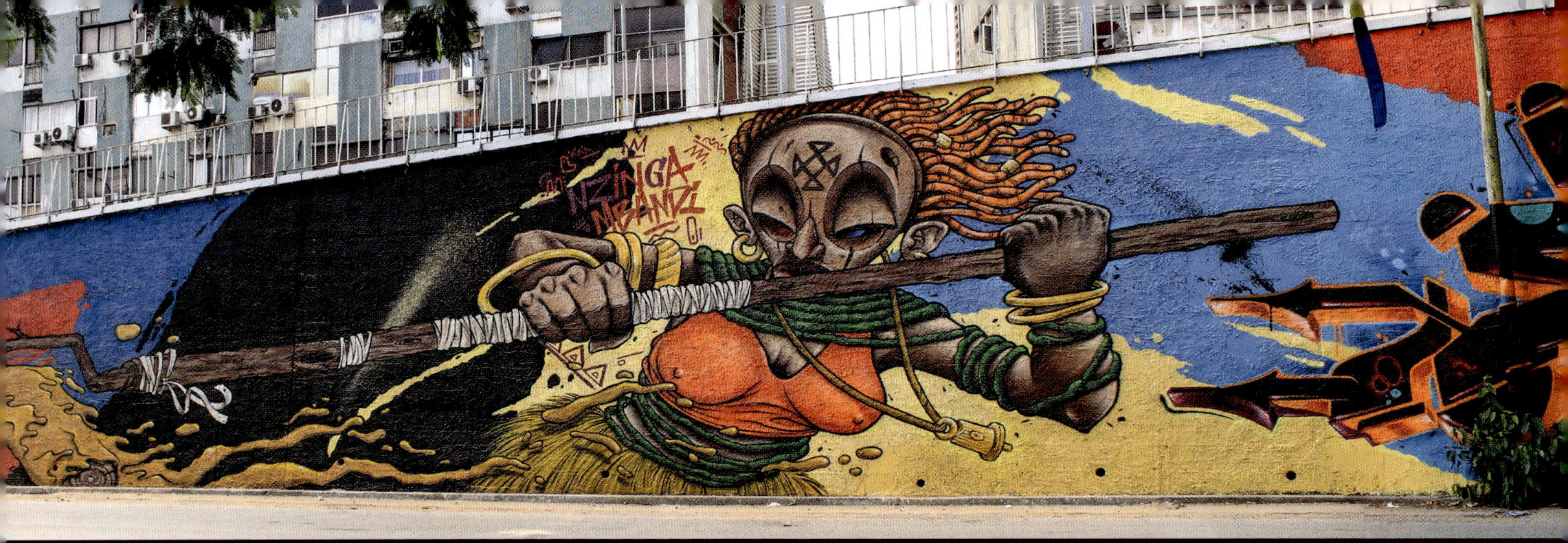

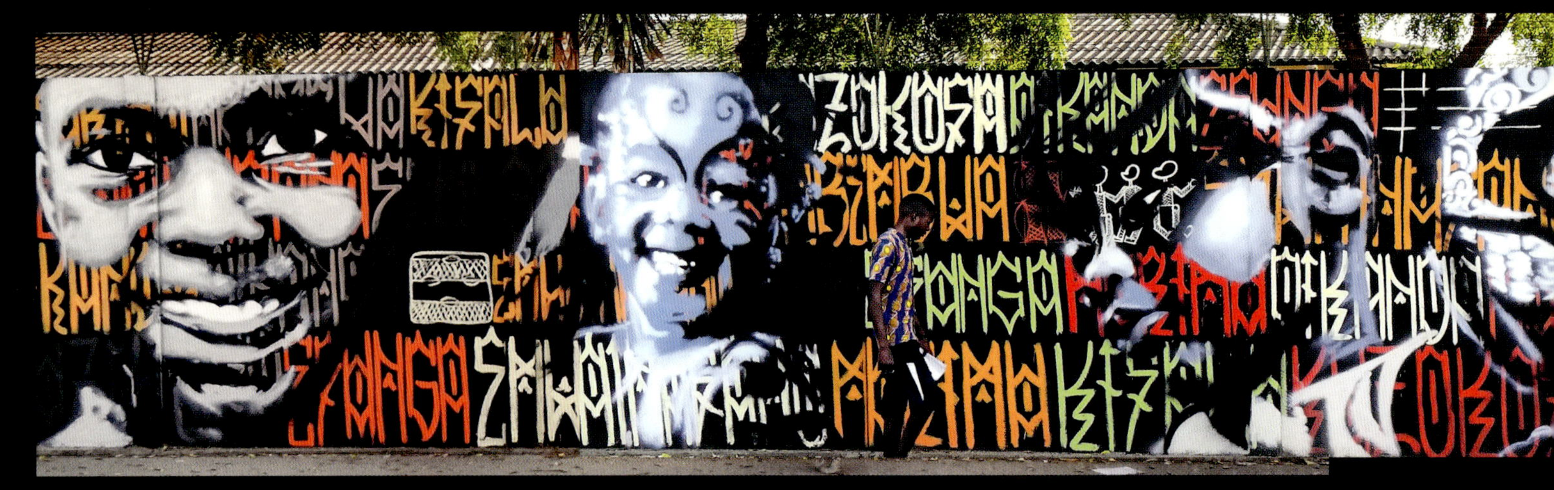
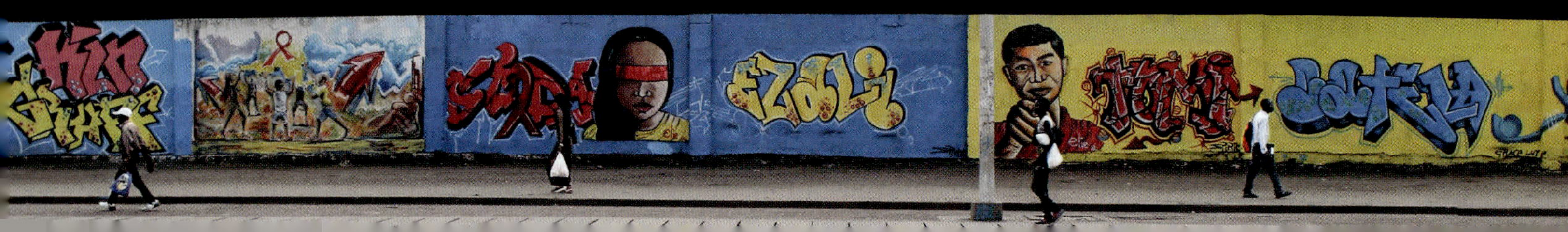

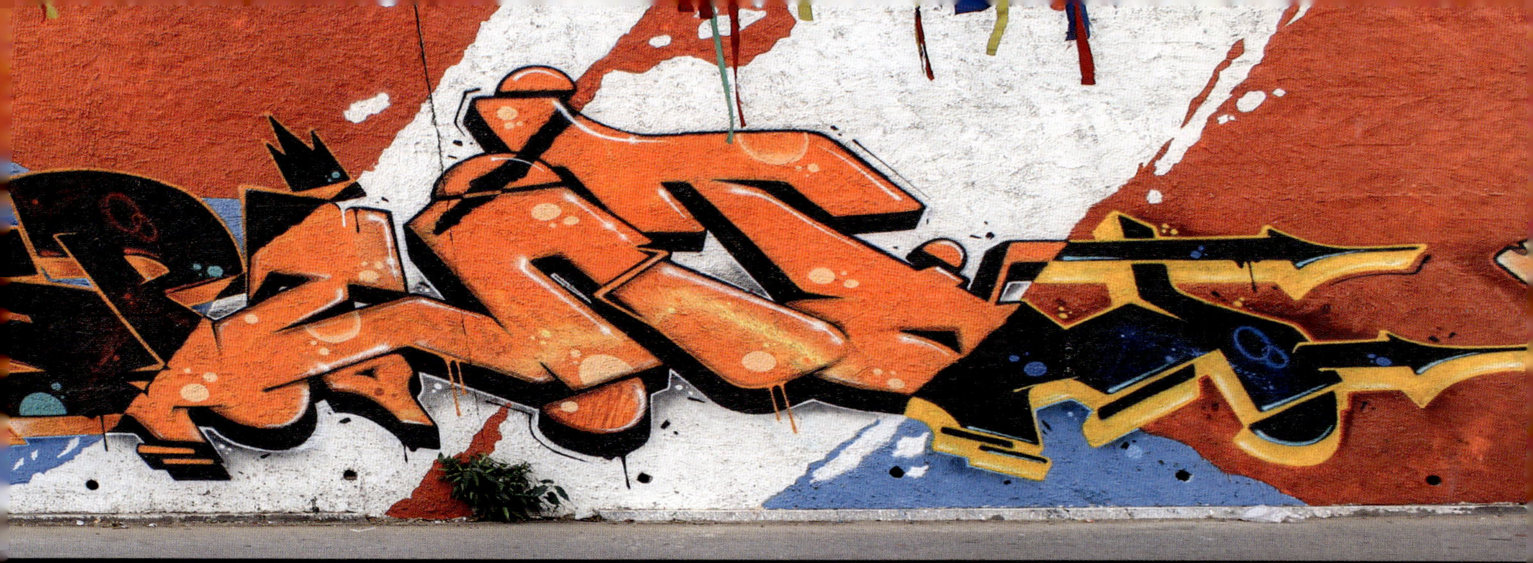

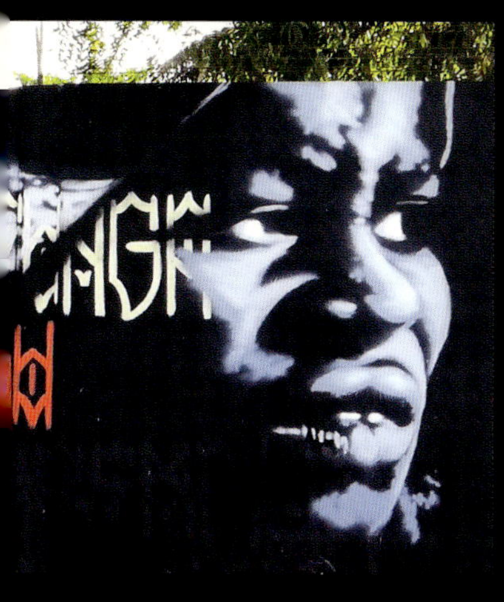

next piece, these artists yearn to produce something rewarding despite the many constraints. The end goal is to spark a dialogue and have as many people as possible relate to it. Content is limited only to their own artistic adroitness and mental paradigms. These artists are beacons of light in the world in which they exist, and they are gradually exploiting this sense for the betterment of their society. In many countries graffiti work is not frowned upon and projects are easily funded. Graffiti is a powerful tool which targets multiple spheres with a high impact; projects often focus on social ills. Artists are committed to the craft and openly express their love for street art culture by not standing behind a mask – rather, they flaunt their identity and want to be praised for their good work.

In the Democratic Republic of the Congo (DRC), a small scene was introduced by Togolese street artist Sitou Matt Imagination (SMI). Over a number of years, Sitou, who has a master's degree in finance, lived and worked in the country's capital, Kinshasa. While living in the megacity, having been inspired by initiatives in Senegal, he decided to create his own graffiti event. Sitou wanted to raise awareness of public health issues, as well as share the merits of the as yet nonexistent graffiti culture. The result was the first Kin-Graff festival, co-founded by Yann Kwete, which debuted in December 2013. Artists from surrounding countries, as well as their peers from other continents, were invited to

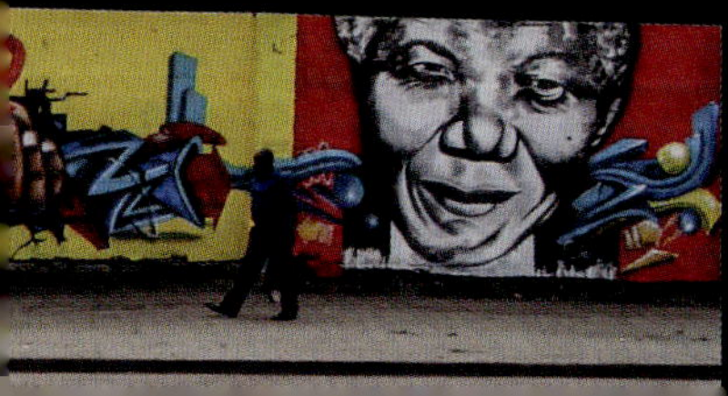

'Our collective memory makes African graffiti unique.
I believe Africans exist in an inspiring circle of events
and deep social crises, but we are careful to record
our history, culture, accumulation of knowledge
and information. We transmit this knowledge from
generation to generation in various ways – and graffiti
is one of them. We have inherited a very particular
and strong artistic and aesthetic sense, which we
see on the street today.' THÓ SIMÕES

Opposite
**Thó Simões. Namibe,
Angola, 2017**

participate in Kin-Graff, with themes focusing on AIDS and STD awareness and anti-violence. Subsequent editions in 2014 and 2016 continued to expand the event while at the same time stimulating the development of cultural diversity and promoting healthy living.

Today graffiti artists are sharing their knowledge with young people, using their medium as a tool for education and social upliftment. Art on the street can create public awareness about any subject and is a powerful way to encourage cleanliness and respect for one's environment. Collectif Moyindo Tag from the DRC and Regis Divassa from Gabon craft bold murals to inspire change in their respective countries. The government of Gabon is supportive of mural arts, having invited Monk.E from Canada to paint the front exterior of its Ministry of Culture building in 2015. A few months later a second trip by the artist followed, this time to adorn the walls of different schools, supported by the Ministry of Education. Another cultural exchange programme in 2017 with South Africa's Department of Arts and Culture, seeking to bolster relationships of trade and talent between the two nations, saw a mural by Buntu Fihla being realized at the Gabon National Museum.

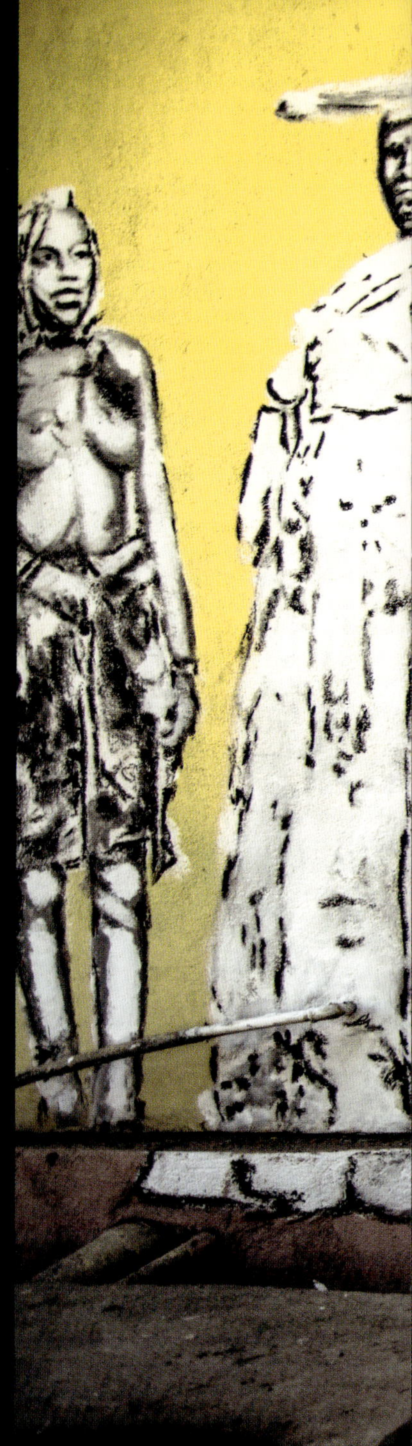

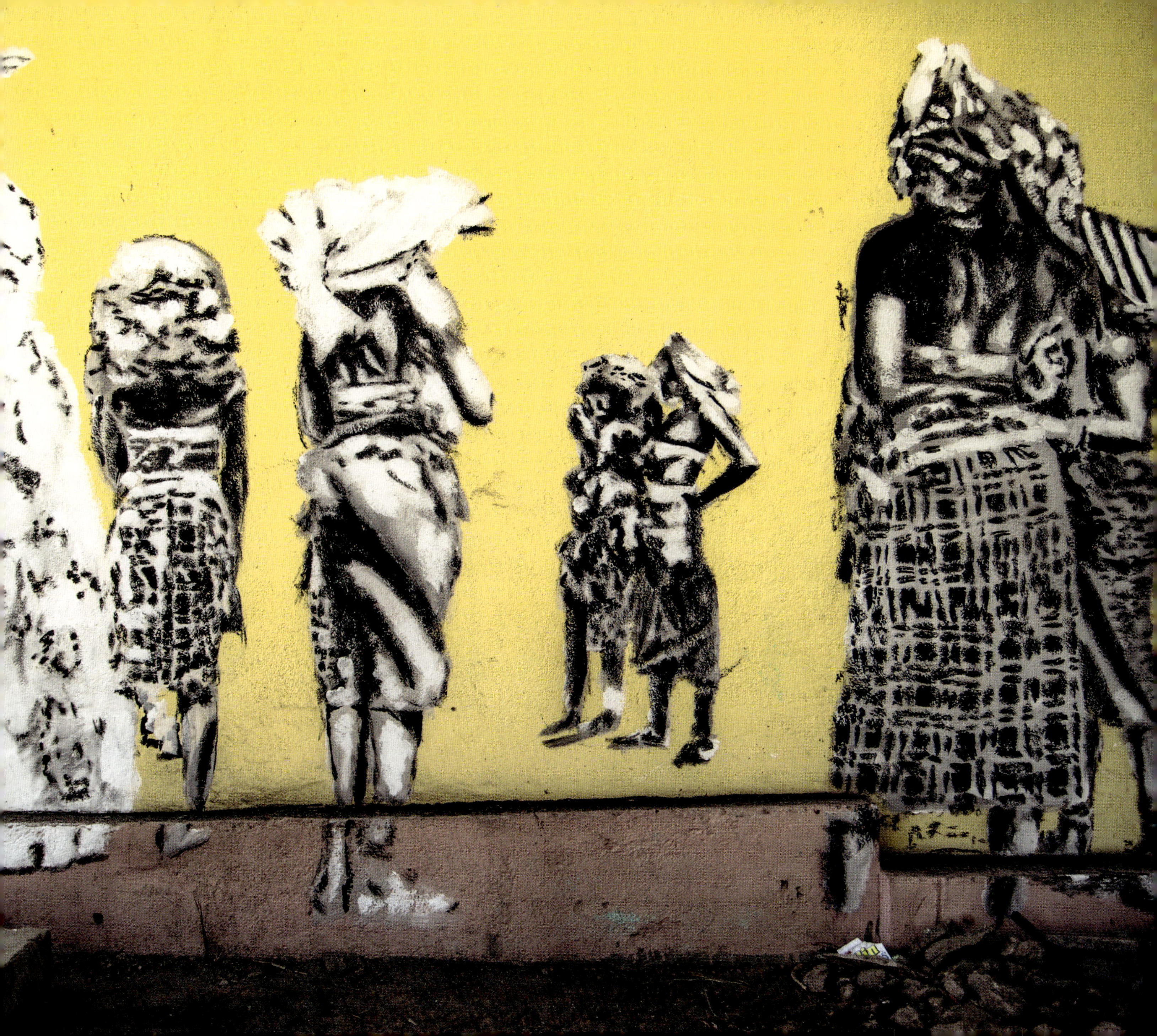

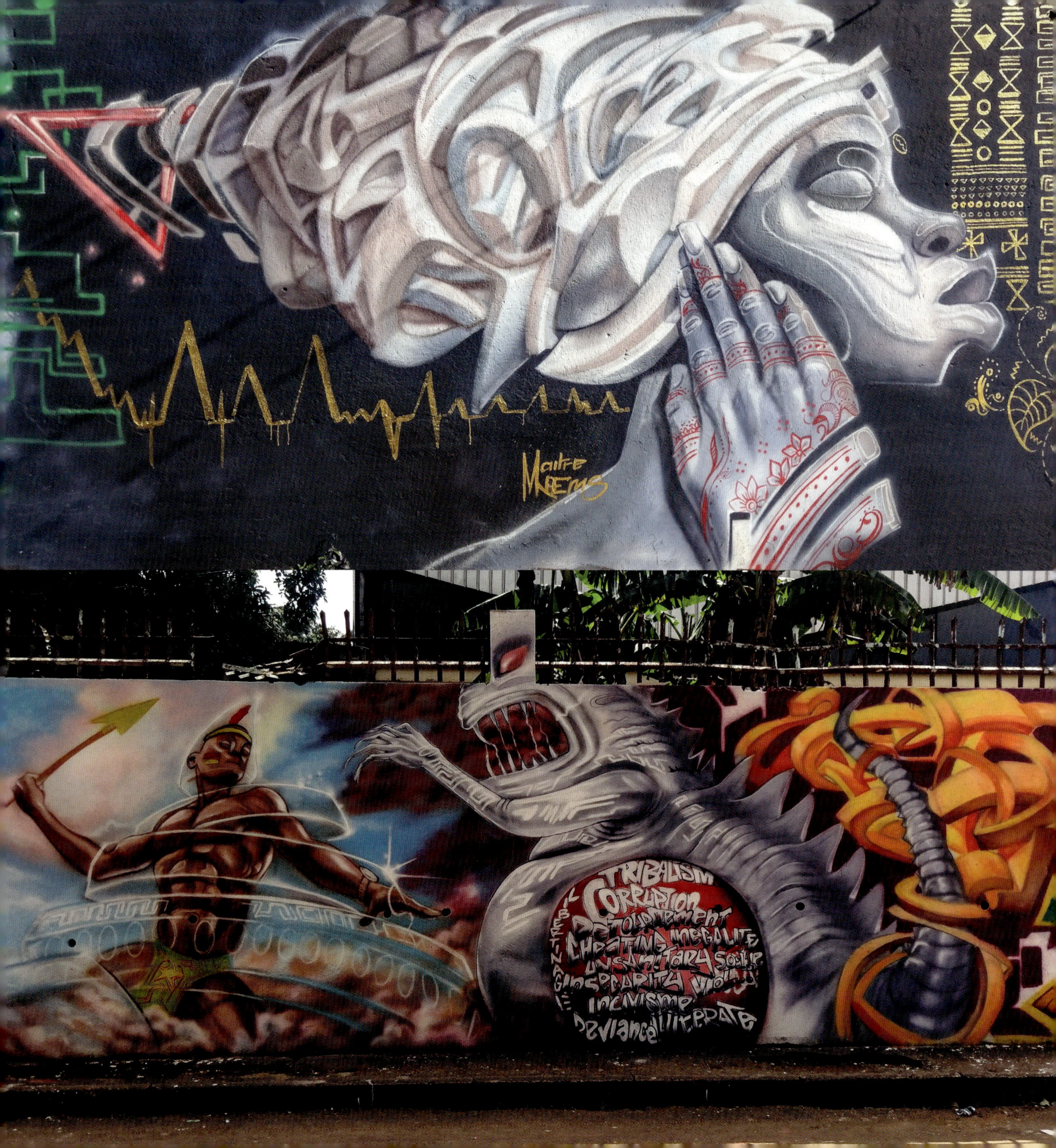
Maître
Meems
TRIBALISM
CORRUPTION
Détournement
Cheating inégalité
insanitary social
insécurité viol
incivisme
Deviance illiterate

CAMEROON

Cameroon's street art scene is coming of age with a new wave of urban artists and muralists who are inspired to continue the legacy of those before them. The late Meric13 (taken from his family name Eric Mouellé) from the city of Douala pioneered the country's graffiti movement in the late 2000s. An avid canvas painter and sketch artist, with skills in graphic design and T-shirt printing, he was inspired to pick up a spray can through his love for hip-hop music. The multitalented artist brought others along on the journey, and this was key to its success. Christo Beks, a young artist who had studied screen printing, started following Meric closely after the two met in 2010, and developed a love for spray painting. In the wake of his mentor's death in 2013, Beks continued to be an advocate for the arts, pursuing a professional career as an artist and organizing Remember Meric events in 2014 and 2015, with the support and collaboration of his fellow graffiti artists. In December 2017, he established Graff Up Festi in Douala, the first fully-fledged festival dedicated to urban art and graffiti in Cameroon, an ode to Meric's legacy and a way of marking their scene on the world map. Beks invited artists from other cities, including the capital, Yaoundé, and they painted three murals during the inaugural festival. The aim was not only to raise awareness of urban mural art and bring similar artists together, but also to challenge and enhance society while highlighting the opportunities available in the arts. These Cameroonian street artists continued their practice through 2018, and a second successful rendition of the festival was held. Three more diverse murals came to life, with little financial support, yet cementing their presence and adding an exciting development to the African graffiti circuit.

Self-driven artists, including Boni, Ensa, Graftu HD, Kayaman, MOC, Nems and Tong, are producing rich content with African themes and subject matter, often with limited resources. Among many handicaps was a government-enforced

Opposite, top
Nems. 237 Five Colors Festival, Yaoundé, Cameroon, 2019

Opposite, bottom
Nems. 237 Five Colors Festival, Yaoundé, Cameroon, 2019

'Public spaces are not always granted because administrative leaders still consider our movement as an art of thugs or rebels. But nobody can stop me because the messages I convey in my graffiti appeal to everyday citizens.' CHRISTO BEKS

Internet blackout in English-speaking areas in 2017 and 2018 that lasted more than 200 days – a lifetime in today's rapidly changing world that is so heavily dependent on online resources for communication and inspiration. The country's ethnic and post-colonial tensions have caused a serious divide between English-speaking and French-speaking sectors. Revolutionary symbols, such as clasped hands covered in the colours of the national flag, are represented in one of the works by Tong as a symbol of solidarity. MOC blends contrasting colours into experimental wildstyle forms and touches on deeper subject matter by incorporating masked faces and other African motifs. He calls his style 'Le Skeum', a diminutive of *skema*, which means 'mask', to depict the way people often put on a façade in front of others. Kayaman, who has been painting since 2006, also paints similar masked characters but sticks to using brushes, blending a mix of bright hues to form kaleidoscopic figurative paintings – colours are his trick and symbolize a united Africa. The gifted artist Nems (behind 237 Five Colors Festival) brings depth to realism with his innovative portraits, incorporating intricate details and shading.

Beks himself is also an innovator, aspiring to create his own unique graffiti alphabet concept known as 'Thilandi Ndem' (character writing) – which is also the name of his adopted crew. Thilandi references ancient texts and Egyptian hieroglyphics, and is entirely created by Beks to contribute to the improvement of Cameroon's artistic and cultural landscape. While the style features triangular shapes with intricate patterns inspired by the civilization of ancient Egypt, the concept draws inspiration from the various ethnicities in the country as well as the cultural diversity of the Cameroonian territory and greater African art history. It remains abstract, but within a graffiti context. This type of bold thinking is a fresh breath in a medium that is often built on referencing other artists' personal styles that metamorphosize naturally. It is also a nod to those who previously reinvented the graffiti wheel in cities such as São Paulo, where *pichação* is a unique visual code. It will be interesting to see others engage with this home-grown font, and how it performs in other countries where Beks has travelled, such as Chad further north.

Opposite, top
Christo Beks. 'Boukarou', Douala, Cameroon, 2018

Opposite, bottom
Nems. 237 Five Colors Festival, Yaoundé, Cameroon, 2019

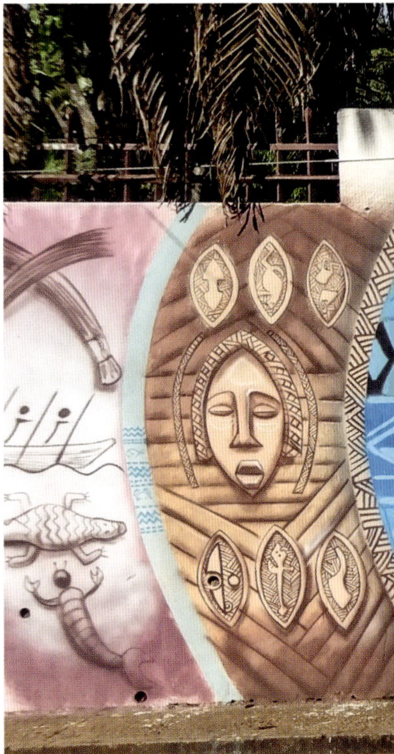

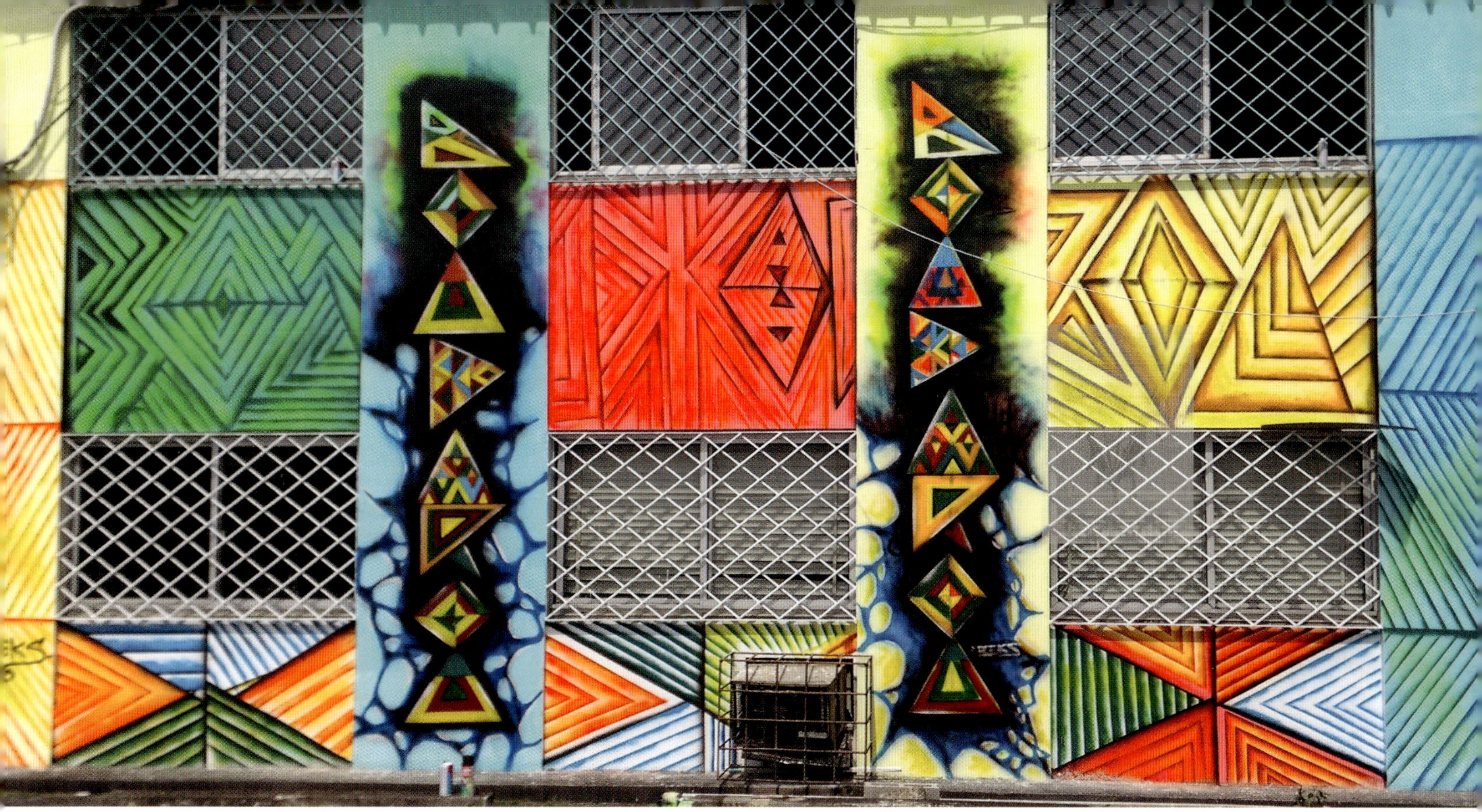

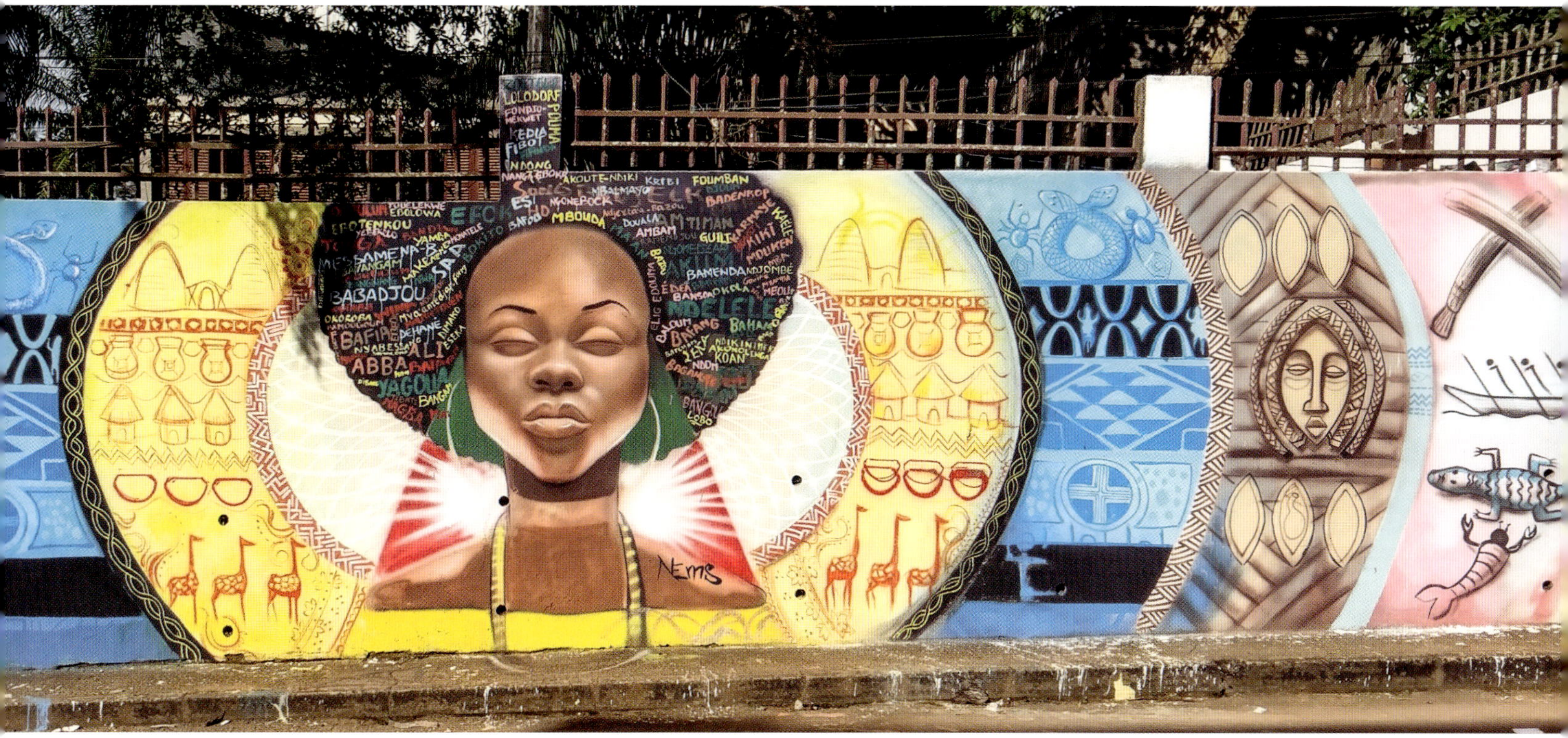

LOLODORF
FONDJO-MEKWET
POUMA
KEDIA
FIBOT
NDONG
AKOUTE-NDIKI
KRIBI
FOUMBAN
MBALMAYO
BADENKOP
ESI
NGONEPOCK
EBOLOWA
MBOUDA
DOUALA
AMBAM
GUILI
KIKI
MOUKEN
TENKOU
YAMBA
BAMENA-B.
BAMENDA
NDJOMBÉ
BABADJOU
ÉDEA
NDELELE
OKOROBA
DEHANÉ
BALOUM
BAFANG
BAFIA
NYABESSANG
ALI
KOAN
ABBA
YAGOUA
BANGAM
LOBO

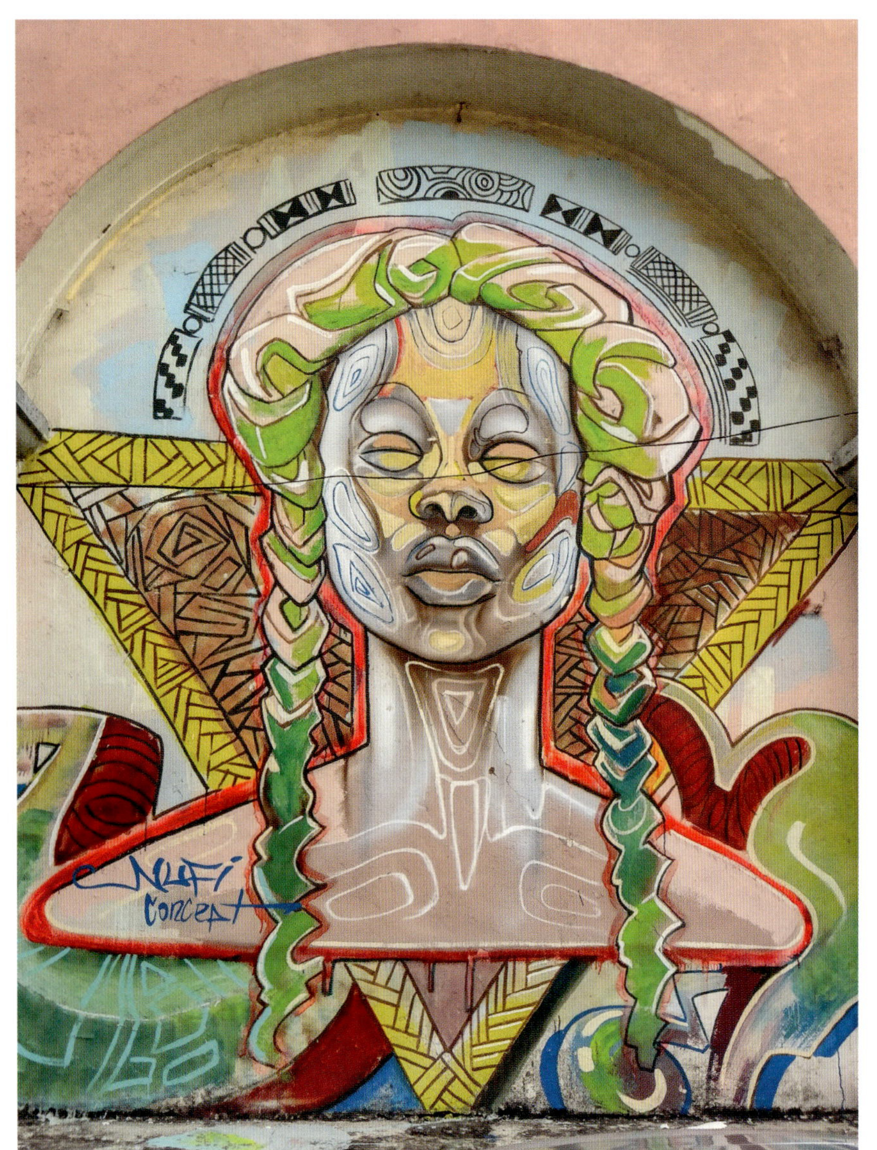
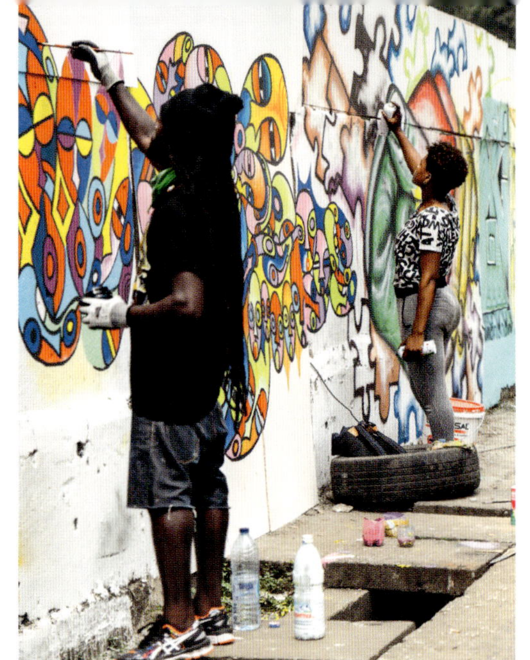
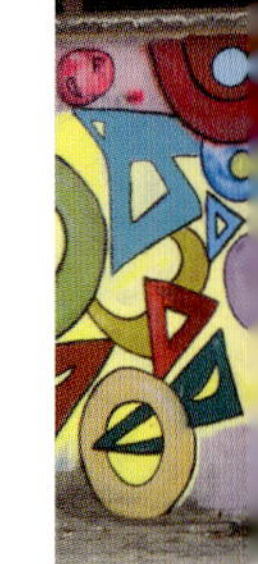
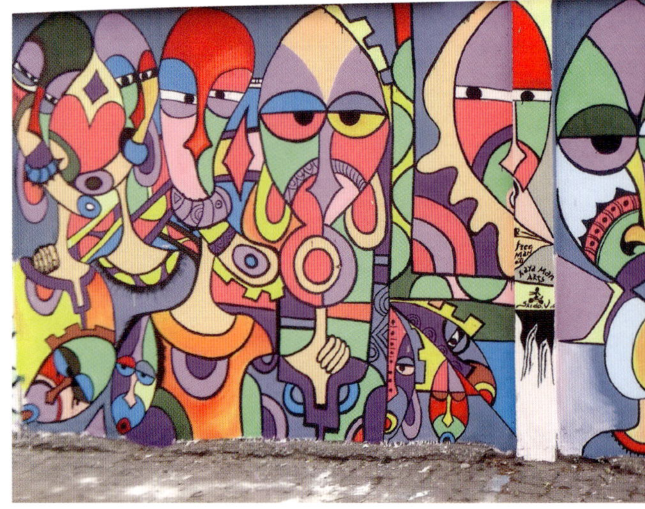
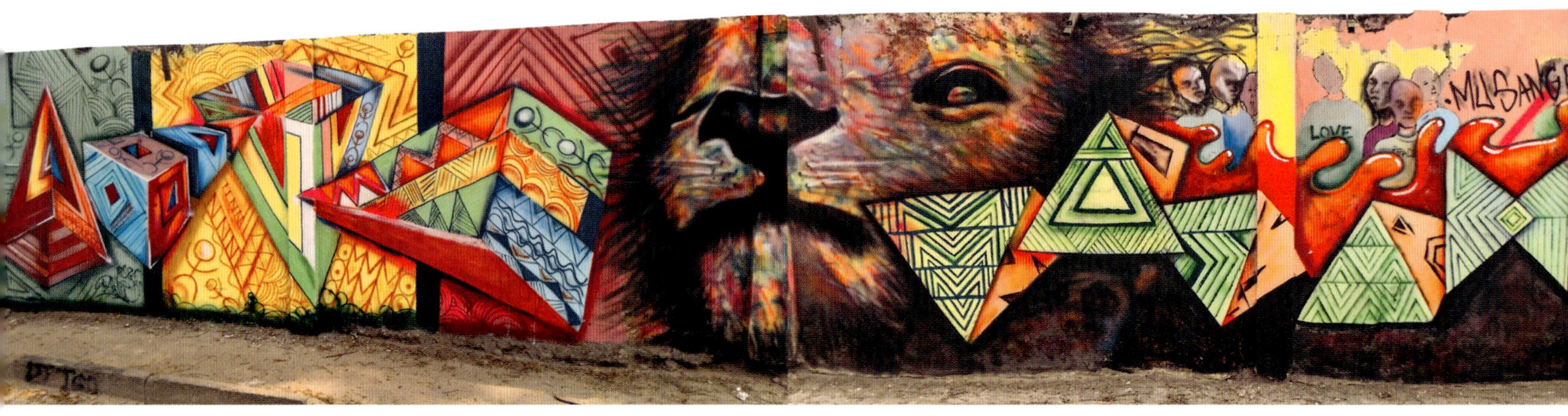
LOVE
MUSANGO

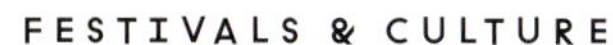

GRAFF UP FESTI

FESTIVALS & CULTURE

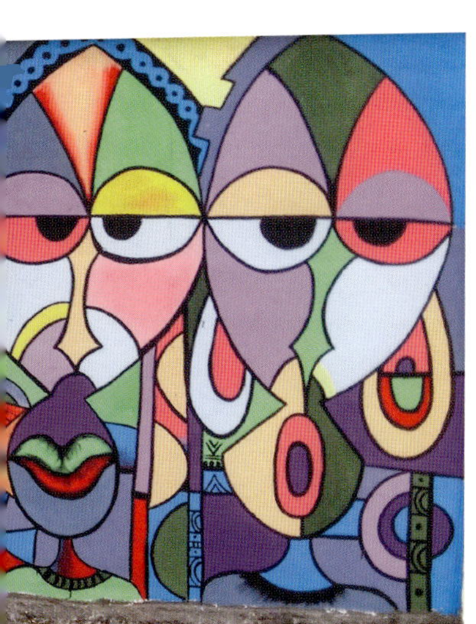

Established in 2017, Graff Up Festi is a graffiti and street art festival in Douala, Cameroon's largest city and its economic (though not political) capital. As an *al fresco* gallery, the event brings artists from multiple cities together to promote urban art in the region and beyond. This united expression of art is also a drive for the enhancement of a country that is currently facing ethnic tensions. Most of the participating artists dedicate themselves to the arts full-time, both as a means of showcasing their skills in public and to encourage others to view art as a way to earn a living.

Clockwise from top left
Nems. 2dn edn, Douala, Cameroon, 2018

Kayaman, Tong. 2nd edn, Douala, Cameroon, 2018

Ensa. 2nd edn, Douala, Cameroon, 2018

Kayaman. 2nd edn, Douala, Cameroon, 2018

Graftu HD, Christo Beks, Nems. 2nd edn, Douala, Cameroon, 2018

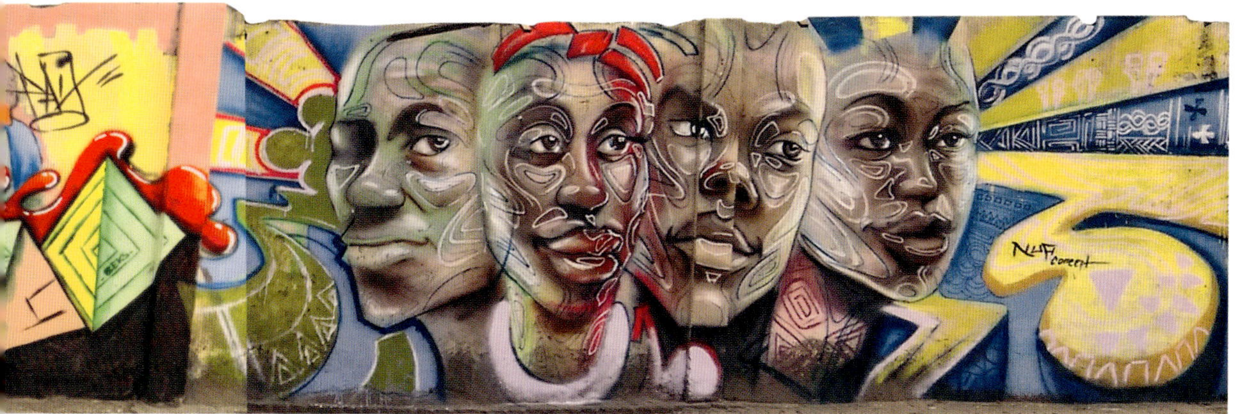

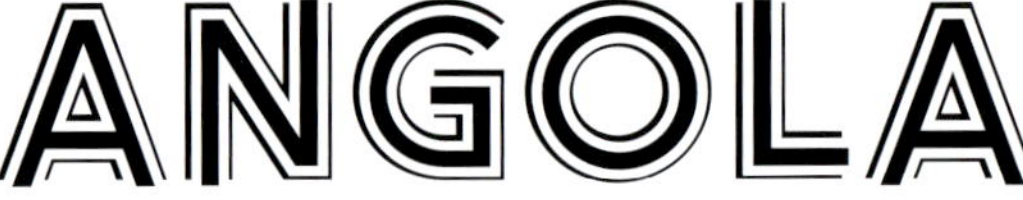

ANGOLA

IN FOCUS

An energetic urban arts playground is unfolding in Angola, making it the largest graffiti scene in Central Africa. Although the country is partly underdeveloped because of a protracted civil war that ended in 2002, its economy is growing rapidly. Expensive paint is often blamed for hindering any rapid growth of the graffiti culture, although this is never a total deterrent. Many crews have formed from their association with hip-hop culture, including BAW (Best Angolan Writers), MUG (Movimento Urbano de Graffiti), MAL (Movimento de Arte Livre), 300 Crew and Crazy Crew. Spent (BAW, PEF, TDI), a pioneer of the movement since 2003, trailblazed his tag across the capital, Luanda, utilizing his experiences of painting in Europe and South America to his advantage. Solidifying his position as Angola's leading graffiti artist, Spent and his crew, BAW, which consists of young talents he recruited and mentored (including AbiOne, Jkob, Señor Poste, Res.One, Rhamzi and Vars), are prolific within the country, decorating many surfaces from walls and roadside furniture to abandoned buildings and the city's railway network. Most painting takes place during the day rather than as a night-time cloak-and-dagger operation because it is safer and the police are less likely to suspect you of doing something illicit. This, however, attracts passers-by, who often request to have their own name added to the wall or ask the artist to teach them how to spray. Artists can face serious jail time when caught painting illegally, but the police have been known to request the artist's phone number to have their own property painted with a personal graffiti commission.

Now, in the second generation, with fewer than forty active graffiti artists, the rising stars include Rafa Invencible (MAL), Noop (MAL), Zbi (MUG) and Sombra Andgraff. Angola's urban art arena also comprises other visual artists, including airbrush maestros such as ArtMore, Els Graf Tridimensional, Lundu Art, Serafim Serlon, Stone Kasiala and Thó Simões, as well as genre-bending plastic artists

Opposite, top
Rafa Invencible. Luanda, Angola, 2019

Opposite, bottom left
Señor Poste. Naxixi Street Festival, Luanda, Angola, 2019

Opposite, bottom right
Verkron Collective, Rafa Invencible. Luanda, Angola, 2019

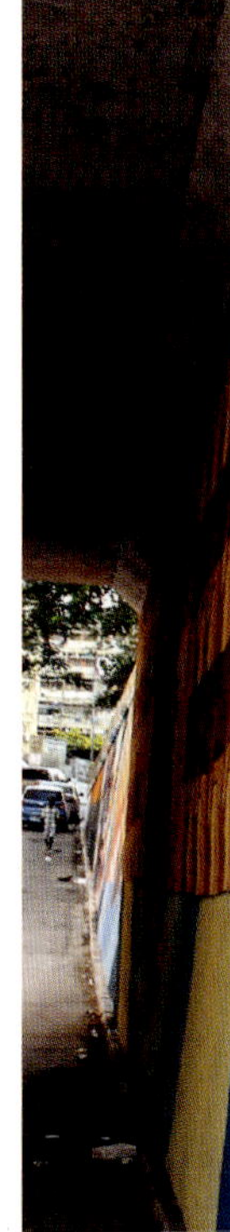

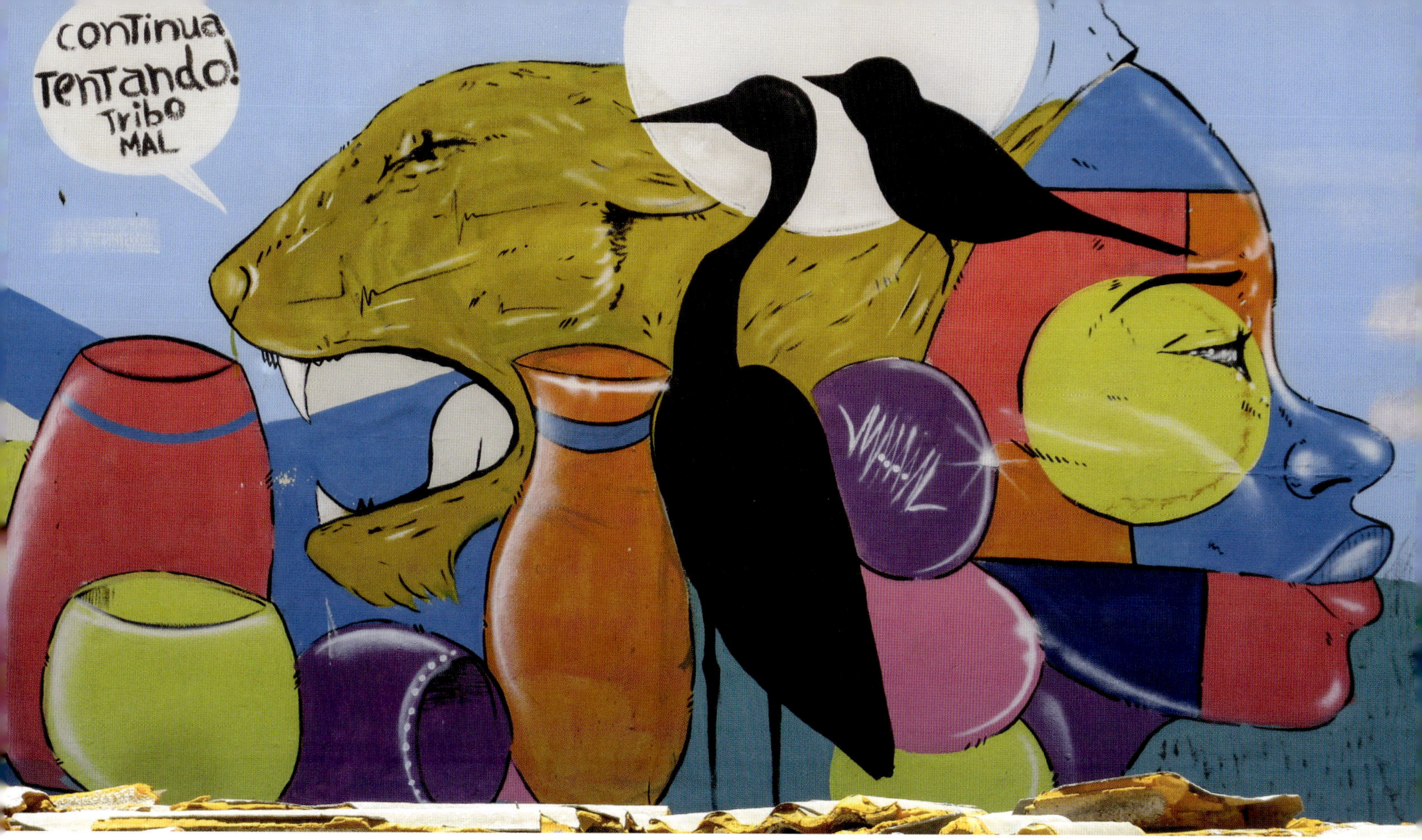

conTinua!
TenTando!
Tribo
MAL

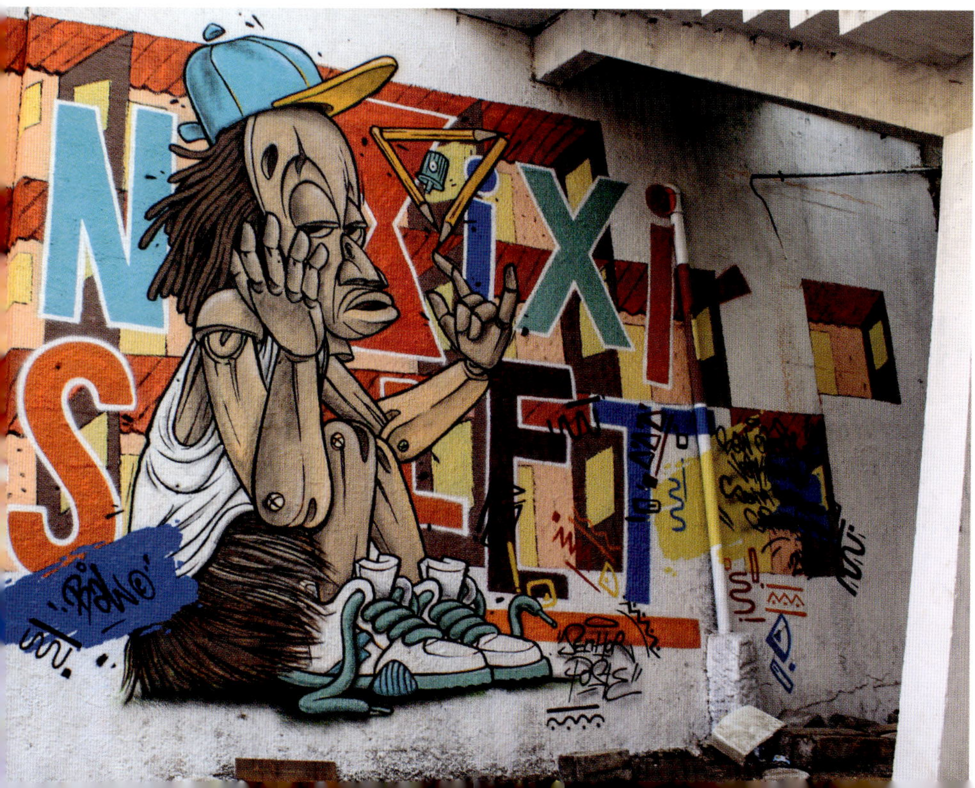

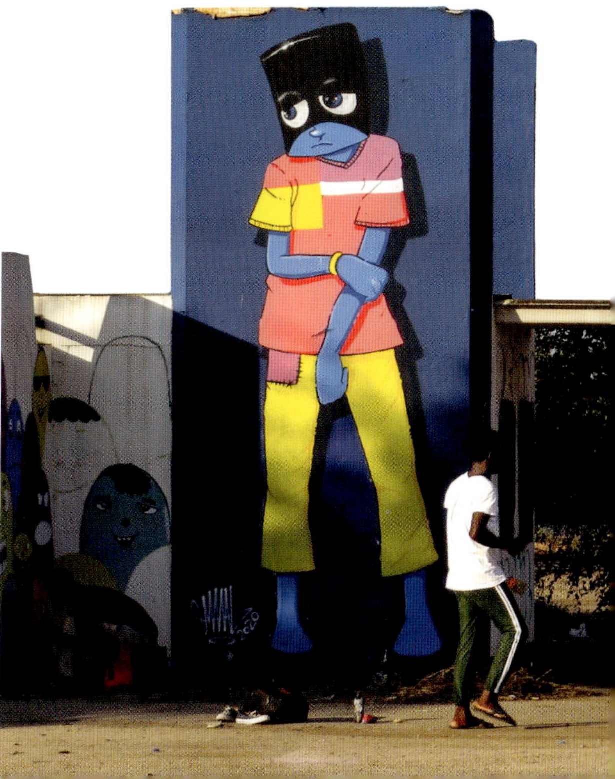

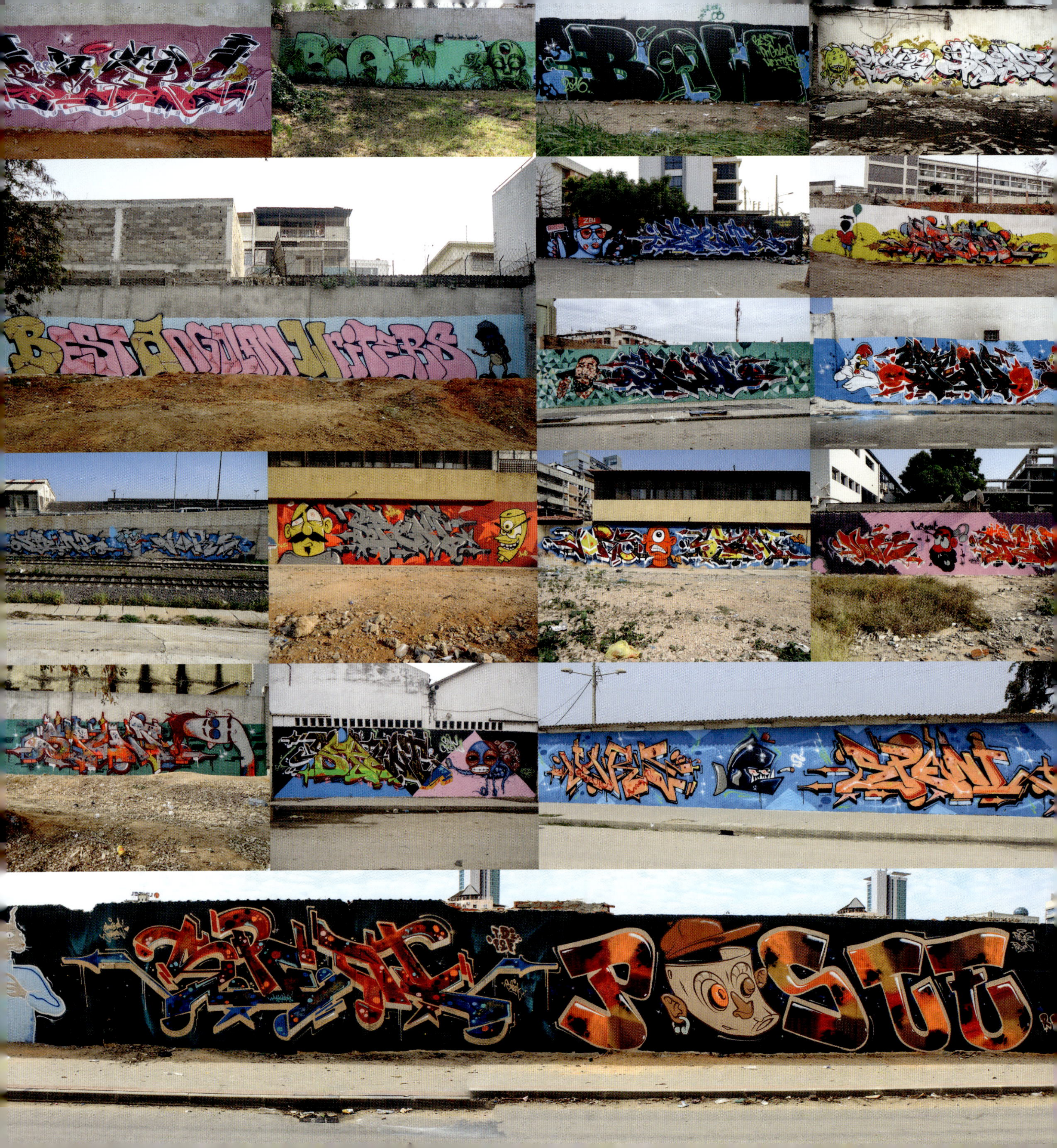

'There is little knowledge about graffiti culture in Angola and sometimes I have to explain what it is. But artists are developing their style and are now getting recognized at an international level. Graffiti and hip-hop is a real lifestyle.' SPENT

such as Colectivo Verkron (Verkron Collective). This collective, founded in the late 2000s, consists of several painters, each with different strengths; Hemak, Resem, Chadrac, Sarhai, Irad, Mac33 and Jafeth. Verkron Collective also enlists additional members who practise other forms of art, including music, literature and crafts, together forming a dynamic family under one umbrella. Utilizing street art as a form of expression, the artists paint both walls and canvases for personal and commissioned projects. They understand the importance of working outside the gallery space to bring their work to everyday people. The name means 'true colours/coloured truth' and was fused from words in Latin and Greek to emulate the group's shared philanthropic belief that an inner light exists in all human beings and, through self-awareness and spiritual awakening, a person can use this notion to better themselves and others. To encapsulate these ideas and feelings Verkron often render abstract characters with complex patterns.

Thó Simões, a renowned fine artist, is building a name for himself both locally and abroad. Possessing skills to channel his creativity into any medium of choice, including urban street art, Simões is taking graffiti to new heights in the country. Meeting the journalist Vladimir Prata led to the creation of one of the most interesting projects on the African continent: Murais da Leba (Murals of Leba). This concept, green-lit by the government, brought together the best artists and later resulted in a cultural exchange programme with Brazil, which shares

Portuguese as a common language with Angola. Thó Simões continues to add
to the walls of the Serra da Leba highway with his invited guests, while also taking
part in international exhibitions.

Zbi (a derivative of his old nickname, Zumbi) is open and willing to dispel any
myths surrounding the art form by talking to people when he is out painting
graffiti in Luanda. Graffiti is still new here and he often imports his supplies from
friends in Brazil and Portugal because of the lack of spray paint resources, the
main reason why many use an airbrush – himself included. Zbi embarked on his
personal graffiti journey in 2012 with the support of the Universidade Hip Hop
(U2H), an institution committed to educating young people through hip-hop.
Rafa Invencible is another young artist who began his journey around the same
time as Zbi, becoming more recognized in 2014 after he started painting with
some members of the first generation. Various projects have successfully
facilitated artistic collaborations, such as the Naxixi Street event in Luanda in
2019, which aimed to bring life back to the capital city streets. Naxixi Street
and Murais da Leba have added further momentum for the burgeoning Angolan
graffiti scene with their impressive large-scale artworks.

Opposite
**Spent, Señor Poste. Murais
da Leba, Serra da Leba,
Angola, 2015**

Below
**Thó Simões. Serra da
Leba, Angola, 2014**

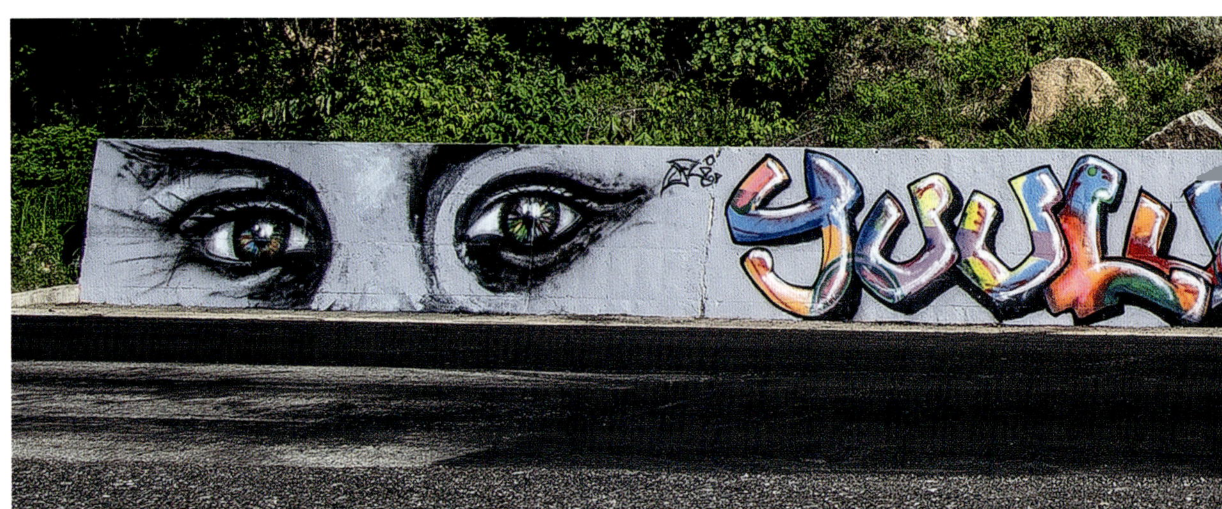

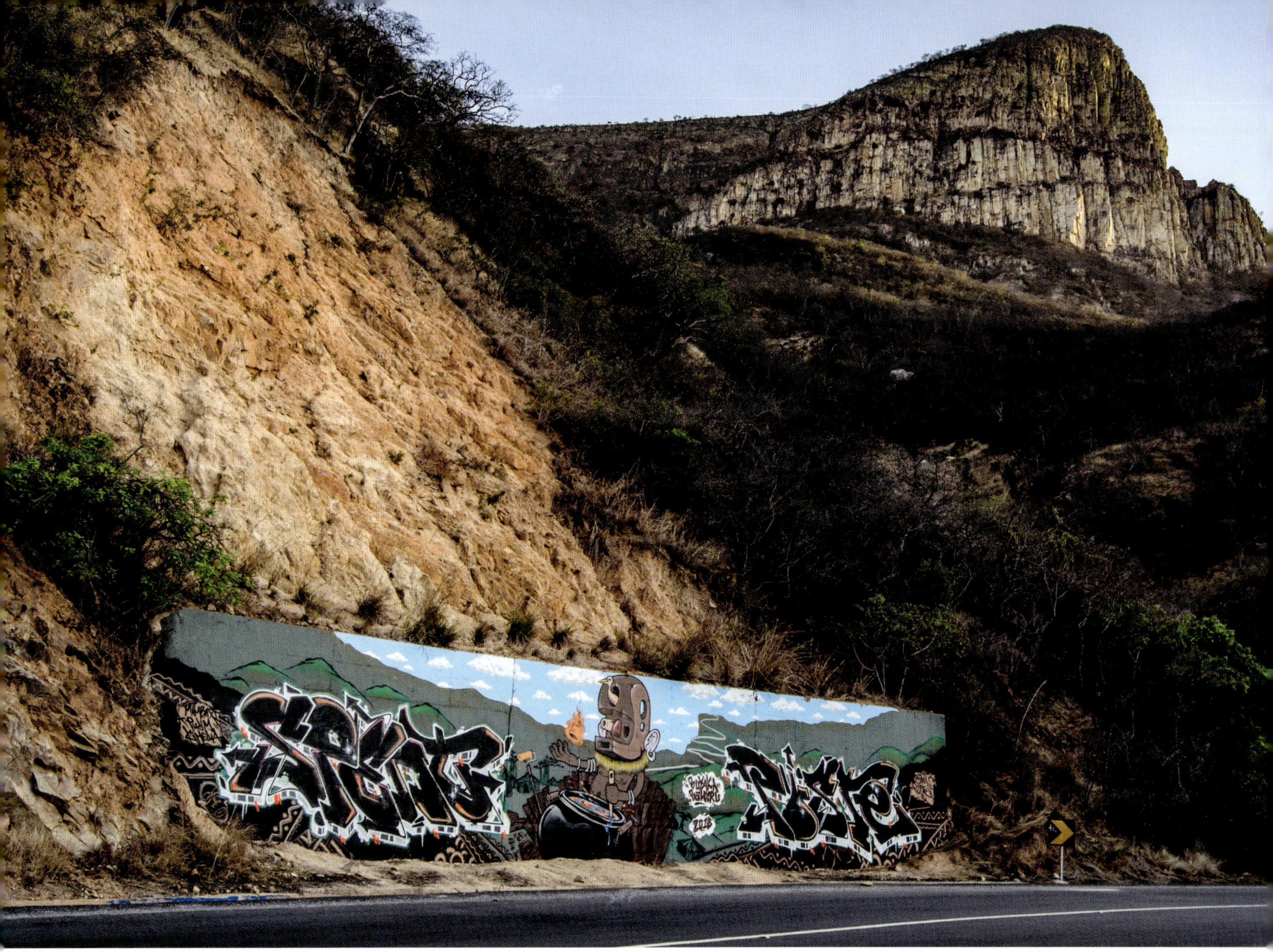

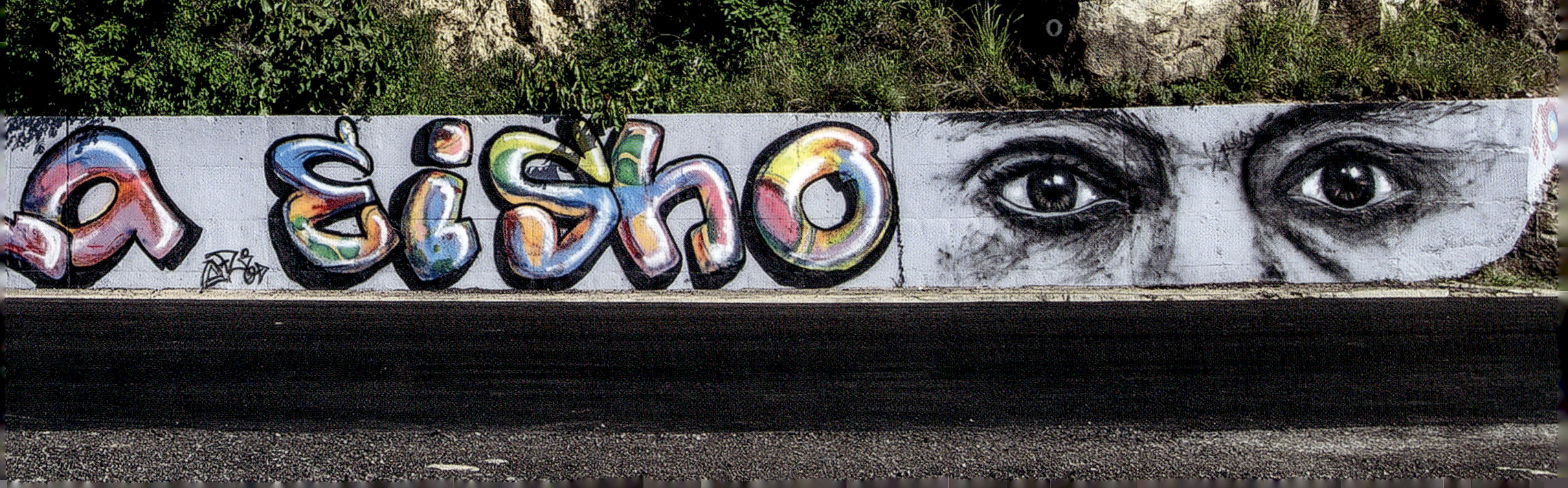

VERKRON COLLECTIVE

Tell me about your introduction to graffiti.
We started doing graffiti in 2008. The ability to communicate with people and the constant evolution of the medium inspired our interest. We have made people aware of our work ever since.

Tell me about the collective.
Verkron is much more than an artist name because it is an existential movement linked to our inner existence. We do not designate ourselves as a crew but rather as a movement, where we never present ourselves separately. We are unique, a single energy, the union between beings: we are a cordoned movement which shares much more than art – we share life and want to colour the streets with the truths of our beings.

Tell me about your style.
Our style is neo-muralism. Our work addresses the existential questions of humanity related to our spiritual being. The message we bring to our art is related to the reconnection of our human roots with the divine being; a work of conscientization [consciousness-raising] about our spiritual essence. We paint with various materials, essentially with plastic paints, and we complete it with touches of spray paint. For some works we only use acrylic paint.

Tell me about the graffiti scene in Angola.
Something is always happening in Angola; active politics, the repression of the system, and a very centralized economy. Graffiti – or street art – assumes the role of resistance and reminds people to focus on other, deeper things. What makes graffiti unique in our country is the sociopolitical climate and the lack of proper material. We use acrylic paint with almost no access to spray cans. We do not have a single store that sells material for street art.

Can you compare African graffiti to that of the rest of the world, places like Europe and America?
African street art is growing and is now garnering visibility around the world. In comparison to Europe and America it is still a little behind because many artists try to reproduce work they see over the Internet. We need to reinvent and reappropriate it for the African climate. Graffiti is evolving and we must create with locally available materials to make a positive difference.

The Internet is a useful tool for graffiti and street artists. What is the importance of

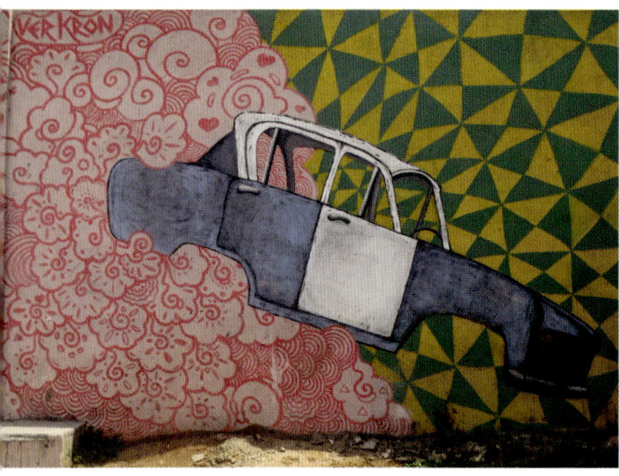

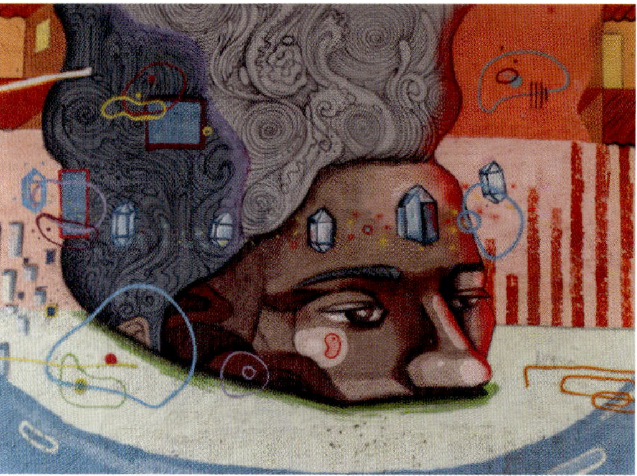

Far left
Verkron Collective. 'Chimboke Verkron', Luanda, Angola, 2017

Left
Verkron Collective. Naxixi Street Festival, Luanda, Angola, 2019

Opposite
Verkron Collective. 'Anarquia 33', Luanda, Angola, 2018

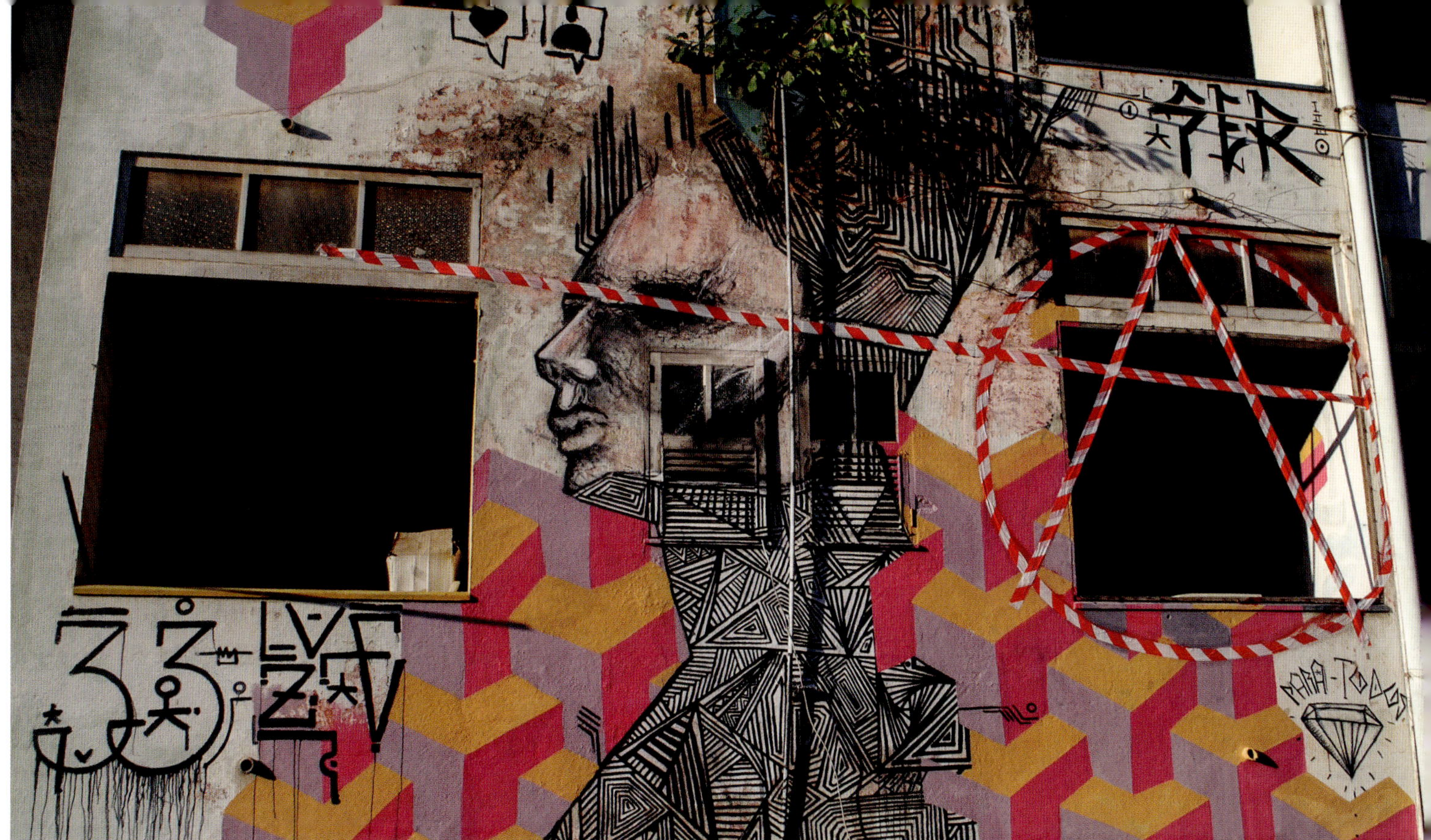

having an online presence for your work?
Work online can be seen outside of our country, in all parts of the world. We feel comfortable with social media, but do not know if social media feels comfortable with our work. We believe everything that demonstrates an escape from the system is of extreme importance in the construction of the human consciousness. If the media manages to maximize this information, then it is important.

How has graffiti affected your life?
Graffiti has directed our whole life. If it was not for graffiti, the Verkron Collective would not have been born. It is through this movement that we create solid foundations for a more humanitarian conscience.

What sort of reactions have you received from people about your art, especially on the streets?
We have never been badly received on the street. People understand the message right away and they change with it. Sometimes the police stop and complicate things, but we paint by day and without fear Painting on the street is a multi-sensory experience, and there is more than one definition. The feeling of gratitude is simply unexplainable.

How is your work evolving?
Our work has evolved into more technical muralism. We dream of painting larger walls and hope to take our African street art to other parts of the world.

Verkron is a collective of artists based in Luanda, Angola. Through spiritual concepts and an array of styles, the group produces enchanting, dream-like figures that combine contemporary fine art with the street art aesthetic. They enjoy being able to communicate with people through their abstract artistic concepts.

Page 102
**Verkron Collective.
Naxixi Street Festival,
Luanda, Angola, 2019**

Page 103
**Verkron Collective.
'Fluir', Luanda,
Angola, 2018**

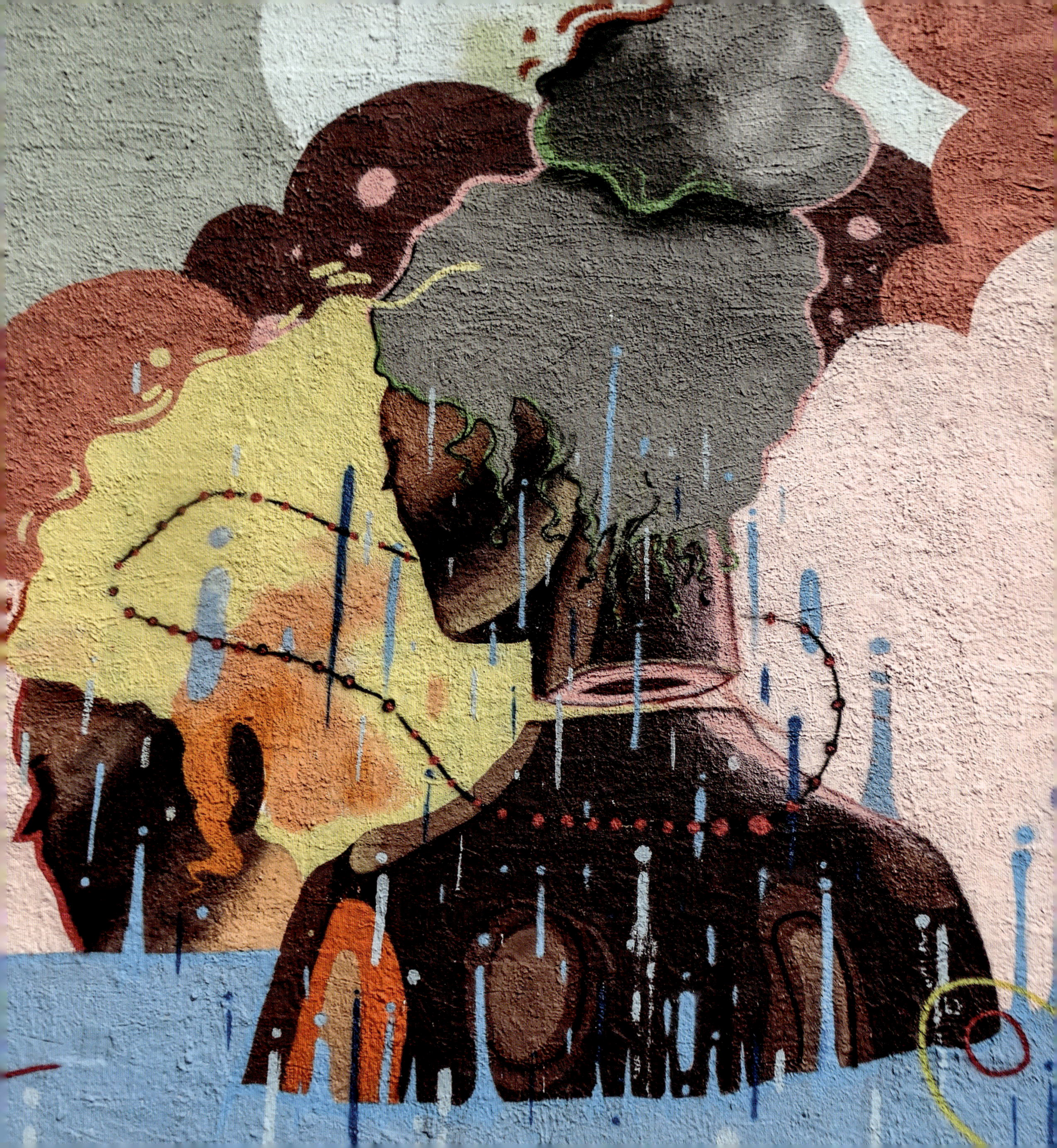

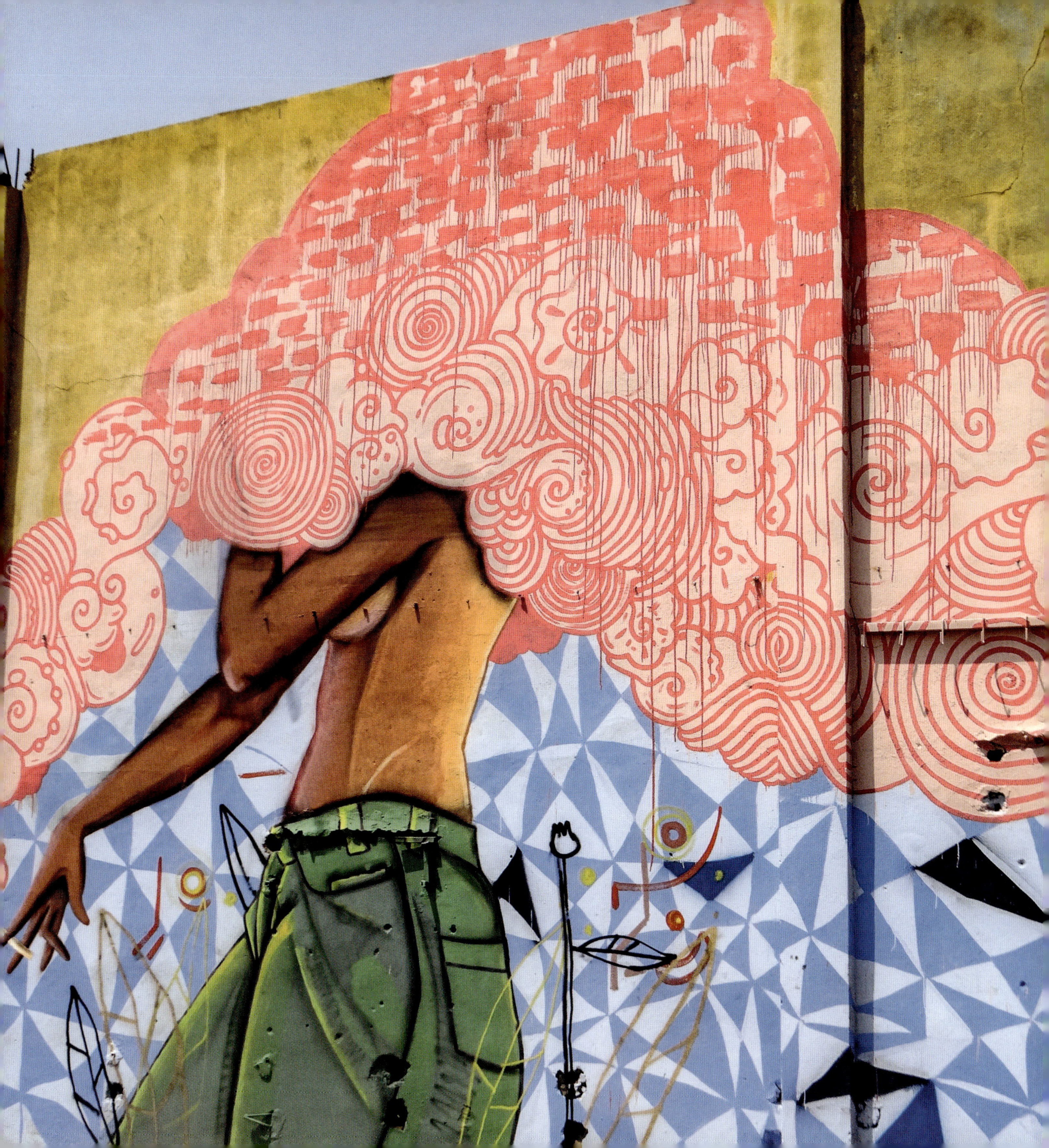

MURAIS DA LEBA

The Murais da Leba project is located along one of Angola's most iconic landmarks, the Serra da Leba mountain pass in Namibe Province. A feat of modern engineering in a spectacular natural landscape, the road snakes across the hillside for more than 18 kilometres (11 miles). Along the route is a series of walls erected to control rockslides, which were often targets for graffiti tags and other vulgarities. The goal is to repurpose the 6,000 square metres (64,500 square feet) of wall with large-scale murals by Angola's talented artists, thereby creating a name for the country's relatively unknown public art movement across the globe. Acquiring the right group of artists and maintaining equilibrium within the glorious setting and its nearby communities was a monumental but worthwhile undertaking.

With support from the Ministry of Culture, provincial governments and other sponsors, the official painting of the murals began in 2015 in conjunction with the country's fortieth anniversary of independence. About half of the allocated wall space has now been covered by local and international graffiti and visual

Opposite
Calangos (Brazil), Thó Simões, Rafa Invencible, Annie Ganzala (Brazil). Serra da Leba, Angola, 2018

Below, left to right
Verkron Collective. Serra da Leba, Angola, 2015

Els Graf Tridimensional, Rafa Invencible. Serra da Leba, Angola, 2015

ArtMore. Serra da Leba, Angola, 2015

Zbi, Fabio (Death). Serra da Leba, Angola, 2015

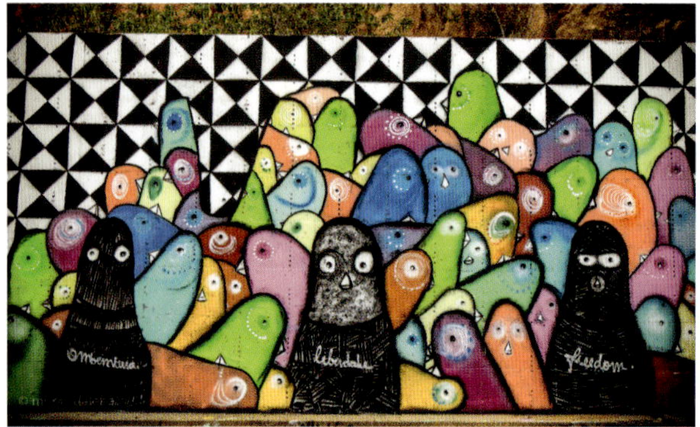

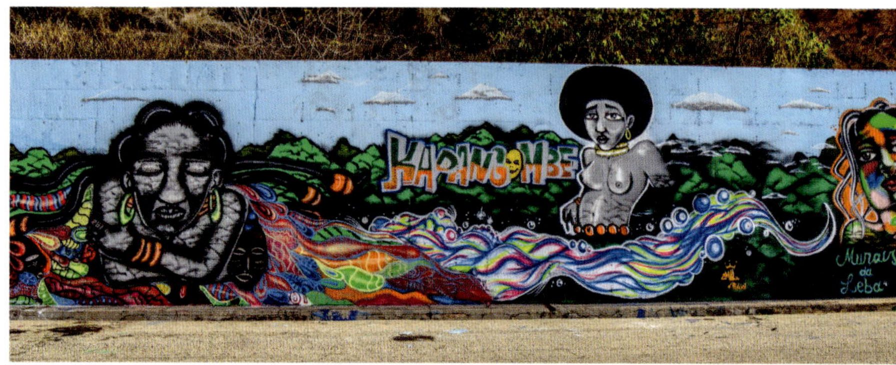

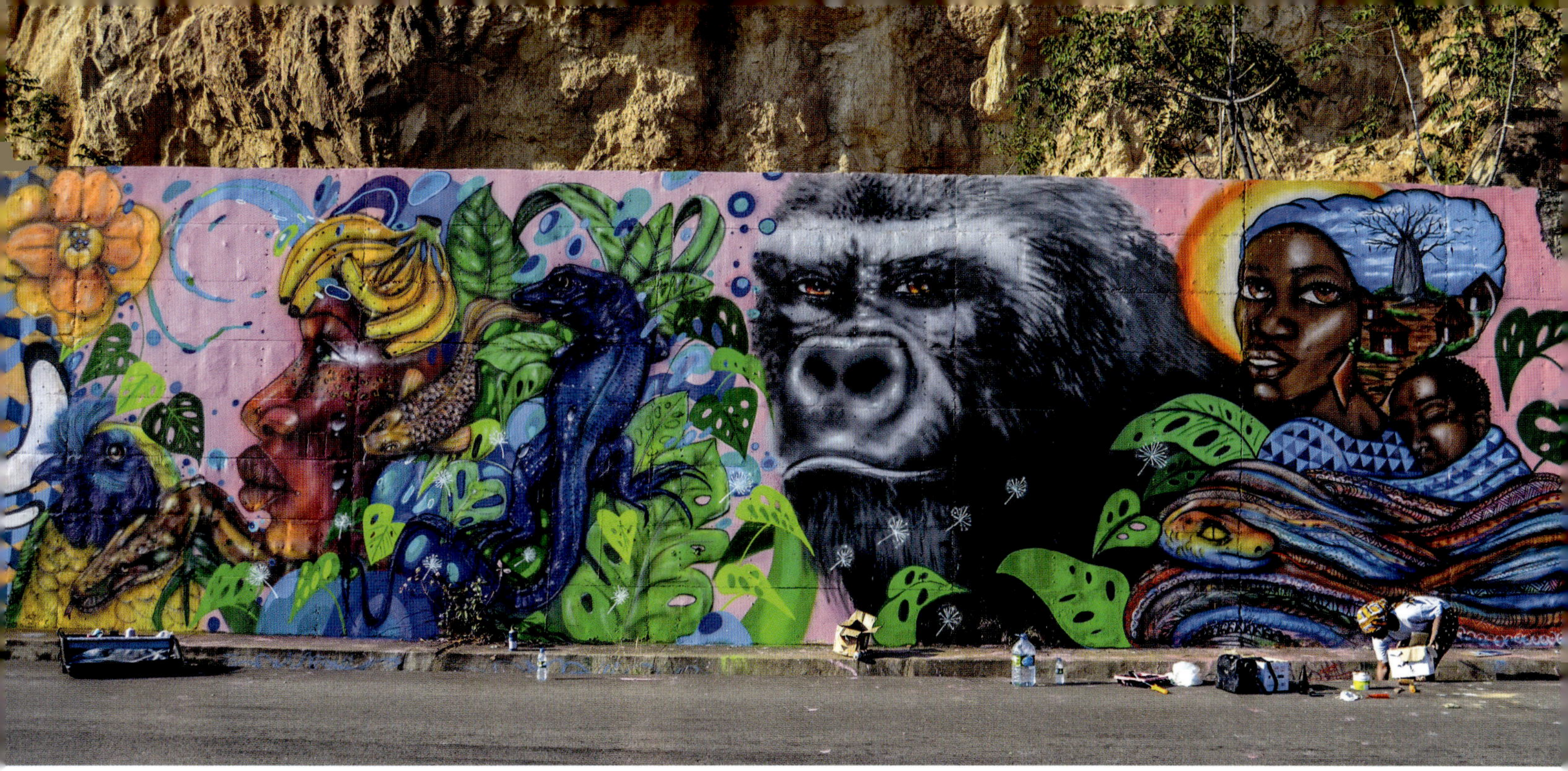

artists, including Angolan artists Rafa Invencible, Zbi and Verkron Collective with themes relating to their own ancestry. Groups of students who had participated in preparatory workshops were also invited to share the experience of expressing themselves at an elevation of 1,845 metres (6,050 feet) above sea level. More than ten murals have been completed, the second phase in 2018 by visiting Brazilian artists Calangos, Annie Ganzala and Srt.as (aka Ananda Santana) as part of an arts exchange programme, and the third in 2019 with Zéh Palito and Diego Mouro. The open-air museum hopes to create an imprint in the tourism sector and is a stepping stone to more government-funded mural projects.

Following spread
Verkron Collective. Serra da Leba, Angola, 2015

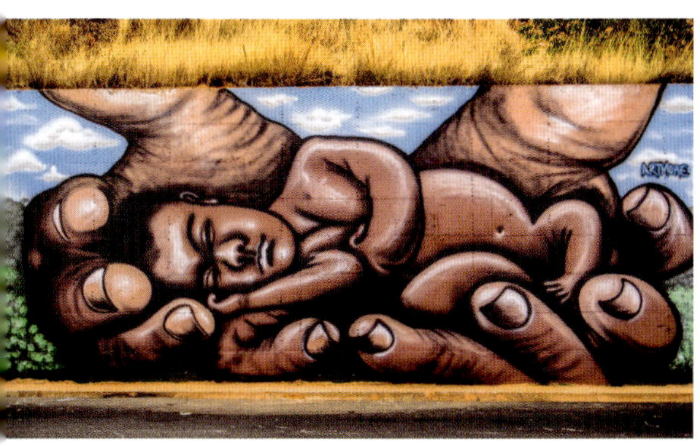

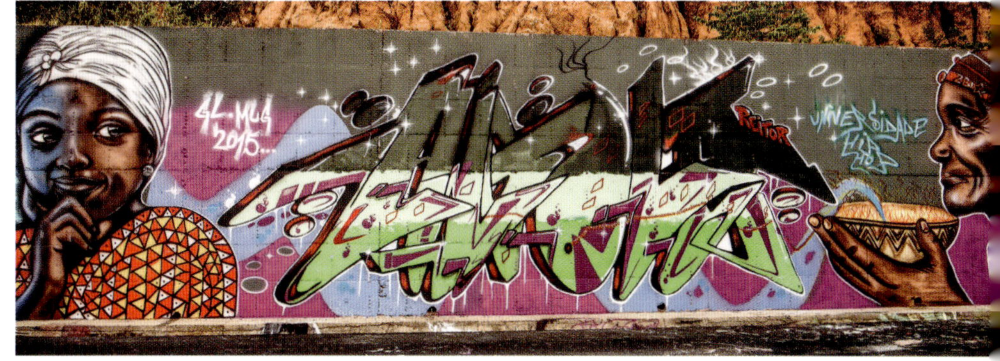

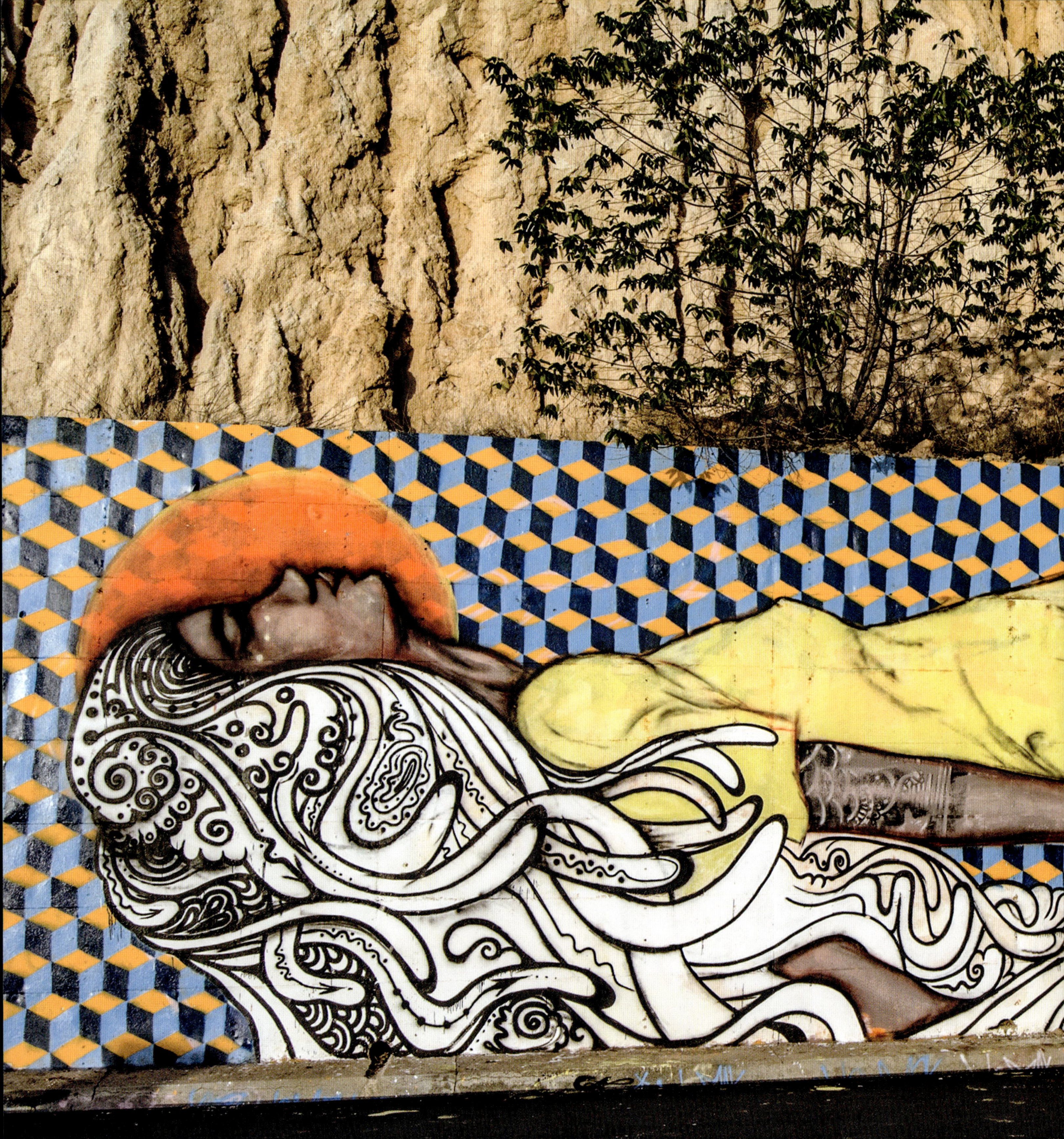

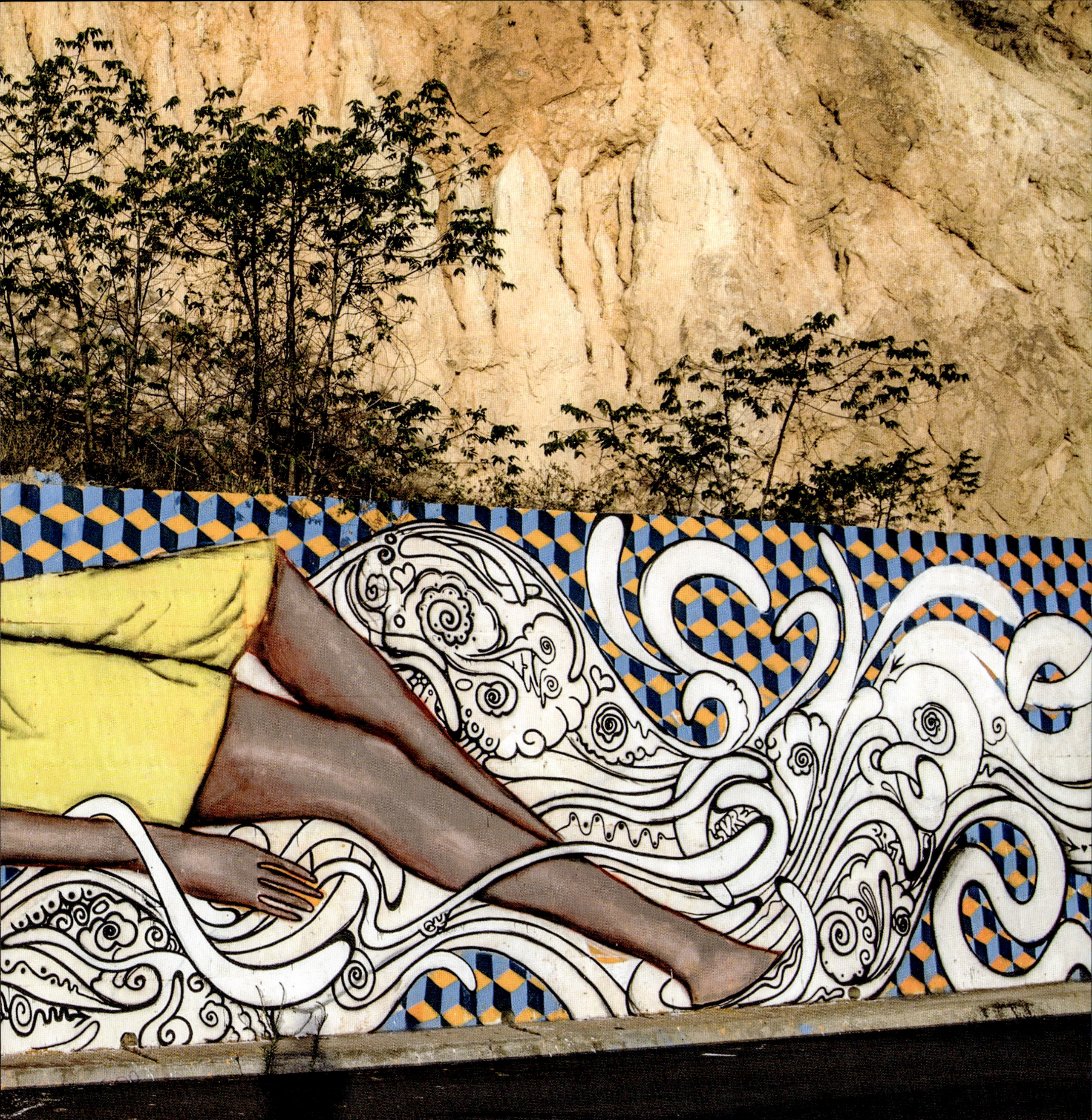

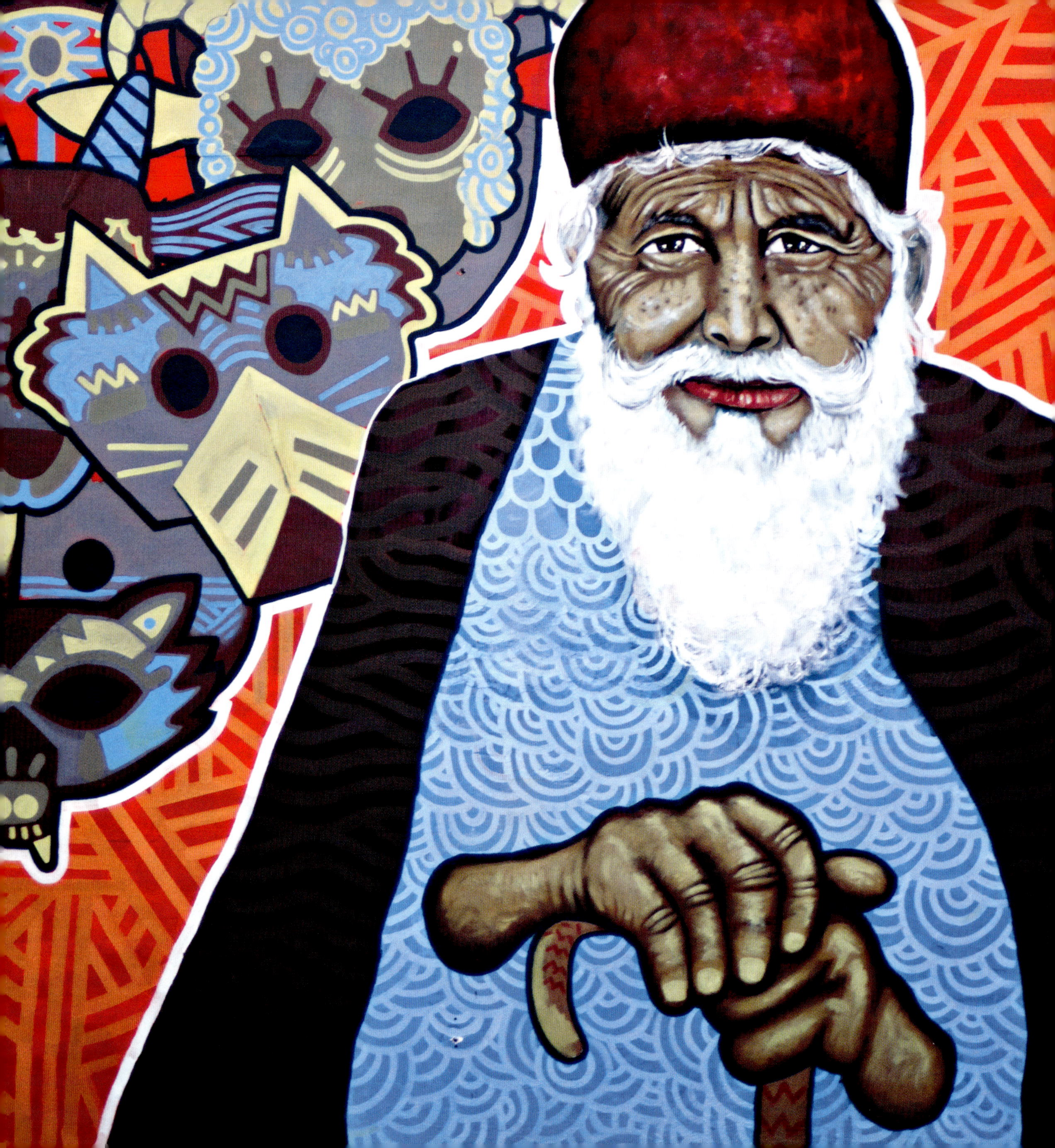

NORTHERN AFRICA

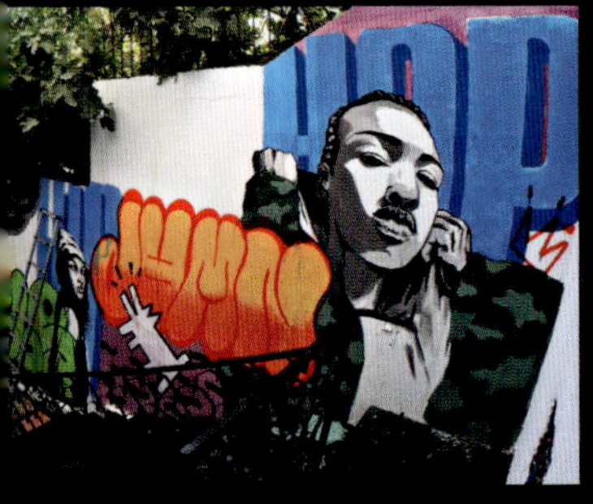

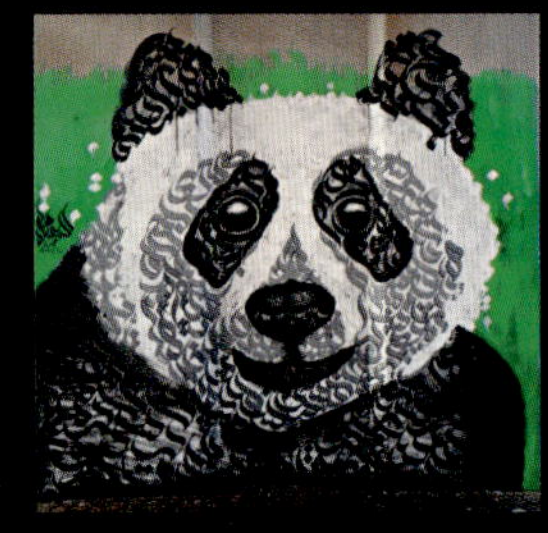

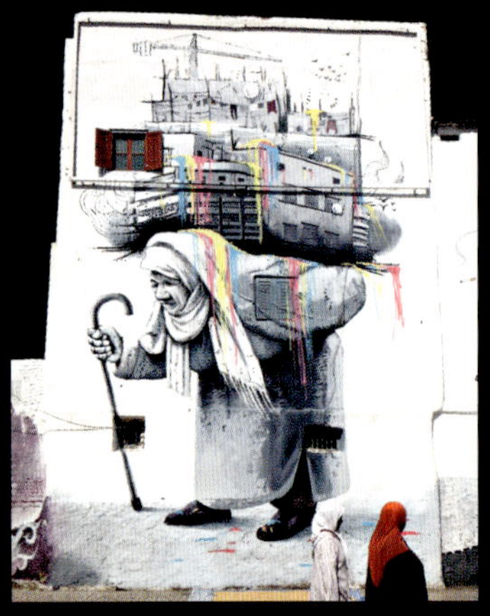

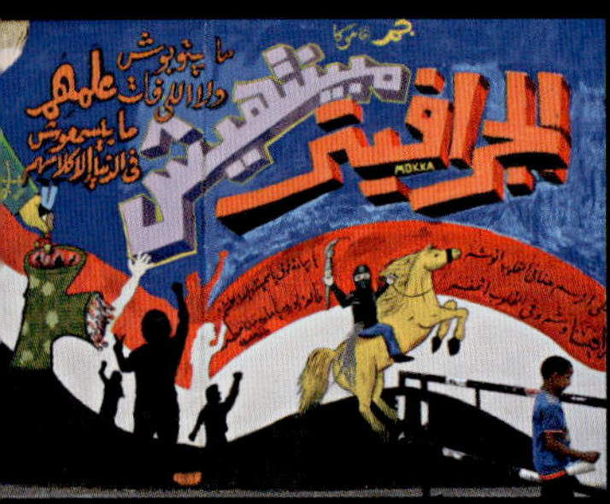

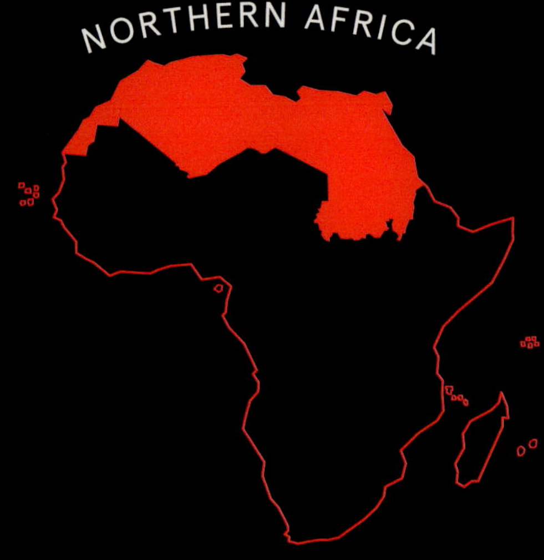

Page 108
Serdas, Slimensay, El Panchow. 'Le Marchand des Masques', Action Citoyenne project, Béjaïa, Algeria, 2016

Left, from top
El Panchow. Algiers, Algeria, 2016

Elbohly. Tripoli, Libya, 2018

Simo Mouhim. Sbagha Bagha Festival (1st edn), Casablanca, Morocco, 2014

Unknown artist. Cairo, Egypt, 2012

Opposite, left to right
Vajo. 'The Big Blue', Tunis, Tunisia, 2017

Various artists. Tunis, Tunisia, c. 2017

Galal Yousif. Khartoum, Sudan, 2019

Psycho (249 Writers). Khartoum, Sudan, 2018

Lmnt. 'Freedom Is Not Given', ARTifariti, Sahrawi refugee camp, Tindouf, Algeria

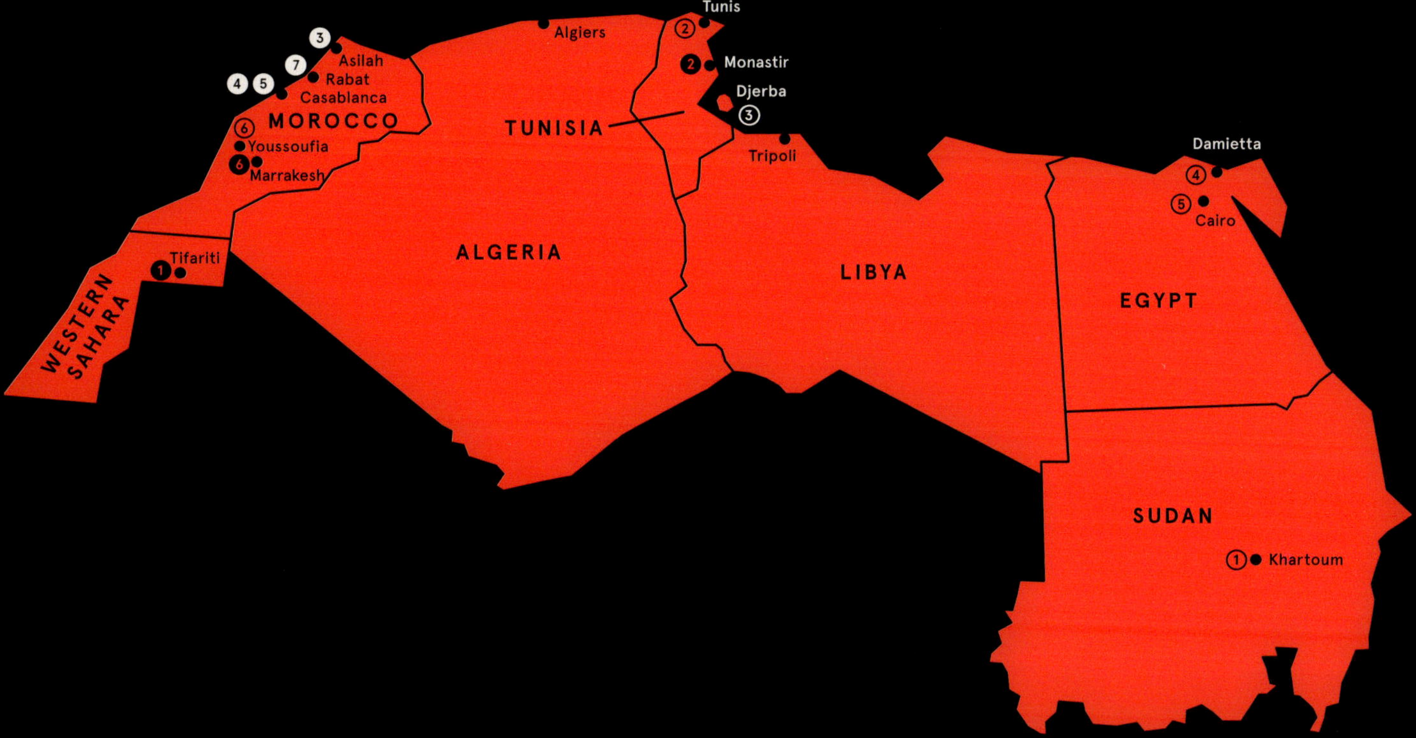

Tunis
Algiers
3
7
Asilah
4 5
Rabat
Casablanca
2
2
Monastir
Djerba
3
MOROCCO
TUNISIA
Damietta
6
Youssoufia
6
Marrakesh
Tripoli
4
5
Cairo
ALGERIA
LIBYA
EGYPT
WESTERN
SAHARA
1
Tifariti
SUDAN
1
Khartoum

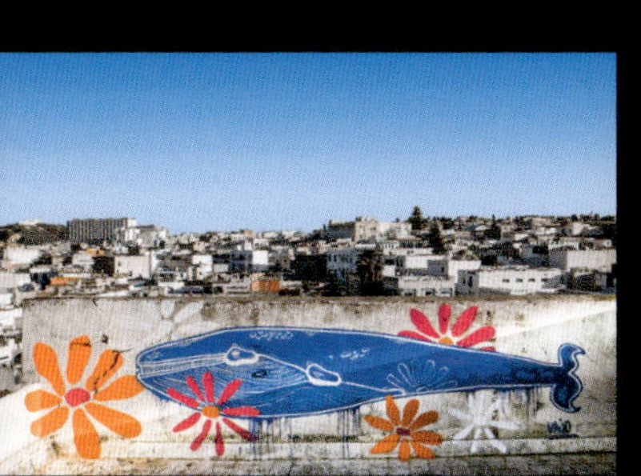

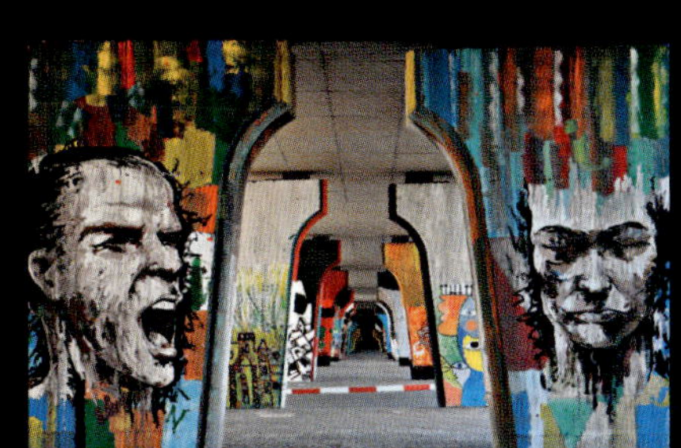

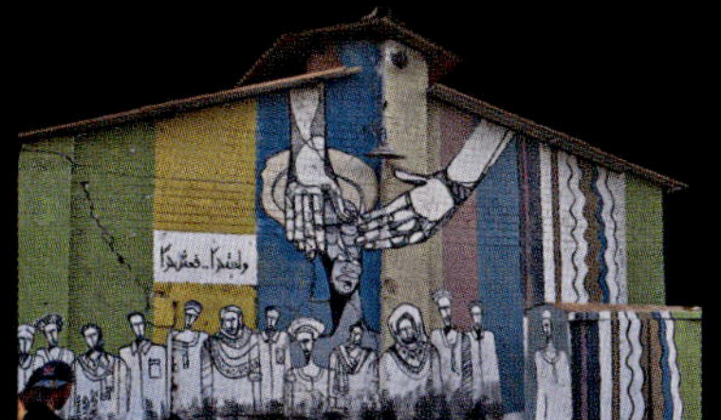

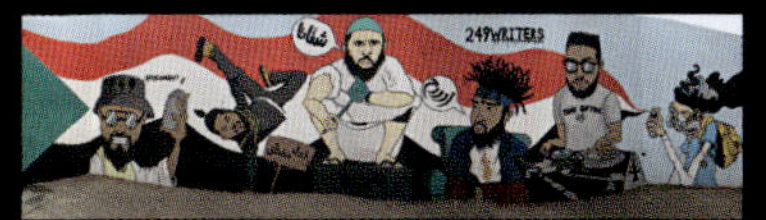

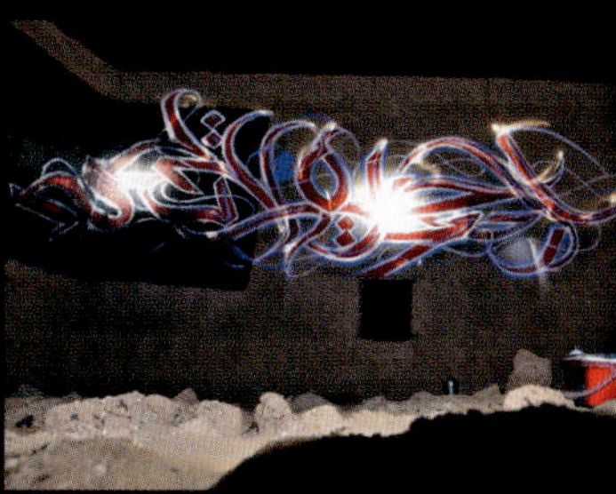

NORTHERN AFRICA

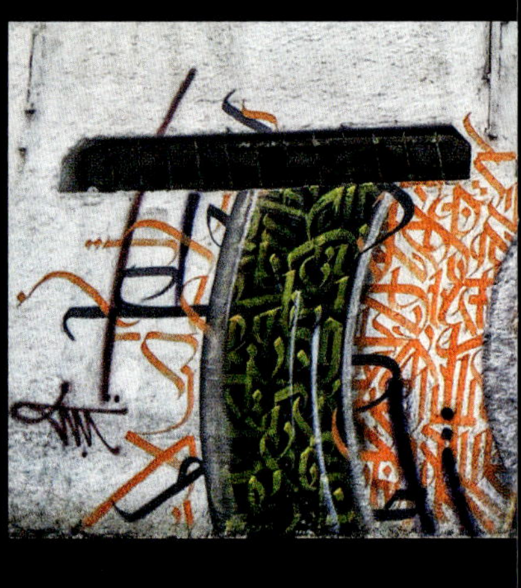

Stretching across the Sahara desert lie the countries of Morocco, Algeria, Tunisia, Libya, Egypt and Sudan. Over its deeply etched history, Northern Africa has been ruled by great powers including the Phoenicians, the Carthaginians, the Romans and the Ottomans. The indigenous Berber people were conquered in the Middle Ages by Arabs, and today the area is largely Arabic and Berber, with Islam being the predominant religion. This distinction has set the region apart from the rest of the African continent and Arabic calligraphy is an abundant visual graffiti style.

Artists such as Nofal O-one (Egypt) and Machima and Ed One (Morocco) are in tune with their native roots, integrating iconic imagery relating to past traditions and facilitating a common dialogue with the viewers and environment. The calligraphers are also intermingling, although their works could be misinterpreted as political messages, and, as in most countries around the world, graffiti is illegal. Much of the region has been engulfed in political tensions, with major upheavals taking place in late 2010 and early 2011. Known as the Arab Spring, these uprisings unleashed a series of radical events for such countries as Tunisia, Egypt and Libya.

The Arab Spring started in Tunisia and catapulted graffiti into the public eye. Reacting against issues such as high unemployment, inflation, corruption and political repression, citizens took to the streets to protest. The demonstrations featured a wave of urban guerrilla artists who chose to boldly express themselves in the city's chaotic streets. In their dedication to the cause they wielded aerosols, brushes and cardboard stencils, turning walls into bulletin boards, telling tales of truth amidst the lies being distributed by state-owned media. Social media was also a powerful tool to steer the revolutionary actions, while the movement amassed a global following through international media attention.

Unlike Tunisia and Egypt, where leaders were quickly deposed, neighbouring Libya's revolution broke out into a full-scale civil war in 2011, lasting from

Above
**Lmnt, Say. Annaba,
Algeria, 2018**

Opposite, top
**Normal. Casamouja:
Urban Art Wave, Casablanca,
Morocco, 2017**

Opposite, bottom
**El Med, Sadik, Ledis
(France). Oran,
Algeria, 2018**

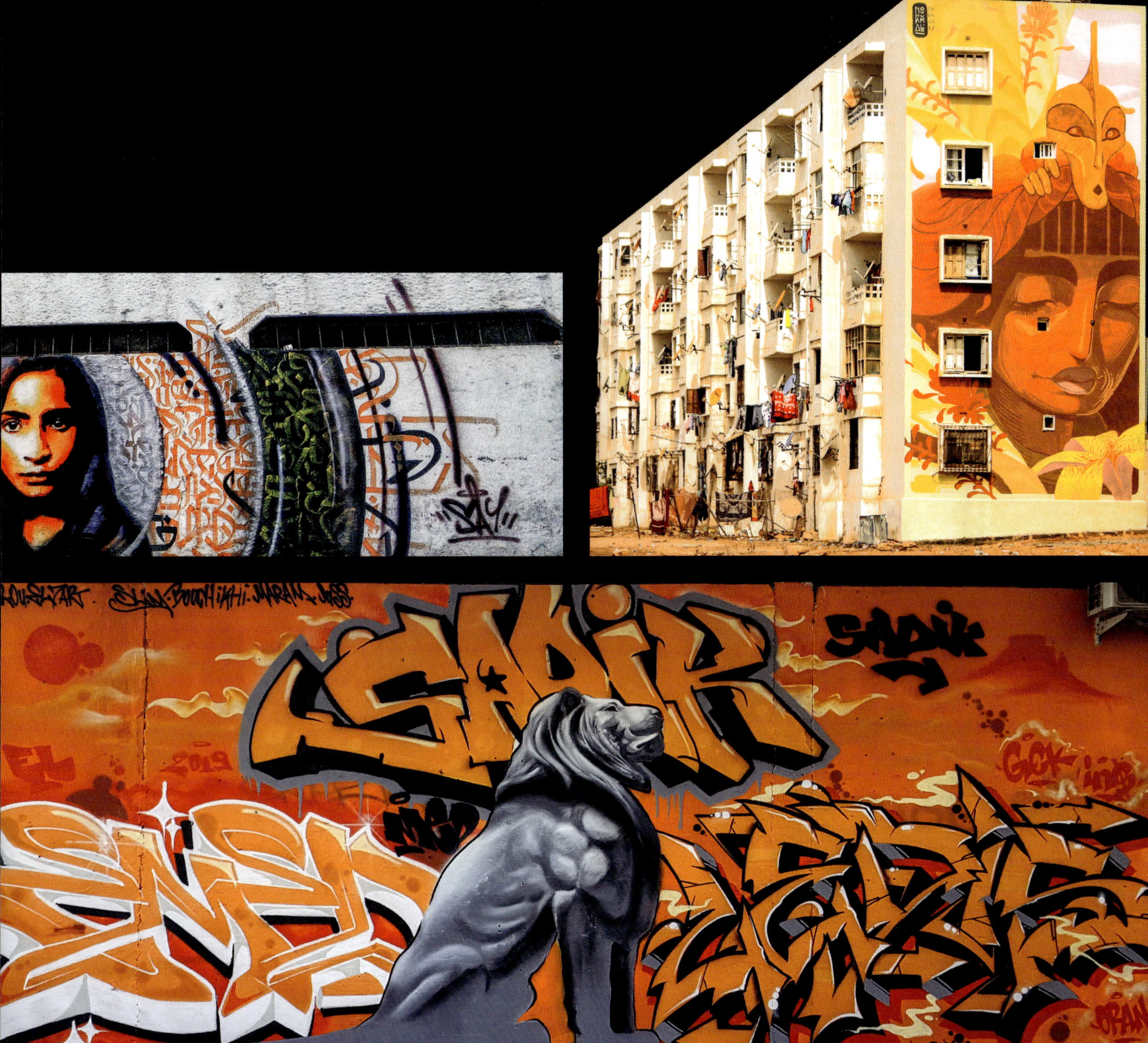

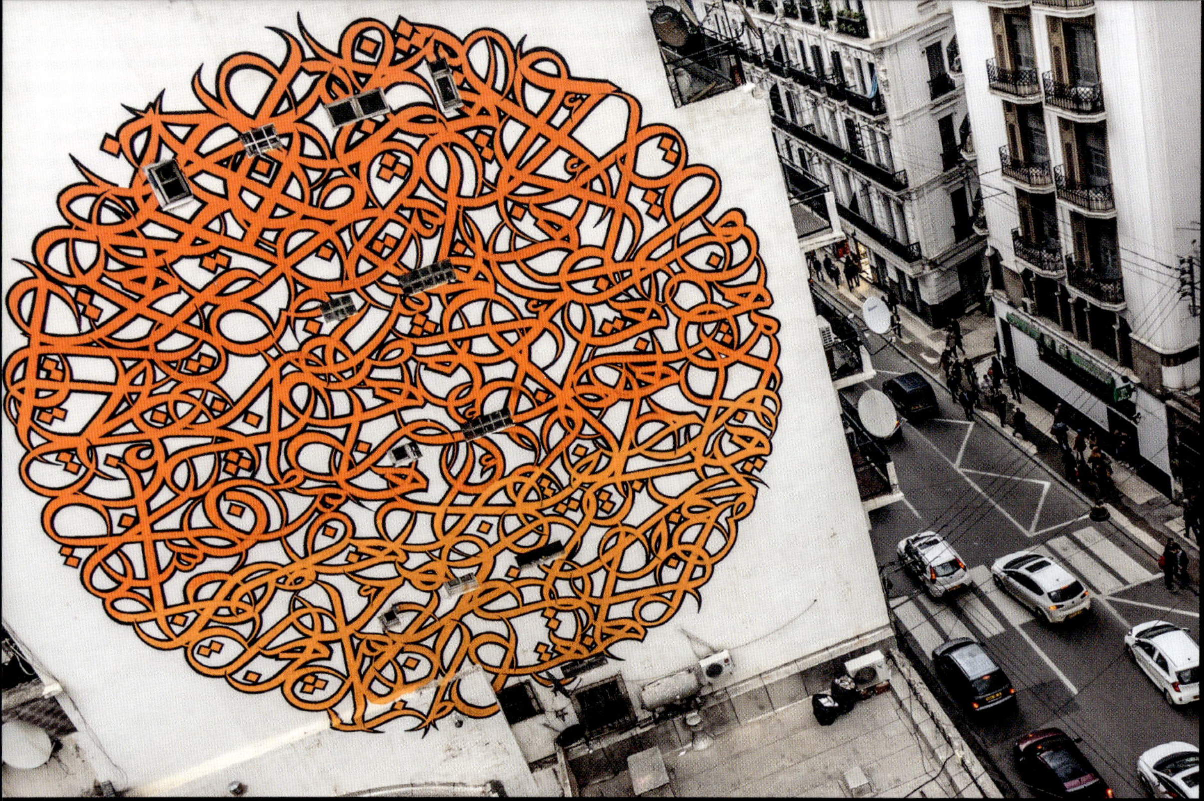

February to October, with a second conflict occurring in 2014. Graffiti and freedom of speech were rare during Colonel Gaddafi's long rule, especially when politically motivated, but during the unrest the streets of Tripoli became canvases for many demonstrators. Although most of the quality was rudimentary, it was responding to circumstances and uncensored, generating a public dialogue that had been absent through four decades of tyrannical rule. In December 2013, a series of workshops against torture were held across Tripoli in celebration of Human Rights Day, with more than a dozen Libyan graffiti artists taking part, including Ej, Sek2 and Elbohly. Egyptian muralist Ammar Abo Bakr and Tunisia's Meen One and Willis from Tunis were invited to facilitate the graffiti workshops.

Algeria is the largest country in Africa and home to some of the oldest-known African cave paintings, on the Tassili n'Ajjer plateau. In recent times, Algeria has experienced a turbulent political scene with many citizens and justice movements taking to the streets to express themselves with messages on the walls, including the phrase 'one, two, three, viva l'Algérie'. Graffiti was a common sight in the 1990s during the country's civil war, which ended in 2002. Today Algeria is home

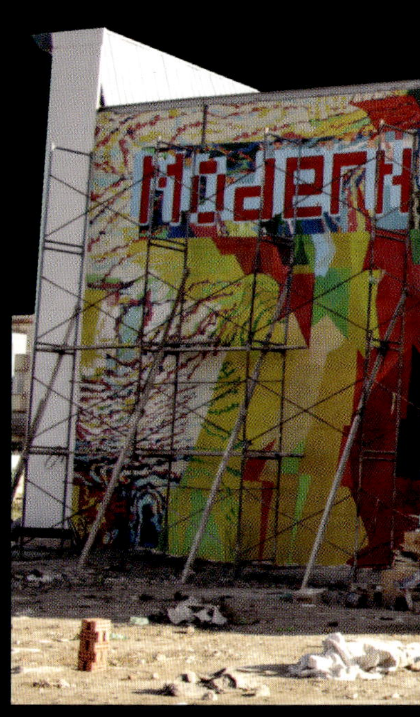

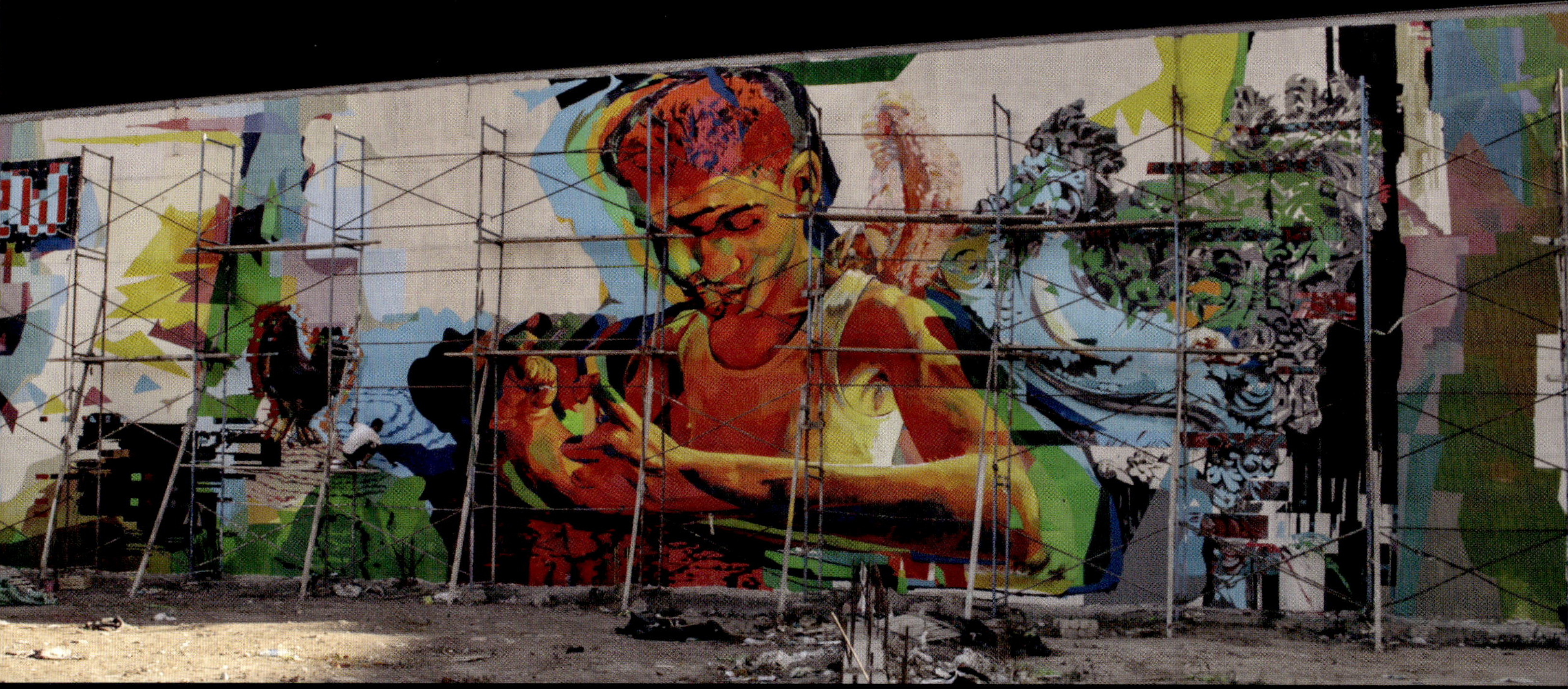

foundation to round up the year 2010. Although the country was not affected by the Arab Spring, social media and the Internet were catalysts for the burgeoning graffiti movement. Further artists began to appear, including Gs Jocker, L'Homme Jaune and TOXYGENE (Sneak Hotep and El Panchow aka DHMN). They adapted graffiti to their context, and by the mid-2010s, collectives such as LIKIP (Vato, Serdas, El Panchow, BLS, Belda, Resna), 213 Writerz (BBKR, El Panchow, Sneak Hotep, Belda, Serdas, TBC) and Inkindustriz (Lmnt, KMNone, Say) were active around the country, including in the cities of Oran and Constantine.

With the growing presence and understanding of street art culture today, urban artists in Algeria can paint more freely, especially when adorning walls with script pieces. There is a solid graffiti culture at play as writers get up on trains and tracksides. Sneak and Lmnt, ACR's Cris, Deas and Tilos, El Med and Sadik have all been busy. A new wave of visual artists is also present, including Say with his pochoir-style stencils, Ouss with his vivid murals, El Woujouh with his deconstructed photography paste-ups, and La Main Du Peuple (Hand of the People) with his deformed, fluorescent finger graphics that aim to highlight the problems of modern society – how people will always be trampled by the regime. Many of the Algerian artists have participated in ARTifariti, an art residence and cultural meeting to support human rights in Tifariti, Western Sahara.

Since its independence from colonial ties in the 1950s, Sudan has been relatively unstable in terms of governance, and its diverse mix of cultures and ethnicities

Following spread
**Bakr. 'Childhood',
Casablanca,
Morocco, 2019**

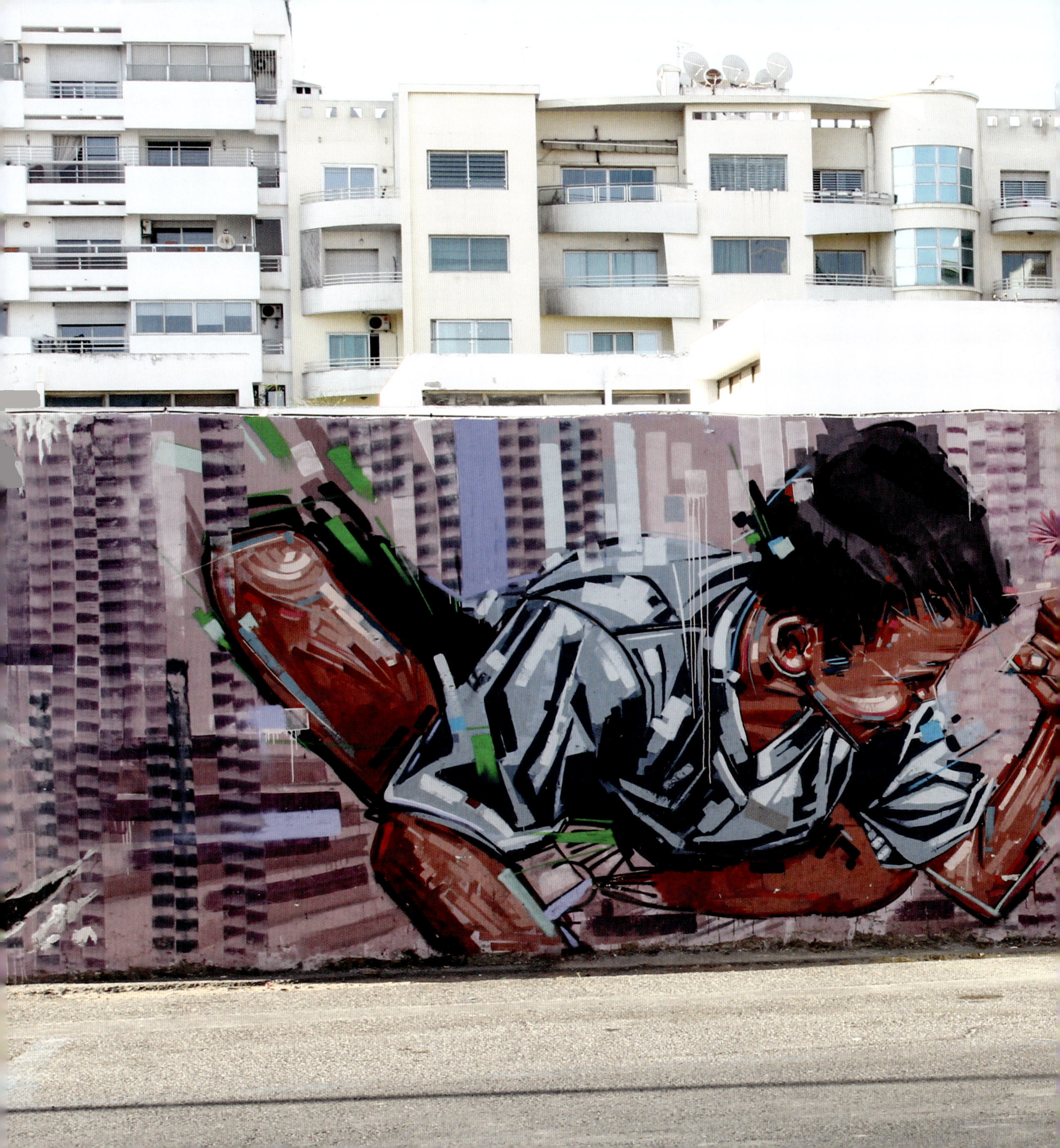

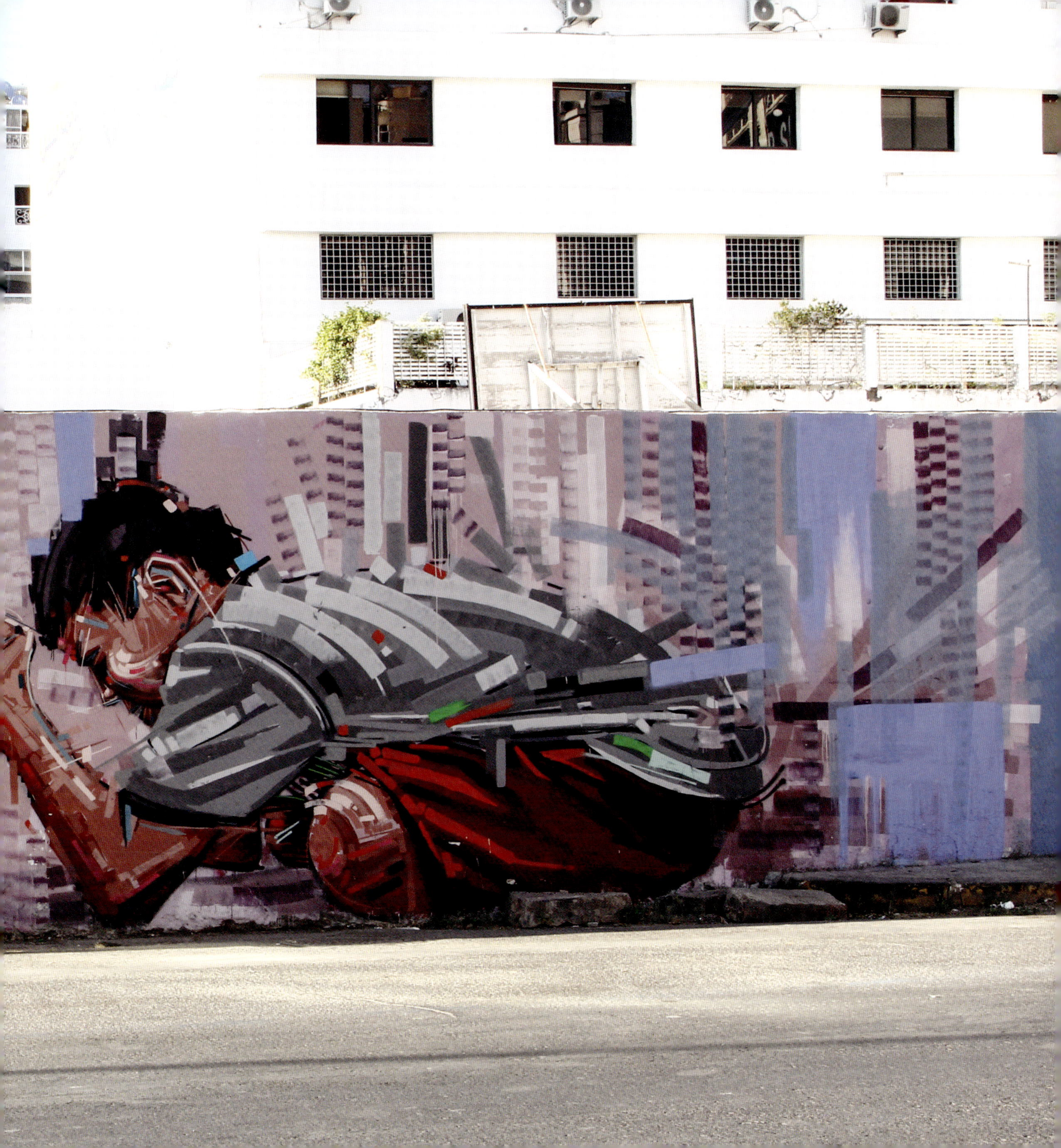

resulted in the formation of South Sudan in 2011. Sudan is vastly rural, with a long
tradition of oral story-telling (especially for those who cannot read and write),
while other arts including music and written literature are plentiful in urban
centres, although they are often suppressed. Many Sudanese writers, poets and
now graffiti artists are becoming known outside the country's borders.

Yalla! Khartoum is a community-based initiative in the capital, Khartoum,
founded in 2013 to promote urban culture among young people, focusing on
music, skateboarding and mural art. Through workshops and other forums,
the centre acts as a platform for Sudanese youths to explore creative ideas and
develop their own outlets. The first graffiti crew, 249 Writers – a reference to
the Sudanese dialling code – was formed in 2016. Flyboy, Teratoma, Graffiti Zool,
Honda, Bash, Psycho, Caesar and Swar Jr. complete the energetic collective
of street artists, calligraphers and graffiti writers. A passion for graffiti culture
brought them together and today they are influential in the evolution of the scene.

Yalla! Khartoum often facilitates mural paintings across long stretches of walls
with international guests as coordinators and mentors. Select local artists
involved in their successful interventions include Ahmed Elradi Mahmoud,
Ghassan Albaloola and Khaish Gallery members Elhassan Elmuontasir, Galal Yousif
and Hazim Alhussin. Their large-scale murals and graffiti productions, rendered
with brush paint, aim to beautify the streets while promoting the culture. In April
2019, after new developments on the political front, ongoing demonstrations and
a mass sit-in, artists and protesters took to the streets to create murals for the
revolution akin to the Arab Spring. Assil Diab (aka Sudalove), the country's leading
female urban artist, based between Khartoum and Doha, Qatar, advanced things
further by memorializing those killed during the conflicts. She also risked her
life with the military lurking in the background to stand up for her people and
challenge societal norms, specifically the stereotypes surrounding women in the
Arab world. Alaa Satir is another active female muralist and illustrator from Sudan.

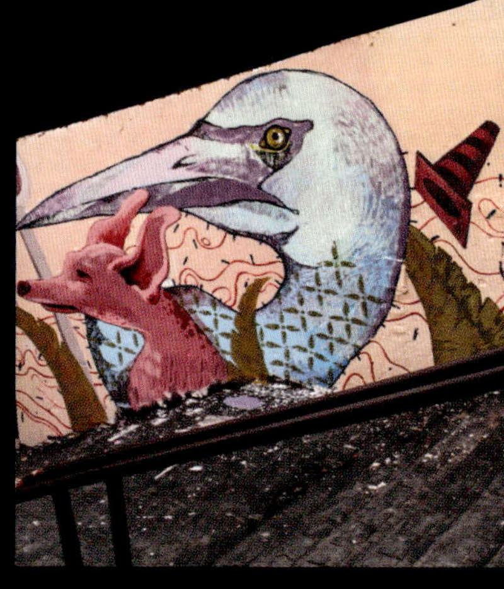

Street art culture emerged only recently in Morocco but has quickly developed
to dominate all other countries in the Northern Africa region. Its closeness to
Europe and its pool of immensely talented artists inspired a string of festivals
to further advance the field. Artists are being fostered through these initiatives,
painting large-scale pieces of quality art and learning via the intercultural
influence of visiting foreign artists. The highly promising circuit is strongly
affiliated to the current contemporary mural movement worldwide. Moroccan
crews such as SMC, TRZ, NOD and the infamous Trick 54 are leading the field.

Opposite, clockwise from left
Ouss. Algiers, Algeria, 2019

El Panchow. Algiers,
Algeria, 2015

Dynam One. 'You Will Shine',
Mur Collectif at JIDAR –
Toiles de Rue (5th edn),
Rabat, Morocco, 2019

249 Writers: Flyboy,
Honda, Graffiti Zool, Bash.
Khartoum, Sudan, 2015

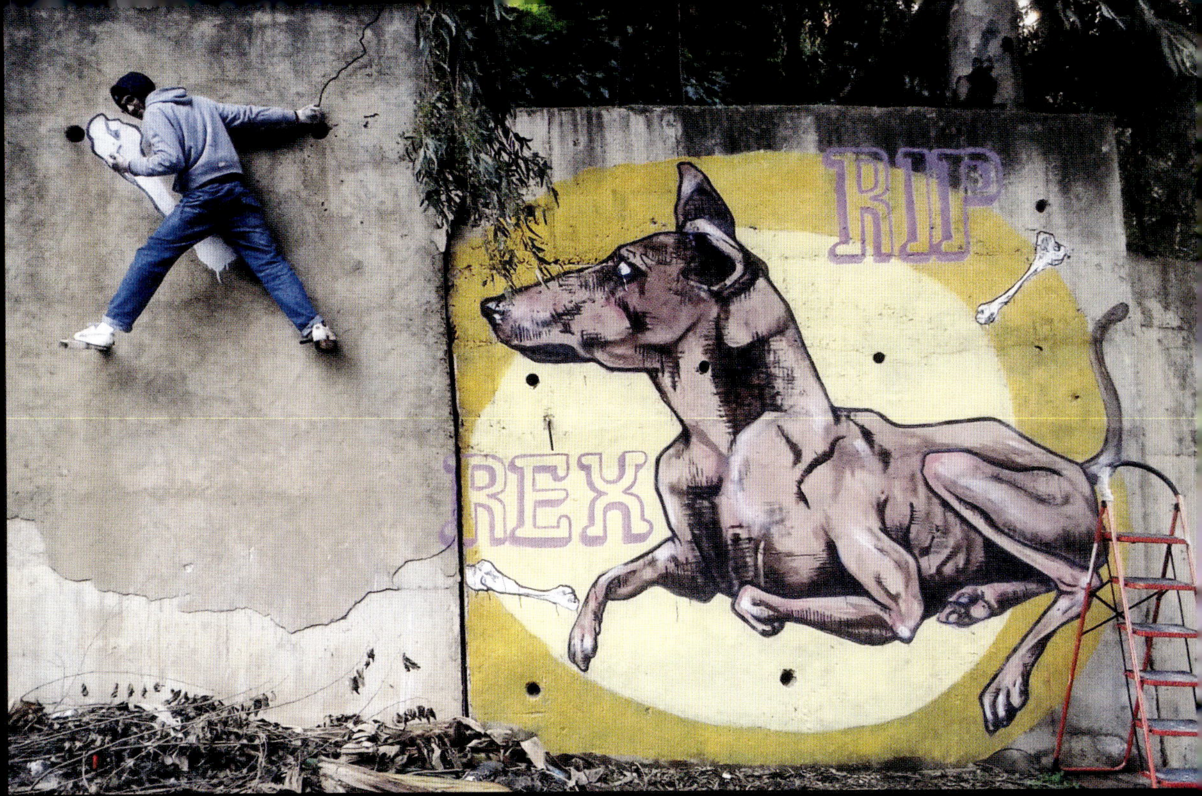

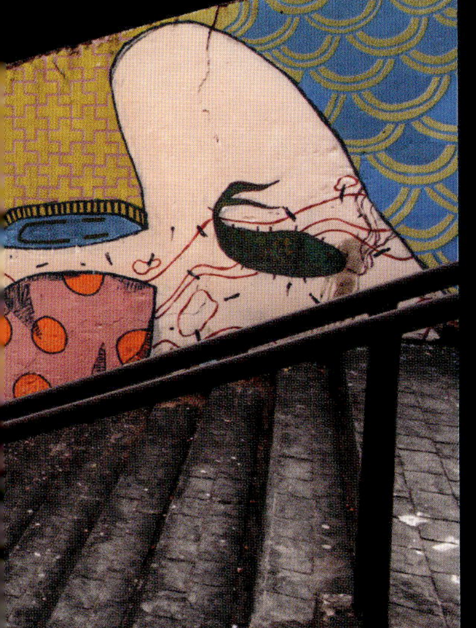

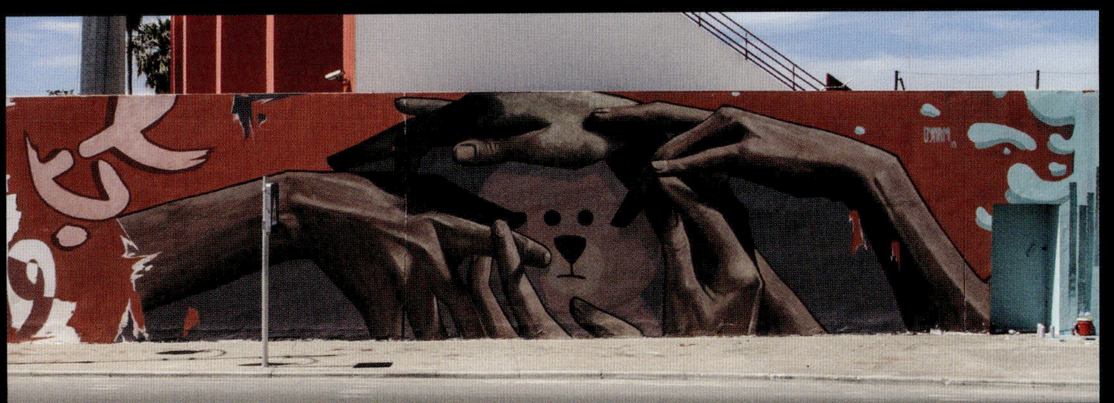

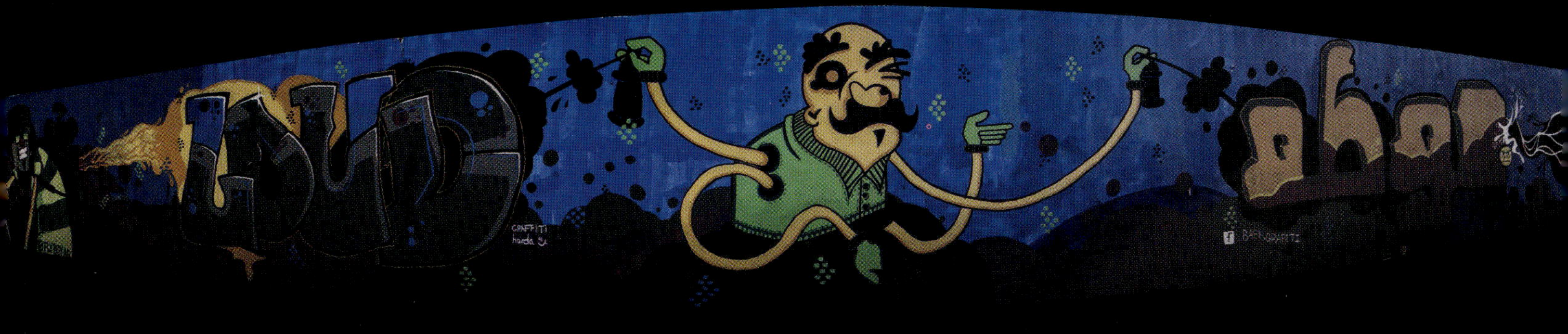

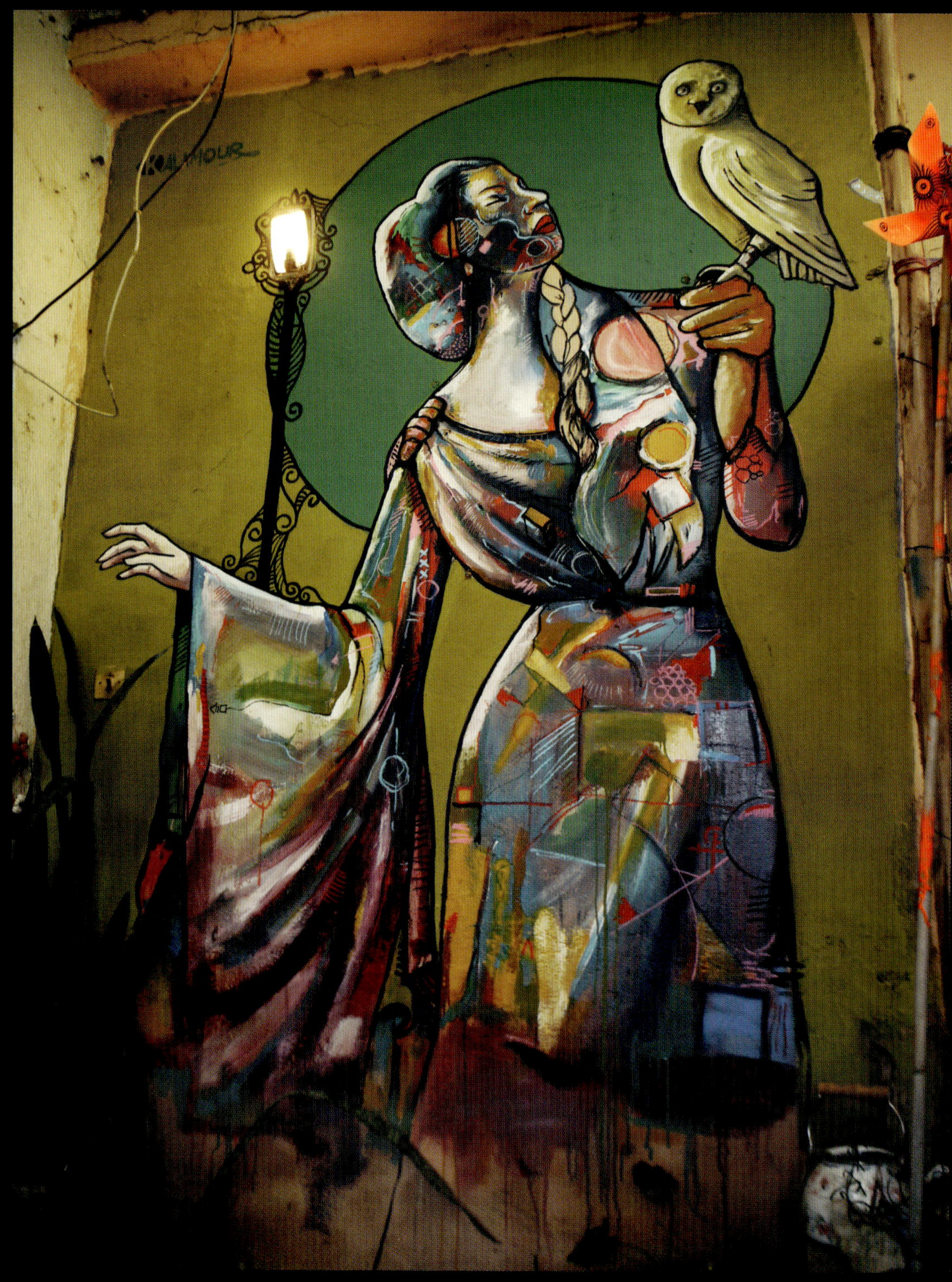

Left
Kalamour. Marrakesh,
Morocco, 2017

Opposite
Senzo Clouds. 'Inner Peace',
Casablanca, Morocco, 2018

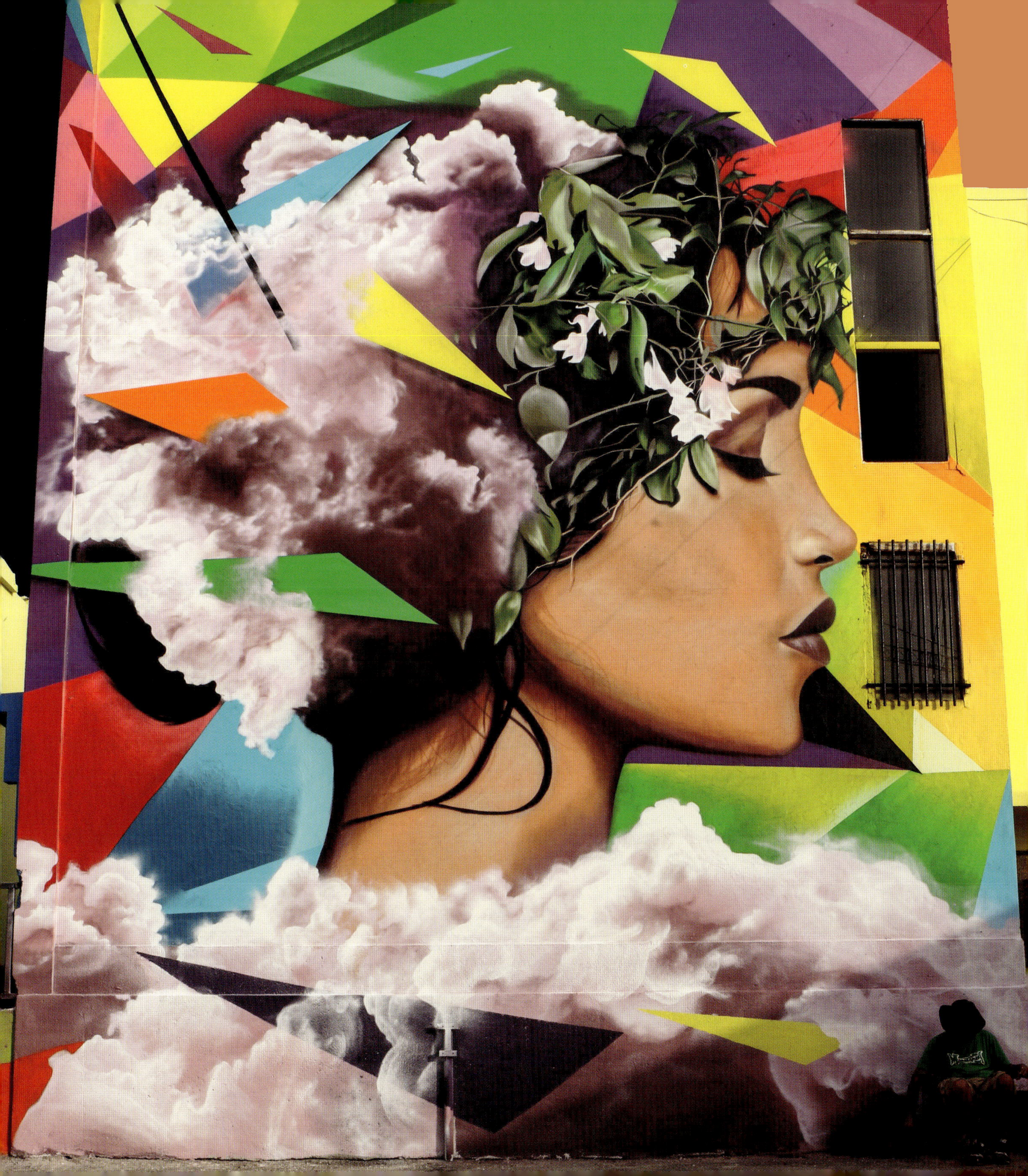

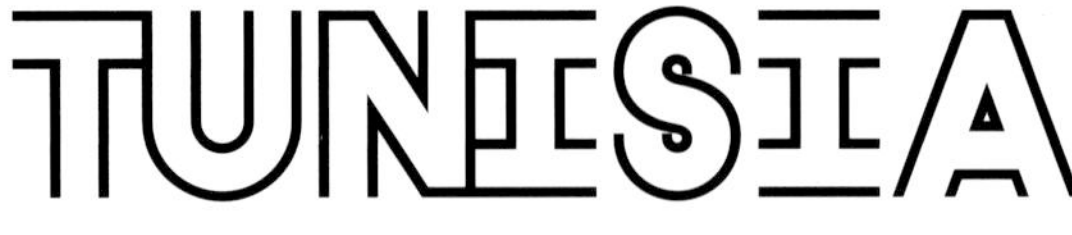

TUNISIA

Tunisia's scene was relatively unknown before the revolution. Artists such as Sk-one, Vajo and Meen One were painting graffiti in the early 2000s, but the revolution enabled them to showcase their talents extensively and brazenly weave their work into the now less restrictive streets. Sk-one, who maintains a strict classical graffiti style, began his graffiti journey around 1997 and was a participant in the country's first graffiti exhibition in 2009. After the mass protests that erupted in Tunisia in December 2010 – the first events of the Arab Spring – President Ben Ali was rapidly ousted. Graffiti artists moved in on the ransacked and destroyed mansions owned by the dictator and his wife. Many graffiti artists, including Sk-one (also Eska-one) and his collective ZIT (Zombie Intervention Tunisie), with Meen One and Willis from Tunis, freely utilized the abandoned luxury homes as the canvas for their art in this ironic turn of events. The regime had alienated its people and provoked fear with its authoritarianism. The act of the graffiti artists, although not always overtly political, united with the visual poetry of other revolutionary graffiti and shone within the communal landscape, becoming a welcome reminder of the country's successful transition.

A host of events further stimulated the culture after the revolution. From 2012 to 2015, vibrant exhibitions, graffiti jams and mass public art projects took place in Tunisia. Kif Kif International and Open Art Tunis hosted Vajo, Inkman and various French urban artists, bringing graffiti to the fore – a disused Boeing 727 plane was even reimagined for Kif Kif's Mourouj Airlines project in a landfill-turned-communal park with a travel theme. Vajo, a street artist from the town of Gabès, was first attracted to the art form by T-shirt graphics featured on clothing, but switched from letters to figurative pieces in 2013. What Vajo ('VA' standing for visual art and 'Jo' for his nickname) enjoys most is the painting process itself – the meditative aesthetic it evokes – as well as the way that art can change the perception of a place. His work has evolved from more colourful, child-friendly bubble characters to a mature illustrative style of street art, and

Opposite
**Shoof. Djerbahood project,
Djerba, Tunisia, 2014**

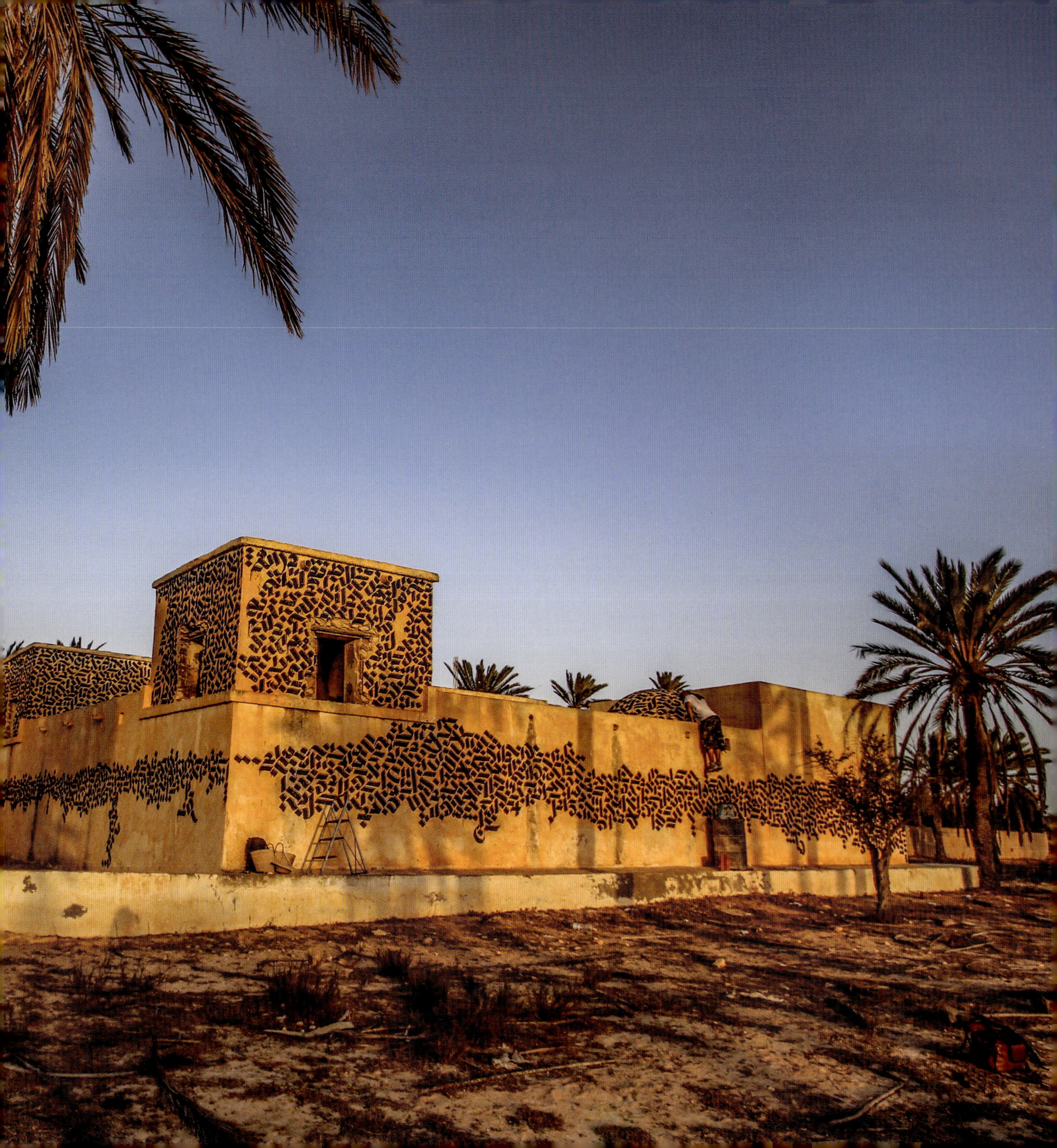

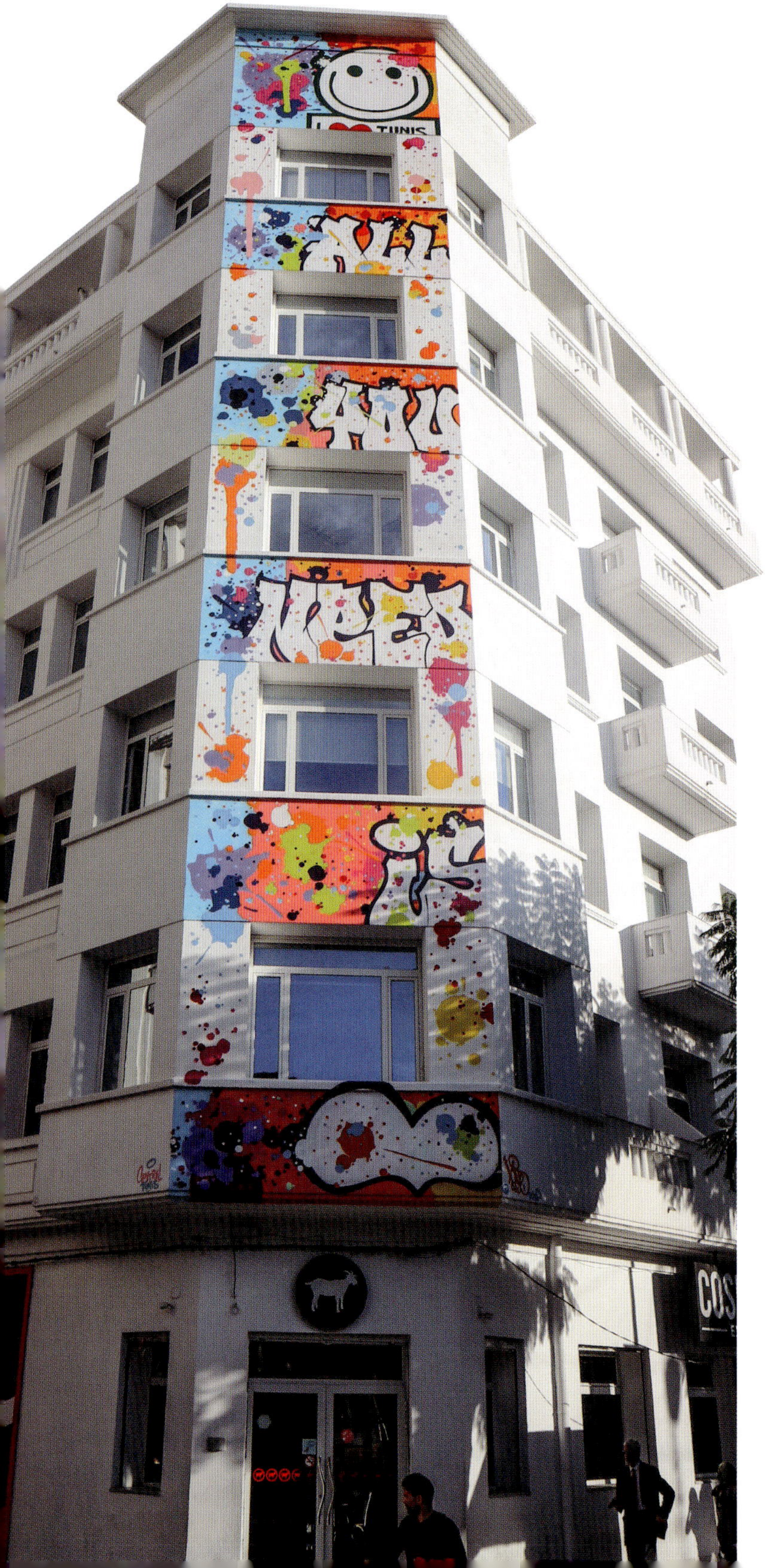

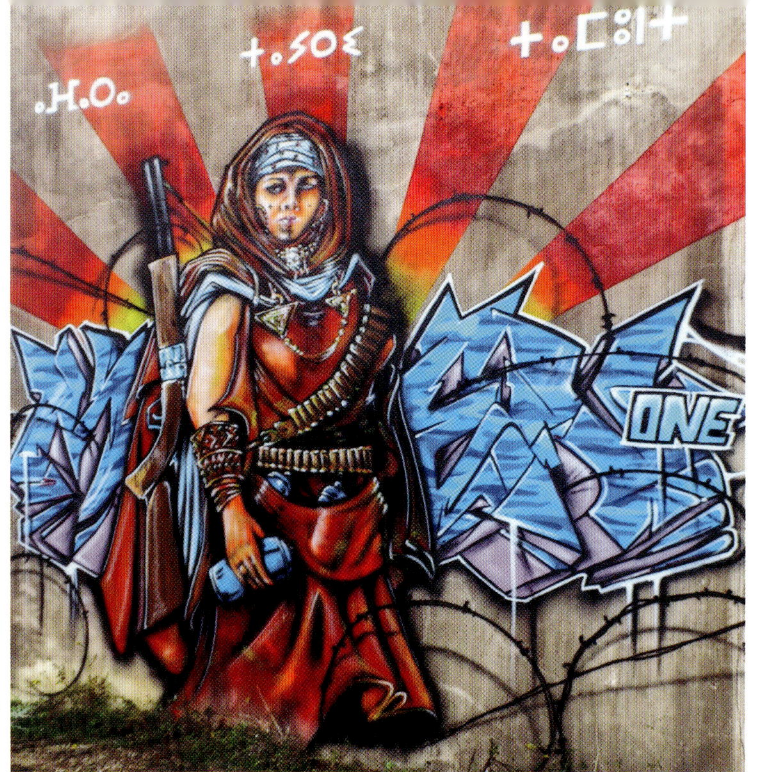
.H.O.
+oⵙoƐ
+oⵎᴐ1+
ONE

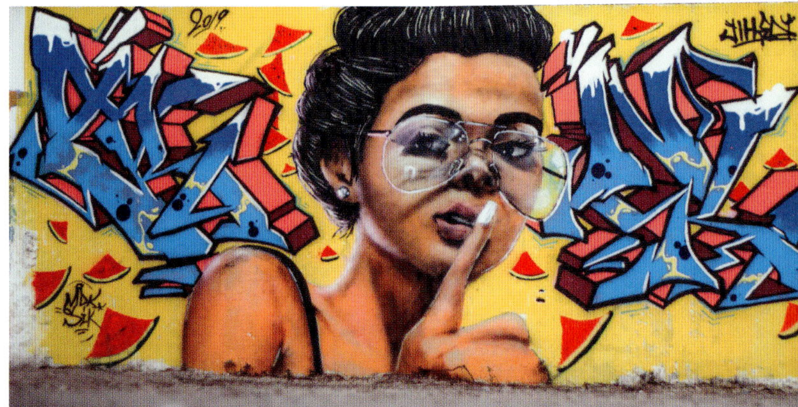

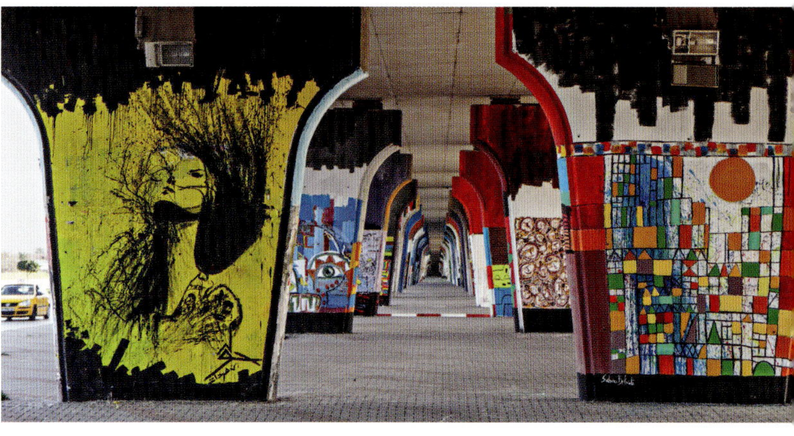

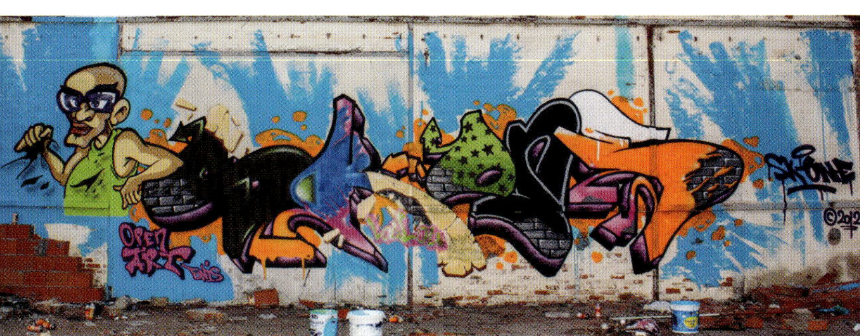

Opposite, clockwise from
far left
**Jaye de Tunis. 'All You Need
Is Love', Tunis, Tunisia, 2019**
**Meen One. 'Berberitta',
Tunis, Tunisia, 2014**
**Trank, Jihedy. Gammarth,
Tunisia, 2019**
**Various artists. Tunis,
Tunisia, c. 2017**

Above
**Sk-one. Open Art Tunis,
Tunis, Tunisia, 2012**

he continues to explore other mediums such as digital art. Inkman, who first began writing under the alias Kim around 2011, is a master of typography and has become a rising star in the world of calligraffiti. His poetic work borrows from both the Latin and the Arabic alphabets, while good values shape his output. Like Vajo, Inkman believes art needs to coexist with its environment and have a greater purpose.

International artists such as Jaye de Tunis and eL Seed also played a vital role in enhancing the Tunisian graffiti arena. Jaye, a member of TVA, TNB and VMD crews, has lived in Tunisia's capital, Tunis, since 2012 and actively paints and sculpts while also hosting visiting artists. eL Seed was born in Paris to Tunisian parents and embarked on a road trip across the country in the summer of 2013 to engage with his heritage through his Lost Walls project. The idea for this journey grew in him after he completed painting the minaret of the Jara Mosque in Gabès, his ancestral home, in 2012. At roughly 50 metres (165 feet) high, the tallest minaret tower in Tunisia had been left unfinished for nearly two decades and eL Seed secured the imam's permission to graffiti it. After a month of painting the artwork was complete: featuring a verse from the Qu'ran, it highlighted the convergence between art and religion. The later Lost Walls project was not solely about the artwork, but also about sparking a dialogue through interactions with everyday people, and overall aimed to represent post-revolution Tunisia. Each of the twenty-four pieces incorporated a relevant quote and eL Seed happily engaged with the locals about it. The project was always about cultural exchange and human interaction at its core, and this approach would set the tone for more ambitious projects in the future (such as 'Perception' in Egypt). Today eL Seed is a world-renowned calligraffiti artist who continues to build bridges with work that is universal.

Other graffiti artists such as Amen and Saif of 94 Crew, Psyko, Trank (MDK, SIK), Sim/Marek and Karim Jabbari also contributed to the Tunisian graffiti scene. Streets Urban Festival took place in the city of Kasserine in 2013, spearheaded by Karim Jabbari, who also completed the longest wall in the country for his Towards the Light project. Jabbari's quest with Towards the Light was to steer young people away from the adversities of society and encourage them to cherish their language and identity, especially in an impoverished city where many youths felt suppressed and marginalized. In Sfax, the second biggest city, the duo of ST4 the project (formerly ST4 Crew) came together to enhance graffiti's mark in their city. Yassin Bouzid and Sadk Kaffel felt inspired by the energy succeeding the revolution and, after experimenting with tags and traditional graffiti lettering, they created their own fusion of styles. Owing to the influential street art scene abroad where artists incorporate their own dynamics, ST4 the project combined Arabic typography with stylistic graffiti forms to meld a new configuration of abstract shapes. By taking individual letters and experimenting with layouts they find endless possibilities, and because they do not write specific words viewers are free to interpret the pieces in their own way. Amplifying their creative ventures, the duo are now interested in exploring public space through installations as they incorporate a mix of muralism, photography and customized objects, ushering in a more mature outlook on urban contemporary art.

In 2014, a highly ambitious project, Djerbahood, took place in and around the small village of Erriadh on Djerba island in the Gulf of Gabès. More than 150 murals by world-leading urban artists of over thirty nationalities came to life. Many Tunisian talents, both fine-art muralists and graffiti artists, were also recruited as Parisian gallery Galerie Itinerrance created an authentic open-air museum. The project is one of the biggest in global street art history and the

Opposite
**Faith XLVII. 'Hunt Her',
Djerbahood project,
Djerba, Tunisia, 2014**

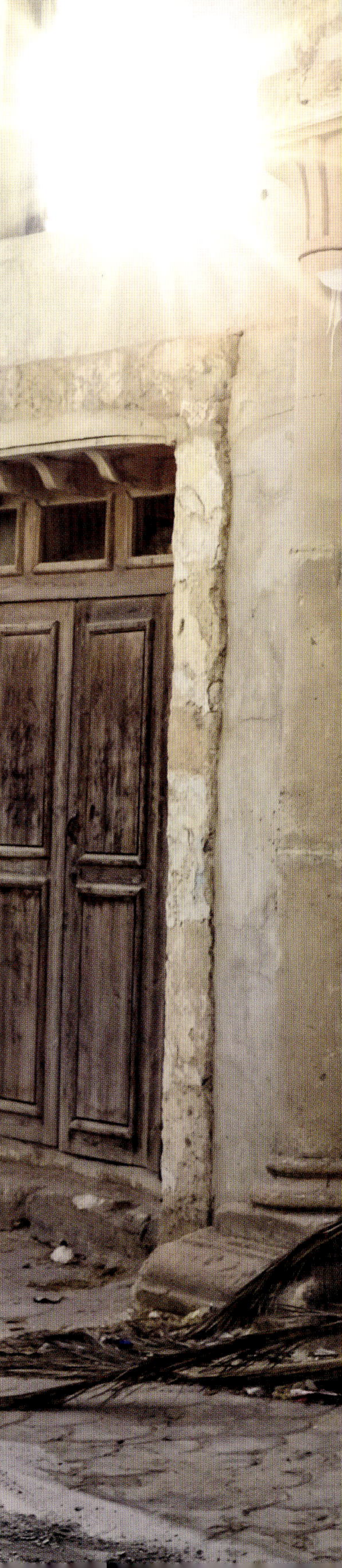

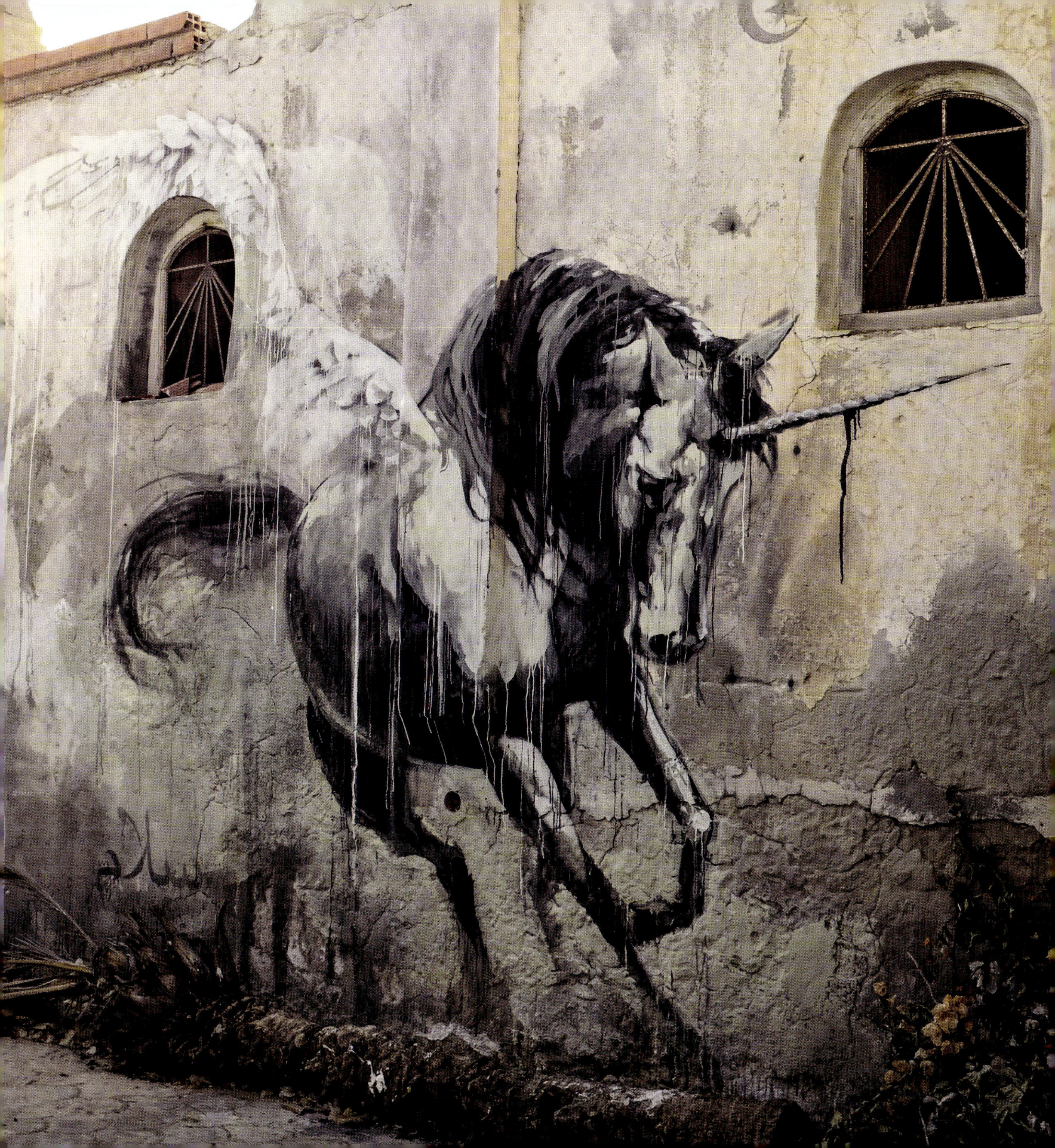

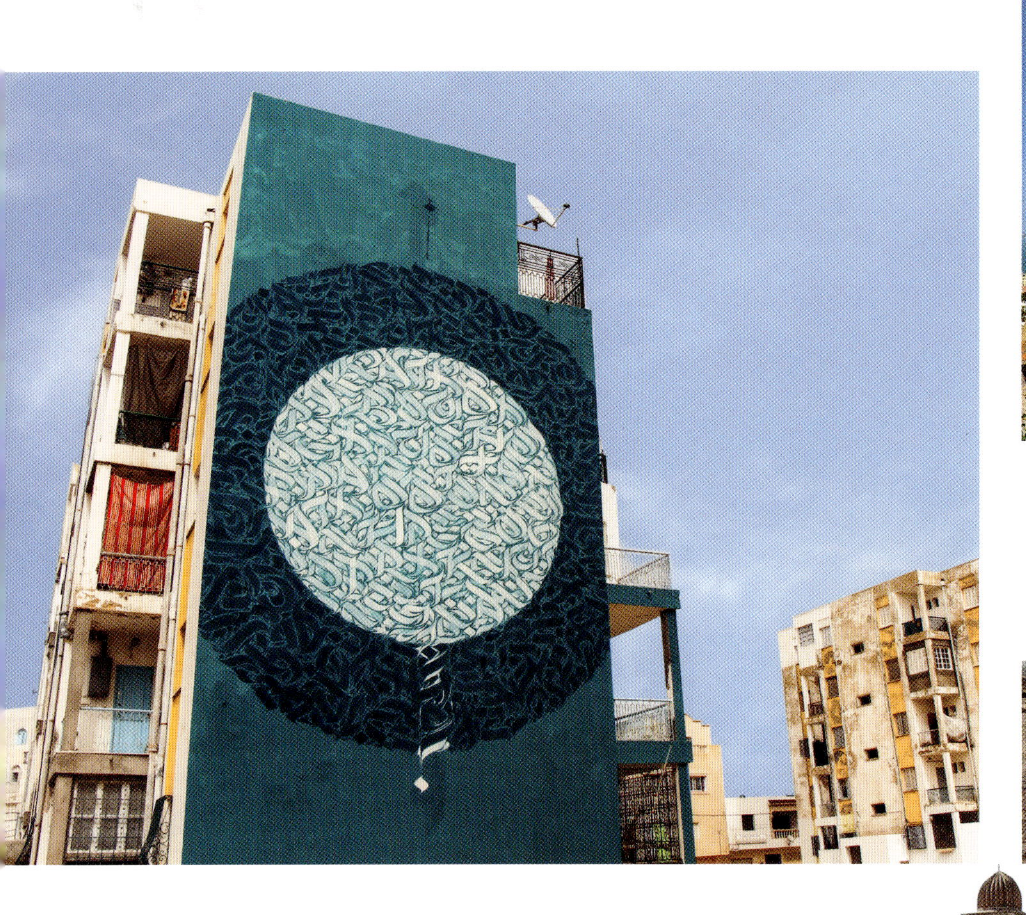
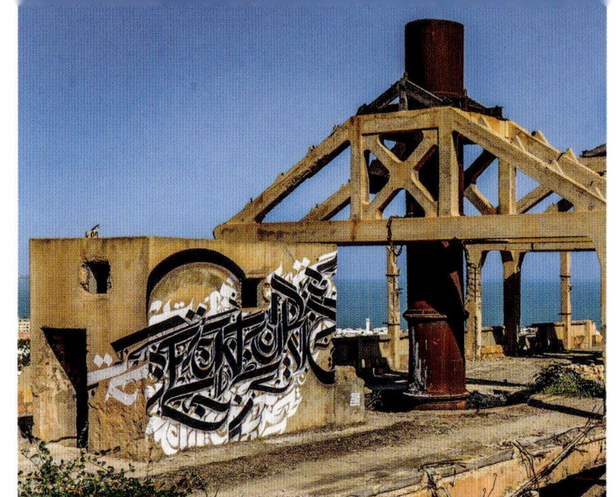
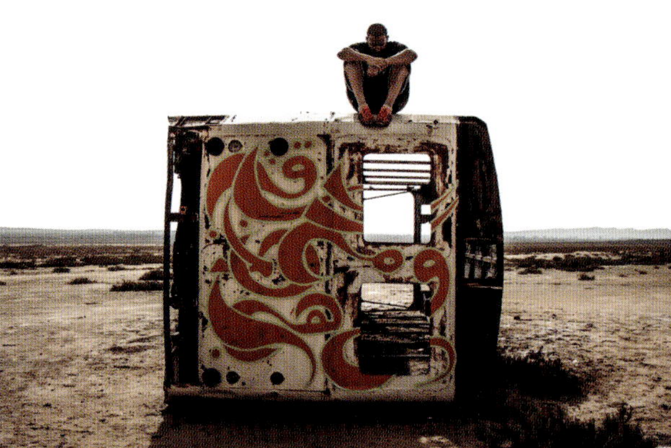

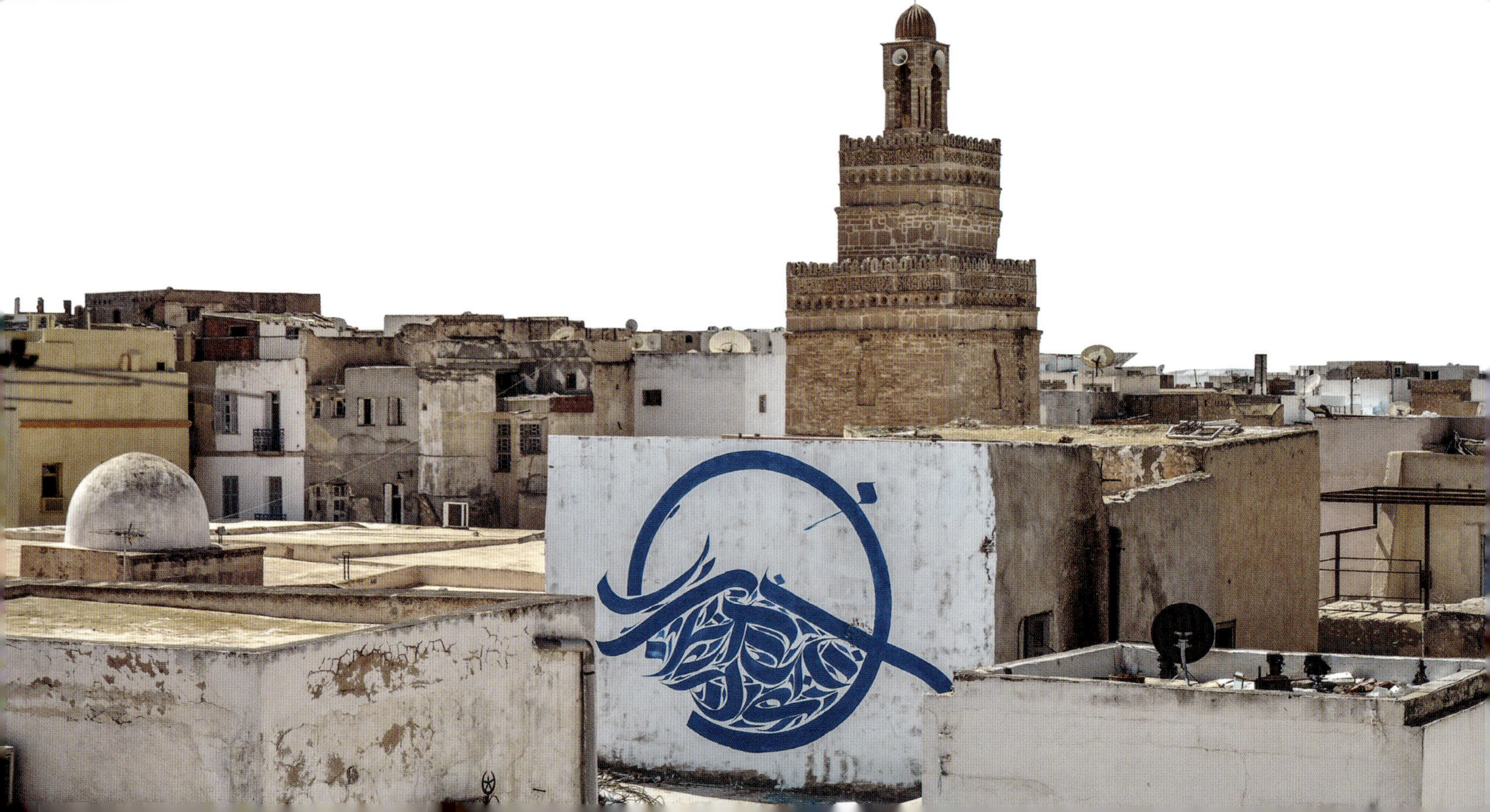

'There was something spiritual that drew me to Arabic calligraphy and its beauty; it has a soul, you can fall in love without even knowing the meaning.' INKMAN

village became a favourite tourist destination. Monastir'IN: Street'IN, in the coastal resort of Monastir, also acted as a platform for local street artists, notably calligraphy enthusiasts such as Inkman, Shoof and visiting artist Tarek Benaoum (France). With all this activity around, a younger generation was gearing up for its spin on the culture. Enter Brotherhood Art, a collective from Sousse that aims to enrich the walls of Tunisia. Brotherhood Art initiated their own style of calligraffiti and created a crew based on family bonds. They also focus on the Mediterranean colours of blue and white, their Tunisian identity and a reference to the town of Sidi Bou Saïd on the northern coast. Members include Alex Hassine Maalel, Boutheina Messous, Manga Hela, Ahmed Mejbri and Abdelhadi Bouzir (The Minister). Ex-members Pesko and Kero have taken a more typographic approach, often merging their styles in interesting collaborative designs.

By 2016 the Tunisian scene was proving itself a key player on the international circuit. Sk-one and Meen One had emigrated, while Inkman was participating in large-scale projects in such places as Dubai. The first dedicated spray paint store was also set up in Tunis to cater for local artists and nurture additional growth. Other artists, including Feddo, D-zy, Gat One, Tunizinho, Jihedy (aka Brella One), Koom and Mezone and female graffiti artists Mylow and Ouma/Oumema, immersed themselves in the culture and steered the movement forward.

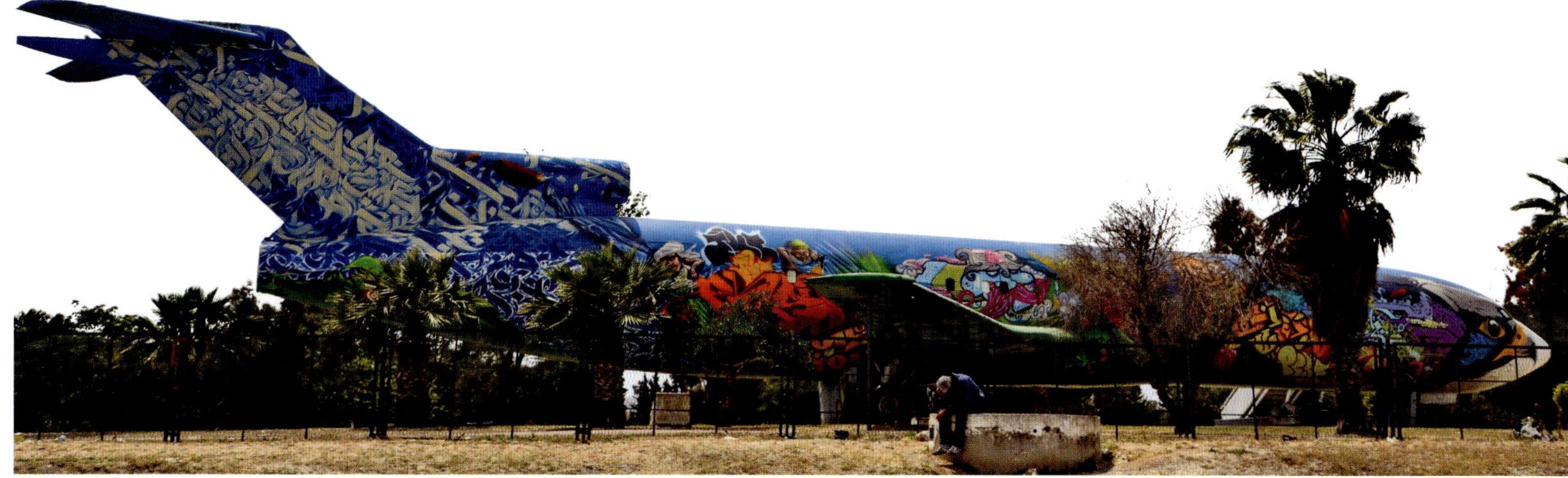

ST4 THE PROJECT

ARTIST PROFILE

Tell me about your introduction to graffiti and how you decided to collaborate.
We consider ourselves post-revolution street artists as we were influenced by the creative atmosphere after the Tunisian revolution. Graffiti was a means of self-expression. We met in 2013 after each of us had been working individually for a while. There was no street art scene in Sfax, Tunisia, so we thought we should work together.

What was the importance of the revolution, especially with regard to art and expression?
After the revolution there was more freedom to paint outdoors and people were supportive because they wanted to see change.

Tell me about your style and how it evolved.
We began by doing tags with old-school graffiti lettering but soon started looking for other ways to express our identity. At the same time street art was becoming more developed around the globe and we were influenced by the way people create their own culture. We started fusing Arabic letters and typography with graffiti style because it was very important for us to create a new shape of the letters.

Tell me about the graffiti scene in Tunisia.
Tunisia has a special atmosphere because of its untouched landscapes and scenery, that is why we want to paint here. We first started painting at night but realized we want to interact with the people. It's illegal to paint in the street but when you ask for permission people are usually very accepting. We have made paintings in a variety of sizes, mediums and locations, each having a different atmosphere. The scene in Tunisia is growing and a lot of good things are happening now.

The words you write: are they significant in any way? Is it words or poetry?
We don't write words or phrases of any kind. We take individual letters and use them as a tool to experiment and create an abstraction. We are not trying to send a message through language but rather to express through it.

How do people on the street react to your artwork when they see it?
It varies a lot. Many people enjoy it and are interested in it, but there are also people who do not care about it or reject it. We really enjoy it when people come to talk to us and appreciate our work. Of course we cannot know exactly what everyone thinks because after the piece is completed we leave and the work stays.

Does the environment play a role in what you choose to paint?
Of course. For example, when painting in the old town or in a deserted place, the colours and the compositions change depending on where we work. We always respect the place we work in.

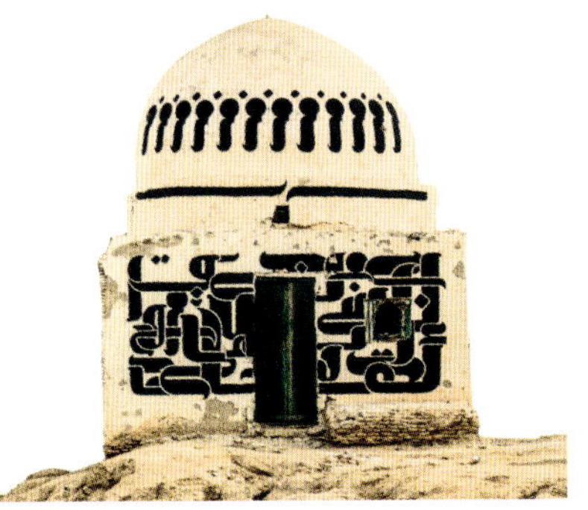

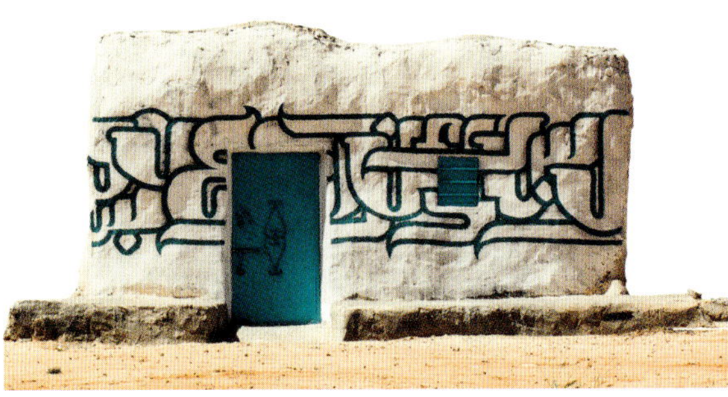

Far left
**ST4 the project.
Naftah, Tunisia, 2018**

Left
**ST4 the project.
Tataouine, Tunisia, 2018**

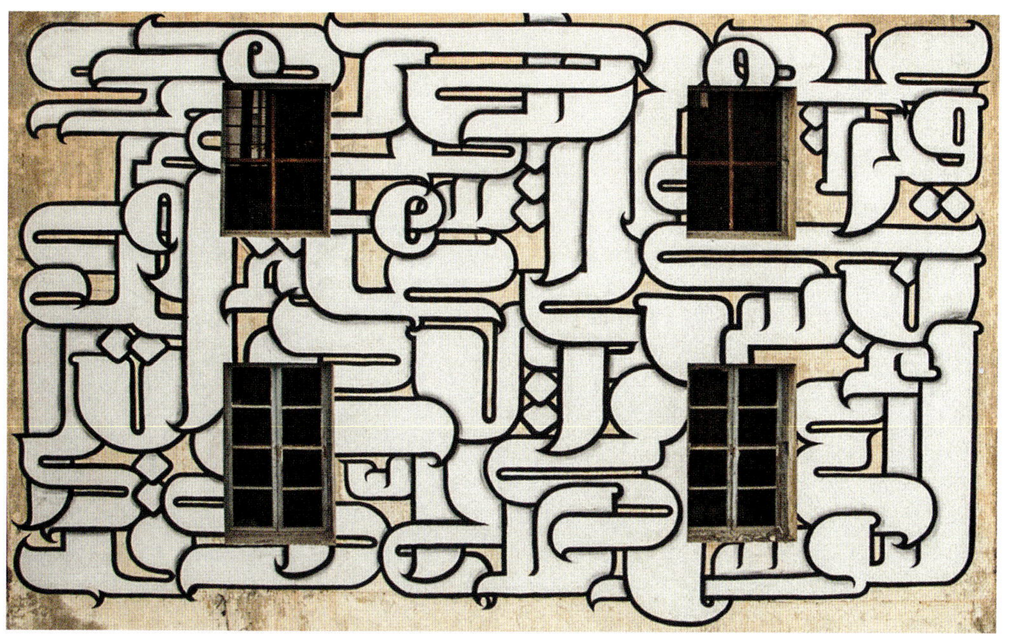
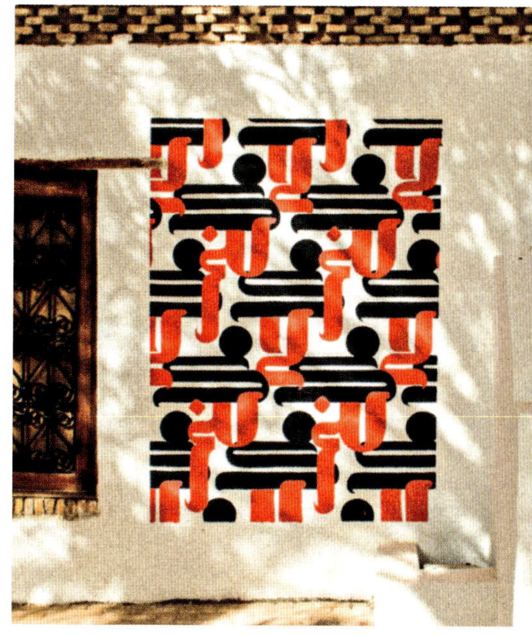

How has graffiti affected your life?

Graffiti has changed our lifestyle and the way we look at the streets and people around us. There is a big reason as to why we started painting graffiti in the first place: we wanted to have more chances in life, to see different places, cultures and people. We feel like we are fulfilling our existence and using more of our potential.

Do you have any particular meaning behind your work?

There are many meanings to our work and we feel that behind every experience is a new interpretation. We like sharing the process with people and giving them the space to make their own interpretations based on their experiences.

Do you feel that graffiti in Africa is unique?

Africa is special and the world is now looking at us. We think the new generation of African street artists is going to do great things in the global art scene.

ST4 the project is a Tunisian duo that formed in 2013, consisting of Yassin Bouzid and Sadk Kaffel. Fusing their existing graffiti styles, which had an Arabic twist, the artists crafted a unique, graphic street style for their murals. Often set in rural locations, the works hold a broad meaning as they are wordless and open to interpretation.

Top left
ST4 the project. Sousse, Tunisia, 2018

Top right
ST4 the project. Naftah, Tunisia, 2018

Below
ST4 the project. Tunis, Tunisia, 2018

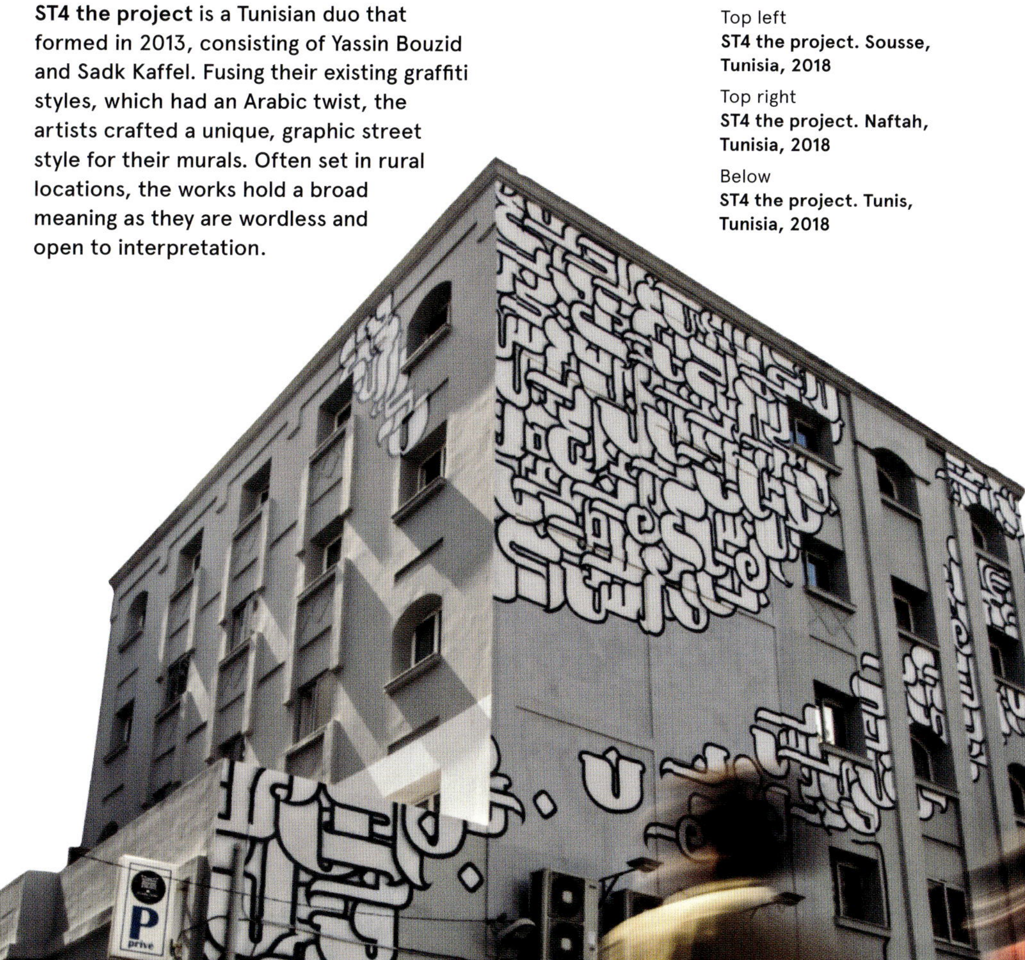

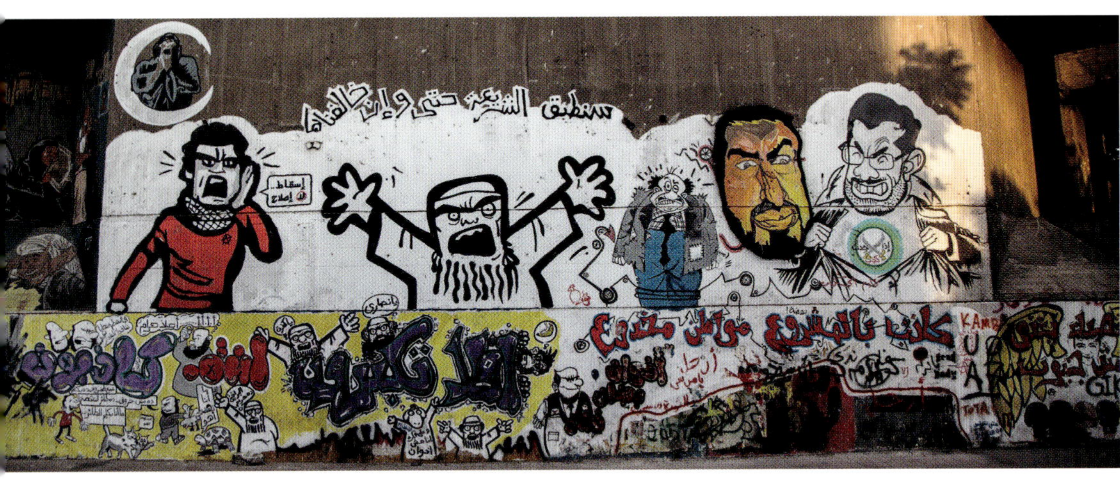
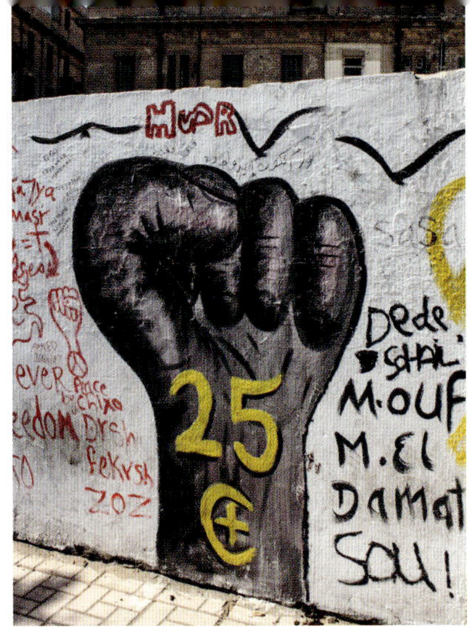
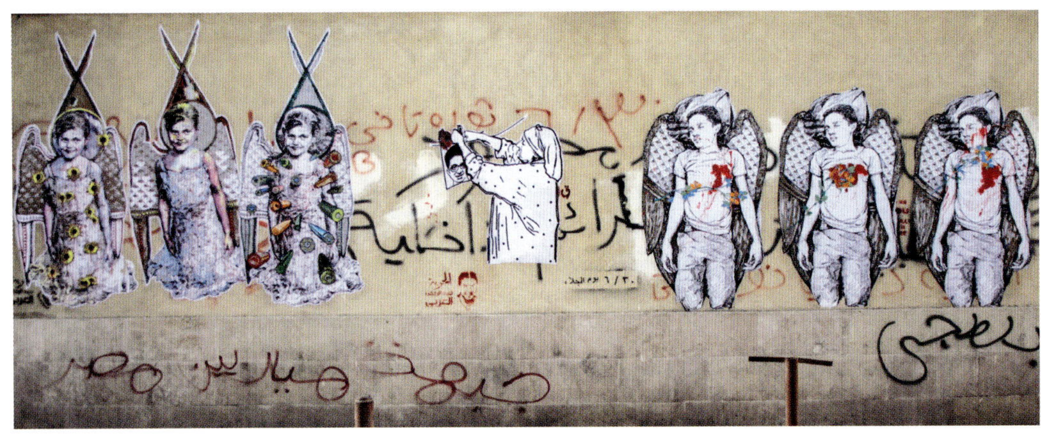

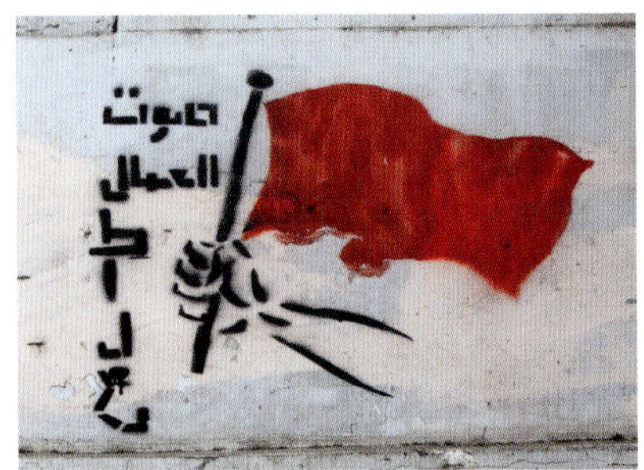
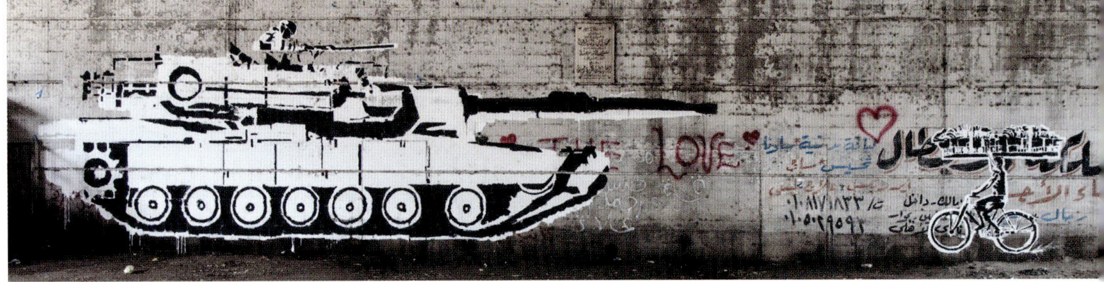
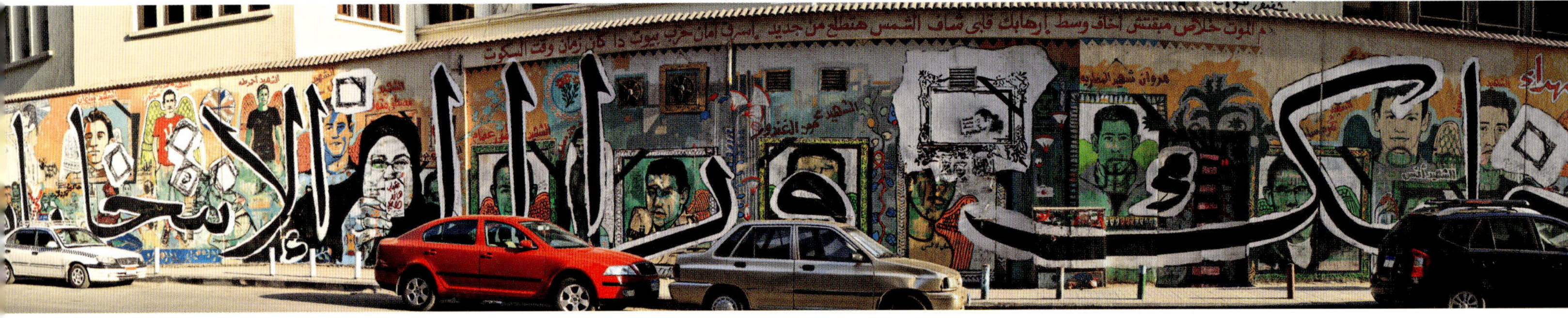

REBELS AND REVOLUTIONARIES

ART ON THE GROUND

Graffiti is often rebellious in nature, a way to air a grievance publicly or even spark a revolt of sorts. This was the case during the Arab Spring, the period of mass protests and uprisings against governments that spread across the Middle East and North Africa region in the early 2010s. Commencing in Tunisia in December 2010, demonstrators used graffiti to spread messages of protest against the oppressive regime. The outburst spread to Egypt with the revolution of 2011 beginning on 25 January. Protesters occupied Tahrir Square in downtown Cairo for eighteen days, where many anti-government inscriptions were added to the walls of nearby streets. Stencil and wheatpaste artists began to flood the country with artworks, often taking inspiration from international street art heroes such as Banksy (UK) and Shepard Fairey (USA), to create an artistic onslaught in aid of the rebellion. Many of these artists were picking up the spray can for the first time, creating martyr murals and fulfilling their desire to get involved in some way or another. Other revolutionaries in Egypt attempted to impact their homeland through initiatives such as El Zeft and Nazeer's #ColoringThruCorruption campaign and the Hekayet Gedar project by Takatol El Fenoon (United Artists) in the Imbaba slum, or, in the case of NeMo, with solo paintings that consistently advocated for the less fortunate. Street artists in Libya joined the ranks of the revolutionaries in February 2011, while more recently Algeria and Sudan have seen similar works on their streets in 2019.

Opposite, left to right, top to bottom
Aboud. Cairo, Egypt, 2013

Unknown artist. Cairo, Egypt, 2011

Ammar Abo Bakr, El Zeft. Cairo, Egypt, 2013

El Teneen. 'Checkmate', Cairo, Egypt, 2011

Unknown artist. Cairo, Egypt, 2011

Ganzeer. 'Tank vs Biker', Cairo, Egypt, 2011

Ammar Abo Bakr, with Alaa Awad, Hanaa el Degham and others. The 'Martyrs Mural' on Mohammed Mahmoud Street went through various stages, culminating in Abo Bakr's large pieces of black and white script, Cairo, Egypt, 2012

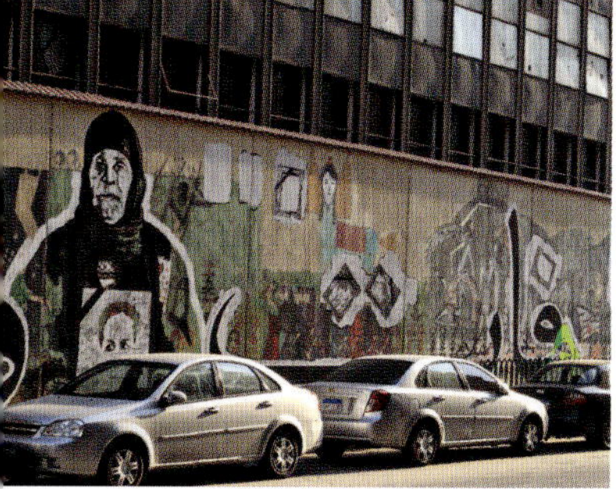

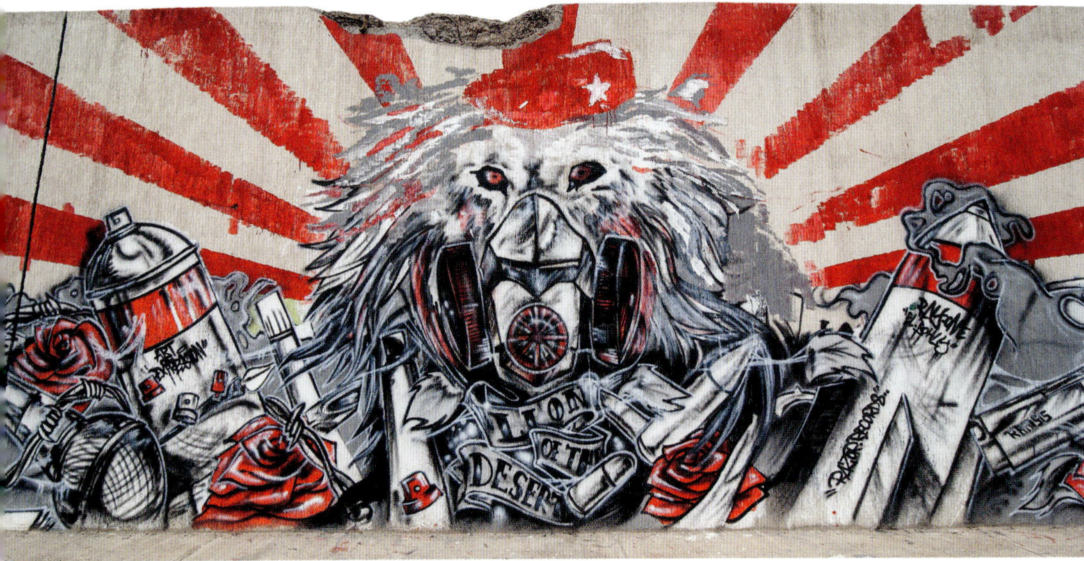

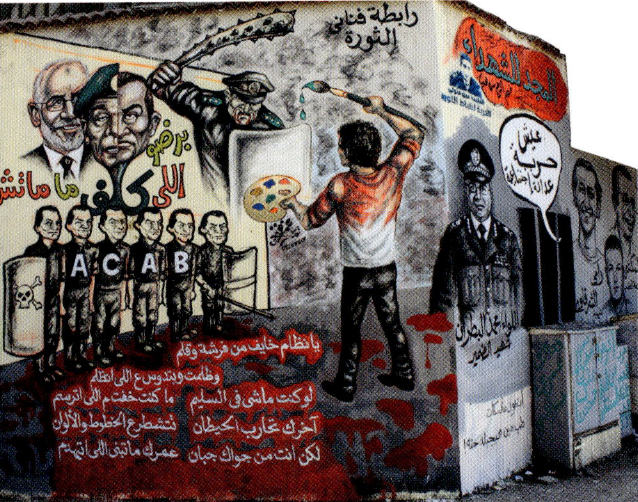

Above
Meen One. Tripoli, Libya, 2013

Left
Omar Fathy. Cairo, Egypt, 2012

Below
Alaa Awad. 'The Battle Mural', Cairo, Egypt, 2012

Opposite
Aboud. 'Governor and Freedom', Cairo, Egypt, 2013

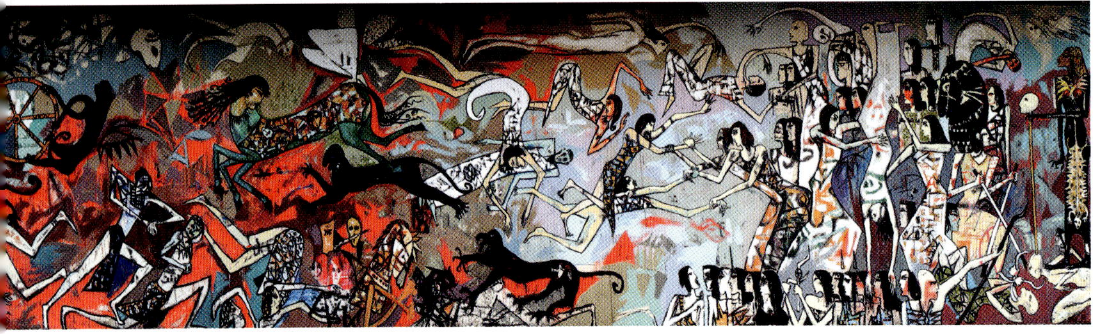

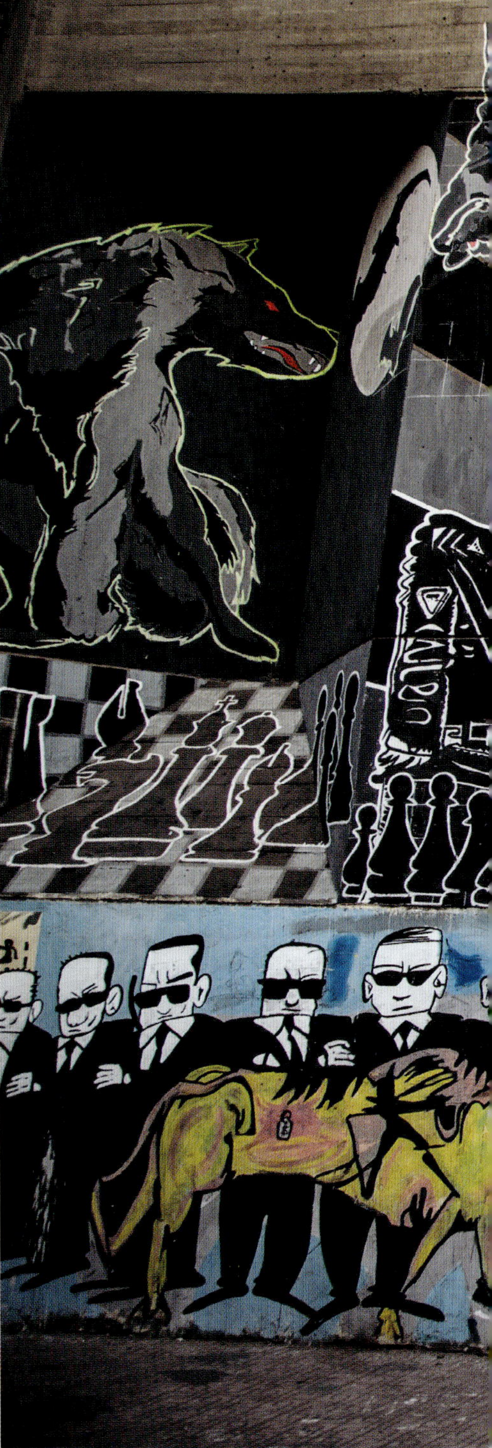

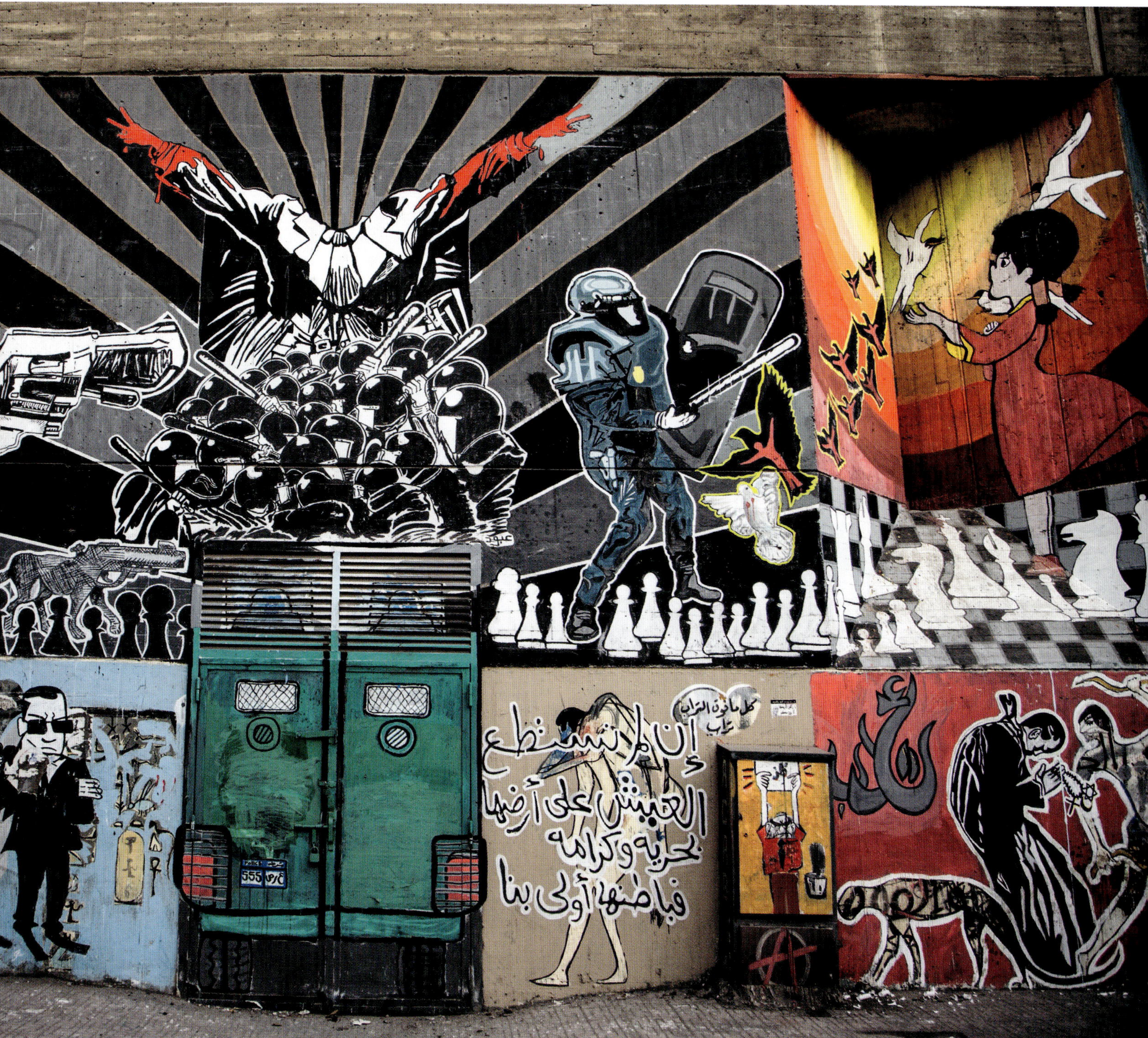
أن لم تستطع
العيش على أرضها
بحرية وكرامة
فباطنها أولى بنا

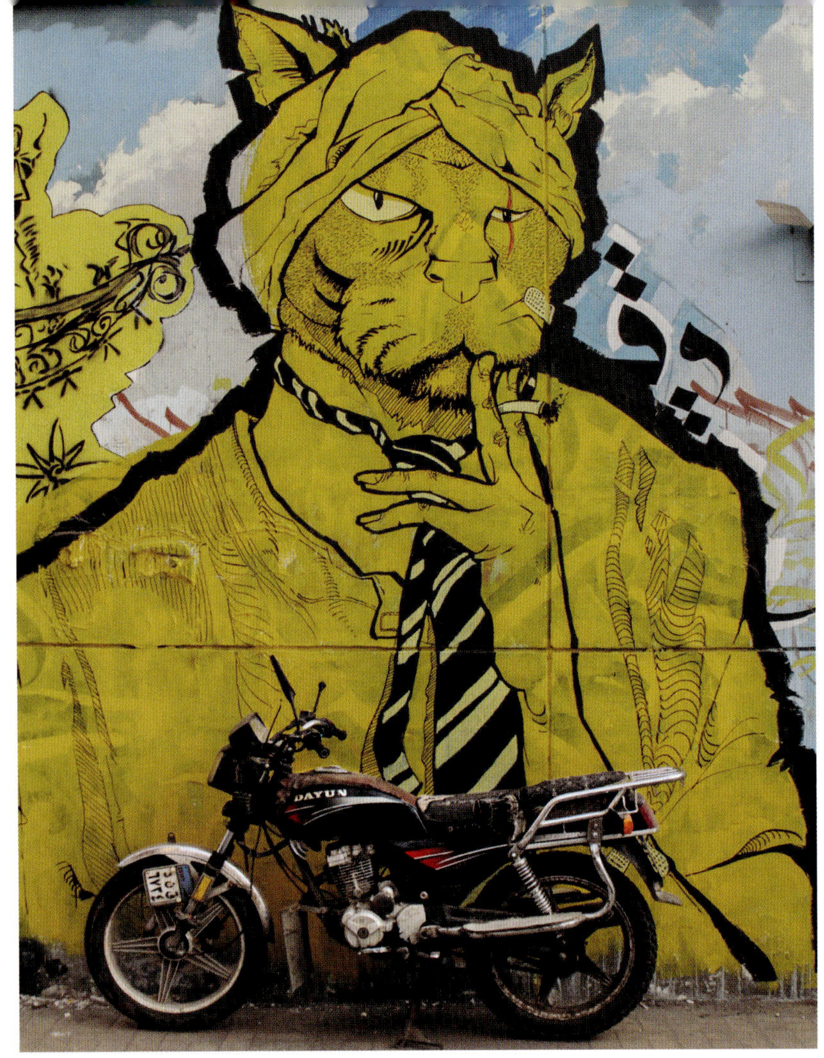
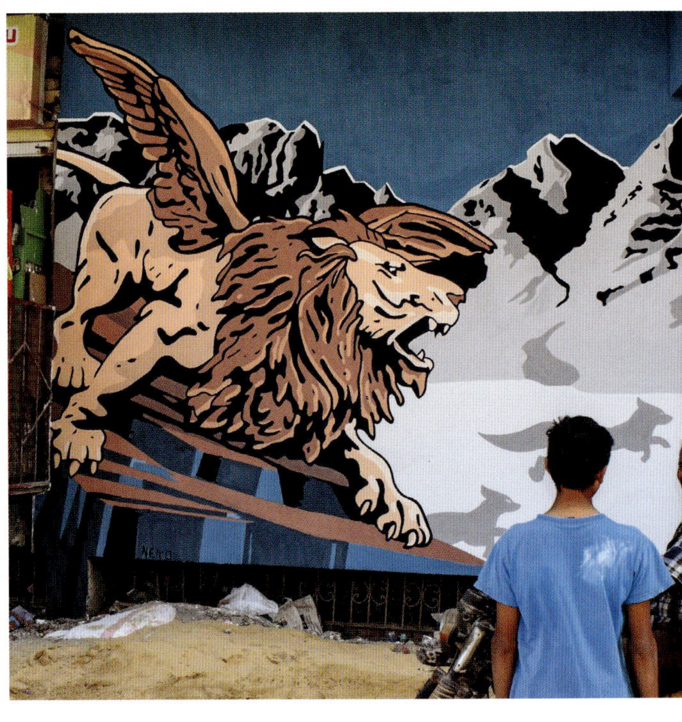
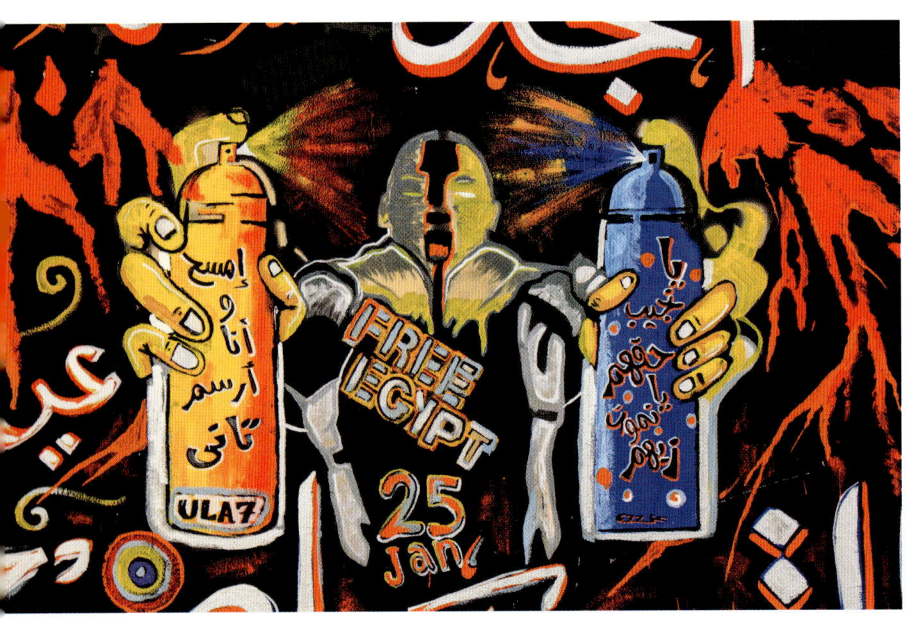
امسح وأنا أرسم تانى
ULA7
FREE EGYPT
25 Jan
يا حبيب يا حقوق يا نموت زهور
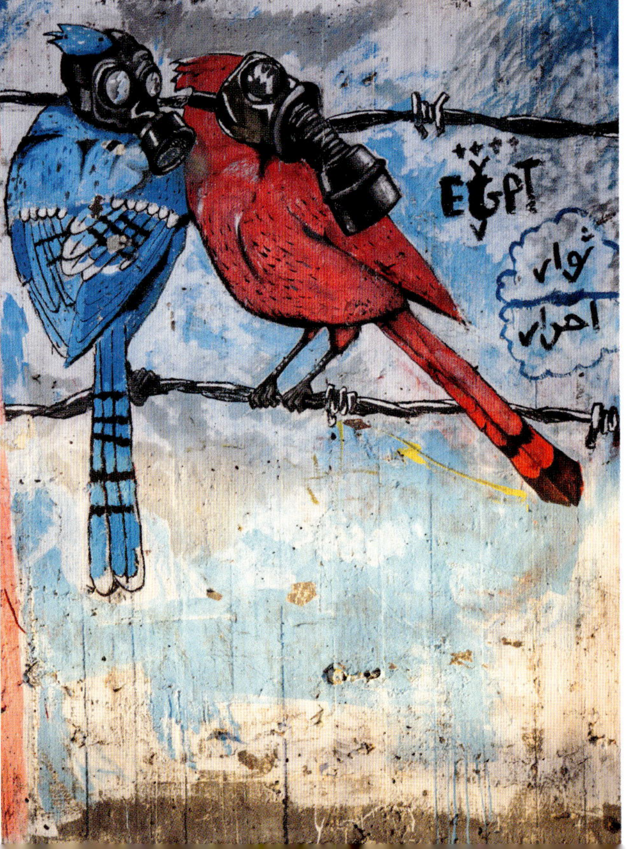
EGPT
ثوار
احرار

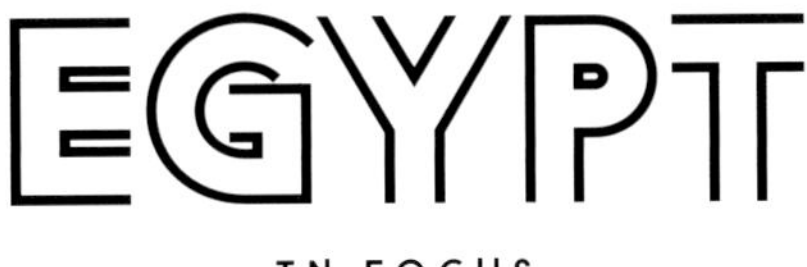

EGYPT

IN FOCUS

Street artworks made waves across the world during the Egyptian revolution of 2011. Following the events of Tunisia's so-called Jasmine Revolution, demonstrators, students and inspired artists rampaged through the streets of Cairo during the January 25 uprising to make their voices heard. The people were tired of the autocratic regime and wanted President Mubarak to step down. The walls leading to Tahrir Square where everyone would gather became prime targets for graffiti tags, stencils, murals and paste-ups. More layers of unsanctioned urban artworks and heart-wrenching thematic productions were to be carried out over the next few years as the reins of power shifted.

Around 2010, most of the visible graffiti in Egypt was the work of Ultras soccer fans, although a small urban art scene was beginning to take shape. Despite the Ministry of Culture monitoring forms of public expression, artists such as Aya Tarek were producing work in the streets of Alexandria, while a few other graffiti paintings were visible on trains in Cairo, but street art was relatively uncommon. When protests broke out, graffiti became a weapon and many first-time graffiti artists became key figures in the establishment of a true street art movement.

Ganzeer quickly rose to fame as the face of Egypt's graffiti artists by creating thought-provoking works, such as his 'Tank vs Biker' piece and his series of martyr murals. He asked people at the rallies to fill in his survey forms, assembled other artists for his Mad Graffiti events and dispensed his own alternative propaganda in the form of graphic posters. He was fully immersed in the cause and wanted to do his bit to drive it in the right direction. With his name translating as 'bicycle chain', Ganzeer believes that artists are vessels to forge new ideas and propel society forward. He was gunning for social justice and used art to promote activism. Social media was another major driving force of the revolt; demonstrators could mobilize through live updates and visual artists could spread their work across the globe. Ganzeer distributed his stencils, stickers

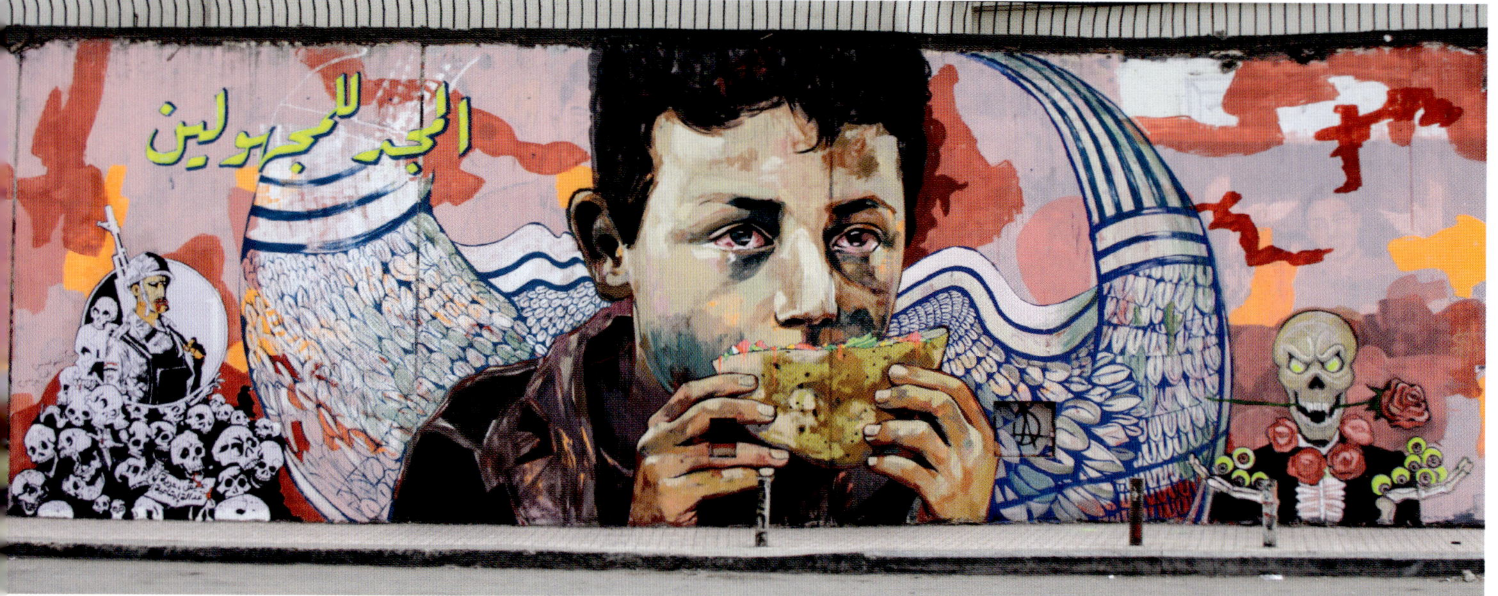

and posters online for people to freely use and his Mad Graffiti events caused a surge of graffiti action. Mad Graffiti Weekend took place in Cairo in May 2011 and over the forty-eight hours artists intensified their efforts to confront the growing number of military tribunals. Ganzeer managed to pull off some large works with a team of volunteers and fellow artists. Mad Graffiti Week followed in January 2012 as a country-wide initiative (even gaining traction in other countries worldwide).

Throughout the Egyptian crisis, from 2011 to 2014, many other artists came out to work in the streets. El Teneen, Keizer, Sad Panda, El Zeft and Zook were some of the most active stencil and wheatpaste artists, their work spilling across Cairo. Mural artists also stepped forward and began to express themselves downtown on the walls of Mohammed Mahmoud Street, especially around the American University in Cairo (AUC). Ammar Abo Bakr, Winged Elephant, Alaa Awad, Omar Fathy (aka Picasso) and others used their brushes to create momentous pieces of public art. They worked alone or together, dividing walls into sections or collaborating on one diverse mural. During and after the revolution they incorporated current events, political dissent and themes of Egyptian heritage. They painted on all occasions – while the streets were empty or when protesters marched into Tahrir Square, during the day or under the cloak of darkness, and for weeks on end. Their dedication was unrivalled and their work became a symbol of the revolt. Artists such as Aboud, The Mozza, Hanaa el Degham, Mohamed Elmoshir, HeMa AllaGa, the Mona Lisa Brigades and the art students of the university also rendered expressive murals and street art in the vicinity.

Ammar Abo Bakr played a vital role in Egypt's graffiti movement during the revolution and is one of the country's greatest street artists today. His elaborate murals would often feature martyrs, including Khaled Said (killed in police

Above
Ganzeer, Ammar Abo Bakr, Salma Samy, featuring a portrait of Khaled Said, a young man whose brutal death ignited pre-revolutionary protests. Cairo, Egypt, 2013

Opposite, top
NeMo. Gedary project, Damietta, Egypt, 2017

Opposite, bottom
NeMo. Mansoura, Egypt, 2014

Following spread
Ammar Abo Bakr. Portrait of Bassem Mohsen, Cairo, Egypt, 2013

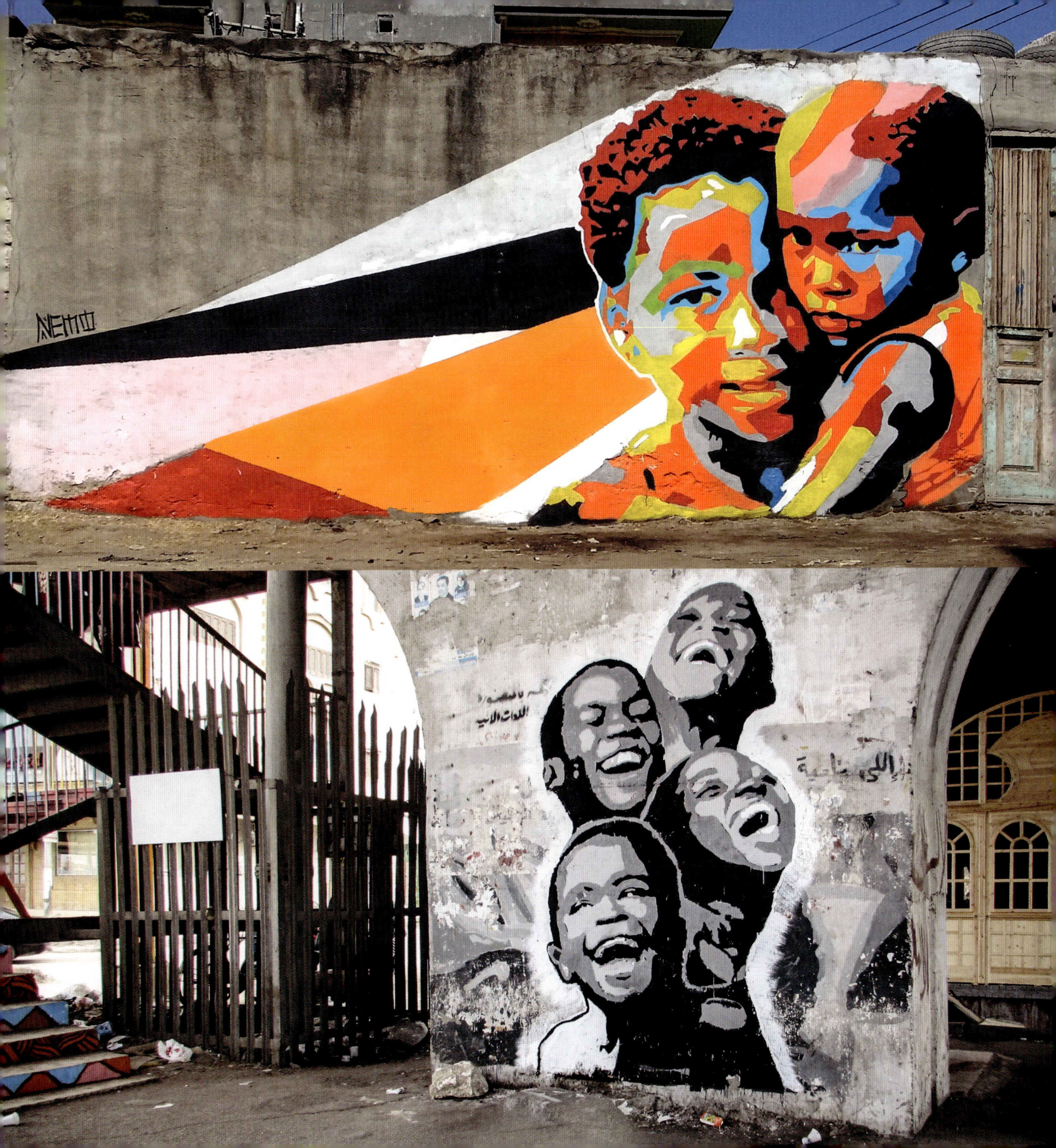

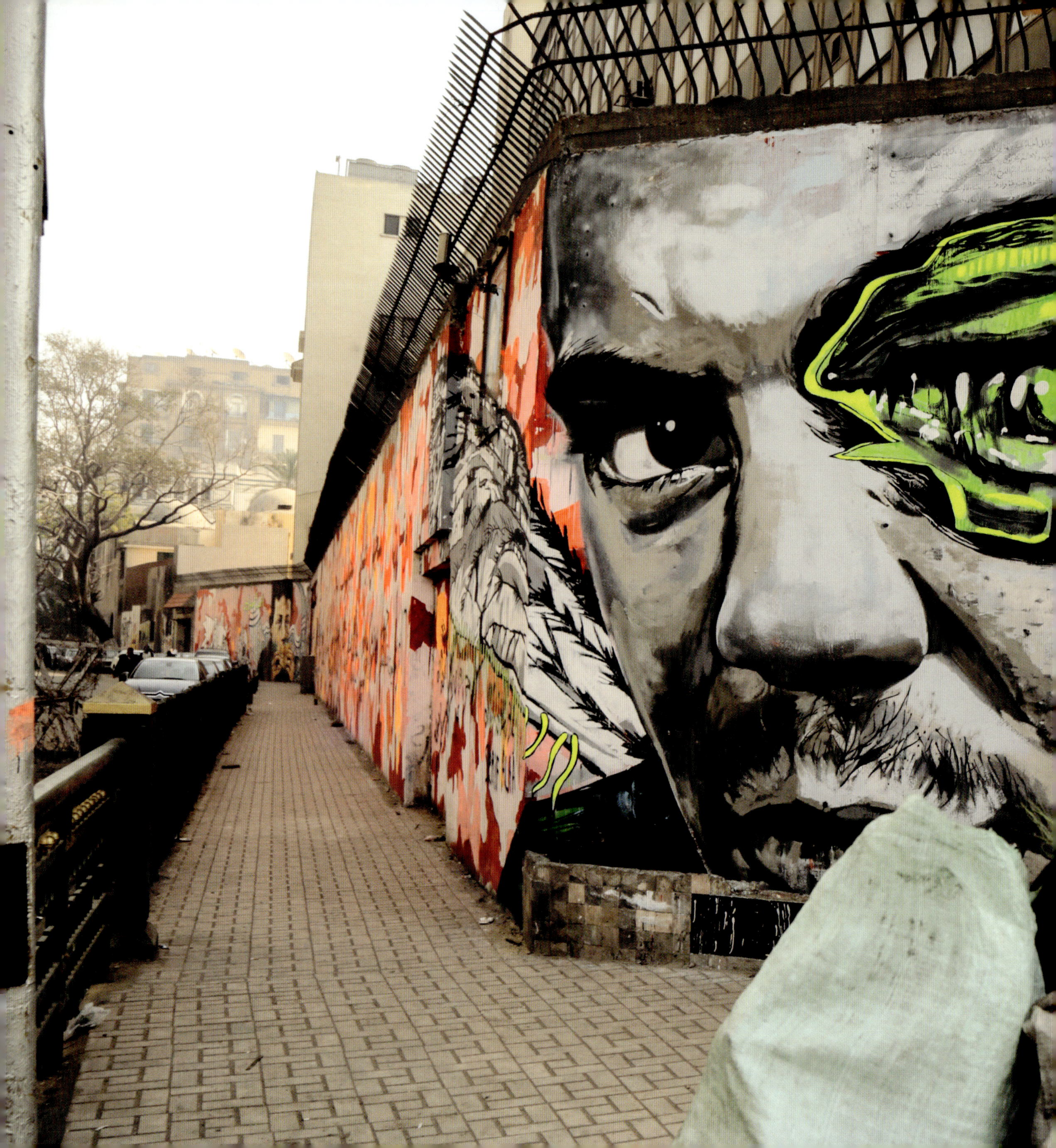

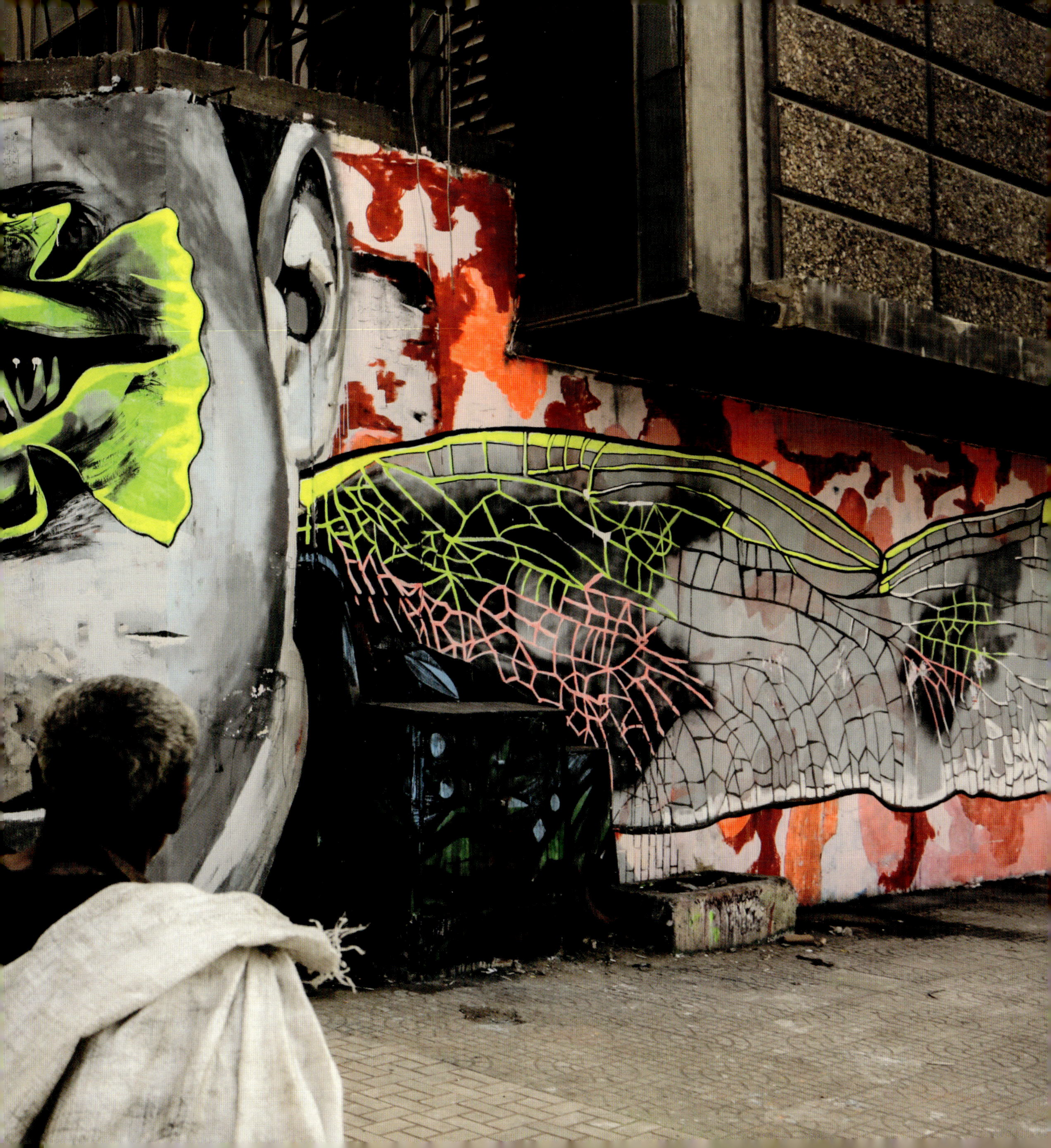

'The ancient Egyptians translated social events and politics into art. Their way of illustration and philosophy inspires my desire to create stories and secrets in my work. There are many things in this life that will not exist if thought about in a realistic way – some things can only be communicated through symbolism.' ALAA AWAD

custody) and the victims of the Port Said football massacre. He wanted to be a conduit to expose the truth and defend Egypt. Working in layers, Abo Bakr paints with feeling and allows the painting to decide where it wants to go. He has an interest in art and wall-writing traditions of the past, especially with Egypt's history of the practice, as well as in folkloric motifs and Sufi, Coptic and Islamic cultures. Ammar Abo Bakr was also involved in the No Walls project by Revolution Artists Association with other artists including El Zeft, Hanaa el Degham and Alaa Awad – who is a frequent collaborator. Through this initiative, the group sought to disguise the concrete blockades installed along the roads leading to Tahrir Square with *trompe l'oeil*-style paintings, allowing the walls to merge into the environment by creating an optical illusion of what could be beyond them.

Despite the risk of being arrested or shot, Abo Bakr continued to paint walls in downtown Cairo and around Mohammed Mahmoud Street over the years, even though the city council often removed the artworks. While his work is often controversial, it is immensely powerful and has accorded him many opportunities to travel to Europe and talk about his experiences, and to paint large-scale murals on the sides of buildings. Recently he has painted some of the biggest murals in Egypt, including a massive wall in Damietta in a glitch-art style, and a mammoth 900-square-metre (9,700-square-foot) hand-painted advertisement in Cairo in 2019 to promote rooftop gardening.

Another classically trained artist, Alaa Awad, joined Abo Bakr to paint walls during the Egyptian crisis. Alaa Awad is passionate about keeping the Egyptian

Alaa Awad. 'Memorial for Maat', Luxor, Egypt, 2016

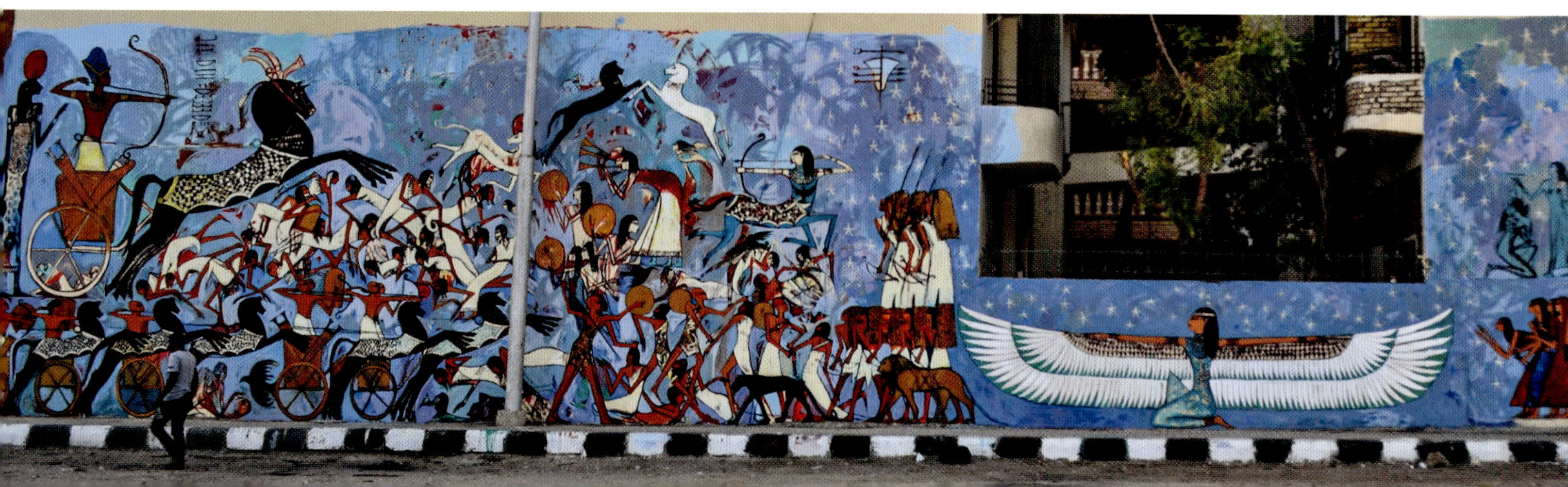

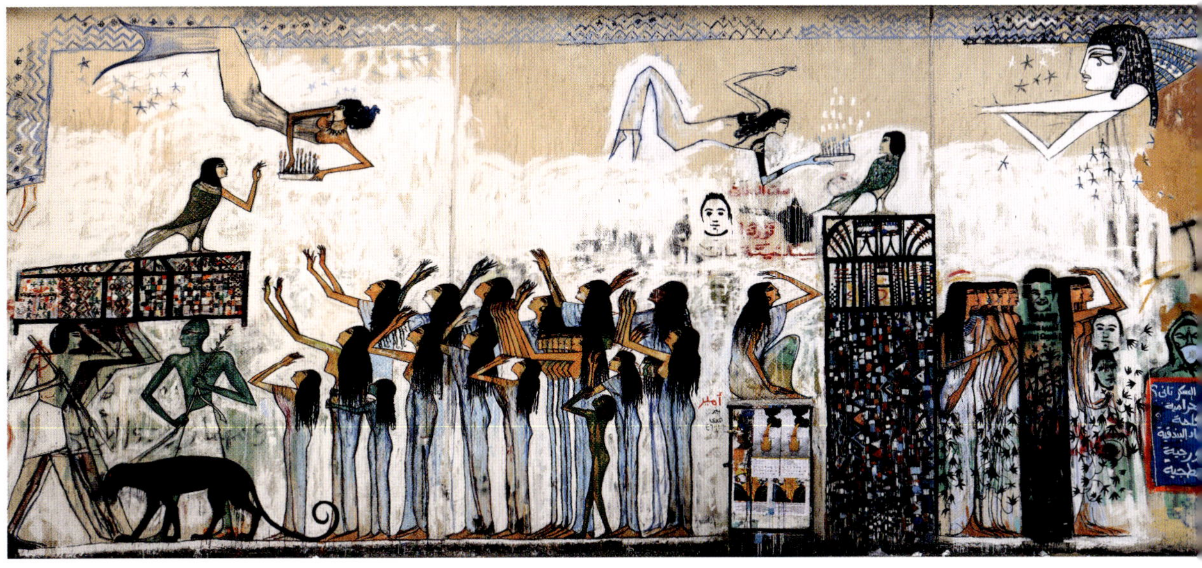

Alaa Awad. 'The Mourners', Cairo, Egypt, 2012

identity alive and paints in a neo-pharaonic style. He bases his murals on historical paintings but presents the work in a contemporary context. The new symbolism spoke to the events of the revolution and highlighted the female revolutionaries, corrupt leaders and chaotic battle scenes. Awad wanted to connect Egyptians with their heritage through public art as well as pay tribute to those who participated in the uprising. On the streets, in a war zone, the heterogeneous artworks were refreshing and striking, regardless of people's political or religious affiliations.

Most of the work from the revolution has long been erased; however, a growing love for arts and culture and for classic hip-hop graffiti has inspired the next generation in both Cairo and Alexandria (now with international spray paint distributors on shore). Graffiti artists such as Fada, Shazly, Sober, Toxic and Nofal O-one have drawn inspiration from occidental street art scenes and are painting funky, hip-hop characters and writing their names in stylized fonts, entirely non-reminiscent of the generation before them. Nofal O-one stands out because he incorporates Egyptian symbolism and has represented Egypt at JIDAR – Toiles de Rue festival in Morocco, along with Ammar Abo Bakr.

Ahmed Gaber (aka NeMo) from Mansoura has been active since 2008 and raises awareness of social issues such as poverty, illiteracy and sexual harassment. With murals and wheatpastes, his work often includes inspiring quotes in Arabic. In 2016 he initiated the Gedary project in Damietta, bringing various artists from other cities to the village to create uplifting works and showcase graffiti as a valuable art form. Elna2ash and Amr Diwan attended the 2017 edition, and are also responsible for several commercial decor projects today. From sheets of papyrus to the graffiti spray can, Egyptian art has come full circle and continues to defy those in power.

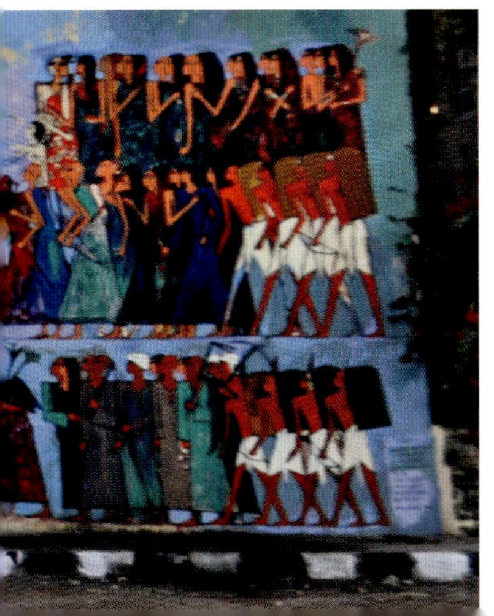

NOFAL O-ONE

Tell me about your introduction to graffiti.
I started practising art in 2009, influenced by hip-hop culture. I found that graffiti represented me best and began to integrate stories of ancient Egyptian civilization. As I dug deeper into urban art I painted larger and manifested a contemporary outlook for the streets of today. I incorporated my culture and the civilization of my ancestors but formulated a modern version through my imagination. This helped me become a painter and designer with a purpose: to deliver a message. I am expressing my love for hip-hop culture through colours on walls.

Tell me about the Egyptian themes in your work.
Ancient Egypt is rich with stories based on life and death and the gods. Mostly engraved on stone, old stories described the way of life and this inspired me to translate them into modern street art. I believe the ancient Egyptians are one of the oldest civilizations who recognized the idea of real public art. I have also been influenced by the culture, customs, traditions and events in upper Egyptian villages, an extension of ancient Egyptians, who draw on the walls of their homes to tell their life stories. These expressions showcase their connection to their cultural heritage, just like me. I was born and grew up in these neighbourhoods and am proud to follow a similar approach, representing our stories on the walls for all to see.

Are there many street artists in Egypt?
There are not many street artists in Egypt, although the situation on the street is uncomplicated. Art on the street is still new and only really appeared after the revolution in 2011. The walls of the revolution highlighted the times, strongly influencing society with free expression, telling vigorous stories of violence that were offensive to the government. This was the first appearance of modern street art and led to the development of laws around the idea of expression on walls.

Tell me about your graffiti name.
My last name is special and I decided to make it my graffiti name. It is simple, distinctive and different. I began to write on walls in a lot of different forms, but was most excited when drawing characters. I soon started replacing letters with figurative objects, for example the letter 'O' had a face because it is circular, and the letter 'F' represented the movement of the hand and fingers. With this approach the letters had personality and there was a story, although it still features my name at the same time.

What is it like to paint in Egypt?
Painting on the walls in Egypt is not difficult unless it has a political aspect or is on private property. It is an emerging modern art form that people wish to spread far. Public art changed the perception of the street, from boring to colourful and full of beautiful stories. But, I must discuss my intentions beforehand because a wall cannot be

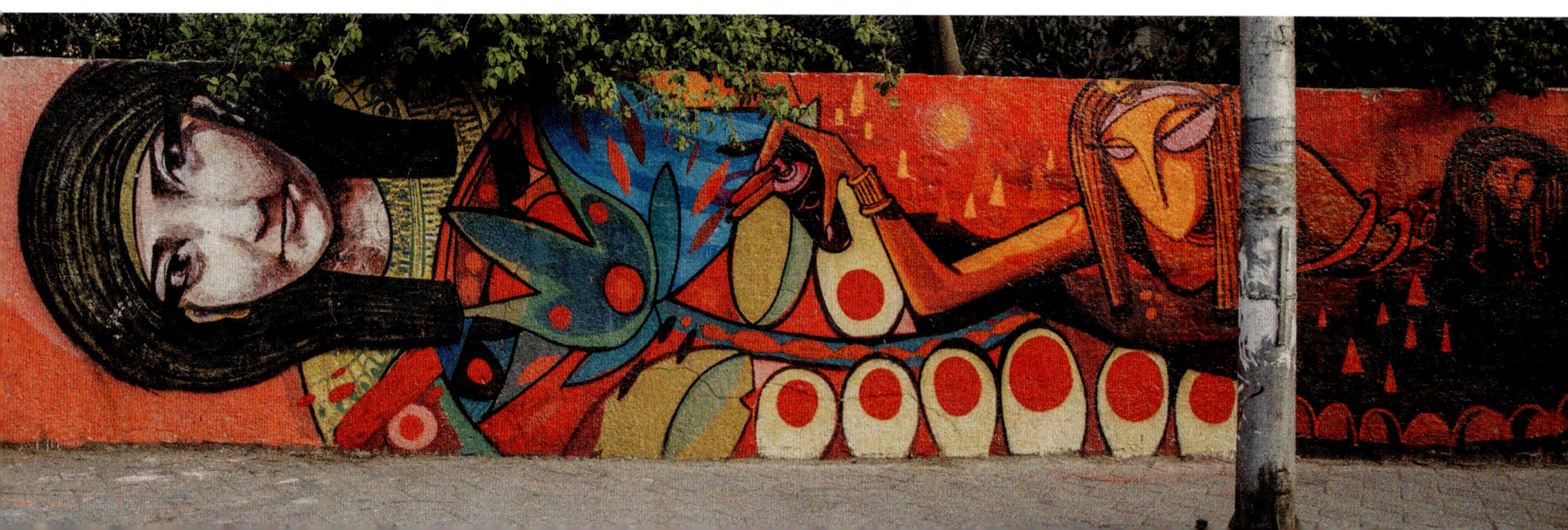

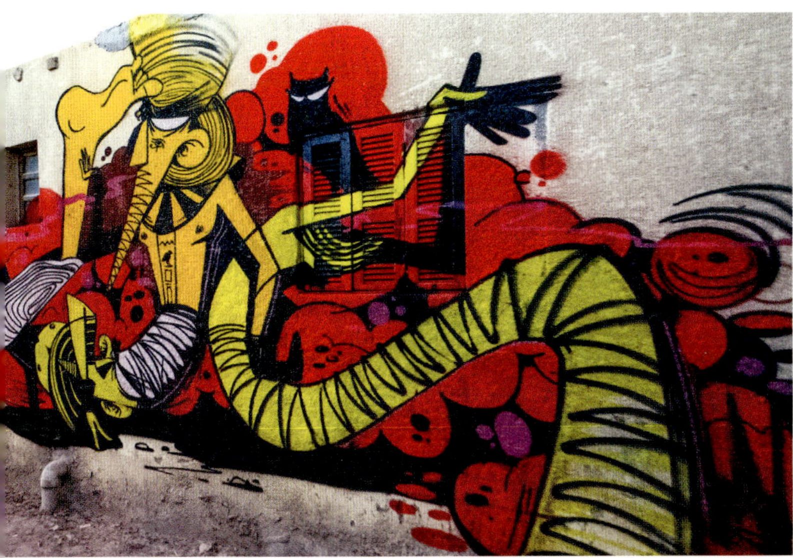

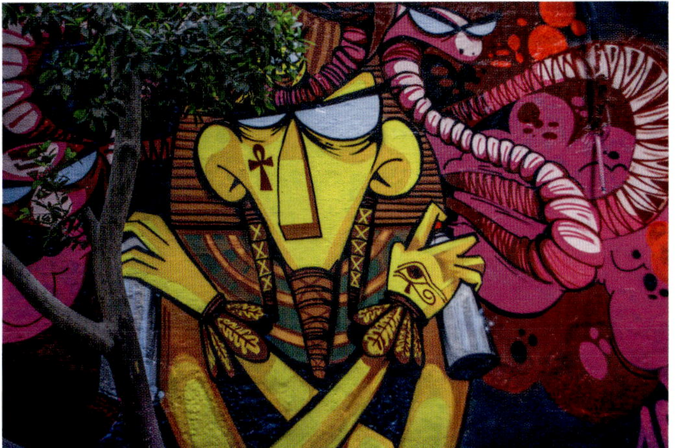

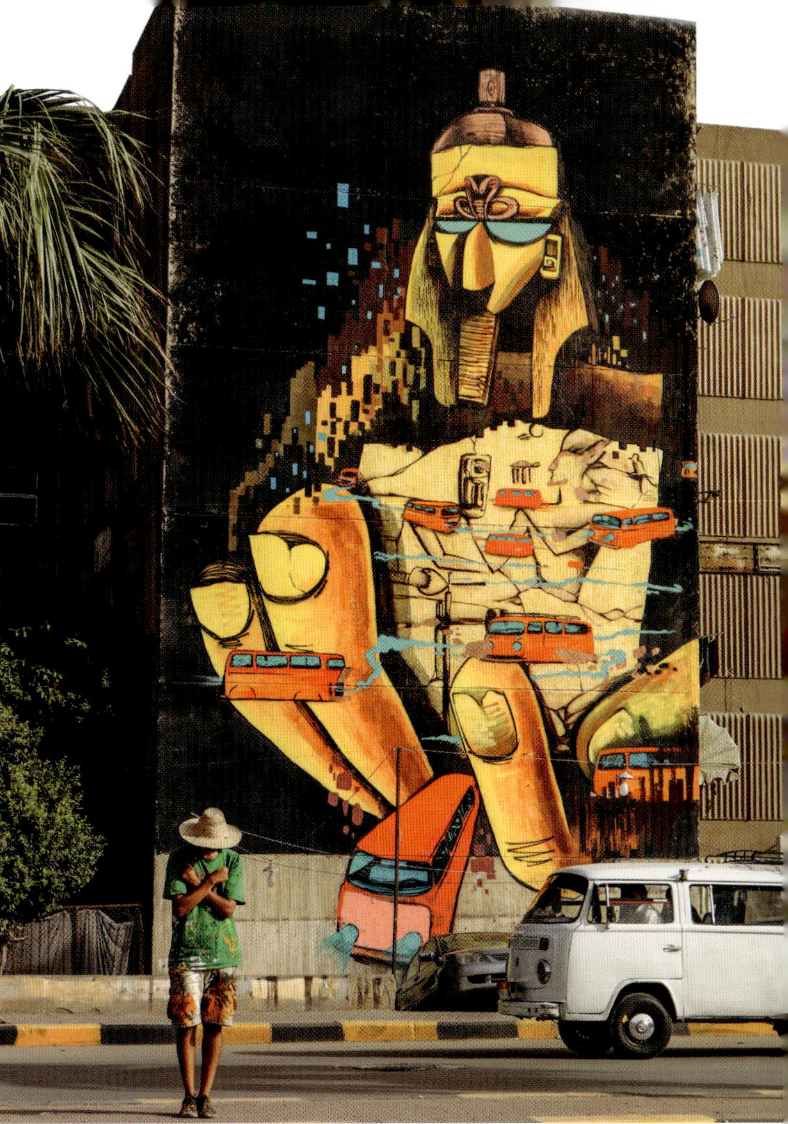

painted without the owner's knowledge or consent. One must remain polite and take the time to uplift.

Why do you love to paint street art?
I love street art because it is free for people of all classes to see and experience. All walks of life exist in the street and artists do not have to wait for exhibitions to display their artworks. Artists can utilize the walls immediately instead of being imprisoned inside a gallery.

Nofal O-one, based in Cairo, took inspiration from his heritage when he began to write on walls. First experimenting with graffiti letters, he later developed a modern take influenced by global graffiti culture and his own imagination, formulating a modern rendition of ancient Egyptian art.

Opposite
**Nofal O-one. 'Miminhottoub',
Cairo, Egypt, 2019**

Above, top left
**Nofal O-one. 'The Ancient
Dance', Faiyum, Egypt, 2015**

Above, bottom left
**Nofal O-one. 'King Tut the
Little Pharaoh', Cairo,
Egypt, 2018**

Above right
**Nofal O-one. 'Ramses',
Cairo, Egypt, 2018**

BEAUTY OF THE SCRIPT

STYLES & TECHNIQUES

Artists in Northern Africa have incorporated Arabic script into their works. It is believed that writing developed independently in many different parts of the world, but the earliest forms stem from Mesopotamia (the Middle East) and ancient Egypt. Signs and symbols were used to create pictures to communicate, especially by means of trade. More characters were invented as time progressed and needs arose, leading to the phonetic, syllabic and alphabetic writing systems. Scribes studied and practised the craft for years and were respected for it, often keeping the tradition in the bloodline. Cursive hieroglyphs, and later hieratic and demotic scripts, were implemented in the writing of religious texts in ancient Egypt and later led to Arabic script being used for the holy Qur'an.

There are many different styles and dialects of Arabic script, but all are written from right to left. Today many artists, designers and graffiti writers apply

Below, from left to right
Brotherhood Art: Alex Hassine Maalel, Fadi Zayeti, Abdelhadi Bouzir (The Minister). Sidi Bouzid, Tunisia, 2017

Kero. 'Rules Are Made To Be Broken', Sidi Bouzid, Tunisia, 2019

Sneak Hotep. 'Sadalmelik', Algiers, Algeria, 2018

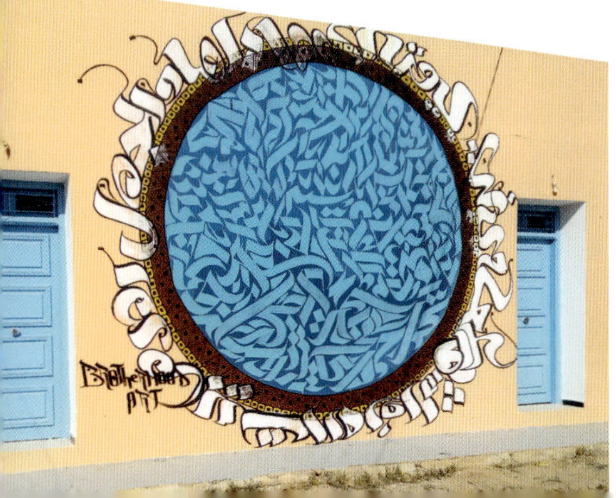

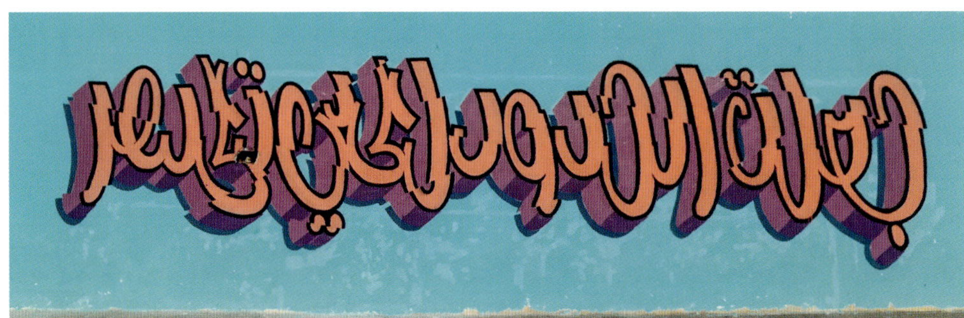

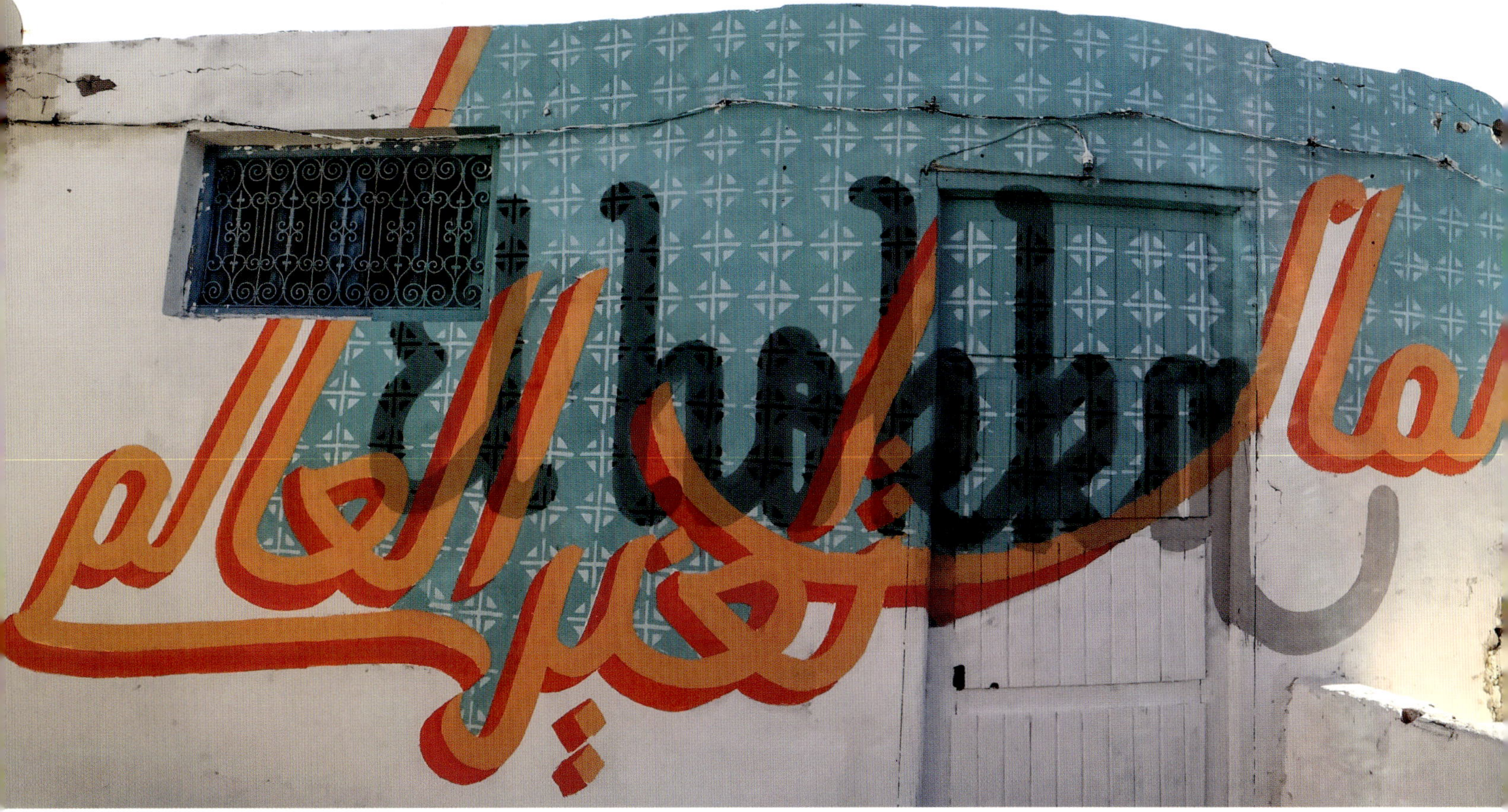

the techniques of Arabic calligraphy in their artworks, mixing traditional and modern styles with more abstract and conceptual compositions. Using brushes, concentric circles and traditional graffiti elements, they majestically flaunt their love for their own language. Sneak Hotep fuses geometry to form a more indecipherable code, while fellow Algerian artist Lmnt constructs his name with the Latin alphabet. Tunisians Pesko and Kero combine their styles for a more graphic effect, and Karim Jabbari and Brotherhood Art are more linear, using a classical script style with their own personal touch – often referred to as calligraffiti, a term coined by Dutch graffiti pioneer Niels 'Shoe' Meulman to highlight the urban use of the format (especially when writing one's name).

eL Seed's 'Perception' is a grand example of calligraffiti, and one of the most significant street art projects of all time. Over multiple weeks, the Franco-Tunisian artist painted an anamorphic mural, visible from one specific spot, which stretches across more than fifty buildings. The powerful nature of this piece opened new dialogues and brought the story of Cairo's Zaraeeb neighbourhood to the world. The area, home to most of the city's rubbish collectors, was often viewed locally as dirty and inferior, but it is equally home to an efficient recycling system, proving how people should not judge things upfront as beauty exists when the background story is revealed.

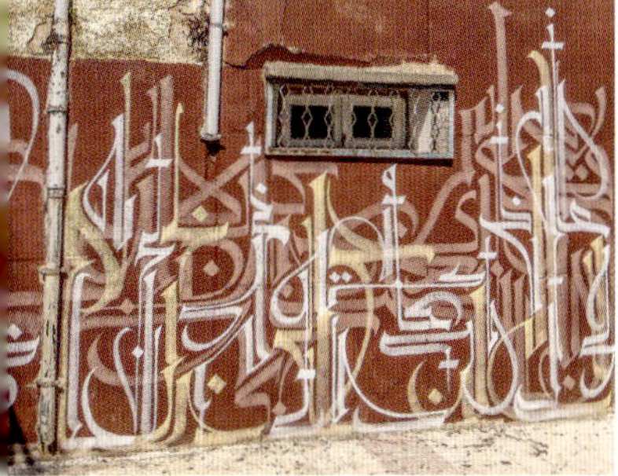

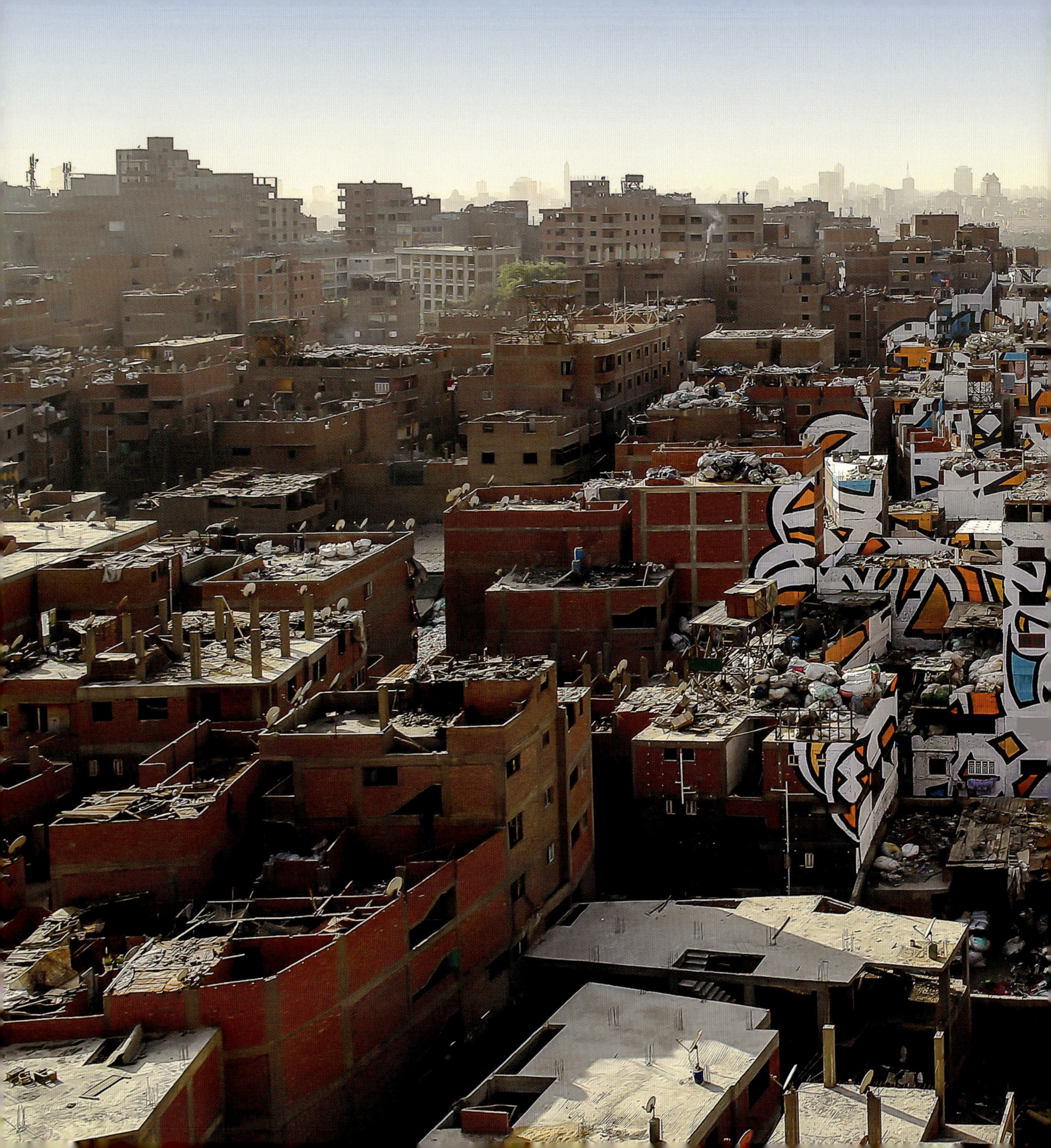

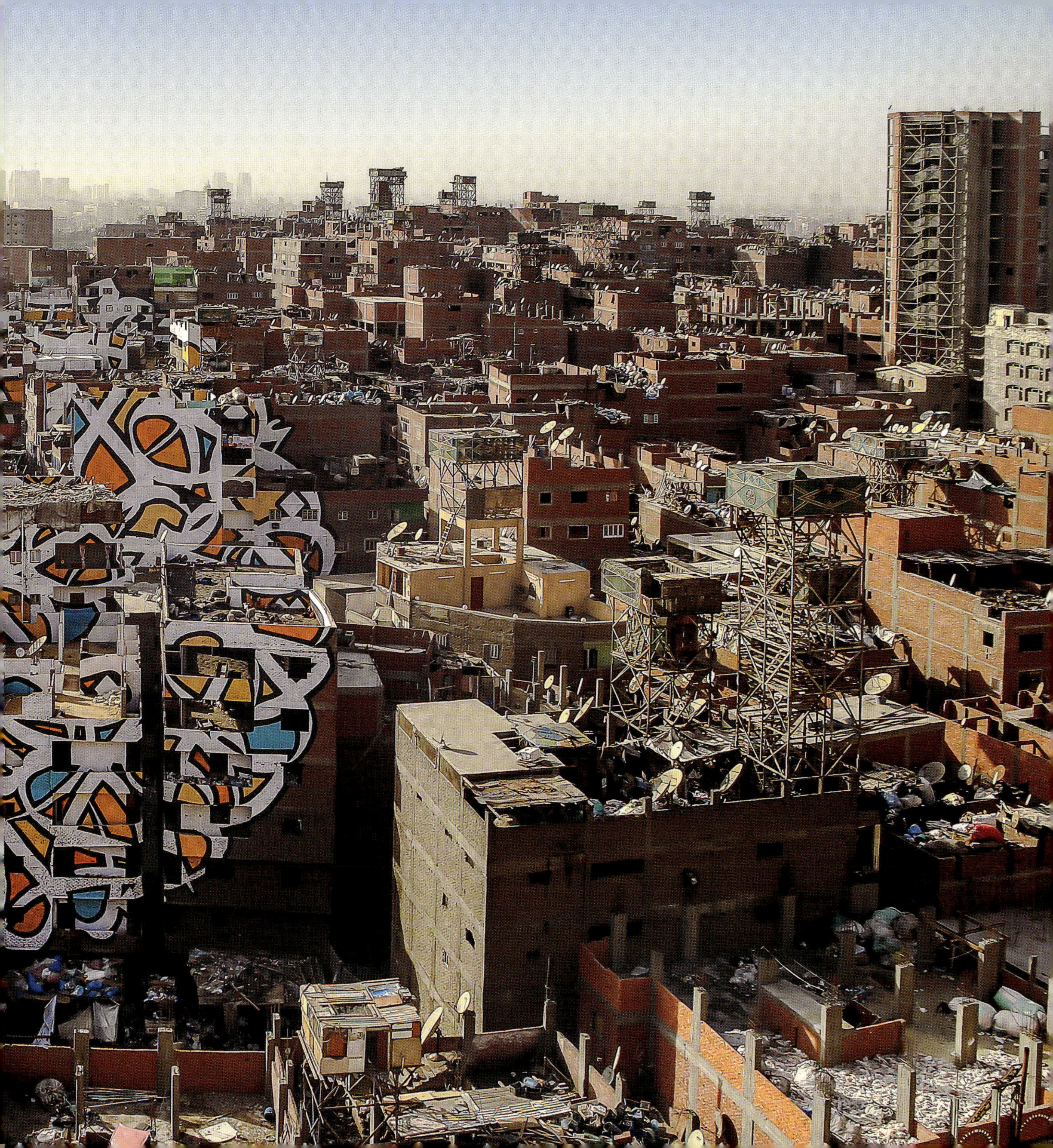

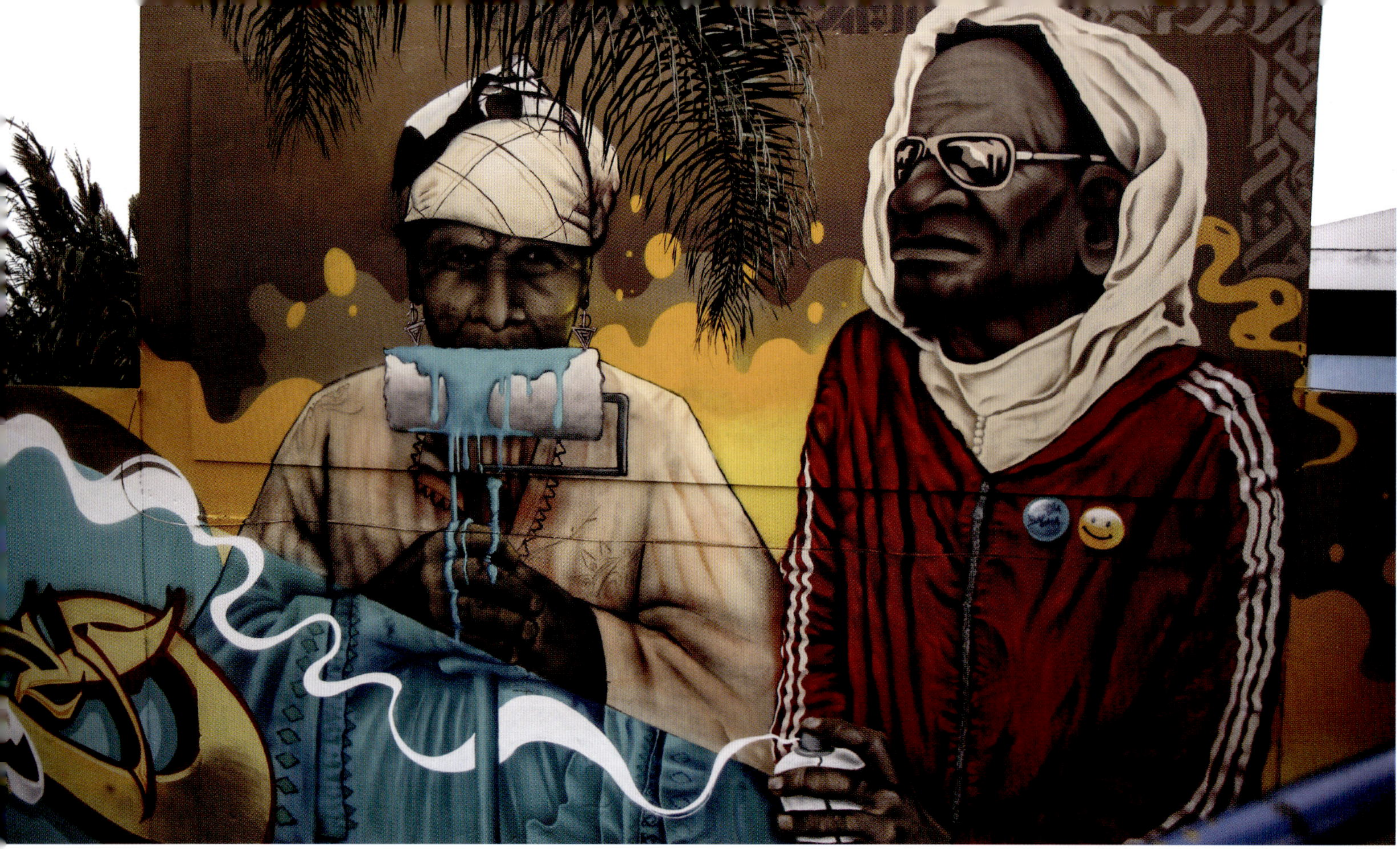

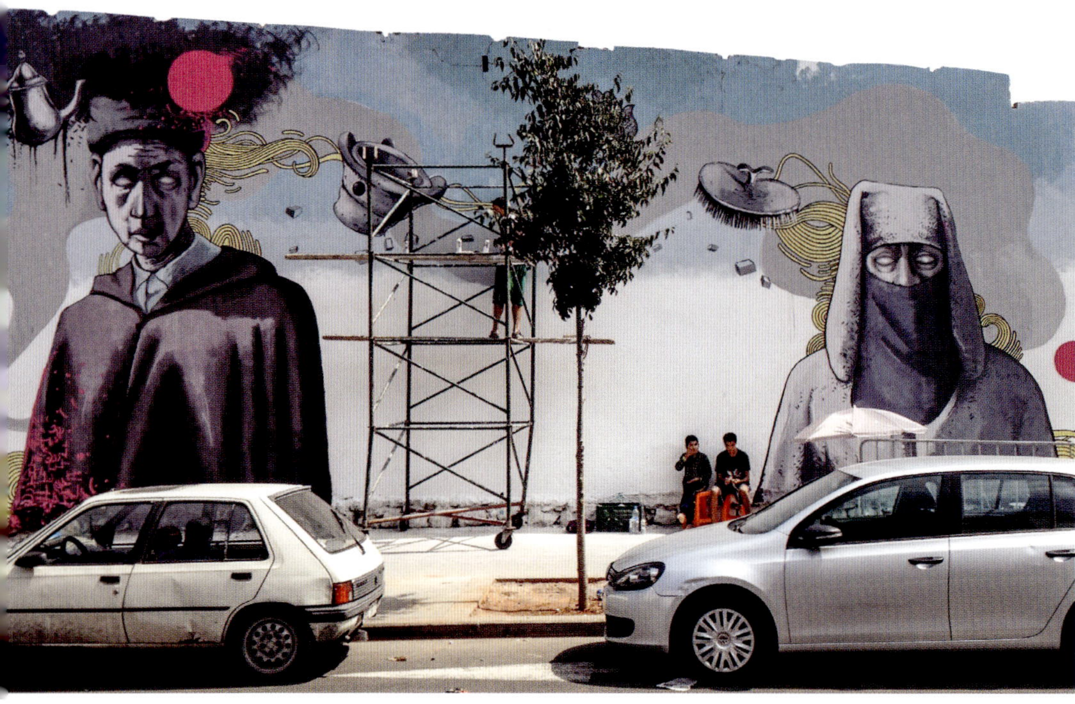
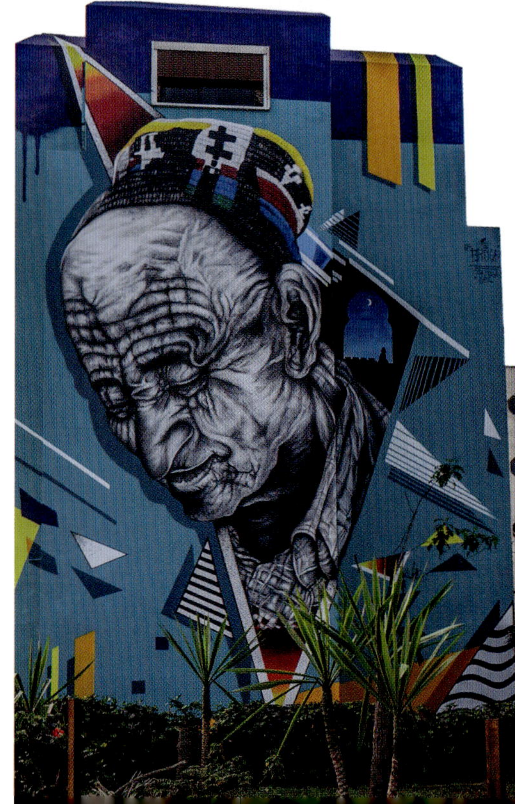

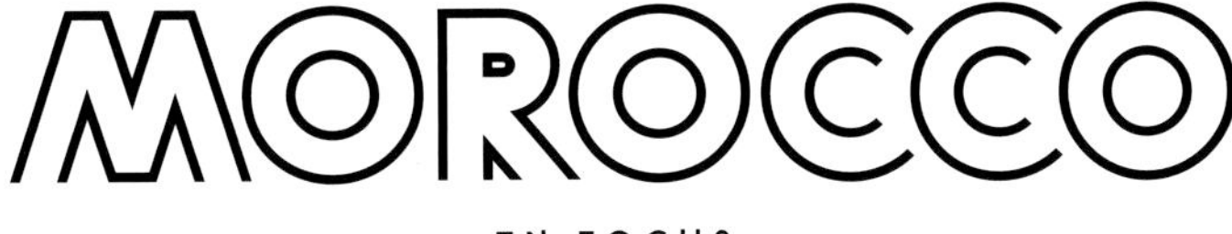

MOROCCO

IN FOCUS

Opposite, top
**D'Et, Brush. Sbagha
Bagha Festival (5th edn),
Casablanca, Morocco, 2017**

Opposite, bottom left
**Simo Mouhim, Dani Tabasco
(Colombia/Spain). Sbagha
Bagha Festival (2nd edn),
Casablanca, Morocco, 2014**

Opposite, bottom right
**Brush. Casamouja: Urban
Art Wave, Casablanca,
Morocco, 2019**

The Kingdom of Morocco, in the northwestern corner of Africa, has long been
a destination for migrants and explorers. Ancient settlers from Arab lands
brought with them the Islamic culture, and a new civilization came to thrive as
the native Berber tribes adopted Islam. Over time – and involving many power
struggles – Europe developed an interest in the region because of its proximity.
In 1912 Morocco became a protectorate of France, but the country gained
independence in 1956, conserving much of its architecture, its traditions and of
course its monarchy. Attracting many Western writers, painters and musicians,
modern Morocco became a burgeoning cultural hub.

In 1978 an arts and culture festival was initiated in the seaside town of Asilah
to effect urban renewal and cultural exchange. The Cultural Moussem of Asilah
implemented murals as a driving force to beautify the medina (old Arab quarter)
and encourage the tourism industry while nurturing inter-country relations
through invited guests. Since then the event has occurred annually, placing an
emphasis on the growing public arts sector in Morocco. Street art is a relatively
new phenomenon in the country, only truly blossoming thirty years later.

A precursor to the development of Morocco's urban arts movement are the
expressive murals painted by its football fans. Known as Ultras, these devoted
members of soccer fan clubs express their allegiance on town walls – a similar
phenomenon exists in other football-crazed countries such as Spain and Italy.
Tangier, Morocco's third-largest city, located just across from the Spanish coast,
is home to one of the nation's most prosperous graffiti scenes, while Meknes
is renowned for harnessing many pioneering writers. Casablanca, Rabat and
Marrakesh have followed suit with the implementation of street art festivals.

Initially graffiti was limited, but with artists such as Rabie setting the example it
quickly began to take shape. Based out of Meknes, Rabie and his Perfect Crew

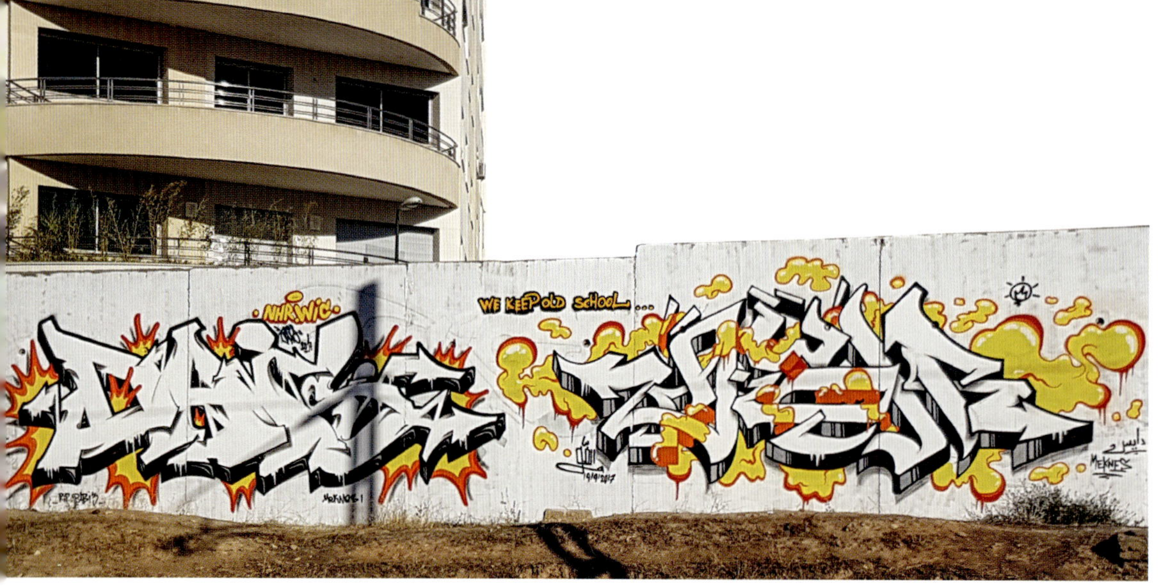

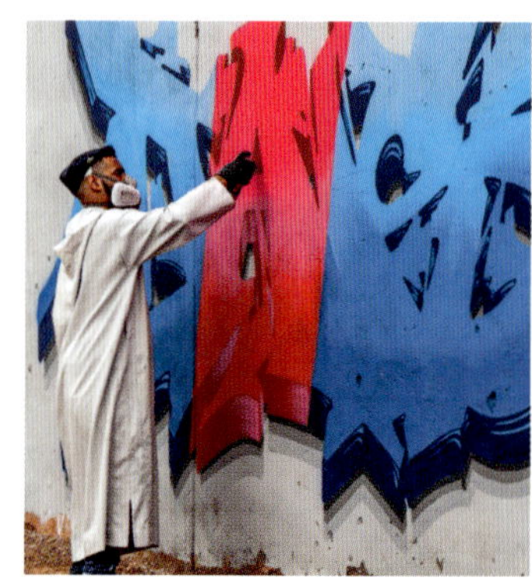

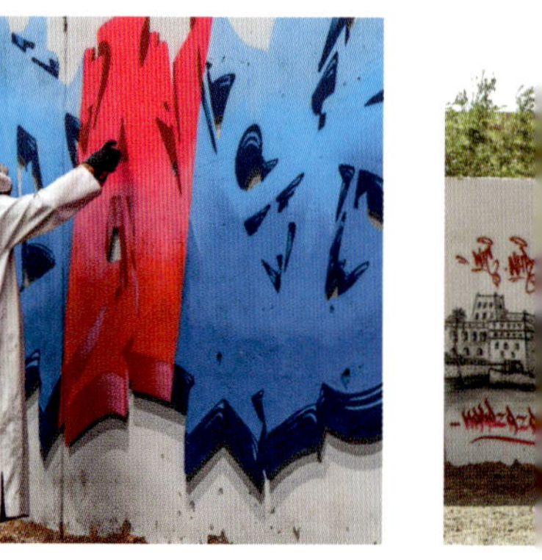

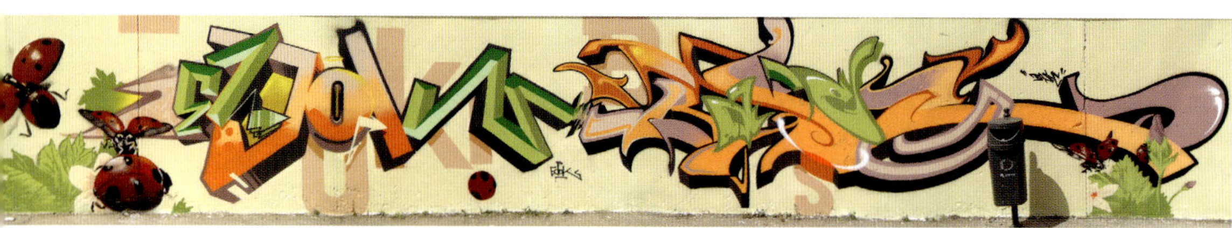

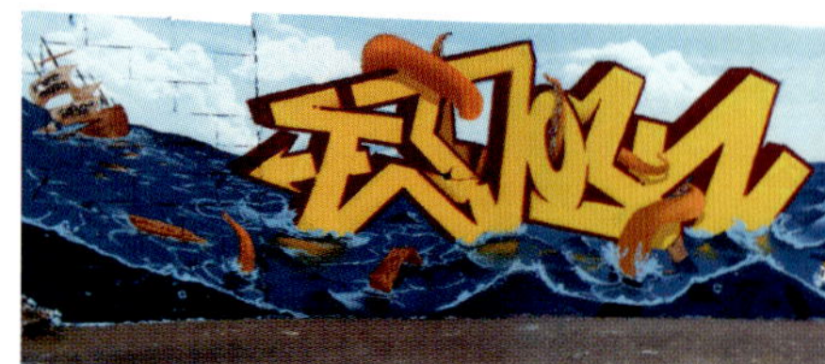

began to explore the art form in a myriad of ways, including airbrush and spray paint, divergent characters – cartoon and realism – and an array of lettering – wildstyle, bubble-style, 3D and Arabic calligraphy. Along with fellow graffiti artists like Issam Refki and Zorg, Rabie made Meknes the country's centre for urban art. Dais (fka 2Es), member of NHR, PRG and WIC (with Keber from Agadir), began his graffiti career in 2003 and continued Rabie's legacy in the wake of his untimely death. Dais, whose style is equally diverse, has represented his city across the country as well as abroad. Dou, another urban artist from Meknes, has added his input, although other cities have now taken over the top spot.

Every metropolis has played a contrasting role in the broadening of graffiti's scope, much as Morocco's imperial cities (Fez, Meknes, Marrakesh and Rabat) were each at one time of central importance. Mevok was one of the originators out of Tangier, first exploring the art form in the mid-2000s. He created 2SC (2step Crew), one of the country's few crews. Only a handful of active street artists operate in each city, although they tend to travel regularly between them. Around 2010, more artists felt enticed by graffiti's lure, including those from other visual art backgrounds. Morran and Aouina are part of the early foundations in Casablanca, the most populous city and now the biggest urban arts producer. Casablanca's graffiti and street art movement is expanding at a rapid rate with astounding, sizeable murals from both local and visiting artists. Trick 54 from Mohammedia and Soul are important figures in terms of street bombing; their names are emblazoned on many surfaces in many cities.

Top row, left to right
Dais, Dou. Meknes, Morocco, 2017

Dais. Ouarzazate, Morocco, 2018

Dais, Dou. Ouarzazate, Morocco, 2018

Trick 54, Kongo (France), Hamgeo, Neok (France), Colorz (France), Morran, Oksir (France), Soul. Anciennes Abatoirs, Casablanca, Morocco, 2012

Bottom row, left to right
Edok (Ed One), Basec One. Rabat, Morocco, 2017

Edok (Ed One), Basec One, Gero, Mevok. Rabat, Morocco, 2017

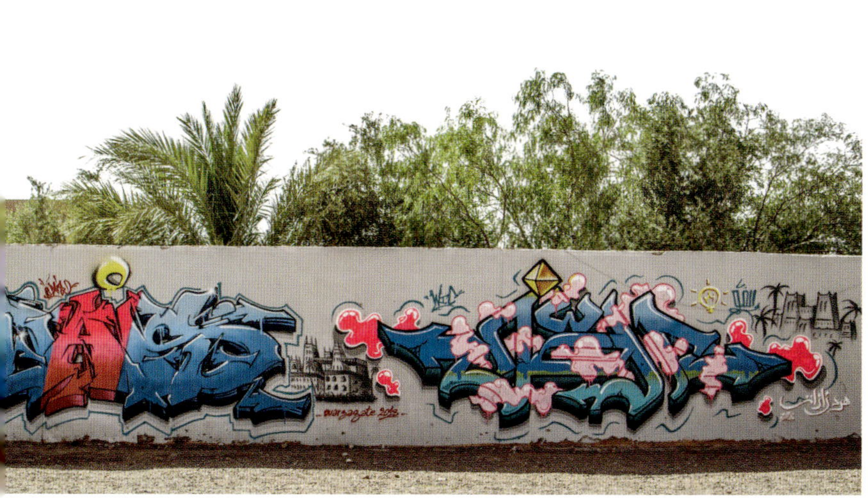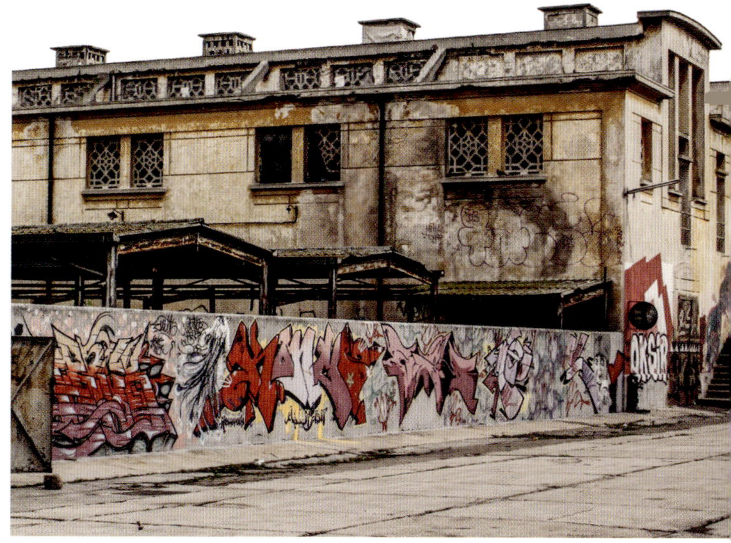

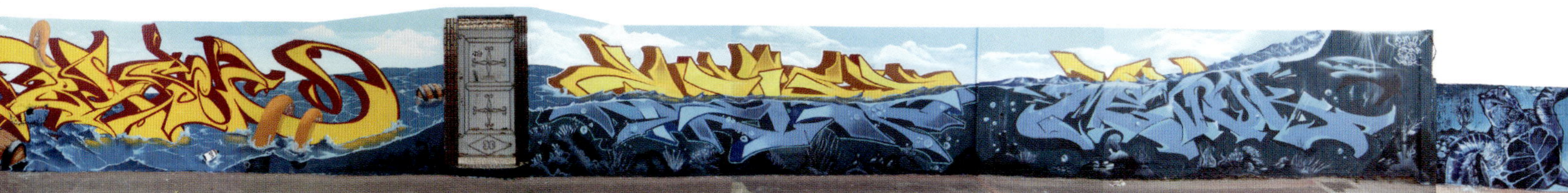

Artists began to upload their work to the World Wide Web, creating a national network and inspiring a new generation. Professional spray paint brands began to appear on the market and the scene started to boom with many expatriates (such as Abid) returning. In Berrechid, a town on the outskirts of Casablanca, high-schoolers Ed One (aka Edok) and Basec One were intrigued by the mystery surrounding the art form and its underground nature, and began to immerse themselves in it. They painted their first graffiti pieces in 2011 and were soon sharing wall space with visiting artists inside Casablanca's abandoned abattoir, Les Anciens – a playground for graffiti artists. The Mafoder foundry also became a favoured home, as artists were welcome to paint in and around the industrial factory to liven up the space. Edok and Basec continue their exploration of the alphabet and beyond as two of the most active visual artists, also helping to inspire a new generation through practical graffiti workshops in Casablanca. Beni-Mellal, another small town, has produced Majic and D'Et, both respected within the scene. Their personal styles often incorporate elements of Moroccan culture, bringing walls to life with evocative portraits. They have been included in many of the country's leading street art events.

The rise of these graffiti gatherings has been primarily responsible for the urban art explosion in Morocco. Not only have they further encouraged cross-participation and skill sharing, but they have also brought the underground art form closer to the public as it seeks further legitimacy. The average person often does not understand the meaning behind the intricate letter forms, instead

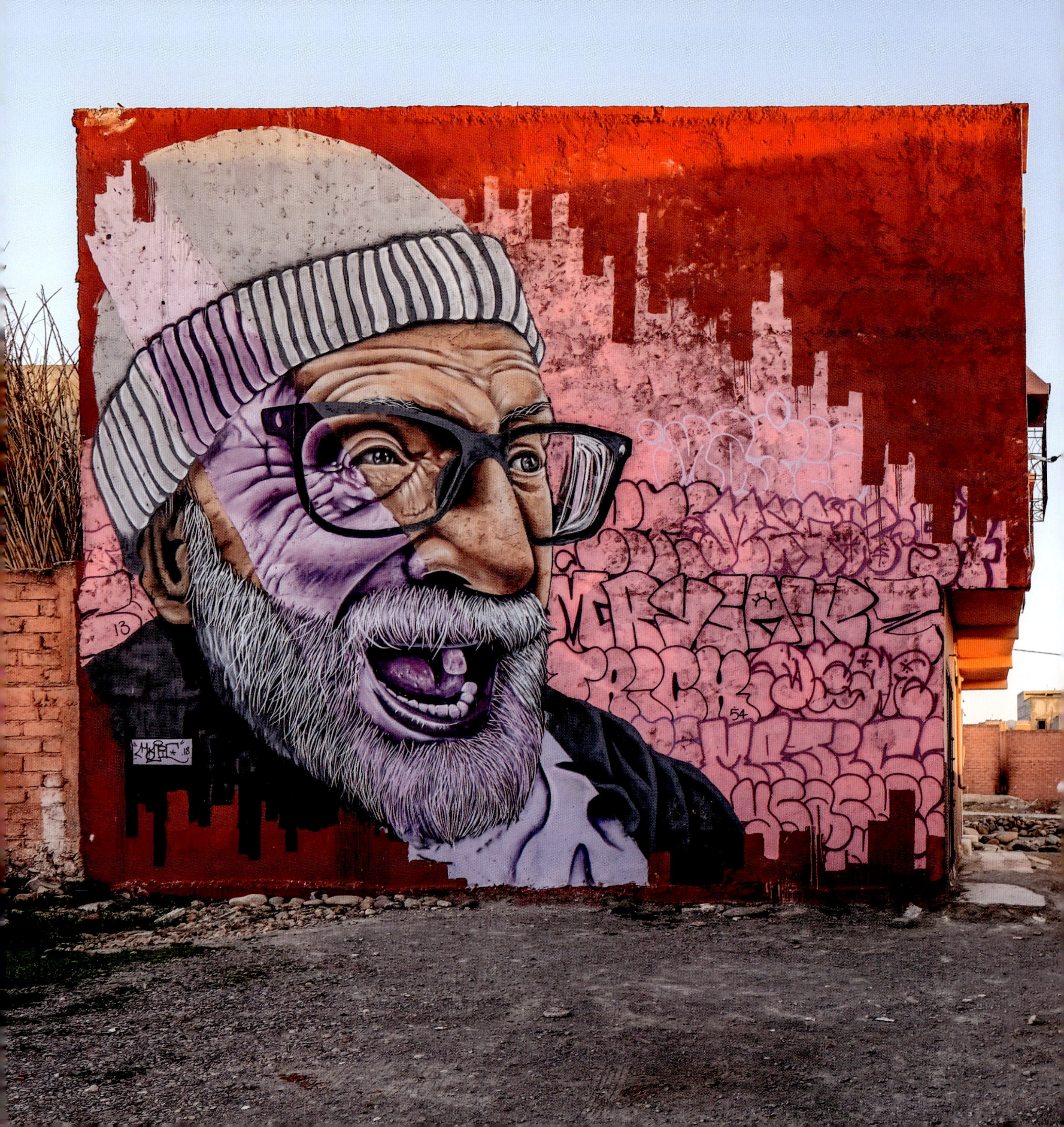

'I paint for pleasure; for myself, for freedom. I also paint for the next generation, to create a base for them and a graffiti history for Morocco. I want to leave my mark behind.' TRICK 54

linking traditional graffiti lettering to drugs, crime or gangsterism. However, through the transparent channels of bigger events, artists are positioned to dispel negative stereotypes while beautifying communal space. With paint provided and more time to act, they can execute expansive, complex pieces, often embedded with content that can be universally embraced. By late 2012 the scene was expanding, with Gero/Gerone, Zores, Enil, Exose, RDS, Hams in Fez, Senzo Clouds and Yann Chatelin (aka Poze) from France, visual artists Simo Mouhim, Kalamour and Rebel Spirit, and crews 219, MGM, FMG, among others.

Held in May 2013, Remp'Arts Festival in Azemmour was one of the first major graffiti festivals – an amalgamation of national and international artists at work, cultivating a lively showcase for a broad audience. Later that year, the debut edition of Sbagha Bagha (loosely meaning 'paint desires' in Maghrebi Arabic) was organized by EAC (Education Artistique et Culturelle) L'Boulvart, which was established in 1999. EAC L'Boulvart was fostering other areas of alternative culture and urban expression but wanted to celebrate graffiti and street art through a formal vehicle. Under its umbrella it began to promote the art form and nurture local artists – some of whom were not even from a graffiti background – to effectively construct a unique model for Moroccan urban art festivals. After the success of each instalment, Sbagha Bagha would continually reinvent itself by adding more elements, such as new districts, more high-profile international guests and a graffiti battle.

With this framework, organizers of EAC L'Boulvart were behind the next development – a festival in Morocco's capital city, Rabat. In 2015, JIDAR – Toiles de Rue (Walls – Street Canvas) was devised. Gigantic murals were scattered throughout the cityscape, involving many of the biggest names in the urban muralism circuit today. A complementary group exhibition was housed at the Mohammed VI Museum of Modern and Contemporary Art, Morocco's first large-scale gallery (founded by the King of Morocco, who also financially supported the festival). The ten-day festivities around JIDAR attract artists and enthusiasts

Opposite
Majic. Festival des Arts de Rue de Tameslohte (1st edn), Tameslouht, Morocco, 2018

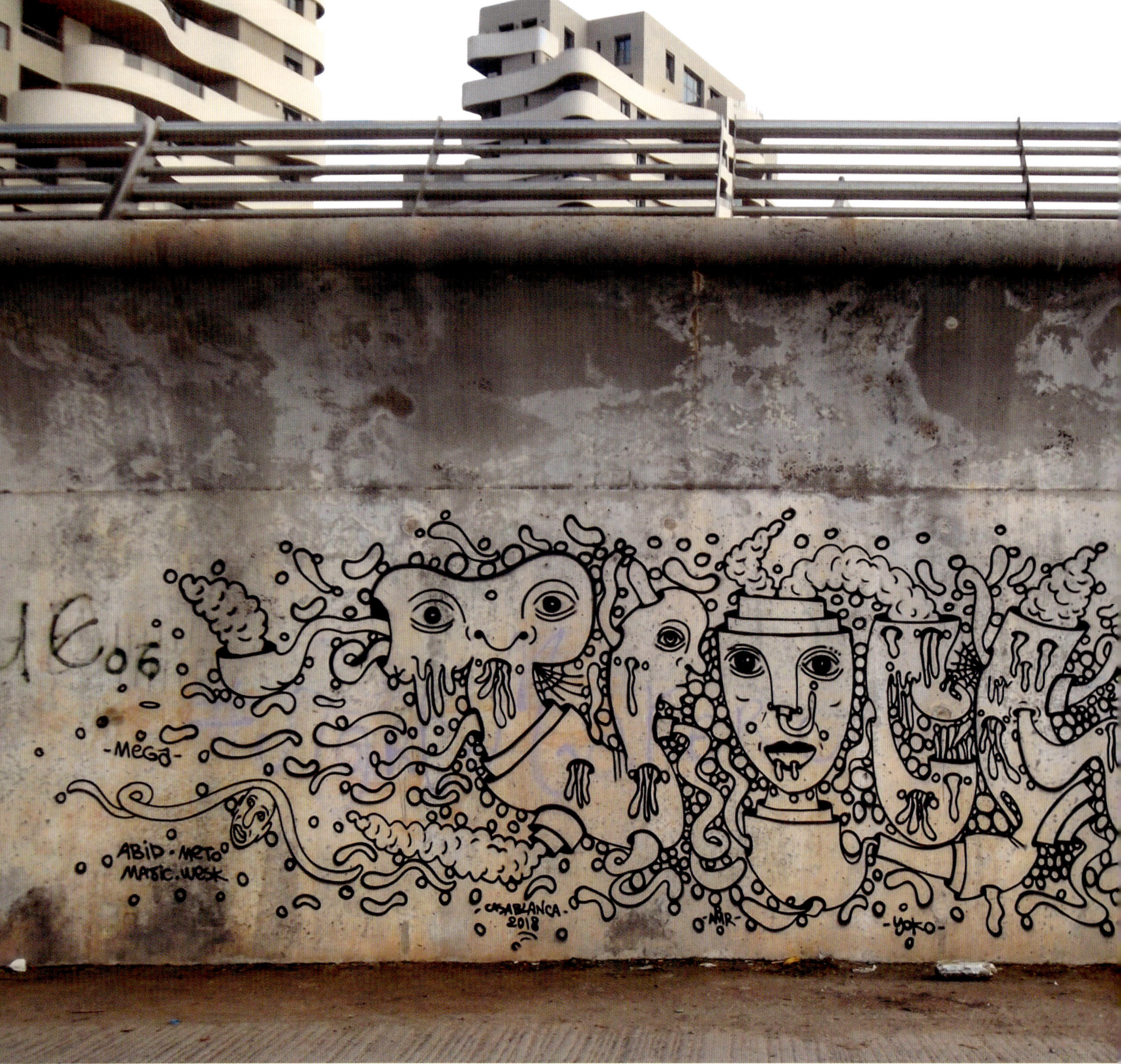

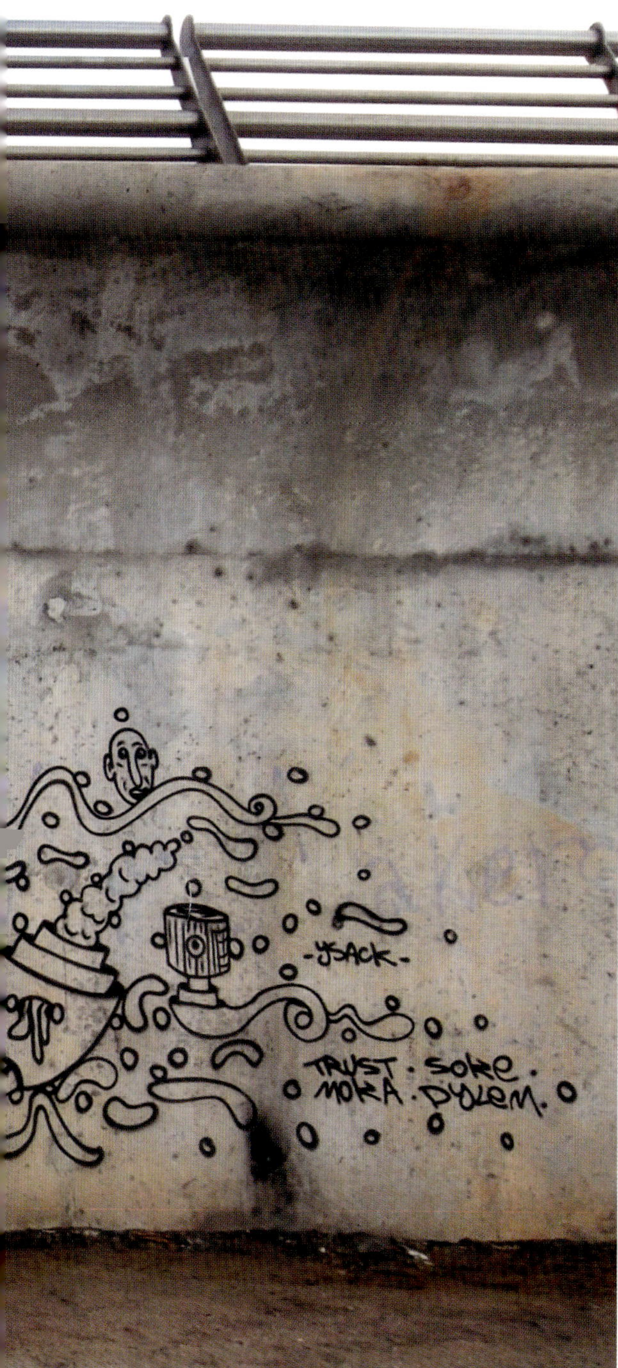

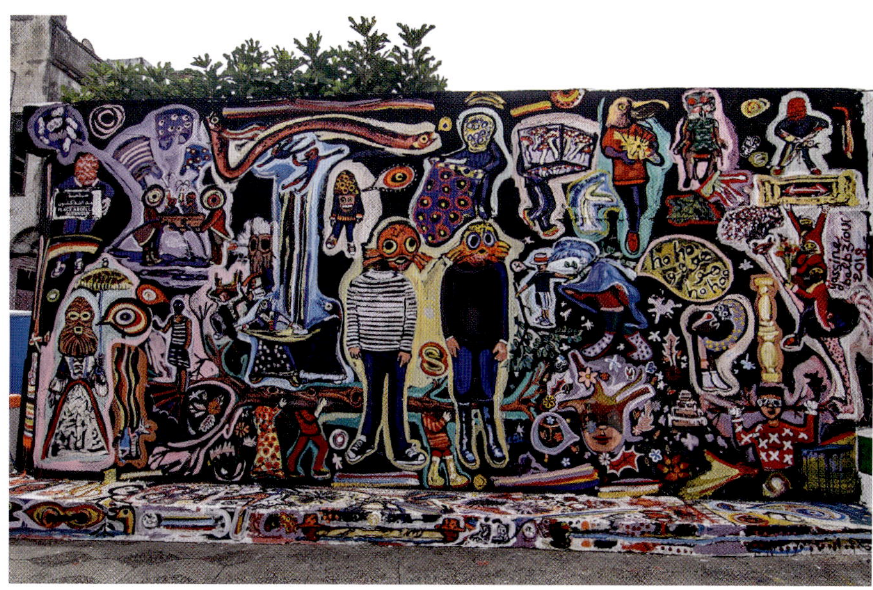

Left
**Trick 54. Casablanca,
Morocco, 2018**

Above
**Yassine Balbziou. Asilah
Festival (40th edn), Asilah,
Morocco, 2018**

Below
**SMC by OTM, Gero.
Casablanca, Morocco, 2018**

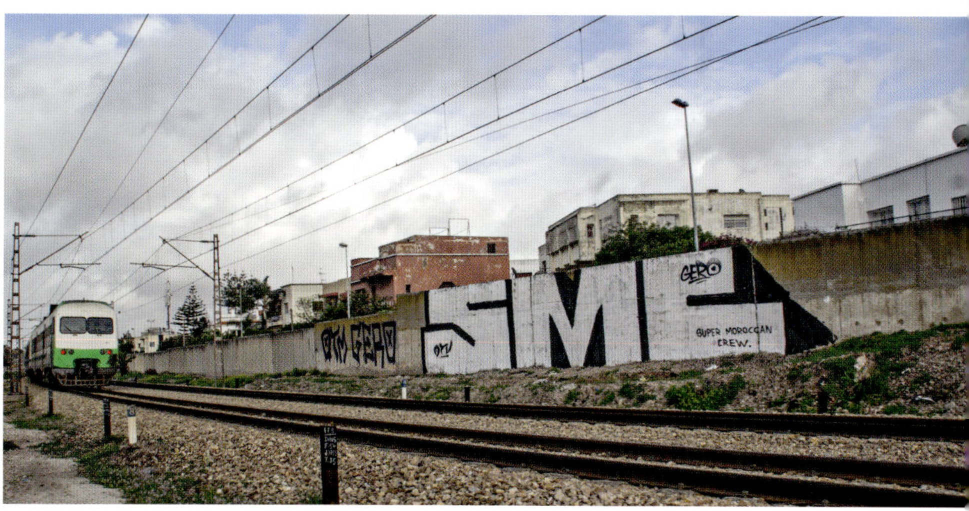

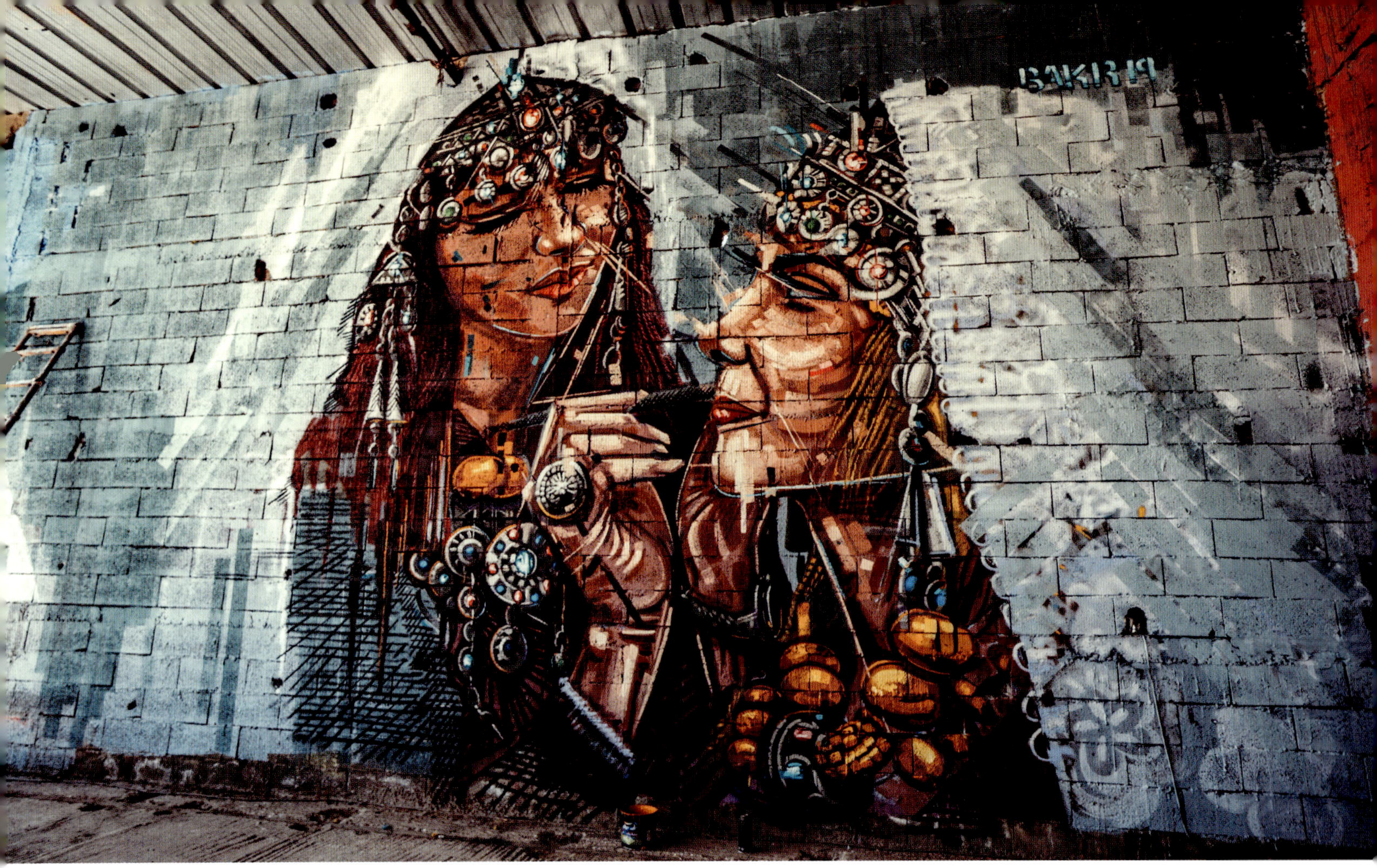

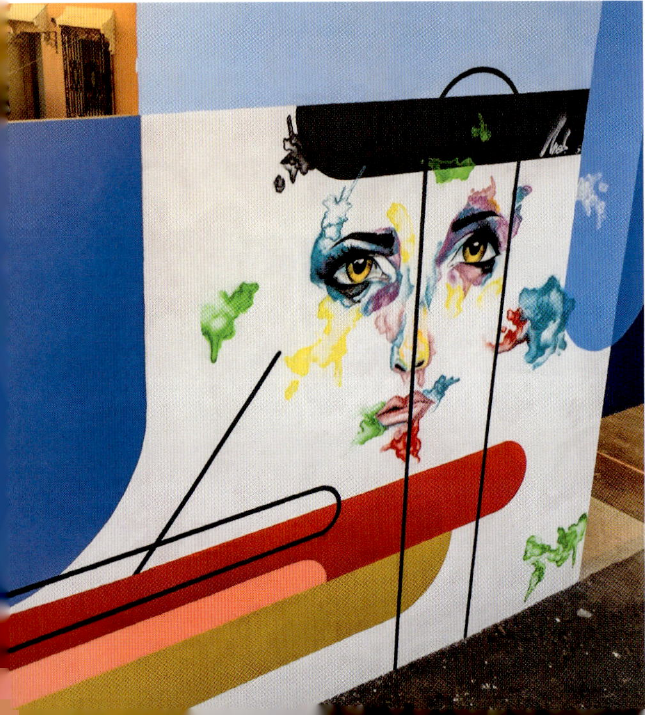

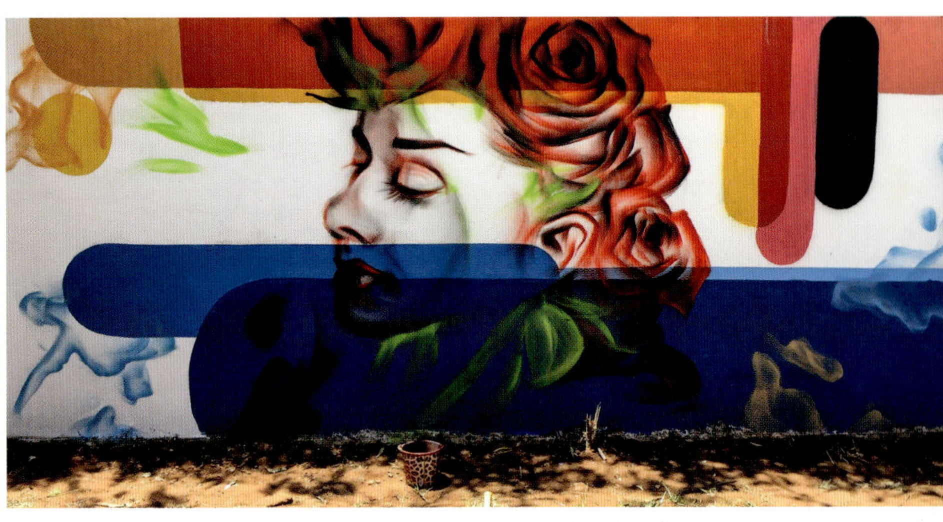

alike. Many graffiti artists descend on the capital each year to paint their own works on the sideline during the event (as a local Rabat scene has not fully developed, yet). The curators of the festival keep a close eye on promising artists and empower them in future editions, either giving them opportunities to learn techniques by assisting the international artists on larger walls or allotting them a wall of their own. Casamouja: Urban Art Wave (by WeCasablanca) is another platform in Casablanca promoting art in public spaces, also breeding artists and challenging perceptions around visual art.

Graphic artist Machima scored his big break when an invitee could not attend the 2016 edition of JIDAR festival, resulting in his first foray into mural painting. This was the catalyst for a new chapter in his artistic career and he has excelled ever since. Iramo Samir and Dynam One entered the world of street art in a different way. They adorned walls with slogans for Ultras and were scouted through their output. Exciting street artists began to appear, including Normal and Med.z, as well as the Placebo Studio art agency. More rendezvouses took place to position the country as a true open-air museum: Street Art Caravane in three cities during 2016 (Youssoufia, Safi and Ben Guerir), the Meeting of Moroccan Graffiti Writers in Casablanca (in 2015 and 2016), and the Festival des Arts de Rue de Tameslohte, inaugurated in 2018 in Tameslouht, outside Marrakesh. Other get-togethers and graffiti jams, including Tanja Street Art Fest in Tangier (created by street-pop artist Mouad Aboulhanain), have also stimulated the underground art sphere.

In Marrakesh there is a lack of local artists, but no shortage of elaborate works. The David Bloch Gallery and the Montresso* Art Foundation's Jardin Rouge artists' residency foster an influx of international artists every month. Huge names in the world of street art and graffiti have visited these institutions to participate in their art exhibitions and residencies alike. The David Bloch Gallery

Opposite, top
Bakr. 'Amazigh Beauty' (the Amazighs, or Berbers, are an ethnic group native to Northern Africa), Mediouna, Morocco, 2019

Opposite, bottom left
Med.z. Marrakesh, Morocco, 2018

Opposite, bottom right
Med.z. Casablanca, Morocco, 2018

Below
Iramo Samir, Majic, 310310310, Okuda (Spain). Casamouja: Urban Art Wave, Casablanca, Morocco, 2018

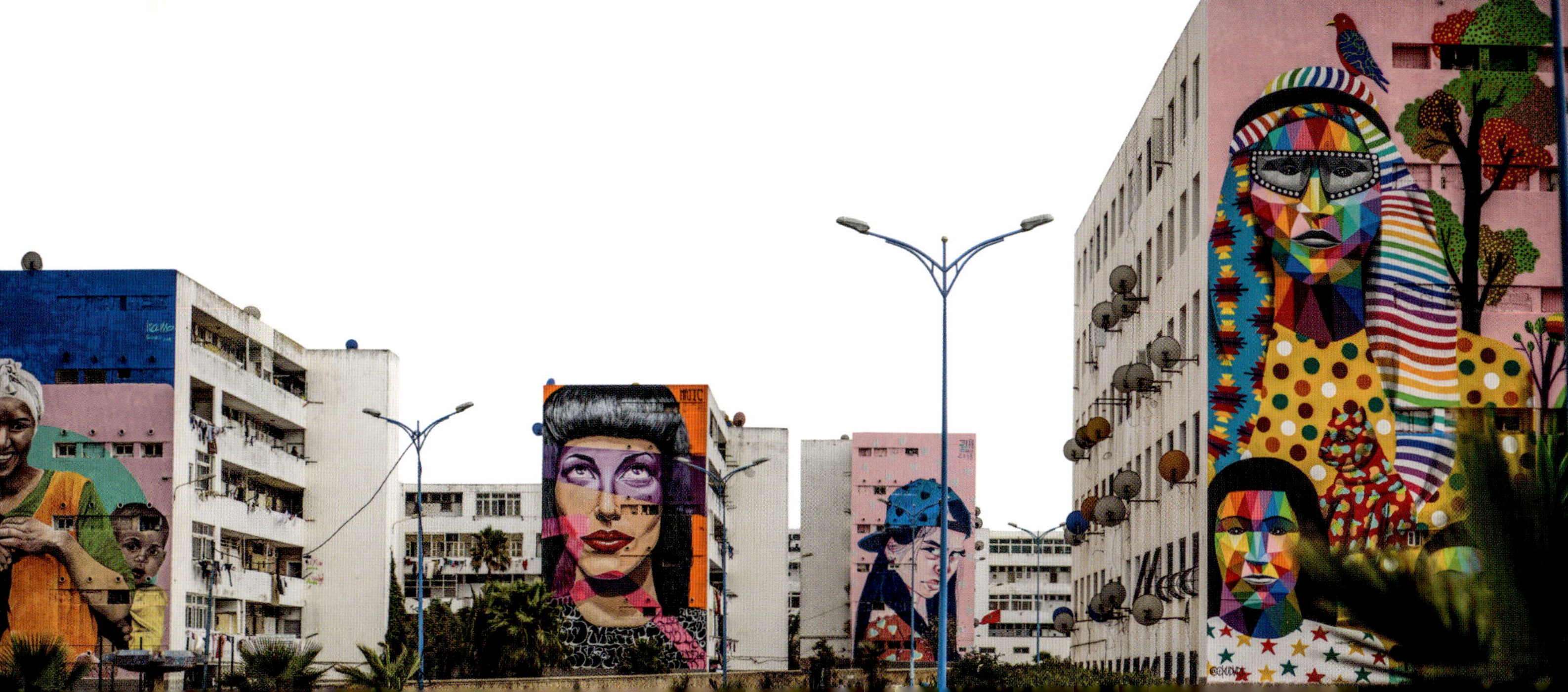

has a focus on post-graffiti (often dubbed 'graffuturism'), curating shows with many of the elite in this field. The buildings in and around the Jardin Rouge (on the outskirts of the city) are adorned with treasures left by resident artists, and the foundation also funds the Outside the Walls mural project. MB6: Street Art, an independent feature of the sixth Marrakech Biennale, was held in 2016 in Marrakesh and Essaouira with eleven international artists present.

Now, with an abundant supply of professional graffiti spray paint and references abounding as to what street art can achieve, artists are finding it easier to locate wall owners who will give them permission to paint. The remaining challenge is to find more legal spots. Amin Brush has a hall of fame in Casablanca's Riviera district, while the Alouane Bladi association has semi-legalized the Marina. There are more walls in Tangier and Meknes and a new generation of artists is appearing across the country, such as Dakon, Atmos, Sez, Dio, Maed, Relk, Zen Zone, Mao, Jeka MBF, Mchimich, Reda Bahrani, Moët and MAM, and females Rose, Gosm, Drobys and Roksy One. Crews are also becoming more relevant and include SMC (Street Masters Crew) – Bosta One/B6, Mevok, Glad, Neval, Omba, Gero, Sako Seven/Aink, Zores, Brush, OTM, Snop and Zest 48; ZMR (Zoo Moroccan Rules) – Abid, Meto, Wesk, Majic, Sker and Brams; TRZ (Taraza) – Normal, Machima, Basec One, Ed One and DaJ3; and NOD (Nodawanod, local slang meaning 'Stand up, come on, stand up') – Senzo Clouds, Iramo Samir, Dynam One, Bakr, Oldr, Abid, Roksy One, Drobys and Meto.

Graffiti remains illegal and artists regularly utilize abandoned and remote spots to avoid hassles, continuing to propel their work into all corners of the country, while at the same time knocking on European shores across the strait. With the artists' ability to create meaningful murals in all styles, the age of Moroccan urban arts and culture has dawned.

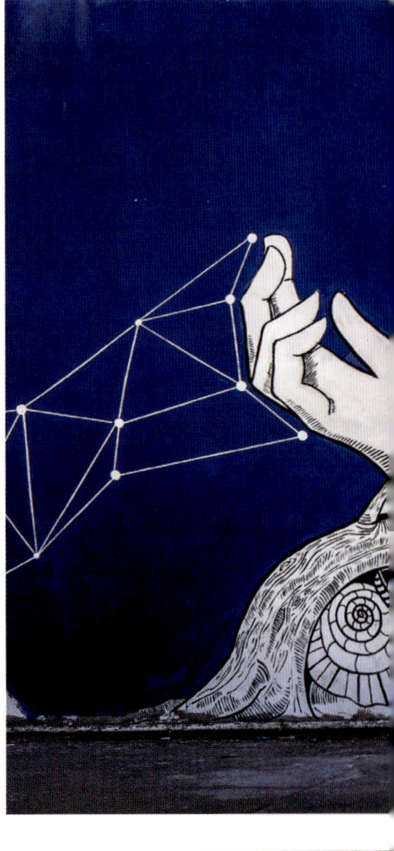

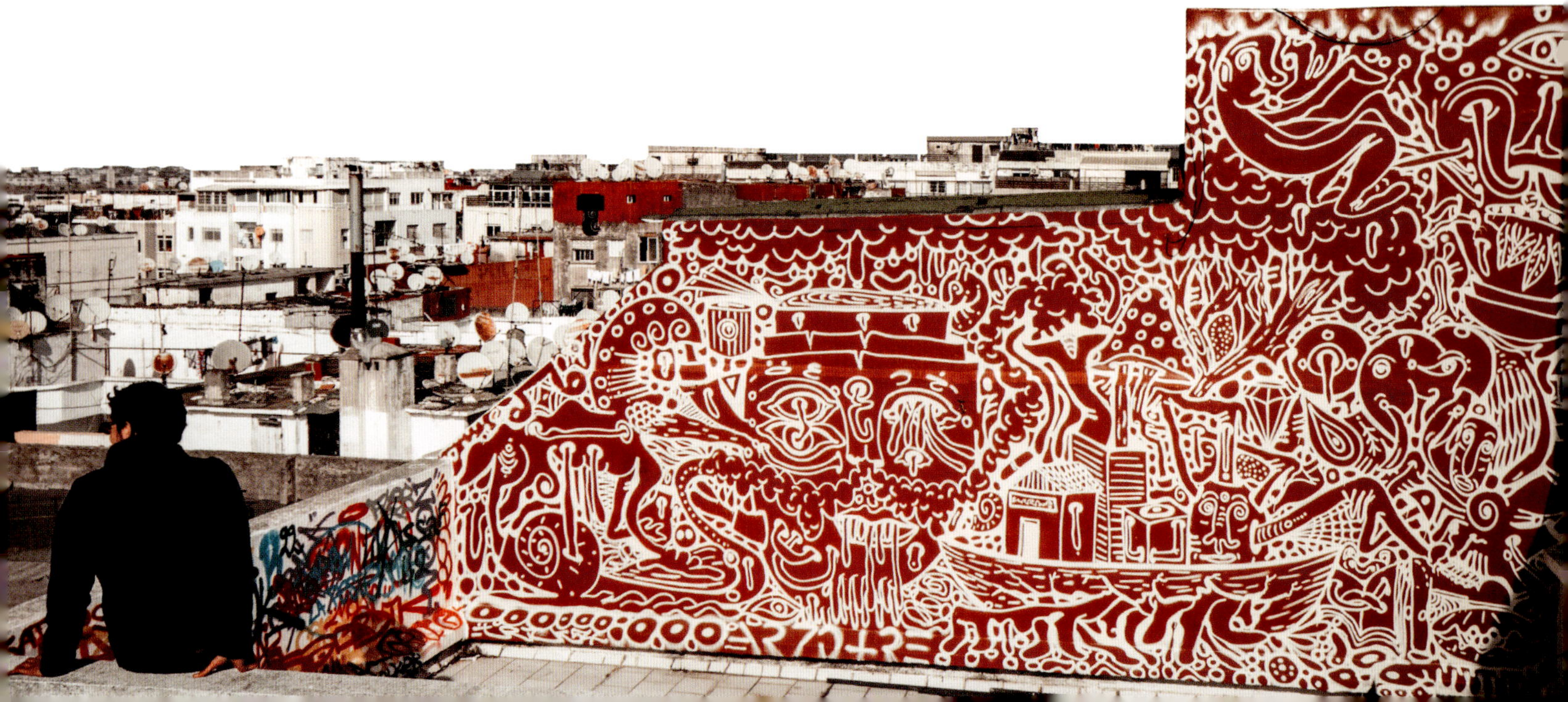

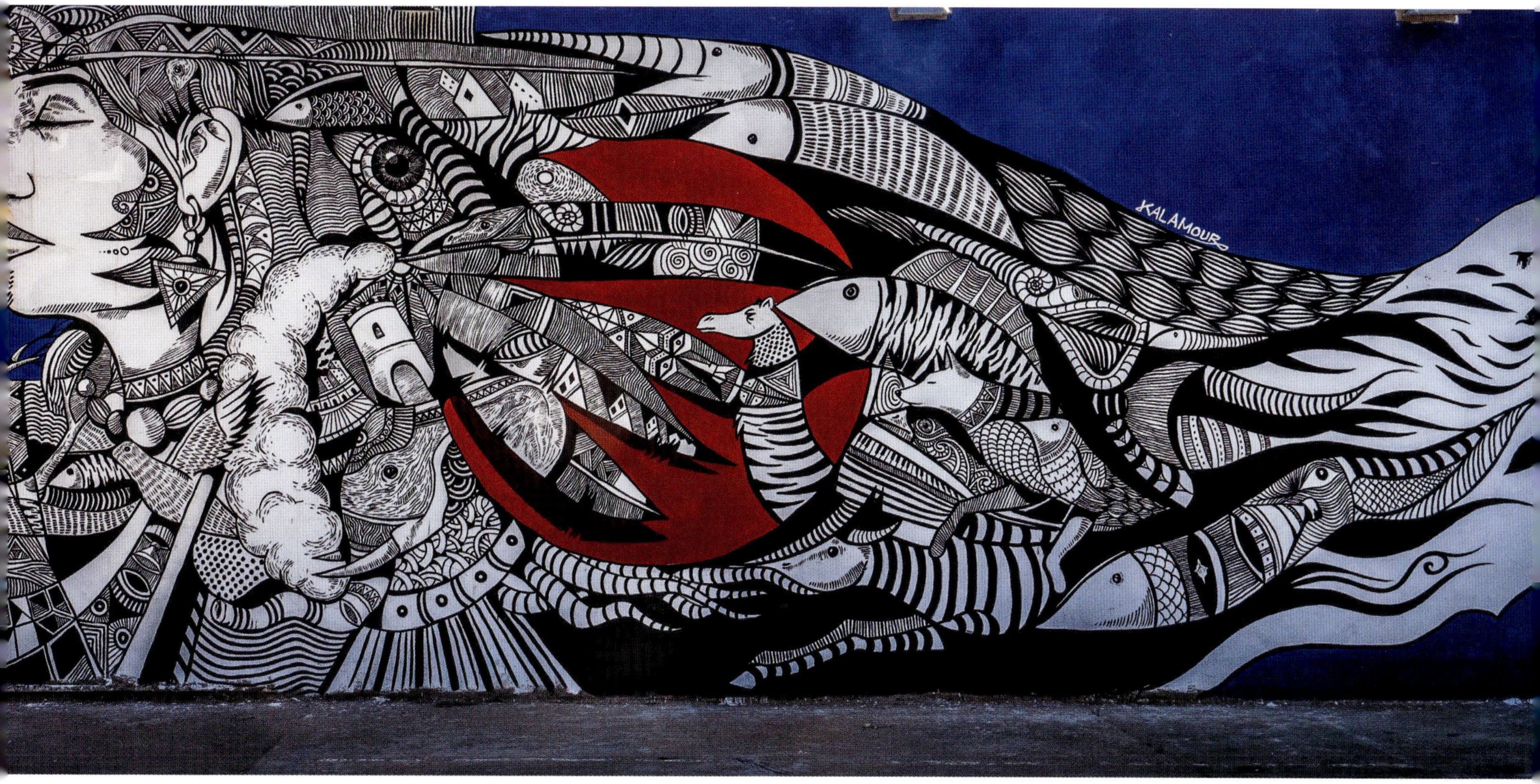

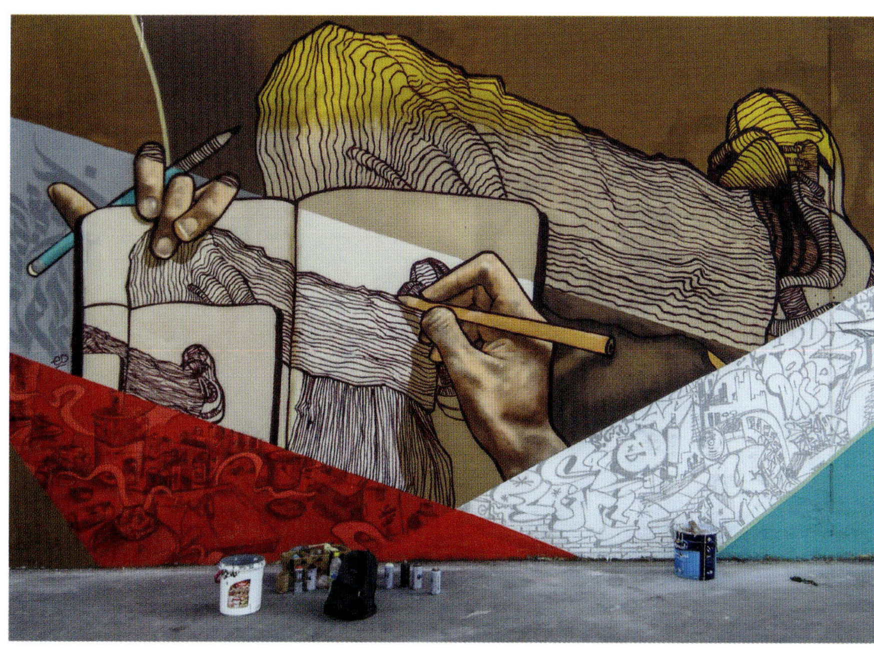

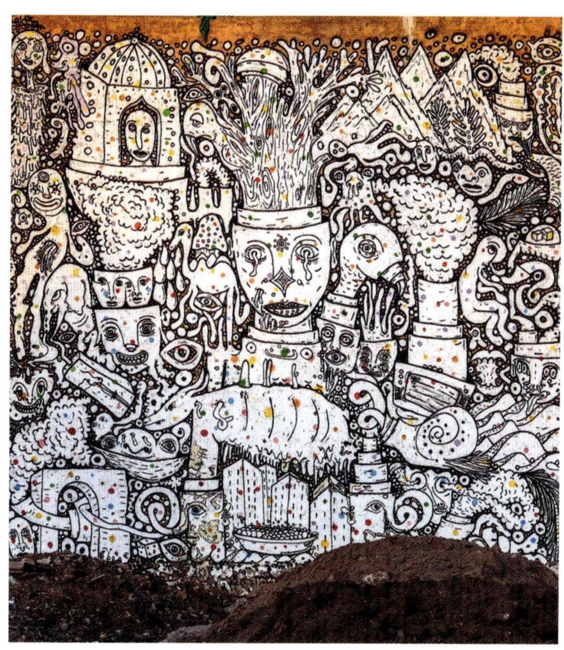

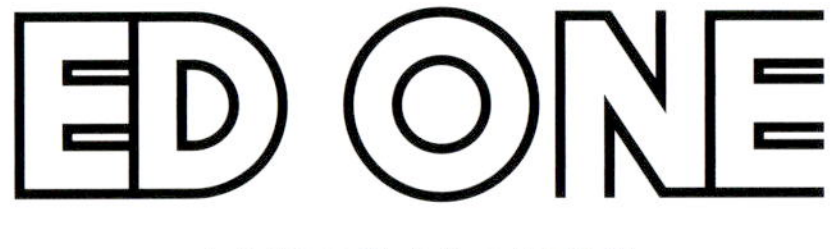

ED ONE

ARTIST PROFILE

Tell me about your introduction to graffiti.
I was influenced by my classmates while studying applied arts in high school. I saw some of my friends sketching and they always had paint on their fingers. I quickly became interested and started sketching and painting with them at the end of 2011.

Why do you enjoy painting in the public space?
The public space is for all, and I offer my art to all people. They can like it and leave it as it is, hate it and buff it, or add something they think is better; it's part of the game and sharing is the main objective. I still paint illegally for a good rush of adrenaline too.

Are you part of a crew?
I am in Taraza Crew, a collective of five people of which three stem from a comic and illustration background (Normal, DaJ3, Machima) plus graffiti writer Basec One.

Where does your graffiti name come from, and does it mean anything?
My first name is Mohamed and the abbreviation is MED, but it is popular and therefore not interesting. I decided to only keep the letters E and D, which is easy to pronounce and remember – and it also reminds me of the cartoon 'Ed, Edd n Eddy'. Sometimes I add letters to play with, forming new names like 'EDS', 'EDONE' and 'EDOK'.

What do you like to paint and how has your style evolved in recent times?
I started doing letters in the best geometric way I could find, using rectangles, triangles and circles – simple shapes that can lead to more complex forms and the addition of 3D and effects. I am now more interested in characters because I love to draw them. Every time I get the chance to paint with the guys I do some letters, but I am currently focused on figurative drawing.

Tell me about your creative process.
My creative process starts with thinking, maybe going out and getting inspired by people living their daily lives, or from the Internet and movies. After getting an idea in mind, I start sketching digitally or on paper. I also visualize walls that could be the perfect fit, and then the action begins.

Lately I am interested in Moroccan culture, which is special. We are always distracted by everyday problems, technology, politics, etc., so people don't always see the beauty

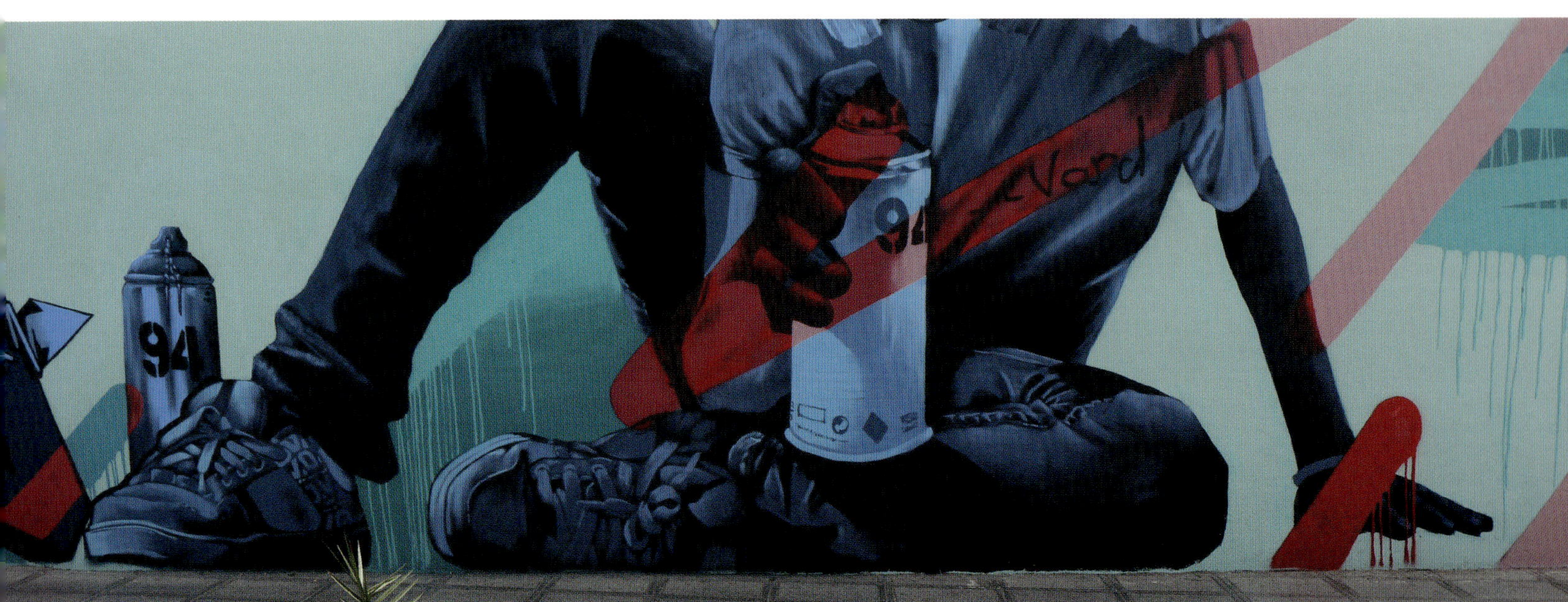

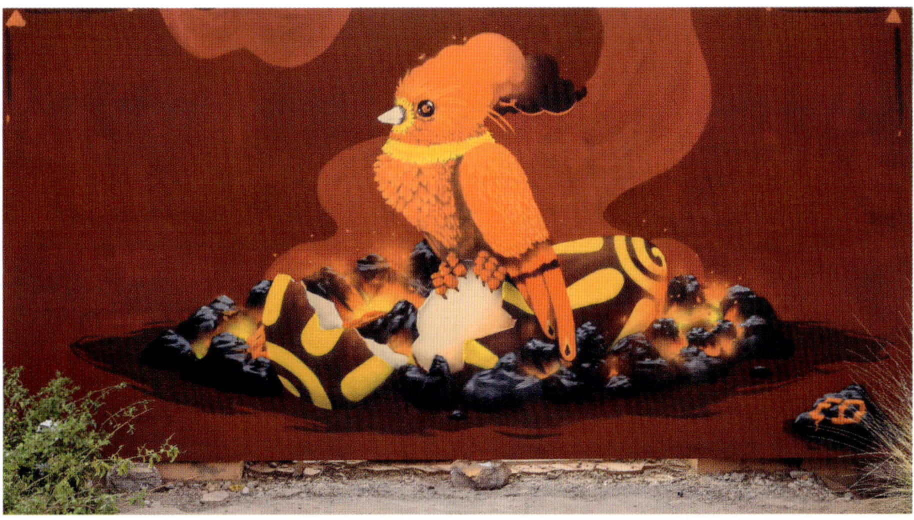

around them. When I see something beautiful I draw it or I take a picture that can be transformed into a drawing or wall painting later.

How different are large-scale outdoor artworks from smaller walls or illustration work?

Large-scale murals are complicated because you need to invest more time and money. The thinking process is harder too, but you don't regret it. When I get an idea I start sketching and developing the colours to see if it fits with the placement of the wall. The painting process is more physical and working all day in the sun is not easy.

Give me a glimpse of the street art scene in Morocco.

The scene is expanding to a higher level and new artists are appearing constantly. I try to help in this evolution by doing workshops where I invite people to develop their talents. The public appreciate street art more and more, as shown by the amount of murals we have in the cities and, of course, the quality.

What are some highlights for you as a street artist in Morocco?

Graffiti events. You meet other artists and learn, all while sharing a common passion. Also when I go out to paint for myself in an abandoned place – music in my ear, paint in my hand, everything I need to be in a great mood.

Ed One epitomizes the rise of Morocco's urban artists. His work continually matures into new territory as he expands his horizons to strengthen his artistic adroitness. From letters to character portraits and abstract studies, Ed is passionate in building his portfolio and passing on his knowledge to others.

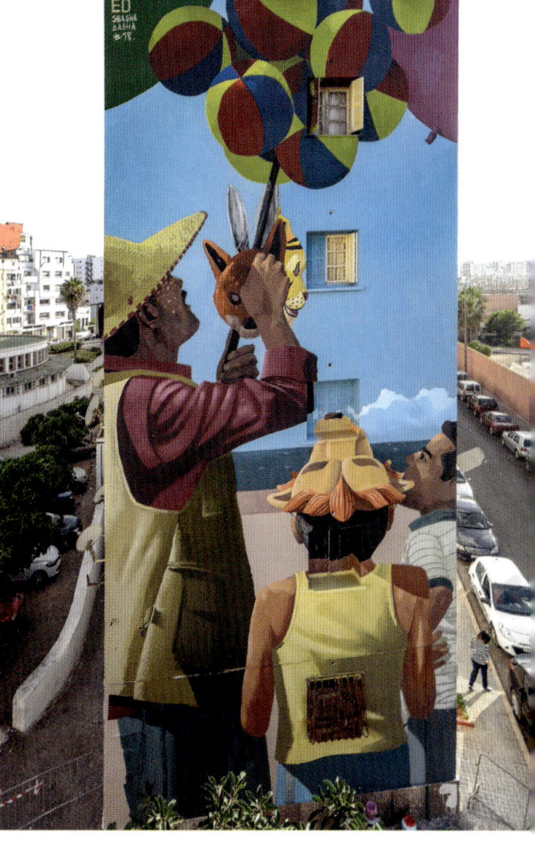

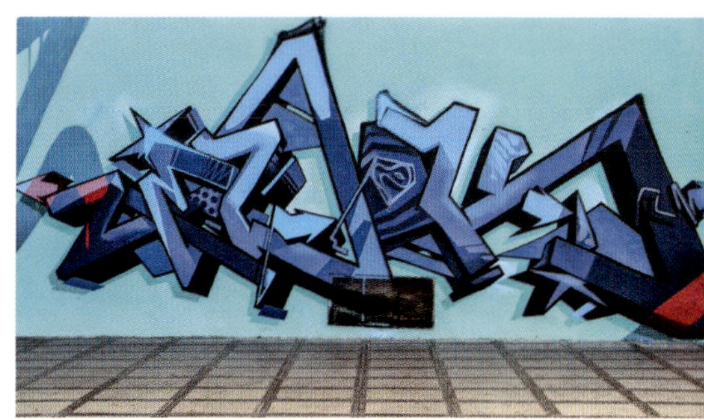

Opposite
Ed One. Casablanca, Morocco, 2017

Top left
Ed One. Maroc Solar project, Ouarzazate, Morocco, 2016

Top right
Ed One. Sbagha Bagha Festival (6th edn), Casablanca, Morocco, 2018

Bottom right
Edok. Casablanca, Morocco, 2017

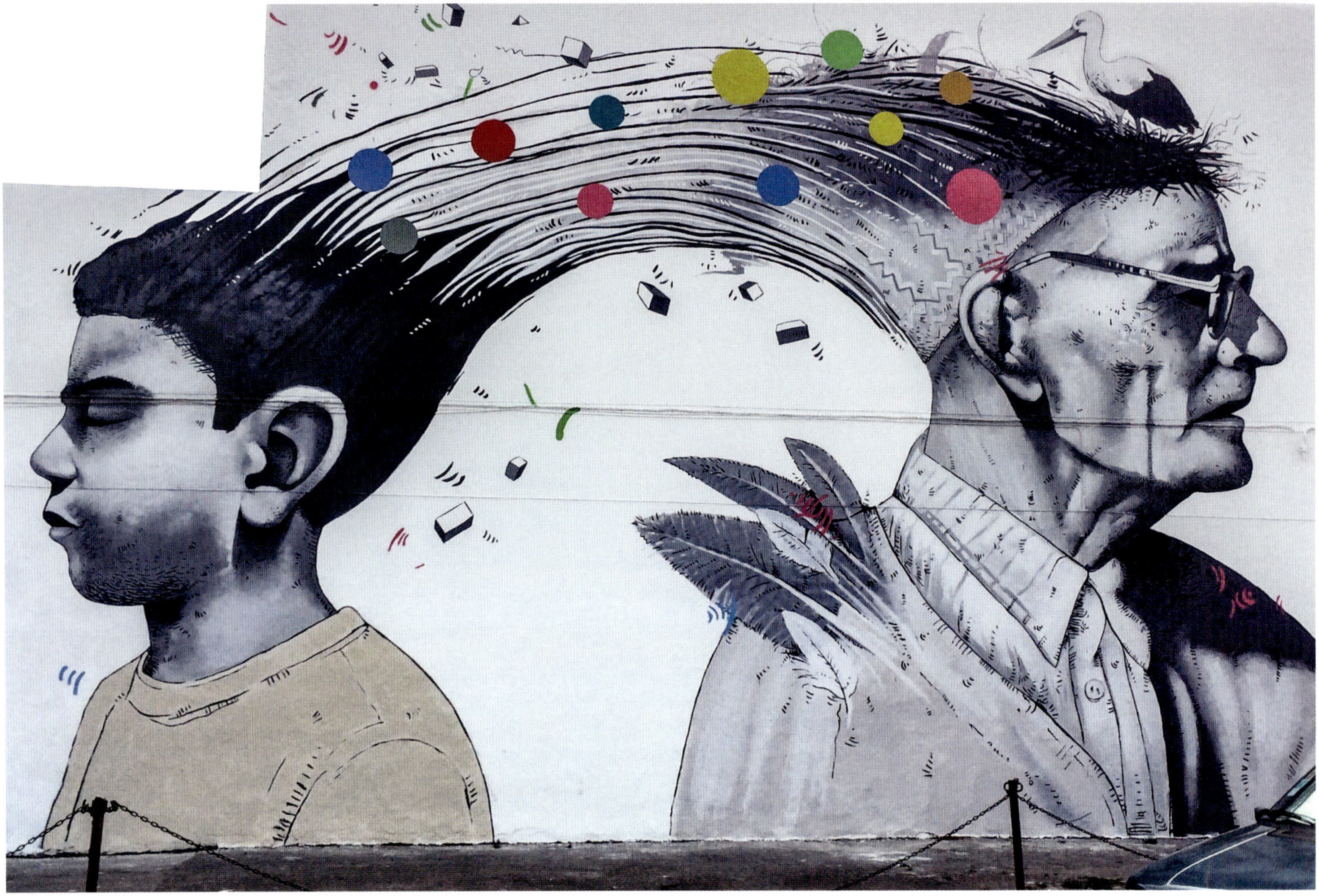

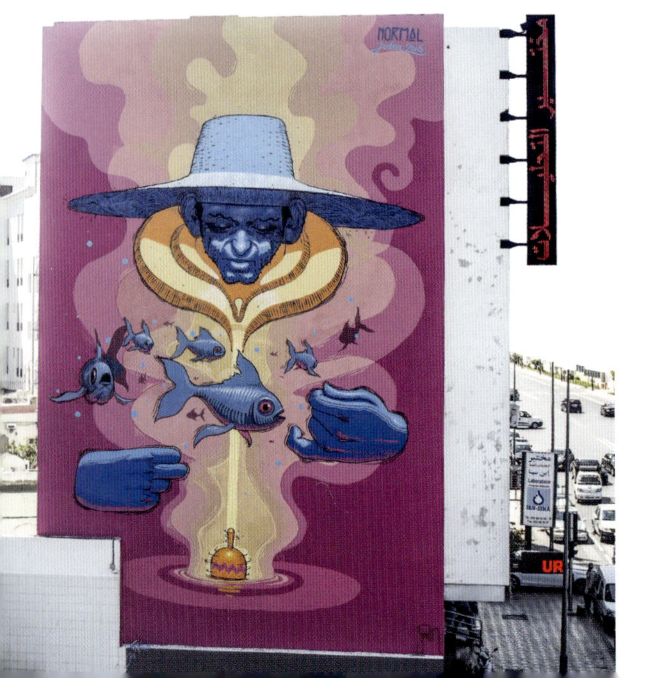

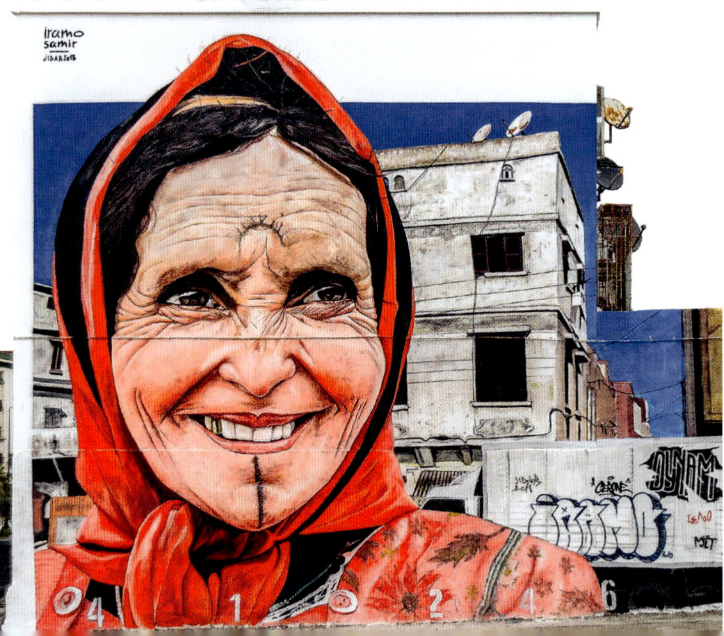

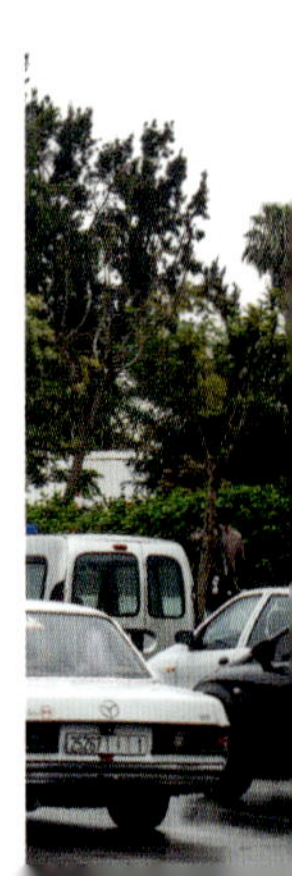

JIDAR – TOILES DE RUE

FESTIVALS & CULTURE

A leading urban art and mural festival on the continent, JIDAR – Toiles de Rue (Walls – Street Canvas), takes place in the Moroccan capital, Rabat. The city's street art scene was nonexistent before the inauguration of the event in 2015. During each edition a series of around a dozen large, multistorey murals are painted by both local and international artists, with outstanding contributions from some of the world's greatest urban artists. Other activities include a group exhibition and various street-level graffiti productions to accommodate local graffiti writers. The Mur Collectif (Collective Wall) element also aims to nurture young, emerging Moroccan muralists under the supervision of selected international guests.

The week-long festival has been blessed with outstanding international contributions from the likes of Saner (Mexico), Zoer (France), Franco Fasoli aka Jaz (Argentina), Decertor (Peru), Nelio (France), MurOne (Spain), Sainer (Poland), Dire 132 (France), Pixel Pancho (Italy), Inti (Chile), Remi Rough (UK), Zepha (France), Peeta (Italy), Case Ma'Claim (Germany), Deih (Spain), Low Bros (Germany), WaOne Intersni Kazki (Ukraine), Fikos (Greece), 3TT Man (France), Hyuro (Argentina), Phlegm (UK), Does (the Netherlands) and Mina Hamada (Japan).

Opposite, top
Simo Mouhim. 1st edn, Rabat, Morocco, 2015

Opposite, bottom row, left to right
Normal. 2nd edn, Rabat, Morocco, 2016

Iramo Samir. 4th edn, Rabat, Morocco, 2018

Ammar Abo Bakr. 2nd edn, Rabat, Morocco, 2016

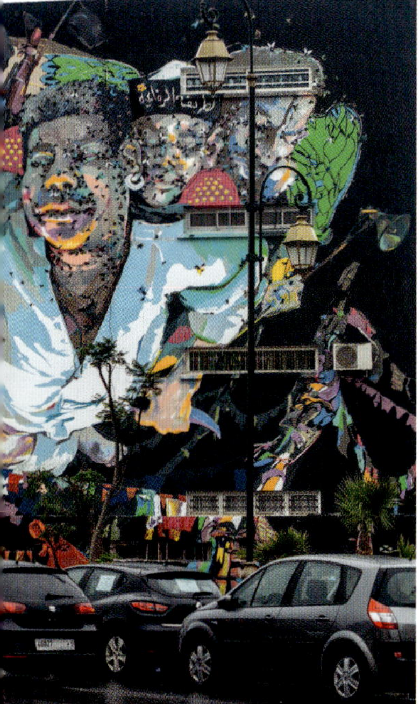

INTERNATIONAL INFLUENCE

The influx of multiple international artists travelling and painting throughout Africa is crucial to its street art growth. Visitors help to inspire and upskill local artists, while highlighting Africa as a global graffiti destination. Morocco has become a major hub and world-renowned artists from nearby countries such as Spain and France have created riveting murals. Events and festivals encourage cultural exchange and showcase the art form in a good light to offset any negative connotations. The foreign influence also has a positive effect on the environment as the work fosters community development and teaches valuable life skills in a new way, through art and interaction.

African artists often assist or collaborate with international artists who are commissioned for various projects by embassies and institutions. This has resulted in a tremendous rise in African graffiti talent. Conversely, African artists are invited overseas, where they often manage to produce some of their best works. A common language is a thread that connects many artists as they travel, making inter-country relationships thrive, especially between French-speaking European countries and those in Africa. Some foreign nationals have immigrated to Western Africa because of this, including, from France, El Marto, who has based himself in Burkina Faso for the past decade to explore his family roots, and Sagés, who moved to Senegal for the sake of adventure. South Africa is also a popular destination for international travellers. Other French artists who have realized multiple projects on the African continent include Seth Globepainter, Invader, C215, YZ, Tilt, Remed, L'Atlas, Marko93, Lazoo and Zepha.

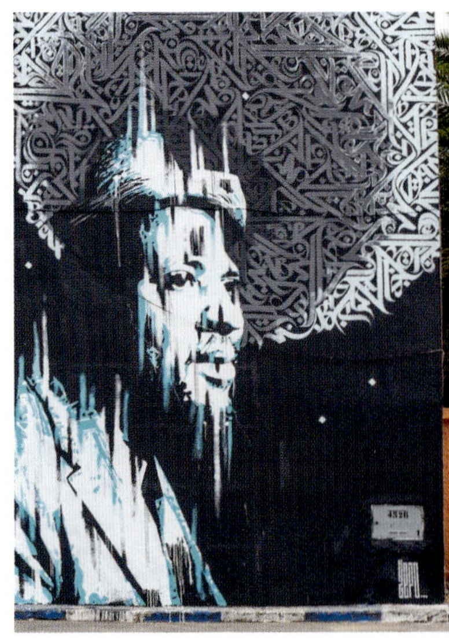

Clockwise from top left
Poze (France). 'Wangari Maathai', Casablanca, Morocco, 2019

Poze (France). JIDAR - Toiles de Rue (5th edn), Rabat, Morocco, 2019

Sagés, Docta, HMI (Belgium), Dema One (Belgium). Festa2H, Dakar, Senegal, 2015

Poze (France). Street Art Caravane, Youssoufia, Morocco, 2016

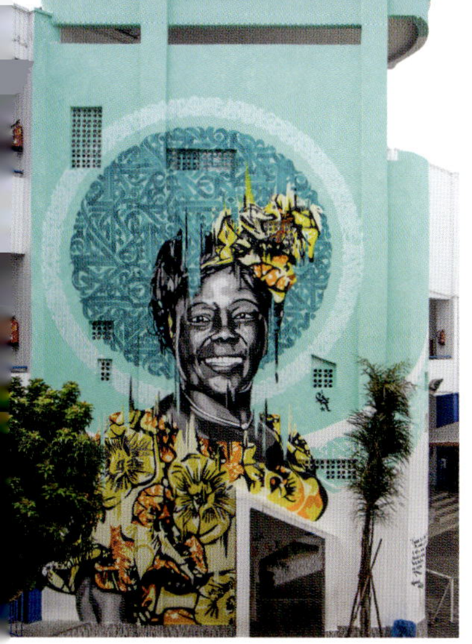
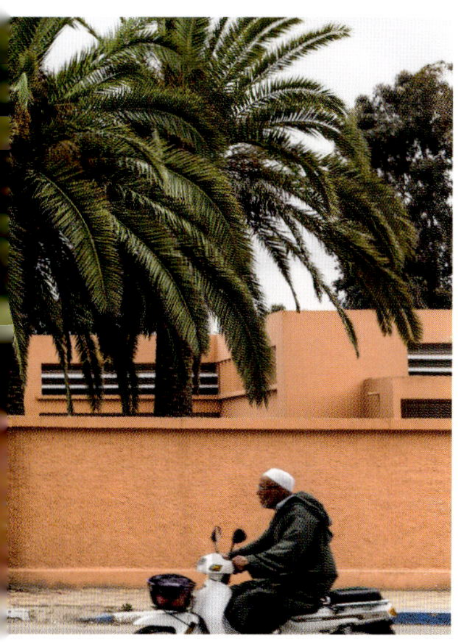

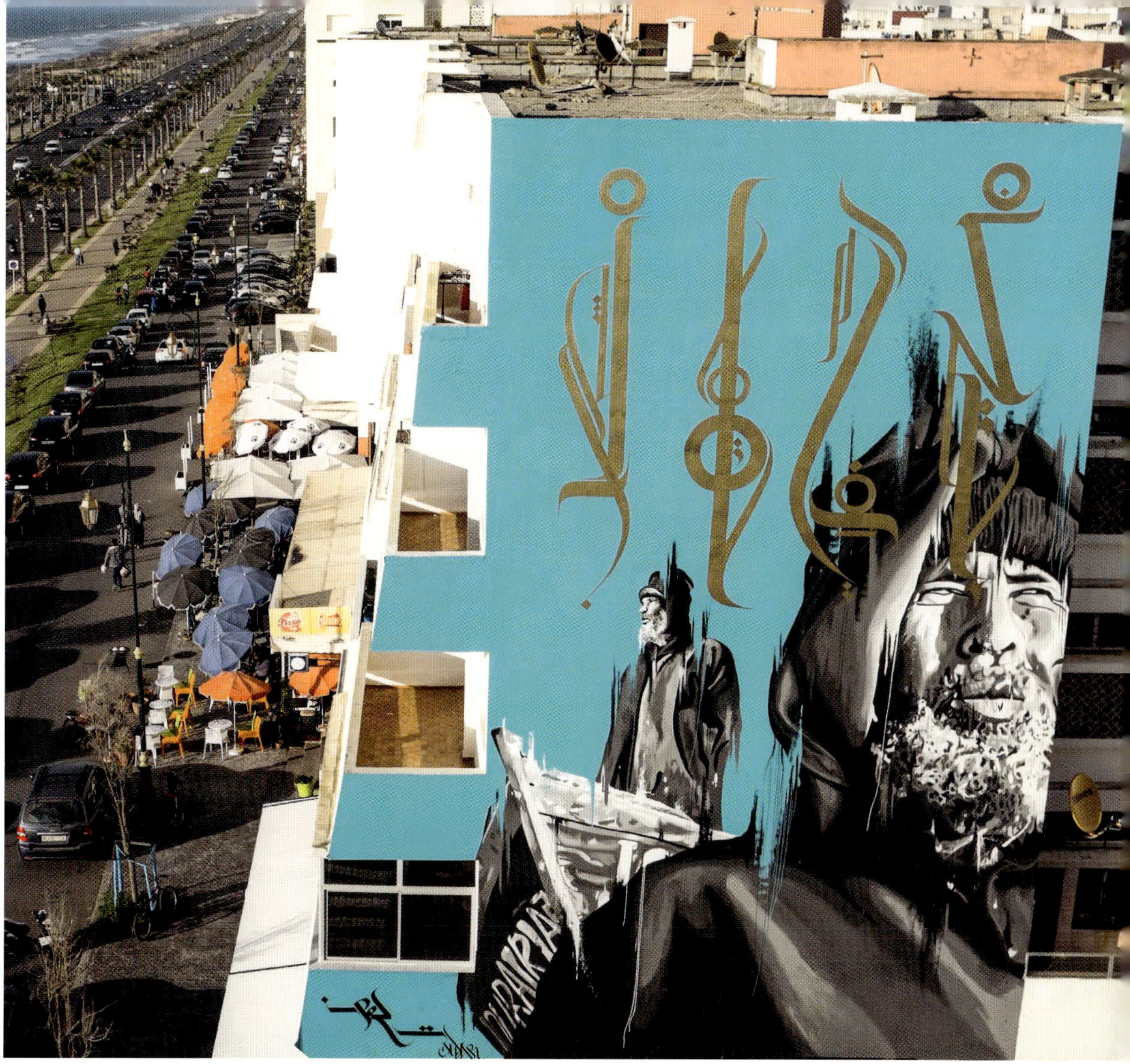

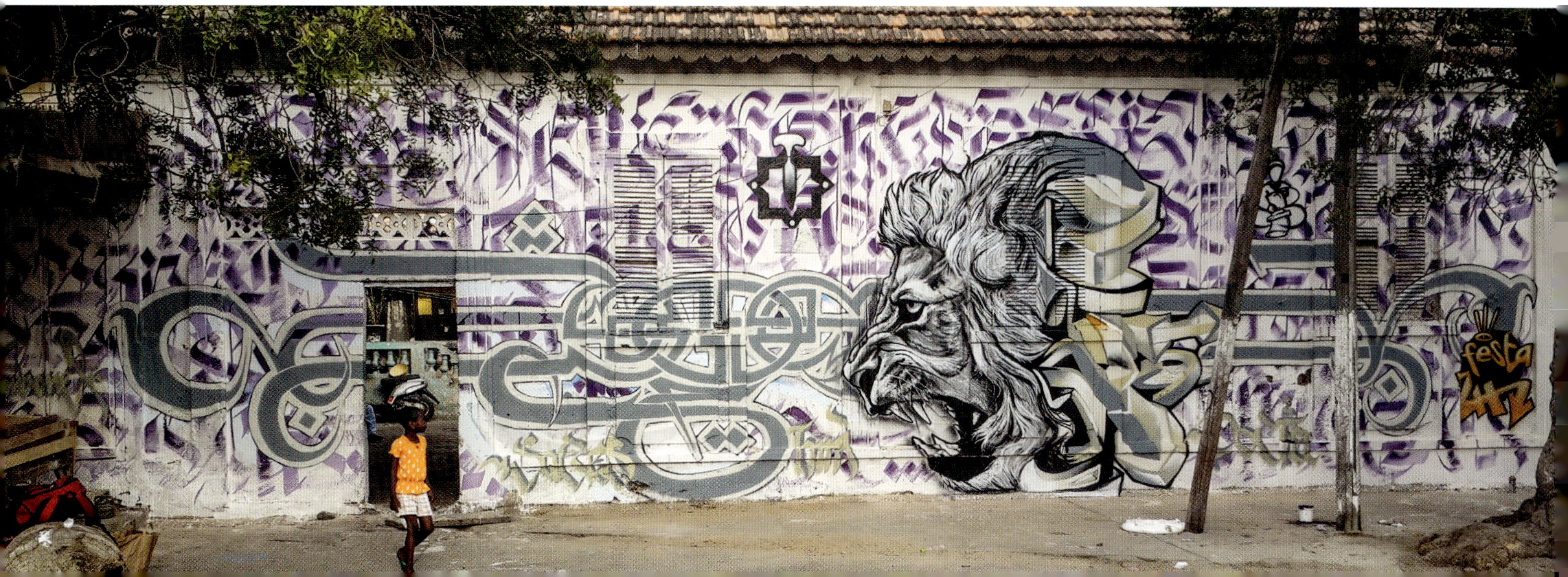

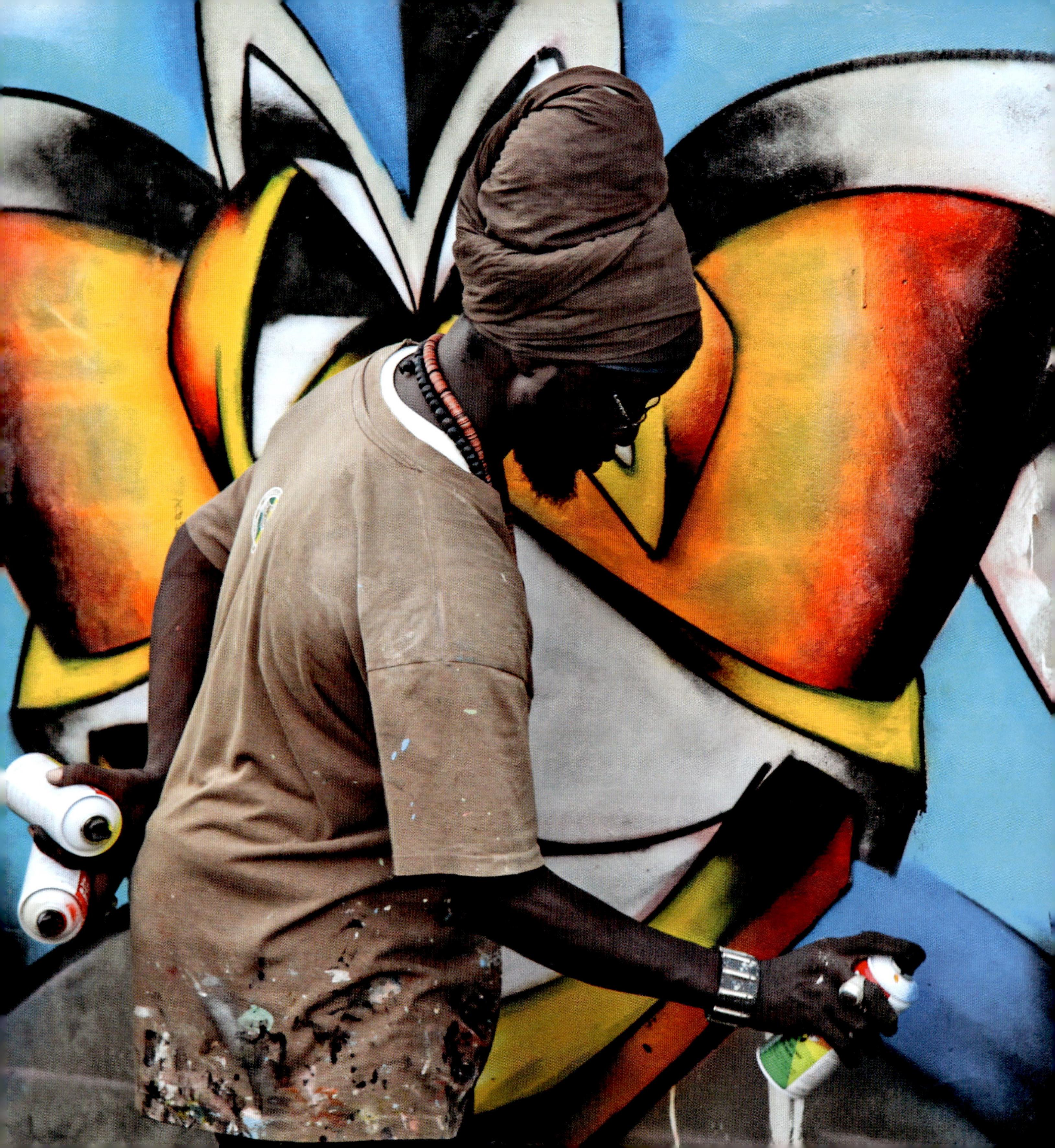

WESTERN AFRICA

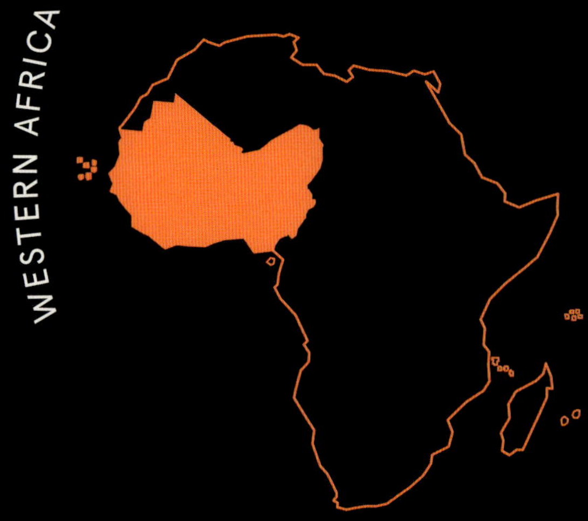

Festivals

Projects

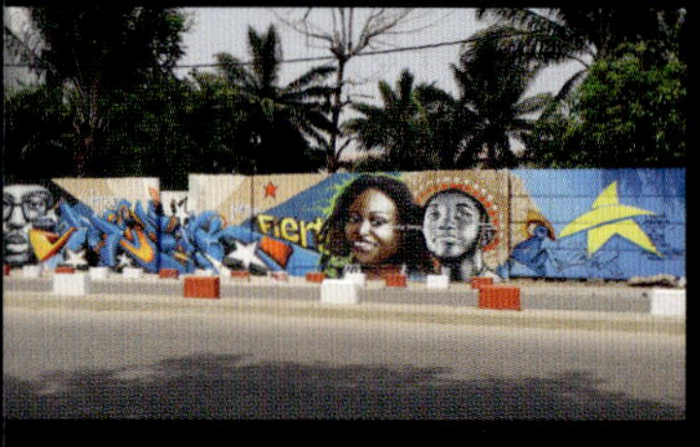

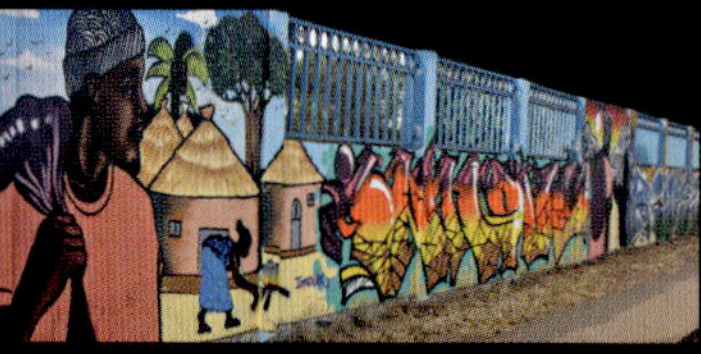

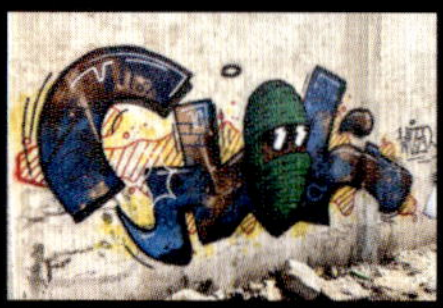

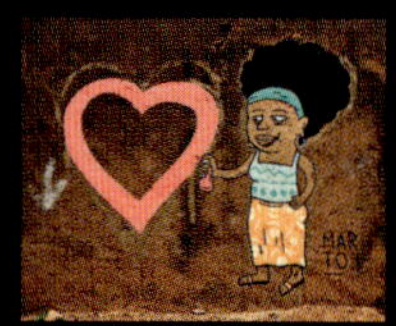

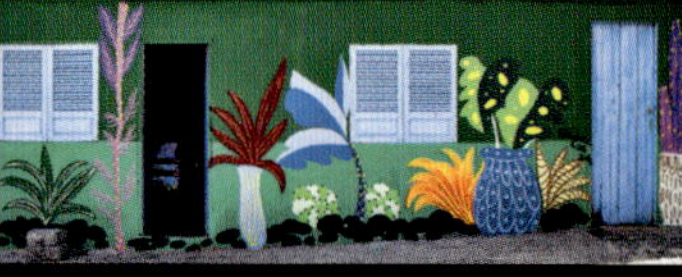

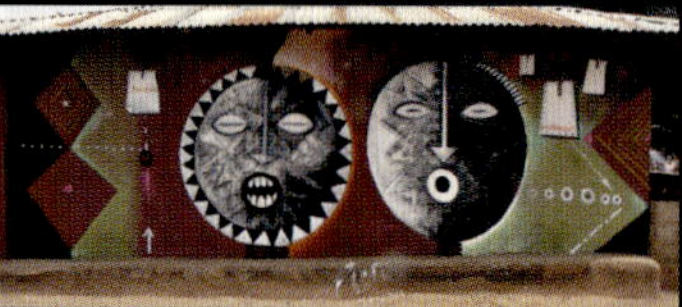

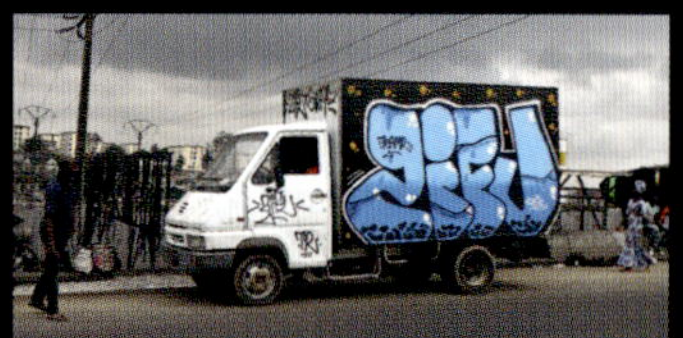

Page 168
Docta. Regraff Festival (2nd edn), Cotonou, Benin, 2013

Left, from top
Line (Switzerland), Mr Stone, Patriot, Dr Mario and others. Effet Graff (5th edn), Cotonou, Benin, 2019

Chimere. Lassiry Graffiti Festival (2nd edn), Conakry, Guinea, 2019

Glok by Lazer. Nouadhibou, Mauritania, 2014

El Marto. 'Tantie Love', Ouagadougou, Burkina Faso, 2018

Gildoca. Kriol Urban Fest (1st edn), Porto Novo, Santo Antão, Cabo Verde, 2018

Njogu Touray. 'Jamma Gain and Munair Gain' (Peace and Patience), Wide Open Walls, Galoya village, The Gambia, 2014

Zifu. Abidjan, Côte d'Ivoire, 2017

Opposite, from top
Marco Conti Sikic (Italy). 'Wings for All', Bamako, Mali, 2015

Nicholas Wayo, Tetebotan Kali. Akropong, Ghana, 2019

Ernest Ibe. 'Flower Girl', Abuja, Nigeria, 2019

Deris, Docta. 'The Wall', Logone Graffiti Festival, Lomé, Togo, 2013

Sangue, Mbautta, Evok1 (France). Festigraff (8th edn), Dakar, Senegal, 2017

Tetebotan Kali. King Dus Arts Festival, Freetown, Sierra Leone, 2018

CABO
VERDE
Praia
THE GAMBIA
GUINEA-BISSAU
Bissau
SIERRA LEONE
Freetown
LIBERIA
Monrovia
MAURITANIA
Nouakchott
SENEGAL
Thiès
Dakar
GUINEA
Conakry
CÔTE
D'IVOIRE
Yamoussoukro
Abidjan
MALI
Bamako
BURKINA
FASO
Ouagadougou
GHANA
Accra
TOGO
Lomé
BENIN
Cotonou
Porto-Novo
NIGER
Niamey
NIGERIA
Abuja
Lagos

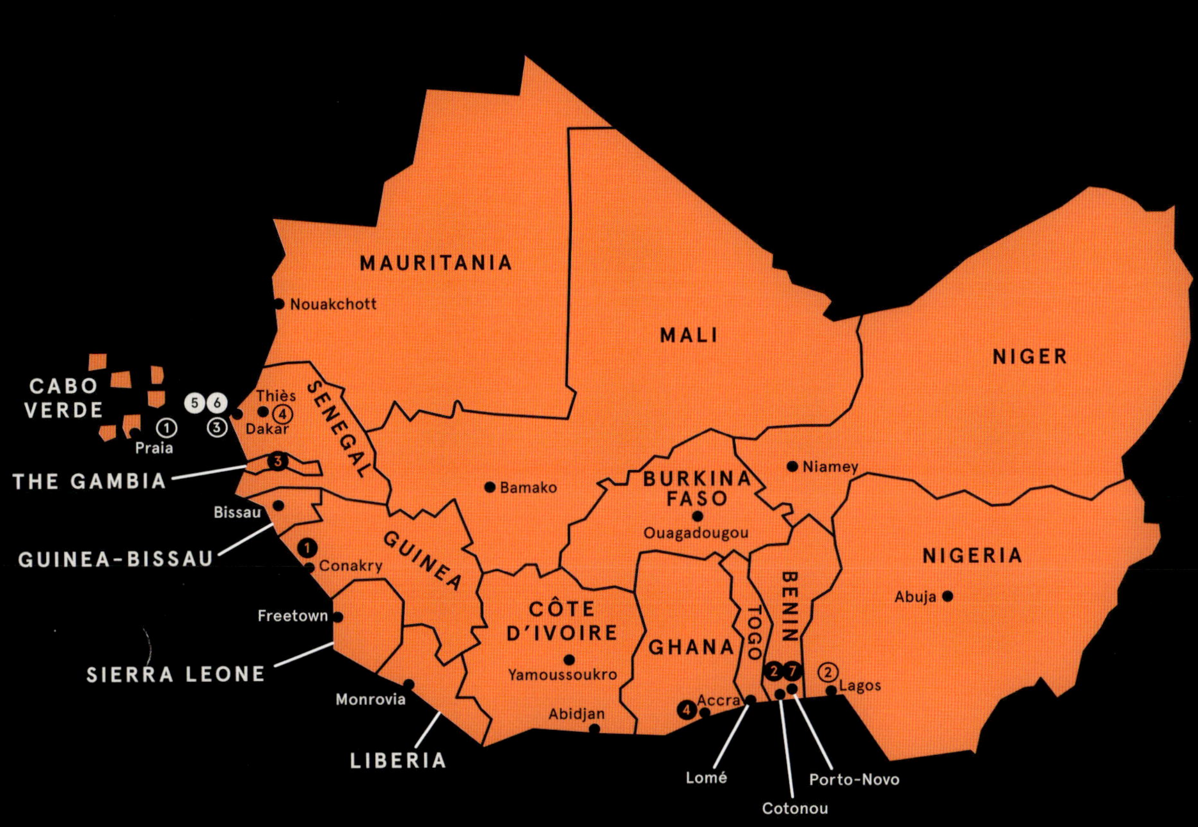

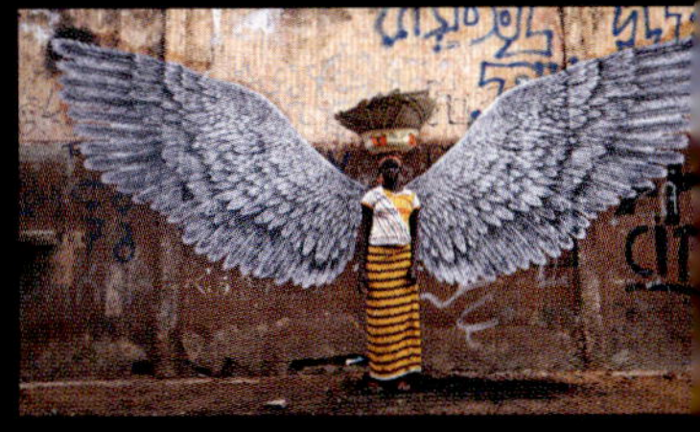

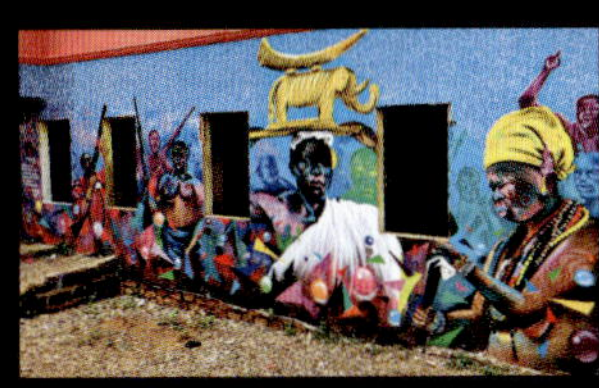

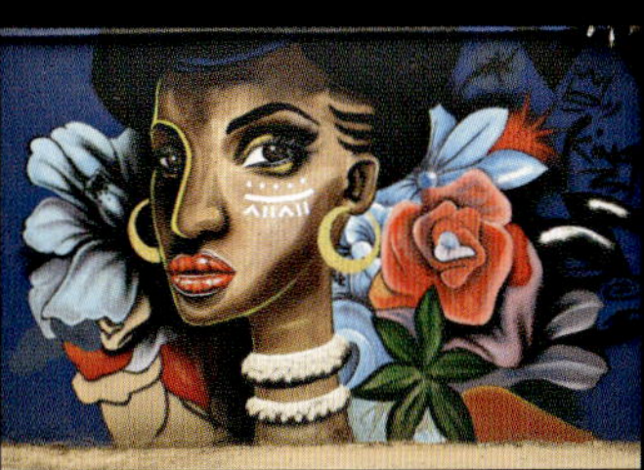

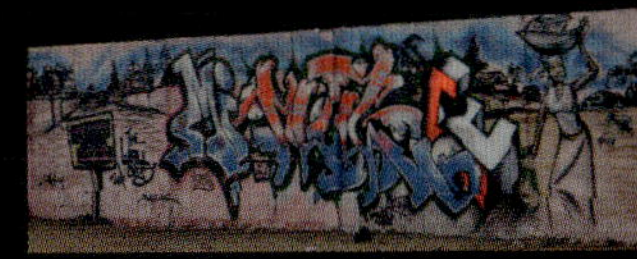

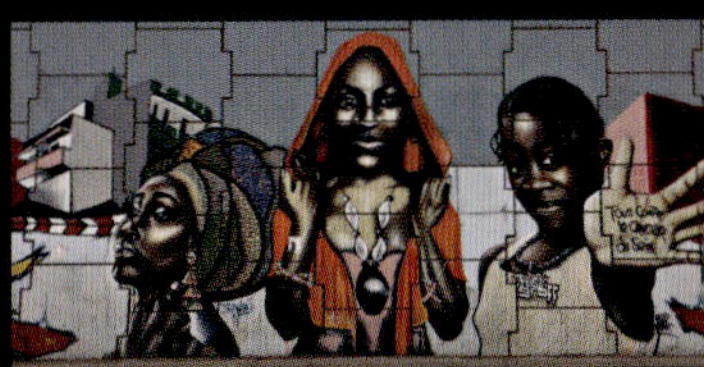

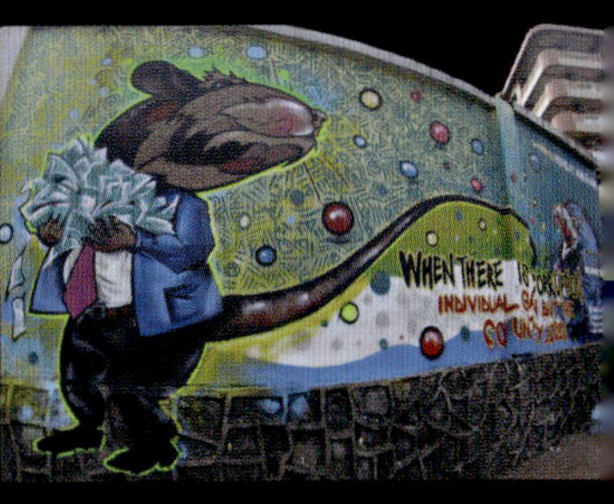

WESTERN AFRICA

With its unique ethos and multitude of artistic styles, the graffiti and street art scene in Western Africa is on an unprecedented trajectory. Western African states – including Senegal, Ghana and Benin – share cultural similarities and a rich history of art that dates back centuries. Although a relatively small number of practising urban artists exists in each territory, their proximity enables them to build meaningful alliances and shape their own identities. Plagued by memories of the transatlantic slave trade and later colonialism, in 1957 Ghana was first to gain independence in sub-Saharan Africa, with other countries soon following suit. A similar revolutionary spirit has infiltrated the graffiti world; walls depict newsworthy topics and issues, fostering dialogue in the public space. Touching on a range of subjects from health and education to female empowerment and black history, artists fuse key words and historical figures into their murals, which are often legible or with notations for the public to understand the context. Western African artists are also emphasizing the importance of their existence by knocking on doors of the international scene.

Several collectives are behind graffiti-based festivals that dominate the year, including Festigraff and Effet Graff (Graffiti Effect). These platforms advocate graffiti as an alternative art form and stimulate practising artists, both amateur and advanced. Through this network the movement has grown steadily, revealing some of Africa's most talented artists and crews – from Doxandem Squad and RBS Crew in Senegal to Burki Graff, Collectif 75, Ghana Graffiti Crew and others. Many have presented their work at festivals and exhibitions around the world, continually adding to and defining the look and feel of African graffiti. By introducing African motifs and iconography they are presenting an indigenous visual style. Visiting international artists, mainly from Europe, are actively involved and the shared exposure steers the African scene to new heights. In Senegal, the government does not see graffiti as a threat, and uses it to promote campaigns such as road safety in the capital, Dakar. Artists are at liberty to paint graffiti, as

Opposite
**Docta, Bandi (Switzerland).
Regraff Festival (2nd edn),
Cotonou, Benin, 2013**

Below left
**Osa Seven. 'Eko Tag',
Lagos, Nigeria, 2017**

Below right
**Mr Stone, Manoos,
Seencelor, SMI, Patriot,
Dr Mario. La Scène Festival,
Lomé, Togo, 2016**

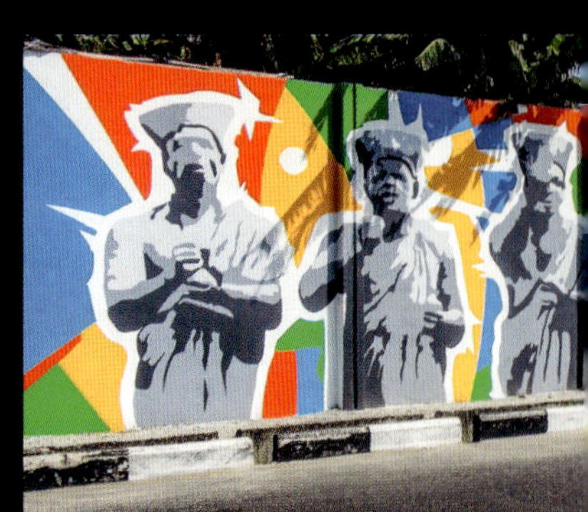

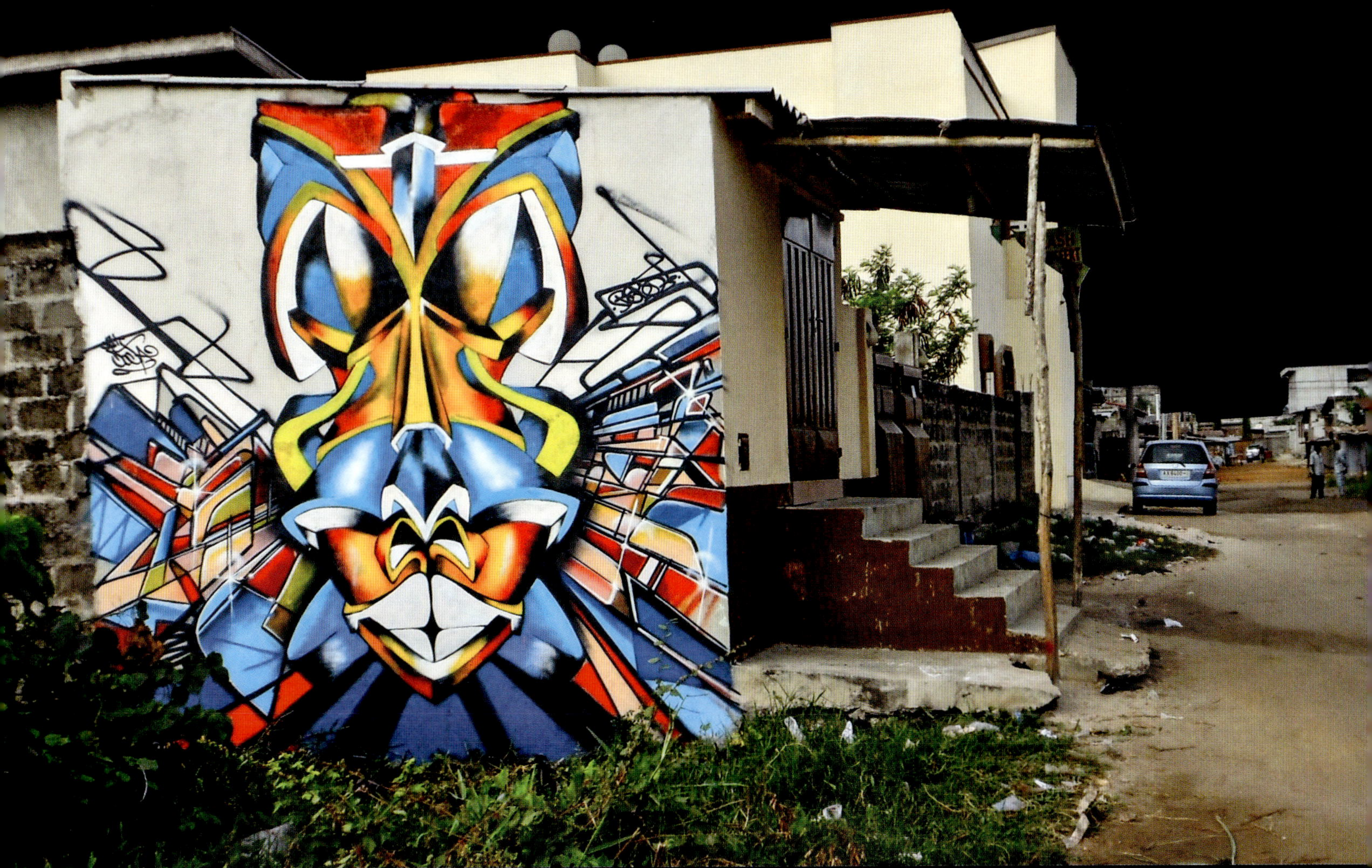

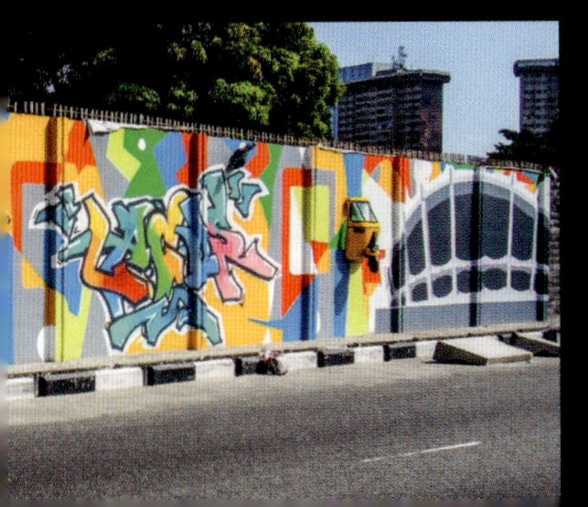
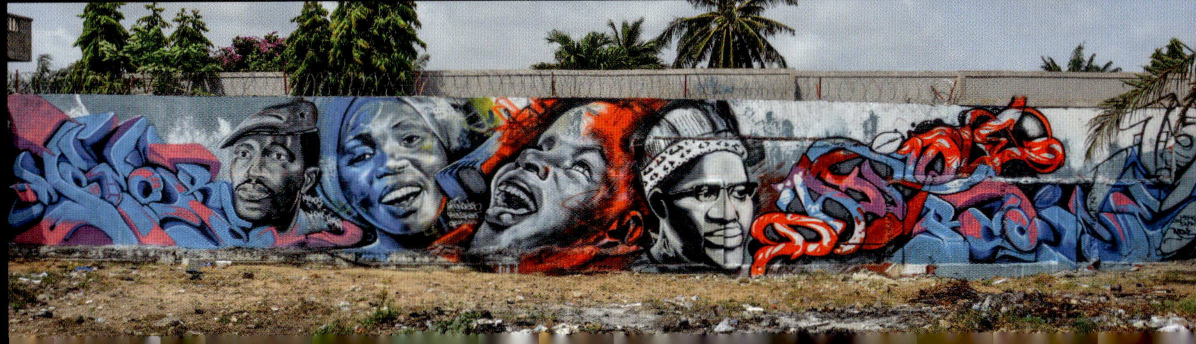

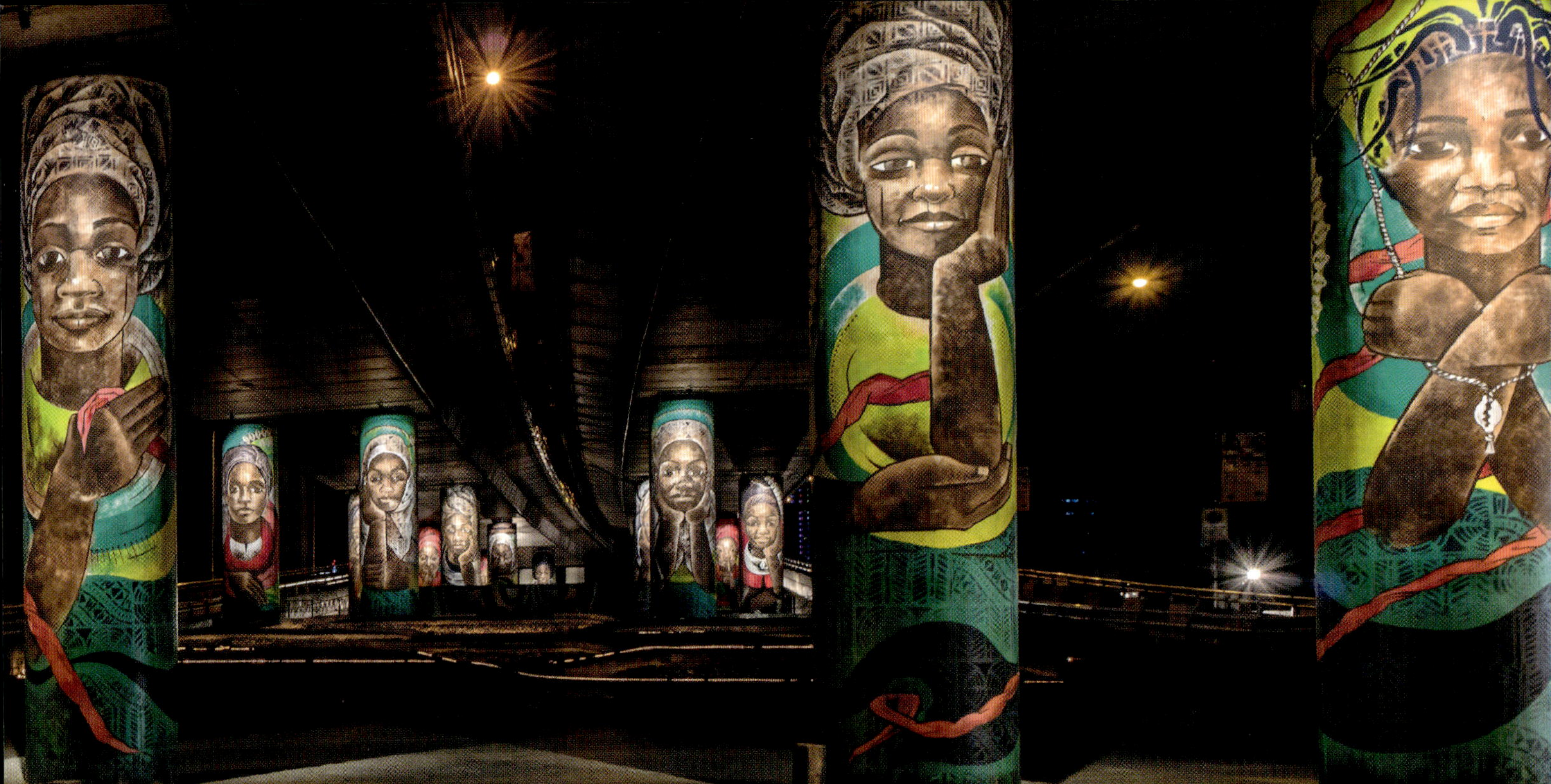

few people oppose it. Many collectives have used their entrepreneurial skills to become professional graffiti artists, turning their passion into a business model.

Known for its ancient and masterly craftsmanship, especially in mask-making and sculpture, Benin has a growing arts industry. Some of the most influential African urban artists are at work throughout the country. Various initiatives serve as a platform to reach unexplored destinations and introduce self-empowerment through art to the youth. Each with their own distinctive styles, Mr Stone, Seencelor Labombe and Dr Mario lead the movement in Benin and are familiar names within regional graffiti circles. All three collaborate with other Western African artists and represent many crews, including their own: Collectif 75. Their formal endeavour, ASSART (l'Association Sèna Street Art), now facilitates graffiti workshops and is behind the event Effet Graff. Another event etched in Beninese urban art history is Regraff, established in 2012 by fine artist Rafiy Okefolahan and graffiti artist Sitou Matt Imagination (SMI). The festival introduced the idea of travelling to multiple cities to elevate the graffiti movement in the country. Along with regional artists, Regraff hosted guests from abroad including Line, Seika One and Bandi from Switzerland, as well as the illustrious Belgian crew CNN 199. The Regraff events took place between 2012 and 2016.

Some countries in Western Africa have a minuscule presence of graffiti, although political messages are common. Guinea's graffiti is limited to events such as the Lassiry Festival, established in Conakry in 2018 under the influence of next-door

Polly Alakija. 'Oluwarantimi' (My God Do Not Forget Me), Lagos, Nigeria, 2017 restaurants, clubs, hotels and theme parks have all supported his artistic journey. International project Street Art Sans Frontières (Street Art Without Borders) has brought bands of colour to public spaces such as bridges and walkways in places like Guinea-Bissau and Niger, while in Liberia Apartial enlisted local surfers to replicate works of some of the world's most credible street artists. Famous French photographer and paste-up artist JR also completed projects in Liberia and in neighbouring Sierra Leone. Since 2015 King Dus Arts Festival in Freetown has been involved with the expansion of public art in the conflict-driven nation.

The Gambia, a small, densely populated nation with a thriving tourism industry, is renowned for Wide Open Walls, a festival forged in 2010 by UK-born globetrotter Lawrence Williams and top Gambian artist Njogu Touray – jointly known as Bushdwellers. Across the way, in the mid-Atlantic Ocean, lies an archipelago of ten islands forming the Republic of Cabo Verde (Cape Verde). Colonized by the Portuguese as a trading post in the 15th century, the islands are a mix of European and African ancestry, a heritage that influences both language and culture. Street art is emerging on the larger and more populous isles, such as Santiago Island, as young creatives and established fine artists like Tutu Sousa explore other canvases. Thanks to initiatives such as Projeto Xalabas (Xalabas Project), mural art is evolving faster than ever. Acting as an art residency, Xalabas invites international urban artists to live within the community, paint murals, host lectures and train promising local artists. The scene continues to develop swiftly with other events, such as Festival Sete Sóis Sete Luas, Kriol Urban Fest and S-Fest, also catering for expressive public murals. Young Cabo Verdean artists and muralists alike are set for a prosperous future, including Gildoca, Zurc, HJC, Yuran Henrique, Talin, Astro Boy, and the Rabelarti artists Fico and Sabino.

Burkina Faso, whose name means 'Land of Incorruptible People', is roughly located in the centre of Western Africa. An avid group of graffiti artists called Burki Graff is based in the capital, Ouagadougou, where they diligently work

Below left
Njogu Touray. Wide Open Walls, Galoya village, The Gambia, 2014

Below right
Bushdwellers. Wide Open Walls, Makumbaya village, The Gambia, *c.* 2011

Following spread
Ian Partikles, Tetebotan Kali, Moh Awudu. Chale Wote Street Art Festival (8th edn), Accra, Ghana, 2018

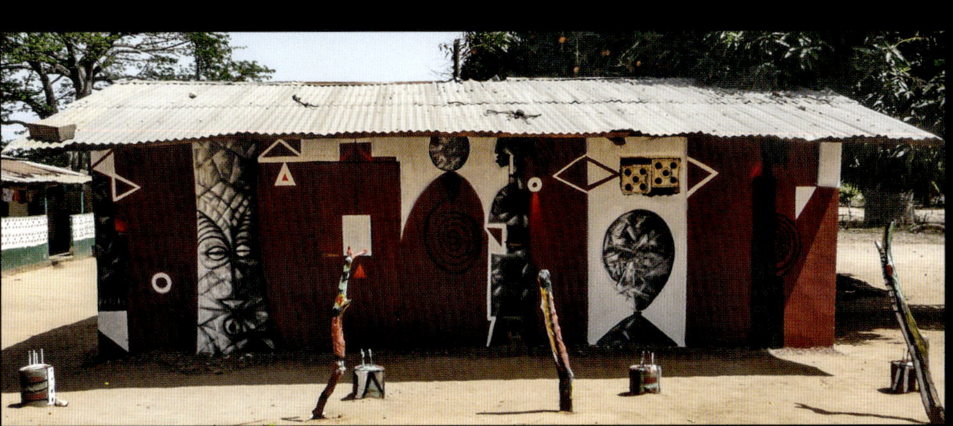

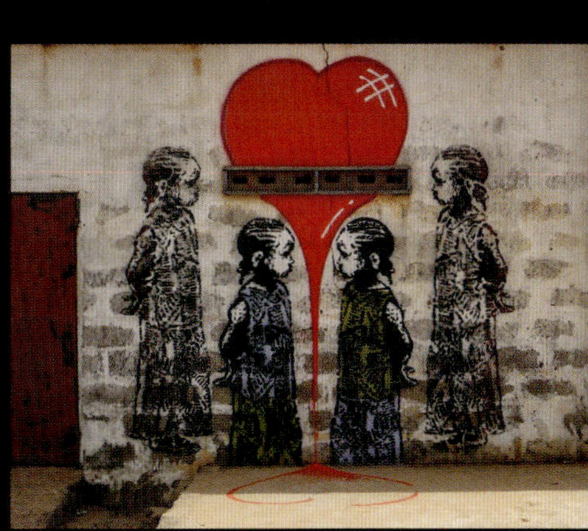

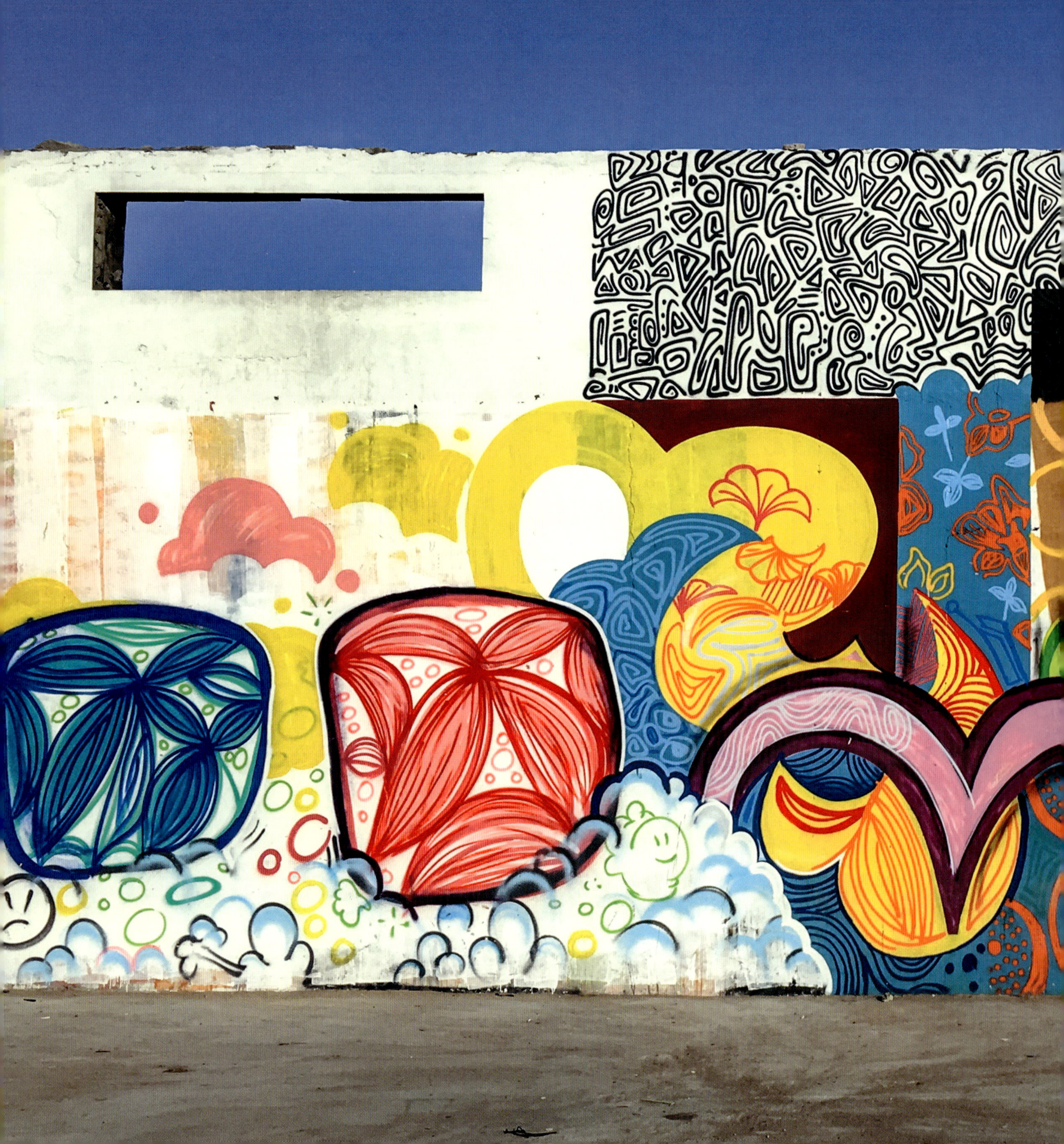

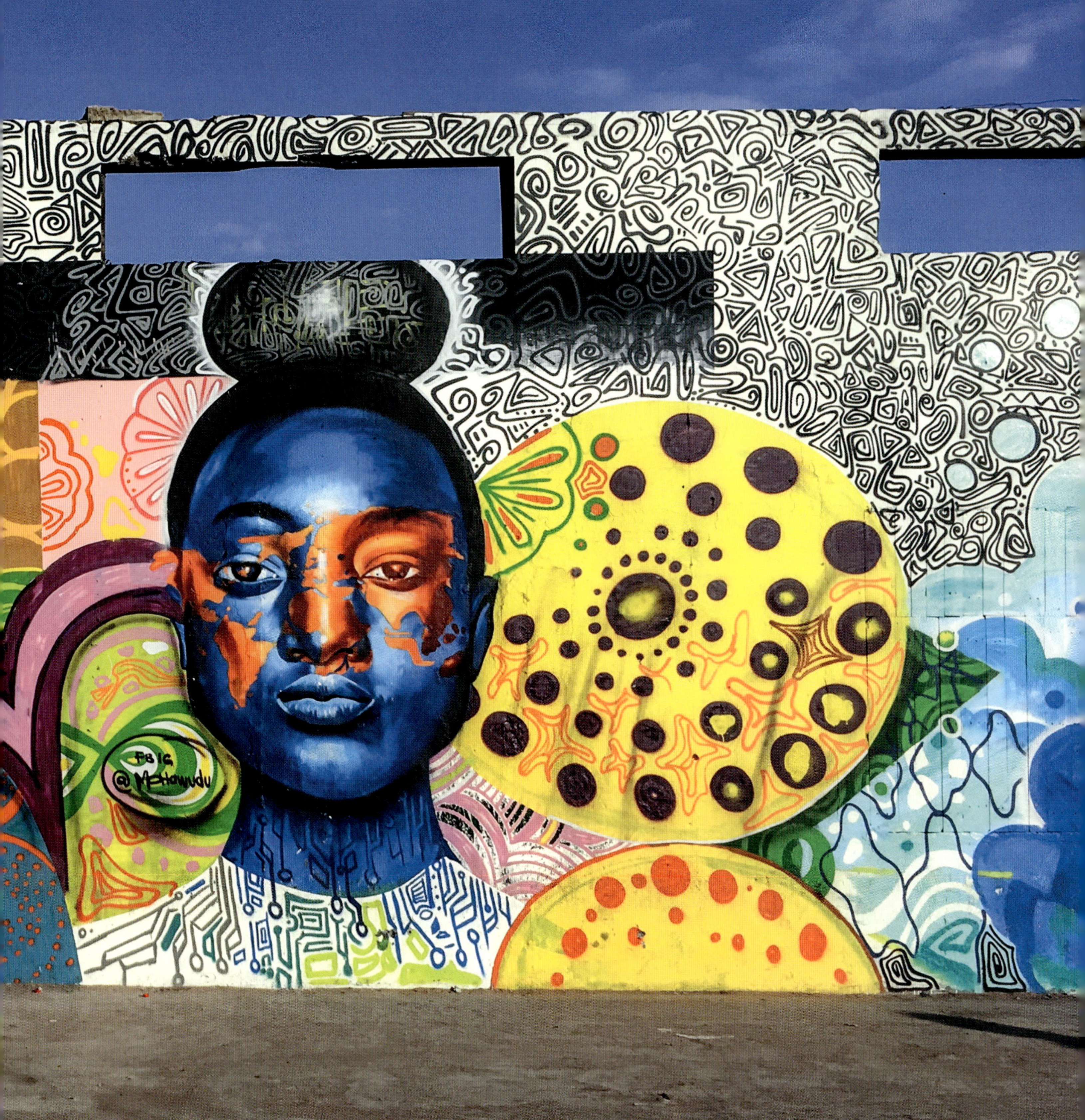
FB 16
@Mohawudu

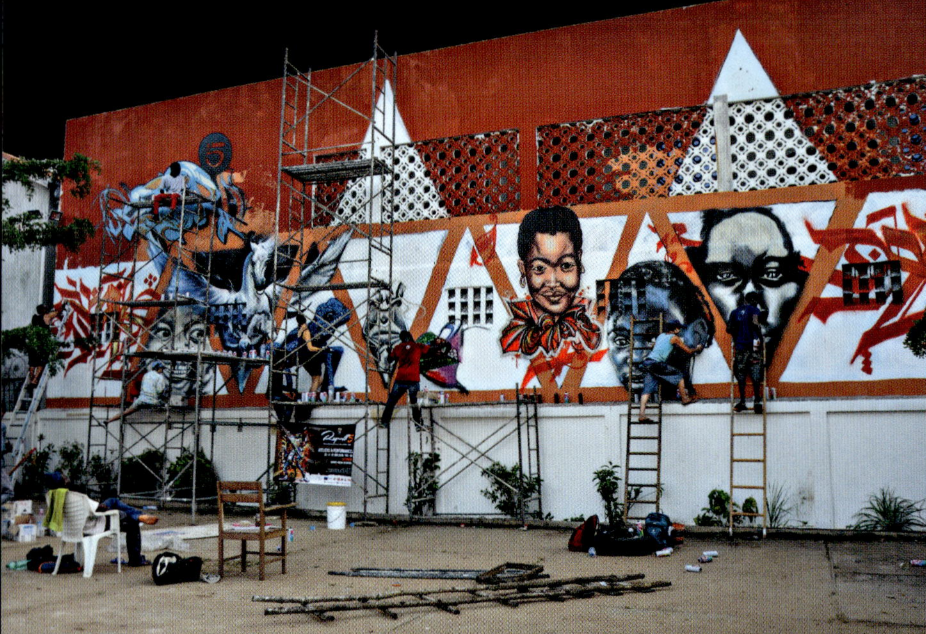

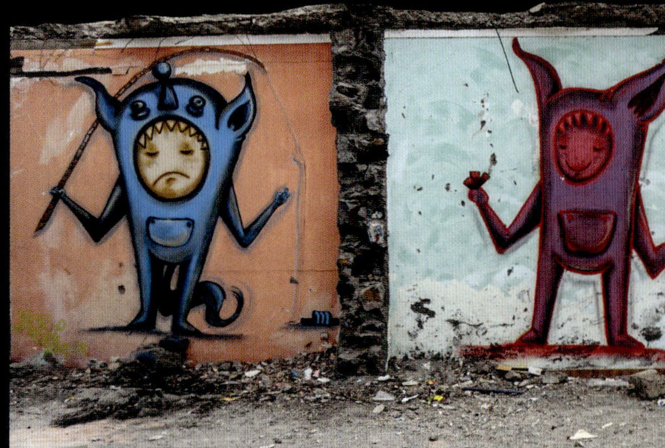

on commissioned works and the promotion of urban art. The collective
is comprised of various members including Deris, Manoos and Sié Decor.
Finding inspiration in each other as well as in revolutionary figures of recent
history, these Burkinabé artists enjoy painting photo-realistic portraits on
walls, canvases and T-shirts, sometimes with airbrush. Nearby Togo is a
formidable force in African graffiti thanks to its handful of progressive urban
artists, including Patriot, Trez, Sitou, Baby and others. These impassioned men
discovered graffiti through their love of hip-hop culture in the early 2000s
and have since managed to popularize the art form. They took inspiration from
abroad and painted their own names and characters in overlooked spaces of
their city, Lomé; locally they had only witnessed revolutionary muralists such as
Max Decampos (who later participated with them). After wrapping their heads
around such concepts as wildstyle, they began fusing African elements and
themes into their pieces. Their progression was slow owing to the high cost
of materials, but their enthusiasm was endless, as were spots to paint. In 2013
they instigated a festival called Logone, a name taken from their collective,
LGC (Logone Graffiti Crew), which later featured as a tour through the adjoining
countries of Benin and Ghana. Fast-forward a few years and budding artists
such as Sitou have cemented the foundation for generations to come.

Sitou created and coordinated graffiti festivals in other African countries
while dedicating time to his own signature look. His style evolved rapidly,
from 3D letters and mask characters to his current vibrant kaleidoscopic style.
Sitou became an exemplar for the region, inspiring new generations of graffiti
artists in Togo, Benin and the DRC, at the same time as making a name for himself
in Europe as a result of the international visitors he befriended. Now based
in Paris, France, Sitou is granted opportunities to paint much larger walls with
suitable spray paint. His latest works are an amalgamation of colours that aim to
represent cohabitation, inspired by the chameleon – a harmonious mix of colour

Above left
**Dema One (Belgium),
Dr Mario, Line (Switzerland),
Seencelor, Veneno (France),
Mr Stone, SMI, Manoos,
Seika One (Switzerland),
Patriot. Regraff Festival
(5th edn), Cotonou,
Benin, 2016**

Above right
**Astro Boy. Xalabas Project,
Praia, Santiago, Cabo
Verde, 2019**

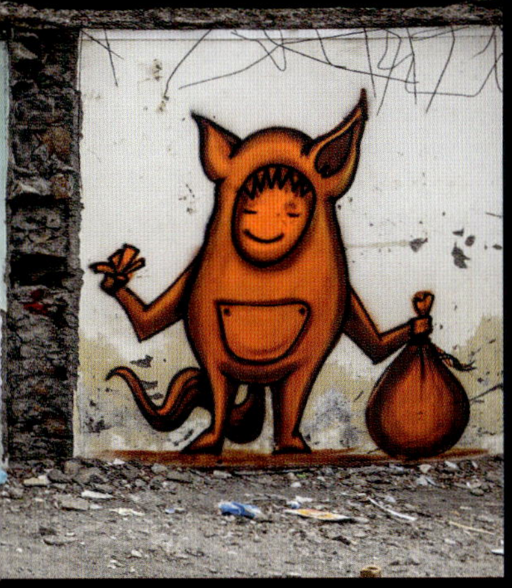

and possibilities, for a perfect unity. Back in Togo, Patriot continues on the roster of local events in the region with his comical characters and realist portraits, while Trez has opened his own festival, Graff Education, to the world. This event aims to emancipate the youth through graffiti.

Ghana presents an entrancing wave of urban expressionism through various festivals full of African dynamism. From 2011, Chale Wote Street Art Festival, one of the key events, has attracted large crowds for its ebullient showcasing of street dance, street theatre, fashion, poetry, photography, film, body painting, music and graffiti. Revellers in outlandish dress fill the streets of the Jamestown neighbourhood in Old Accra for the high-octane carnival. The event snowballs each year, gathering momentum as a world-leading arts festival. Many of the active graffiti artists in Accra, the capital, come from a fine arts background, with Chale Wote acting as a catalyst. During the festivities local and foreign artists show their best works while promoting themselves and the street art movement.

Ghanaian artists such as Mohammed Awudu (affectionately known as Moh) are being recognized overseas. Recently he was invited to Brazil for the International Graffiti Biennial and to France for Festival Ourcq Living Colors. A trained artist, he almost gave up his craft because of peer pressure, but persevered to become a full-time art virtuoso and an indispensable representative for African graffiti. Having grown up in Nima, an impoverished district in Accra, Moh Awudu dreamed of changing the conceptions about the area with striking murals, a goal that he accomplished by dotting artworks around his neighbourhood, including many collaborations with renowned international guests. As the founder of Ghana Graffiti, Moh, with his crew, showcases the power of wall murals to the public. Fellow crew mates, including Hamid Nii Nortey Noi, Tetebotan Kali, Ian Partikles and Jah Power, take on large commissions and government-funded projects, setting the bar high for future generations to follow. Their positive impact has put Ghana on the map for African graffiti. Tetebotan Kali is a multidisciplinary

Below left
Drissa Konaté, with Issa Konaté. 'Donko' (Knowledge), Bamako, Mali, 2012

Below right
Drissa Konaté, with Issa Konaté. 'Africando', Bamako, Mali, 2018

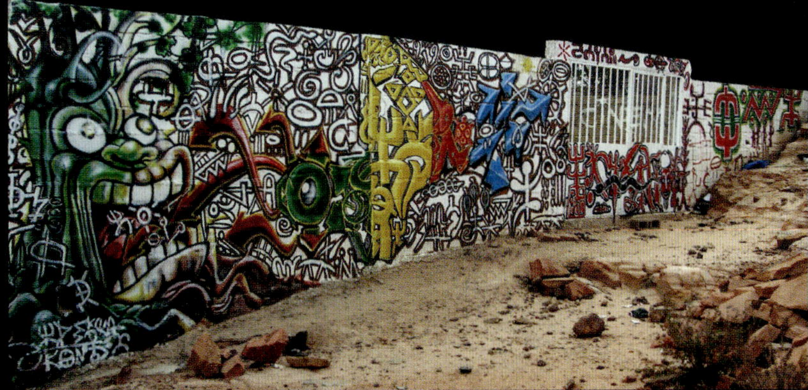

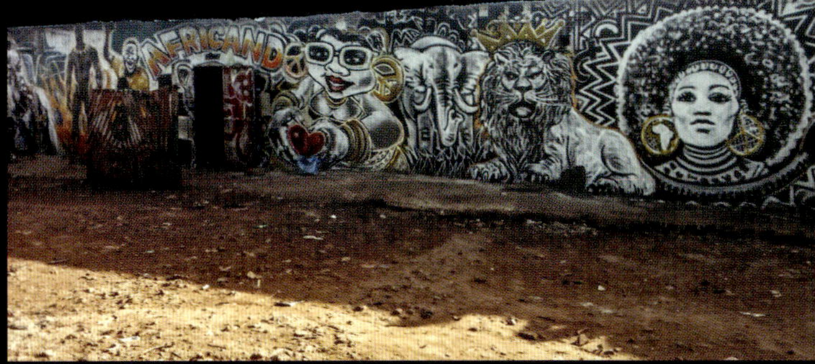

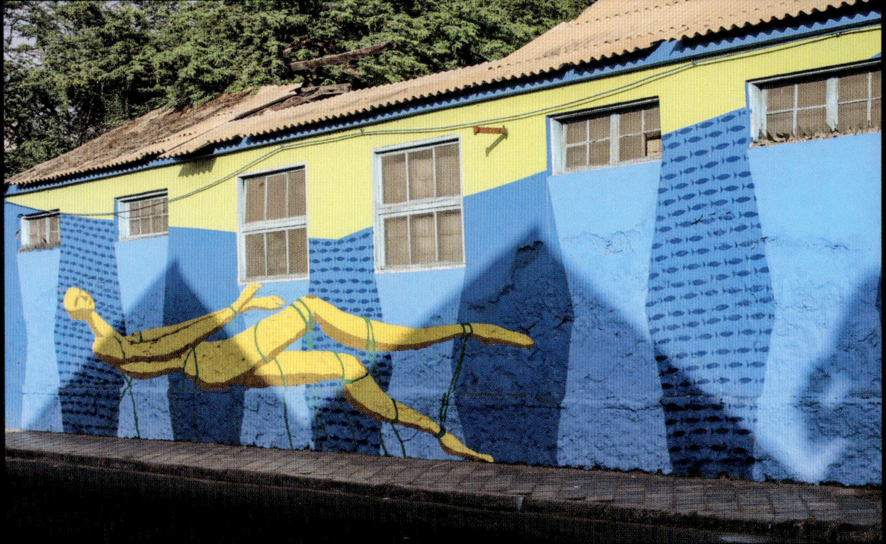

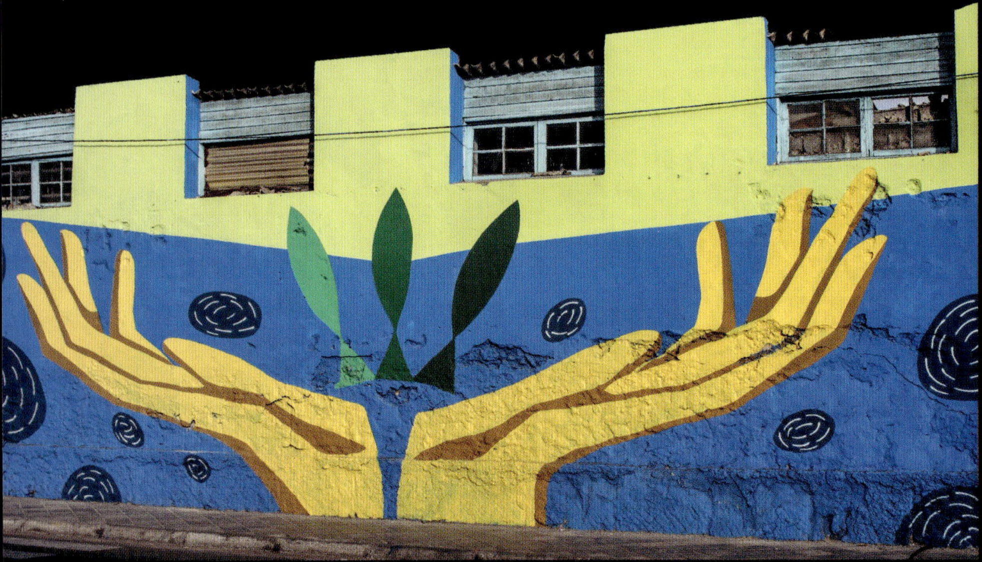

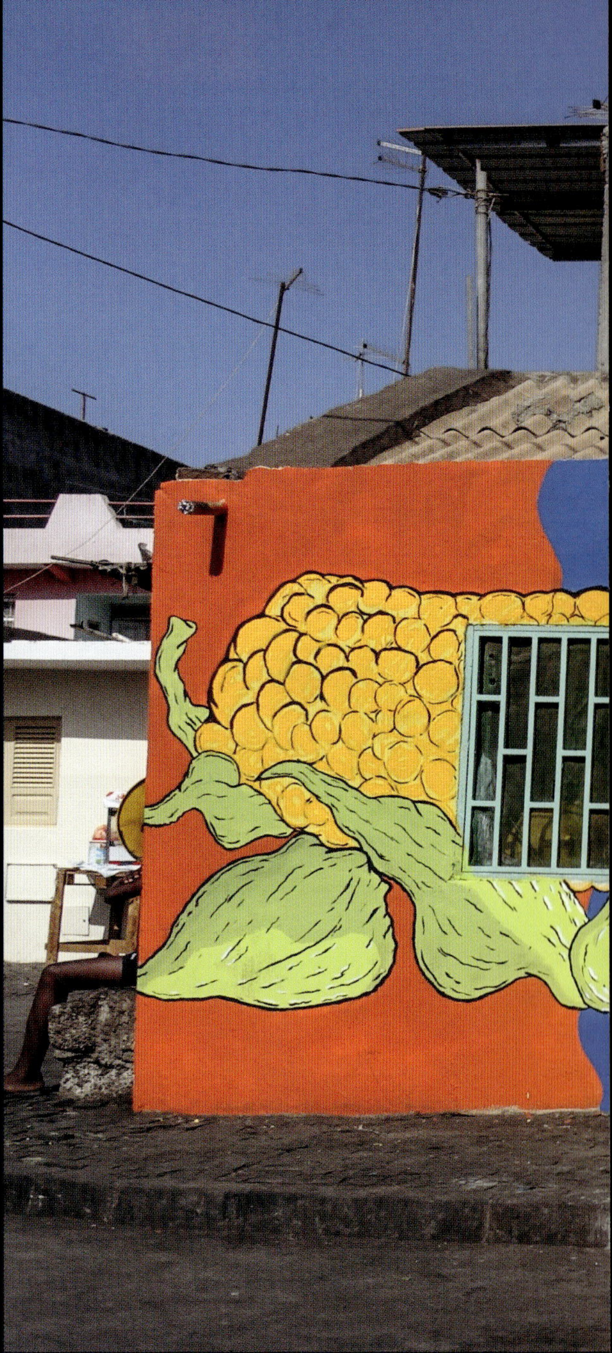

Top
Gildoca. Mindelo, São
Vicente, Cabo Verde, 2018

Above
Gildoca. Mindelo, São
Vicente, Cabo Verde, 2018

Right
Yuran Henrique. Xalabas
Project, Praia, Santiago,
Cabo Verde, 2019

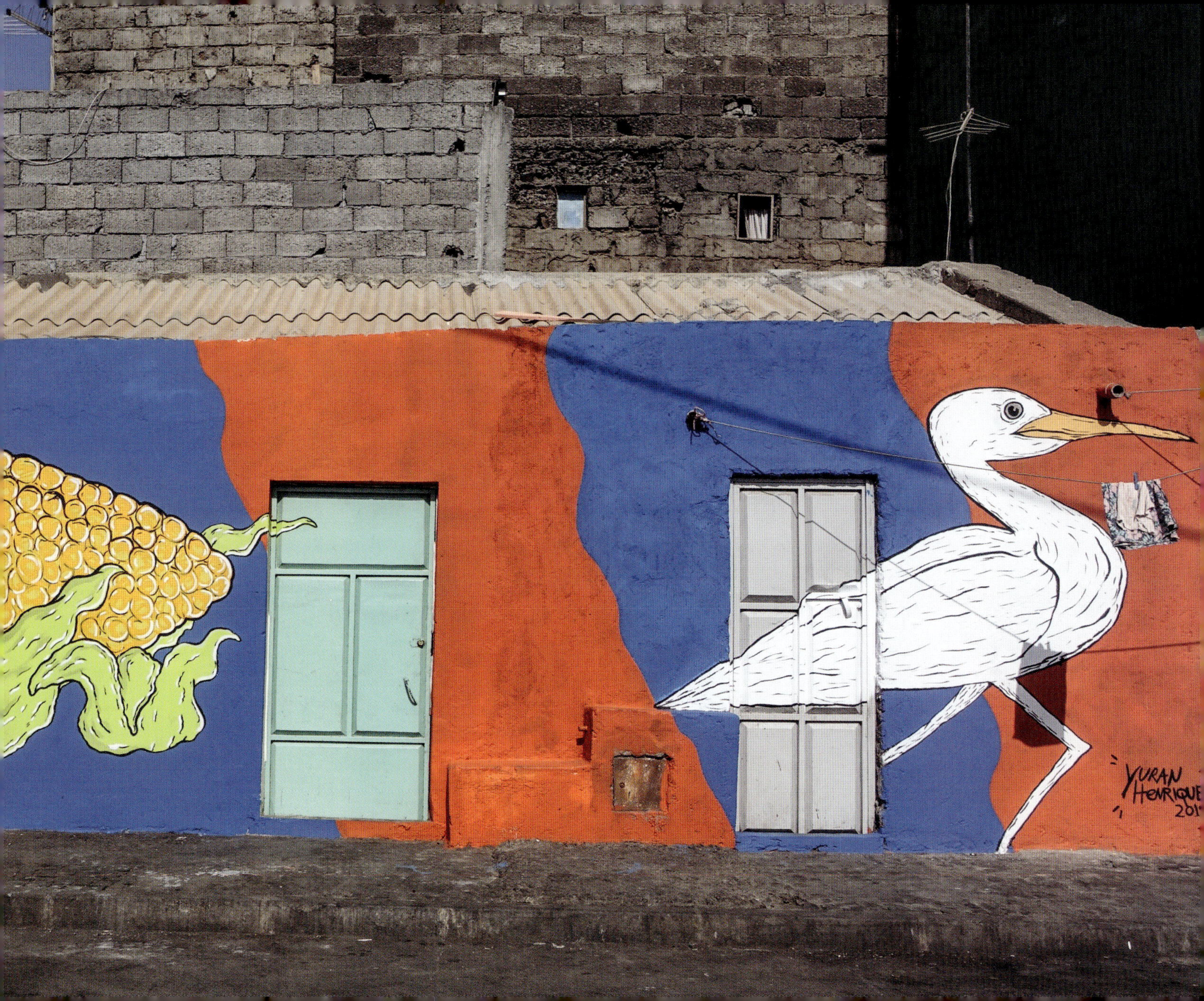
Yuran
Henrique
2019

African graffiti artists have signed up to bring something new that adapts and integrates easily into their community. We paint our realities, our experiences, our history. Even if we do it for ourselves, we do it much more for others. Graffiti is the most noble art form I know. The sensation it provides is what makes me live.' MR STONE

artist with a street style that includes maze-like patterns that give his work an African stamp. Hamid Nortey has a heterogeneous oeuvre, while the likes of Deff Art, Saddiq, Scarecrow, Scrapa 2020 and Wil Quartz are entering the scene. Other visual artists including Nicholas Wayo, Muhasim Hamzagiwah and Rufai Zakari are bridging the worlds of contemporary street and fine art.

Nigeria, with its constant hustle and bustle, has the biggest population in Africa with a thriving economy and film industry to boot. So-called Nollywood is one of the largest producers of movies in the world, a sign of a soaring creative industry. Arts and crafts are abundant, but graffiti and street art is still a new sphere. In a project to rehabilitate the public space under the Falomo bridge in Lagos, Polly Alakija painted forty pillars with inspirational portraits of girls for the 'Lagos at 50' celebrations, while Osa Seven, a local creative with an interest in street art, was also commissioned for the same city-sanctioned public art project, resulting in his 'Eko Tag' mural. There is an ever increasing awareness of public art, but proper channels to obtain permission are hard to navigate and authorities like to oversee the content. Other artists from various genres such as graphic design, fine art, sign writing and customization are beginning to break out into the graffiti scene. Ernest Ibe, Shaygo (Jesse Josh), Oghenedoro Styles, Fada, Gahbrivah, Olatunde Alara and Amina (P.U.T. Studio) are among them.

In Côte d'Ivoire (Ivory Coast), Koungolo (or Koun) has been tagging since 2013, later joining the crew Team R (Team Royale) with Zifu and Tsé. Zifu grew up in Côte d'Ivoire but went abroad to study because of the civil war and picked up graffiti as a hobby. On his return he began to plaster his name on walls with basic paints, importing proper cans whenever possible. A common sight within Abidjan city limits are the delivery trucks painted with graffiti. These trucks are imported from mainland France because they are cheaper to buy, and are often covered with pre-existing tags and throw-ups. Team R use this to their advantage, giving the vehicles a makeover by respraying the side panels with their own work. Traditional painters Zoro Zipa and Dévé Epik have now descended on the small Ivorian graffiti scene. Zipa utilizes motivational words such as 'fo bara' (it is necessary to work), while Dévé formulates the saying 'fo pa te tcha' (don't depigment your skin) to address the cultural crisis of skin-bleaching.

Opposite, clockwise from top left

Zoro Zipa, Dévé Epik. Abidjan, Côte d'Ivoire, 2018

Team R: Koun, Tsé, Zifu. Abidjan, Côte d'Ivoire, 2018

Zifu, Koun, Overe (France). Abidjan, Côte d'Ivoire, 2018

Trez, Mr Stone. 2 Jours 2 Graff, Lomé, Togo, 2018

Team R: Zifu, Koun, Tsé. Abidjan, Côte d'Ivoire, 2018

Koun. Abidjan, Côte d'Ivoire, 2018

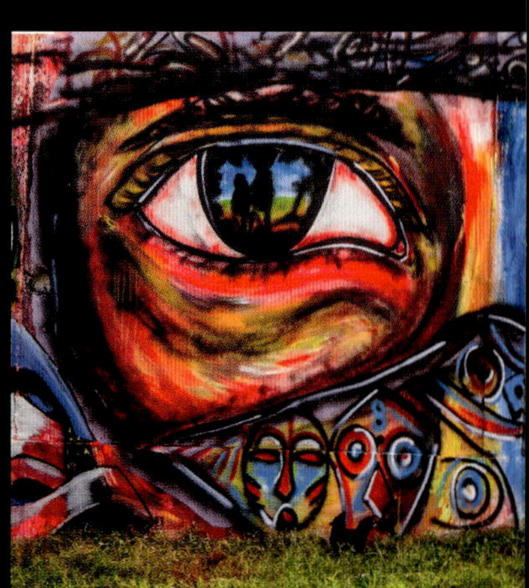

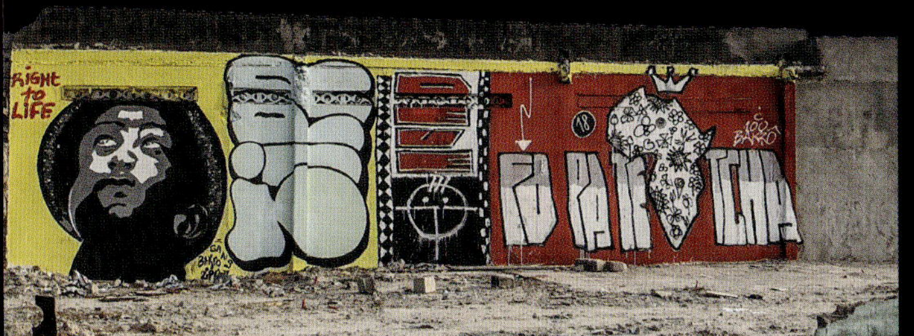
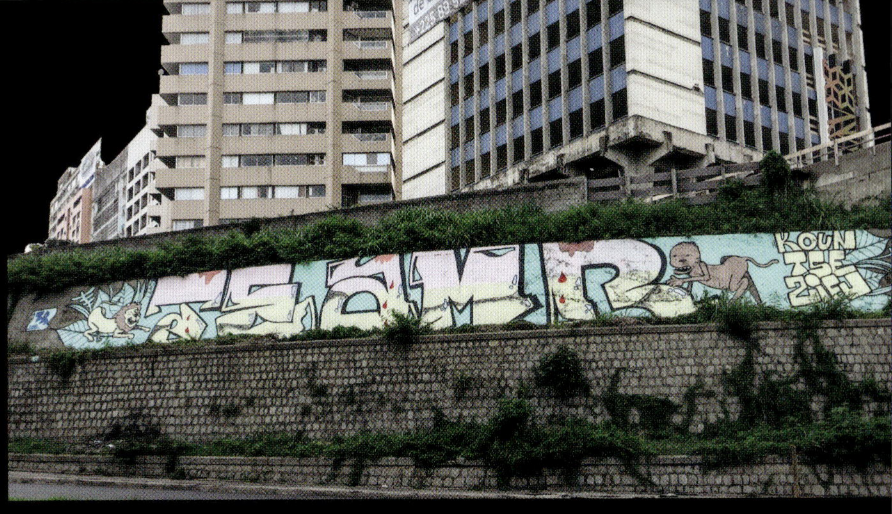
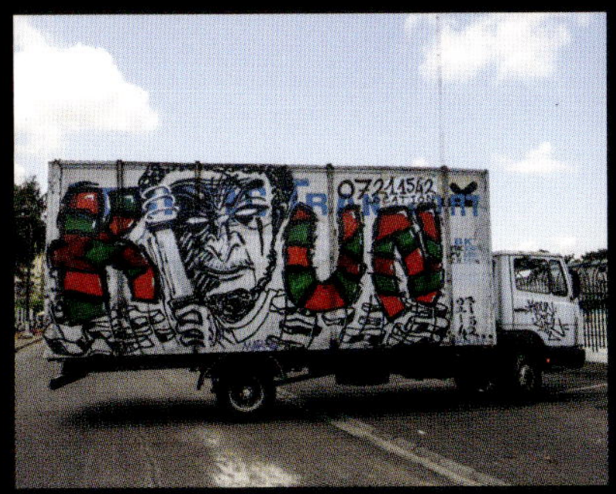
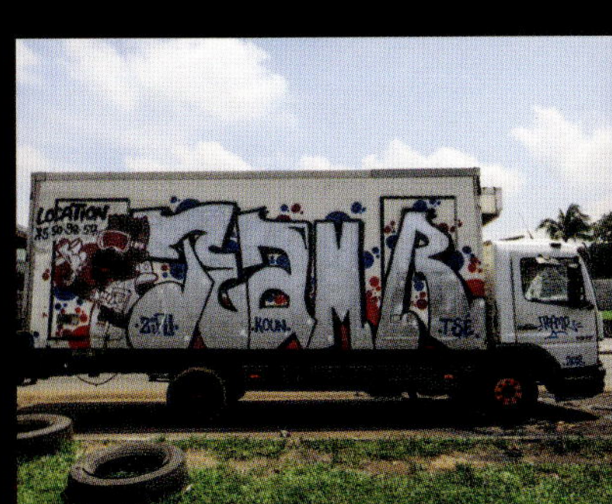
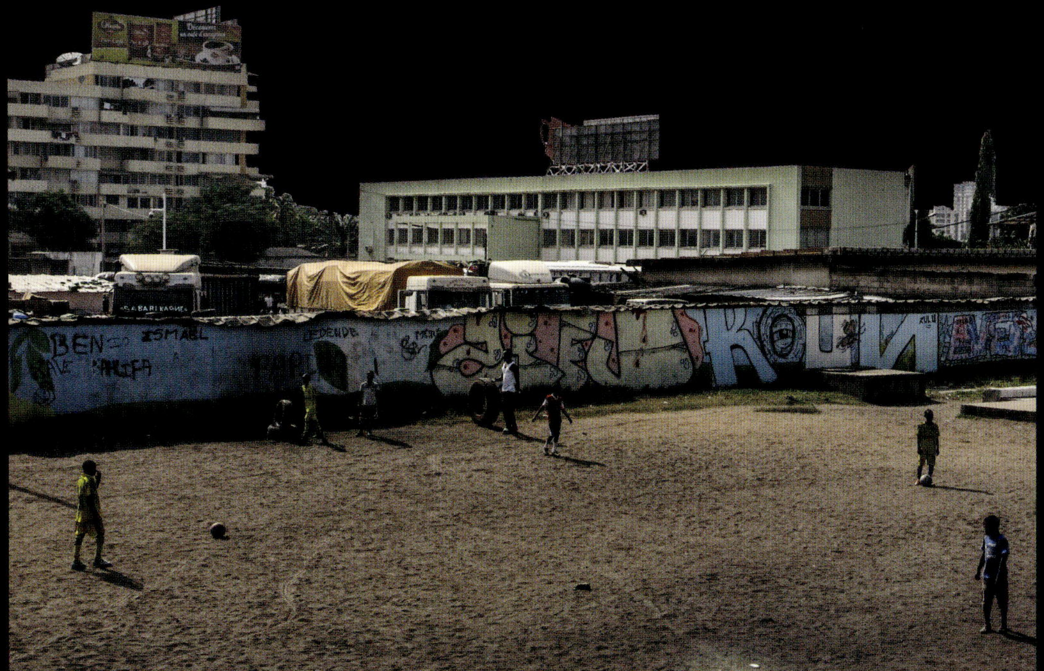
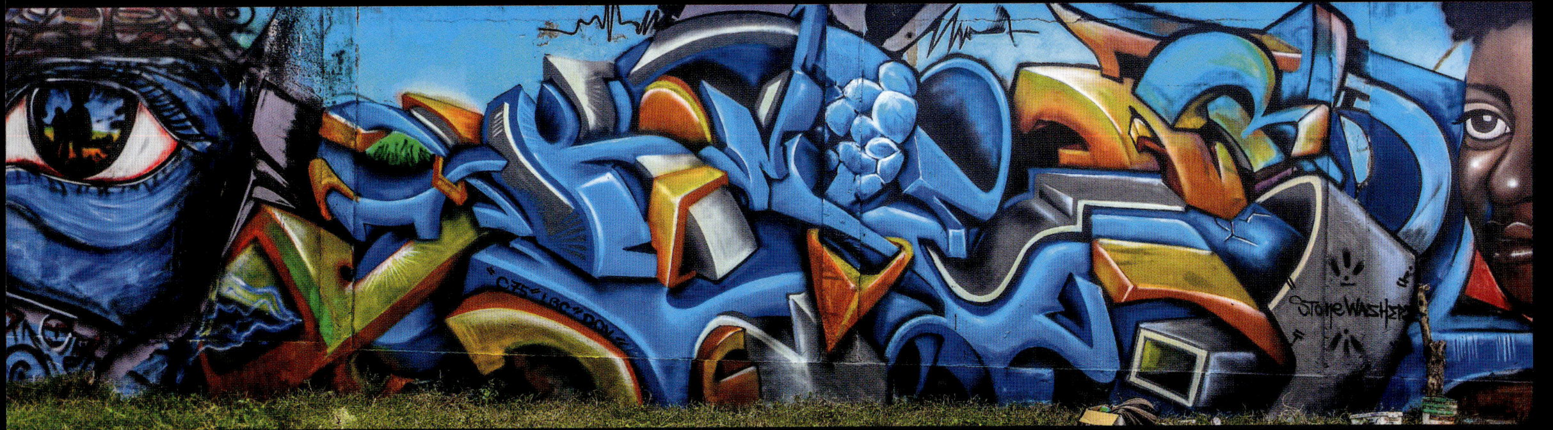

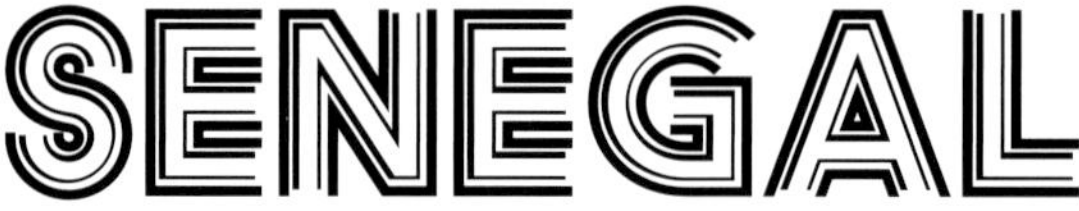

SENEGAL

IN FOCUS

With its highly motivated assemblage of artists, rich history and distinctive approach, Senegal has become a powerhouse boasting the largest concentration of active graffiti writers in Western Africa. Art, fashion and music have a lively presence, especially in Dakar, with the biennale taking place since 1990, and museums and institutions oriented around African artefacts and heritage. The graffiti scene plays a key role at all levels of society, allowing for values and belief systems while also being a catalyst in its own right.

The late 1980s saw the rise of a formidable movement led by the youth of the country during a time of political adjustments. The movement, known as Set Setal ('to make clean'), was born out of necessity following the state's failure to provide basic services, resulting in an overwhelming amount of visible filth, affecting the people's physical and mental well-being. Dakar was becoming a cesspool and the only way to overcome the situation was to actively clean the city oneself. With brooms and brushes in hand, residents began to rehabilitate their environment, picking up garbage, organizing rubbish collections, restoring communal gardens and painting walls. The murals were talking points addressing various issues that had contributed to the decline. Often emblazoned with the movement's title, these exemplary artworks with their optimistic iconography generated further awareness of Set Setal. Religious figures were sometimes incorporated to discourage people from leaving rubbish nearby, and artists such as Papisto Boy became well established. The overall collective endeavour set a pulsating example of a virtuous value system, in which numerous inhabitants participated. The campaign was working and the government acknowledged it. Health, safety and social conditions were improved, as well as the school system. The scheme remained embedded in the moral compass of future generations of Dakarois.

The murals relating to the Set Setal movement became widespread and served as visual reminders of a successful intervention for years to come.

Opposite, top
FéTicHe. Dakar, Senegal, 2015

Opposite, bottom
Diablos. Dakar, Senegal, 2018

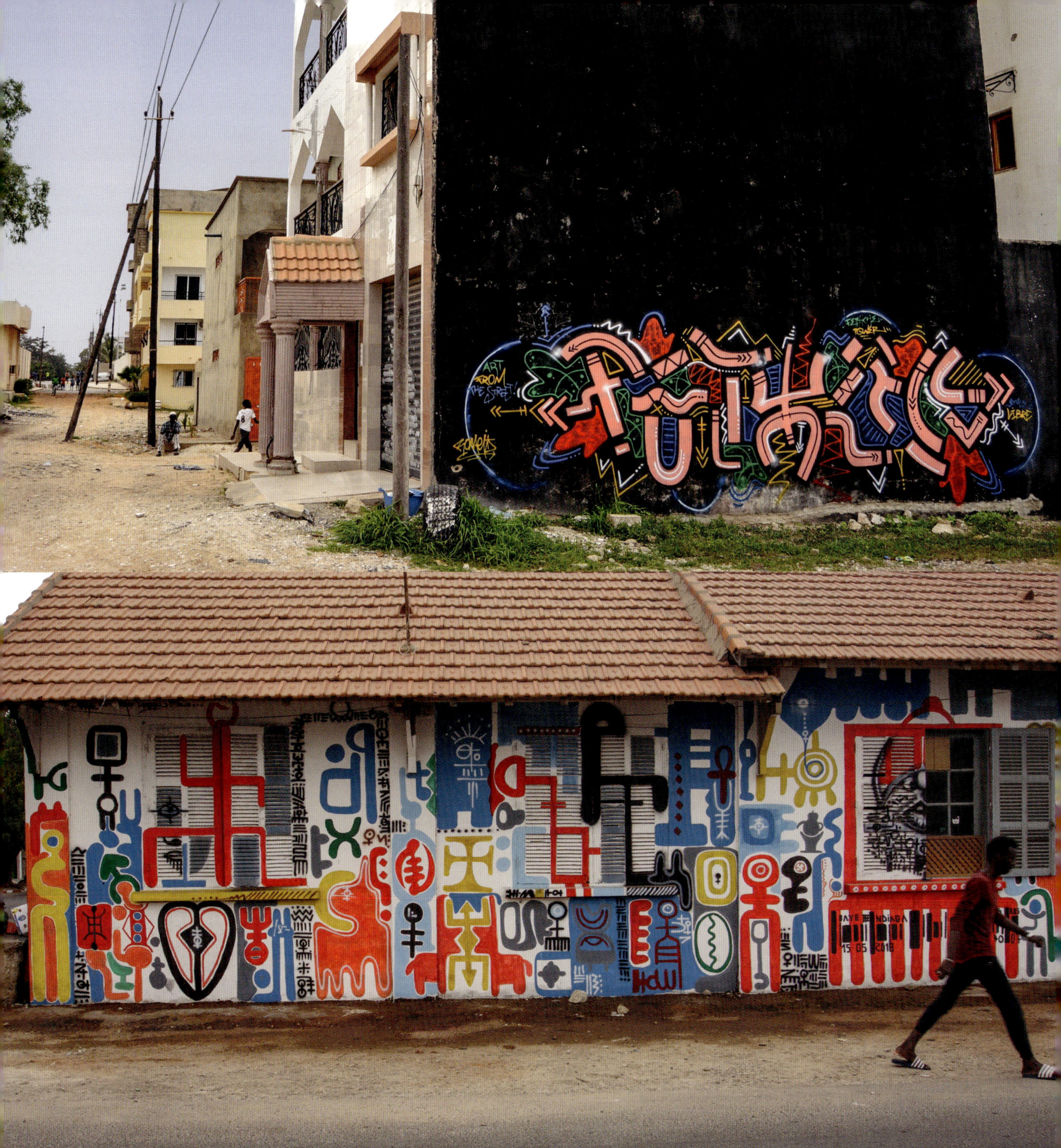

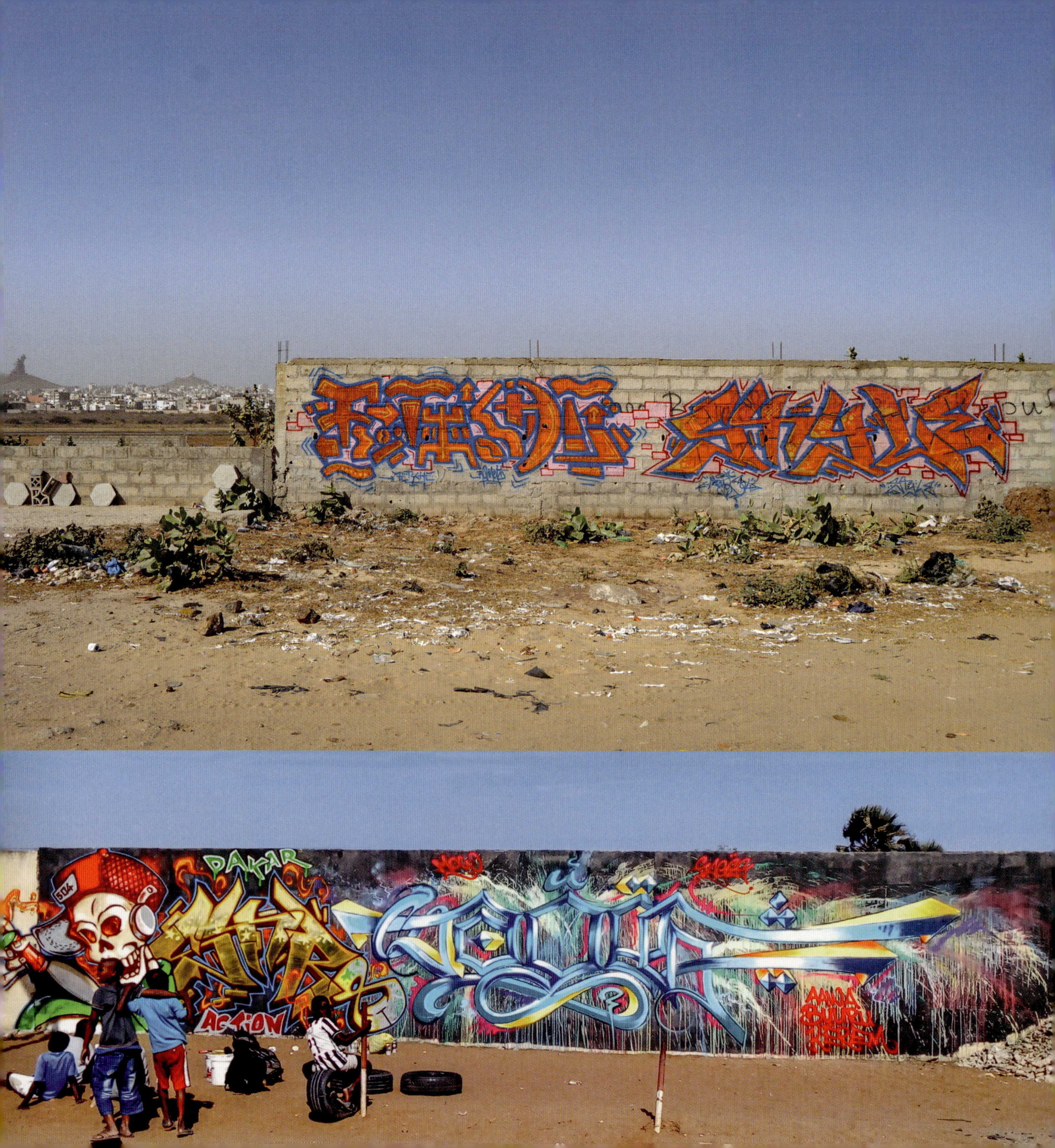

'Graffiti saved my life and now
I can do something useful for
my community. The world is sick,
we need more art and less war.
Give me enough colours and
I will change this world.' MOW 504

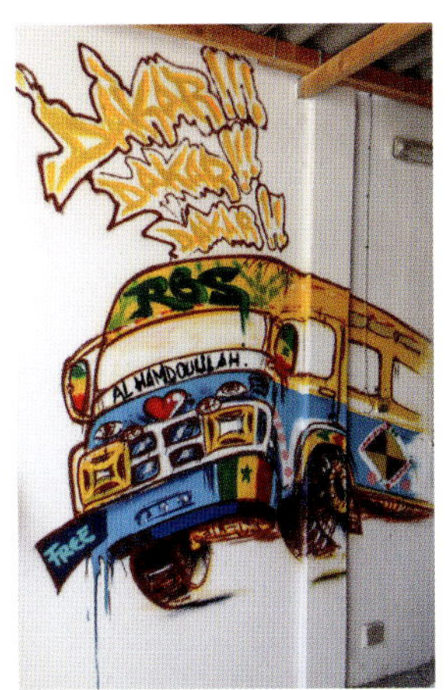

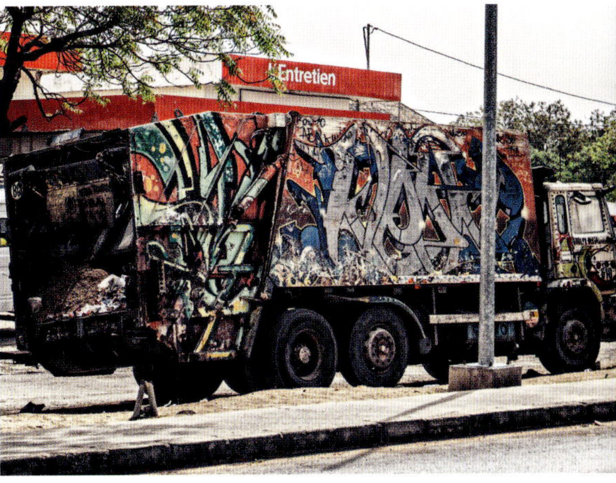

This foundation of revolutionary public art was to become the basis of and
entry point for the graffiti wave that followed. In 1991 hip-hop was in its teething
stage on Senegalese shores. Graffiti was present in the form of lyrics scattered
on the walls of makeshift rap studios, and soon made its way into Dakar's sandy
streets. Underground rappers such as Dippi Depp (Les Wagëblë) and Matador
(Wa BMG 44) wanted to cross lines and assert their mark, adding colour to the
walls for the people. Their experiments and their obsession with the alphabet
were the first traces of traditional graffiti. In the early 1990s, Docta, who would
later become a renowned cultural figure and ringleader for Senegal's graffiti
boom, began to paint graffiti inspired by the elders who were producing Set Setal
murals. Already familiar with rap and breakdancing, Docta was keen to explore
a new avenue along with his love for comics and drawing. Fascinated with the
capability to spread messages and bring colour to the world, he began a journey
that would become his way of life.

At the very beginning, Docta believed art to be a voice; a tool for social
empowerment, something that should coexist with the populace. In this way,
his work ethic in the public domain was to fight social ills and add worth. In 1994,
as a committed graffiti artist, he established DSG (Doxandem Squad), a vessel to
carry out all his projects. The association grew to comprise multiple generations
of graffiti artists and cemented Docta's place as a pioneering African graffiti artist.
DSG, with more than twenty members, became the backbone of Senegal's graffiti
community. The collective managed to promote graffiti as art while enlisting
eager minds through their tutelage. Through an array of styles, like-minded
youths were taught the ins and outs of the subculture, and the apprenticeship
structure remains in place today. Togetherness is an important element as many
artists and crews work together, often presenting a more united consciousness
as part of the alternative art form.

Above left
**Akonga. Dakar,
Senegal, 2017**

Above right
**Big Key. Dakar,
Senegal, _c_. 2010**

Opposite, top
**FéTicHe, MOW 504 ('Style
08'). Dakar, Senegal, 2014**

Opposite, bottom
**MOW 504 ('Str8'), Sagés.
Dakar, Senegal, 2016**

Following spread
**Serdas, Diablos. Dakar,
Senegal, 2018**

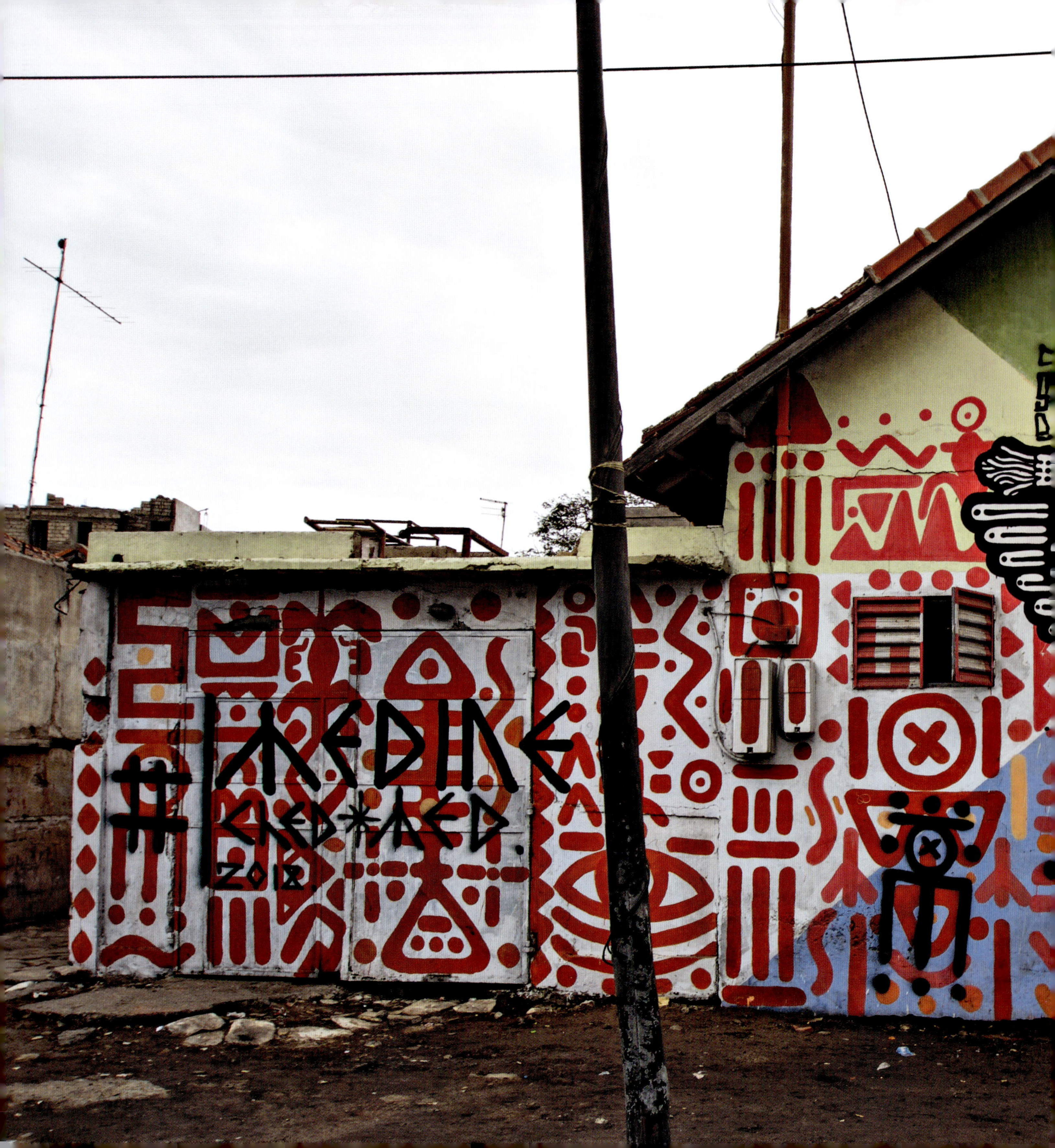

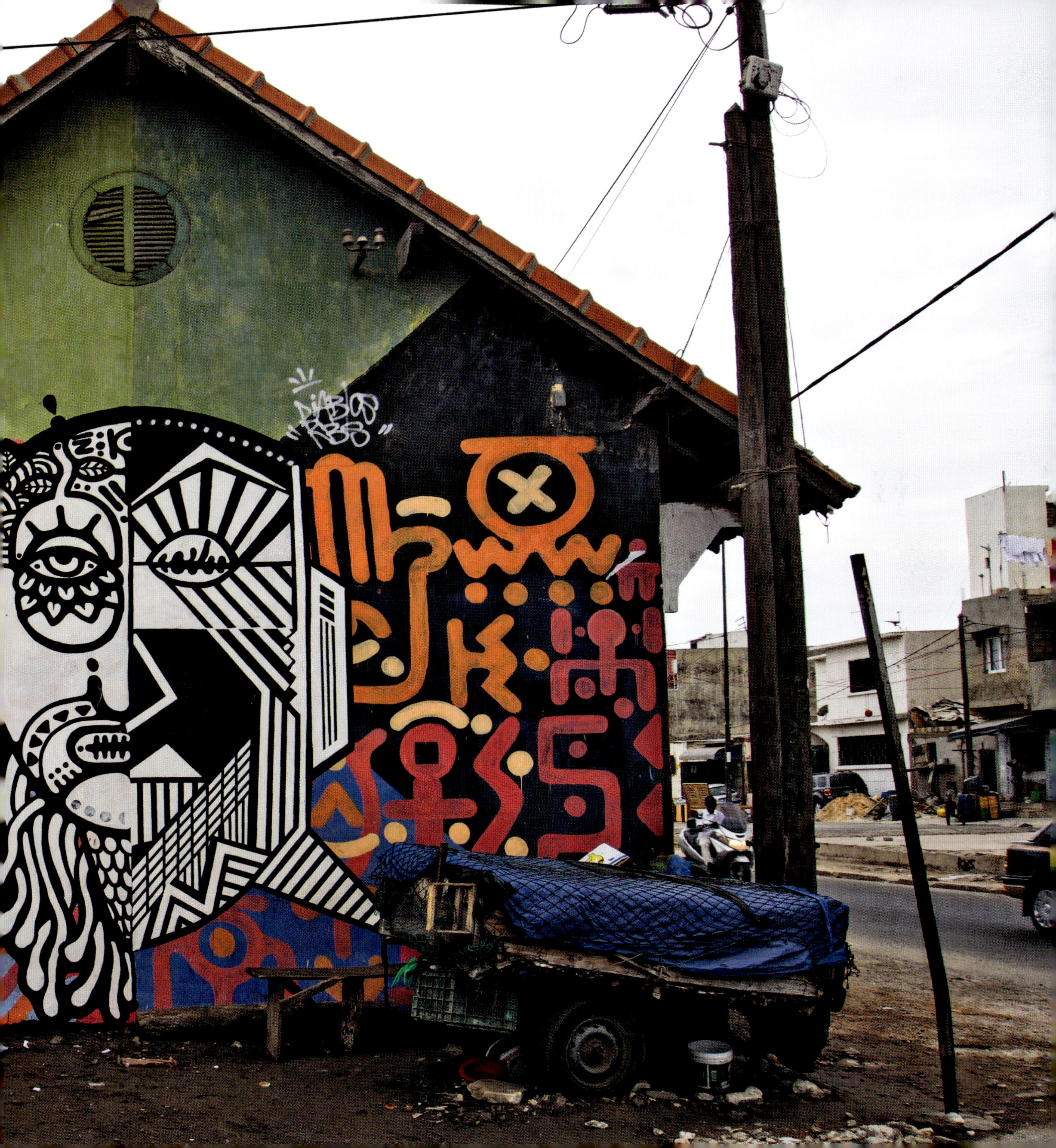

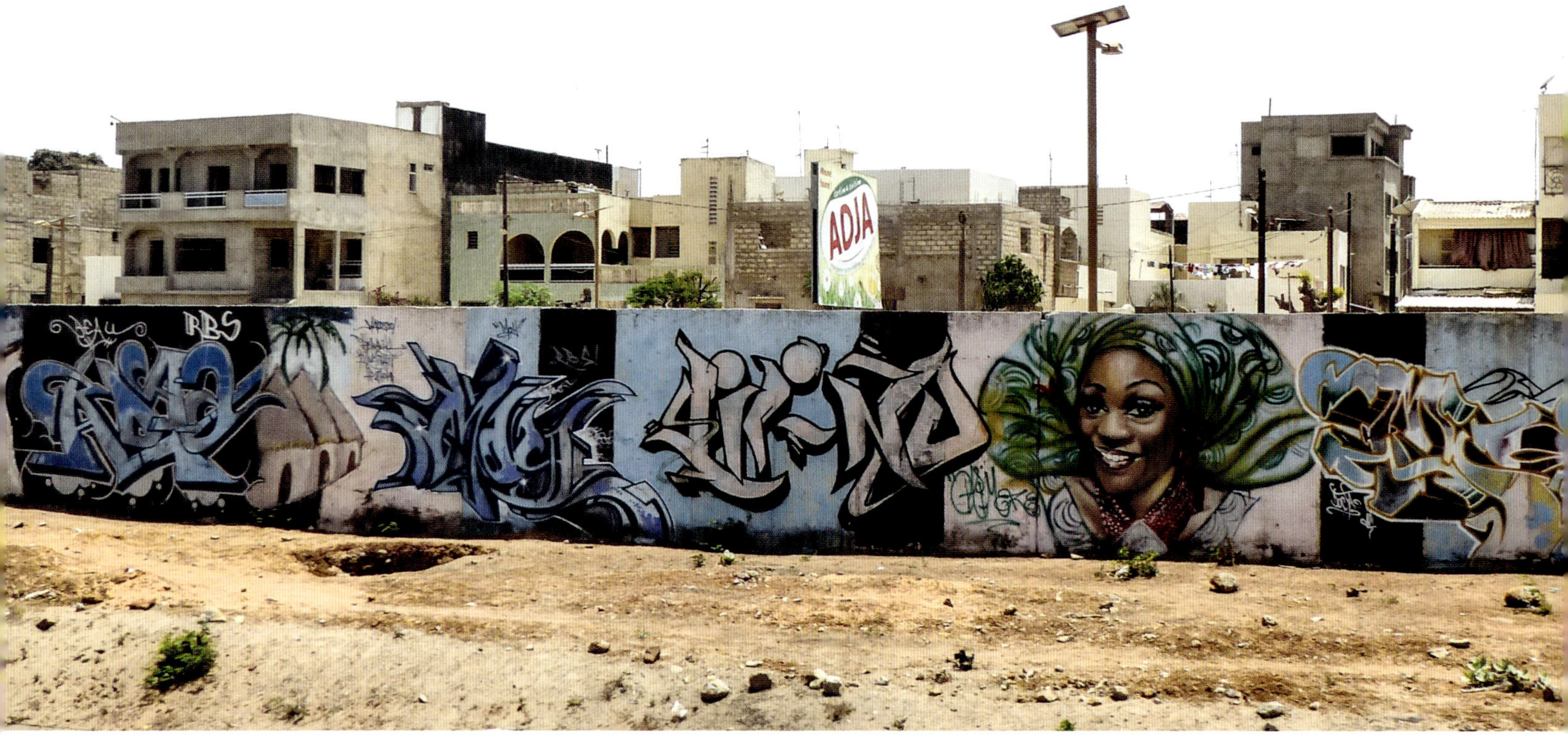

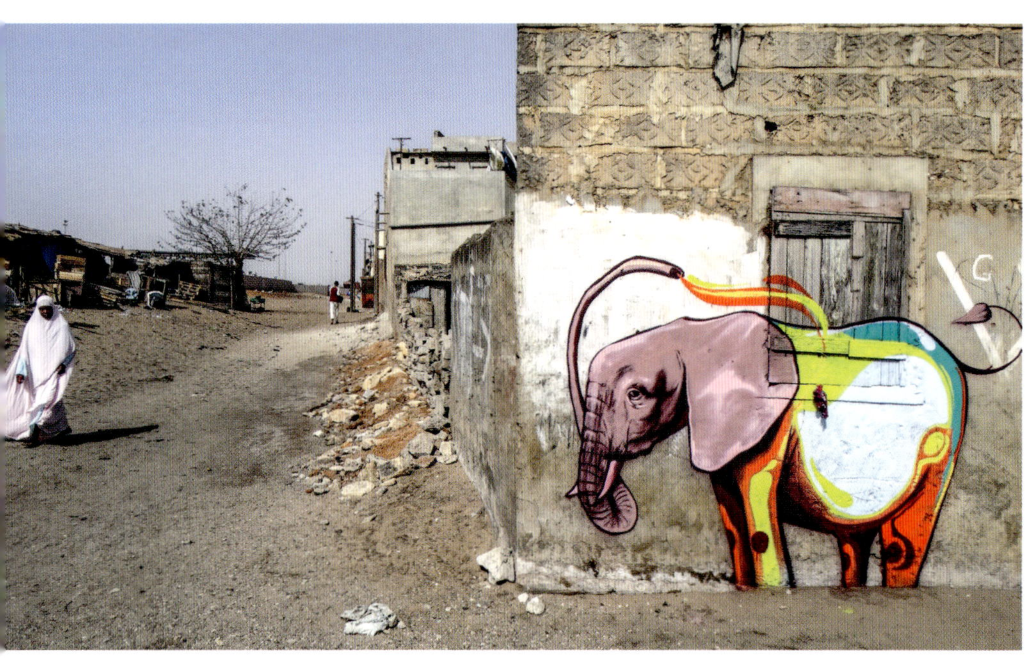

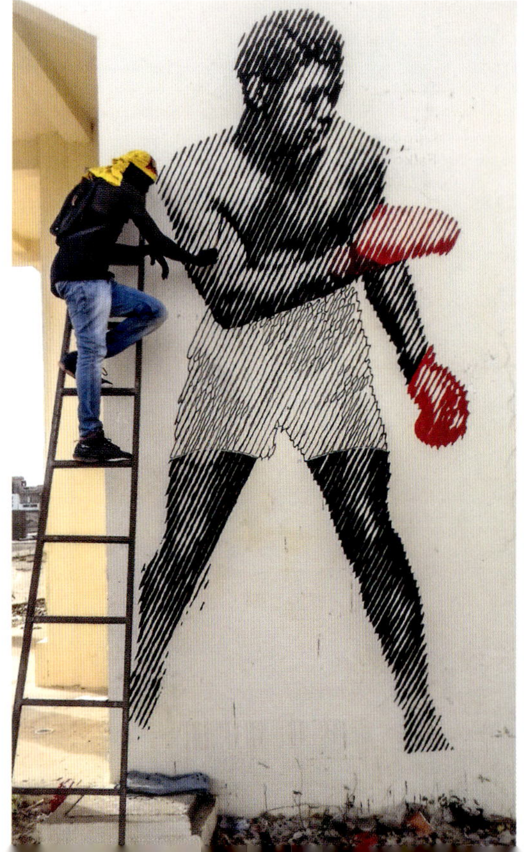

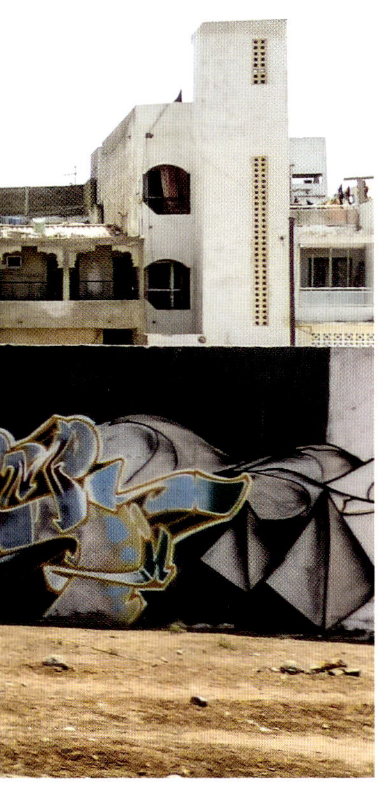

In 2008, Docta established Graff et Santé (Graffiti and Health), an awareness campaign focusing on humanitarian aid amid a range of topics, from illnesses and sanitation to information sharing. Street-side check-ups are performed by professional doctors among the painters while they are diligently at work on their murals, thus harnessing the potential of graffiti as a forum to elevate society. Docta went on to establish Festigraff (Festival International de Graffiti au Sénégal) in 2010, a fully-fledged graffiti festival and the debut event of its kind on the African continent. Another crucial development was the formation of Mizérables Graff, a crew made up of Big Key and Deep. In the absence of suitable materials (their name references their feelings about debilitating factors), the duo began to use charcoal and makeshift ladders to express themselves in the late 1990s. In advancing their practice they too have been recognized as important figures in the Senegal scene, creating a solid link between graffiti and hip-hop, and later becoming mentors to the next generation.

Around the turn of the new millennium, other urban artists and crews included Almukhtar Graffixx, Willy Kemtane, Syndikate 21, Art2Clan, Guiso, Elso and PPS. Soon the movement would witness the arrival of many of the newer-generation street artists who would rapidly enhance the collective spirit. Mad Zoo TRK (The Radikl Killuminati) was introduced to Big Key and asked him to draw the titles of his comics; through these interactions Mad Zoo grew fond of the attractive letters and began practising graffiti himself. As an academic with an interest in conscious thinking, Mad Zoo realized his vocation. While much of the pre-existing scene was based around the clichés of hip-hop, with added functions to educate and uplift, Mad Zoo wanted to incorporate a deeper, more focused message: awakening ancestral values. With this mindset he co-founded RBS (Radikl Bomb Shot) Crew in 2012 with fellow thinkers MOW 504 (Master of Wisdom, aka King, aka Ekzo 1, aka Style 08) and Krafts the Artistik One (fka Kraftsman). The crew was the perfect platform to express the artists' outlook and it quickly rose to fame.

Recruiting other impassioned individuals, some from the fields of graphic design and illustration, RBS Crew amassed a membership of about thirty active artists in 2020, with representatives in other African countries, as well as in France and Switzerland. Like Docta's Doxandem Squad, with its members in multiple countries and frequent projects, RBS decided to organize their own event-cum-festival: The Last Wall Tour. As dynamic as their desire for profound artworks, the members exhibit numerous talents. From comical characters to photo-realism, wildstyle and 3D, each artist is gifted with their own style and approach. Many are not limited to one specific trait, especially Krafts the A.O. and Mad Zoo, who tend to explore all elements of urban art – letters, characters and even elaborate pencil sketches on paper. Beau Graff is also advanced on paper, while MOW 504 was the first in Senegal to render a digital piece.

Opposite, top
Beau Graff, Mad Zoo TRK, MOW 504, Chimere, Docta. Dakar, Senegal, 2012

Opposite, bottom left
Falko One. Dakar, Senegal, 2014

Opposite, bottom right
2mgraff. Portrait of Senegalese World Boxing Champion Louis Mbarick Fall (aka Battling Siki), Nioro du Rip, Senegal, 2019

'Street art is a powerful means of communication. It adapts to all media. It is decorative and deeply enigmatic. It is a positive, message-bearing movement that awakens, educates and cultivates.' KRAFTS THE A.O.

In terms of portraiture, the magicians of RBS include Chimere, El Memf, BK, Nohine, Man Innov and Seika One (based in Switzerland), while Akonga, Freemind, Kromagnon, Enigmatik, Daiinzo, Guiso, Elviz the Warrior, Triga, ZeUs Design, Nourou Zaman, Kaire, Eldo the Ghost, Xalima, Diablos and others make up the rest of the group. Diablos, a long-time graffiti artist, started his practice through the influence of Senegalese streetwear culture and clothing customizations in the 2000s, soon becoming one of the most active and distinctive urban artists in the country. Throughout the early Festigraff editions he rocked his mark with semi-wildstyle lettering, later developing his signature Diablos character with tags and girdled Afrocentric motifs. More recently he has stripped away his graffiti background to reveal a more studied artist, embracing the global street art wave. Much of this is driven by natural artistic growth and his desire to keep reinventing himself. Another factor in the growth of local artists such as Diablos, and the local graffiti scene in general, is the impact of visiting foreign street artists. Manoos in Burkina Faso, P3pe Art2dieu in Cameroon and Sparrow in Uganda are also members of RBS Crew.

The decade beginning in 2010 saw the arrival of French immigrants Sagés and RoMeiJ (aka FéTicHe) and the formation of other local crews such as AM-O-Niak. More solo artists, including 2mgraff (aka Kemp) from the city of Nioro du Rip, Sangue, Diaz, El Pacino, Graff Systems (aka Jama Wear) and Mbautta, also stepped into the arena. Mbautta rubbed shoulders with Docta and Doxandem Squad, joining the ranks of Undu Graffiti collective with Charlestyle, O'markrak and Ounda Ndiath in 2018. A recurring issue in most circles of graffiti is the distinct lack of women artists. Dieynaba Sidibe, better known as Zeinixx, is hailed as the first female graffiti artist in Senegal. She began to paint graffiti in 2007/8 under the wing of her mentor, Graffixx. During this time she began to work for Africulturban, a hub that promotes hip-hop and urban cultures that was founded by graffiti pioneer Matador (who is now an established MC) in 2006. Africulturban is responsible for many social events, including Festa2H. Zeinixx is highly gifted behind the microphone with her slam poetry, and uses her position to advocate women's rights and environmental activism.

Truly independent and with their own perspective, Senegalese 'graffeurs' remain committed to reshaping the present and shaping the future. Their unity has helped to demystify the art form, gaining it a semi-legal status as graffiti has never been condemned by the authorities. Autonomous and impassioned, the movement will endure much as the Set Setal movement of the past.

Opposite
Top row
Man Innov, Mad Zoo TRK, Sagés, MOW 504. Dakar, Senegal, 2019

Second row
Korsé (France), Krafts the A.O., Mad Zoo TRK, Akonga, Freemind. Dakar, Senegal, 2018

Third row, left
Beau Graff, Mad Zoo TRK. Dakar, Senegal, 2019

Third row, right
Diaz. 'Fraternité', Dakar, Senegal, 2018

Fourth row
Krafts the A.O., Akonga. 'Street Messengers', Dakar, Senegal, 2015

Bottom row
Chimere, Big Key. Festigraff (4th edn), Dakar, Senegal, 2013

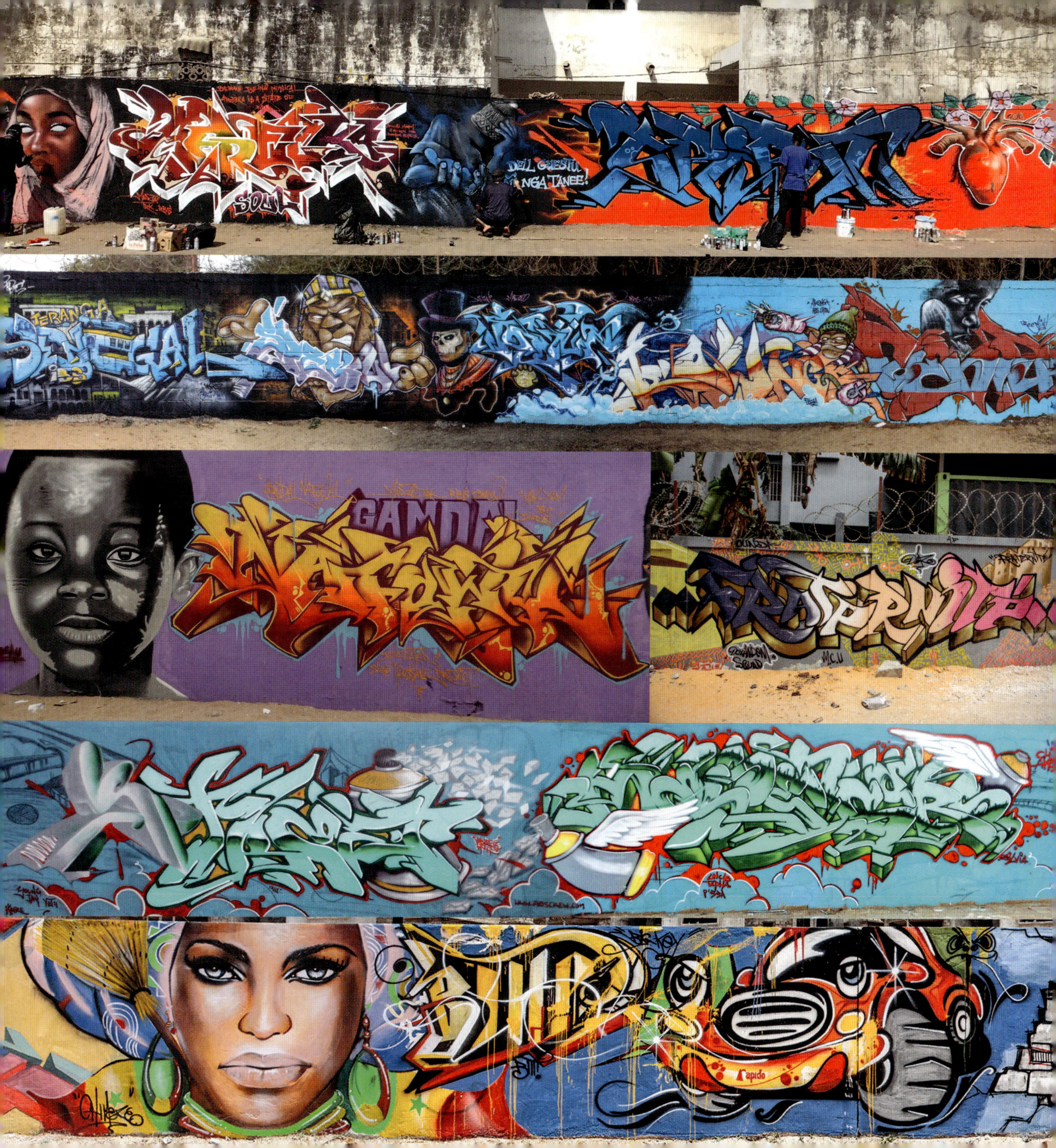

FESTIGRAFF

Festigraff is a landmark graffiti festival in Dakar, Senegal. With an overarching theme each year, often paying tribute to a historical cultural figure, the spectacle attracts visitors from abroad and aids the growth of the art form in the vicinity. During the ten days of festivities, many walls are collaboratively enhanced and artists paint words (often in native Wolof or French) relating to the chosen theme for the day. Senegalese graffiti artists embrace the freestyle nature of this method, maintaining their personal styles across the various letter-sets to remain identifiable in group productions. Making use of whatever material is available, the overall practice becomes beneficial to their repertoire. Celebrating its tenth anniversary in 2019, along with a vibrant showcase of live music, craft markets, hip-hop culture and more, Festigraff is now the longest-running festival of its kind on the continent.

Below
Shem (Peru/Switzerland), Sekit (France), Onemizer (France), Mad Zoo TRK, Baro (Switzerland), Refa One (USA), Kicey 1 (France), La Kase (Switzerland), Docta and others. 7th edn, Dakar, Senegal, 2016

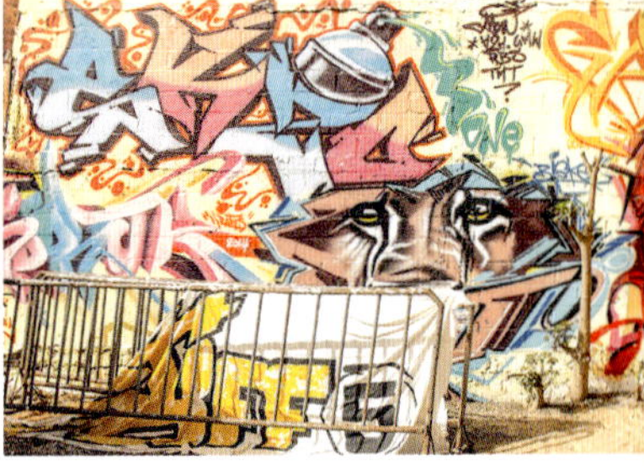

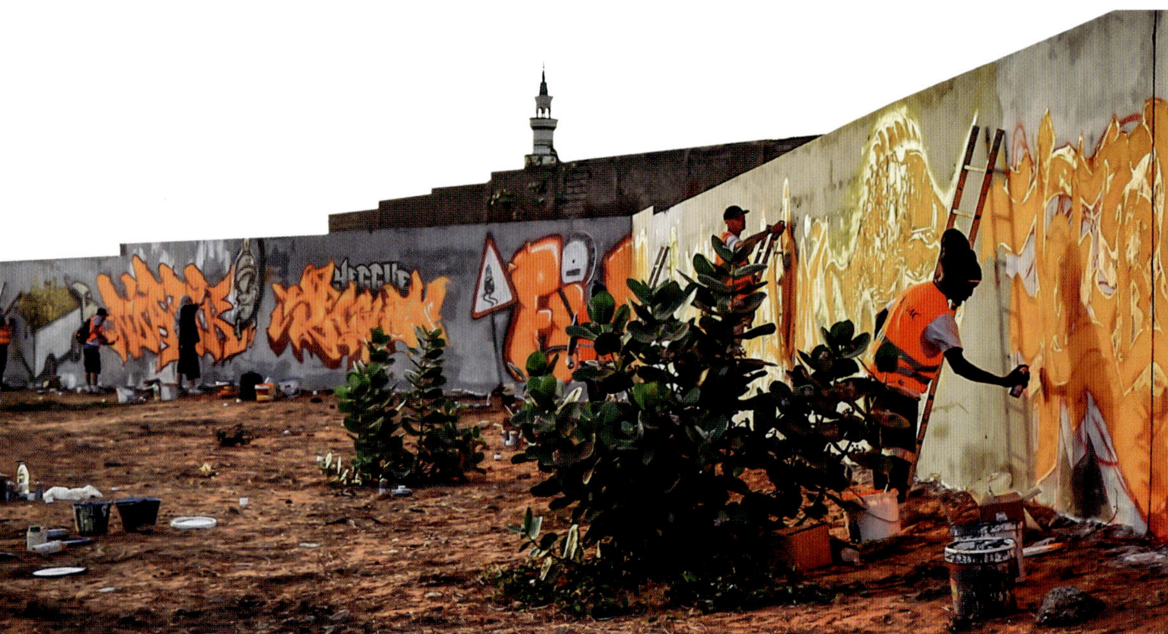

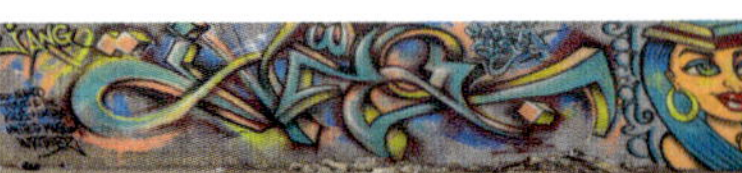

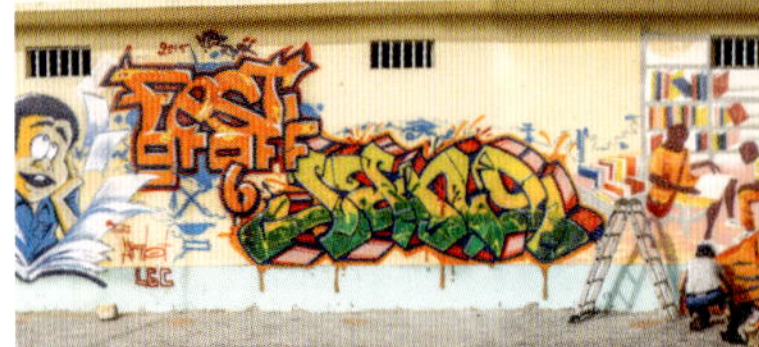

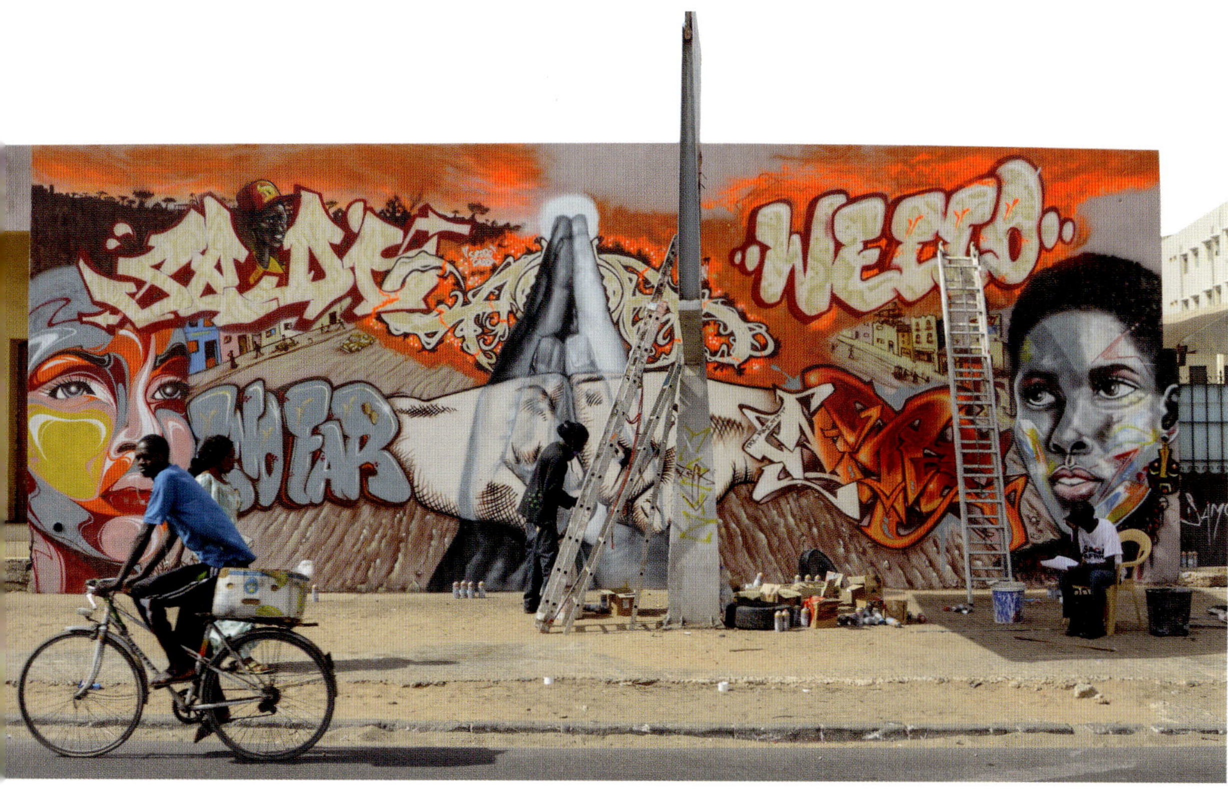

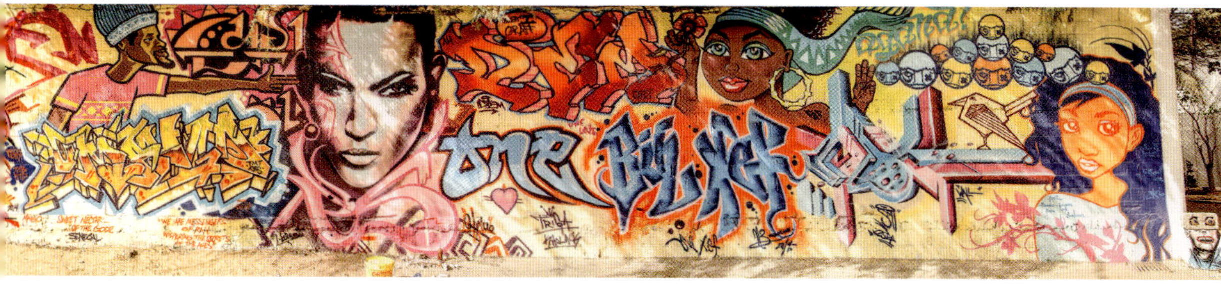

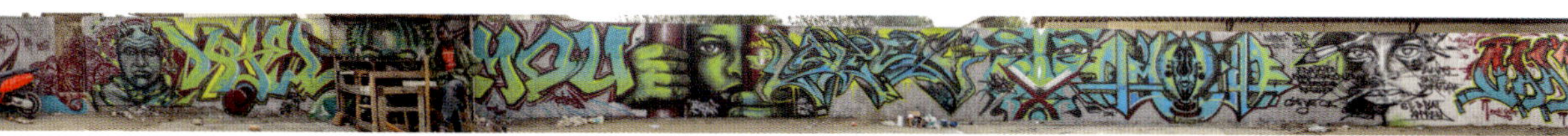

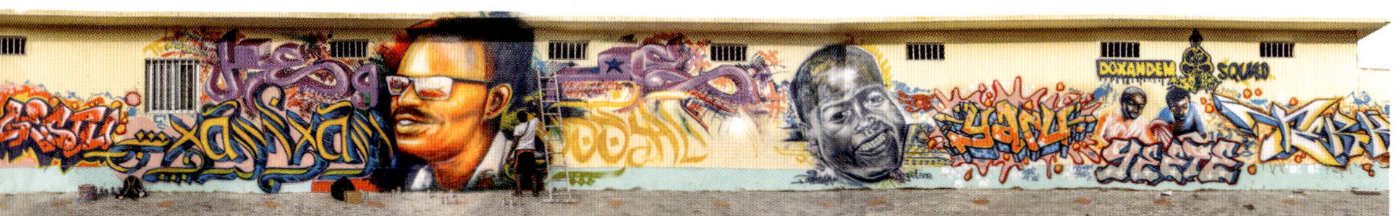

Left, from top

Onemizer (France), Encr (France), Baro (Switzerland), Ozas (France), Shem (Peru/Switzerland), Aspe (Spain), Veneno (France), Mad Zoo TRK, SMI. 7th edn, Dakar, Senegal, 2016

Krafts the A.O., MOW 504, Big Key, El Memf, Refa One (USA), Farm Prod (Belgium), Diablos, Chimere, Triga, Diem One (Belgium), Nourou Zaman, Agana (USA), SMI, IPNS One (France), Monsieur Cana (France), Lady Alezia (France), Waf (Belgium) and others. 5th edn, Dakar, Senegal, 2014

Sagés, Agana (USA), Triga, Waf (Belgium), SMI, Seika One (Switzerland), Diem One (Belgium), Krafts the A.O., Mad Zoo TRK, El Memf, Diablos, Big Key, Manoos. 5th edn, Dakar, Senegal, 2014

Patriot, O'markrak, Kufue One (USA), Mbautta, Seika One (Switzerland), Sagés, Seencelor, Bankslave, Refa One (USA), Diem One (Belgium), Mr Stone and others. 6th edn, Dakar, Senegal, 2015

Following spread

Batsh (France), Refa One (USA), DeeDee (USA), Monsieur Cana (France), Mr Stone, Diem One (Belgium), Triga, Krafts the A.O., Joule (Switzerland), Manoos, Seencelor, Just One (Switzerland), Trez, SMI, Bandi (Switzerland), Seika One (Switzerland), MOW 504, RoMeiJ, Beau Graff, Chimere, Guiso, Falko One, El Memf, Mbautta, Deris, IPNS One (France), Pi80 (France), Louise Thiongane, Mad Zoo TRK, Docta, Sagés, Kromagnon, OliScrat (France), LayeDesign, Big Key, Diablos, Agana (USA), Waf (Belgium), Lady Alezia (France), Farm Prod (Belgium) and others. 5th edn, Dakar, Senegal, 2014

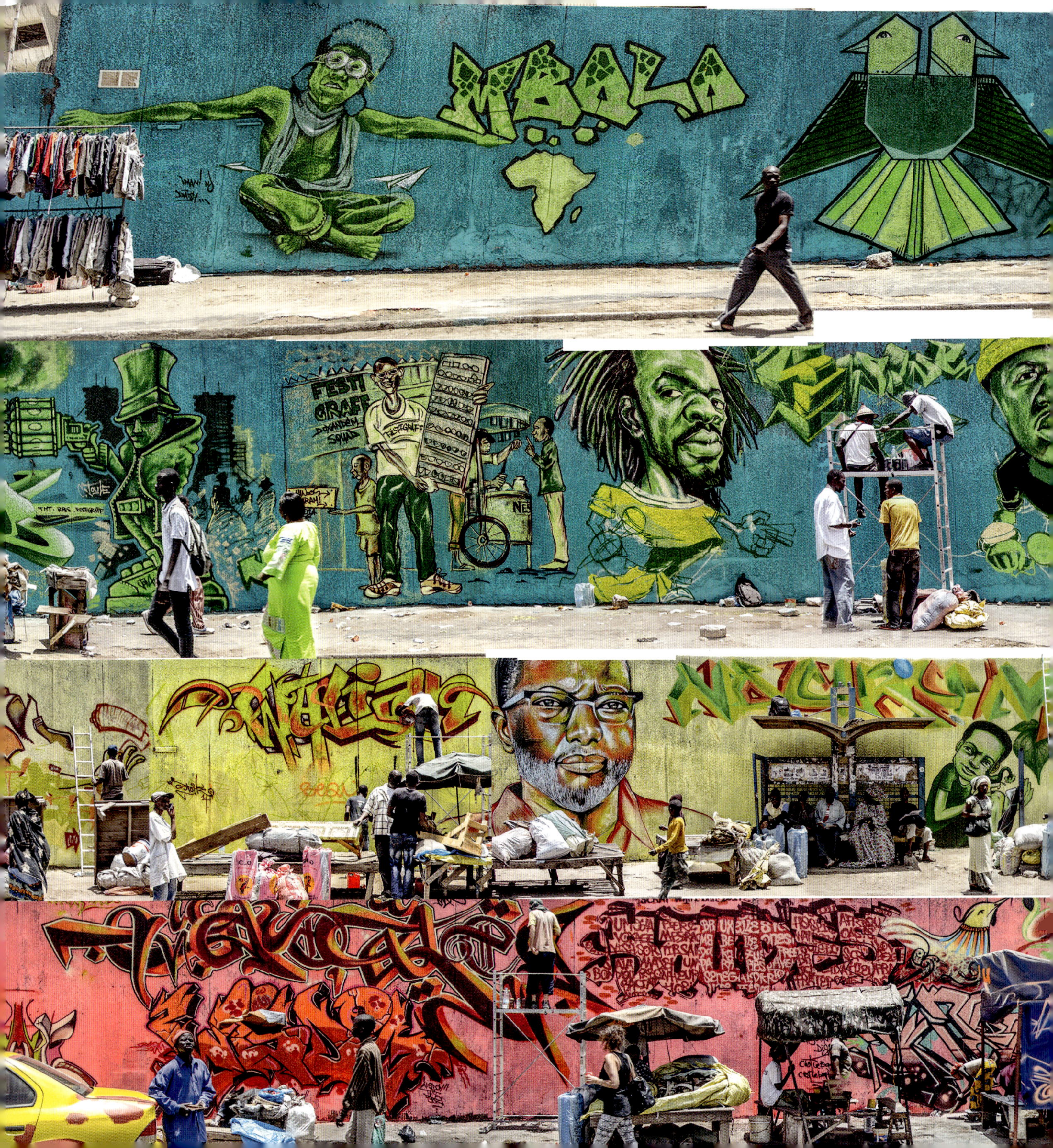

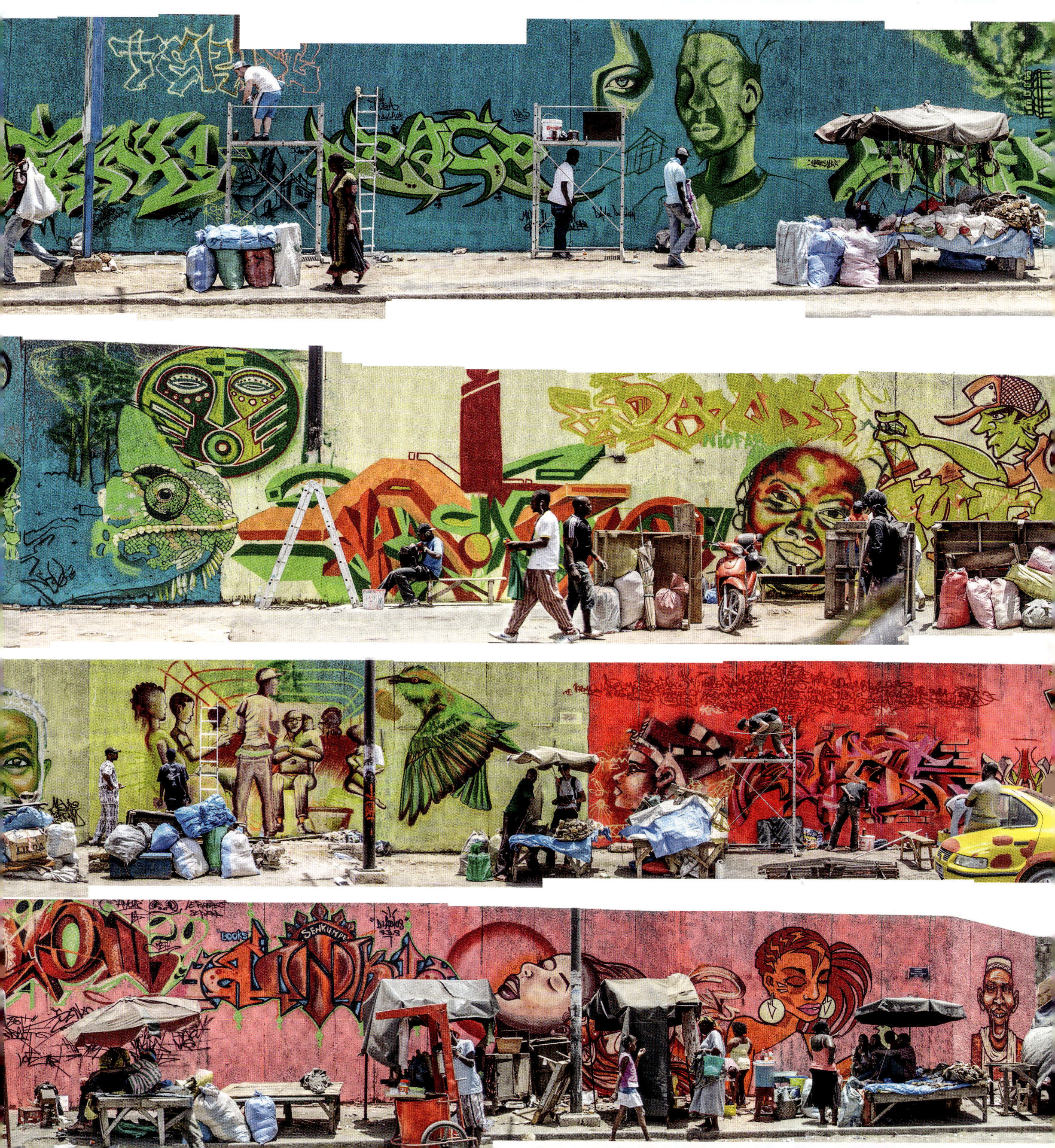

MAD ZOO TRK

Tell me about your crew, RBS.
What started out as a group of friends who all shared the same passion soon grew more conscious. We realized our art could drive change and that most of us were academics. The culture of knowledge became the bedrock of our commitment and our desire to help out the young people who asked us to integrate them into our crew. RBS became a sort of pan-African movement that cultivated self-determination and self-knowledge, and the will to return a sense of dignity to African people by restoring their historical cultural values.

Tell me about graffiti and its place in Senegal.
The definition of graffiti is a vast one. For some, it's an art practised with a spray can, whereas for others, the association with rock art is more prominent, regardless of the techniques used. With this in mind, we could say that the roots of graffiti in Senegal go back way further than the first graffiti artists. Graffiti in Senegal begins after colonization, which sees a freer expression of the Senegalese people who paint religious figures on walls as symbols of resistance and sovereignty, way before the advent of the hip-hop movement towards the end of the 1980s. The Set Setal ('clean up') movement reinforces this thesis; generally taking place on Sundays, these great popular gatherings were organized around sanitation and the fight against insalubrity. People would go out and clean the streets to some music; to keep them durably clean, they had the ingenious idea of inviting local artists to come paint on walls. They would paint religious figures, which was a way to dissuade the population (who was profoundly religious) from littering these newly cleaned places. This way of representing figures on walls gave way to graffiti as it is known today, with the emergence of Senegalese hip-hop. We then witnessed the birth of an artistic movement beyond hip-hop dance and rap.

Tell me about your graffiti philosophy.
Compared to our elders, we were lucky to stay longer in school, and most of the members of RBS are intellectuals and academics. We had the advantage of understanding the world and its challenges and communicating well when it came to our artistic practice. A deep awareness of the great struggles of our African people combined with the influence of a deep-rooted popular culture around comics, new technologies, film culture and hip-hop music: this multicultural cocktail – rooted in its African values – is what determines our graffiti today. This is conveyed by the increasingly frequent representations of pan-African figures in a tribal African graphic style, with a level of skill that equals international standards and which has given Senegal its status as a graffiti hotspot. Styles range from wildstyle to 3D, cartoon characters and realism.

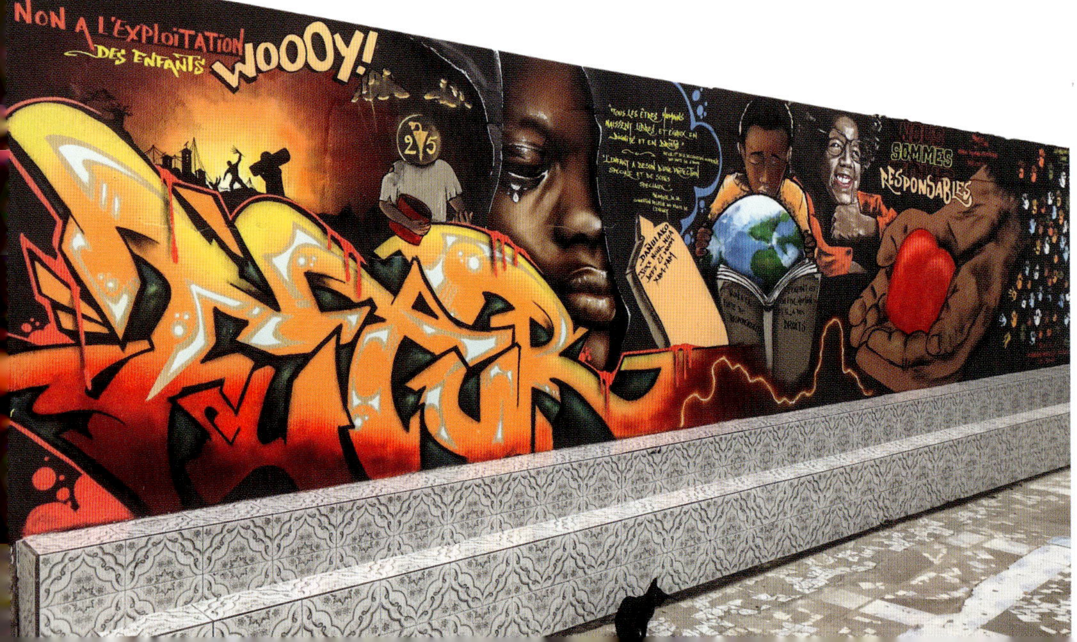

Left
Mad Zoo TRK, Akonga, Freemind, Kromagnon. Saint-Louis, Senegal, 2018

Opposite
Mad Zoo TRK. 'Yandé Codou Sène', Festigraff (8th edn), Dakar, Senegal, 2017

What limitations do you encounter as a graffiti artist in Senegal?

The only limitations we often encounter here are logistical ones. The necessary materials are not really available and this prevents us from reaching our full potential in a way, even though we still succeed in expressing it with what we have. Solutions are being carried out to allow us to exercise this art with all necessary conditions met.

Why is it important to send positive messages through graffiti art?

Senegalese graffiti art was born with the notion of commitment and social responsibility. We have a legacy to protect, with our art as much as with our way of living in society. The street is our preferred space, to reach everyone. We are brought to the fore as leaders of opinion, so we have this duty to be aware of our responsibilities more than our privileges. Art has always played this fundamental role in the shaping of consciences around certain ideologies – this means artists have a great responsibility. Some run away from them and dedicate themselves to making profit; we are just deciding to do our duty according to our conscience, in the steps of our ancestors who showed us the way.

Tell me about working together as a united graffiti community.

We live in a world where human foolishness would have us all competing against one another – I personally find this absurd. I find it rather idiotic that artists who share the same art form, but distinguish themselves by their own sensibility, should fight each other for privilege. I see the complementary nature of differences, rather than comparing or confronting them

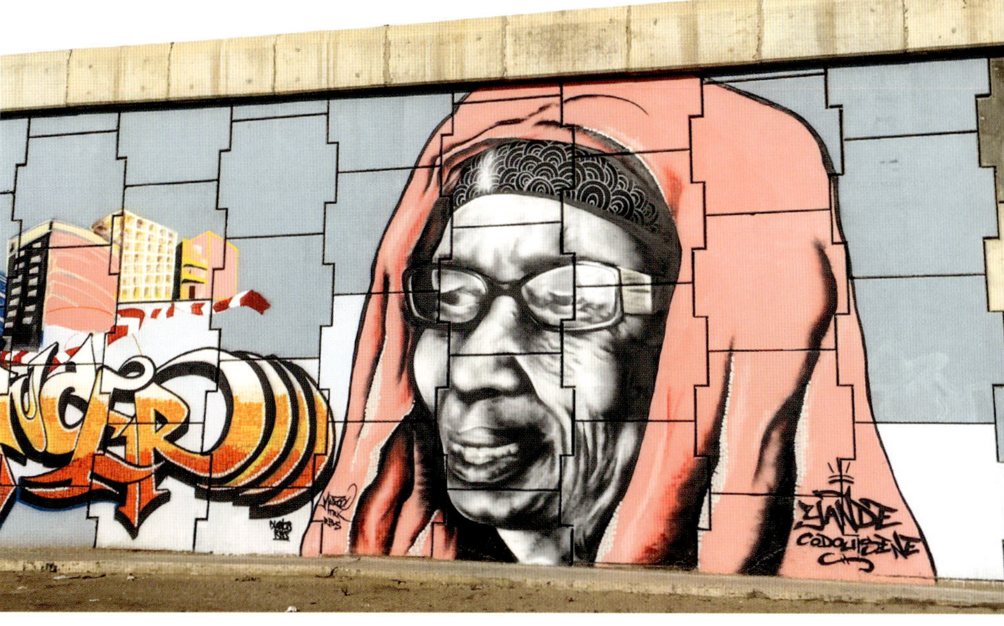

to one another. As I often say, we can be totally fine on our own, but we are better together. The greatest challenge will be to leave the absurdity of competition behind and for each of us to accept the other person's skill, in a complementary dynamic. To build human relationships beyond differences, RBS is first and foremost a family, a community where everyone is linked, beyond the simple practice of the art form. Everyone has a role to play in it, regardless of their level. It's an *art de vivre* (art of living), one which is reflected in our murals when we fuse our styles.

What do people think of graffiti when they see it?

People's reactions make us really happy because they are always amazed by what we do. The most important is when they understand the meaning of our messages and when they are proud to still see artists who are not just interested in money, and who fight for noble causes – this really fills us with comfort. Sometimes they come with presents, or just say prayers to show their satisfaction with what we are doing. It is

an art at the service of the people, and they really give back. It is in these moments that we feel the full meaning of our battles.

What is the best thing about being a graffiti artist?

I would say that for us, the best thing is to be recognized, to be respected by our people and to continue to inspire future generations. That the people we are fighting for recognize the sacrifices made for their well-being, that the causes we are fighting for find their inspiration again and again in future generations, for them to know that great power involves great responsibility, and to know the value of respect.

Growing up in the Guédiawaye area of Dakar, Senegal, Mad Zoo TRK (The Radikl Killuminati) surrounded himself with comic books and educated himself in philosophical concepts such as pan-Africanism. His love for illustration merged with graffiti and he passionately shares his ideologies in his artworks to elevate African society.

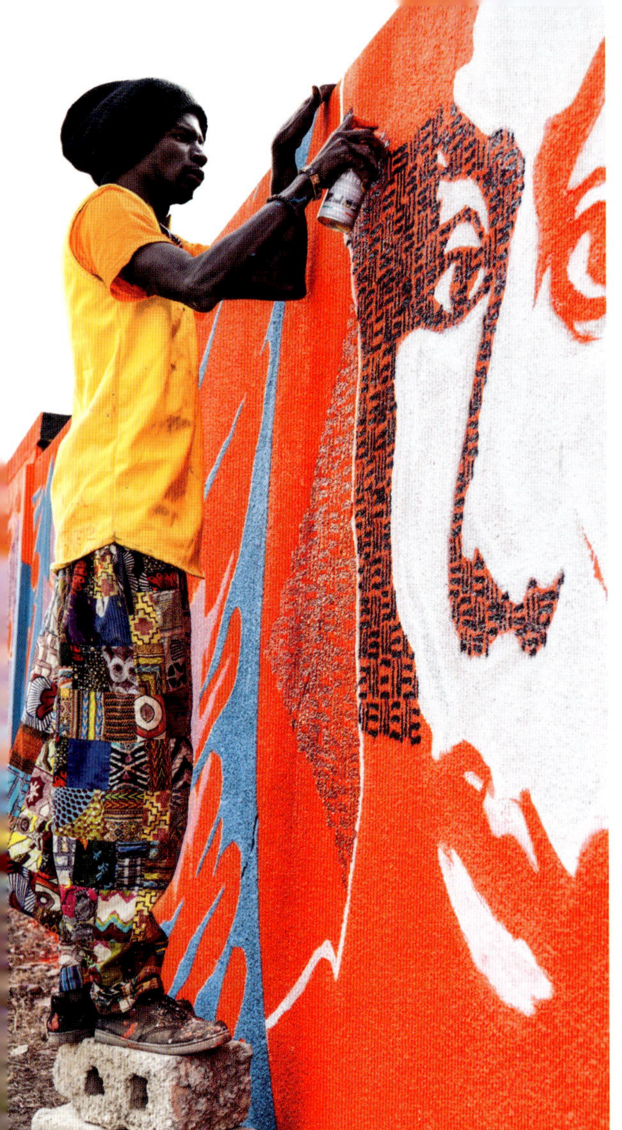

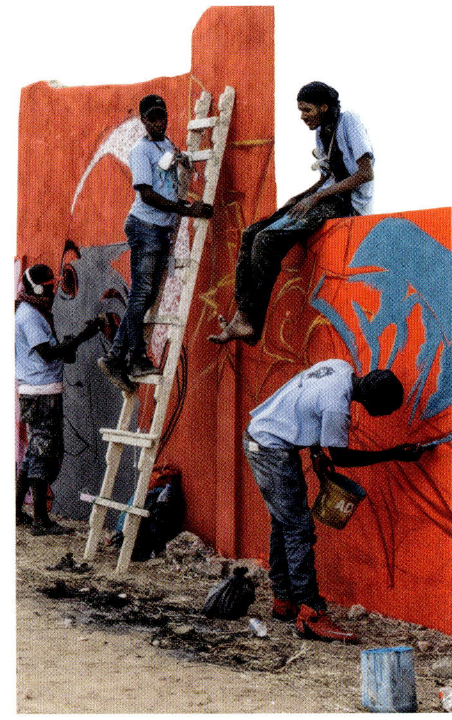

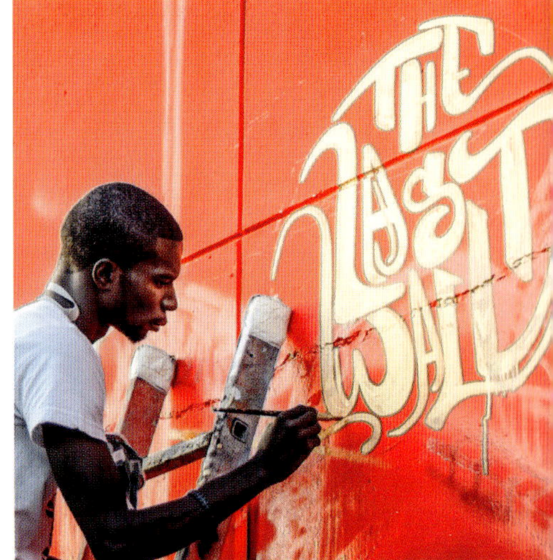
THE
LAST
WALL

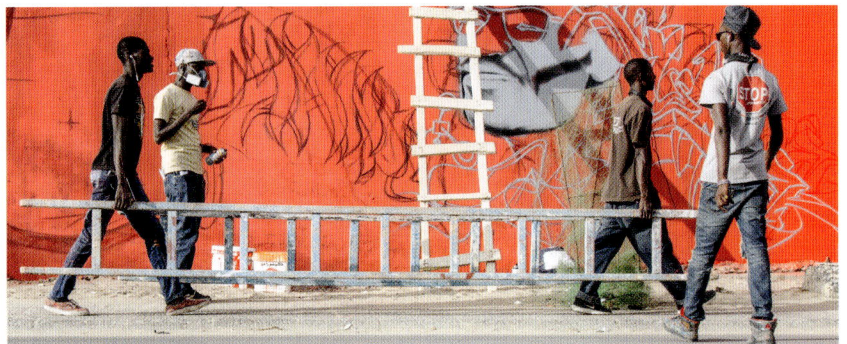

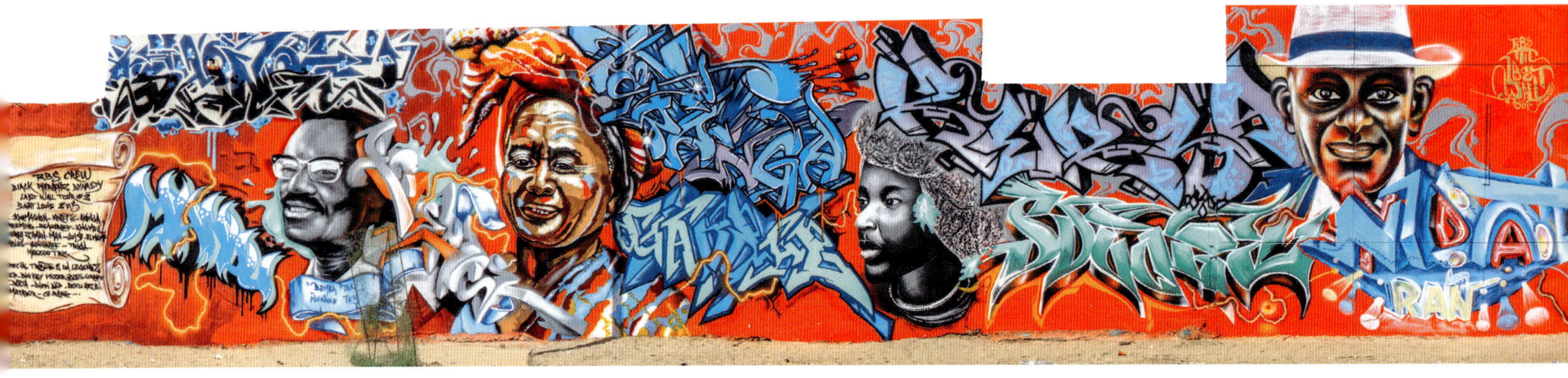

THE LAST WALL TOUR

FESTIVALS & CULTURE

The Last Wall is an annual touring event produced by Senegal's RBS Crew. The Dakar-based graffiti collective launched the event in the city of Thiès in 2014. Every year they travel to a different town to produce a monumental, collaborative mural with members of the crew and invited guests. The tour aims to take their graffiti – and their pan-Africanist approach – to unexplored territories, where they spend a few days enhancing the landscape. Successive productions were painted in Saint-Louis (2015), Kaolack (2016), Kaffrine (2017), Louga (2018) and Thiès again (2019).

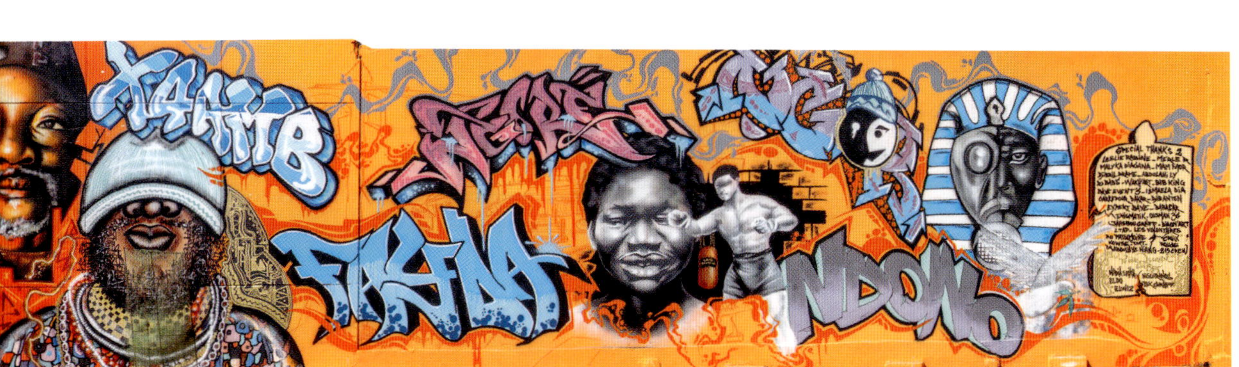

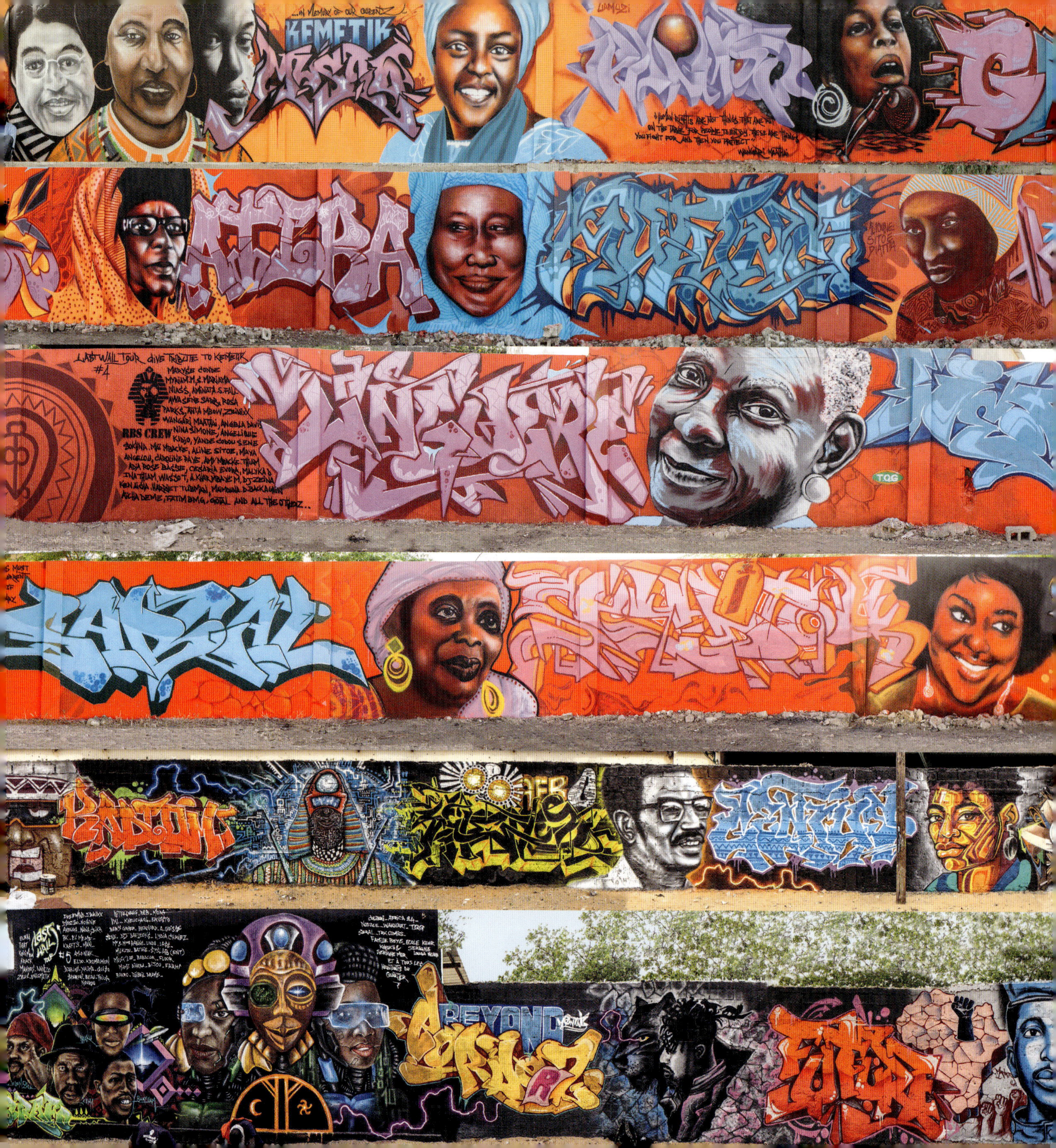

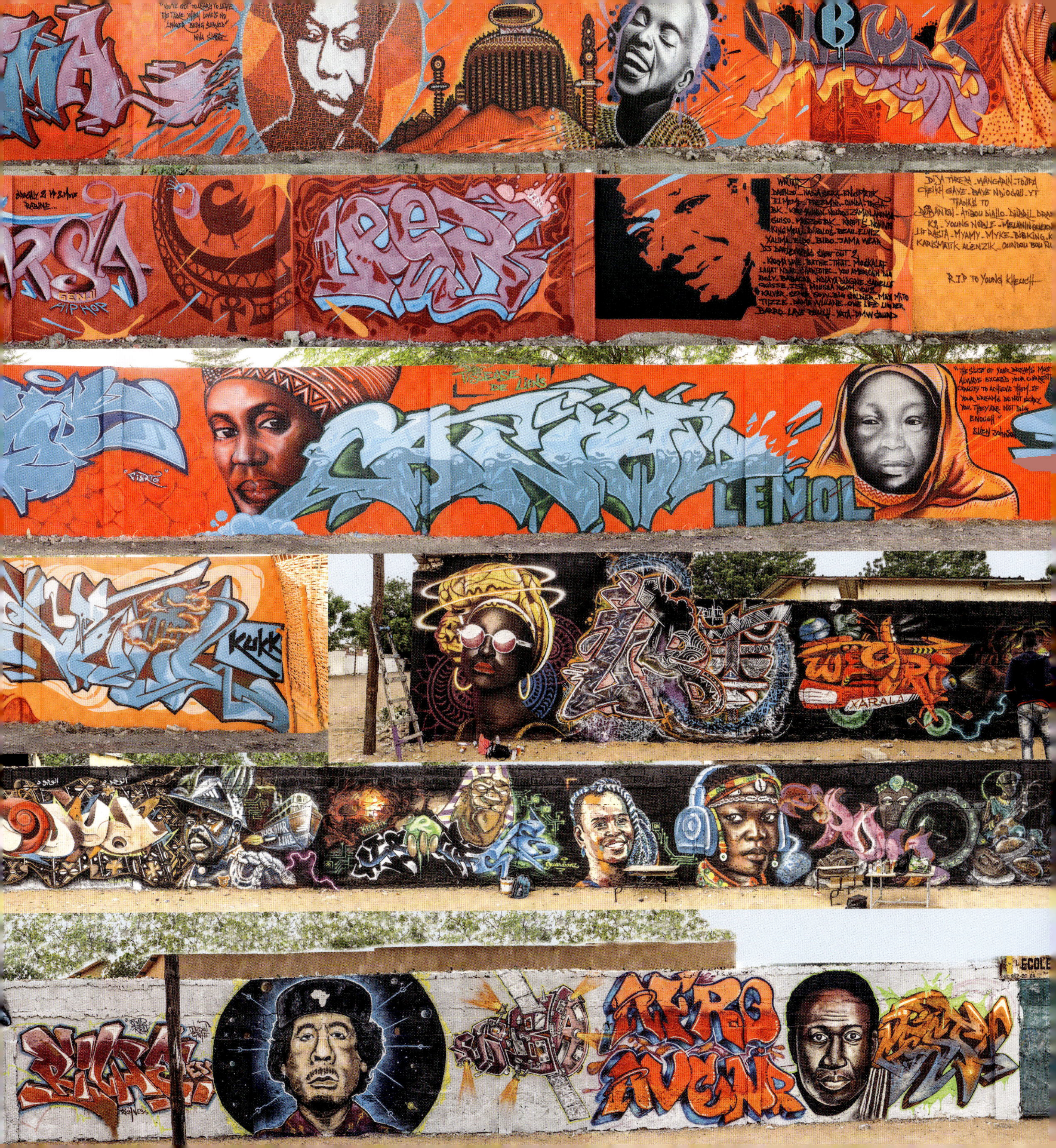

MOH AWUDU

Tell me about your introduction to graffiti.

I fell in love with graffiti through the influence of hip-hop. I loved the airbrush T-shirts and graffiti walls that you did not normally see around Ghana. I decided to start doing it myself from pictures I found in magazines – there was no Internet at that time. I finally noticed graffiti is a medium where you can send messages to the public. There are a lot of topics that I want to bring attention to through graffiti.

Tell me about your style.

My style is representative of my culture – African tradition, and my experiences in everyday life. I like to empower women because they are very strong. My parents play a big role in my personal life and art life. My mom did a lot, she is so supportive, and my wife really inspires me. Art is in me. I like to represent geometric structure and African symbols, culture and fabrics in my works. I also try to imagine Afro-futurism where women have equal power to men. Graffiti is beautiful and I can bring light to social issues to educate. I want to promote my African culture and connect with different people around the world. It's my life now, and I enjoy doing it.

Tell me about graffiti in Ghana.

Graffiti and street art is going from strength to strength in Ghana. The public love it and I am using it to create a tourist attraction. The government likes it too, and more public events invite graffiti artists to paint live. We have about ten active artists, but more younger artists are ready to learn from us.

What would you say is unique about graffiti in Africa?

African graffiti art is growing. Artists are now making a living from their artworks and are creating their own styles influenced by historical, cultural and ethnic backgrounds, all while inspiring others.

The Internet is a useful tool for graffiti and street artists. What is the importance of having an online presence for your work?

The Internet is a great revolution, especially as an artist, because previously one could only get inspiration through magazines. The World Wide Web is a great tool to easily share your visions and connect with people.

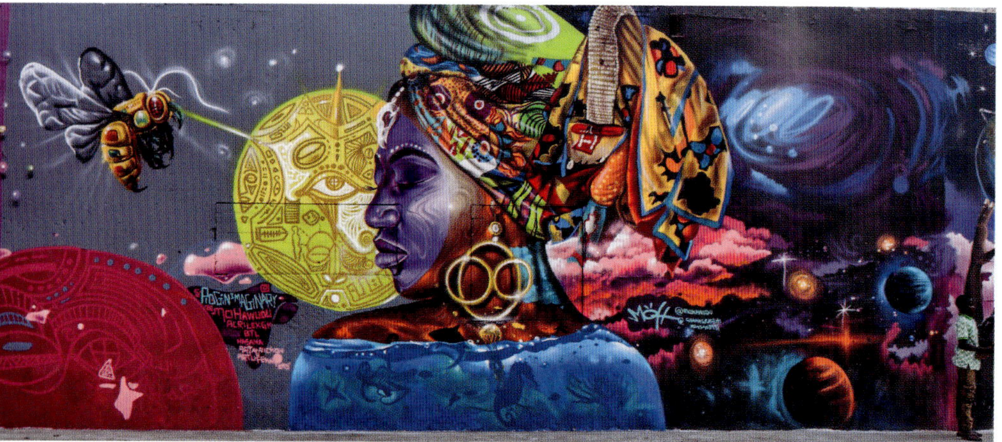

Moh Awudu. Chale Wote Street Art Festival (9th edn), Accra, Ghana, 2019

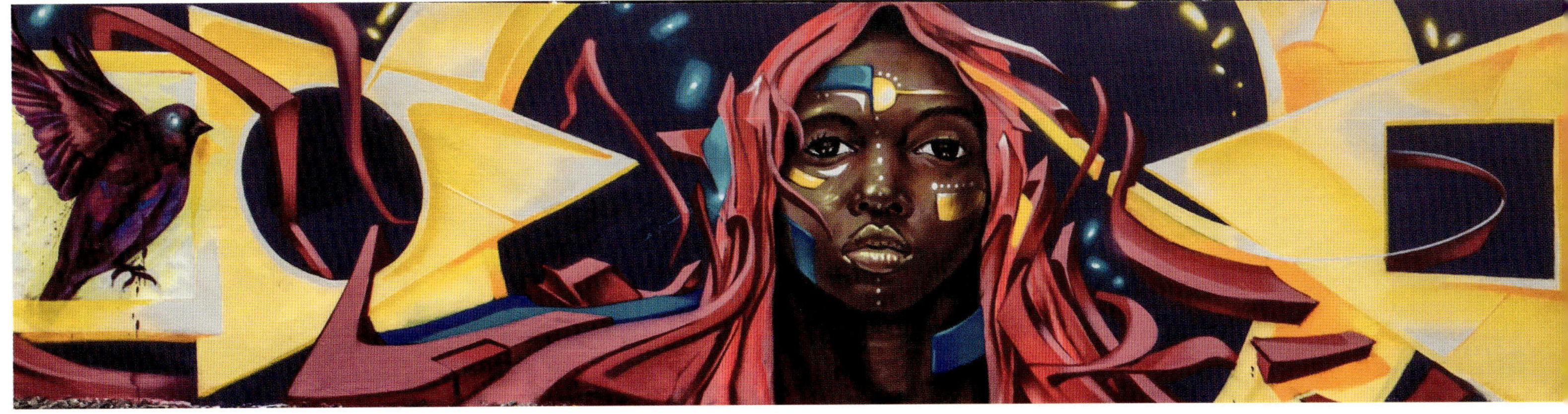

How has graffiti affected your life?

Graffiti has changed everything in my life. I go to places I only wished to be and hang out with people I dreamed of meeting. Through coverage in TV news, magazines and documentaries, I get to change the narrative about my community and inspire young people around the neighbourhood and the world.

I want to be a global ambassador through art and travel, teaching the youth to believe in themselves and inspiring them to take responsibility. You don't have to hold a big position in society before you can make a change in life, you can contribute from your small corner and make a positive change in the world. It is amazing how people just love and appreciate everything I do. People believe in me and see great potential from my street art.

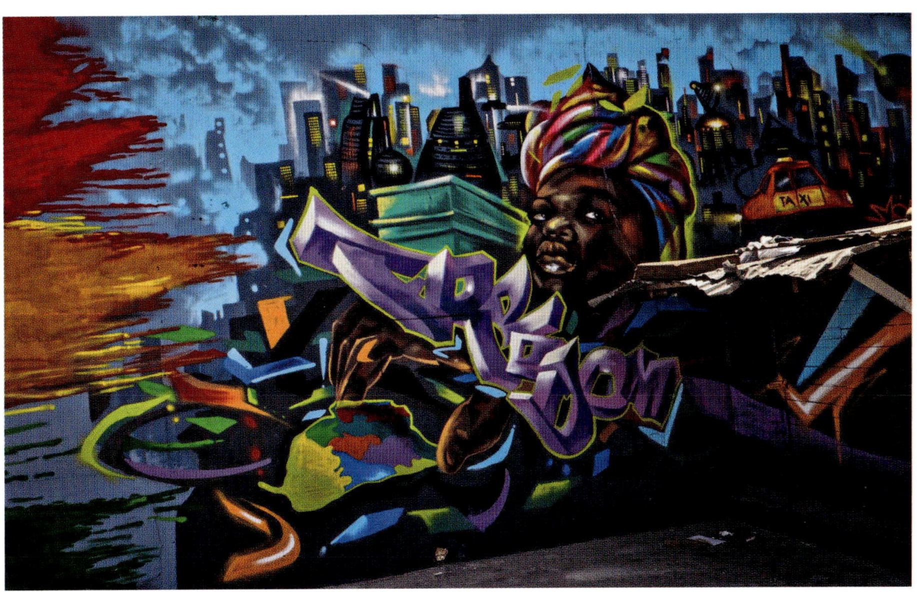

Moh Awudu, aka Freestyle 233, trained under Hashim Mozzay before attending art school to obtain a degree. Working as a graffiti and fine artist from Accra, Ghana, he exerts himself in multiple disciplines; from canvas and brush work to airbrush and street art. His realist portraits are exquisite, incorporating strong African imagery, and his murals are now present on six continents.

Top
Moh Awudu, with Raphe (France). Accra, Ghana, 2017

Above
Moh Awudu. Accra, Ghana, 2018

Page 206
Moh Awudu. Chale Wote Street Art Festival (7th edn), Accra, Ghana, 2017

Page 207
Moh Awudu. Bienal de Graffiti Fine Art, São Paulo, Brazil, 2018

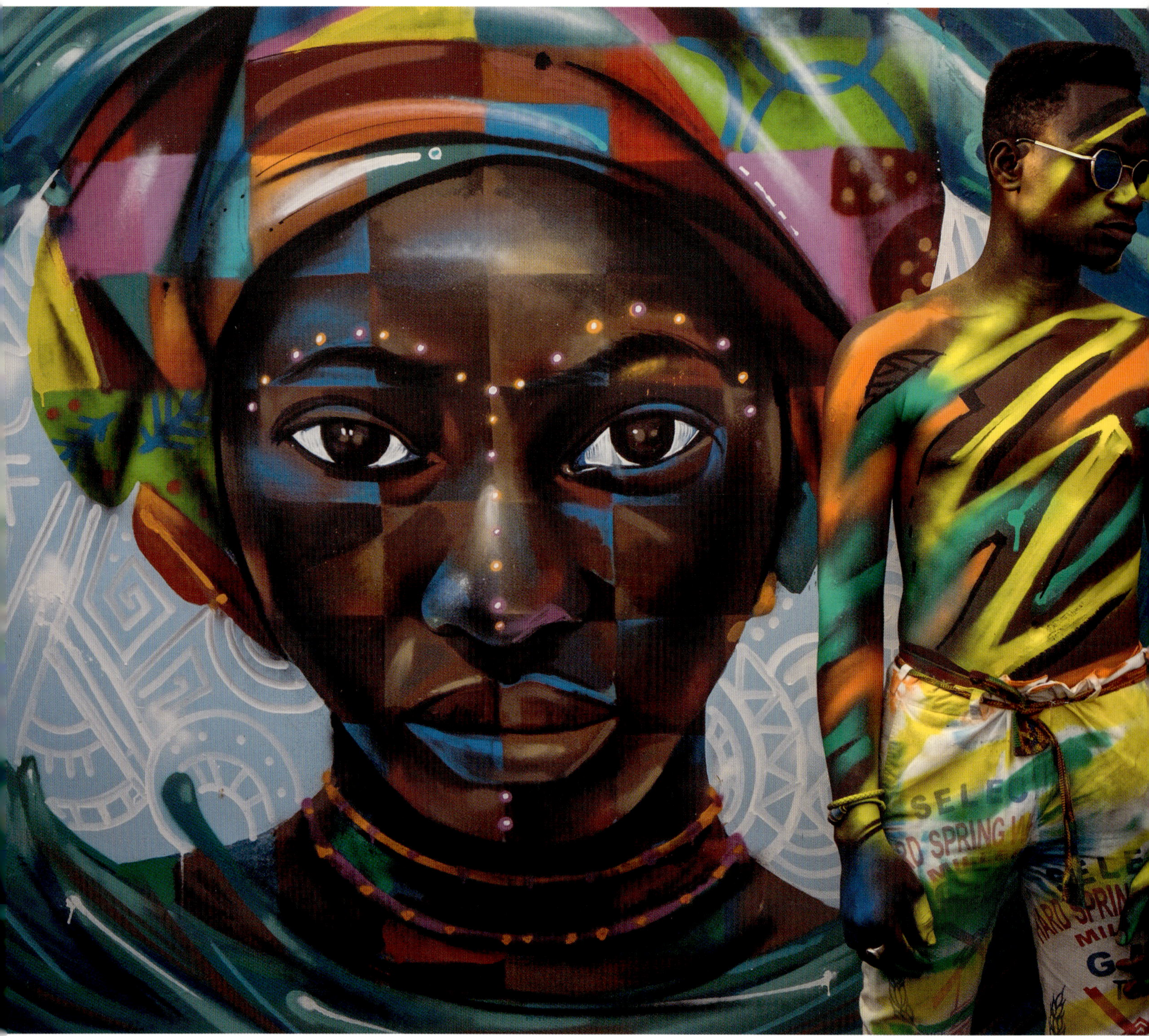

WESTERN AFRICA

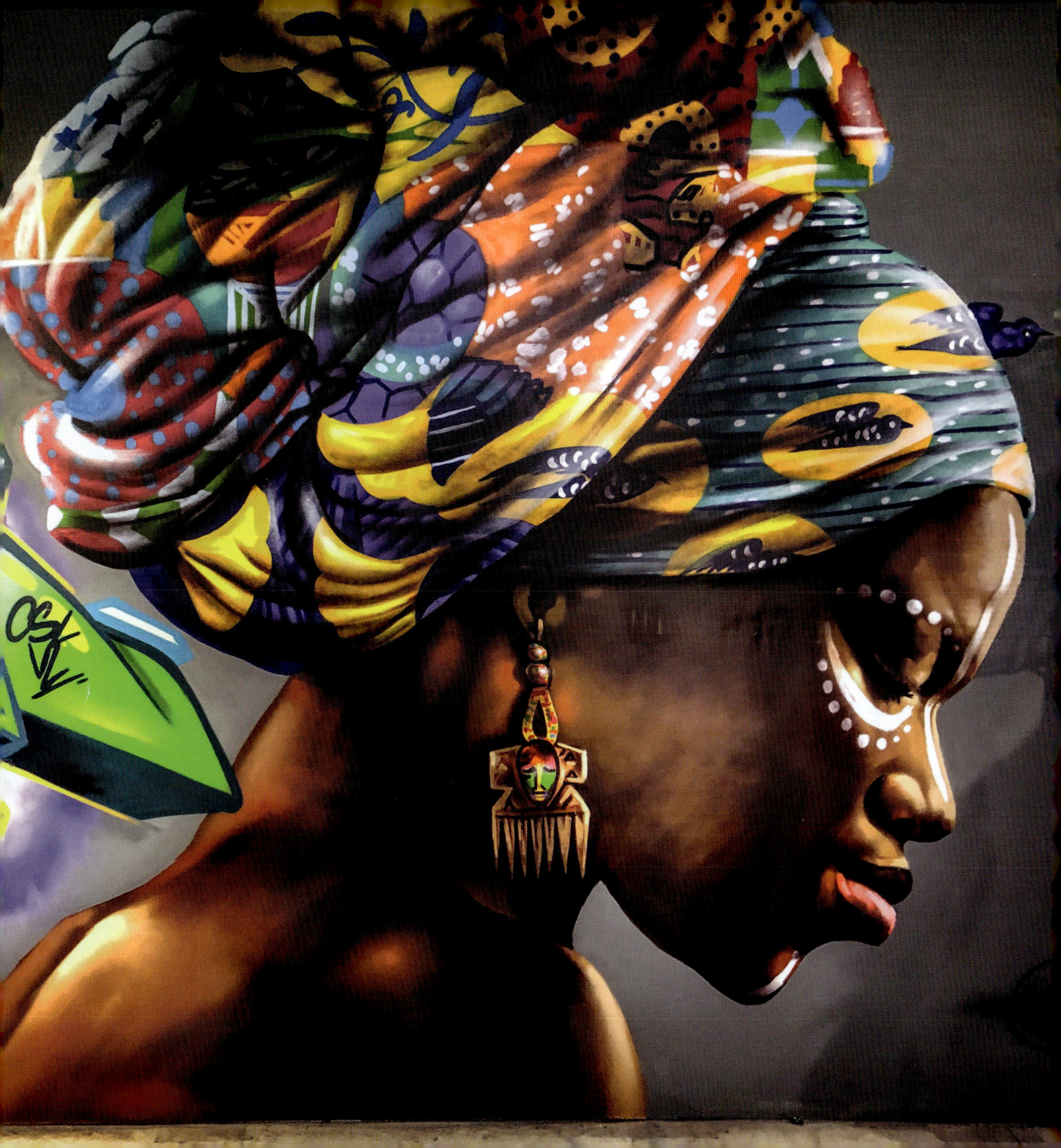

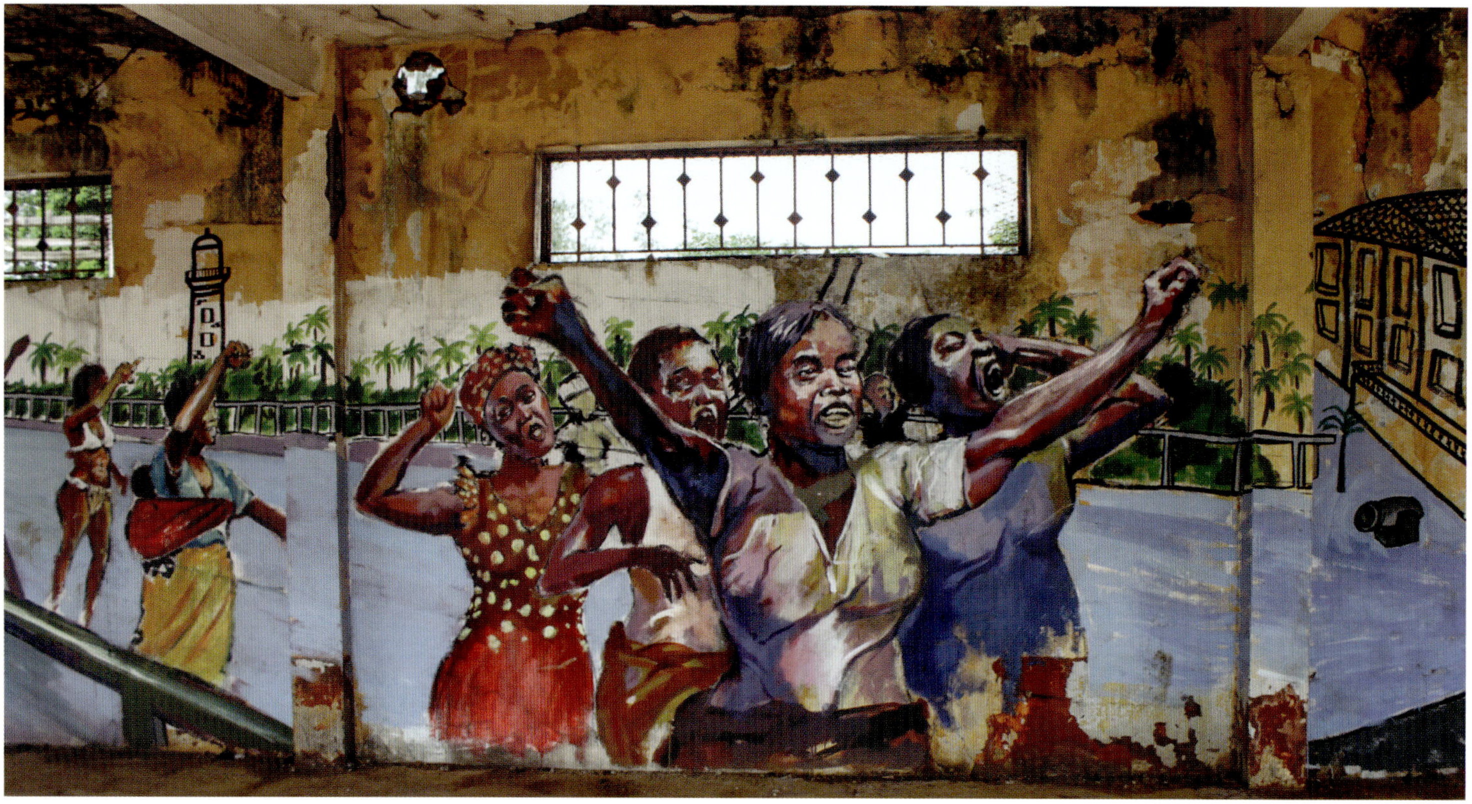

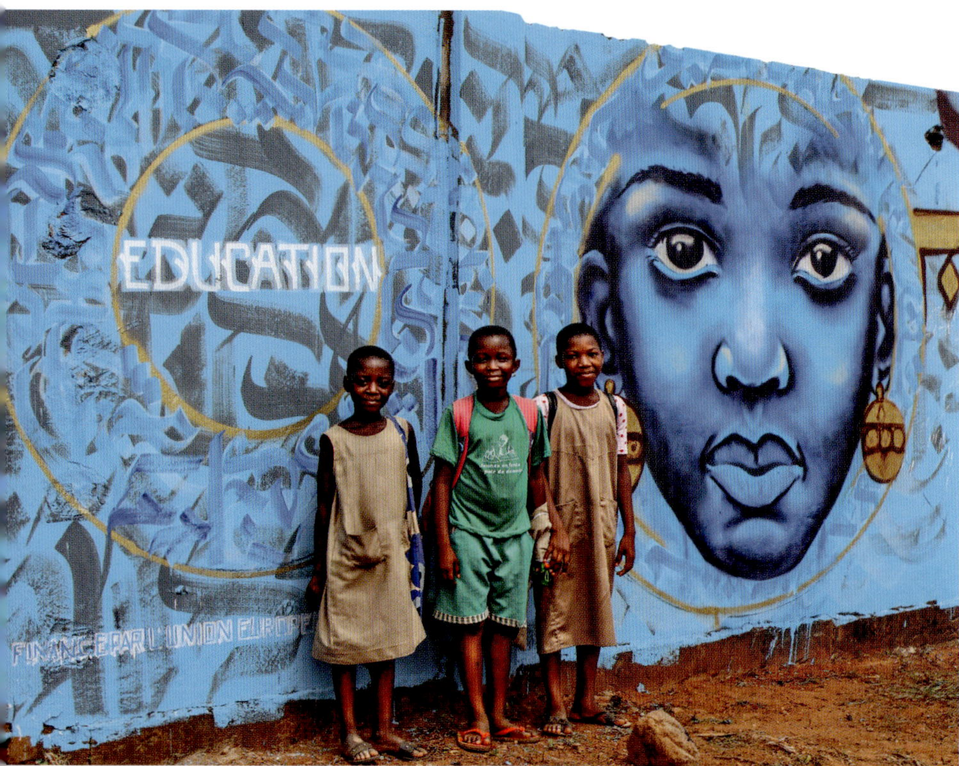

EDUCATION
FINANCE PAR L'UNION EUROPE

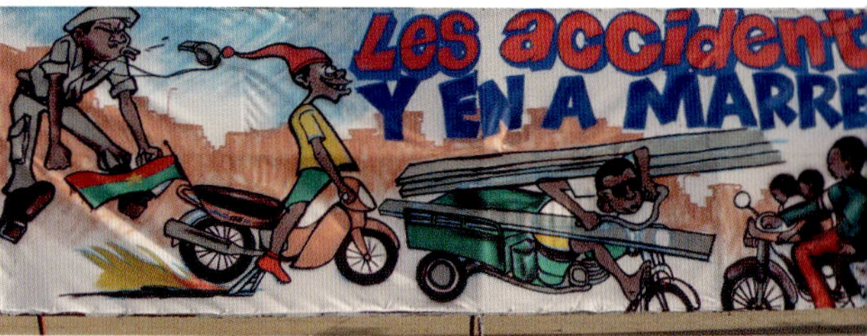

Les accident
Y EN A MARRE

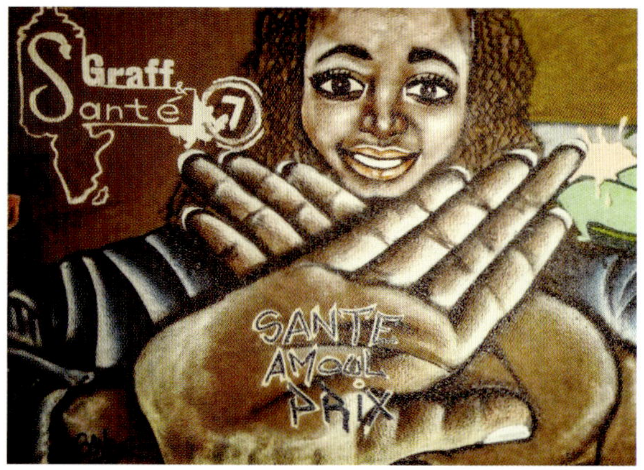

Graff
Santé
SANTE
AMOUL
PRIX

EDUCATE AND UPLIFT

ART ON THE GROUND

Various projects across the continent relate to education. Graffiti interacts like few other art forms and easily breaks down barriers between people and places. It is an important tool for social stimulation as it connects, empowers and encourages profound thinking. It can even impact those who were not directly involved in the process – the simple addition of colour on a wall can act as visual stimulation, sparking ideas, changing the perception of how one identifies with a space, inspiring or altering one's understanding of a specific subject, or enhancing one's capability to unleash a series of positive events. Over the years, many projects have been established to tackle issues and generate change. Through the support of select institutions, African artists can earn a living from their passion and teach others a myriad of topics using their art form. The enrichment of young minds and the transformation of communities is the end goal of many facilitators. Artists also reflect on their own stories in the process.

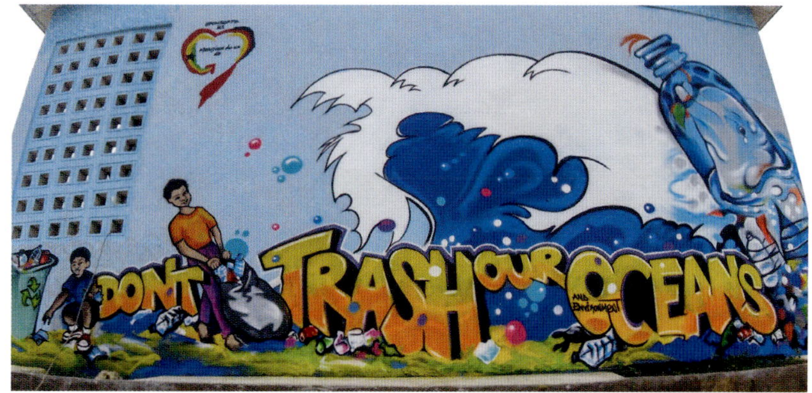

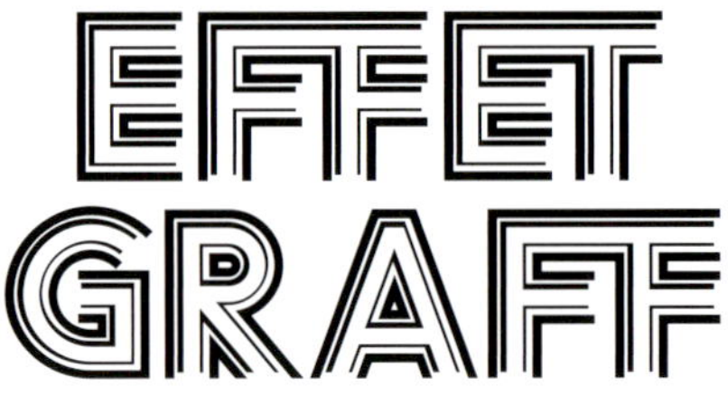

EFFET GRAFF

FESTIVALS & CULTURE

Below
**Freemind, Mr Stone,
Dr Mario. 5th edn,
Cotonou, Benin, 2019**

Opposite, top
**Mr Stone. 4th edn,
Grand-Popo, Benin, 2018**

Opposite, centre left
**Patriot, Dr Mario,
Lionel DaVinci, Afart,
Freemind, Seencelor, Line
(Switzerland). 5th edn,
Comè, Benin, 2019**

Opposite, centre right
**Patriot, Freit'Arts, Lionel
DaVinci, Mr Stone. 5th edn,
Ouidah, Benin, 2019**

Opposite, bottom
**Freemind, Mr Stone,
Dr Mario, Afart. 5th edn,
Cotonou, Benin, 2019**

Effet Graff (Graffiti Effect) is a graffiti tour in Benin where participants paint walls in multiple localities, aiming to make art more accessible. A number of intricate wall murals were produced during the fifth edition in 2019 as artists travelled to four cities in ten days, from the home base in Cotonou. Every wall was based around the chosen theme – modern heroes – while workshops held at participating cultural institutions offered classes in diverse fields, from calligraphy and comics to music, dance and photography. The public and other admirers were drawn to each intervention as the graffiti artists brought new life to bare walls with their colourful expertise. Having freedom to articulate themselves and a platform whereby to popularize urban expression, the artists facilitate the expansion of their street art scene.

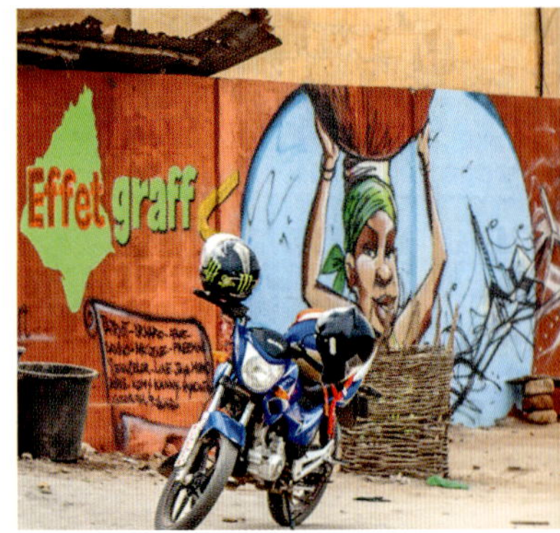

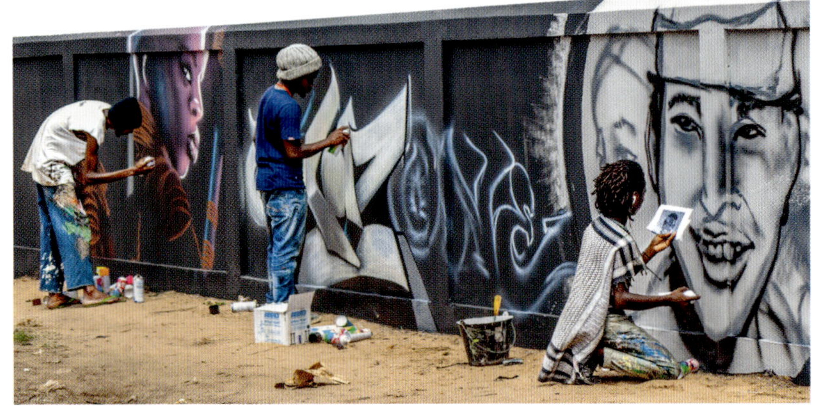

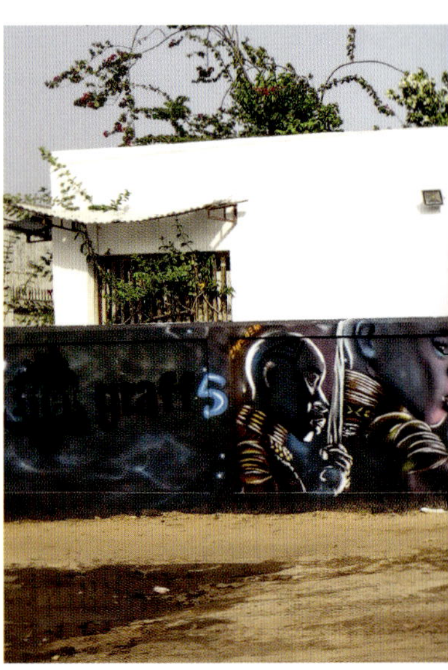

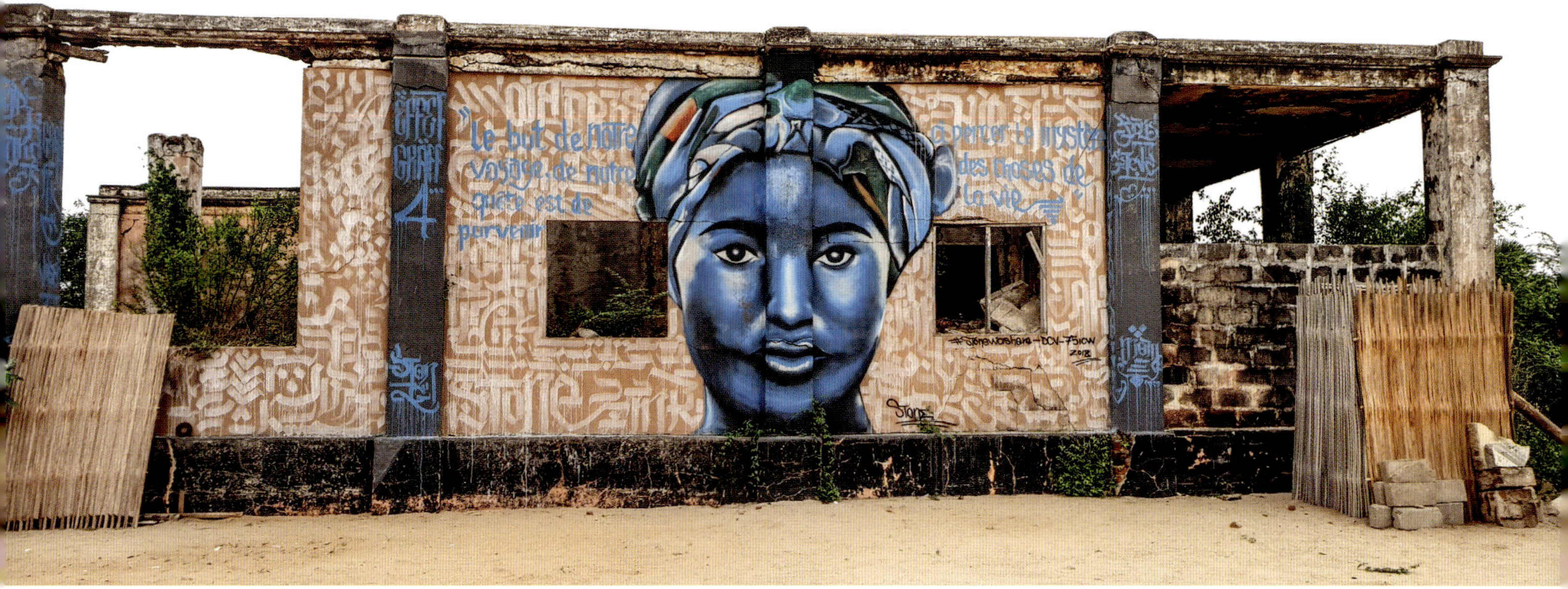

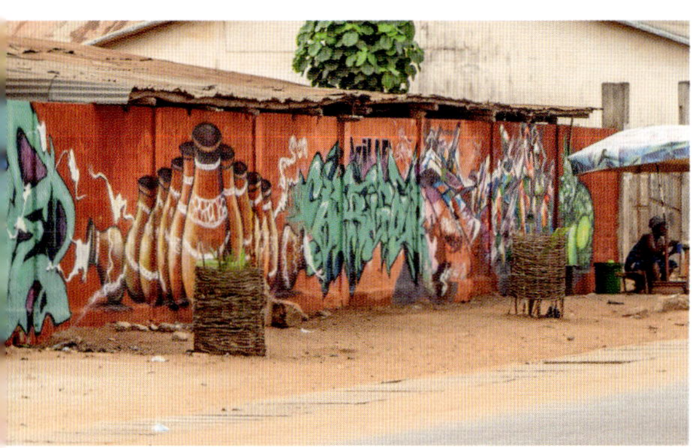
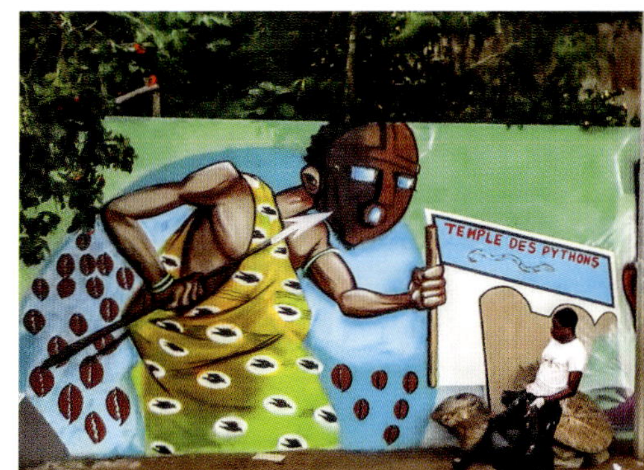
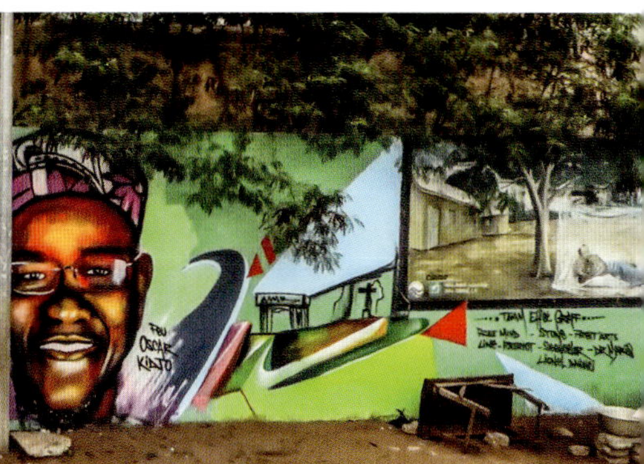
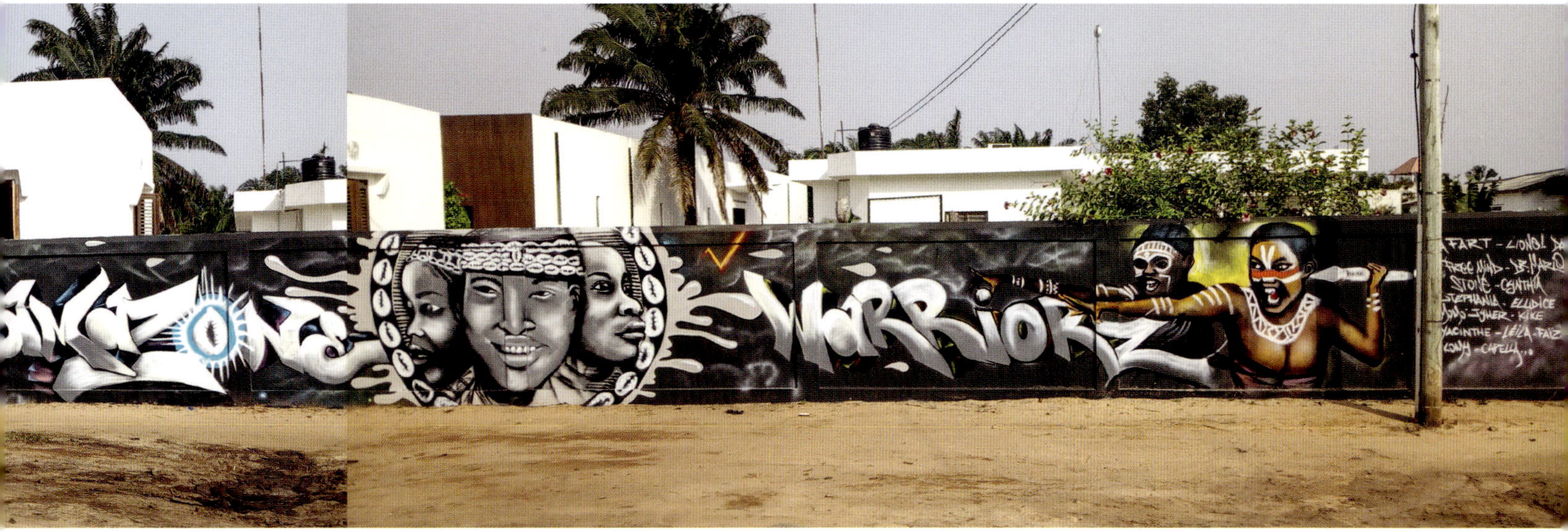

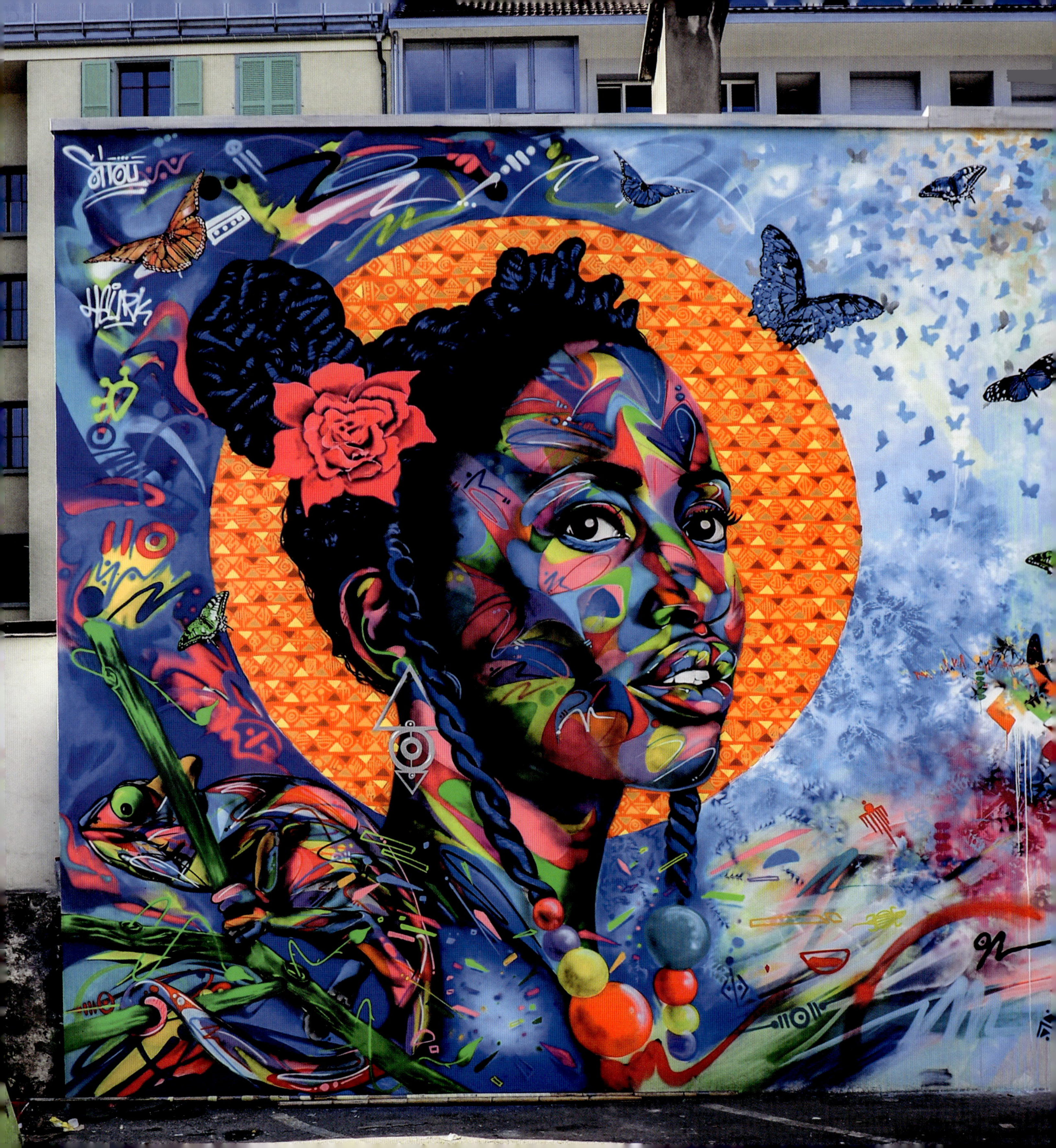

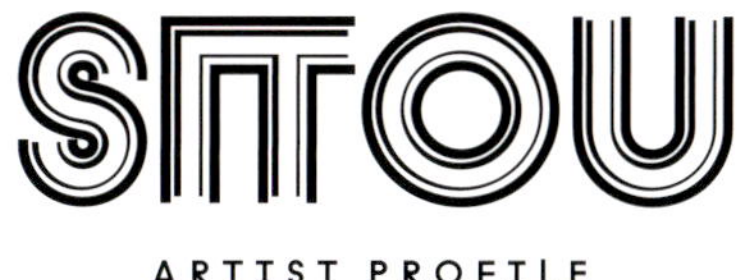

Tell me about your introduction to graffiti.

My friends and I threw ourselves head-first into the hip-hop movement in the 2000s. I danced, I rapped. Then I saw some graffiti in magazines and music videos and I told myself: that's mad, I need to start doing this. I began reproducing exactly what I saw. I started on my first wall in 2003. However, at the time I was not considering turning this into a career. In parallel with my studies, I trained myself in graphic design using online tutorials. It was only after I participated in the Waga Hip-Hop Festival in Burkina Faso that I realized my passion had worth. Instead of handling spray cans and brushes, I could very well have ended up behind a desk, working with numbers – I have a master's degree in finance and banking. My real passions are drawing and hip-hop; that is why I said goodbye to numbers and chose to focus exclusively on urban culture.

Tell me about your graffiti artist name.

My graffiti artist name is Sitou, which means 'blessing' in my language (Ewe, the language spoken in Togo). My grandmother gave me this name and I am attached to it – it keeps her by my side and reconnects me to my roots and memories.

Tell me about your style and painting process.

My style is very colourful and is tied to the chameleon, an animal that represents an African divinity called Agama in Ewe, or Lira in Voodoo, which announces change, mutation, adaptation and diversity. The colours that I work with represent our cultural differences above all: their wealth, beauty and complementary nature. These colours are connected by lines which link each element together, in a perpetual search for harmony. It seems to me that these values should be the bedrock of our societies, to enable us to move towards a more beautiful, united world.

Painting in an environment means enhancing the colours of that space, blending them and adding a few more to convey emotion, and a positive and communicative energy. First, I apply flat tints to represent a range of emotions. Then, I add strong black and white lines, which bring the artwork together and add power, light and dynamism. Finally, I shade off the flat tints with additional colour lines, which reinforce the work and allow a harmony between the colours.

What is the graffiti and street art scene like in Togo?

When I started in the 2000s, Togolese graffiti barely existed. Only one person was doing it: Max de Campos. He was my role

Opposite
Sitou, with Heurk One (Switzerland). 'MONAFRICA', Geneva, Switzerland, 2018

Right
Sitou. Casamouja: Urban Art Wave, Casablanca, Morocco, 2019

Far right
Sitou. 'Human & Technology', Lomé, Togo, 2018

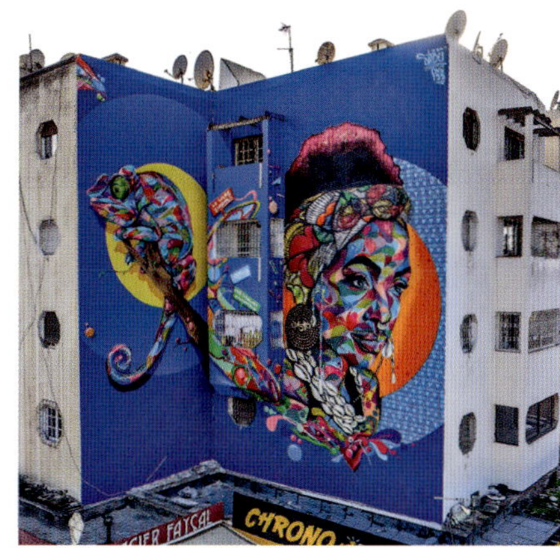

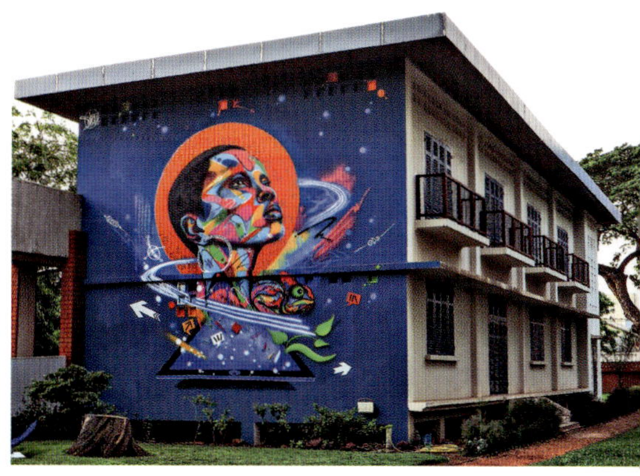

model. He really won us over with his work. Today, aged thirty-five, I am one of the pioneers who helped develop the scene in Togo, alongside Trez and Patriot, two other street artists. Young artists are rallying to take the helm in Togo and neighbouring Benin, such as Mr Stone, Seencelor and Dr Mario, who I have supported for several years. They are developing their own styles, forming crews and organizing events.

But it remains difficult to support the new generation; spray paints are expensive and this passion is still hardly accessible. Young people need to be creative and adapt to the materials available. A positive point is that popular opinion is now changing. What was previously viewed as vandalism is now seen as an art form and inhabitants are happy to offer their walls to artists.

What is the difference between African graffiti and that in the rest of the world?

In Africa, graffiti is not only an artistic style. Graffiti is used as a tool of communication, to convey messages on themes that are central to young people's lives, such as raising awareness about STDs, the importance of education, even rules of basic hygiene. This medium speaks to all, from urban centres to villages where literacy rates are low. I have organized festivals on these various themes in Togo, Benin and the DRC, where each time the message gets through. I am always surprised by the power of this art form!

Tell me about the paint you use.

When I started, I did not have good-quality paints, they were not distributed in Togo and materials were expensive. I started with spray cans with low coverage, using acrylic paints on the wall for flat tints and a darker spray can for the finishes. Today, I have access to various brands and I am used to working with different types of spray cans. There are big differences between each one, but I do not have any preferences.

What reactions have you received from people while painting on the streets?

People stop and share their opinions, positive or negative. Communication is established, a discussion is launched, and social ties are strengthened. Children are the most expressive, and that's amazing. They have no filter – they love it or they hate it, and most often they want to try it out themselves. It is not uncommon for people to offer us food or drink to thank us for enhancing their environment, and that really brings us joy.

How is your work evolving? And what do you think you'll be doing in the future?

These last few years, my style has evolved a lot. Travel and dialogues with various graffiti artists have allowed me to access new sources of inspiration, to develop my technique and to refine my style. My goal is to continue my research, to explore new techniques, new colour combinations, new media. It is like cooking – I always want to discover new dishes!

What is the most important thing about painting?

The most important thing for me is the approach and the creative cycle. This process is not tangible at first, but eventually it comes to life on a wall. Obviously the result is important – it is what others will see – but I am never satisfied, I always want to go further.

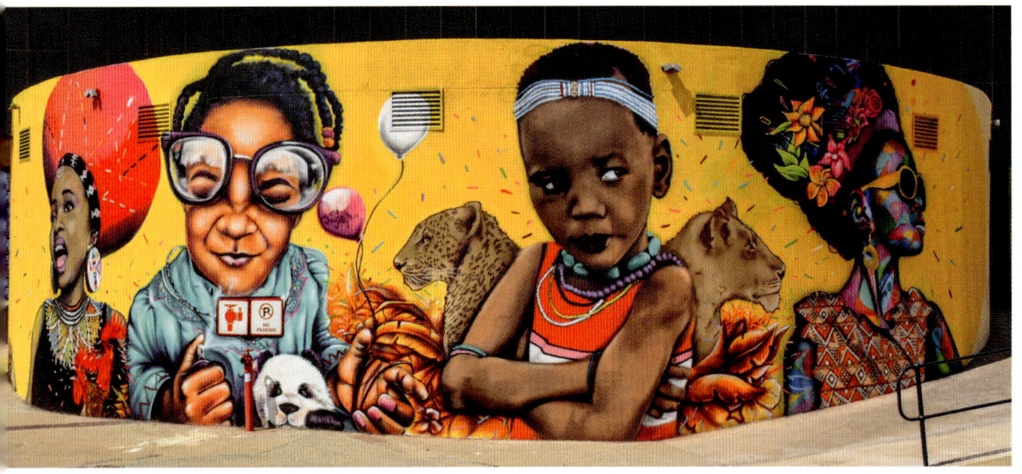

Sitou Matt Imagination (SMI) is a graffiti and street artist from Togo, and member of several crews including Doxandem Squad from Senegal and CNN 199 from Belgium. After traversing the African continent, inspiring other young visual artists through festivals and murals, he is now based in Paris, France, and awarded bigger opportunities to carry out his unique Afro-urban offerings.

Left
Mr.ëksê, Doudou'Style (France), Breeze Yoko, Sitou. Ubuhle Bendalo project, Soweto, Johannesburg, South Africa, 2019
Opposite
Sitou, Moh Awudu. Accra, Ghana, 2018

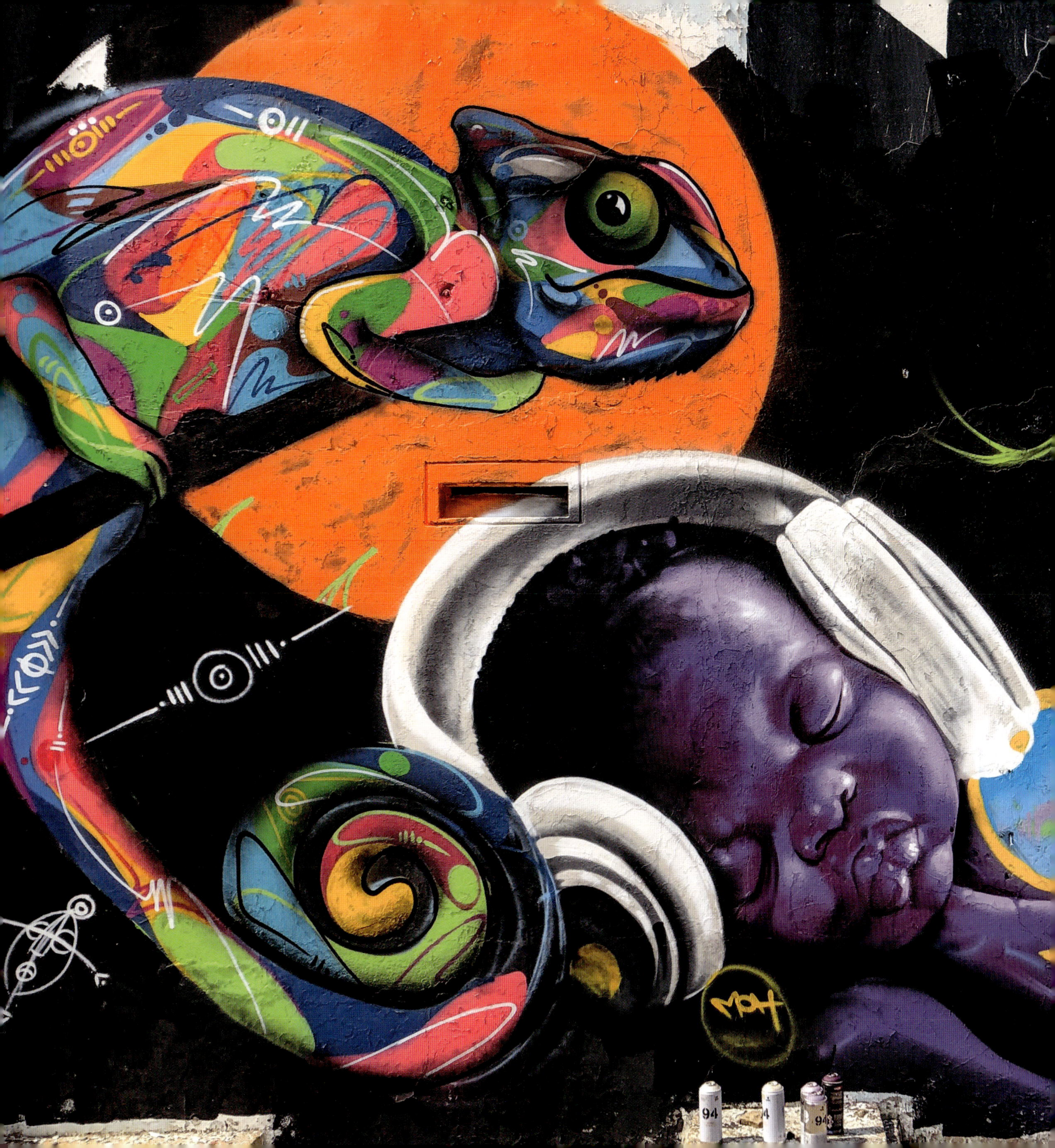

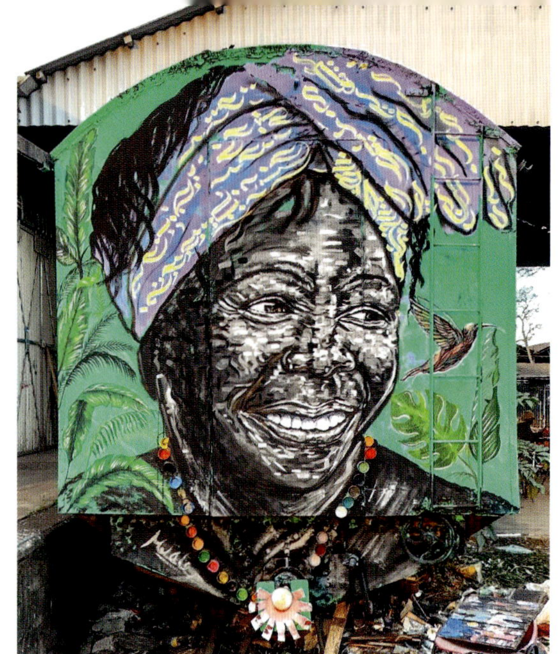

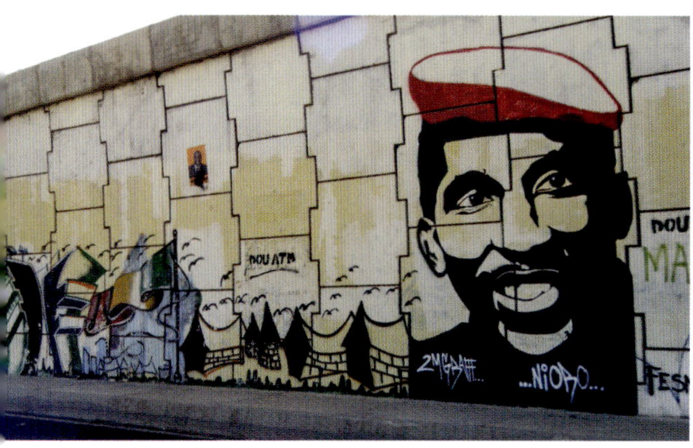

DOU ATM
MA
DOU ATM
2MGRAFF... ...NIORO...
FES

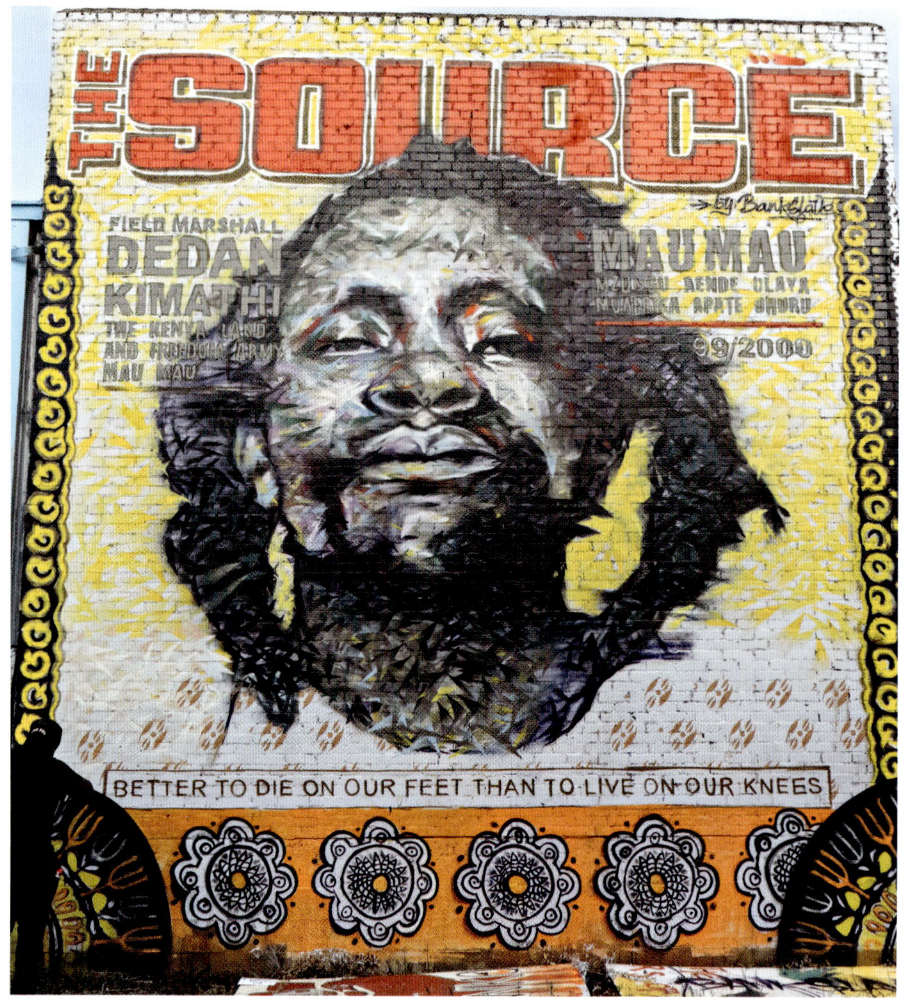

THE SOURCE
by BankSlate
FIELD MARSHALL
DEDAN KIMATHI
THE KENYA LAND
AND FREEDOM ARMY
MAU MAU
MAU MAU
MZUNGU AENDE ULAYA
MWAFRIKA APATE UHURU
99/2000
BETTER TO DIE ON OUR FEET THAN TO LIVE ON OUR KNEES

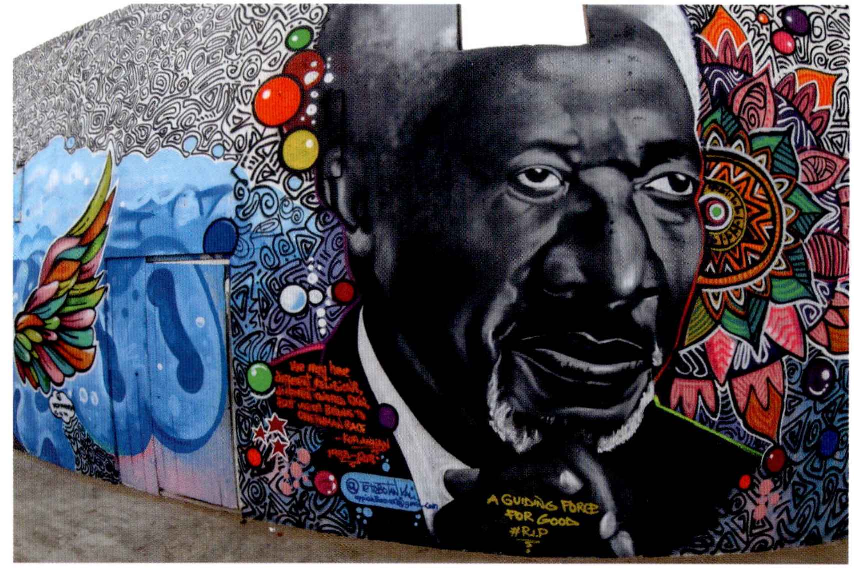

A GUIDING FORCE
FOR GOOD
#RIP

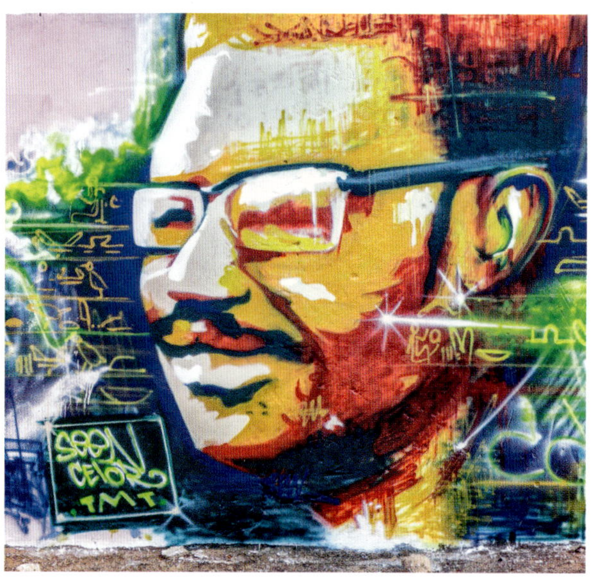

SOON
CELOR
TMT

AFRICAN HEROES

ART ON THE GROUND

Opposite, clockwise from top left
Msaleh. 'Wangari Maathai' (Kenyan activist and first African woman awarded the Nobel Peace Prize), Nairobi, Kenya, 2019

Bankslave. 'Dedan Kimathi' (leader of the Mau Mau Uprising during Kenya's struggle for independence), New Orleans, USA, 2018

Seencelor. 'Cheikh Anta Diop' (Senegalese visionary who shared ideas about a united Africa), Festigraff (6th edn), Dakar, Senegal, 2015

Tetebotan Kali. 'Kofi Annan' (seventh Secretary-General of the United Nations, who advocated for peace), Chale Wote Street Art Festival (8th edn), Accra, Ghana, 2018

2mgraff. 'Thomas Sankara' (revolutionary Burkinabé figure often likened to Che Guevara), Dakar, Senegal, 2010

Right
Mad Zoo TRK. 'Winnie Madikizela-Mandela' (anti-apartheid activist and wife of Nelson Mandela), Dakar, Senegal, 2018

African artists place strong emphasis on their culture, their roots and their identity. They find great importance in creating work that encourages dialogue and fortifies their collective history. Emotive portraits of well-known politicians, activists or leading figures in entertainment, as well as inspirational quotes, are often embedded in wall murals. This appreciation highlights the importance of independent thinking within art, especially as a means of free expression. Throughout history there are leaders who have an impact on society, becoming role models or agents of change. In African graffiti circles, some of these heroes include Thomas Sankara, Nelson Mandela, Marcus Garvey, Angela Davis, Martin Luther King, Kwame Nkrumah, Wangari Maathai, Patrice Lumumba, Steve Biko, Kofi Annan, Dedan Kimathi, Winnie Madikizela-Mandela, Cheikh Anta Diop and Maya Angelou.

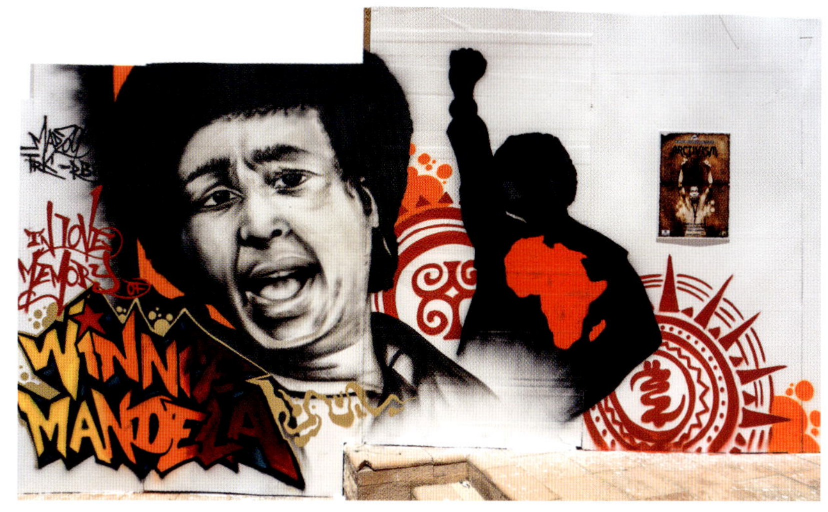

Following spread
Sonny. 'Nelson Mandela' (first black president of South Africa and global icon for peace), Johannesburg, South Africa, 2018

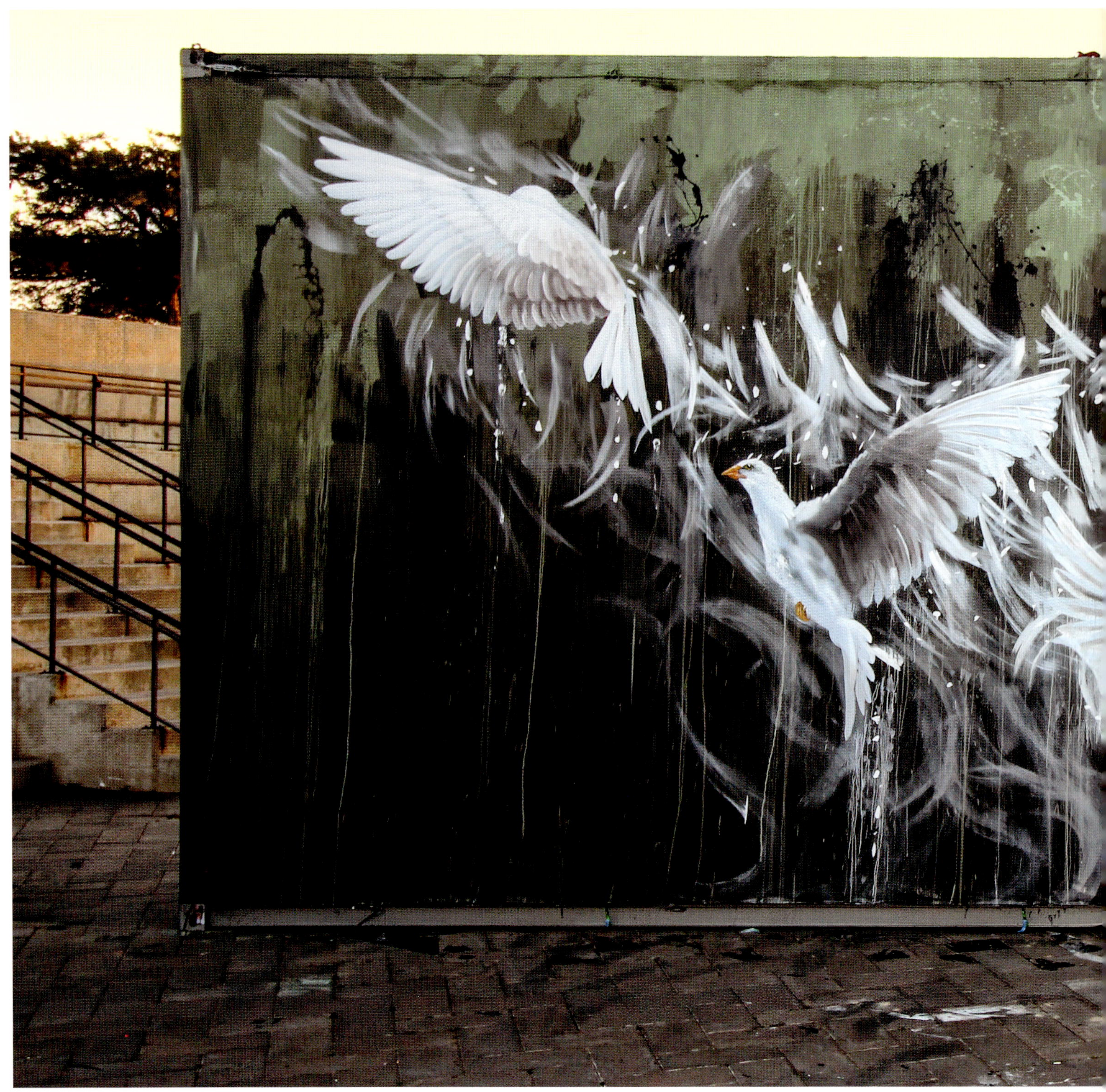

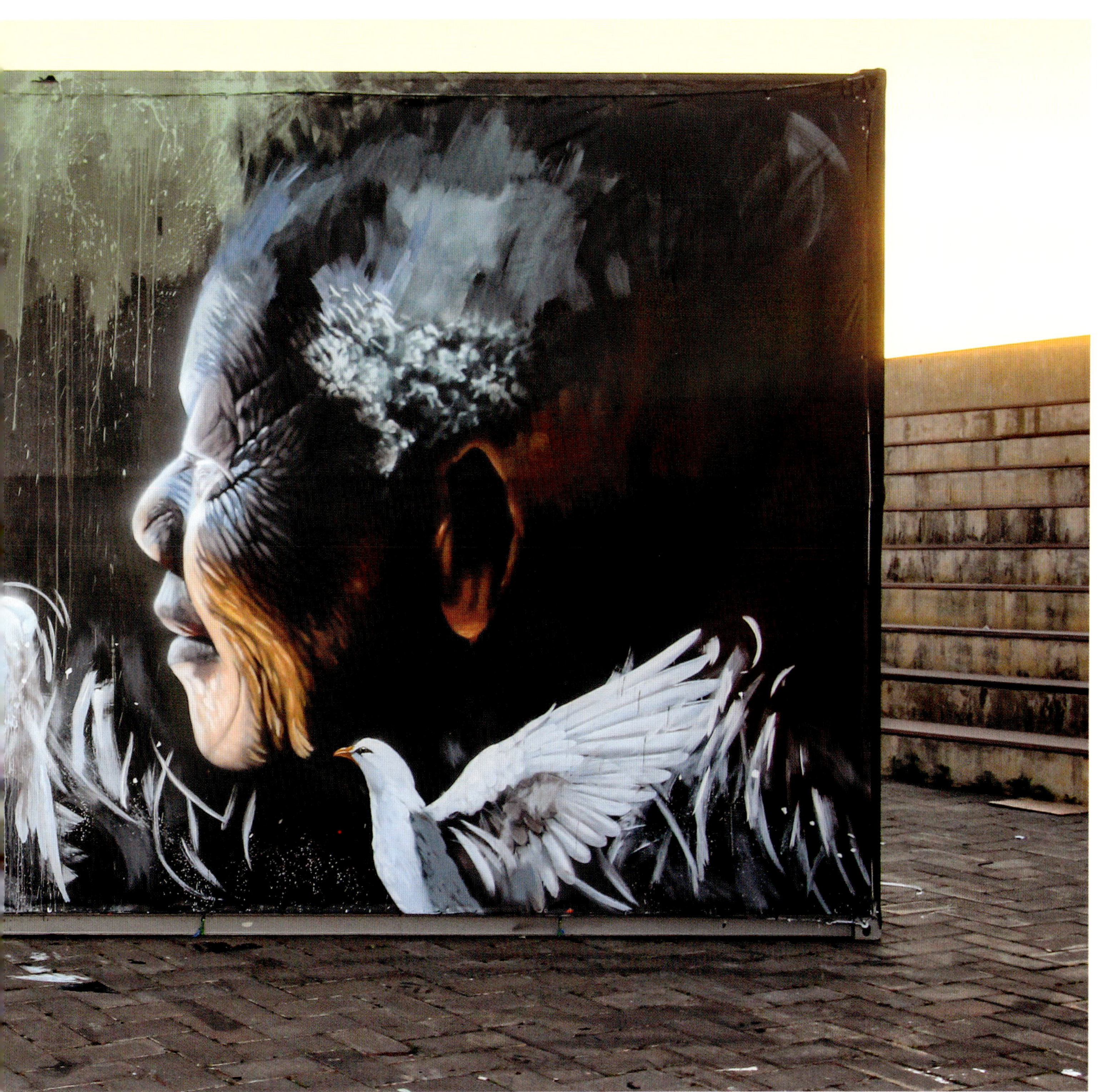

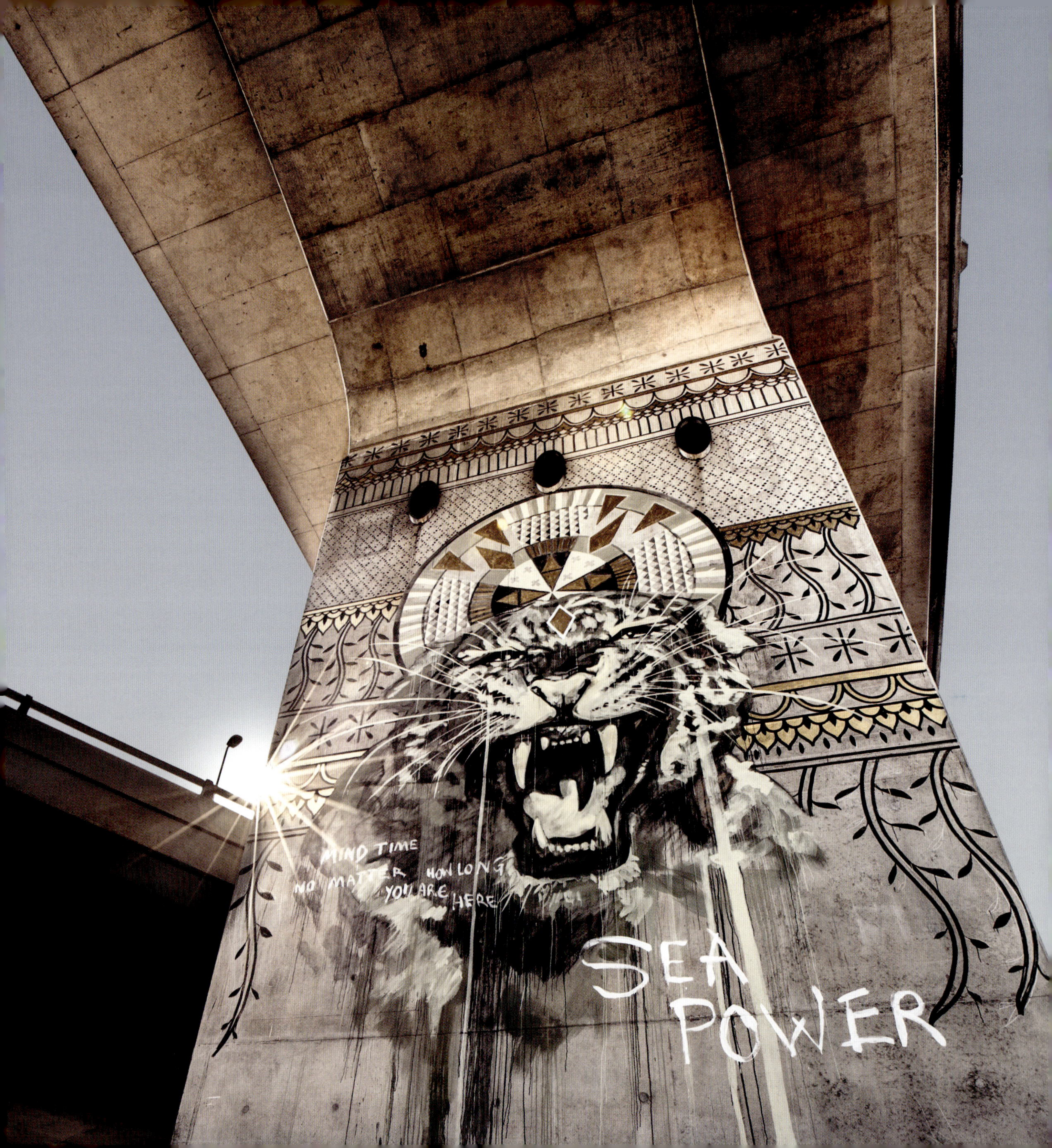

MIND TIME
NO MATTER HOW LONG
YOU ARE HERE
SEA
POWER

SOUTHERN AFRICA

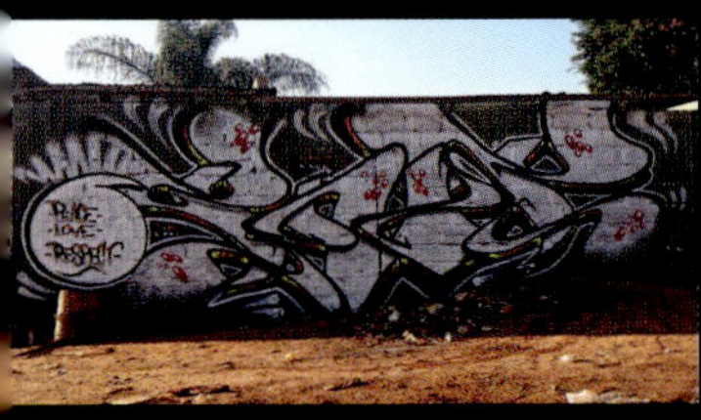

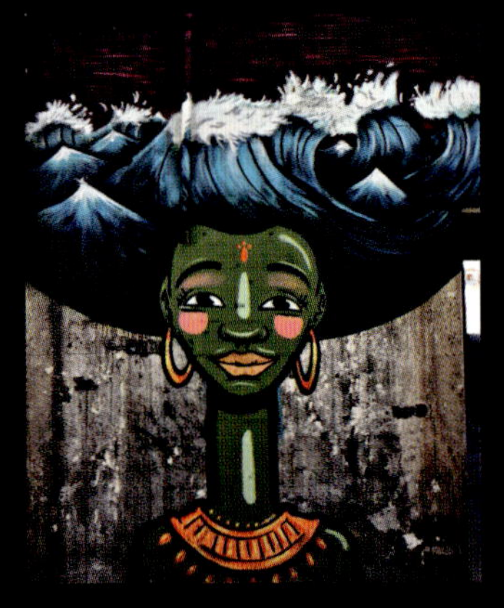

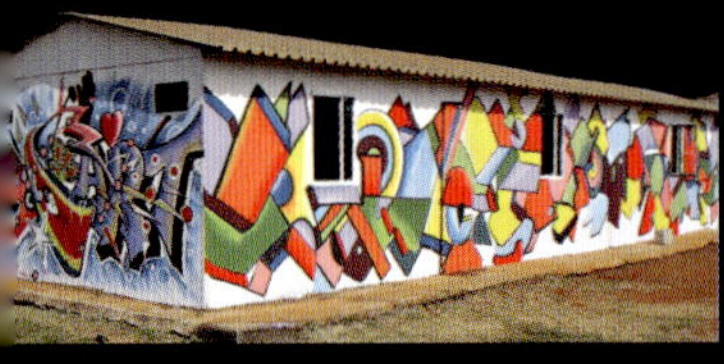

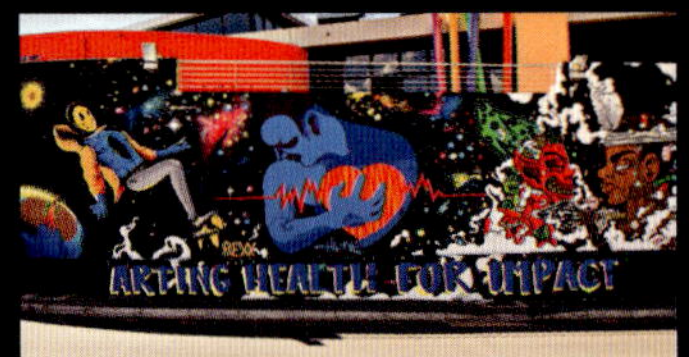

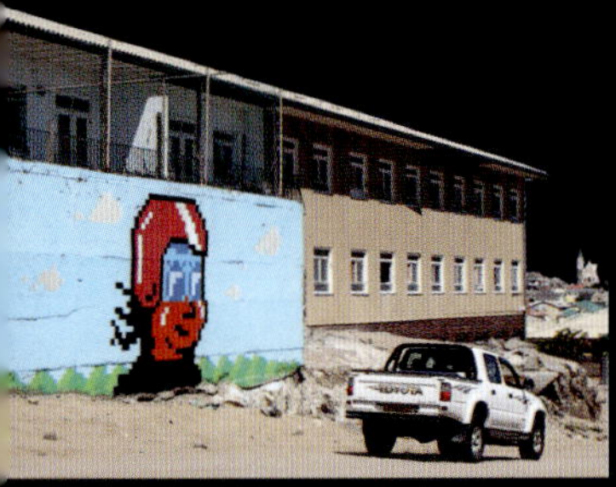

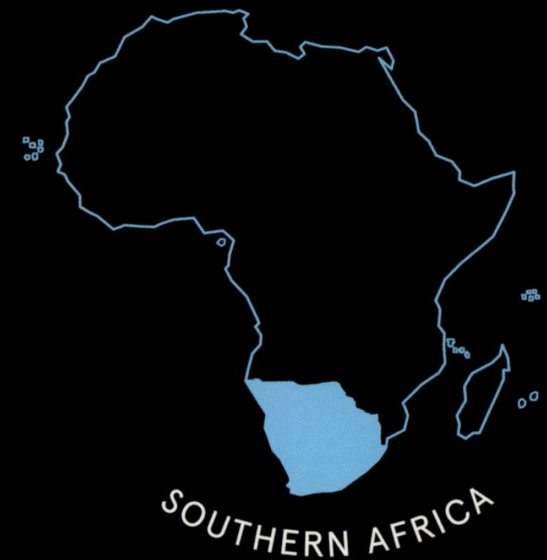

Festivals

❶ **Back to the City Hip-Hop Festival** p. 245

❷ **IPAF (International Public Art Festival)** p. 246

❸ **City of Gold Urban Art Festival** p. 250–53

Projects

① **Arts for Change** p. 231

② **Colour Ikamva** p. 234

③ **Yebo ArtReach** p. 234

④ **The Bridge Tour** p. 235

Page 220
Faith XLVII. 'A Study of Warwick Triangle at Rush Hour', Durban, South Africa, 2014

Left, from top
Snot420. Lobamba, Eswatini, 2016

FOK. Cape Town, South Africa, 2017

Thabo Lukhele, Fela Dlamini, Celimpilo Dlamini. Mahlanya, Eswatini, 2014

Rexx, Khwezi, Fifi Wale. Arting Health for Impact project, Gaborone, Botswana, 2018

Pixel Monster (Spain). Lüderitz, Namibia, 2011

Opposite, from top
Sub-0. Windhoek, Namibia, 2013

Dbongz. Mohlakeng, South Africa, 2019

OptOne. Maseru, Lesotho, 2012

Mook Lion (assisted by Ourspace Mural Crew: Sakhile Mhlongo, Kev7, Sphephelo Mnguni and Tyran Roy). Durban, South Africa, 2014

Senzart911. Johannesburg, South Africa, 2018

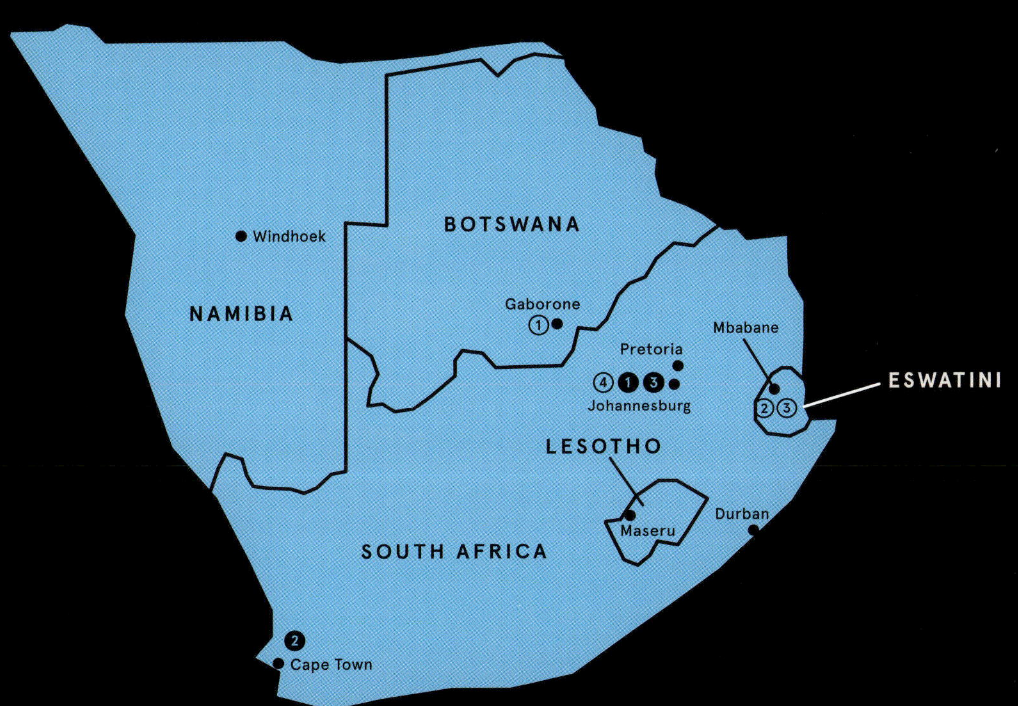

NAMIBIA
BOTSWANA
Windhoek
Gaborone
Pretoria
Johannesburg
Mbabane
ESWATINI
LESOTHO
Maseru
Durban
SOUTH AFRICA
Cape Town

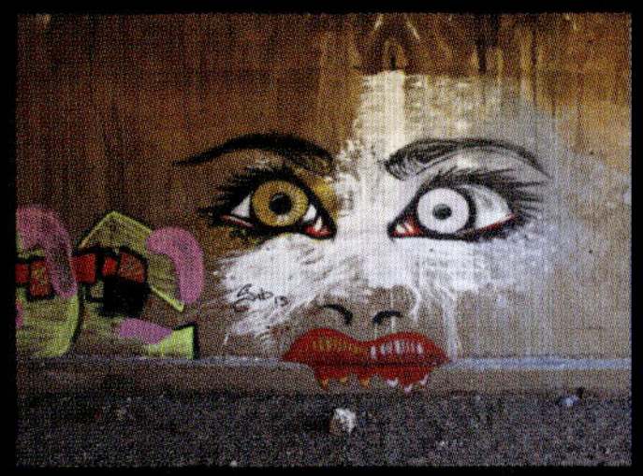

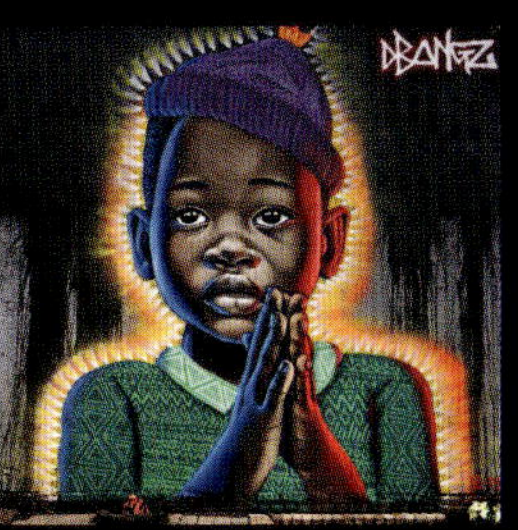

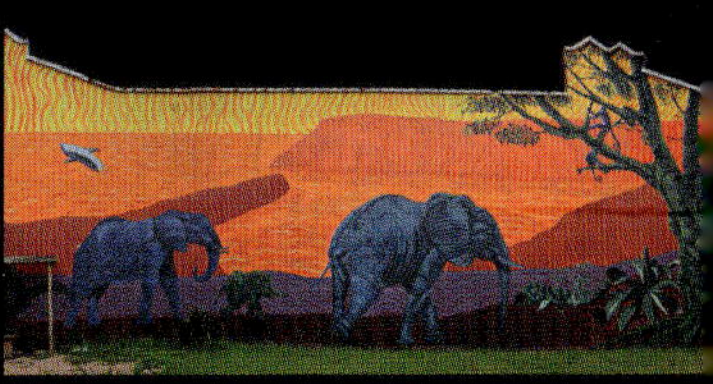

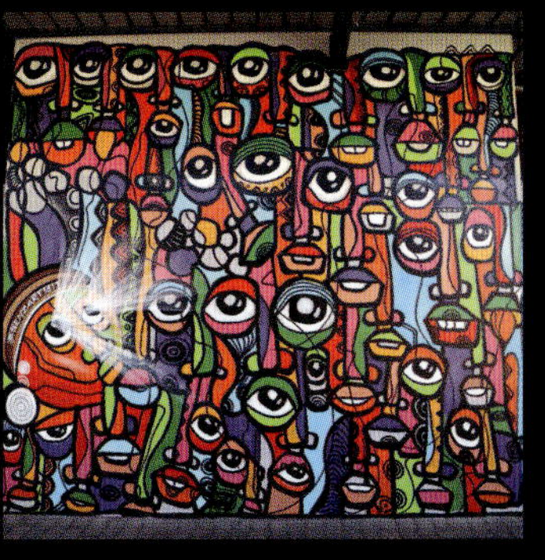

SOUTHERN AFRICA

Graffiti and street art in Southern Africa are dominated by South Africa, thanks to its many active artists. South Africa's rise is primarily linked to its development as a fully-fledged urban centre. As the region's economic hub it boasts an established and growing arts and culture circuit, with exponential growth since a democracy was formed in 1994, after the abolition of apartheid. Graffiti is more accessible, and recently more widely praised because it often assimilates the notions and trends of its international counterparts. After hip-hop culture successfully spilled over into South Africa, the craft appeared in neighbouring states such as Namibia and Botswana, although graffiti there remains low-key with a modest output.

Some of the earliest remnants of art can be traced back thousands of years to the rock art produced by the San people of the Kalahari. The San are hunter-gatherers known for their language composed of clicking sounds, and were the original people of Southern Africa before the arrival of the Bantu speakers. Another people, the Southern Ndebele, have used art for centuries to reinforce their cultural identity as well as for aesthetic reasons, with, for example, women painting intricate patterns on their homesteads. By the 1960s, the paint was advancing from primitive inks and the application techniques had gone from painting with fingers to using chicken feathers. The Ndebele style evolved to what we know today: bright, bold hues and thick black outlines, on a predominantly white background. This form of decoration brought them renown and is possibly the earliest known form of organic public art in the region.

From rural to urban, a very small number of public art murals were created in major South African cities during the 1970s and 1980s. The country was experiencing the height of its oppressive apartheid system and more common political scrawls were a direct response to what was happening in the social environment. Walls were difficult to source and artists risked arrest. Some artists found it easier to express their resistance via fine art shows in galleries.

Opposite, top
Faith XLVII. 'A Study of Warwick Triangle at Rush Hour', Durban, South Africa, 2014

Opposite, bottom
Tek1, Kid Kreol & Boogie (Réunion), Khwezi. Arts for Change, Gaborone, Botswana, 2013

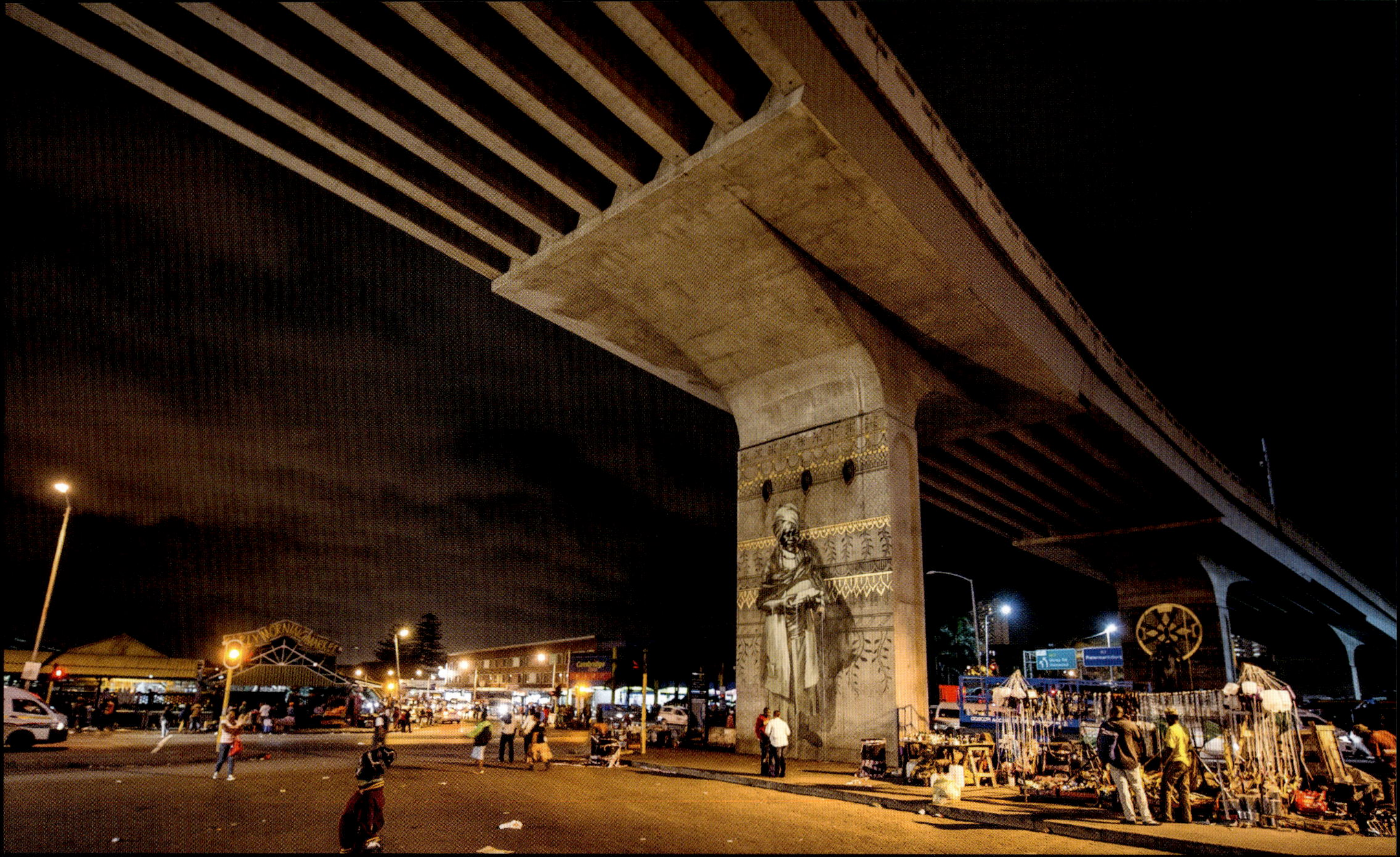

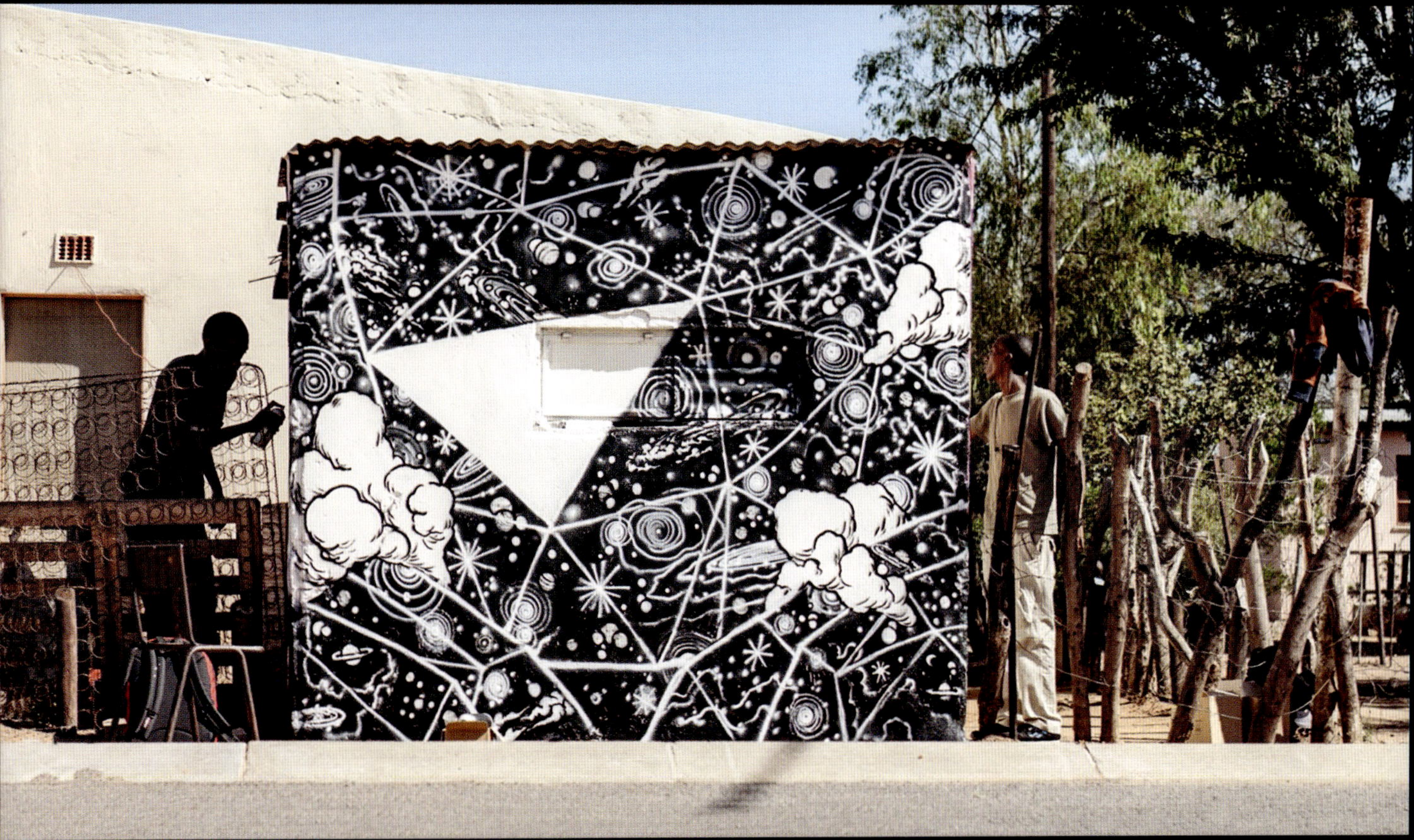

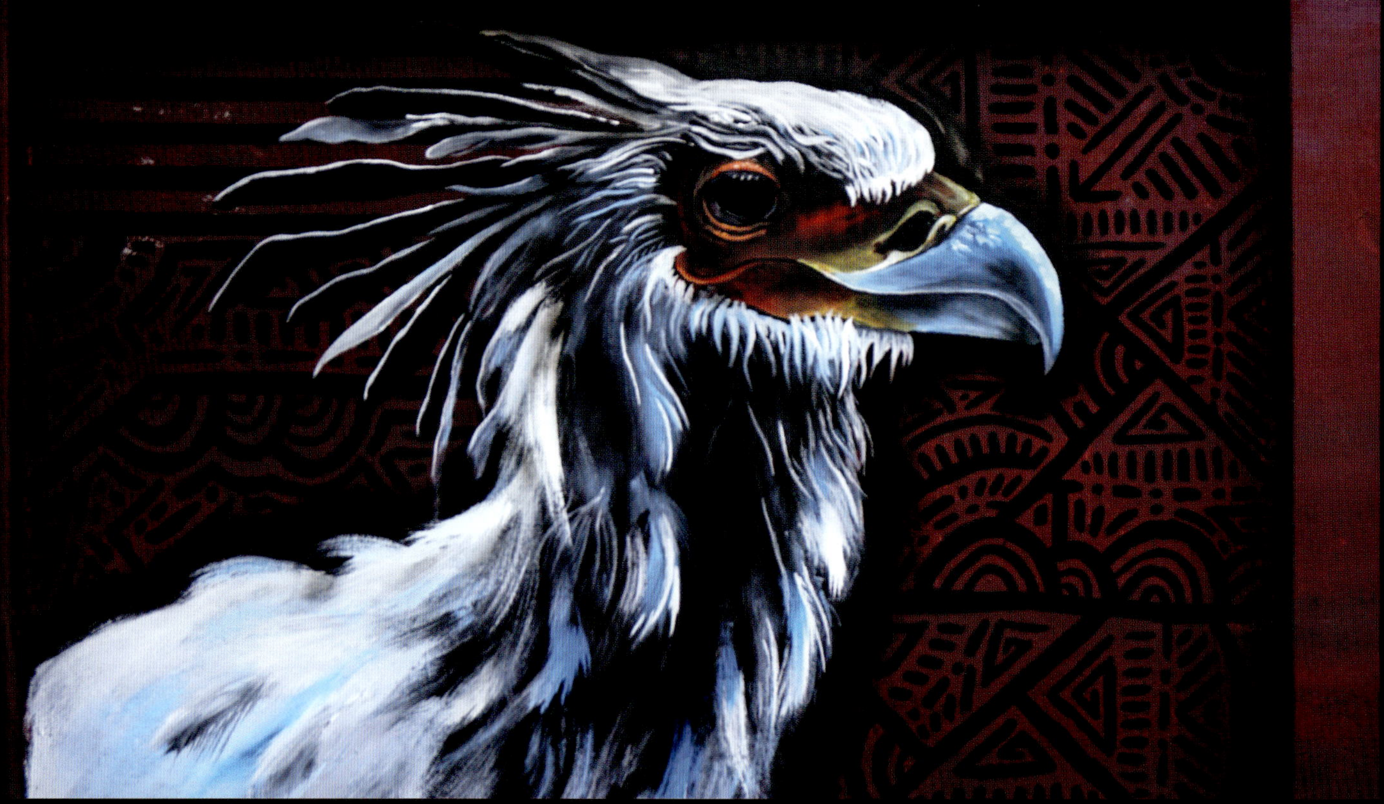

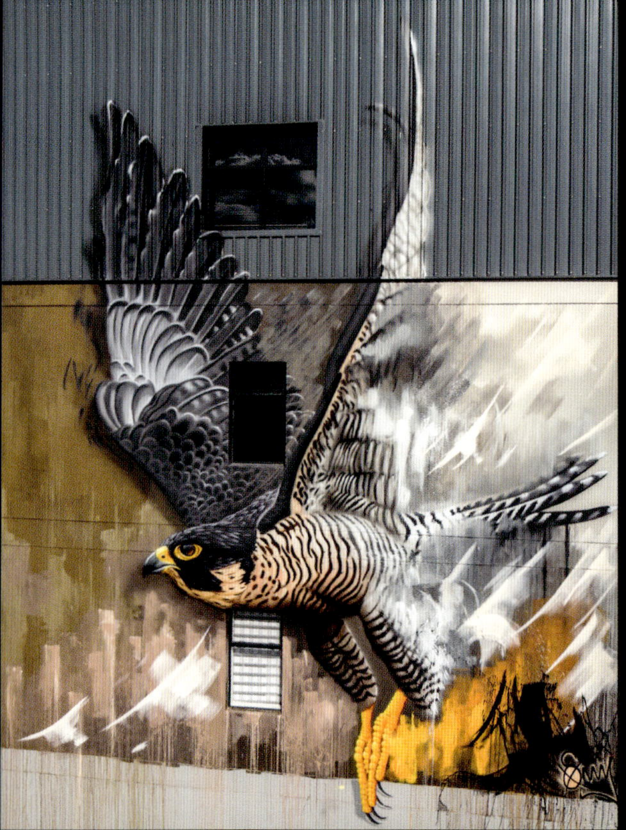

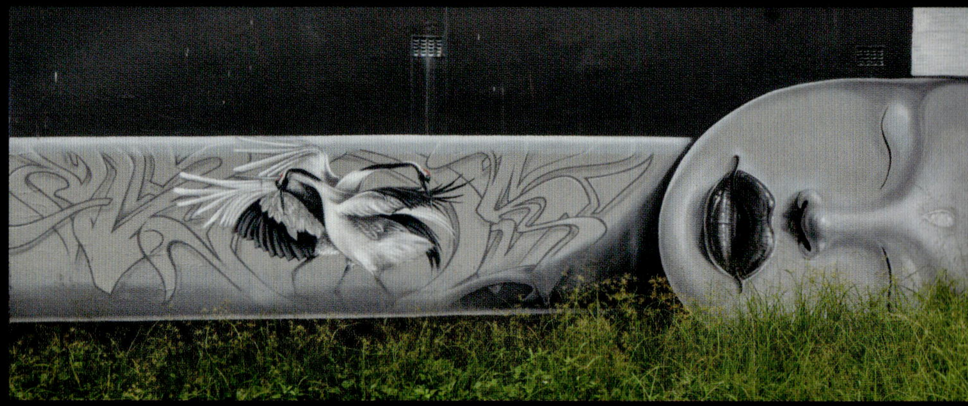

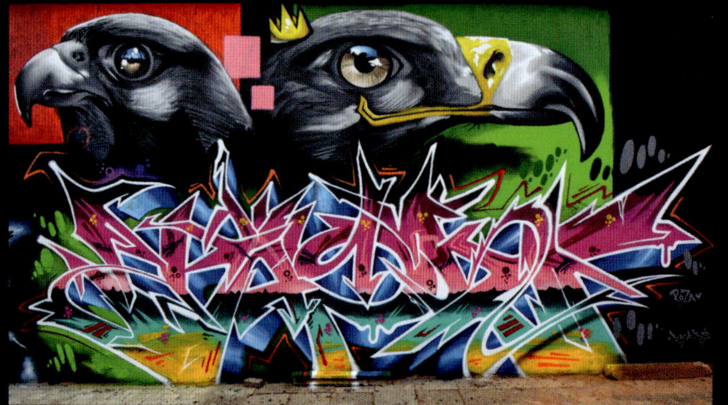

I explore different mediums and techniques within the same context, making beautiful spaces out of forgotten places. I inform and motivate in a beautiful way, the language of the heart. I've always been interested in showcasing my neighbourhood and the small details of township life.' MR.ËKSÊ

Murals were well promoted only in the 1990s as South Africa ushered in a new chapter, often through art programmes or community engagement projects with themes focusing on human rights, AIDS awareness and other educational topics. Traditional graffiti was slowly emerging thanks to popular culture; however, this has largely remained separate from art with overt political connotations.

South African youths began to imitate what they saw in New York City, soon breaking ground and spreading the graffiti gospel. The Cape Flats, an apartheid designated area outside Cape Town, became a mecca for South African graffiti artists, who later infiltrated greater Cape Town as they met practitioners in the city's Southern Suburbs. Artists such as Falko One, Gogga (aka Devastator16), Mak1one and later Wealz130 played integral roles in building the scene. Graffiti culture was soon present in Johannesburg and Durban at the turn of the century, with artists including Rasty, Tapz, Dreadr, Ewok and 2kiler. There was a raw energy present in all creative fields as society began to normalize. By the mid-2000s, South African graffiti culture was booming and an assortment of paraphernalia was available. The advent of cross-country crews such as EM (Evil Minds), FSU (Fuck Shit Up) and WK? (What Kind?) meant that cities were linked, while graffiti jams and battles became important fixtures on the social calendar. The Internet soon became a tool to reference styles, showcase work and connect fellow artists. Further afield, in Botswana and Namibia, the scene has been hindered by the insignificance of the culture, mainly owing to the shortage of active artists as well as the high cost and lack of tools. Many practitioners spend time creating work in sketchbooks, which does not advance the culture at street level, and results in few works in the public domain.

Namibia, in the southwest, is sparsely populated largely because of its arid terrain. The capital, Windhoek, is the heartbeat of the country's business and arts, but graffiti's existence is confined to very few spaces, such as Three Circles, a panoramic viewpoint. Sub-0 began to explore graffiti in 2007 after completing an assignment about the visual art form. He soon partnered with ABC (Another Brilliant Creation) and formed CBV (Comic Book Villains), one of the only graffiti crews from Namibia. CBV linked with Real1, an artist from the UK who lived in Windhoek for several years, and the three were responsible for multiple

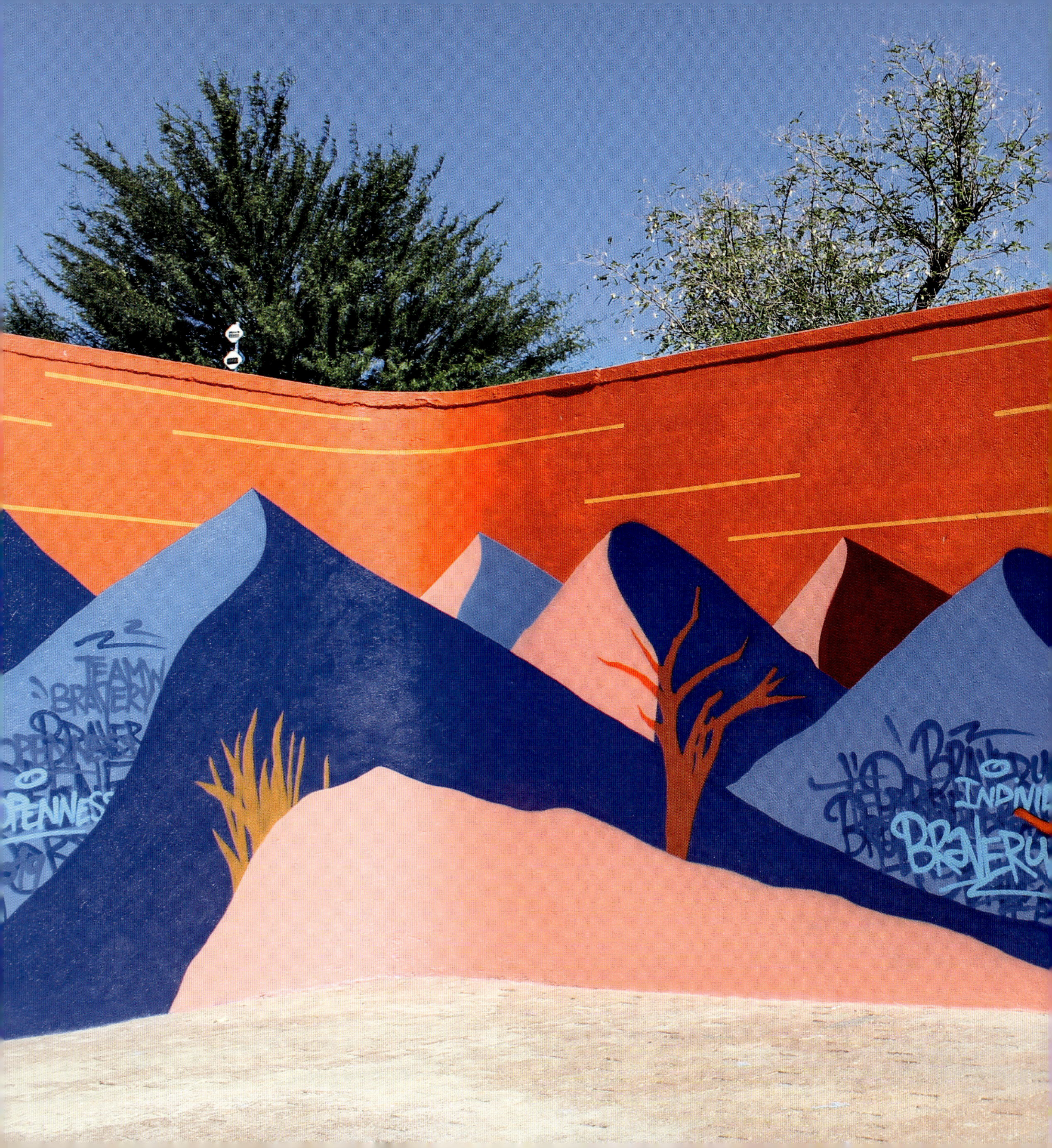

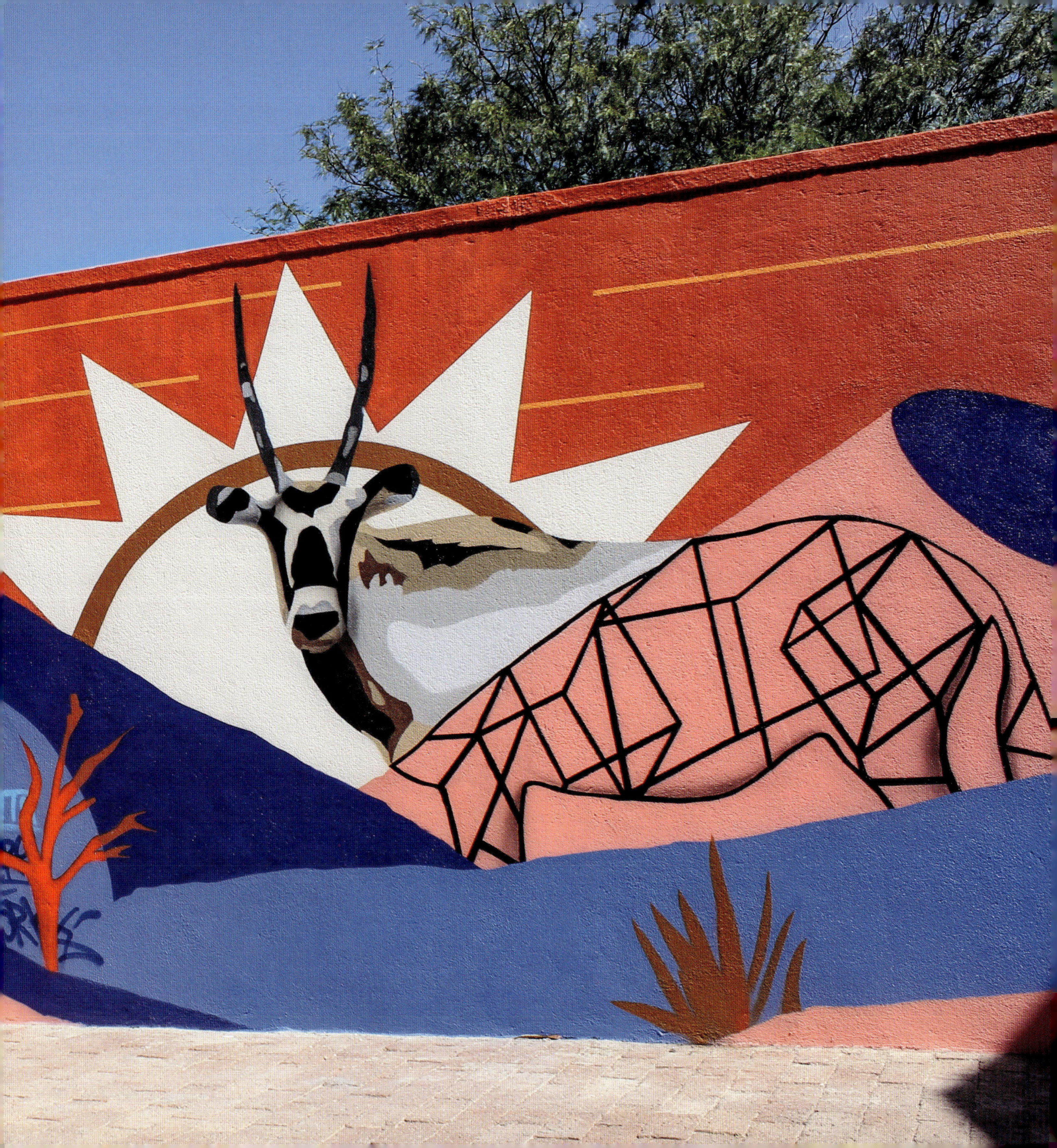

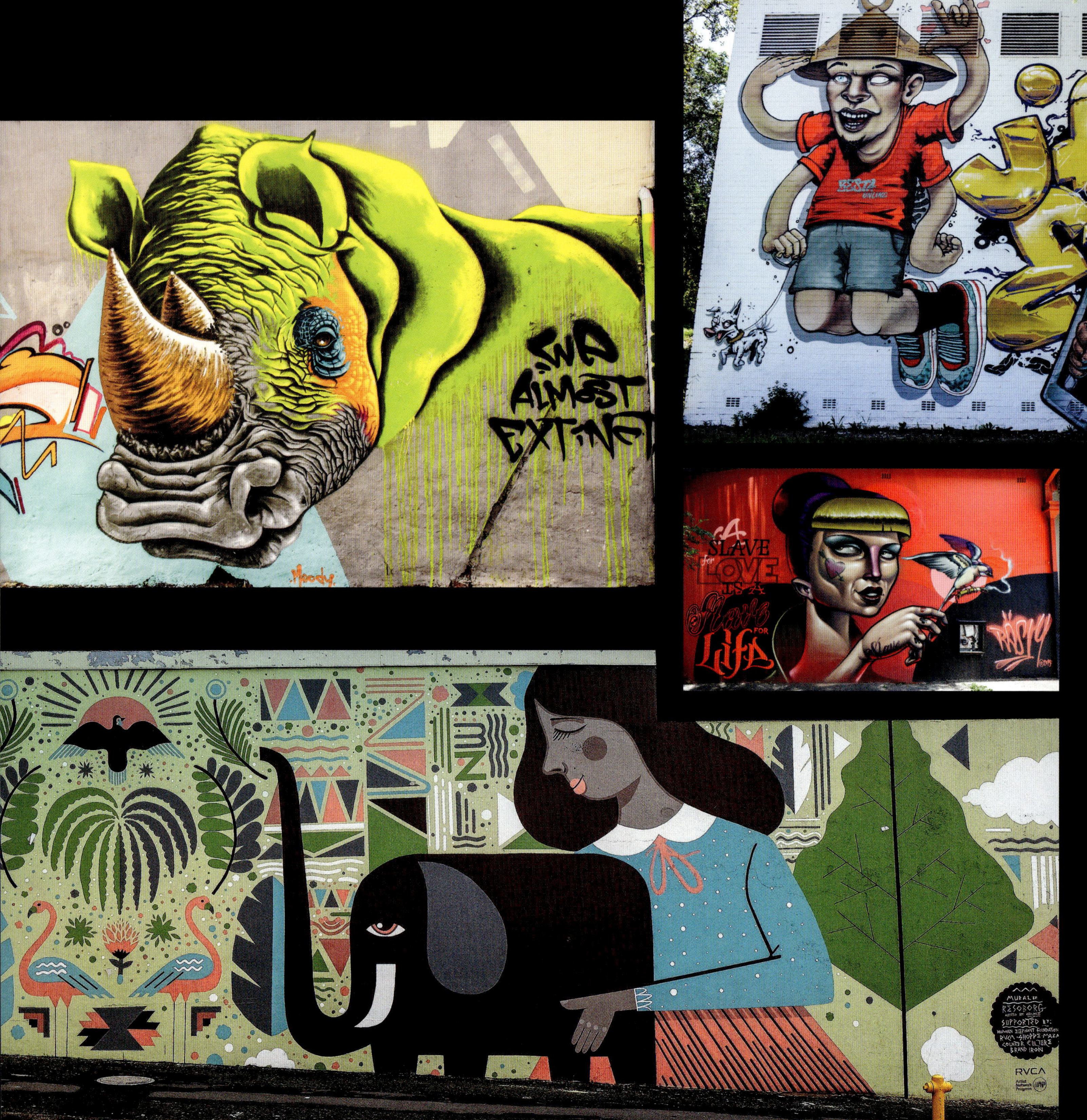
WE
ALMOST
EXTINC
Moody
SLAVE
for
LOVE
Slave for
LiFE
MURAL BY
RESOBORG

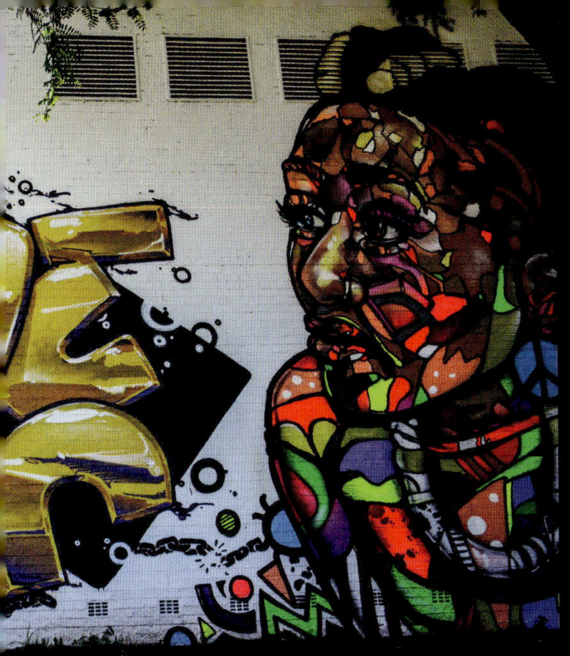

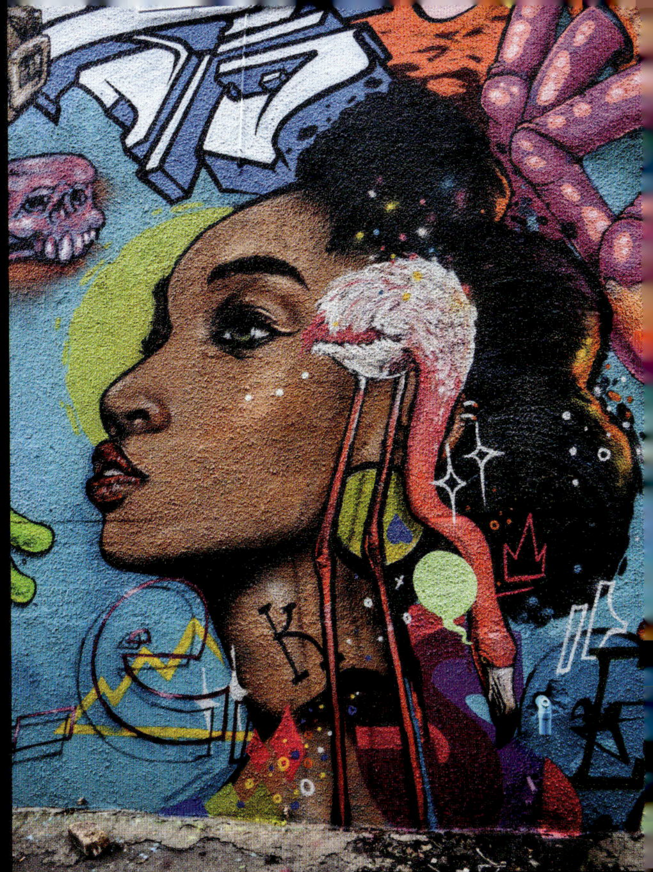

commissioned works from 2009 until around 2013. Another international artist, Pixel Monster, from Spain, made the small town of Lüderitz his home from 2010 to 2015 and painted a wealth of characters in the vicinity.

Botswana, Namibia's neighbouring state, has similar dry climate conditions because of the Kalahari Desert stretching across the country. Gaborone native and accomplished rapper Khwezi (aka khwezididit) was given professional spray paint in 2010 and haphazardly went to work in his studio space, producing his first throw-up. He was quickly hooked and began to focus on an art career that would shape his next ten years. In 2012, he facilitated a graffiti workshop with other local artists, including the now-defunct Siren Crew, and invited special guests from South Africa. Khwezi soaked up all the knowledge he could and proceeded to set up his own creative endeavour, Arts for Change. Informal residences and tuck shops (small food retailers) in the Old Naledi district in Gaborone, Botswana's capital, were decorated during Arts for Change projects in 2013 by Khwezi, Saone, Tek1 and Réunion Islanders Jace and Kid Kreol & Boogie. In 2018, Arting Health for Impact, a new multinational project using street art to engage with health issues, was initiated with Khwezi to bring a message to life in the form of a large-scale mural. Other street artists from Botswana include Smurf One, Sick O and JadeArt from CUP (Concepts Under Pressure).

we need to see art in public spaces, otherwise it becomes a high-society cultural activity that few people get to enjoy. Pushing art in the public sphere and the enjoyment of creating it keeps my passion alive.' MR FUZZY SLIPPERZ

Below
**Pixel Monster (Spain).
Lüderitz, Namibia, 2011**

Right, top to bottom
**Star, Snot420. Mpaka,
Eswatini, 2016**

**Bief37. Alice,
South Africa, 2015**

**Star, Snot420. Mahlanya,
Eswatini, 2016**

Opposite, top
**Mr Fuzzy Slipperz.
Johannesburg,
South Africa, 2016**

Opposite, bottom
**Mr Moris by Mars.
Johannesburg,
South Africa, 2017**

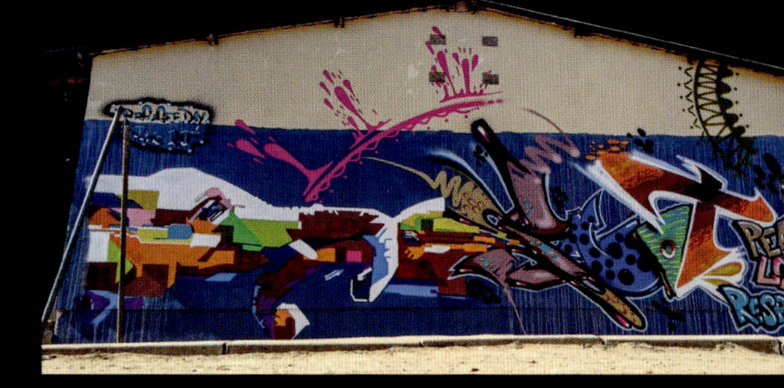

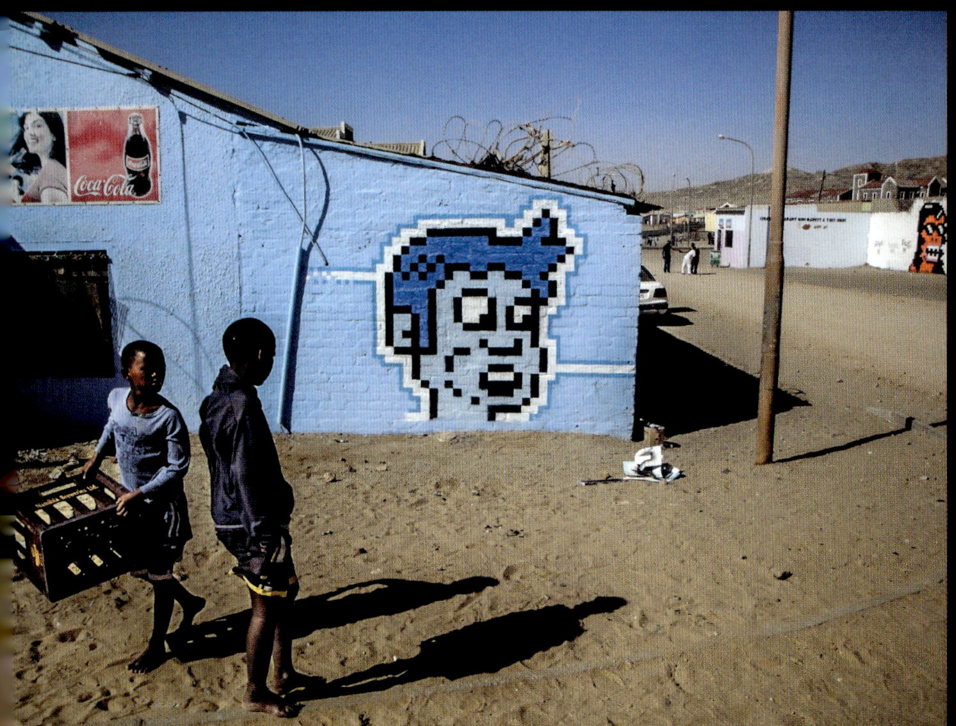

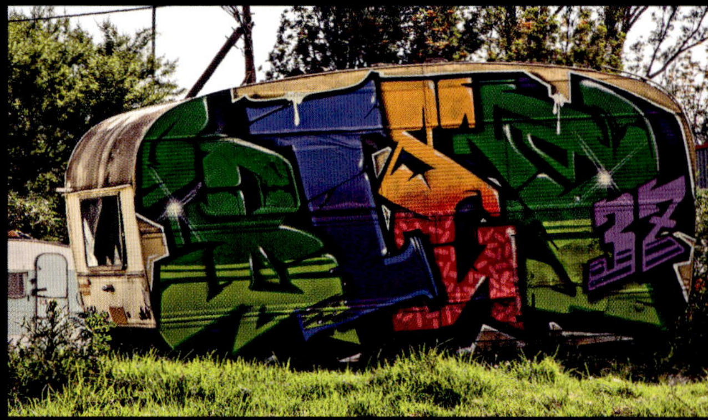

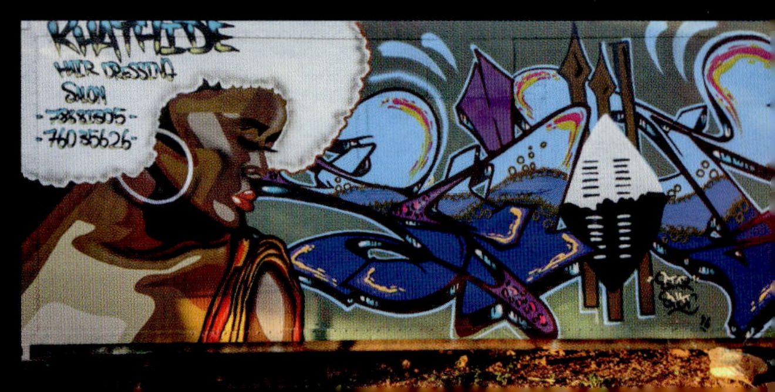

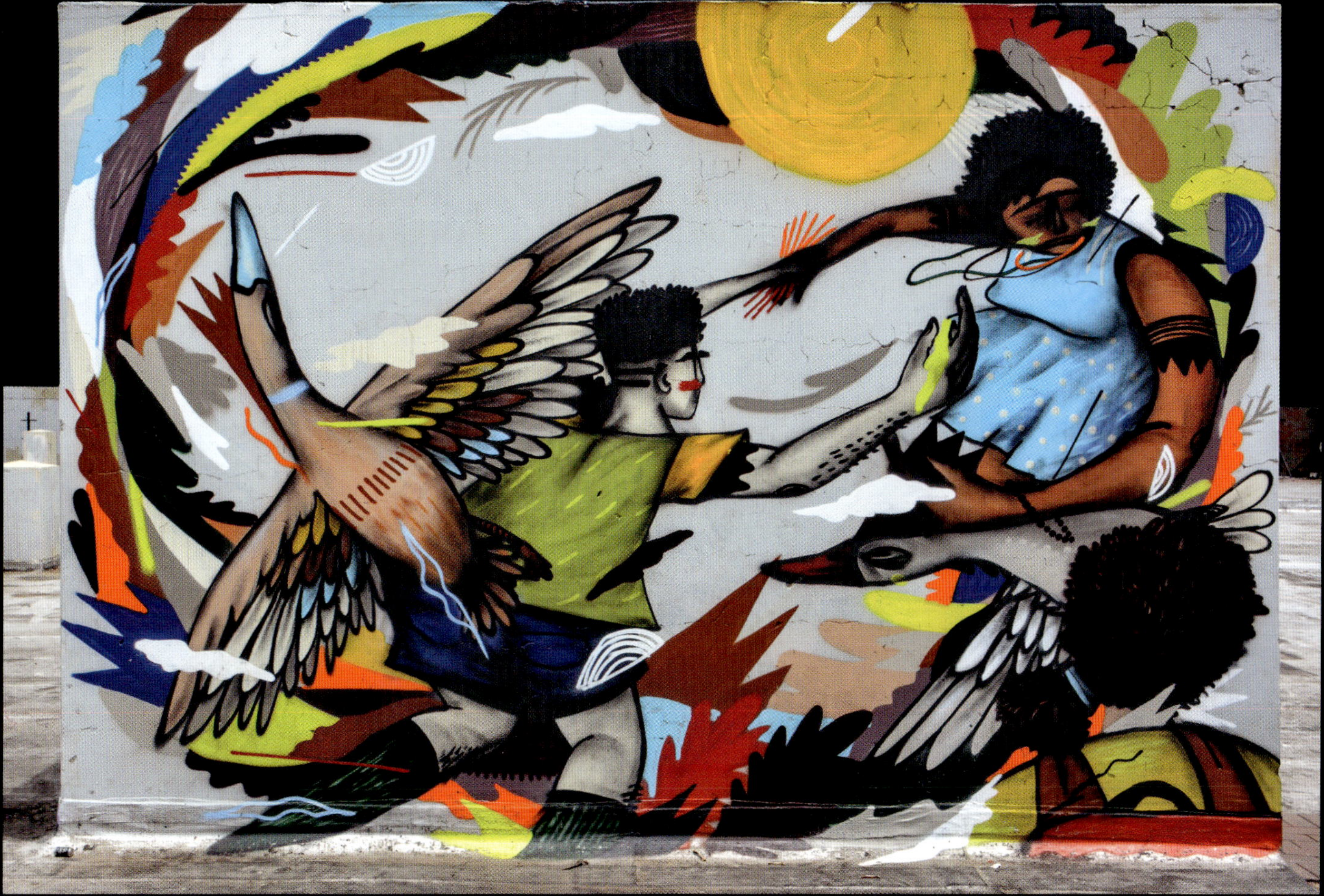

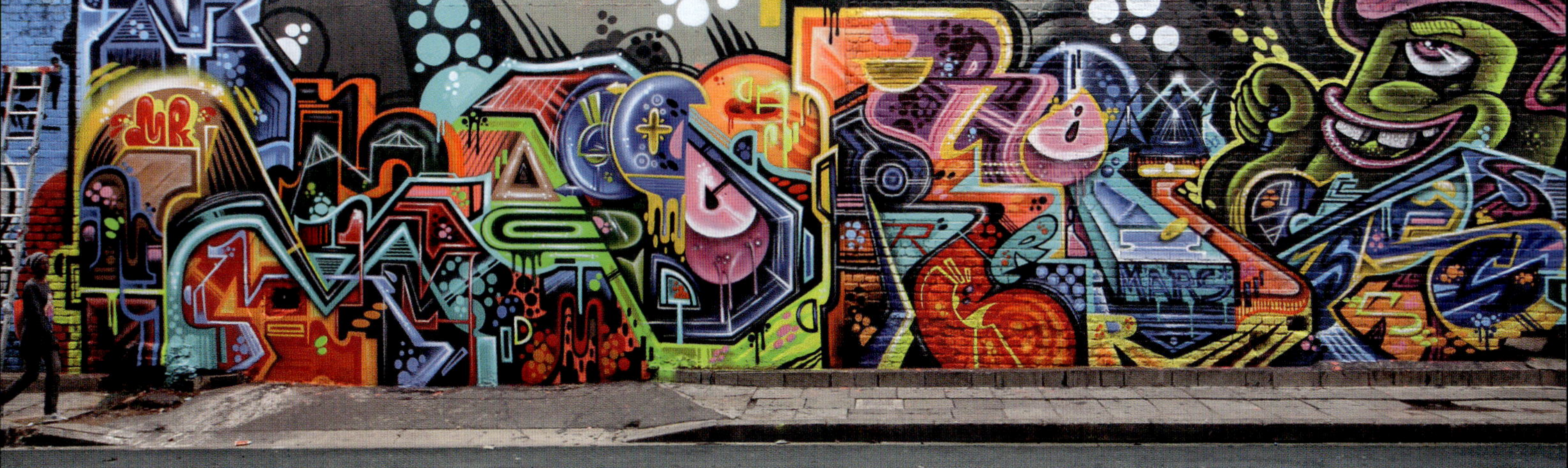

CONNECT AND EXCHANGE

Various community art projects and workshops take place across the continent, and travelling South African artists are influential to graffiti's growth in the southern vicinity. Ricky Lee Gordon (fka Freddy Sam) was involved in various upliftment projects through his /A Word of Art (fka Write on Africa) platform. He painted schools in Eswatini (Swaziland) and later in Zambia in 2014 with a new initiative called Colour Ikamva.

Street art is in its infancy in Eswatini, but Yebo Art & Design has been advocating public art since 2011 with a variety of offshoots and collaborations, including ArtReach (a community arts NGO) and MTN Bushfire (an annual music and arts festival). Numerous community murals and street art projects have been completed over the last decade, much to the benefit of the local community. Participating Swazi artists include Thabo Lukhele, Fela Dlamini, Joseph Mushipi,

Below, left to right
Ricky Lee Gordon. Colour Ikamva workshop, Lusaka, Zambia, 2014

Ricky Lee Gordon. Colour Ikamva workshop, Lusaka, Zambia, 2014

Sakhile Mhlongo. Ezulwini, Eswatini, 2014

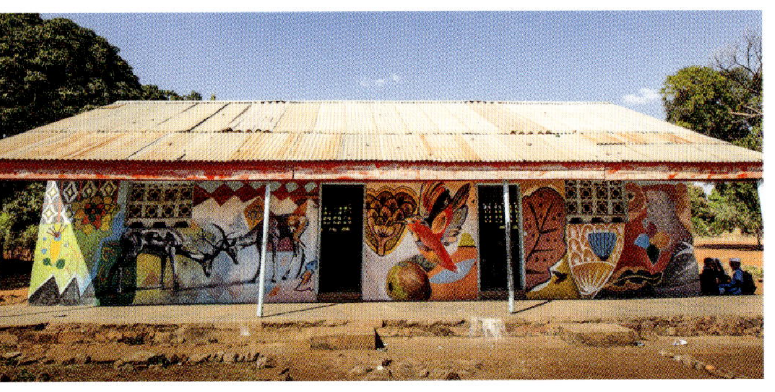

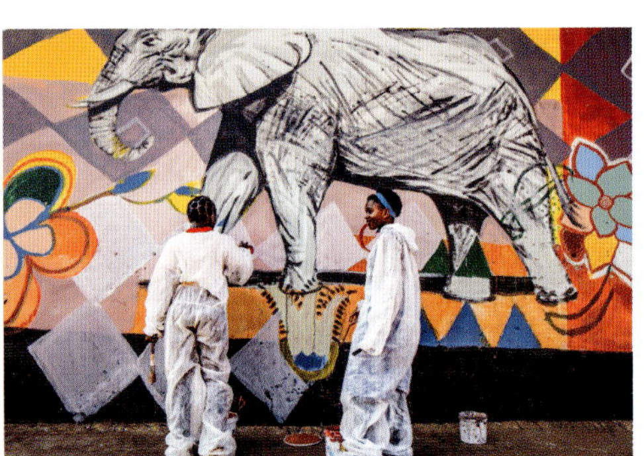

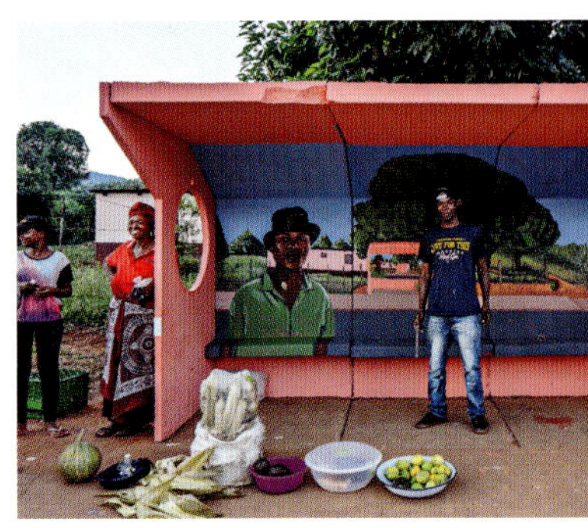

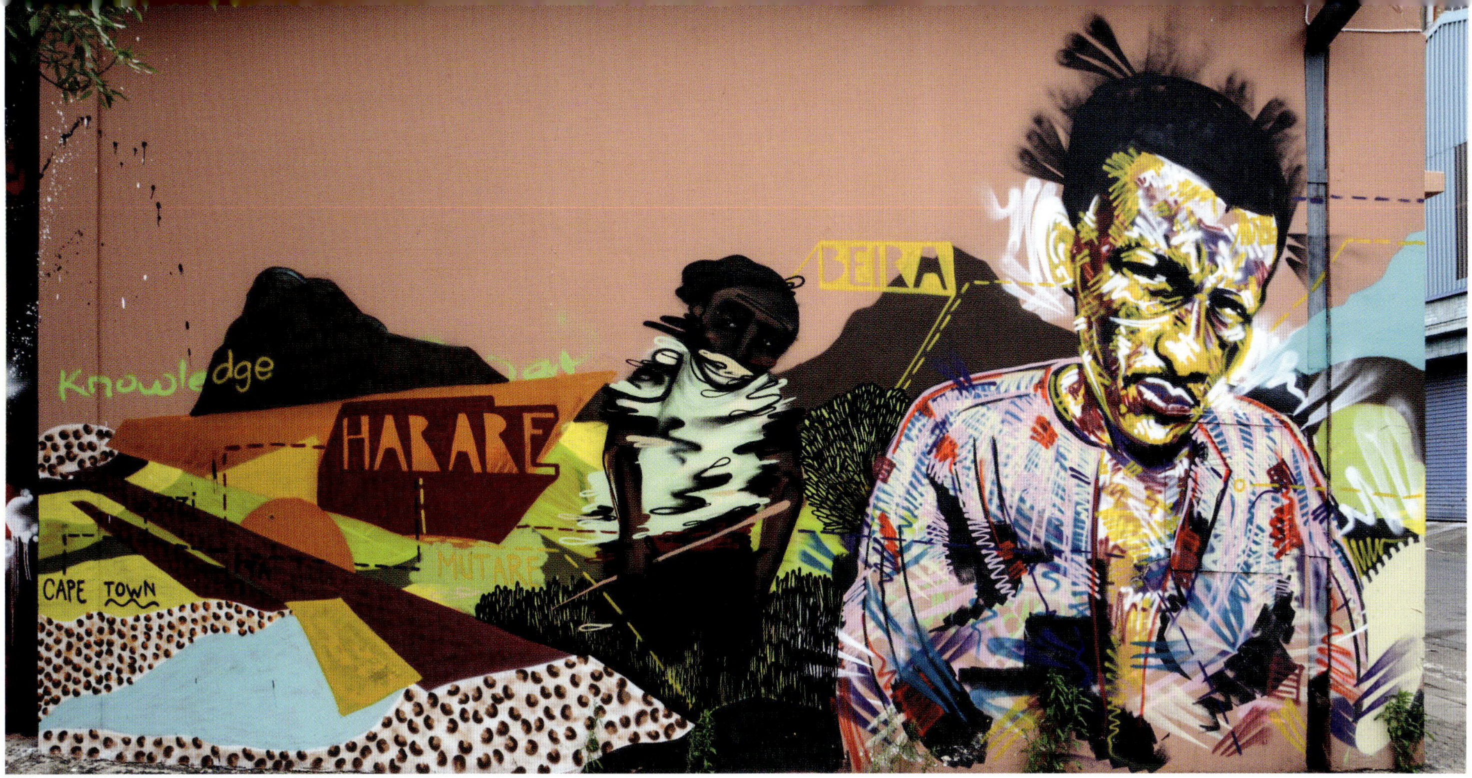

Above
**Isaac Zavale, Magwinya,
Mr Fuzzy Slipperz,
Skubalisto. The Bridge
Tour, Johannesburg,
South Africa, 2014**

Below
**Sven Christian. Ezulwini,
Eswatini, 2014**

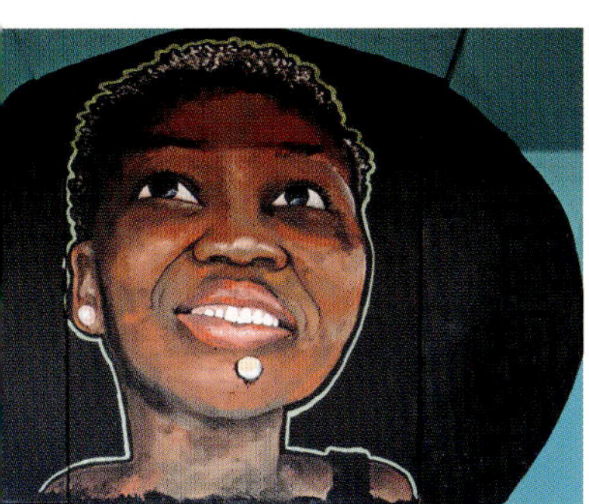

Sunshine Nxumalo, Celimpilo Dlamini, Obed Chipwepwe, Mbongeni Dlamini and Dane Armstrong, while visiting artists also play a key role – South African graffiti artists Snot420 and Star visited twice in 2016 and painter Sakhile Mhlongo visited in 2017 with Sven Christian, who returned in 2019 with Mook Lion.

Christian is familiar with places off the beaten track as his own artistic residency and community engagement programme, Ism-Skism, took place in Clarens, a small town in South Africa's Free State province, near Lesotho, in 2014. This venture brought graffiti artists from larger cities into a rural setting to bridge communities, highlight social issues and transform spaces. It was also a showcase to introduce street art to the bustling art town and challenge any misconceptions about it. The participants included members of the Crate Collective such as Skubalisto, who also ventured into the greater SADC (Southern African Development Community) region with Mr Fuzzy Slipperz for their The Bridge Tour, with similar goals. Street art is a channel that creates engaging dialogue to overcome obstacles, be they interpersonal or geographical. It breaks the rules of conventional art, with few limitations.

SOUTH AFRICA

Located at the southernmost tip of Africa is South Africa, distinguished by its assortment of ethnicities and cultural hubs. Graffiti formally developed in Cape Town in the 1980s with King Jamo, Baby, Peace 26, Falko One, Mak1one and others, then was bolstered by the arrival of foreign artists such as Seemsoe (Germany) and SoloOne (UK) in the late 1990s. The presence of more proficient artists from abroad has continuously nourished the scene. Local artists are spoilt for inspiration, not only from their unique cultural standpoint and the availability of prime surfaces, but also because of the sheer amount of existing work. Since the new millennium, the scene has steadily expanded with multiple generations of practitioners. Each city adheres to its own graffiti history and maintains a distinctive group of artists and crews. The country's semi-conservative character has failed to influence the competitive nature of the artists, resulting in the rampant escalation of the art form. Artists are brazen, dismissing hindrances of public perception, private security and other dangers that are widespread in South Africa's complex environment.

South Africa's graffiti artists generally focus on mastering all aspects of the graffiti game: both tags and pieces, and sometimes commissions. This approach has introduced a high standard within the scene and artists feed off one another's creative explorations. As one's technical dexterity improves, they paint more intricate pieces and mingle with other practising artists to learn valuable tips and the layout and history of the scene. Some choose to focus on illegal activities like tagging and 'getting up', while designers, illustrators and other would-be street artists are now producing world-class murals inspired by the international contemporary mural movement with no tangible connection to the existing local urban art scene. Appreciation from the public is also stimulating further growth.

Cape Town instigated the evolution of South African graffiti with key figures like Falko One, Wealz130 and Toe007. In the 1990s to early 2000s, a large wave of

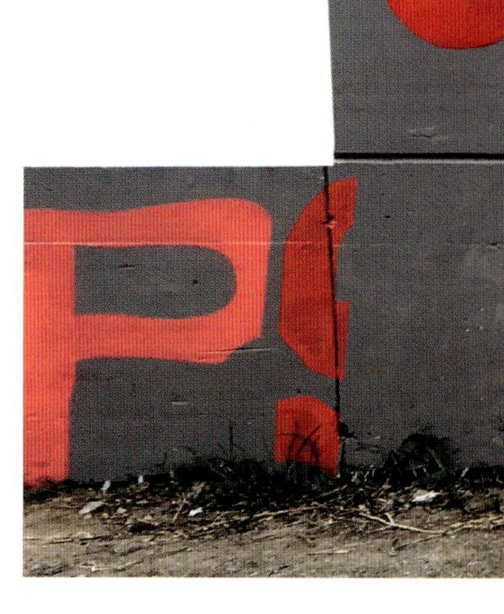"

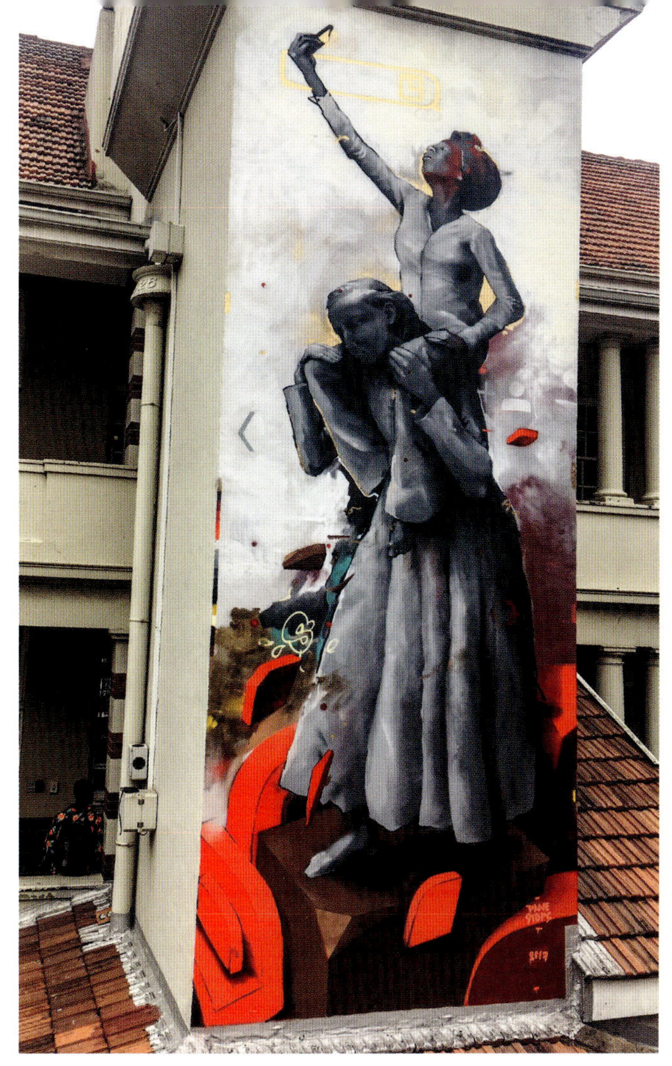

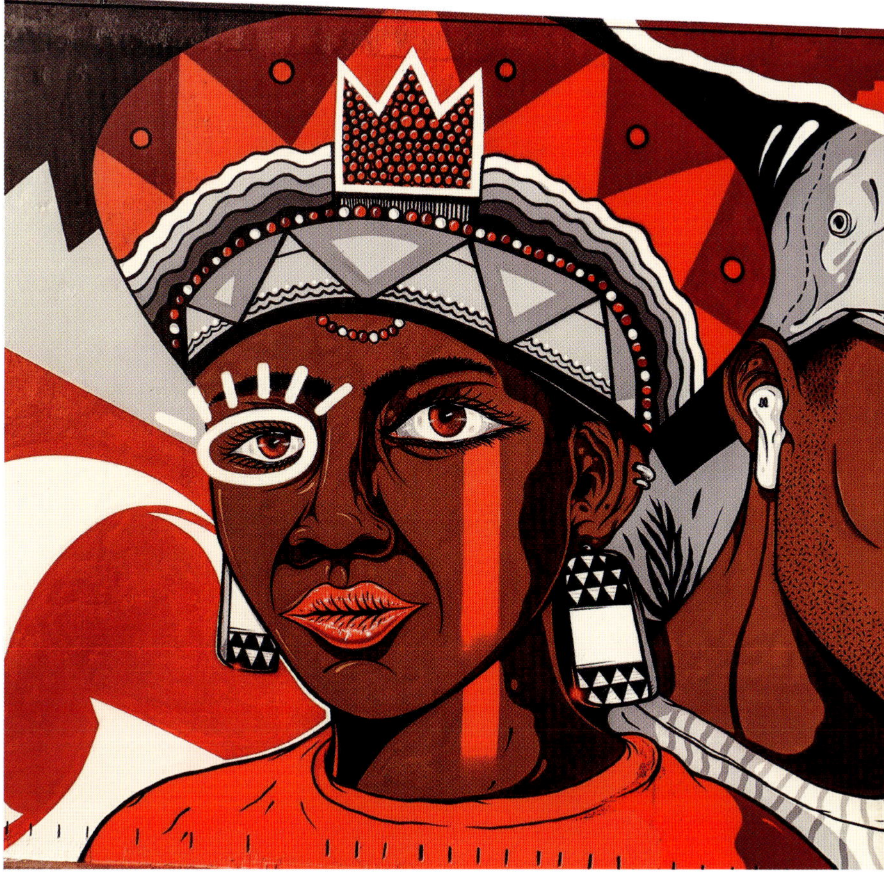

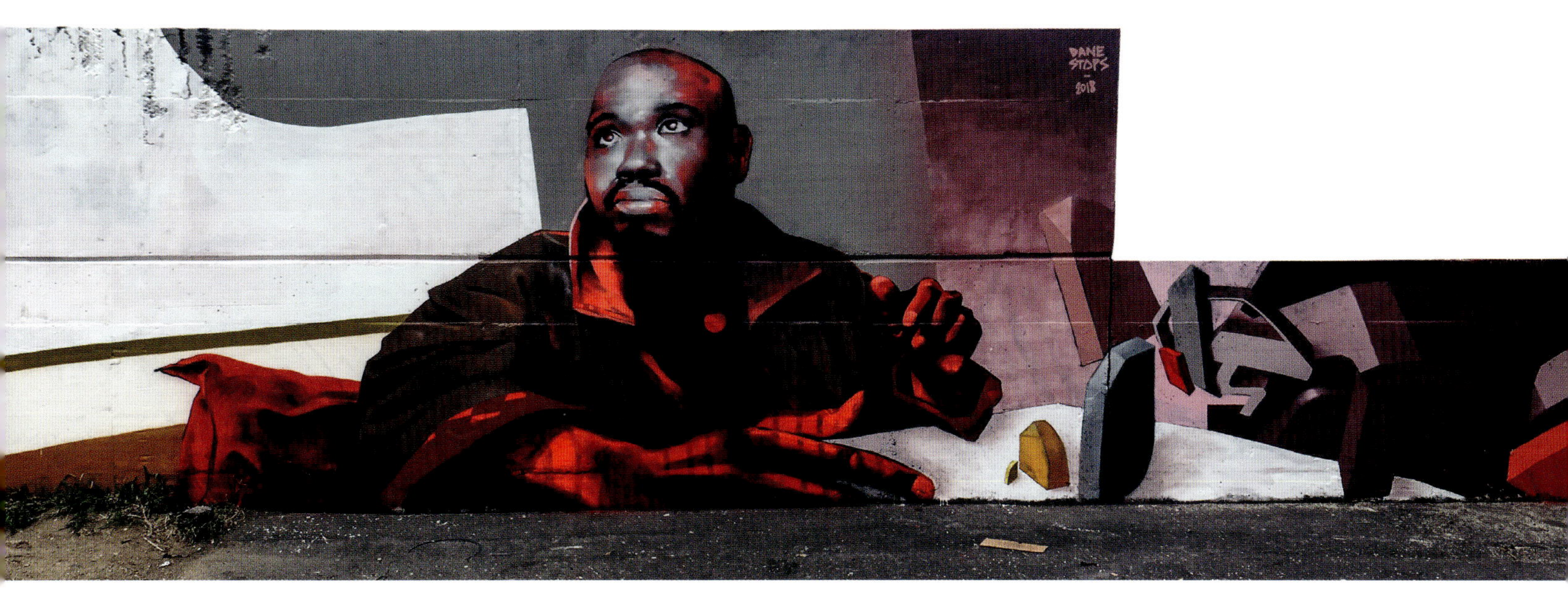

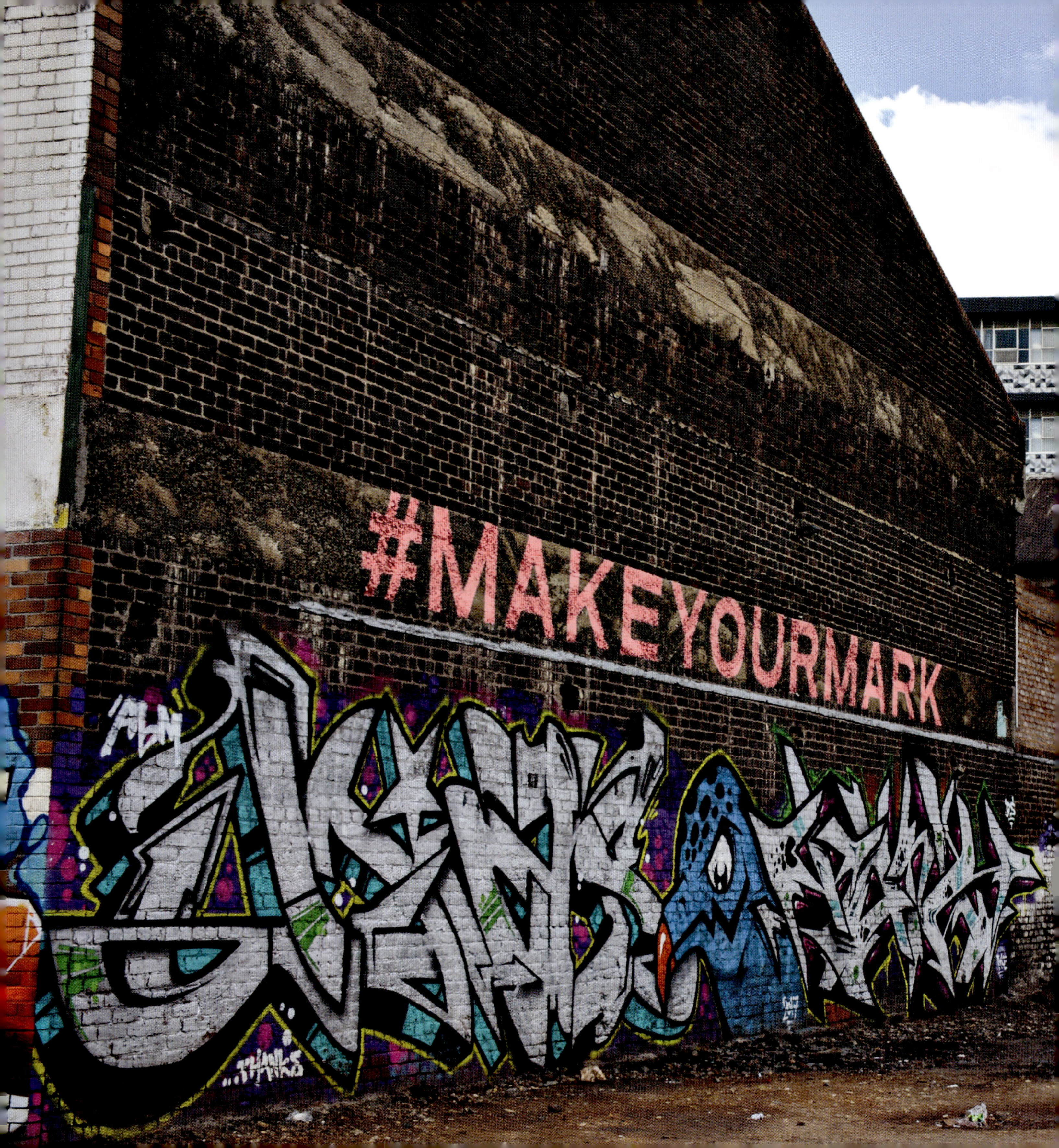

#MAKEYOURMARK

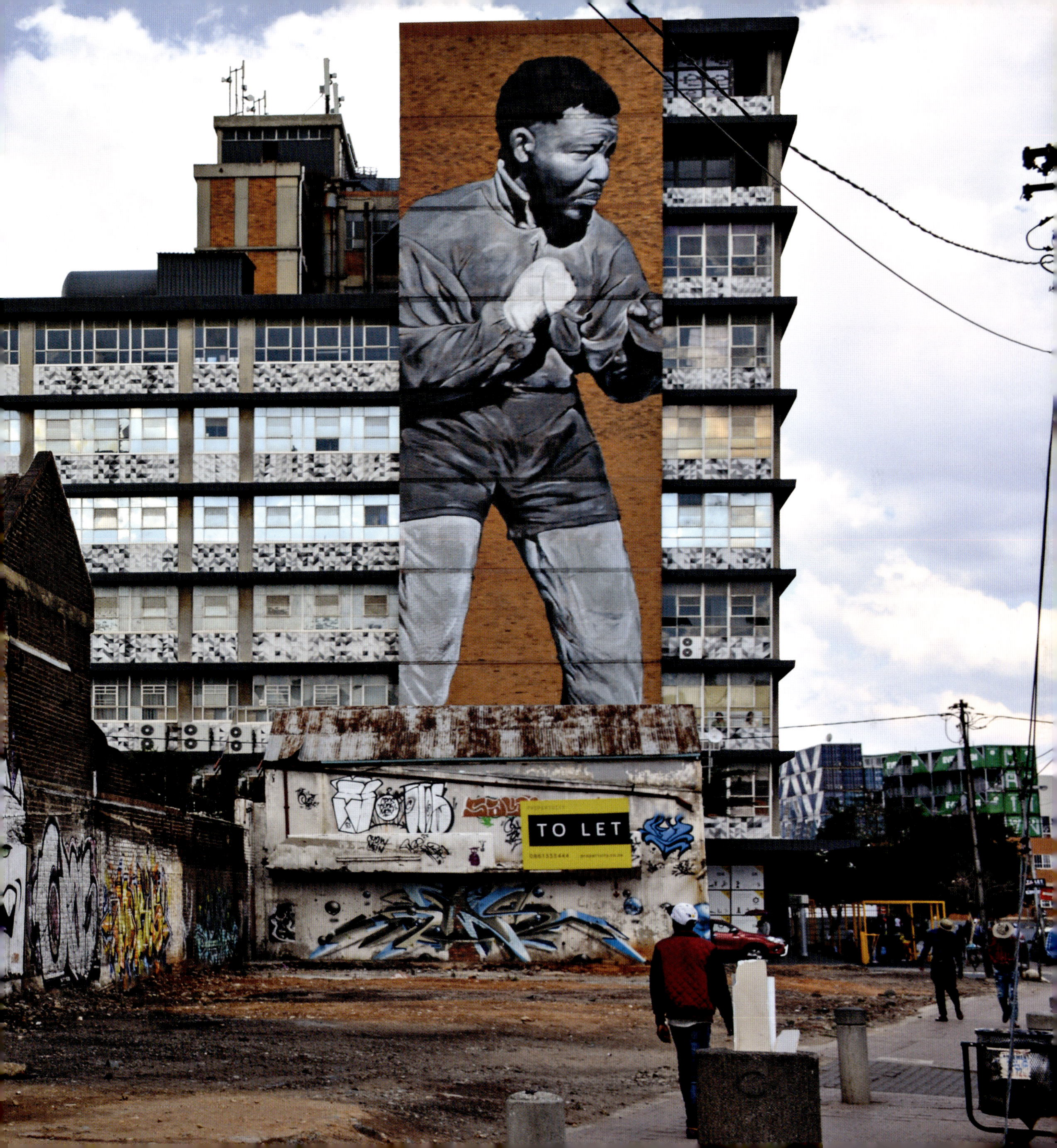
TO LET
peppercity
0861333444
propercity.co.za

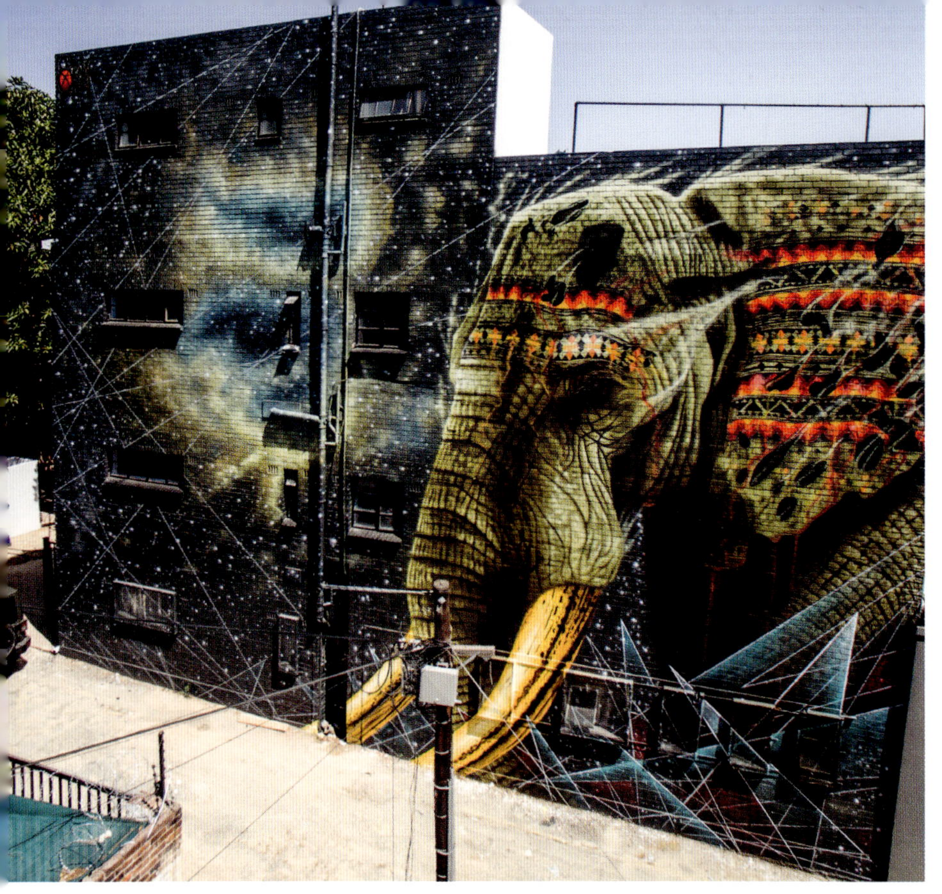
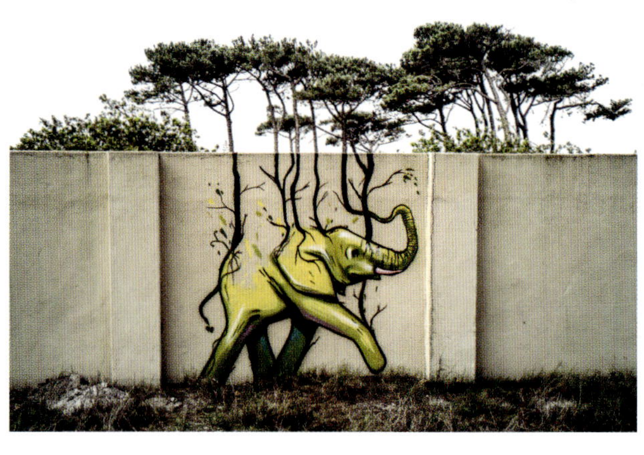
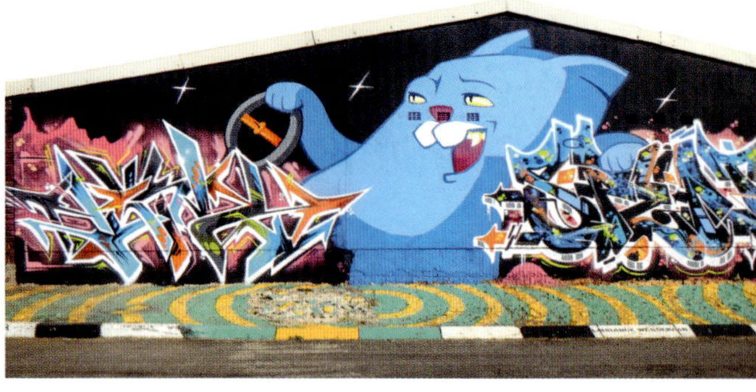

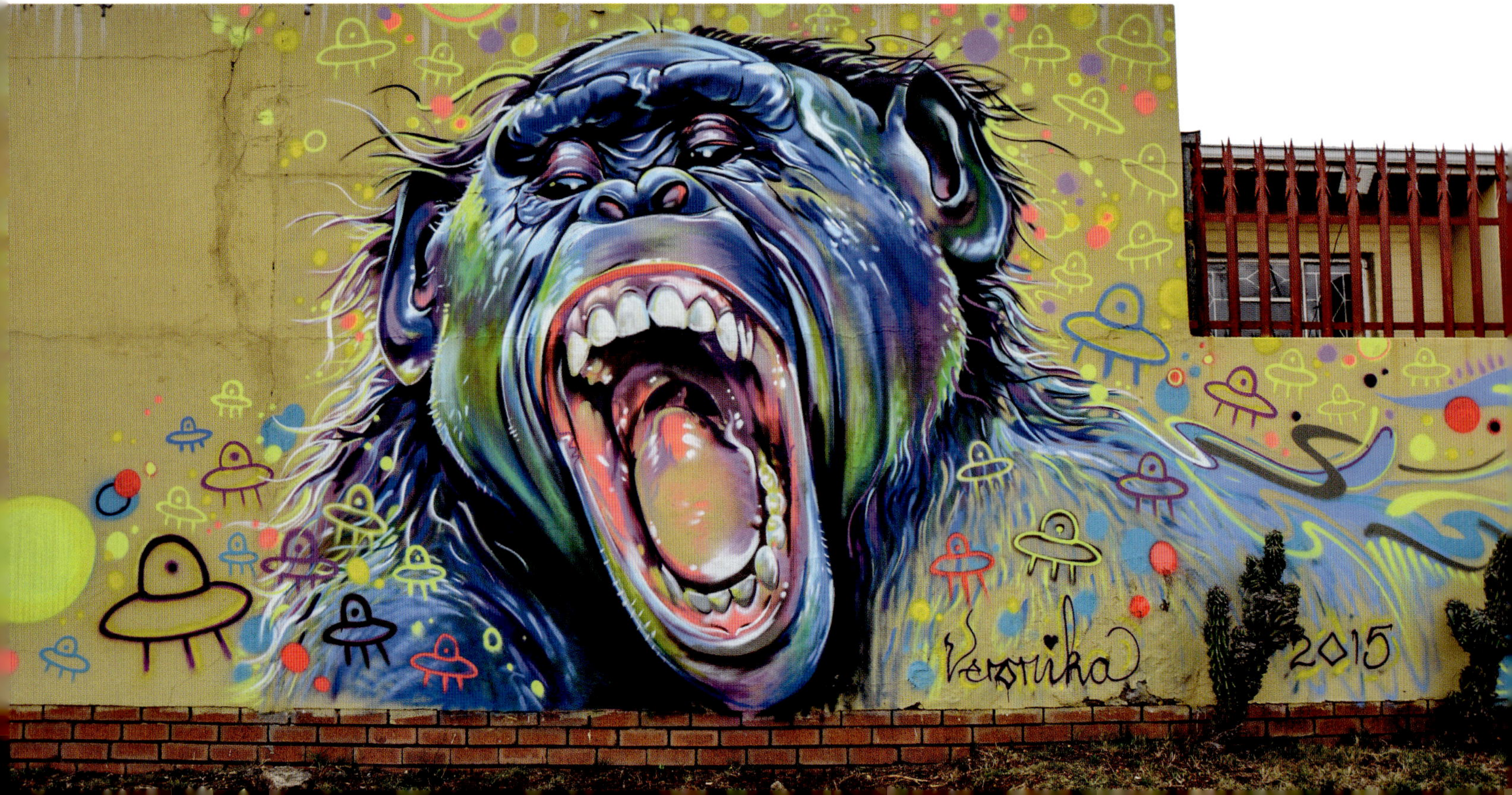

'Street art in South Africa could perform a major role in promoting social cohesion. We still live in deeply divided cities inherited from our colonial and apartheid history. The boundary walls which keep us apart could be the perfect space to get to know each other, our differences and similarities. By stimulating imaginations artists can help people visualize a more unified future.' MOOK LION

crews connected, including TVA (The Villanous Animators), NME (Enemy), WOTS (Word On The Street), YMB (Your Millenniums Best) and RL (Running Lines). Writer's benches, graffiti jams and urban-themed events, such as Battle with Vapours (established in 1997 by Falko), Selfish Vandals Social Club and the Alex Groll Cup, united artists from across the city. Dek3, Mantis, Sect and Disk also played productive roles and a new generation of crews, including WK? (What Kind?), DTR (Down To Rock), MDK (Murder Death Kill) and QK (Quick Killers), formed in the mid-2000s, making contributions to the culture in all forms. The greater metropolitan area overflowed with top-to-bottom blockbusters and unauthorized, thematic productions appeared on motorways and railway lines. The city began to take note of the mass escalation and intervened with a contested by-law deeming all forms of public painting forbidden. The repressive law would dampen Cape Town's graffiti growth for several years. Many artists lost interest because of the council's extensive cleaning campaign and the lengthy processes involved to sanction a mural. In areas like Woodstock and Salt River much of the work endured because of its street art appearance and appeal to a broader audience as international artists were assigned to art residencies and beautification projects in the vicinity. The graffiti scene, however, continued to thrive elsewhere in the underbelly of the city and on commuter trains through writers like Cros, Sure, Enos, Toe007 and QK Crew.

Around 2016, a new wave of artists emerged in Cape Town as the grip of the by-law softened. Graffiti's underground interlude was over and the art form began its ascent to the surface once more. The city of Durban, South Africa's third-largest city, situated on the east coast, remained productive with a steady increase despite a smaller scene compared to Cape Town and Johannesburg. Durban has consistently produced talented artists in all fields and street art is no exception. Graffiti flourished there in the mid- to late 2000s as several active crews shaped the community. OTC (One Two Cru), WK? (What Kind?), QST (Quest Boys), FTO (Forenziks Taking Over), ALT (Aliens Learnt This), TOA (The Only Answer/Taking

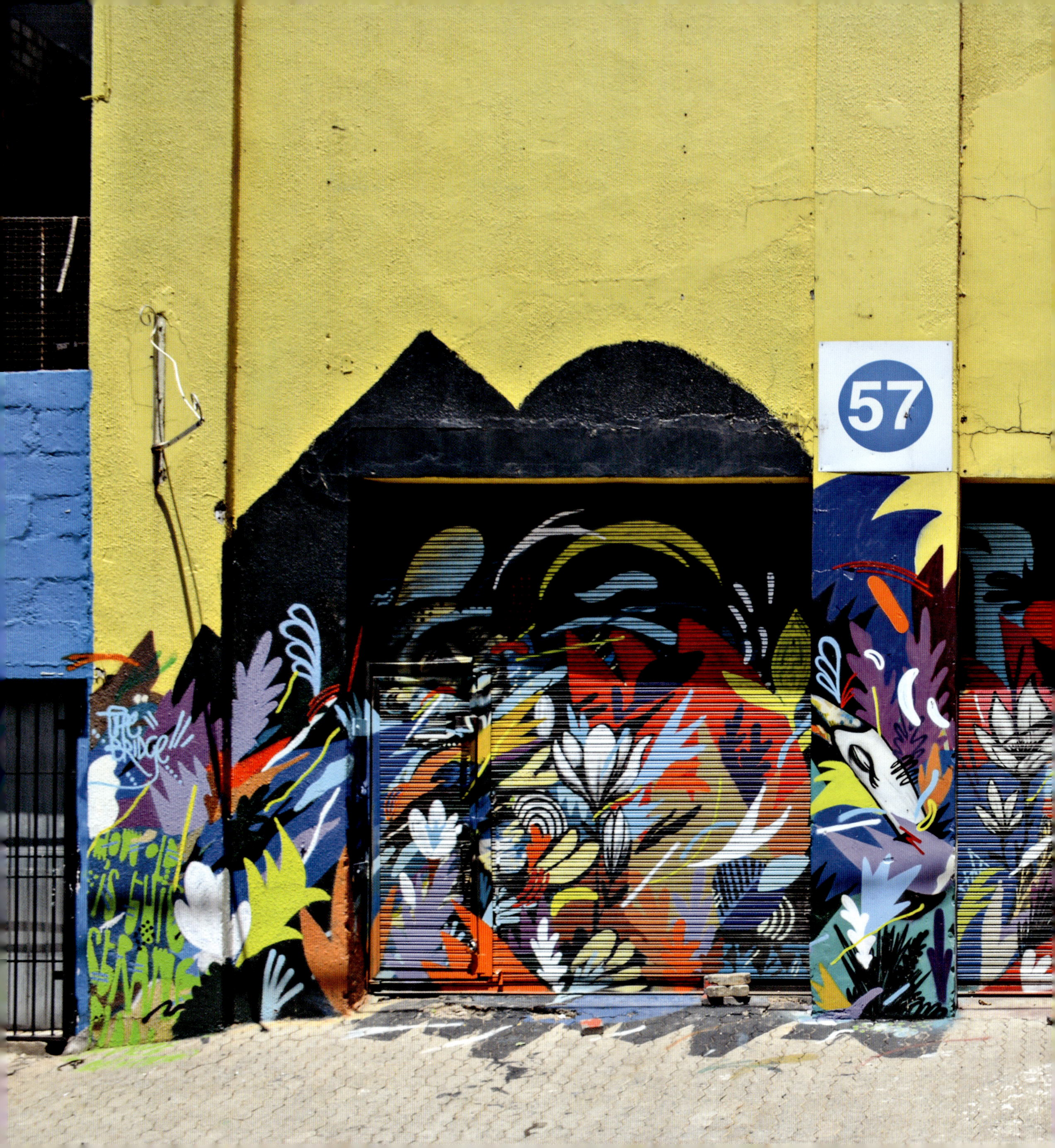

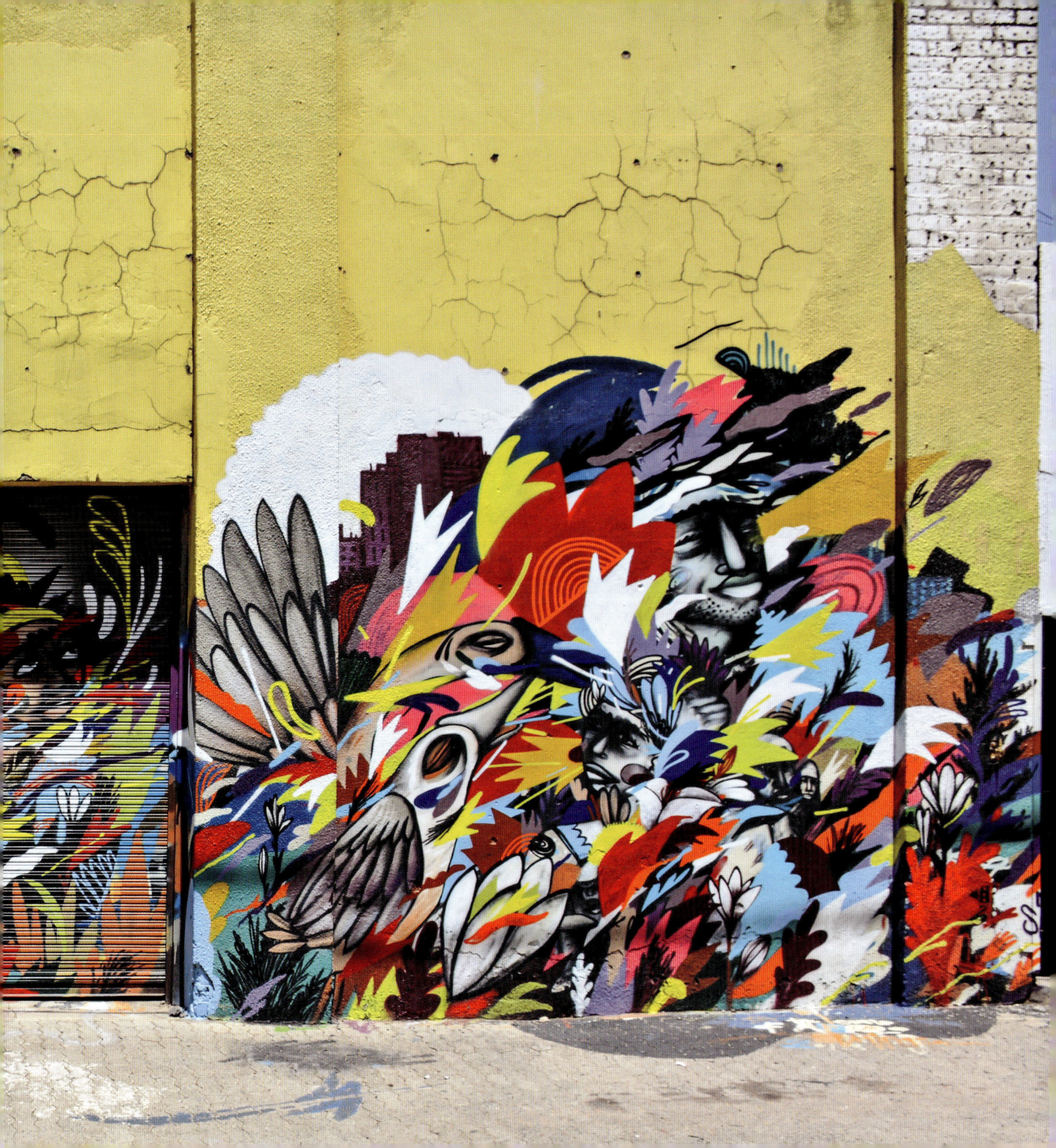

'What I find fascinating about working in the street is the interaction that takes place between the passer-by and the art piece. As soon as you put a piece up it gets a life of its own and becomes open to interpretation. I receive fascinating opinions from very diverse backgrounds.' r1.

On Authority) and DFA (Durban's Fallen Angels/Don't Fuck Around) featured multiple members with varied skillsets. (A large emphasis was placed on crews in South Africa throughout the 2000s, with more solo artists emerging after 2011.) OptOne, 2kiler, Plastik and others from OTC (or 1.2!) were at the pinnacle of the Durban graffiti scene until some members left the city. Quest Boys prevailed with a younger generation, which included Gift, Polizei, Oec/People and FiyaOne. The intermingling of crews yielded many high-standard production walls and select artists came to define the scene, including Damn Vandal, Ewok, Taik, Hoser (fka Sykad), Giffy, Mook Lion, Dane Stops and late greats Pastel Heart and 4givn. Muralists such as Sakhile Mhlongo, Resoborg and WOTS are also at the forefront today.

Johannesburg, South Africa's largest city, outstripped Cape Town as the leading producer of urban art partly thanks to that city's draconian by-law. Its raw and edgy environment has encouraged the formation of a strong graffiti foothold, as in other international cities including São Paulo, Berlin, Paris and Los Angeles. Crews such as FUK (Fukt Up Kids), DS (Demolition Squad), PCP (Pressure Control Projects), TK (Time Keepers) and Soweto's MSE (Msantsi Street Exhibitz) and SEC (Style Elite Crew) became important groups, with members still active in 2020.

Senzart911. Westdene Graffiti Project, Johannesburg, South Africa, 2017

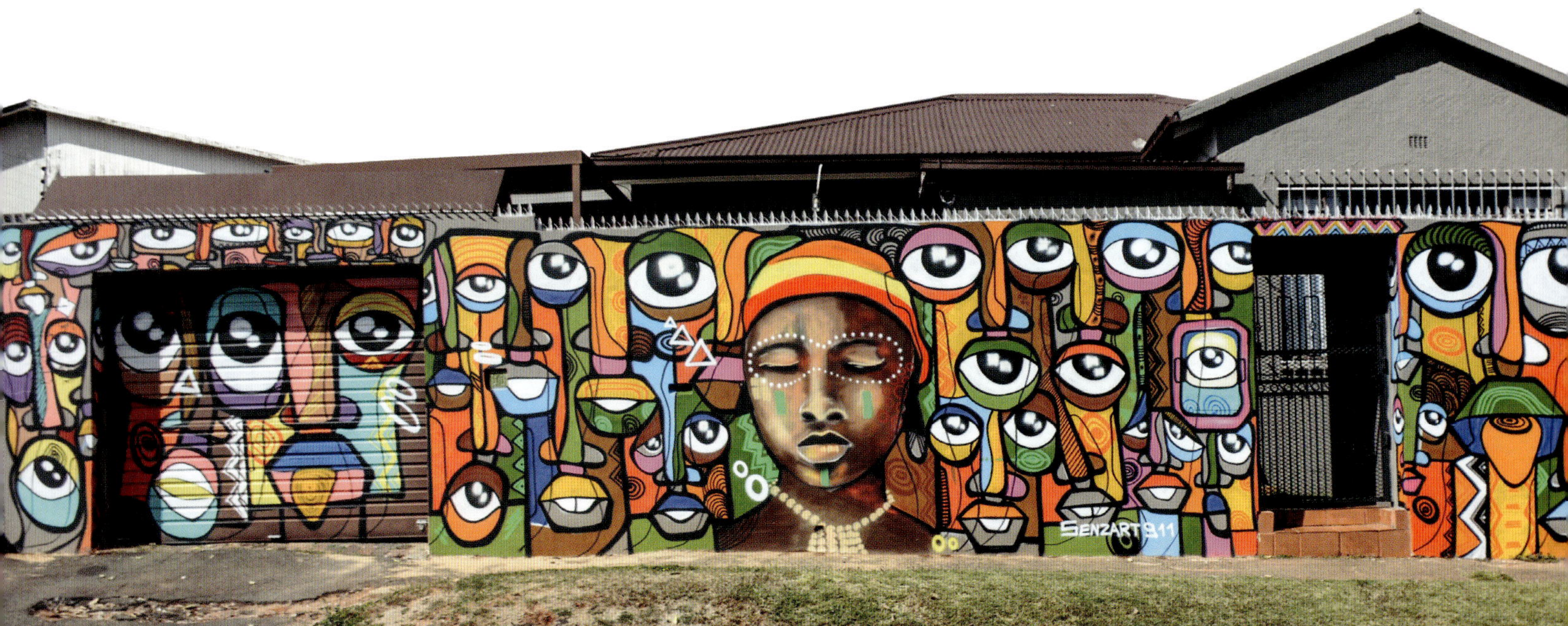

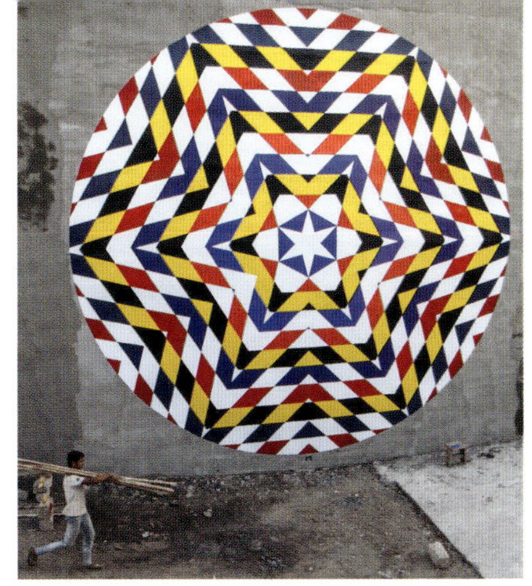

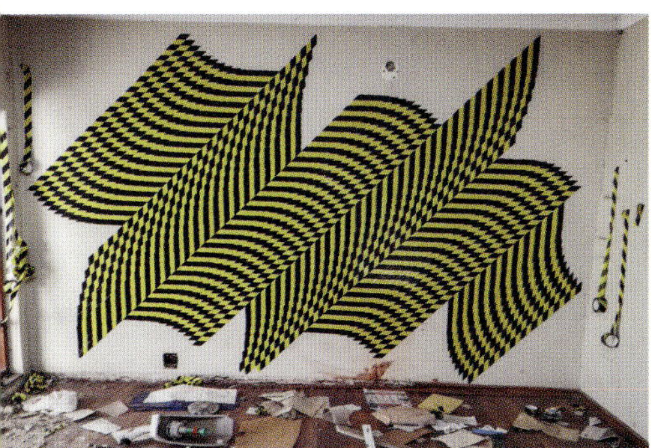

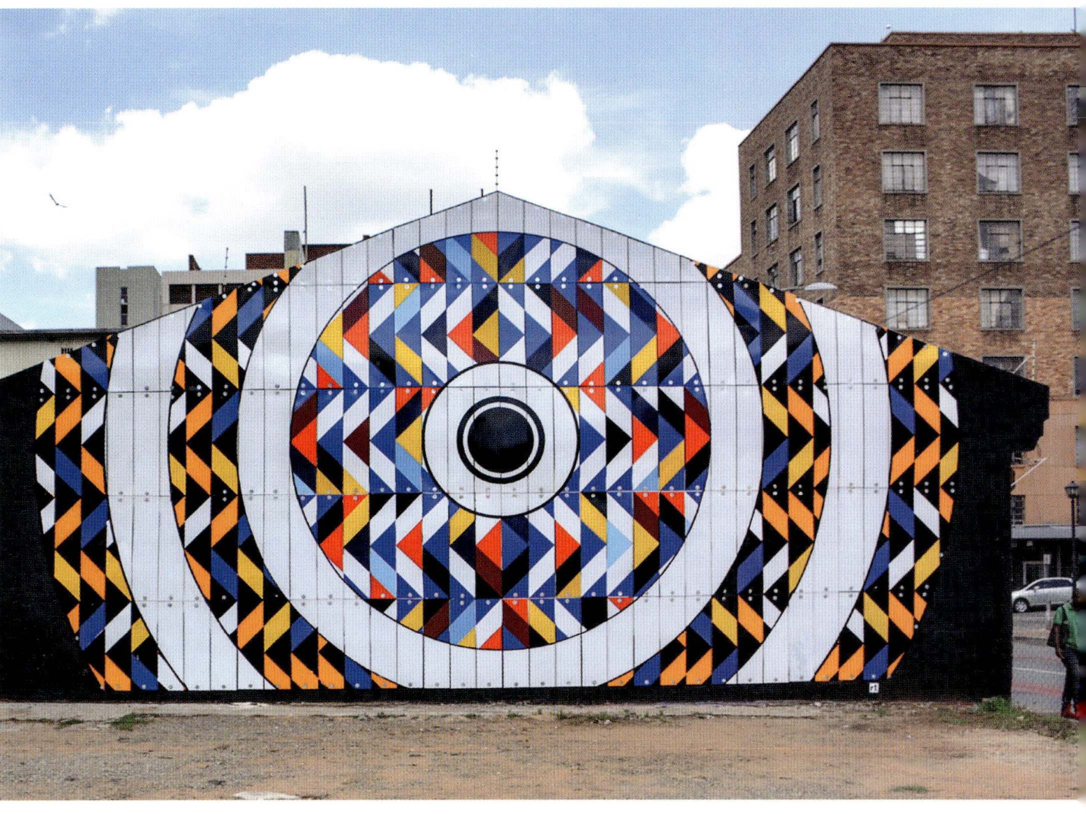

Joburg's urban environment is an important factor in graffiti's domination. Certain areas of the cityscape become prime locations thanks to the prevalence of usable space or the community's engagement with the art form. Suburbs like Newtown, Yeoville and greater Jeppestown have long been visited by graffiti artists. The maze of storm drains and bridges are also explored by artists as these areas are not cleaned by the council. Bias (aka Sloe) is notorious in this area, producing up to five pieces a week. He prides himself on finding untouched spots, often filling entire walls of bridges. Mars (aka Mr Moris) paints regularly with Bias and the two build complex letter forms in an array of layered colours and styles.

When the inner city area of Johannesburg was redeveloped in the 2000s, it brought graffiti artists with it, and has since become an open playground. Many artists paint freely, especially on dilapidated walls. A domino effect led to substantial strips of wall being painted that are perceived as legal. The annual hip-hop festival Back to the City attracts thousands of revellers on Freedom Day (27 April) to its live concert, but began as a predominantly graffiti event. The columns under the highway over Newtown are repainted every year for the festival. Since its inception in 2007, the event has become a staple for graffiti artists. Other projects such as the Westdene Graffiti Project were significant because residents lent their boundary walls to graffiti artists to express

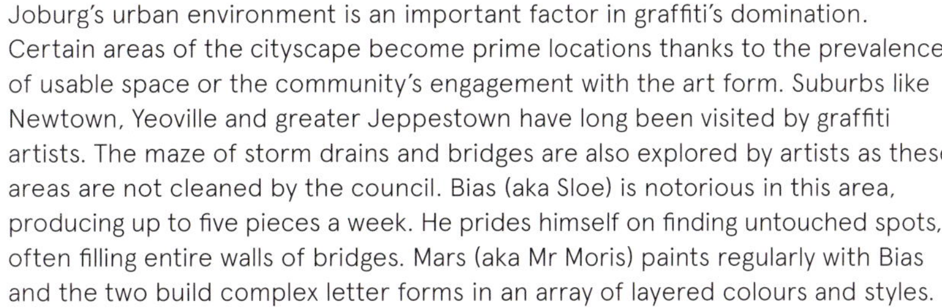

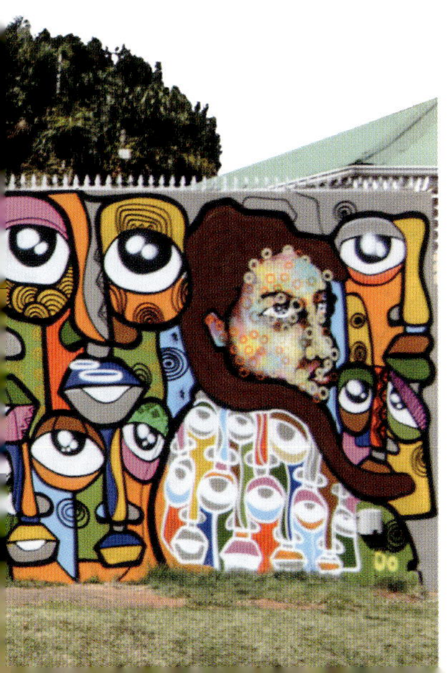

themselves. Work in Johannesburg is widespread, from the East Rand to Soweto, and even sweeping into nearby Pretoria. In 2011, City of Gold Urban Art Festival was established as the first major international mural festival in the country. Recently, IPAF (International Public Art Festival) in Cape Town has endeavoured to encourage a similar aesthetic. The festival engages with residents and street art blends with the environment to act as an agent for change. Smaller cities and towns do not produce as much work, apart from Port Elizabeth and King William's Town in the Eastern Cape, where Joff and Bief37 are based, respectively.

Cape Town's Faith XLVII is a leading urban artist. Since her humble beginnings around 1997, Faith has been on a constant journey of self-discovery. She painted graffiti letters and cartoon characters, but began to express her love for typography and interest in more profound concepts bordering on the spiritual. Her work is powerful and informative, speaking to a multitude of issues and feelings. Her signature style formed after 2010 and she has since travelled the world, appearing at graffiti's biggest gatherings. Today she is based in Los Angeles, but continues to paint in South Africa. Sonny is also gaining fame in international circles from his To the Bone tour in 2017, which highlighted the plight of wild animals. He painted his signature photo-realistic animal portraits in North America, Russia and the UK, raising funds for conservation. Falko One, another global representative of South Africa, has painted graffiti for over three decades. He is known across Africa and embarks on tours to rural areas for his Once Upon A Town project. Falko is fascinated with blending his work into the environment or creating work based on existing architectural elements.

Few artists are dedicated to the crafts of wheatpasting or stencilling, with Burning Museum collective being one of the most historically prominent. In terms of interventions and installations, r1., Hannelie Coetzee and Ralph Ziman (aka Afrika 47) have conducted interesting projects in the urban environment. Numerous South African street artists have explored international territories on holiday or via emigration – the worldwide footprint is greater than ever before, whereas Breeze Yoko is the most travelled on the African continent. Back home new generations of crews, including EDK (Every Day Krooks), Glok (fka Glockstars), MHC (Most Hated Crew), NVS (eNViouS Crew), UDC (Urban Decay Cartel) and KSG (Krew Squad Gang), are now prolific. Standout names include Conform, LoveLeigh, Nardstar*, Fers, AuReT, ChowMein, BobD, Dekor One, Keya Tama, Bushy, SergicalOne, Care, Yonus D, Creative Yeti, Slegh, Beva, Marti Lund, Mr Migo, Senzart911, Rayzer, Dbongz, Empty, Jestr, Khosa, Mr.ëksê, Rekso, Robane, Drake, Veronika, Kevin Love, Page33, Zesta, Seth Onetime, Skubalisto, Mr Fuzzy Slipperz, CoeOne, Dreadr, Tower, Kev7, Nomad, Tykuno, Scabbage, Myza420, Rare, Days, FOK, CORE collective, Anser NineOne, Mister, Reks and the infamous Tapz.

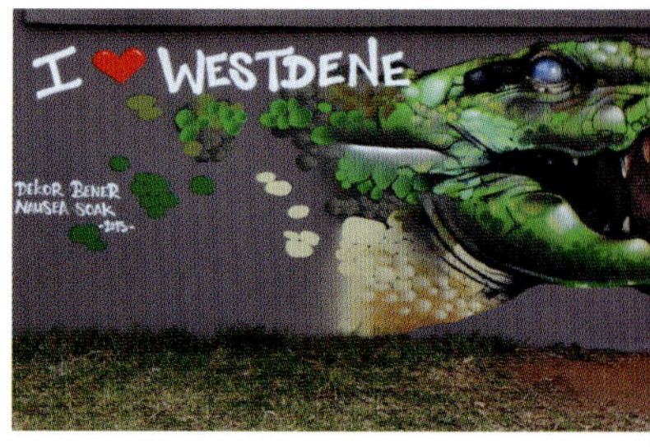

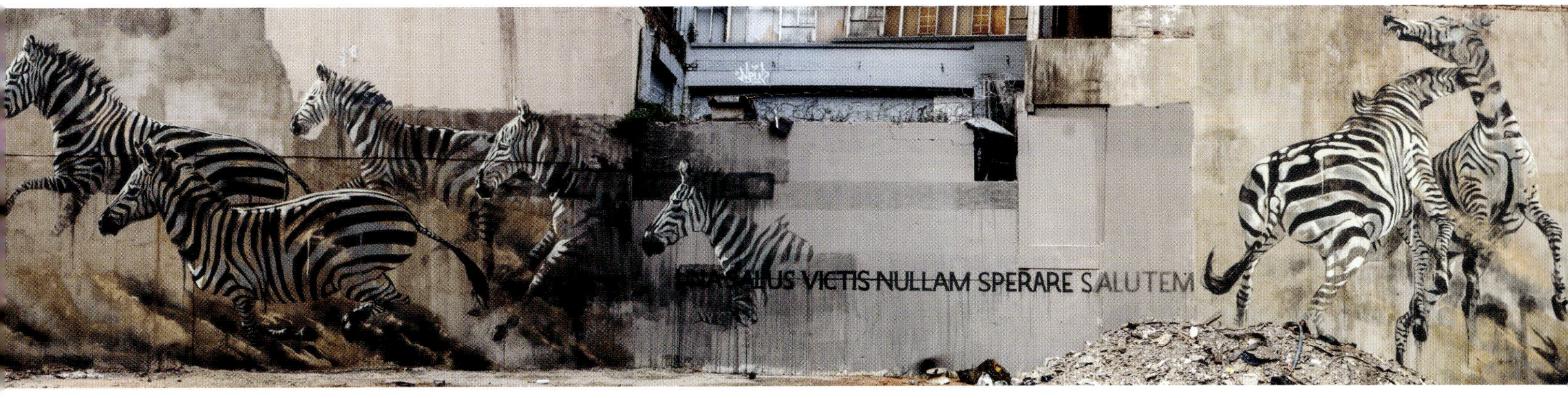
UNA SALUS VICTIS NULLAM SPERARE SALUTEM

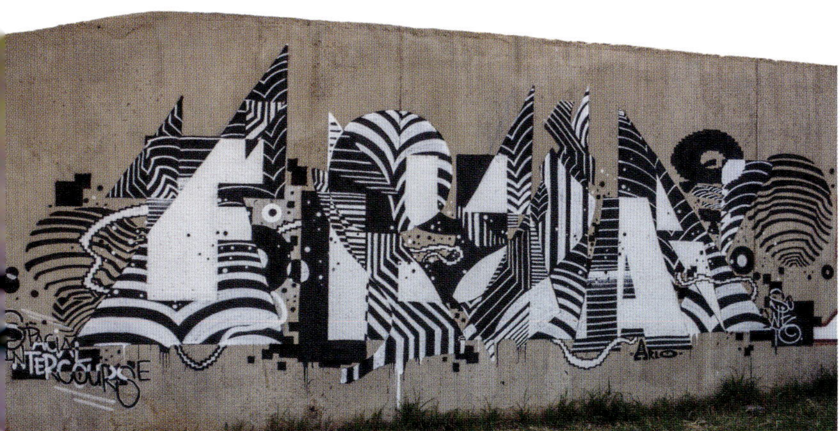
SPACIAL
INTERCOURSE

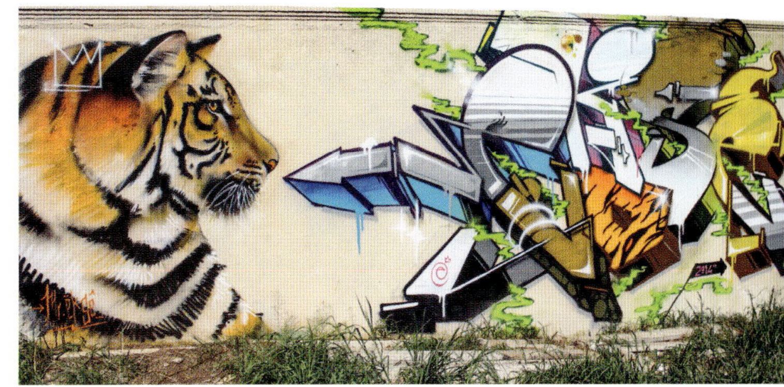

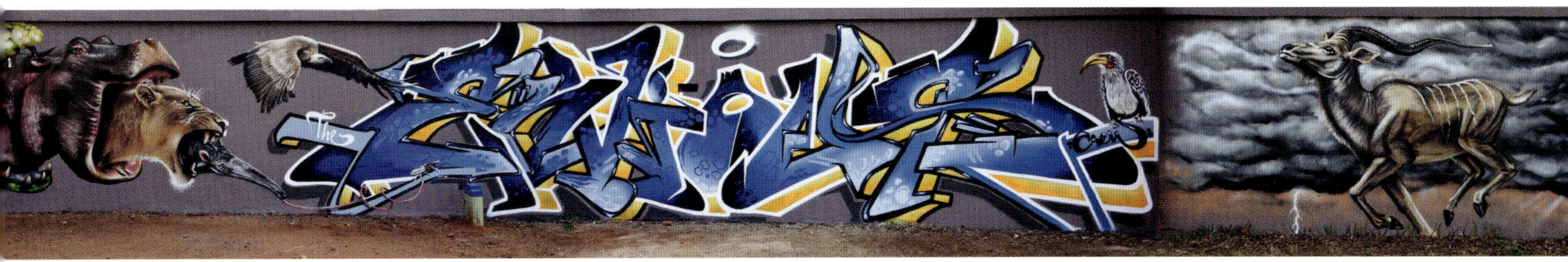

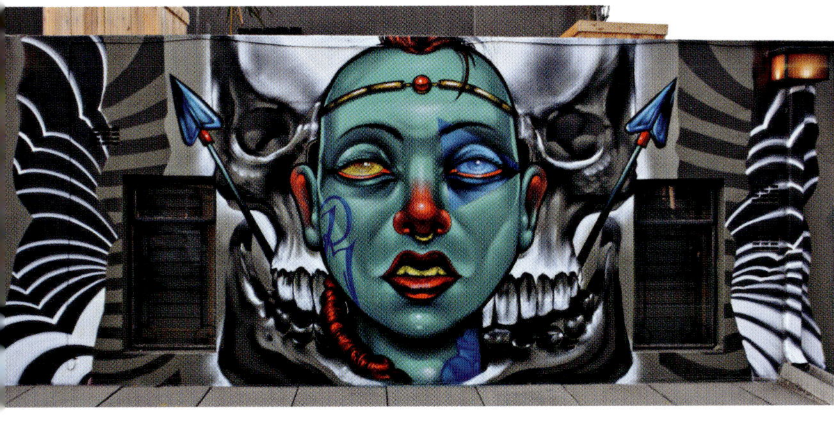

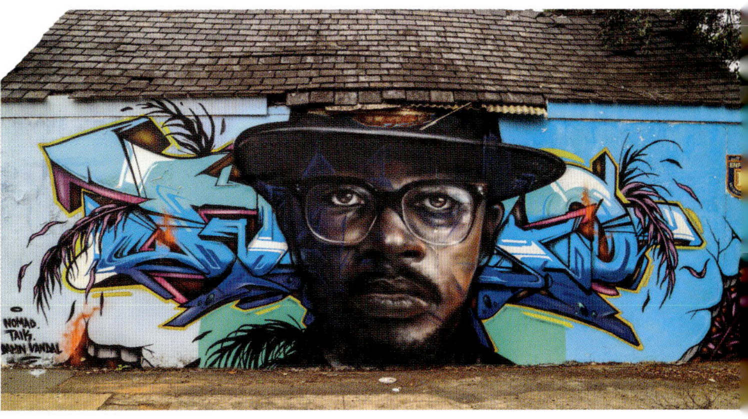

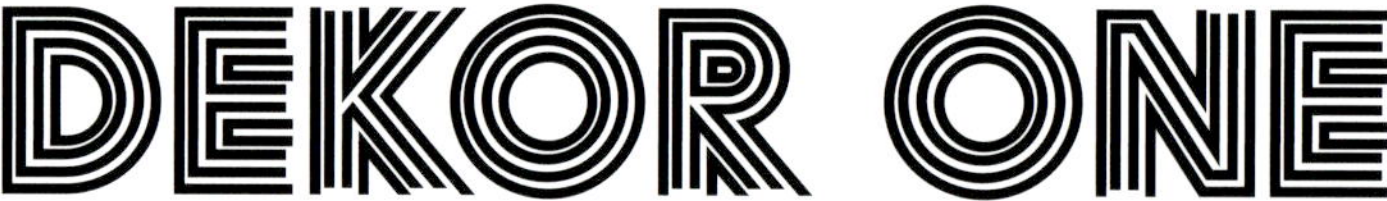

DEKOR ONE

ARTIST PROFILE

Tell me about your introduction to graffiti.
We only had a few magazines and you could count the Johannesburg graffiti artists on two hands. My first dosage of proper graffiti was at a nightclub which brought TVA Crew up from Cape Town – Mantis, Falko One and Mak1one. Their original style was crazy good and that sold me. I had seen graffiti previously and had sketched a lot before I even picked up a spray can – I lived in London for two years (in the early 2000s) when graffiti was blowing up. I went to art school but did not enjoy it because they made us do textbook art, the same still life, so I pursued art in a new direction. I actively started painting graffiti with KWS (Kids With Style) and PCP (Pressure Control Projects), as well as other crews like NN (Nozzle Ninjas), ABC (Assorted Bad Characters) and DOC (Destruction of Cities). There was no weekend where I was not painting. I now represent NVS (eNViouS) Crew.

How did you end up choosing the name Dekor One?
I just like the letters. They seem to fit nicely and I can do a good-size piece. I changed it to a K later, because of decor for interior design and another artist who paints the same name.

Tell me about your style and its evolution.
I started doing cut-back-style pieces when we got access to imported spray paint and more colour gradients – these supplies changed the whole graffiti game. A lot of the early pieces were done with crappy, watery spray paint which was extremely limiting, and I was stuck in a monotonous process: only doing pieces. Going solo definitely opened up a lot of doors because I needed to do commissioned work and things I could not do before. It pushed me in the right direction.

I have matured from general graffiti, although I still enjoy doing it. I like to be ahead, doing my own stuff. I like typography and mixed typography is a style now, everyone is doing it, following trends. What is working for me at the moment are images in vector style, encompassing a little realism, portraits and animals. A lot of people ask me why I do not paint one specific style – it is because I am still trying to find a style, exploring everything and seeing what I like the most. One day when I finally get to that point I will combine everything and that will be my style.

Tell me about working as a full-time artist, and having a studio practice.
It has its ups and downs. It is cool when things are good, but when you do not have work you struggle a bit. The studio has opened me up to more things. I can go and sit there and do my own stuff. I have been experimenting, doing pieces on gallery paper, using brushes and sponges and watered-down paint and inks, markers, all sorts of things. It makes a difference and I can produce interesting stuff. Stepping back and knowing that I am making something off my art is the best feeling.

How has travel and seeing the international scene first-hand expanded your scope?
Everyone needs to go overseas. It opens you up to new techniques and inspiration, and I always come back feeling reborn. You need to hang out with other artists, see how they do things and implement the techniques yourself, otherwise you will be stuck in a one-track world.

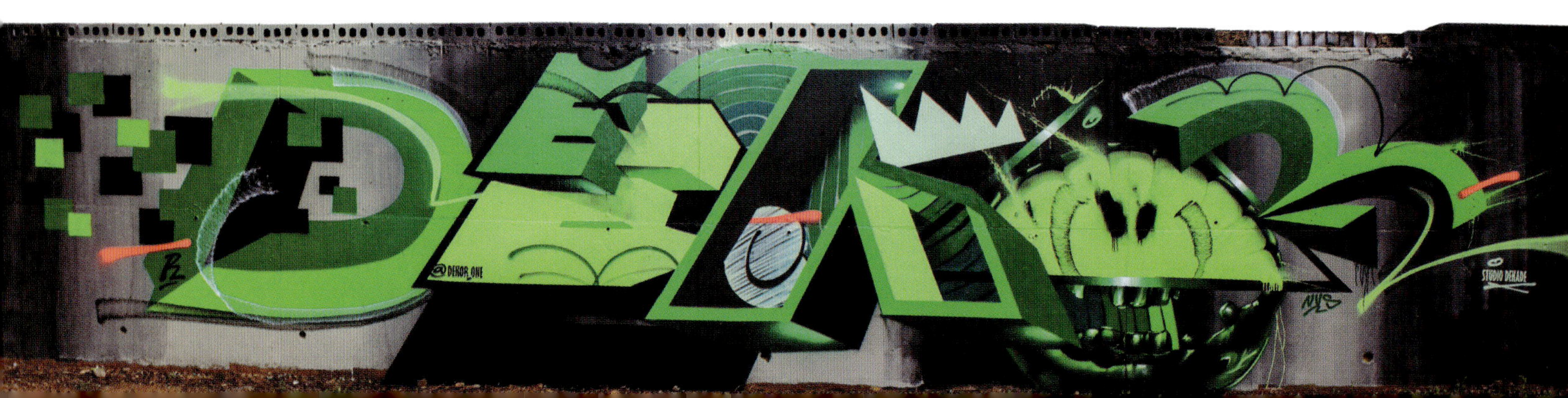

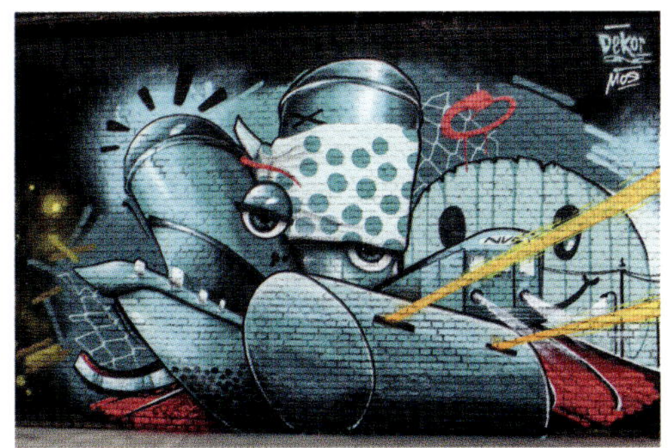

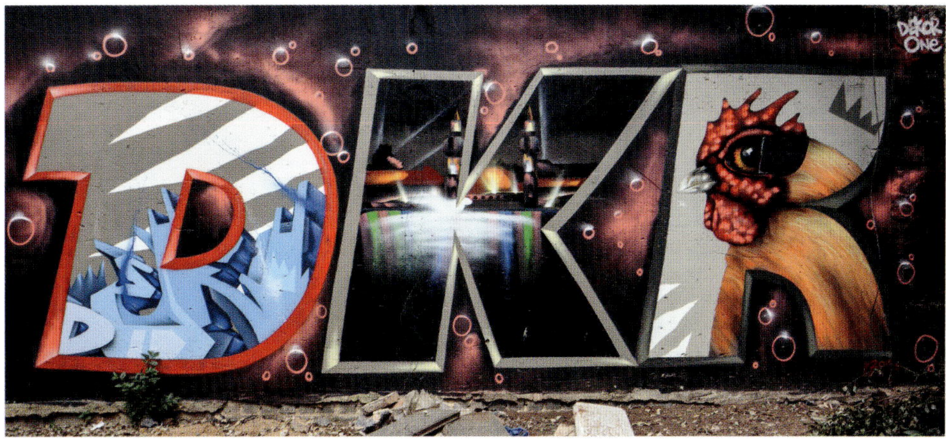

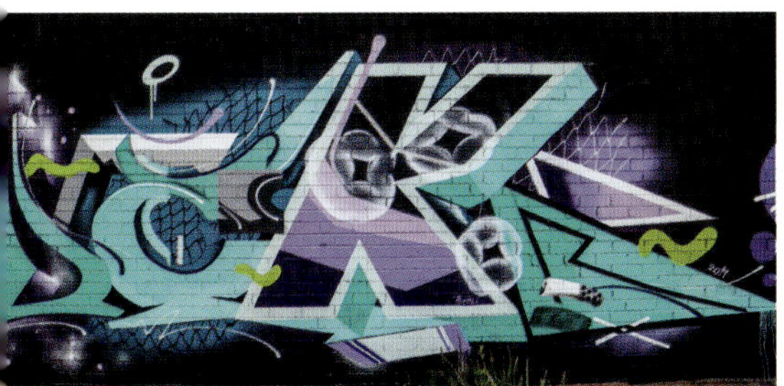

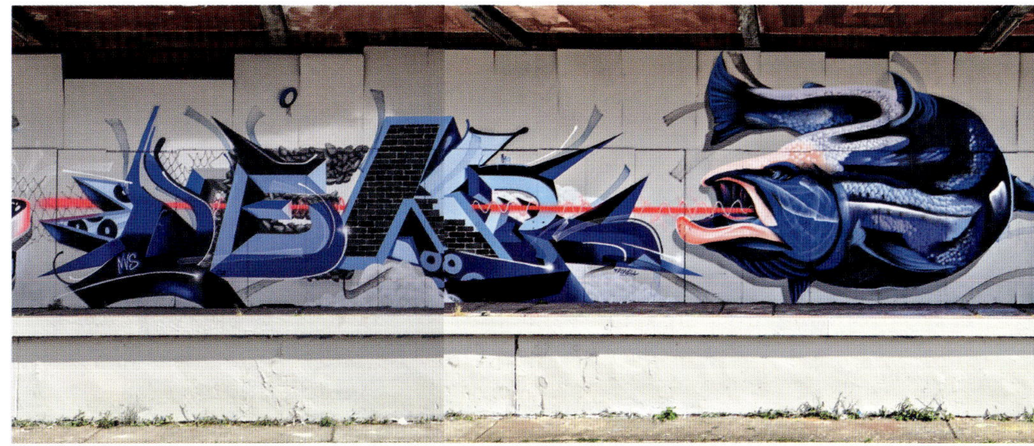

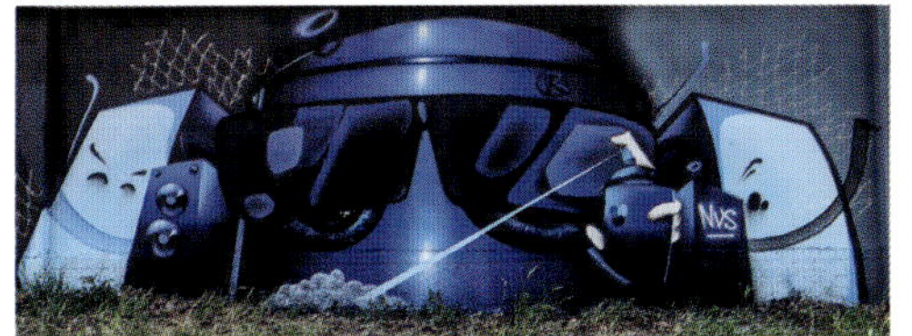

Tell me about graffiti culture today.

I have always done graffiti and I will always do graffiti. I consider myself a graffiti artist, not a street artist who paints pretty pictures. I am up for a challenge and if I was only painting pieces I would be very bored by now. There are a lot of new artists who claim our fame and have nothing to do with the culture. I paint it from nothing, even the parts that are supposed to look like stencils are painted by hand. A lot of people move into buildings because of the graffiti, and I painted it.

Johannesburg's **Dekor One** is a stalwart of the local scene, taking on copious amounts of commissioned works in all forms, while remaining active on the street with his graphic letter pieces. His passion for design and eagerness to stay on top of trends are evident in his artworks, now also appearing on European shores as he works as a member of the international NVS Crew.

Opposite
Dekor One. Johannesburg, South Africa, 2019

Above, clockwise from top left
Dekor One. Meeting of Styles, Antwerp, Belgium, 2018

Dekor One. Johannesburg, South Africa, 2015

Dekor One. HipHop OlymPics, Magdeburg, Germany, 2019

Dekor One. Meeting of Styles, Wiesbaden, Germany, 2019

Dekor One. Johannesburg, South Africa, 2019

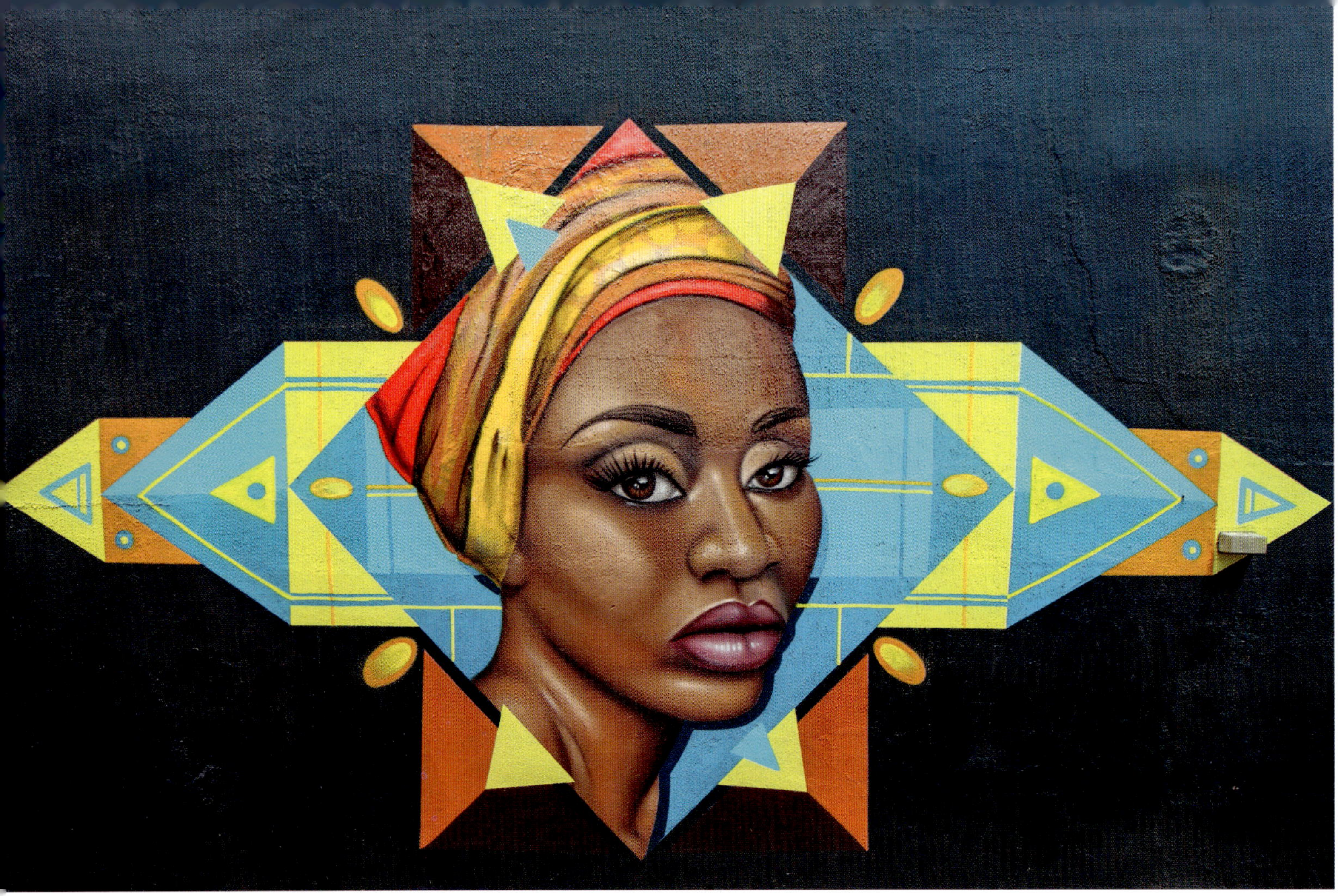

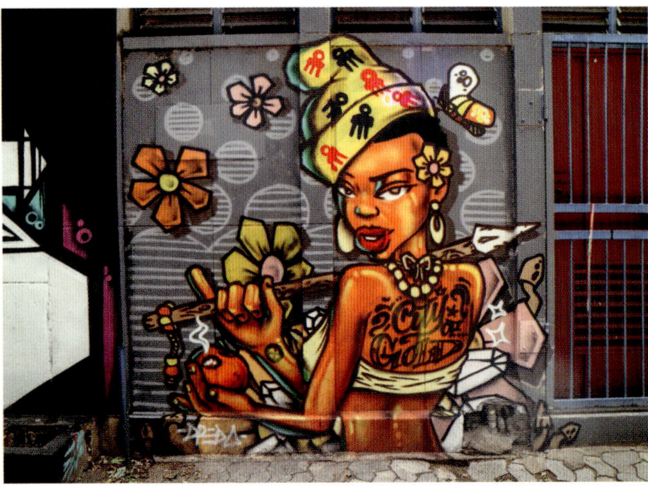

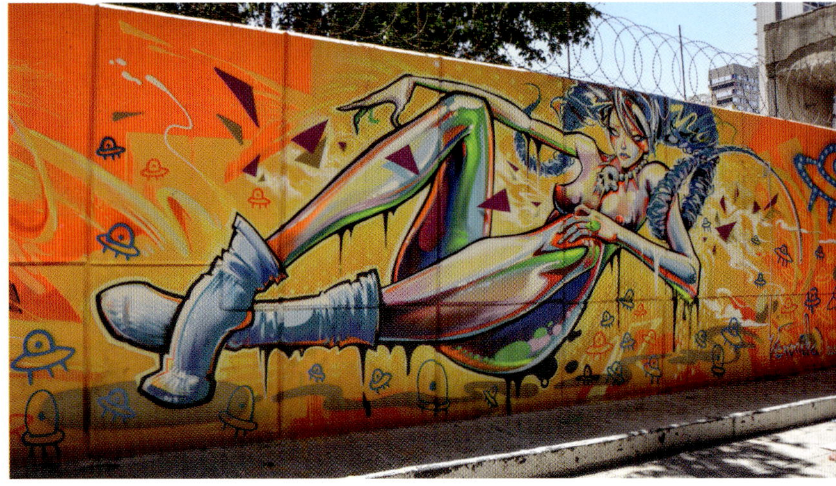

CITY OF GOLD URBAN ART FESTIVAL

FESTIVALS & CULTURE

Opposite
**Mars. 'Precious',
6th edn, Johannesburg,
South Africa, 2018**

**Below, far left to right
Dreadr. 6th edn,
Johannesburg,
South Africa, 2018**

**Veronika. 4th edn,
Johannesburg,
South Africa, 2014**

**Jestr, Zesta, Kevin Love.
'Wild in the Streets',
4th edn, Johannesburg,
South Africa, 2014**

**Myza420. 4th edn,
Johannesburg,
South Africa, 2014**

Johannesburg's City of Gold Urban Art Festival was created by leading graffiti and tattoo artist Rasty of PCP Crew. The event aimed to showcase the scene to a broader audience and stimulate local artists by inviting select global icons. Activities took place in a variety of areas of the city, through exhibitions, film screenings, walking tours and collaborative artworks, turning Johannesburg into a must-visit street art city. Editions were held from 2011 until 2015, and again in 2018.

Following spread
**ChowMein, Zesta, Page33,
Dreadr, Breeze Yoko,
Mr.ëksê, Tyler B. Murphy.
6th edn, Johannesburg,
South Africa, 2018**

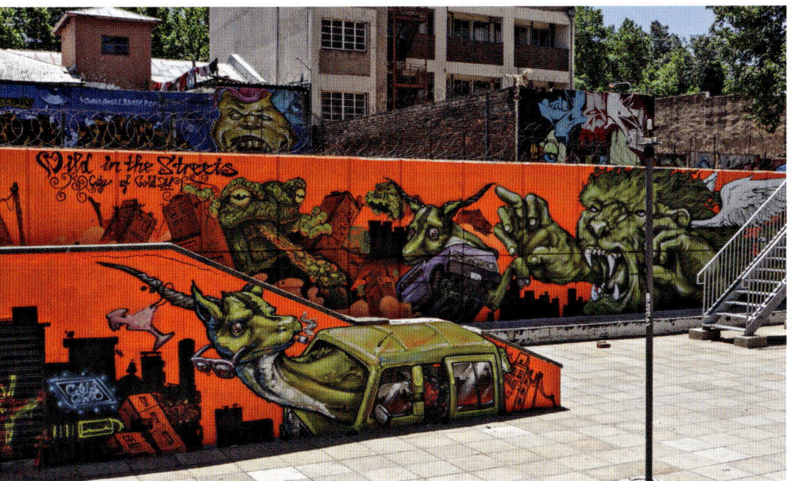

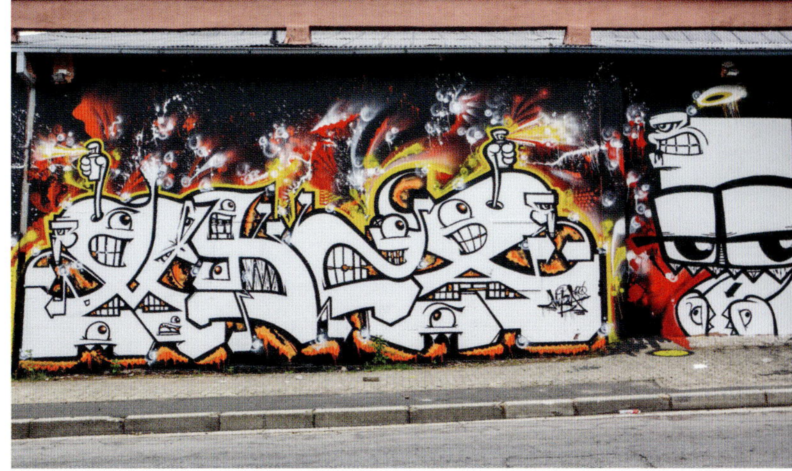

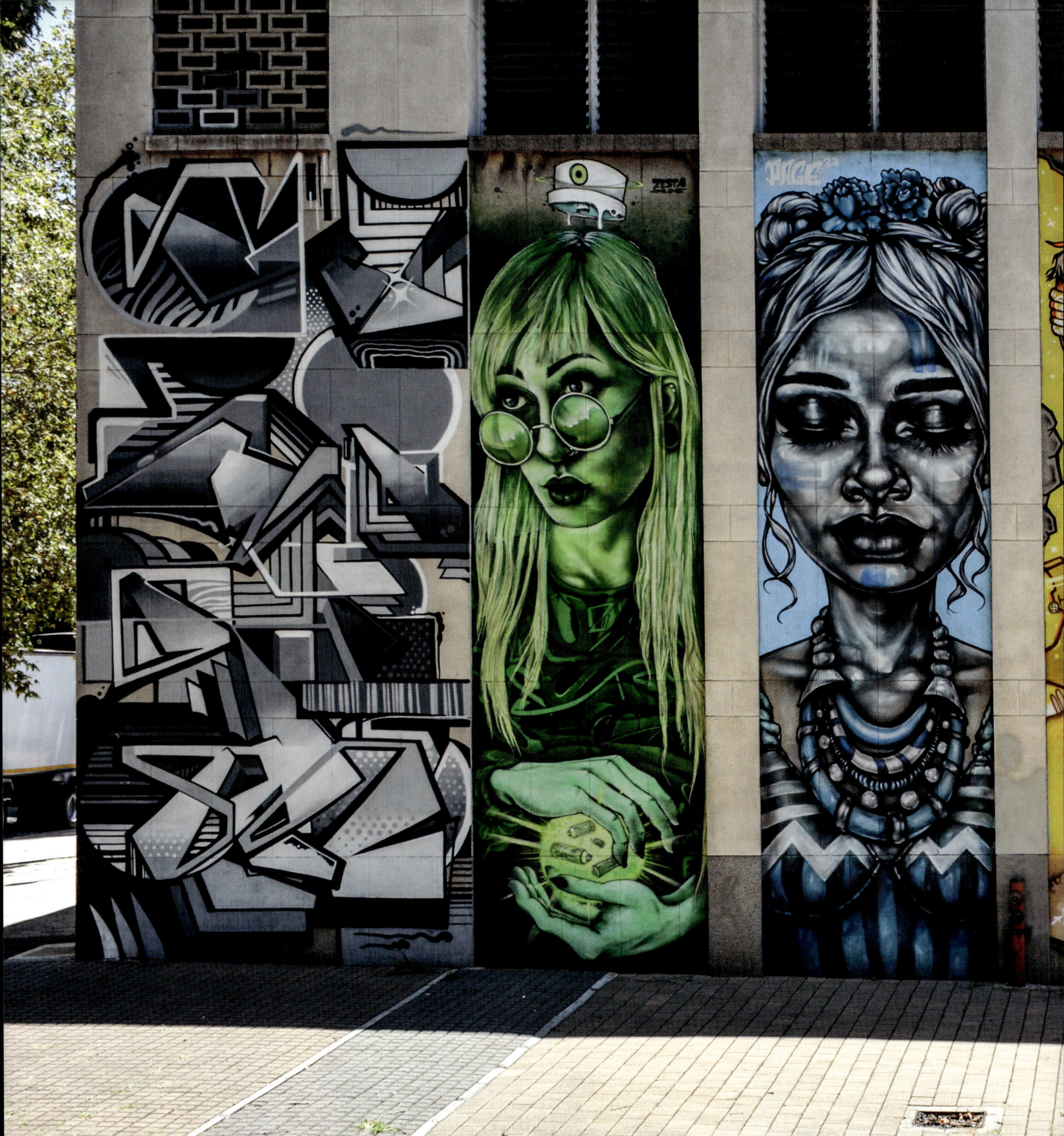

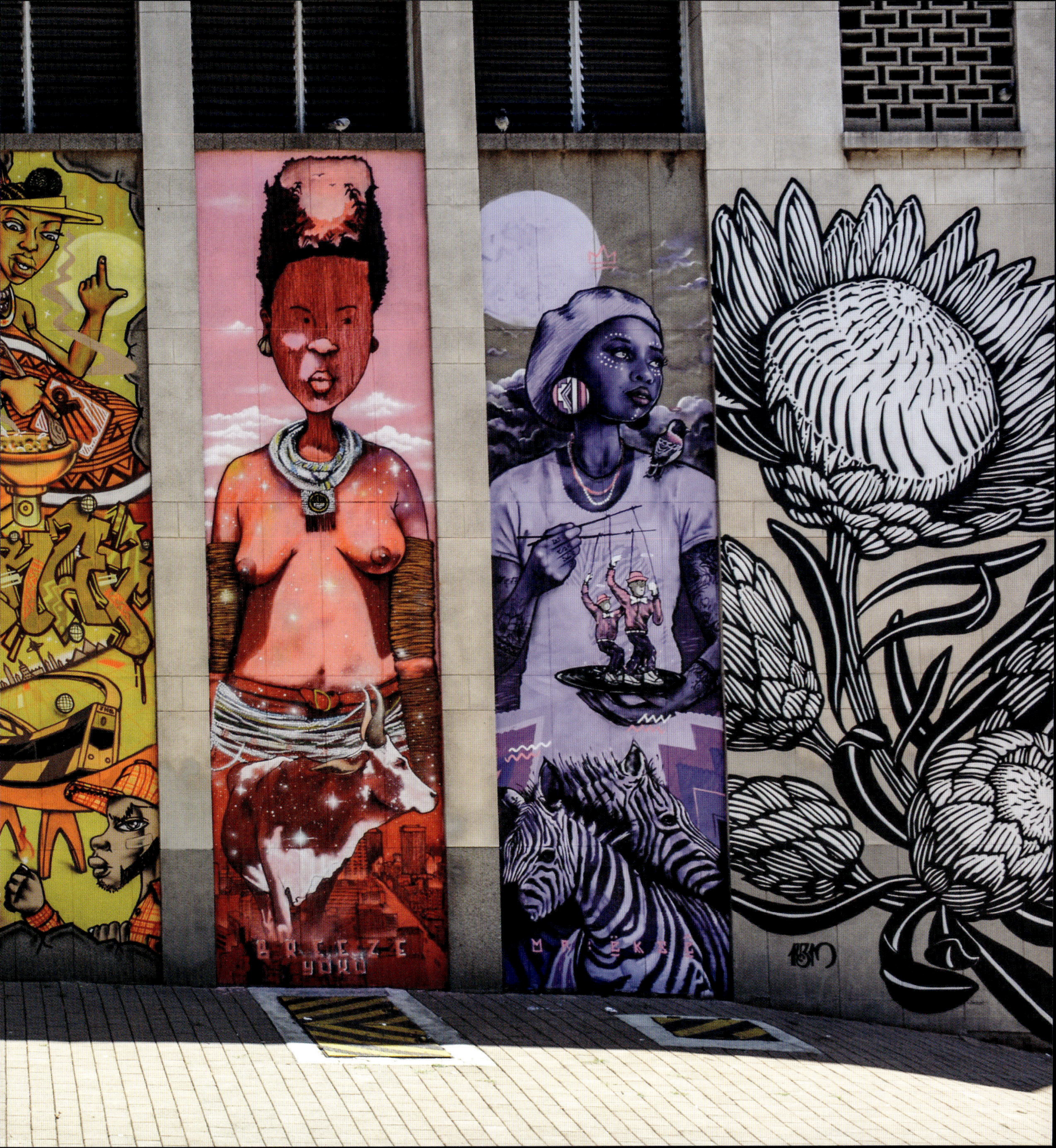
BREEZE
YORK

NARDSTAR*

Tell me about your introduction to graffiti.
I was very into hip-hop culture and started playing around with graffiti in 2004 in Cape Town. I was already a wild child, rolling around the streets on my BMX any time of the day and night. I noticed tags and pieces and was intrigued by the rebelliousness and spray can skills, so I wanted to do it too. I am now addicted to painting walls.

What do you enjoy most about painting graffiti?
The freedom, being outside, seeing weird things, the competition, the scale, the technical difficulty, painting whatever I want to, bright colours and being friends with other graffiti nerds.

Tell me about your style.
My style developed after trying a whole lot of styles early on. I picked out what I liked about different styles, finding one which felt authentic to me. As a kid I was always building puzzles, taking apart and reassembling things, and arranging products in stores. Maybe it makes sense that my style turned out to be a bunch of brightly coloured shapes being arranged in a beautiful way.

How do you approach a new painting?
I paint in phases, based on what colours I am interested in or want to play with, subject matter that I want to challenge myself with or if I just want to flex some letters. I like to create challenges for myself when I am painting – I don't want the walls to feel easy.

Tell me about the commissioned work you do.
I do commissions based on what I paint in the streets or how it fits into what I paint. I do not accept jobs that are not in my style or have subject matter I do not want to paint – like logos or Mickey Mouse.

How has travel influenced you? And what have been some memorable experiences?
Travelling to paint is always weird because I still wonder how graffiti gave me this privilege. It has been cool to see what graffiti looks like in other cities and it also gives me an appreciation and inspiration for painting at home.

Some of my most memorable trips include a project (Grafikama) in France where myself and a team of artists from around Africa transformed an abandoned building into an exhibition space; a graffiti project at the Nike world headquarters in the USA; and a live painting in Chicago at the Obama Foundation summit, where I had the opportunity to meet Barack Obama – the best experience my art has ever given me.

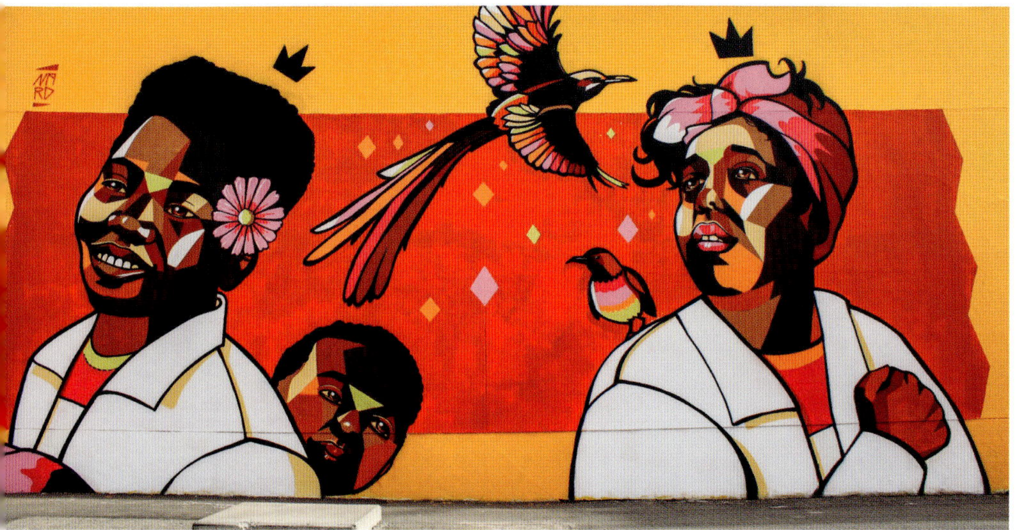

Nardstar*. 'Eyes on the Prize', East London, South Africa, 2019

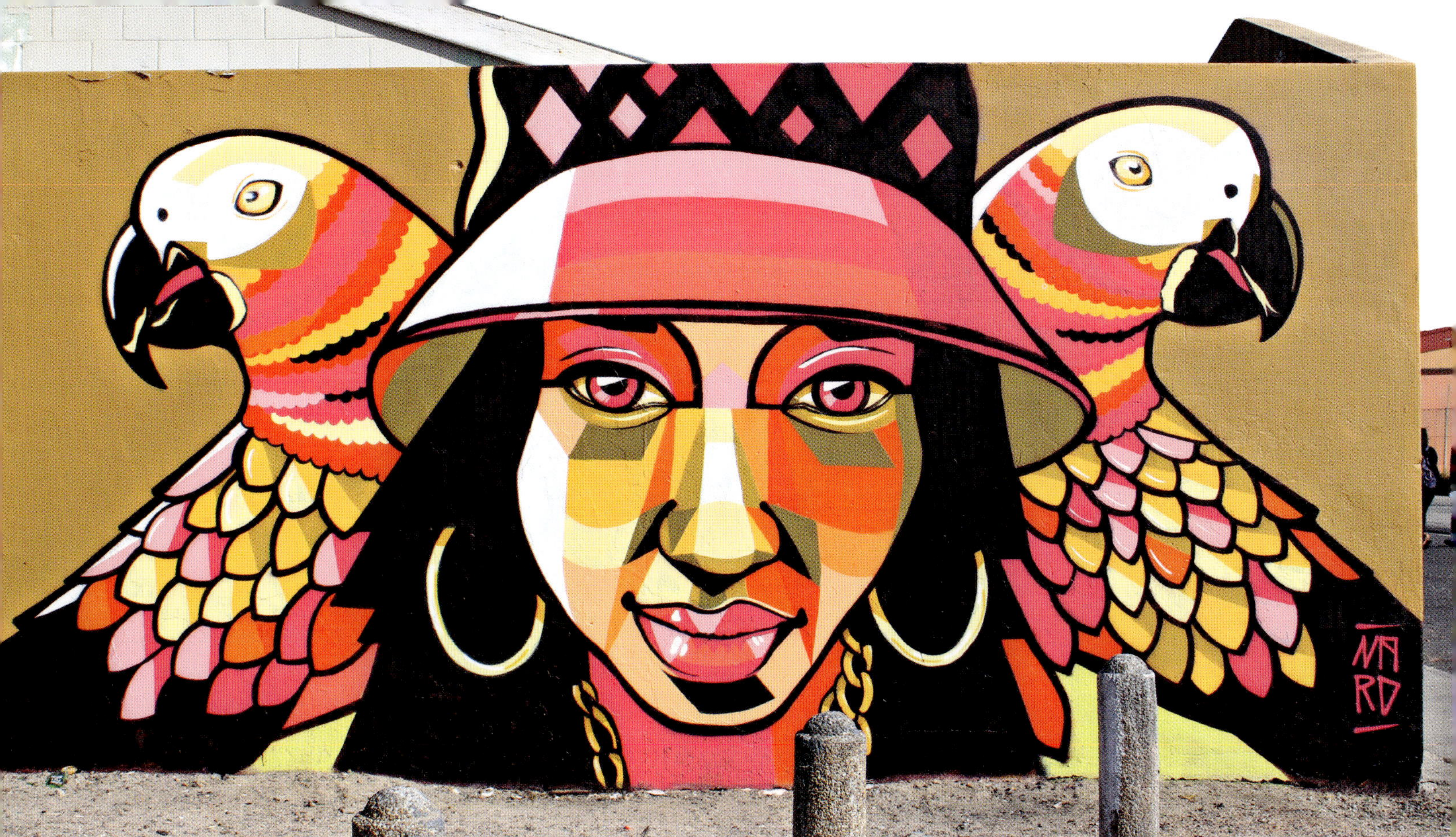

What would you say is unique about your work?

I do not know what singles it out as unique but I just try to paint in a style that I enjoy. I am not trying to imitate anybody and maybe my work shows attitude.

Can you compare African graffiti to that of the rest of the world, places like Europe and America?

Resources are the big difference. Graffiti writers around Africa do not have access to the best paint or governments that appreciate art and are able to provide funding for bigger projects. The graffiti scenes are still relatively new or small, but South Africa is lucky because we have proper spray paint.

The Internet is a useful tool for graffiti and street artists. What is the importance of having an online presence for your work?

Social media helps my art reach more people who are not in my city or out on the streets. The downside is that people who paint only two walls in their life can manipulate reality and present an image of themselves as writers or street artists. Another downside is that social media is very demanding and can make you feel like you constantly need to provide content for your followers.

Nardstar*. 'Think for Yourself', Cape Town, South Africa, 2018

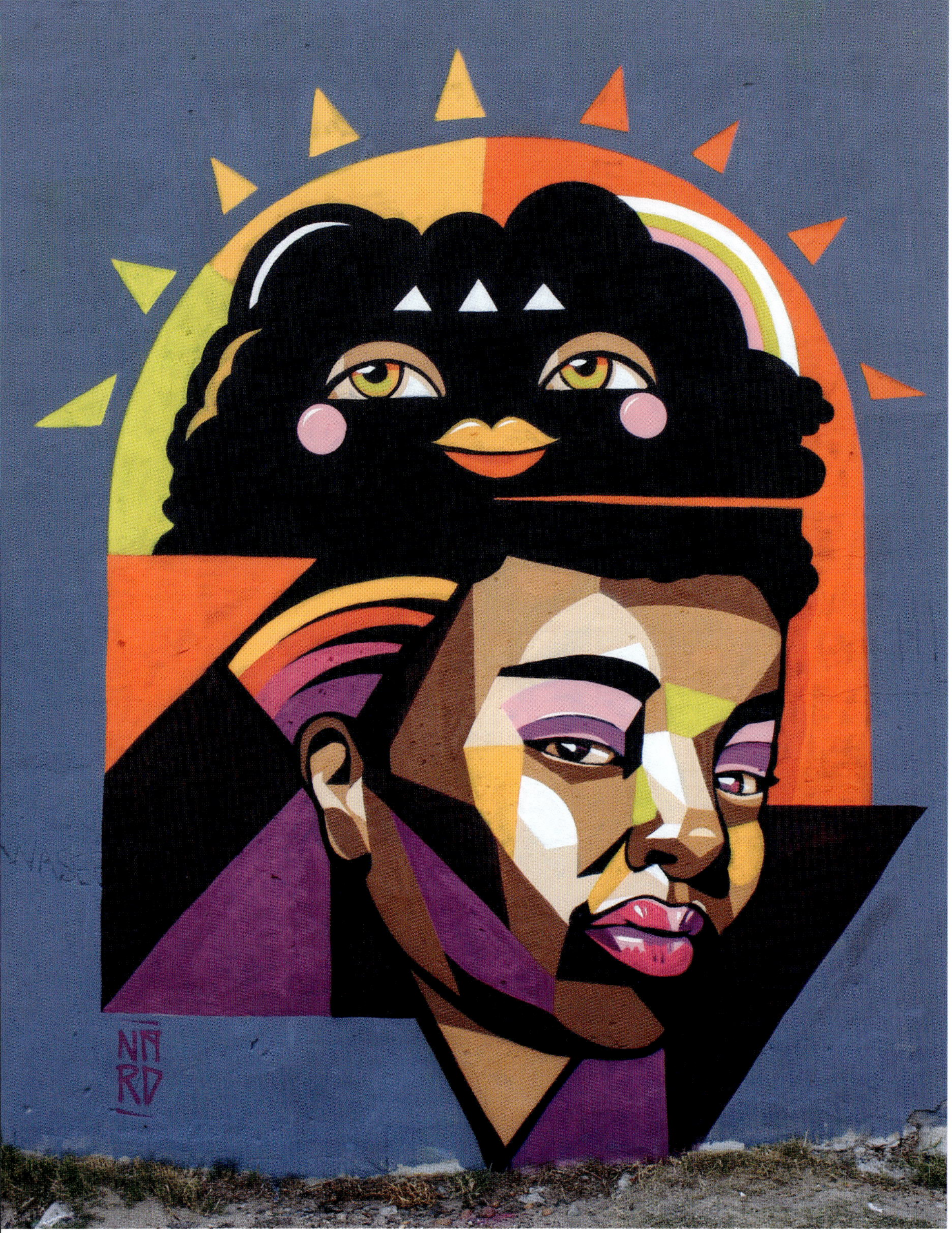

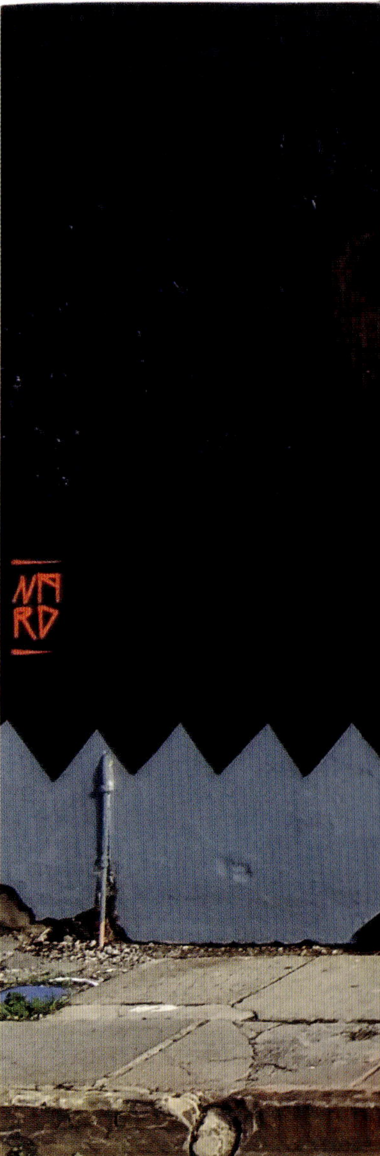

Left
**Nardstar*. 'Daydream',
Cape Town, South
Africa, 2018**
Below
**Nardstar*. 'Lion Queen',
Cape Town, South
Africa, 2018**

SOUTHERN AFRICA

How important is it to convey a message or say something important with your work?
It is not that important for me to have blatant messages in my art. I can be very selfish with my subject matter because I started painting walls as a graffiti writer who was not worried about the everyday human understanding my art. But, as an artist who paints portraits and other subject matter, I am aware of how my walls live in a community and am mindful to add to the space in a positive way. As I further my art career, I have taken an interest in telling my story, even if it is as simple as creating a space for women to be represented on walls.

Nardstar* is a female street artist based in Cape Town, South Africa. Her distinct, colourful and geometric-inspired work features women of colour and fauna and flora, and has afforded her many opportunities to travel abroad to paint. As she elevates the role of female street artists worldwide, as well as graffiti's place in her local community, she still finds time to practise more traditional graffiti lettering styles in the name of fun.

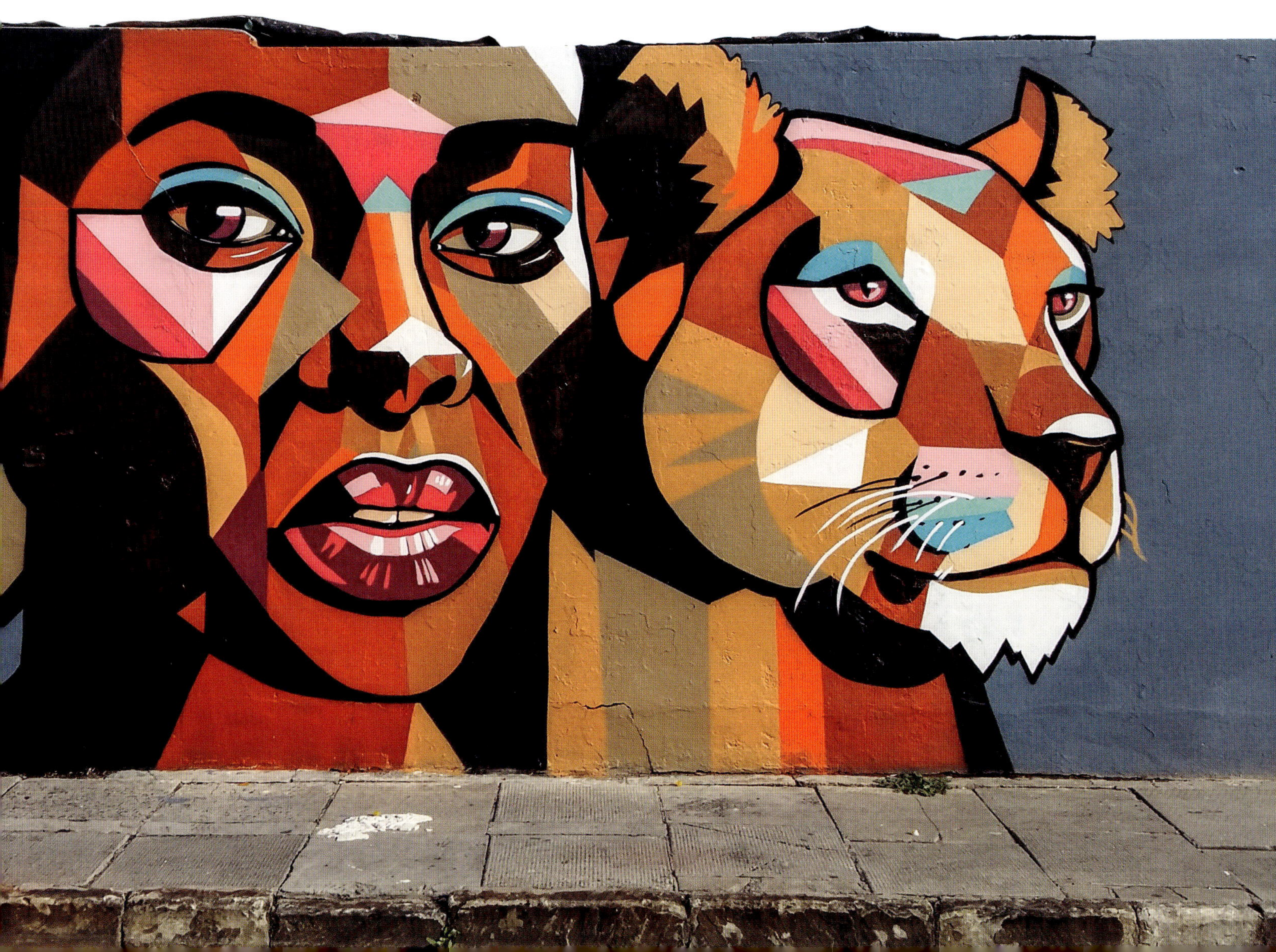

THE WORLD AND BEYOND

The scene is expanding – the world is an endless canvas and more African artists are being offered opportunities to paint abroad. Over the past two decades only a handful of Africans have been featured in publications and events, but today this is becoming more common. Talent in the motherland has risen exponentially and international franchises have tuned in. Festivals are more inclusive and many curate their line-up to focus on global representation, while others take a more developmental approach, deploying influential African artists who can impart what they learn to their countrymen and women.

On home soil, urban cultures are maturing and are less contested. Graffiti is now more often designated as an art form because of its inherent power to do good. It is continually reinventing itself and its ephemeral nature adds to its mystique. Distinct styles are being developed with a focus on African heritage, and inter-regional relations are poised to be the future as artists begin to traverse their own continent with a mission in hand. An exciting dawn has arrived for graffiti and street art in Africa.

Opposite
Sonny. 'Looking to Tomorrow', To the Bone project, London, UK, 2017

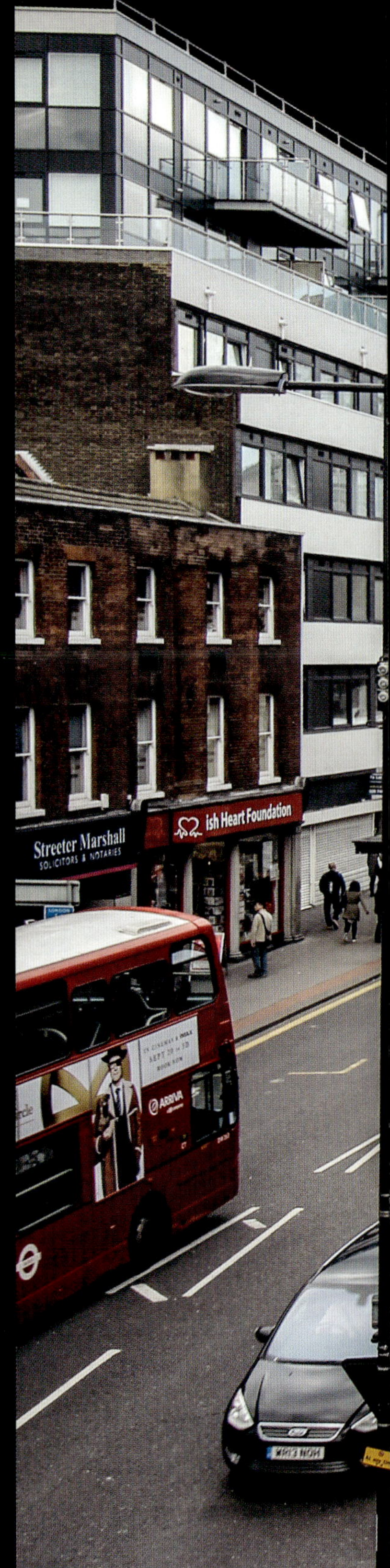

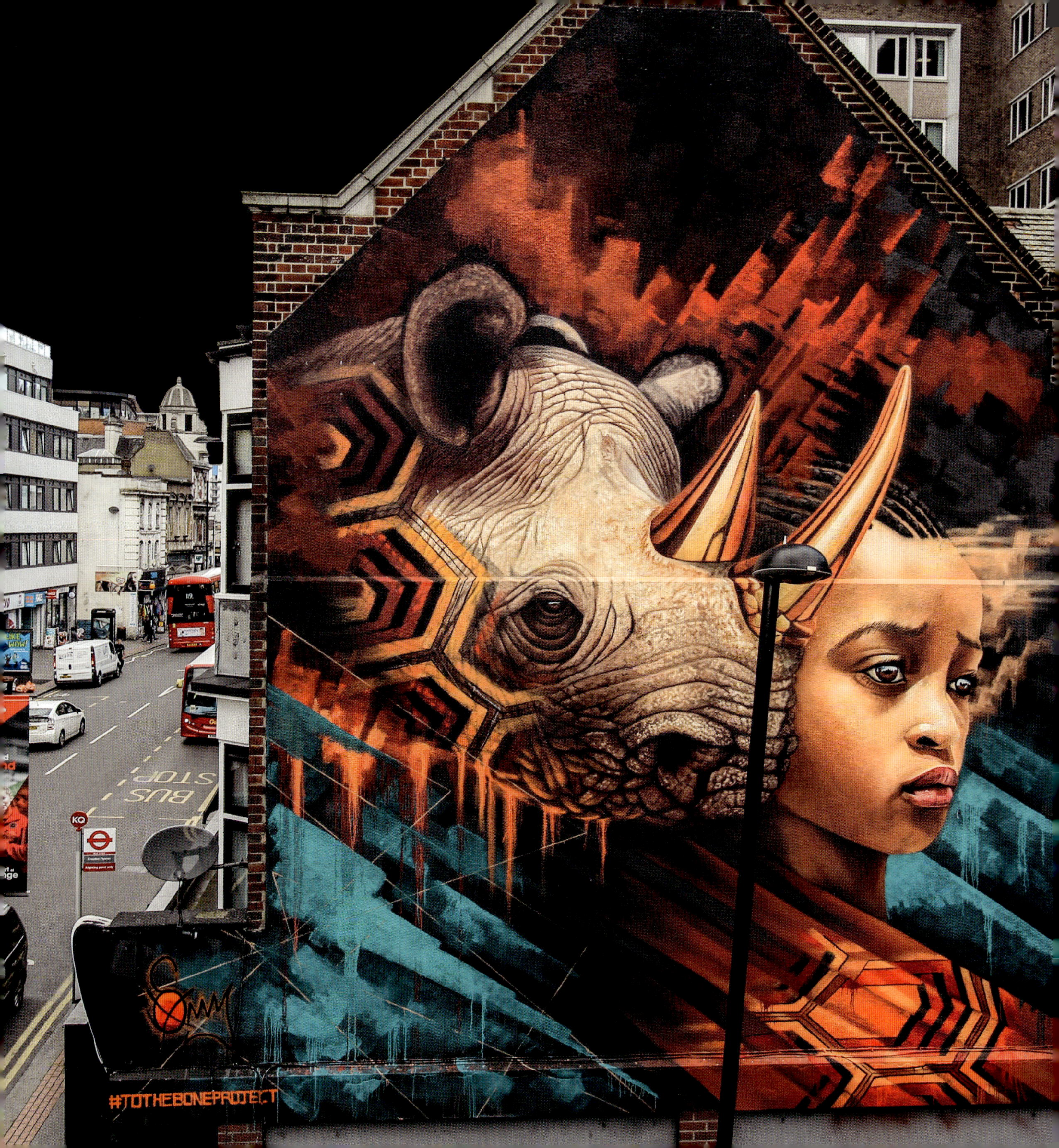
#TOTHEBONEPROJECT

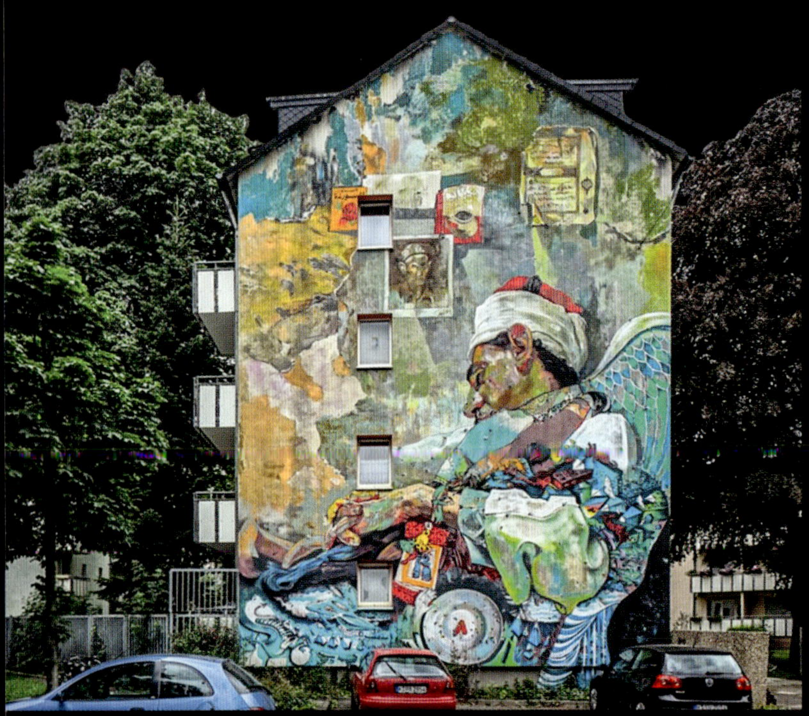

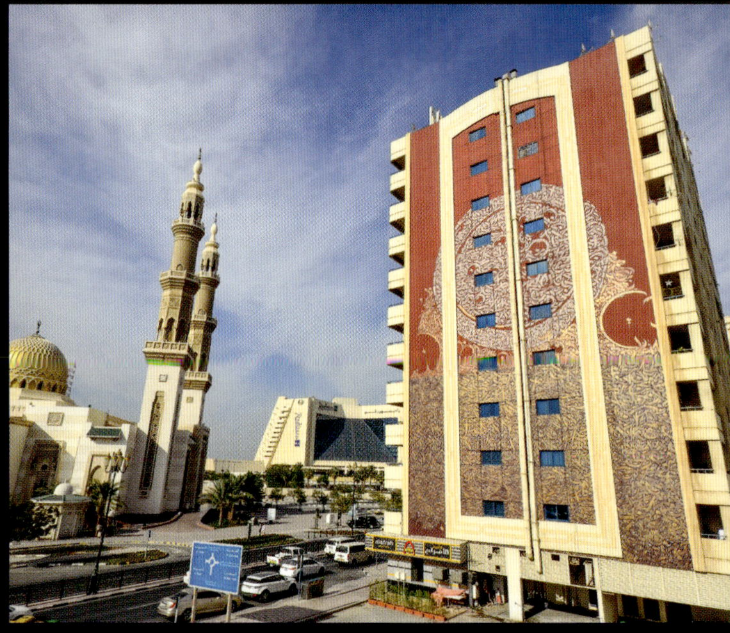

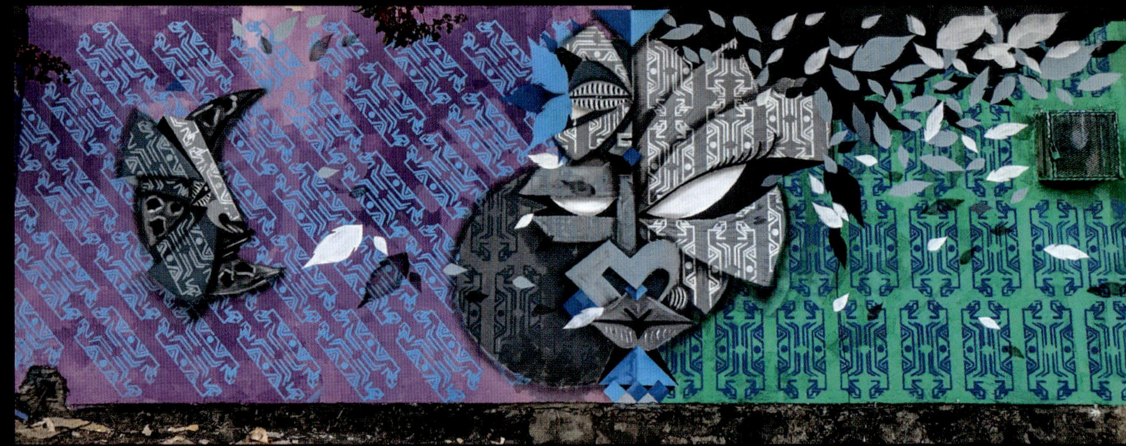

Top left
Ammar Abo Bakr. CityLeaks Urban Art Festival, Cologne, Germany, 2015

Top right
Inkman. Jedariya project, Sharjah, UAE, 2019

Bottom
Wise Two. Malinalco, Mexico, 2017

Opposite, top
Louis Masai (UK), Breeze Yoko, Doudou'Style (France). Ourcq Living Colors Festival, Paris, France, 2018

Opposite, bottom
Vajo. 'Legal Creature'. Barcelona, Spain, 2018

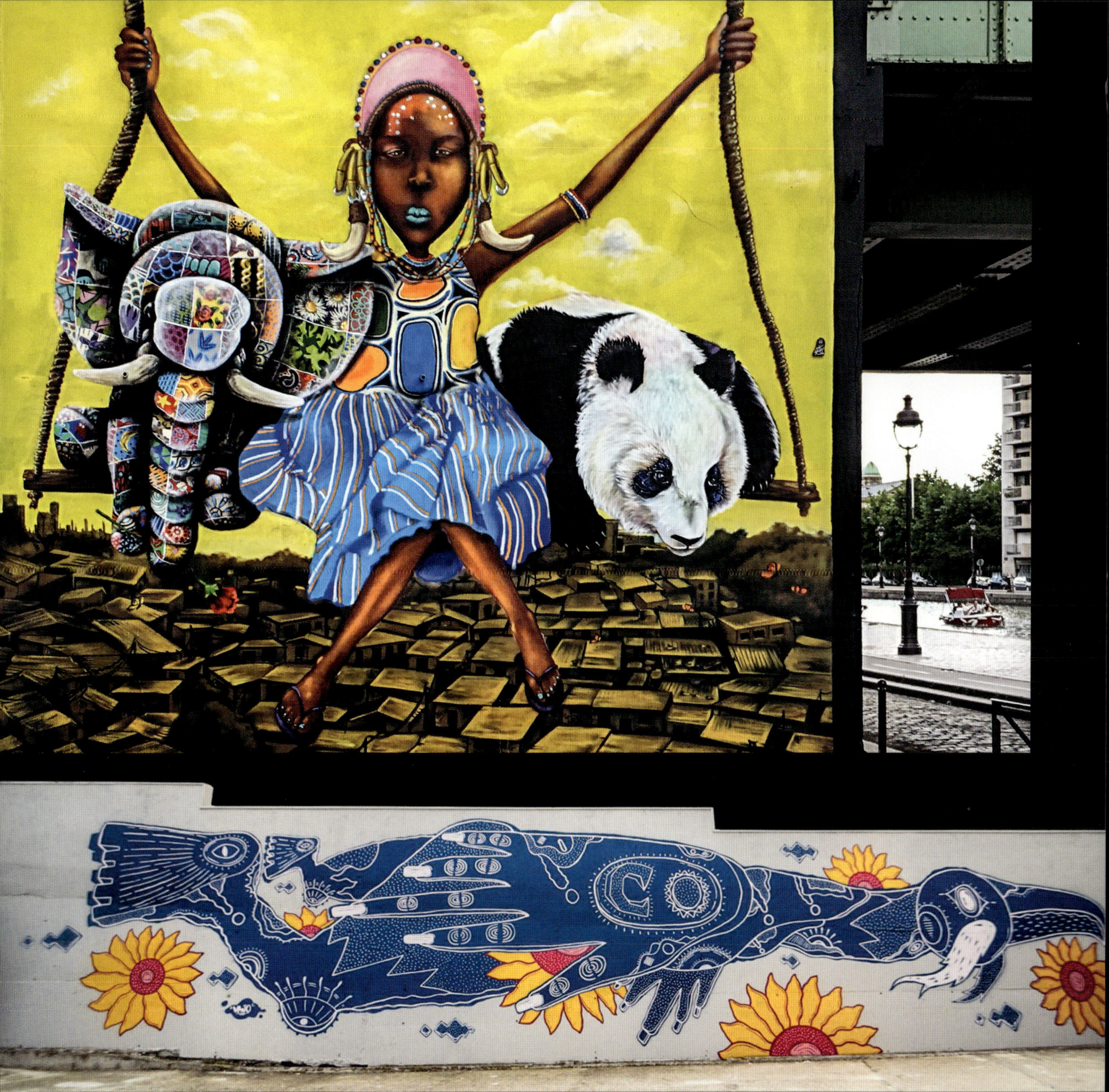

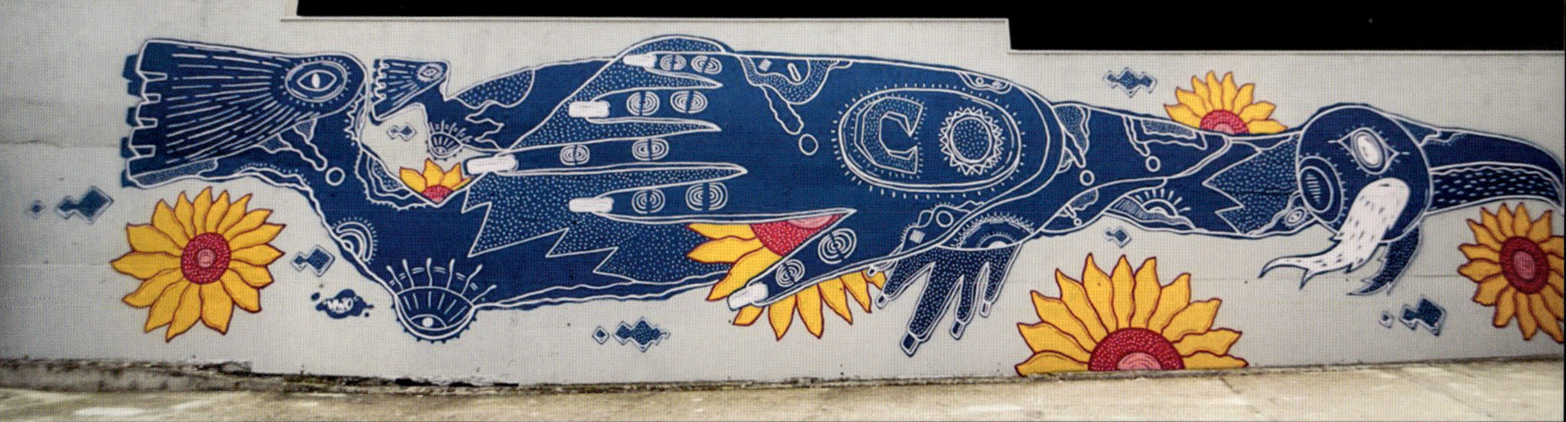

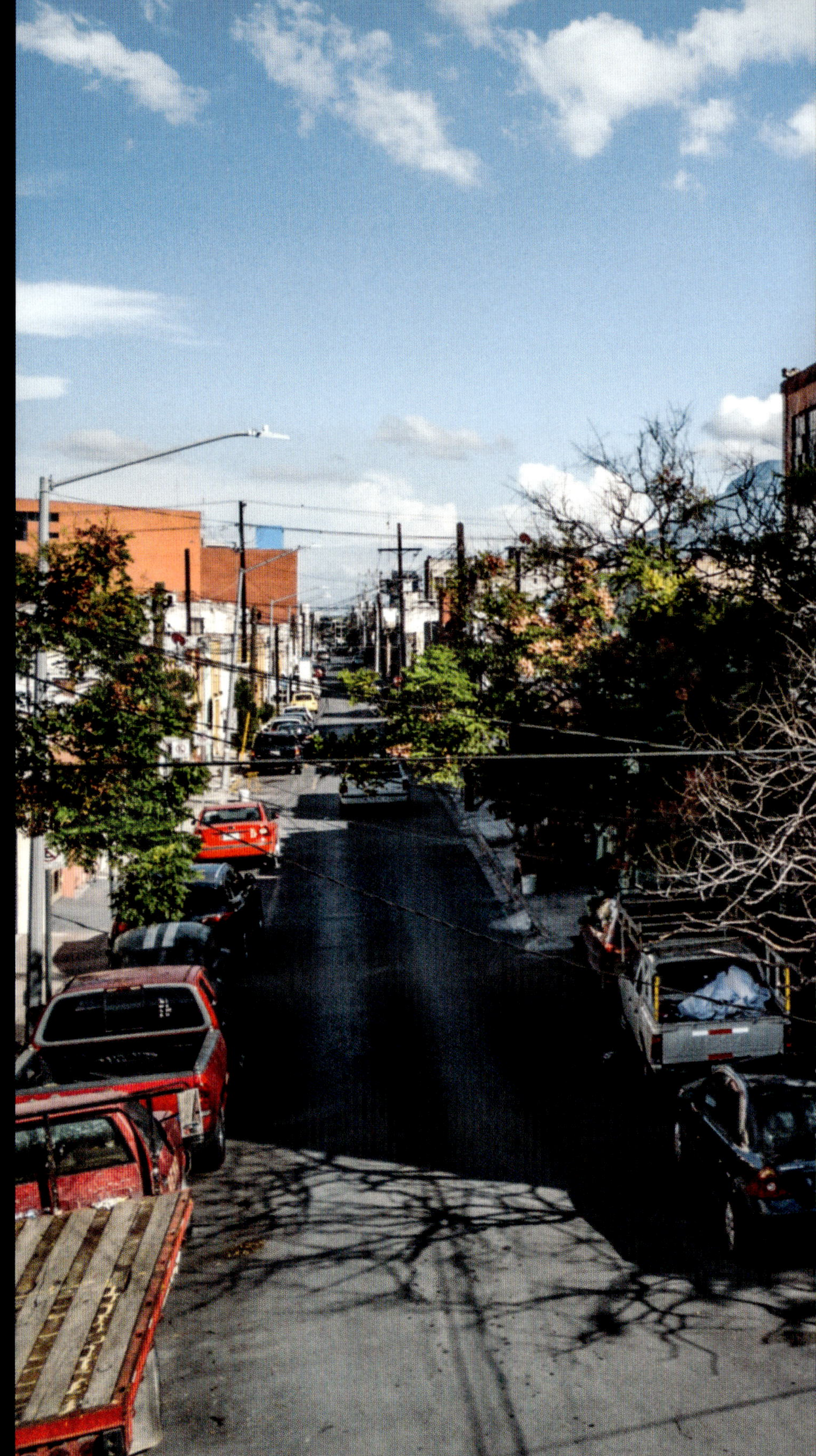

Mars. International Public
Art Festival, Monterrey,
Mexico, 2017

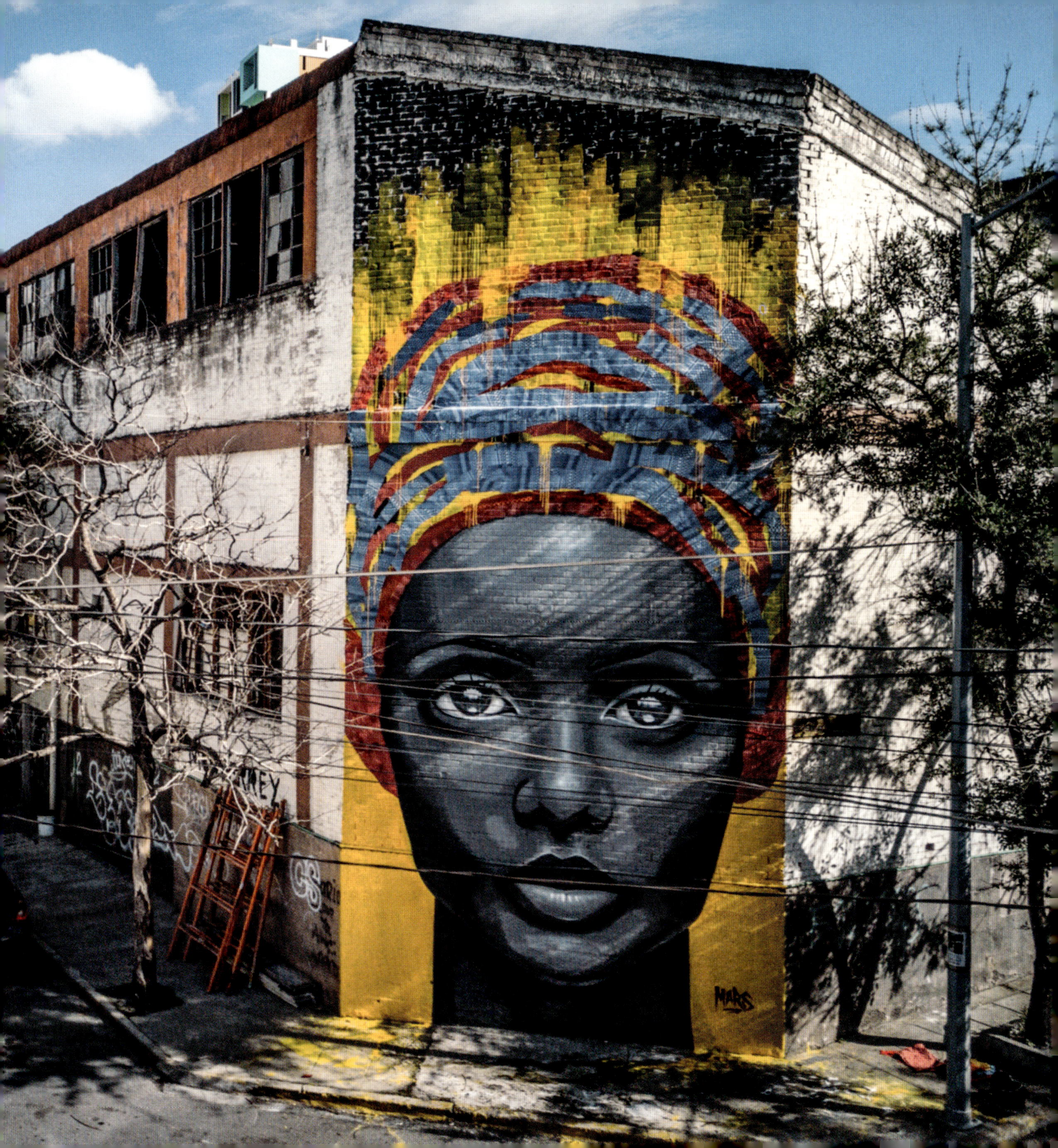

GLOSSARY OF GRAFFITI TERMS

3D
Three-dimensional style of letters for added effects or complexity.

aerosol
Liquefied paint in a pressurized can that emerges as a mist when sprayed.

background
The colour or design painted behind the piece or character, making it stand out or be more appealing.

battle
A competition between two artists or two crews after a rift or disagreement to decide a winner. These skills battles also form part of hip-hop events, often involving a time limit, judges, an audience and knock-out rounds.

benching
When graffiti artists meet up and converse about their culture. This includes sharing ideas and stories, sharing pictures of their work, sketching and planning designs. Also, the practice of observing graffiti, especially that on trains.

blockbuster
Large square letters painted with minimal colours and a roller, often used to take over a spot or be seen from a far distance.

bomb
To go out and paint graffiti illegally, often referred to as 'getting up'. The artist spreads their name or moniker to be seen. This usually involves tags and throw-ups.

breakdancing/B-boying
A dance movement inspired by breakbeats and martial arts, related to hip-hop culture.

bubble letters
A simple, rounded form of graffiti letters that originated during the movement's early stages. Often used for throw-up letters as it is quick to execute.

buff
To remove unwanted graffiti by either painting over it or using chemicals and other instruments.

calligraffiti
A mixture of calligraphy, typography and graffiti. The literal meaning of the script is sometimes hidden to arouse intrigue through a new visual language or abstract compositions.

cap
Any one of the interchangeable nozzles that fit onto the can to project the spray at various sizes. A fat cap releases a thick line, while a stencil cap produces a super-fine line. Also, to paint over another artist's work intentionally.

character
A portrait, either realistic or a cartoon figure.

crew
A group of graffiti or street artists who paint together. The crew name is often an acronym.

getting up
When an artist actively spreads their work in multiple locations, thus developing a reputation and gaining respect in the graffiti community.

graffeur
French terminology for a graffiti artist, especially used in Senegal.

graffiti
Roughly translates to 'scratches' on a surface, but has evolved over time to become its own subculture largely relating to the graphic practice of (mostly urban) lettering. The hip-hop movement has embraced graffiti as a form of visual art and expression.

graffiti jam
An organized gathering or 'bench', where graffiti artists meet up to paint a single wall or location together.

hall of fame
An area that consists of a large amount of graffiti walls or pieces.

hip-hop
A culture that was established in the late 1970s and early 1980s. Elements include rapping, breakdancing, DJing and graffiti.

legal
A work painted with permission.

letter-set
A set of similarly structured graffiti letters, like a font.

mural
A painting executed directly on an interior or exterior wall, and sometimes a ceiling.

old-school
Refers to a previous generation, technique or time frame, usually the early or formative days.

paste-up
Paper glued onto a wall or surface with wheatpaste or wallpaper paste. The paper will usually have a drawing or stencil already on it.

pichação
A unique form of tagging that originated in Brazil. Whole sides of buildings are covered by *pichadores* who riskily climb to untouched spots to paint their name or crew name.

piece
An abbreviation of 'masterpiece', referring to a work of graffiti that is usually large, elaborate and time-consuming to execute. Various effects are incorporated, including 3D and arrows, as well as many colours and colour transitions.

post-graffiti
A term that describes the current evolution of graffiti as it fuses with street art, fine art and abstraction. Also used to define artists who come from a graffiti background and now practise art professionally.

production
A large work featuring multiple artists and a theme.

public art
Art produced or exhibited in a
public space for people to enjoy
freely. Usually installation art,
such as architecture, sculpture,
ceramics, mosaics and tapestry,
as well as performance art. Urban
art (street art and graffiti) also
falls under the umbrella.

roller
A rotating brush to spread paint
on a wall or surface. Also, a
graffiti work made with a paint
roller instead of spray paint,
usually large in size and simplified
in formation.

roller paint
Common house paint available
in a tin or bucket, which is more
cost-effective for large or porous
surfaces. Also referred to as tub
or bucket paint.

script
To write using a specific alphabet,
e.g. Arabic script; the practice
of writing script styles.

spot
A location where one can paint
or view graffiti.

spray paint
Paint in aerosol form: held in
a pressurized can, it is released
as a fine mist by a propellant gas.
This is the main medium used for
graffiti as it offers high coverage
in little time.

spraycation
A play on the word 'vacation'.
Graffiti artists venture to
new places for a so-called
working holiday: to get up
in a new environment.

stencil
An illustration or design that is
cut out from cardboard or other
material. All of the time-consuming
work is done beforehand and
the artist can quickly transfer the
image onto a surface with spray
paint. The ability to easily replicate
the work in numerous places
makes stencils an ideal tool to
spread a message or apply effects.
Multiple layers render a more
intricate design.

sticker
Similar to a stencil, a sticker is
also prepared in advance and can
be executed swiftly and discreetly.
Peel away the protective sheet
to reveal the adhesive, which will
stick to most surfaces. The design
will be showcased and the options
are endless – handmade with
a marker or designed on the
computer and printed in large
quantities.

street art
A blanket term to describe
art found on the streets:
predominantly stencils, stickers
and paste-ups, although
graffiti and other public art are
sometimes included. Generally
it focuses on more illustrative
artworks and murals rather
than lettering.

style
The particular look or aesthetic
visible in the work. Many
graffiti artists give their letters
a unique appearance to be
easily identifiable among other
artists even when working with
alternative names or words.
A good style is well balanced
yet rhythmical.

style writing
When a graffiti artist produces
a letter piece.

tag
As a noun, the stylized signature
or name of a graffiti artist. As a
verb, to write or paint one's graffiti
signature or name, usually with
great speed.

throw-up
A work in-between a tag and
a piece in terms of complexity
and labour intensity. It is
usually executed quickly and
comprises a single-colour
outline with a single layer of fill
colour. Graffiti artists generally
create a fixed throw-up style in
order for their work to be easily
identified, like a logo.

top-to-bottom
First referenced with regard to
a train carriage, a top-to-bottom
is a piece that stretches from
the top of the wall or train car
all the way to the bottom.

trackside
A graffiti work painted along a
railway line, or visible from a train.

traditional graffiti
Refers to the common
practices of graffiti such as
tags, throw-ups and pieces.
Wildstyle, 3D and bubble
letters were part of the early
formation and have since become
the basis for today's graffiti
practitioners. With the constant
evolution of the craft, new,
elaborate and experimental
techniques are classified under
additional categories such as
abstract graffiti.

up
Graffiti artists, or writers, are
considered 'up' when their work
becomes well known. This is
determined by the amount of
visible graffiti they have painted –
taking style, skill and location
into account.

urban art
A blanket term used to describe
art found in urban areas, including
traditional graffiti and street art;
also includes more traditional
artists such as fine artists,
illustrators and designers who
may work at a street level when
an opportunity is presented.

wheatpaste
A basic glue made from flour,
water and sometimes sugar. Used
for wheat pasting or paste-ups.

wildstyle
A complex and highly stylized
form of graffiti that is difficult to
read or decipher. It often features
three-dimensional type with
elaborate connections.

writer
A graffiti artist or practitioner.

PICTURE CREDITS

1 Ayaa Pixels; **2–3** Arsène Zounon (PIX Studio); **6–7** Cale Waddacor; **8–9 Clockwise from top** Zakaria Latouri/Esen/Bouchama Mohamed Kamel/Spent; **10 Left** Chadi Ilias; **10 Right top** Albernais Gonçalves; **10 Right bottom** Cale Waddacor; **11** Chadi Ilias; **12–13** Faith XLVII; **14 Clockwise from top left** Lorenzo Bordonaro/El Marto/Irene McCullagh/Giffy; **15 Left** Falko One; **15 Right** AIRJP Tagman; **17 Clockwise from top left** La Main Du Peuple/Jason Goder/Grocco/Frédérique Binet/Cale Waddacor; **18–19** Abdelrhman Zin Eldin; **20** AIRJP Tagman; **21 Top left** Toni Kaatz-Dubberke; **21 Bottom left** Nii Odzenma; **21 Right** Khwezi; **22–23** See captions on page 271; **24** Kibuuka Mukisa Oscar; **26 From top** Socrome/Behulum/Kaguamba Theuri/Yamiko Yakobe/RinaArt/Jason Goder; **27 From top** Judith Kaine/Mrock/Emily Tibihika/Kibuuka Mukisa Oscar/Lo/Tinashe Charleson; **29 Top** Swift9; **29 Centre** Esen; **29 Bottom** Kahiga Muchiri; **30 Left, right top** Wachata Crew; **30 Right bottom** Seth Markle; **31 All images** Behulum; **32–33** Falko One; **35 Clockwise from top** Felix Magara/Evans Kiiza/Kyeyune/Xenson; **36 Clockwise from top** Mr Fuzzy Slipperz/Judith Kaine/Ismael Anza (Do Pau); **37** Dilayla Romeo; **38–39 Top** Lo; **38–39 Bottom** Tinashe Charleson; **39 Bottom right** Tinashe Charleson; **40–41** Olivia Morel; **42 Left** Monk.E; **42 Right** Shakes; **43 Top** Bantu.Moja; **43 Bottom** Kerosh; **44** Felix Magara; **45** Esen; **46–49 All images** Cale Waddacor; **50** Ray Ndikwe; **51** Lucky Philip Rundu; **52** Robin Letellier; **53 Clockwise from top** Vans the Omega/Mike Gichora/Bankslave; **55 Clockwise from top left** Cale Waddacor/Resko/Smok/Swift9/Cale Waddacor; **56 Top left** Kibuuka Mukisa Oscar; **56 Clockwise from top right** Robin Letellier; **57** Kibuuka Mukisa Oscar; **58 Top, bottom** Kibuuka Mukisa Oscar; **59 Top** Robin Letellier; **59 Bottom** Kibuuka Mukisa Oscar; **61, 62 All images** Socrome; **64–65** Jason Goder; **66, 67** RinaArt; **68 Top, bottom** Matt Tse; **69 Top** AIRJP Tagman; **69 Bottom** RinaArt; **70 Top left, bottom left** Fabio Andriamiarintsoa; **70 Top right** Conor Ralphs; **70–71** Sk4rz Tsijonriake; **71** Fabio Andriamiarintsoa; **72–75 All images** AIRJP Tagman; **76–77** Judith Kaine; **77 Top** Mxko World; **77 Bottom right** Mook Lion; **78** Nems; **80 From top** Buntu Fihla/Monk.E/Tetebotan Kali/David Jouary/P3pe Art2dieu; **81 From top** Spent/Spent/Nadia Seika/Osaré Studio; **83 Top** Thó Simões; **83 Bottom** David Jouary; **84–85 Top** Spent; **84–85 Centre** Thó Simões; **84–85 Bottom** Yann Kwete; **86–87** Thó Simões; **88 Top, bottom** Nems; **91 Top** Christo Beks; **90–91 Bottom** Nems; **92 Top left** Nems; **92 Top right** David Jouary; **92–93 Top, centre, bottom** Christo Beks; **95 Top, bottom right** Albernais Gonçalves; **95 Bottom left** Spent;

96 All images Spent; **98, 99** Thó Simões; **100–03 All images** Verkron Collective; **104–7 All images** Thó Simões; **108** Amine Ait Ouaret; **110 From top** El Panchow/Elbohly/Simo Mouhim/Chris Opila; **111 From left** Hamza Bennour/Georg Höermann/Galal Yousif/Psycho/Bouchama Mohamed Kamel; **112–13** Say; **113 Top** Mehdi Annassi; **113 Bottom** Abderrahmane Ferhat; **114** Hichem Merouche; **114–15** Abdelrhman Zin Eldin; **116–17** Placebo Studio; **118–19** Harrachif Oussama; **119 Top** Youcef Krache; **119 Centre** Hamza Nuino; **119 Bottom** Larissa Fuhrmann; **120** Kalamour; **121** Placebo Studio; **123** Aline Deschamps; **124 Left** Jaye de Tunis; **124 Top right** Meen One; **124 Centre** Jihed Yahyaoui; **124 Bottom** Georg Höermann; **125** Hend Tekaya; **126–27** Faith XLVII; **128 Clockwise from top left** Inkman/Claude Danrey/Houssem Omri/Alba D; **129** Claude Danrey; **130 Left, right** ST4 the project; **131 Top left, top right** ST4 the project; **131 Bottom** Becem Sdiri; **132 Left to right, top to bottom** Abdelrhman Zin Eldin/Chris Opila/Abdelrhman Zin Eldin/Chris Opila/Chris Opila/JoAnna Pollonais/Abdelrhman Zin Eldin; **134 Top** Claudia Wiens; **134 Centre** Chris Opila; **134 Bottom** Alaa Awad; **134–35** Abdelrhman Zin Eldin; **136 Clockwise from top left** Abdelrhman Zin Eldin/Ahmed Gaber/Abdelrhman Zin Eldin/Chris Opila; **138** Abdelrhman Zin Eldin; **139 Top, bottom** Ahmed Gaber; **140–41** Abdelrhman Zin Eldin; **142, 143** Alaa Awad; **144** Samir Ahmed Shafi (Droogs); **145 Left top, left bottom** Mohamed Abd Elgafour; **145 Right** Shady Bahgat; **146 Left** Fadi Zayeti; **146 Centre** Kero; **146–47** Sneak Hotep; **147** Kero; **148–49** eL Seed; **150 Top** Chadi Ilias; **150 Left** Simo Mouhim; **150 Right** Placebo Studio; **152–53 Top row, left to right** Dou/Zakaria Bouatir/Dou/Abdelhamid Belahmidi; **152–53 Bottom row, left to right** Ed One/Gero; **154** Bart van Kersavond; **156–57** Trick 54; **157 Top** Yassine Balbziou; **157 Bottom** Youness Battach; **158 Top** Placebo Studio; **158 Bottom left, bottom right** Med.z; **159** Chadi Ilias; **160** Grocco; **160–61** Fabe Collage; **161 Bottom left** Ed One; **161 Bottom right** Bart van Kersavond; **162** Youness Battach; **163 Top left** Mohamed Amine Nassiri; **163 Top right** Hamza Nuino; **163 Bottom right** Youness Battach; **164 Top** Simo Mouhim; **164 Bottom left** Chadi Ilias; **164 Bottom right** Hamza Nuino; **164–65** Ben Brahim Walid; **166–67** Yann Chatelin; **167 Top left** Yann Chatelin; **167 Top right** Zakaria Latouri; **167 Bottom** Sagés; **168** Nadib Bandi; **170 From top** Vilédé Gnanvo/Lymo Condel/Lazer/El Marto/Melissa Rito/Njogu Touray/Zifu; **171 From top** Marco Conti Sikic/Tetebotan Kali/Ernest Ibe/Nadib Bandi/Samuel Behr/Tetebotan Kali; **172–73** Sola Omobomi; **173 Top** Nadib Bandi; **173 Bottom** Zina Godeau; **174** Tayo Adeoye; **175 Left, right** Njogu Touray; **176–77** Moh Awudu; **178 Top left**

ACKNOWLEDGMENTS

Zina Godeau; **178–79** Lorenzo Bordonaro; **179 Bottom left, bottom right** Drissa Konaté; **180 Top, bottom** Grace Ribeiro; **180–81** Lorenzo Bordonaro; **183 Clockwise from top left** Jolie Derouet/Zifu/Zifu/Boris Esteve/Zifu/Zifu; **185 Top** RoMeiJ; **185 Bottom** Samuel Behr; **186 Top** RoMeiJ; **186 Bottom** Sagés; **187 Left** Akonga; **187 Right** Leslie Rabine; **188–89** Samuel Behr; **190–91** Keith Clark; **190 Bottom left** Falko One; **190 Bottom right** 2mgraff; **193 Top row, second row, third row left, fourth row** RBS Crew; **193 Third row right** Samuel Behr; **193 Bottom row** Leslie Rabine; **194** Mame Mor Seye; **194–95 Top to bottom** Zina Godeau/Leslie Rabine/Leslie Rabine/Leslie Rabine; **196–97** Leslie Rabine; **198** RBS Crew; **199** DJ Cortega; **200–03 All images** Leslie Rabine; **204** Moh Awudu; **205 Top** Raphe HautEnCouleur; **205 Bottom** Nii Odzenma; **206** Nii Odzenma; **207** Rodrigo Fonseca Silva; **208 Clockwise from top** Tsé/Nomwindé Vivien Sawadogo/Sangue/Zina Godeau; **209** Tetebotan Kali; **210** Boris Esteve; **210–11 Centre left, bottom** ASSART; **211 Top** Vilédé Gnanvo; **211 Centre right** ASSART; **212** Sitou; **213 Left** Placebo Studio; **213 Right** Sitou; **214** Cale Waddacor; **215** Moh Awudu; **216 Clockwise from top left** Msaleh/Joshua J. Visuals/Leslie Rabine/Tetebotan Kali/Ashlee Sang; **217** Samuel Behr; **218–19** Sonny; **220** Luca Barausse; **222 From top** Snot420/FOK/Dane Armstrong/Taboka Bachibili Nfila/Pixel Monster; **223 From top** Sub-0/Dbongz/OptOne/Cale Waddacor/Cale Waddacor; **225 Top** Kierran Allen; **225 Bottom** Neo Jasmine Mokgosi; **226 Clockwise from top** Sven Christian/Cale Waddacor/Tapz/Sonny; **228–29** Dekor One; **230–31 Clockwise from top left** Wayne Lee Danker (Righteous Photography)/Cale Waddacor/Cale Waddacor/Derek Smith/Cale Waddacor; **232 Left** Pixel Monster; **232 Right, top to bottom** Snot420/Bief37/Snot420; **233 Top** Cale Waddacor; **233 Bottom** Mars; **234 Left to right** Sarah Isaacs/Sarah Isaacs/Sven Christian; **235 Top** Cale Waddacor; **235 Bottom** Sven Christian; **237 Top left, bottom** Dane Stops; **237 Top right** Damn Vandal; **238–39** Cale Waddacor; **240 Clockwise from top left** Sonny/Falko One/Cale Waddacor/Cale Waddacor; **242–43** Cale Waddacor; **244–45** Cale Waddacor; **245 Clockwise from top left** r1./Cale Waddacor/r1.; **247 Second row right** Mr.ëksê; **247 All other images** Cale Waddacor; **248** Dekor One; **249 Clockwise from top left** Dekor One/Cale Waddacor/Dekor One/Dekor One/Cale Waddacor; **250 Top** Mars; **250–53 All other images** Cale Waddacor; **254–57 All images** Nardstar*; **258–59** Tess Cunliffe; **260 Top left** Bart van Kersavond; **260 Top right** Alba D; **260 Bottom** Wise Two; **261 Top** Nathalie Vallet-Papathéodorou; **261 Bottom** Clara Antón; **262–63** David Sepa

I am extremely grateful to all artists, organizations and photographers for their contributions which made this book possible. To those who answered questions for feature interviews and research purposes – thank you! Special thanks to everyone who went out of their way to gather images and connect me to other artists and organizers, or who helped with verifying facts. Thanks to the team at Thames & Hudson and everyone who supports this book project. Let's grow the African street art community!

Heartiest thanks to my mother, Elaine, for her everlasting wisdom in proofreading my manuscript, and to my beloved wife, Tilana, for her continuous support. Love and light to my daughter, Willow, who was born amidst the book-writing activities, and to my friends and family across the world. I dedicate this book to my father, Michael, who bought my first graffiti book, *Graffiti World*, and inspired it all.

Help to support street art in Africa by funding select projects via our charity drive at http://www.streetartafrica.com/

INDEX OF ARTISTS

Captions to pages 22–23
Left to right, top to bottom

Page 22
Top row
Inkman. Jedariya project, Sharjah, UAE, 2019. Photograph: Alba D

Sistadada. Afri-Cans Festival (2nd edn), Kampala, Uganda, 2018. Photograph: Kibuuka Mukisa Oscar

Ammar Abo Bakr. JIDAR – Toiles de Rue (2nd edn), Rabat, Morocco, 2016. Photograph: Ben Brahim Walid

Maherisoa Rakotomalala. Festival d'Art Urbain (4th edn), Antsiranana, Madagascar, 2017. Photograph: Alliance Française Diego Suarez

Second row
Shoof. Djerbahood project, Djerba, Tunisia, 2014. Photograph: Aline Deschamps

Sié Decor, Deris. Ouagadougou, Burkina Faso, 2017. Photograph: Armel Boris Bonégo aka Yam

eL Seed (France). 'Perception', Cairo, Egypt, 2016. Photograph: eL Seed

MOC. Graff Up Festi (2nd edn), Douala, Cameroon, 2018. Photograph: David Jouary

Third row
Ngabonziza Bonfils, Dolph Kayitannkore. GaraGara250 project, Kigali, Rwanda, 2018. Photograph: Pamela Tulizo Kamale

Brush. Casamouja: Urban Art Wave, Casablanca, Morocco, 2018. Photograph: Chadi Ilias

Nofal O-one. Cairo, Egypt, 2019. Photograph: Samir Ahmed Shafi (Droogs)

Freemind, Diablos, Man Innov. Dakar, Senegal, 2016. Photograph: RBS Crew

Saïd Omar. Moroni, Comoros, 2010. Photograph: Socrome

Fourth row
Lmnt. Mascara, Algeria, 2018.

Photograph: Mahdi Boucif

Momo Relmo assisting with the priming of the wall. Effet Graff (5th edn), Cotonou, Benin, 2019. Photograph: Boris Esteve

Assil Diab. Khartoum, Sudan, 2019. Photograph: Anas Altayeb (Nasca Media)

Swift9. Nairobi, Kenya, 2017. Photograph: Kerosh

Brave Tangz, Isaac Iirumva, Shingiro Ntigurirwa, Gilbert Iradukunda, Dolph Kayitannkore, Viktart, Ngabonziza Bonfils, Jim Rolland. GaraGara250 project, Kigali, Rwanda, 2018. Photograph: Pamela Tulizo Kamale

Fifth row
Socrome. Moroni, Comoros, 2010. Photograph: Hamou

Vajo. 'You Get What You Give', Tunis, Tunisia, 2016. Photograph: Simona Bonomo

Saïd Omar, Keal (France). Moroni, Comoros, 2010. Photograph: Socrome

Amaphiko graffiti workshop by Mostarr (Kuwait), with Jero, CBV Crew and others. Windhoek, Namibia, 2018. Photograph: Jurgen Muller

Page 23
Top row
Akonga. The Last Wall Tour (5th edn), Louga, Senegal, 2018. Photograph: Sparrow

Bushy, Conform. Cape Town, South Africa, 2019. Photograph: Conform

Falko One. Once Upon A Town project, Coffee Bay, South Africa, 2016. Photograph: Luke Daniel

Second row
3rdeyegoof. Afri-Cans Festival (2nd edn), Kampala, Uganda, 2018. Photograph: Kibuuka Mukisa Oscar

Patriot. Effet Graff (5th edn), Comè, Benin, 2019. Photograph: Komy Thomas

Krafts the A.O. Festigraff (5th edn), Dakar, Senegal, 2014.

Photograph: Leslie Rabine

Wise Two. Nairobi, Kenya, 2017. Photograph: Felix Magara

Third row
Bankslave. Nairobi, Kenya, 2015. Photograph: Ashley Beckett

Layla Magued. No Walls project, Cairo, Egypt, 2012. Photograph: Vincenzo Mattei

AIRJP Tagman. Morafeno, Madagascar, 2018. Photograph: Nasu Juinoxin

Sié Decor. Ouagadougou, Burkina Faso, 2016. Photograph: Armel Boris Bonégo aka Yam

Charlestyle. 'Suxali', Dakar, Senegal, 2019. Photograph: Ounda

Falko One. Xalabas Project, Praia, Cabo Verde, 2019. Photograph: Lorenzo Bordonaro

Fourth row
Guiso. 'Ndimaagu', Kaffrine, Senegal, 2017. Photograph: RBS Crew

NSAGAS collaborative mural. Blantyre, Malawi, 2018. Photograph: Bright Simbi

Participatory workshop by Christine Kuhn (USA). Kinshasa, Democratic Republic of the Congo, 2014. Photograph: Yann Kwete

Manoos, Deris. Ouagadougou, Burkina Faso, 2015. Photograph: Sophie Garcia

Skoper. Kotu, The Gambia, 2017. Photograph: Mutar

Sk4rz Tsijonriake. Antananarivo, Madagascar, 2019. Photograph: Laurianne Bitarelle

Fifth row
Tek1. Arts for Change, Gaborone, Botswana, 2013. Photograph: Neo Jasmine Mokgosi

Diaz, Kal3 (Serbia). Festigraff (9th edn), Dakar, Senegal, 2018. Photograph: Samuel Behr

Brave Tangz, Shingiro Ntigurirwa, Gilbert Iradukunda. Kigali, Rwanda, 2018. Photograph: Pamela Tulizo Kamale

Cale Waddacor was born and raised in Johannesburg, South Africa, where he developed a lively passion for visual art and urban exploration. His first book, *Graffiti South Africa,* was published in 2014, and he has since expanded his scope and expertise to document the rise of Africa's extraordinary street art movement.

All images were submitted to the project on request. Every effort has been made to identify artists and photographers correctly. Any amendments will be made in future editions. This book is a documentary record and critique of graffiti as an expressive art movement and does not condone vandalism in any form.

On the front cover
Left to right, top to bottom

First row
Nardstar*. 'Lion Queen', Cape Town, South Africa, 2018. Photograph: Nardstar*

Ed One. Sbagha Bagha Festival (5th edn), Casablanca, Morocco, 2017. Photograph: Chadi Ilias

Krafts the A.O. Dakar, Senegal, 2018. Photograph: RBS Crew

Second row
r1. 'Colour Blink', Johannesburg, South Africa, 2017. Photograph: r1.

Falko One. 'Rock Steady', Cape Town, South Africa, 2017. Photograph: Falko One

Mr Moris by Mars. Johannesburg, South Africa, 2017. Photograph: Mars

Trick 54. Fuzala Festival, Mohammedia, 2016. Photograph: Amr Sabra

Evan Sohun. 'Manghalkan', Curepipe, Mauritius, 2017. Photograph: Jason Goder

Third row
BSQ Crew, Teeoohusee. Nairobi, Kenya, 2019. Photograph: Ray Ndikwe

Kalamour. Marrakesh, Morocco, 2017. Photograph: Kalamour

Spent. Luanda, Angola, 2017. Photograph: Spent

Hatimax256. Kampala, Uganda, 2018. Photograph: Evans Kiiza

Fourth row
Wise Two. Nairobi, Kenya, 2018. Photograph: Cale Waddacor

Verkron Collective. 'Fluir', Luanda, Angola, 2018. Photograph: Verkron Collective

Alaa Awad. 'Memorial for Maat', Luxor, Egypt, 2016. Photograph: Alaa Awad

SergicalOne. Cape Town, South Africa, 2017. Photograph: Irene McCullagh

Senzart911. Johannesburg, South Africa, 2018. Photograph: Cale Waddacor

Fifth row
Ian Partikles, Tetebotan Kali, Moh Awudu. Chale Wote Street Art Festival (8th edn), Accra, Ghana, 2018. Photograph: Moh Awudu

Bankslave. Xalabas Project, Praia, Santiago, Cabo Verde, 2019. Photograph: Lorenzo Bordonaro

On the back cover:

Sitou, Breeze Yoko. Ubuhle Bendalo project, Johannesburg, South Africa, 2019. Photograph: Cale Waddacor

First published in the United Kingdom in 2020 by Thames & Hudson Ltd,181A High Holborn, London WC1V 7QX

First published in the United States of America in 2020 by Thames & Hudson Inc., 500 Fifth Avenue, New York, New York 10110

Designed by Sam Clark, www.bytheskydesign.com

Display Typeface: Grow (Dinamo)

British Library Cataloguing-in-Publication Data
A catalogue record for this book is available from the British Library

Library of Congress Control Number 2020933633

ISBN 978-0-500-02282-5

Printed and bound in China by Toppan Leefung Printing Limited

Be the first to know about our new releases, exclusive content and author events by visiting
thamesandhudson.com
thamesandhudsonusa.com
thamesandhudson.com.au